THE INVENTION OF MARXISM

THE INVENTION OF MARXISM

HOW AN IDEA CHANGED EVERYTHING

CHRISTINA MORINA

Translated from the German by Elizabeth Janik

OXFORD
UNIVERSITY PRESS

OXFORD
UNIVERSITY PRESS

Great Clarendon Street, Oxford, OX2 6DP,
United Kingdom

Oxford University Press is a department of the University of Oxford.
It furthers the University's objective of excellence in research, scholarship,
and education by publishing worldwide. Oxford is a registered trade mark of
Oxford University Press in the UK and in certain other countries

© Oxford University Press 2023

The moral rights of the authors have been asserted

First Edition published in 2023

Impression: 1

Published in the United States of America by Oxford University Press
198 Madison Avenue, New York, NY 10016, United States of America

British Library Cataloguing in Publication Data
Data available

Library of Congress Control Number: 2022950531

ISBN 978–0–19–885208–7

Printed and bound by
CPI Group (UK) Ltd, Croydon, CR0 4YY

Links to third party websites are provided by Oxford in good faith and
for information only. Oxford disclaims any responsibility for the materials
contained in any third party website referenced in this work.

Contents

III. ENGAGEMENT

On Misery, or the First Commandment: The Radical Study of Reality

On Revolution, or the Second Commandment: Philosophy as Practice

Acknowledgments

Thirteen years ago, when I knocked on Norbert Frei's office door in Jena to discuss an idea for my second book, there was no immediately obvious connection between my proposal and his work on the history and aftermath of National Socialism. He nevertheless encouraged my questions about Marxism, the other extremely consequential political worldview of the modern age. He shared my curiosity about how Marxism came to be, how the first Marxists actually "ticked," and about the relationship between their lifeworlds and their politics. Thanks to a fellowship from the Deutsche Forschungsgemeinschaft, I was able to begin my research in the archives of the International Institute of Social History (IISH) in Amsterdam. However, this project would never have gotten underway without Norbert Frei's initial encouragement and critical engagement. I therefore extend my sincere thanks to him first of all.

I am also grateful to the late Helga Grebing for her constructive criticism and unflagging support. She brought the perfect mixture of wisdom and dissent to our many conversations, and she constantly reminded me that political history is indeed history, and that conditions in the world today demand not just scholarly engagement.

In an even more profound way, the expertise, advice, and friendship of Jeffrey Herf has deeply influenced this book, even though our conversations became less frequent after I finished my doctoral thesis with him. The fundamental issue I tackle here, and have tackled in many other projects—namely, how ideas matter in politics—is one of the core questions in his work as a historian, teacher, and public intellectual. I deeply cherish the lessons I have learned from and with him, including how to disagree in mutual respect.

Over the course of this project I received countless suggestions from other scholars—including my colleagues in Jena (Franka Maubach, Thomas Kroll, Lutz Niethammer, and Joachim von Puttkamer), at the Duitsland Institut Amsterdam (Ton Nijhuis, Krijn Thijs, Hanco Jürgens, Moritz Föllmer, and the late Angelika Wendland), and at the IISH (Götz Langkau, Ulla Langkau-Alex, and Marcel van der Linden). I have learned much from Gerd Koenen—not only from his books but in lively dialogue about the historicization of communism, a field in which we have each sought to make our own contribution. And I have benefited from fantastic discussions at the colloquia of Ingrid Gilcher-Holtey, the late Thomas Welskopp, Matthias Steinbach, Ulrich Herbert, and Paul Nolte.

I extend my gratitude to Louisa Reichstetter, Alexandra Stelzig, Daniël Hendrikse, Christian Laret, and David Rieter for their assistance with transcription and editing, and to the staff of the IISH for their unfailing helpfulness. Last but not least, I am immensely grateful to my editor at Oxford University Press, Timothy Bent, and my congenial translator, Elizabeth Janik, for their enthusiasm and professional expertise at every step along the way toward this English edition of *Die Erfindung des Marxismus*.

I dedicate this book to my parents. They raised my sister and me in socialist East Germany, a land of very limited opportunities, and they ensured that questions about what was right, just, and acceptable were a regular topic of family conversation—perhaps not every day, but often at breakfast. Since part of our family lived in the "other," western part of Germany, beyond the Iron Curtain, these questions were always present. My parents gave me a happy childhood but still conveyed their deep discomfort with the absurdities and inhumanity of East German socialism, to which I had to swear an oath of allegiance and accommodate my expression. The history in this book—and thus, in a sense, also my own—could not have been told without the principles they instilled in me.

Thanks to my husband and sons, my home today is full of life. They ground my work and help in difficult moments with gestures large and small. I'm grateful for their presence every day.

My grandmother Marianne Neuber, who has since passed away, helped me incorporate into this project hundreds of letters written in the Sütterlin script. She always listened patiently, even if she was sometimes unsure of what I was up to with these letters. She would have been so proud and pleased about this book, especially now that it has also been published in English.

Abbreviations

Germany

ADAV	General German Workers' Association (Allgemeiner Deutscher Arbeiterverein), 1863–1875
KPD	Communist Party of Germany, 1918–1946
SAPD	Socialist Workers Party of Germany (Sozialistische Arbeiterpartei Deutschlands), 1875–1890
SDAP, or the "Eisenacher"	Social Democratic Workers' Party of Germany, 1869–1875
SPD	Social Democratic Party of Germany, 1890–

Austria

SDAPÖ	Social Democratic Workers' Party in Austria

Russian Empire

PPS	Polish Socialist Party
RSDLP	Russian Social Democratic Labor Party (includes Bolsheviks and Mensheviks; German: SDAPR)
SR	Socialist Revolutionary Party
Kadets	Constitutional Democratic Party
Proletariat	Social Revolutionary Party—in Poland

SDKP   Social Democracy of the Kingdom of Poland
SDKPiL   Social Democracy of the Kingdom of Poland and Lithuania

France

POF   French Workers' Party (Parti Ouvrier Français)

Prologue

The Founding Generation of Marxism

> Politics is an activity conducted with the head, not with other parts of
> the body or the soul. Yet if politics is to be genuinely human action,
> rather than some frivolous intellectual game, dedication to it can only
> be generated and sustained by passion.
>
> —Max Weber, *Weber: Political Writings*

Some historical questions are worth asking over and over again—not
only because satisfying answers to them have not yet been found but
because their answers depend on who is asking and why. The renowned Marxist historian Eric Hobsbawm posed one such question in
the early 1970s: "Why do men and women become revolutionaries?"
His answer at that time was surprisingly personal: "In the first instance mostly because they believe that what they want subjectively
from life cannot be got without a fundamental change in all society."[1]
Revolutionary engagement, Hobsbawm suggested, is inspired less by
grand utopic visions and more by immediate circumstances and social conditions. Closely following this line of argument, this book
explores the early history of Marxism as the story of many individual
attempts to transform the narrow realities of the present into something greater by applying the ideas of Karl Marx. It shows how the
first generation of Marxist intellectuals made these ideas their own
and relayed them across Europe.

Resolving what Marx famously called the "Social Question"—
a topic of debate that assumed growing urgency across all political
camps over the course of the nineteenth century—was at the center
of these efforts to change society from the ground up. Marxism was
one attempt to answer this question. With a passion unrivaled by any
other political movement in what has been described as the "Age

of Ideologies," in the last third of the nineteenth century disciples
of Marx and Friedrich Engels claimed to have found a way to har-
monize their theories about society with practical ways of changing
it.[2] First and foremost among these disciples are the protagonists, as
I call them, for they are the main actors of the story this book tells:
Karl Kautsky, Eduard Bernstein, Rosa Luxemburg, Victor Adler, Jean
Jaurès, Jules Guesde, Georgi W. Plekhanov, Vladimir I. Lenin, and Peter
B. Struve. Born in Germany, Austria-Hungary, France, or Russia be-
tween 1845 and 1870, they all belonged to the founding generation of
Marxist intellectuals.[3]

Combining the history of ideas with that of lived experience, I
investigate how these eight men and one woman created a movement characterized by total political and intellectual engagement.
This group portrait reconstructs the origins of a Marxist worldview
through their individual experiences, showing how they dedicated
their lives to openly addressing the Social Question. Through this
commitment they became the foremost theoreticians *and* practitioners
of Marxist socialism in their respective countries, thereby shaping the
"Golden Age of Marxism."[4] By their mid-thirties each of them had
assumed a leading role in their national movements, published many
of their most important works, and—whether holding formal office
or not—acquired an influential political mandate. For this reason, I
focus on the course of their lives through young adulthood—that is,
on their political coming of age.[5]

Today, more than three decades after the end of the Cold War,
the history of Marxism has become a niche academic field. By contrast, Marx, who lent his name to this worldview, has lately enjoyed a
renewed degree of attention, evident not only in new biographies and
an array of other works in philosophy, political science, sociology, and
art, but also, especially in the wake of Donald J. Trump's presidency,
in more sinister ways, as a revived ideological bogeyman ("American
Marxism"), allegedly threatening Western democracy.[6] *Capital*, Marx's
magnum opus, has been staged as a play and reinterpreted in the popular media. The film *The Young Karl Marx* premiered in the spring of

2017. And the earnestness and verve that has recently informed the academic community's engagement with Marx's writings, and wider public debates over their ongoing relevance, is apparent in the title of the French economist Thomas Piketty's recent book on global income and wealth inequality (an analysis that extends well beyond Marx): *Capital in the Twenty-First Century*.

All this revived interest derives in part from the commemorations that mark all kinds of notable anniversaries and centennials: Marx's birth in 1818, the publication of *Capital* in 1867, the Russian Revolution in 1917. Moreover, the financial crisis of 2008 fueled new discussions about the viability and legitimacy of the capitalist system overall, which made a return to the thought of the forefather of capitalist critique seem altogether plausible. These diverse approaches (despite the fierce attacks by right-wing activists in places such as the United States) are driven by a desire for contemporary relevance—and so it is easy to forget how extraordinary the widespread fascination is with the original texts of the (unintended) godfather of one of the most destructive social experiments in human history. Even the scholarly conferences organized around Marx's two hundredth birthday tended to ask what he "can still tell us today"—as if his work holds eternally valid truth—rather than what had made Marx himself such a singular historical figure. Instead, these approaches are frequently driven by utopian longing, or by a desire to come to terms with the communist past—motives that are legitimate, to be sure, but that tend to obscure rather than foster historical understanding.

For we cannot sufficiently grasp the appeal of Marx's work until we have considered its temporality—the historical time and place in which it emerged. Needless to say, no attempt to historicize Marx is free of contemporary influence. This book, however, seeks to grapple analytically with these influences by posing new questions and reconsidering sources, thereby opening up new perspectives for the historiography of Marxism at the beginning of the twenty-first century. What does it mean in principle, for example, to engage on behalf of a worldview, whether religious, political, environmental, or cultural in inspiration? What is the relationship between everyday life and politics, between experience and engagement, between seeking to understand the world and seeking to change it? How can we explain radicalization? What makes revolutionaries tick?

Moving beyond contemporary scholarship on Marxism that predominantly sees it as an endless series of theoretical and programmatic quarrels, this book explores the origins of the Marxist worldview from the perspective of lived history and by conceptualizing this worldview as a form of modern political engagement. My hope is that this illuminates the social conditions that produced this new intellectual movement. My work thus brings together two recent trends: incorporating biographical perspectives into the history of the workers' movement and situating this movement within the broader history of social movements.[7]

The emerging group portrait of these nine prominent individuals reconstructs their coming of age and—similar to Thomas Welkopp's study of the early years of the German social democratic movement—raises new questions about their numbering among the "usual suspects." What paths of socialization led Marx's first—and perhaps most influential—"epigones" to take up his cause? How were their paths shaped by home and family life, schooling and university education, creative and literary interests, and choice of profession? What kinds of "social knowledge" did these early champions of working-class liberation actually possess about how members of this class lived and worked? What experiences did they hearken back to when contemplating how to solve the Social Question? How did their often eclectic reading—poetry, fiction, philosophy, and science, in addition to the emerging Marxist canon—inform their observations about industrial and agricultural labor and their political engagement in the emerging workers' movements? And, of course, what role did the books of Karl Marx play in all this?[8]

My selection of the nine protagonists is based on several factors: the intellectual and historical influence of their writings and speeches; their role in popularizing and disseminating Marx's works in Germany,

Austria, France, and Russia between 1870 and 1900 (they were among the very first persons to study Marx's works systematically in their respective countries); and, because of this work, their gradual self-identification as "Marxist intellectuals."[9] Furthermore, their political ideas, intentions, and strategies of action were united by a specific Marxist notion of "interventionist thinking." Ingrid Gilcher-Holtey, building upon the work of Michel Foucault, uses this term to characterize those who want to serve as "mediators of consciousness." Based on their understanding of social development, these nine sought to organize, steer, and lead the struggle for emancipation. Their audience was the revolutionary subject.[10] Just as, according to Foucault, Marxist intellectuals saw the proletariat as the bearer of the universal, they saw themselves as the bearers of this universality "in its conscious, elaborated form." They believed that they were, to some extent, "the consciousness/conscience" of the whole world.[11] This peculiar self-image was the source of their claim and their confidence that they were capable of changing it.[12]

When I discuss the engagement of Marxist intellectuals in the following pages, I do not use "intellectual" in the sense of a sociological category or "social figure,"[13] nor do I mean an ephemeral social role. Rather, the term reflects a certain kind of political self-awareness, in conjunction with an understanding of "engagement" that is more precise than in conventional usage. Without such a conception of the intellectual, the emergence of Marxism cannot be properly understood.[14] Marxist intellectuals did not practice criticism as a profession;[15] instead, they followed a calling. Despite their frequent assertions to the contrary, they did not approach the social conditions they critiqued with detachment. Rather, they were "engaged" or "involved," as expressed by Norbert Elias in his critique of the social sciences and their subjectivity. These intellectuals routinely mixed analysis and prediction in their work: how things are and how things ought to be.[16] Their texts bear witness to a "sustained political passion" that grew out of an enduring cognitive and emotional preoccupation with social conditions—a preoccupation that transcended their own lived experience.[17] I therefore also examine Marxism from the perspective of the history of emotions. In so doing, I contribute to a growing field, one that focuses on the individual motives and emotions that drove engagement in political movements in both the nineteenth and twentieth centuries.[18]

The three parts of this book—"Socialization," "Politicization," and "Engagement"—interrogate the relationship between experiencing and interpreting the world among Marx's first disciples. I am inspired by the fundamental assumption that the "radical study of reality" is the first commandment of Marxism.[19] Within the unique laboratory of social ideas that coalesced in nineteenth-century Europe, Marxism clearly distinguished itself from all other political worldviews with its programmatic appeal to "reality." This was one of the most important reasons for its intellectual, emotional, and political resonance—both creative and destructive—that extended far into the twentieth century and continues to function as state ideology in countries such as China and Cuba today.[20] Marxism's distinctive appeal to reality not only warrants an investigation of its origins from the perspective of lived history; it also poses an essential (and thus far neglected) historiographical challenge.

A look back to the very beginnings of Marx's philosophical thinking can help. In 1844 the young Marx introduced one of his most important texts, the *Critique of Hegel's Philosophy of Law*, with a bombastic critique of religion and an appeal to embrace reality. Humans had to abandon "illusions about their condition" in order to establish the premises for "*true* happiness." They had to move to the center of political philosophy. Likewise, theory had to become radical and demonstrate its views *ad hominem*: "To be radical is to grasp matters at the root. But for man the root is man himself."[21] And there it was: Marx's Promethean appeal for thought to become "practice." To Marx, the relationship between classical philosophy and "studying the actual world" was like that between "onanism and sexual love."[22]

He later sought to resolve this appeal in a number of (often unfinished) writings, reducing it to the demonstration of humans as materially dependent beings.[23] What later became known as the "materialist conception of history" was—as a much older Engels warned—"first and foremost a guide to study, not a tool for constructing objects after the Hegelian model." This was nothing less than an epic program of deconstruction, for, as the elder Engels wrote, "the whole of history must be studied anew, and the existential conditions of the various social formations individually investigated before an attempt is made to deduce therefrom the political, legal, aesthetic, philosophical, religious etc., standpoints that correspond to them."[24] This guide to study was not *ad hominem*, but rather *ad societatem*. It corresponded to the fundamental idea that Marx and Engels had already expressed in *The German Ideology*: that "the essence of man is not an abstraction inhering in isolated individuals. Rather, in its actuality, it is the ensemble of social relations."[25] Because of this insight into the social contingency of human essence, both men are still considered founders of the sociology of knowledge, and many of their works have become classics of the discipline.[26]

All nine protagonists in this book felt a sense of duty to this insight and to the challenges it posed. In the following pages, I examine their individual paths of socialization, their readings of Marx, and their documented efforts to meet this challenge in the age of what Wolfgang Bonß called the "factual gaze." Marx and Engels called for an objective, empirical approach to reality. By breaking down the wall between theory and practice, their approach not only promised a realistic understanding of the present but also suggested options for political action for the immediate future.[27] The resulting critique of capitalism purported to be universally valid—a claim that seemed undeniable to many observers and could be verified again and again, given the stark antagonism between wage labor and capital in the second half of the nineteenth century.[28] If we consider both Marx's works and the protagonists' gaze at the social conditions of their time, we can understand Marxism as an attempt, fueled by both intellectual and popular sources, to develop a comprehensive program to change reality.

For the protagonists, the primary appeal of this program was no vague utopia but rather a concrete, "scientific" relationship to the present. Marx's work promised insight into the here and now, not merely faith in a better future. Marxism was an ongoing course of study in the actual world of the past and present. The nine applied themselves to this study, each in their own way and with remarkable endurance. Because their intellectual turn toward Marx took years, we cannot describe it as some kind of sudden "conversion" to a "secular faith," expressions used by Thomas Kroll in his group portrait of communist intellectuals after 1945.[29] It was, rather, an extended process of internalization, a kind of tertiary socialization into a new reality, and the protagonists committed to this process with everything they had.[30] My effort to tell the story of early Marxism as "lived experience"[31] therefore enters uncharted territory.

In the spirit of new beginnings, I treat Marxism not as a closed political ideology but rather as a worldview (*Weltanschauung*). Worldviews are what Wilhelm Dilthey has called "interpretations of reality," which reflect an intimate connection between experiences and conceptions of the world; Dilthey considered Marx's materialism a "philosophical worldview."[32] Following more recent reflections on the history of political worldviews in the age of ideological confrontation, Marxism, too, can be understood as providing a secular context that gave "all specialized knowledge a '*higher*' meaning, subjective perceptions a uniform perspective, and actions a moral value."[33] In a narrower sense, though, Marxism has also been used as a collective term for the "epigonous reception of Marx's teachings."[34] In effect, however, it emerged as a worldview only as a result of this reception, which the nine protagonists of this book themselves understood as both a philosophical and a scientific process of learning and appropriation.

By focusing on their individual paths and their ways of apprehending the world through early adulthood, I observe Marxism as it emerged—in other words, as it was being invented. At the same time, I revisit a crucial question once raised by Hans-Ulrich Wehler, about how the language of Marxism came to dominate German social democracy in the last third of the nineteenth century—and I rephrase it more broadly: Why did Marx and Engels's texts exert such an enduring power of persuasion in so many different places and contexts way beyond Germany, touching the minds of such different contemporaries?[35] In Paris, London, Zurich, Geneva, Vienna, Stuttgart, Warsaw, and St. Petersburg, the protagonists made Marx their own. Their interwoven experiences allow the founding history of Marxism to be told as a generational project, resting on far more than the work of Engels, the alleged "inventor of Marxism."[36]

The members of this founding generation were in constant contact with one another, in writing and in person. They built a transnational network that was grounded in part on discursive or virtual ties, and in part on personal relationships. Although they argued often and intensely, a feeling of like-minded community prevailed until 1914. Even at the height of the fierce debate over revisionism, Kautsky described his party ideal as a "voluntary association of like-minded people."[37] All of the protagonists spoke multiple languages, and through education, exile, and travel they were familiar with life in other countries. They met at international congresses and party meetings, and they communicated with one another in private letters and through the public media of newspapers, journals, and theoretical texts. They translated and published each other's work, establishing an interrelationship that was often lasting and intense, and sometimes only superficial and short-lived. This network became a peculiar manifestation of "proletarian internationalism" in its own right, and it played an important role in their lives. Recent research suggests that a complex history about networking, mobility, and solidarity—personal and transnational, real and imagined—in the first Marxist generation has yet to be written.[38]

The source base for my study is correspondingly diverse. It includes published and unpublished letters, diaries, notes, sketches, and autobiographical texts, as well as published speeches and writings. As I began my research, it soon became clear that I would not merely be revisiting familiar sources. I found an array of personal writings, particularly at the International Institute of Social History in Amsterdam (IISH), that have previously received little or no attention.[39] These include family letters, school essays, sketchbooks, and novel manuscripts in the papers of Kautsky, Adler, and Guesde, as well as political memoirs by Alexander Stein and Paul Frölich that prominently feature Luxemburg.[40] Unearthing lost treasures, however, was not the focus of my archival research. Indeed, many well-known sources and biographies have much to say about the young protagonists' personal, intellectual, and political strivings and how they made sense of the world, offering a wealth of material for a comparative coming-of-age study.

In search of the origins of Marxism, this book dives deeply into the lives and worlds of eight men and one woman—a group of sensitive, highly politicized young people who cared deeply about social and political conditions that extended well beyond their personal lives. They were courageous, ambitious, mobile, multilingual, feisty, idealistic, eager to learn, and confident in their own potential. We could also say that they were probing, pretentious, eclectic, and often doctrinaire activists who were adamantly convinced that they *personally* could solve the world's problems. Always aware of this ambivalence, I examine how the life stories of these nine individuals played out on the political and ideological battlefields of their times.

PART I

Socialization

I

Born in the Nineteenth Century

Origins and Influences

He who is afraid of the dense wood in which stands the palace
of the Idea, he who does not hack through it with the sword and
wake the king's sleeping daughter with a kiss, is not worthy of
her and her kingdom; he may go and become a country pastor,
merchant, assessor, or whatever he likes, take a wife and beget
children in all piety and respectability, but the century will not
recognise him as its son.

—Friedrich Engels, 1841

If you can imagine a group portrait of the nine individuals who are
the subjects of this book, you would see eight men and one woman
from different places and different walks of life.[1] You would notice
their remarkable similarities—and not only because they had all embraced Marxism as young adults, a development that was in no way
inevitable. They had also all undergone similar experiences at home
and at school that shaped how they viewed themselves and society.

In order to get to know these protagonists, as I call them, we
must first consider their early, pre-socialist politicization—family
influences, time at school, what they read when they were young.
Sometimes extensive—if often unsatisfying—biographical literature, and autobiographical writings by the protagonists themselves,

can help us reconstruct their individual paths to socialization. These paths were interconnected, despite their different routes across multiple European countries. The nine were not only children of the nineteenth century by birth; they embraced their era as a personal challenge. Their early letters, diaries, sketches, and notes reveal that they—like the young Friedrich Engels, who later served as an intellectual mentor to many of them—were determined to cut their own swath through the "dense wood" where freedom, like a sleeping princess, was awaiting release.

Eduard Bernstein and Jules Guesde grew up in modest, even impoverished, circumstances, each in the middle of a European metropolis. Bernstein was born in Berlin on 6 January 1850, the seventh of fifteen children in a Jewish family. They were "not part of the bourgeoisie, but not the proletariat, either," according to his own, somewhat ambiguous, wording.[2] Bernstein's father first worked as a plumber, then as a railroad engineer, earning enough to sustain his large family in "genteel poverty."[3] Guesde's background was similarly humble. Born Jules Bazile on 11 November 1845, he grew up in the middle of Paris, on the Île Saint-Louis. His father supported the family of seven as best he could with his earnings as a teacher.[4] Financial worries hounded Guesde his entire life. Despite excellent grades in school, he could not afford to attend university and began to work as a clerk instead. At the age of twenty, he became a journalist. Bernstein completed secondary school with a scholarship from a relative, and so he was able to earn a comparatively secure income as an apprentice at a bank, and later as a private secretary. As children, both Bernstein and Guesde were often sick and somewhat frail. Even as an adult, Guesde's health was always poor.

The other protagonists came from more comfortably situated backgrounds. The parents of Georgi Plekhanov and the parents of Vladimir Ilyich Lenin owned estates tended by domestic servants and other workers. After childhoods free from material worry, both lost their fathers when they were still teenagers and became the heads of their respective households. Both had to liquidate their parents' estates, giving them an early introduction not only to money matters but to rural life. Born on 29 November 1856, Plekhanov was the oldest of twelve children. His family lived in Gudalovka, a village in the central Russian province of Tambov, 280 miles southeast of Moscow. His father was a member of the gentry of Tatar descent who served for decades in the tsar's army before retiring to manage his estate of 270 acres and fifty serfs.[5] Although Plekhanov's mother had brought a dowry to the marriage that had doubled the value of the estate, the family struggled financially after the emancipation of the serfs in 1861.

When Plekhanov was fifteen years old, his father gave up his duties as a landlord and took a position with the local elected assembly (*zemstvo*)—developments that formatively influenced Plekhanov's youth and political awareness. Both the bankruptcy of the estate and his father's move to the civil service were a direct consequence of Tsar Alexander II's far-reaching reforms. When his father died in 1873, the seventeen-year-old Plekhanov helped his mother sell the family property. These proceedings were accompanied by fierce, and sometimes violent, disputes with the local peasants, affecting him deeply.

Vladimir Ulyanov, who later took the name Lenin, was born on 10 April 1870 in Simbirsk on the Volga, 435 miles east of Moscow. He, too, grew up in rural surroundings. His father, Ilya, was a liberal educator who taught physics and mathematics in the local school; he attained the post of school inspector and was even given a noble title. Lenin's mother came from a landowning German-Swedish-Russian family. She spoke multiple languages, and she, too, trained as a teacher, although after marrying she devoted herself to her family and children. Lenin's childhood was marked by relative material security and his parents' encouragement of education, although as a teenager several events fundamentally changed his life. In 1887, one year after his father unexpectedly died of a brain hemorrhage, his older brother Alexander was hanged for revolutionary agitation following an unsuccessful plot to assassinate the new tsar. Like Plekhanov, Lenin became head of his household at the age of seventeen. He had to manage the finances of his family, which included an older sister and two younger siblings. The family was still prosperous but was ostracized socially after Alexander's execution.[6]

Peter Struve and Rosa Luxemburg, too, originally hailed from the Russian Empire—Struve from the province of Perm, more than 700 miles east of Moscow, and Luxemburg from Zamość, a town 150 miles southeast of Warsaw, near the empire's western border. Struve's family had emigrated from northern Germany to Siberia in the early nineteenth century, so his German Danish grandfather, Friedrich Georg Wilhelm Struve, could avoid service in the Napoleonic army. The family later moved to Dorpat (Tartu in present-day Estonia) and then resettled in St. Petersburg, where Friedrich became a celebrated mathematician and astronomer, receiving a noble title and Russian citizenship. Struve's father became a high-ranking civil servant, inheriting the grandfather's loyalty and commitment to the new homeland, although he later wrote that he simultaneously felt like a lifelong foreigner who was not fully accepted. He got into trouble at work and had to change posts frequently. The family moved many times: first to St. Petersburg and Astrakhan (southern Russia), then to Perm (Siberia), and then to Stuttgart, where the nine-year-old Struve acquired his fluent German. His mother—who has been described as unreliable, erratic, and extremely overweight—apparently brought the family little stability.[7] Even so, Struve, the youngest of six sons, grew up with few material worries. The family had the means to ensure that the children were well-educated and poised for promising careers as teachers, diplomats, or scholars.

Like Struve, Luxemburg, who was born on 5 March 1871, grew up with few material worries. Her childhood was unsettled for other reasons, as her family was subjected to pressures from two sides: an increasingly antisemitic mood within mainstream society, and an Orthodox Jewish community that opposed assimilation. These pressures seem to have bolstered the family's "unique cohesion," as one of Luxemburg's biographers put it.[8] Luxemburg's father was a successful timber merchant who traveled frequently. The family could afford a comfortable home close to the town hall on Zamość's central square. By 1873, his business was prosperous enough that the family moved to Warsaw, where Luxemburg, the youngest of five children, grew up and attended school. When she was three years old, she developed a hip ailment that was misdiagnosed and incorrectly treated, resulting in a mild but evident physical disability that gave her a limp for the rest of her life. The family spoke and "felt" Polish, but German language and literature—especially the works of Friedrich Schiller, beloved by Luxemburg's mother—held a special place in their home. Her father occasionally brought home foreign newspapers, and both parents nurtured their children's early interest in literature and politics. Luxemburg's biographers continue to debate the relative strength of the family's Polish, German, and Jewish influences; however, all agree that she was an intellectually curious child whose parents were attentive to her education.[9]

Karl Kautsky shared the privilege of a comparatively well-situated family that encouraged education. He, too, grew up in a home with a keen interest in current events and critical social thought. Despite some lean times, his parents were able to support themselves as artists; his father painted scenery in theaters, and his mother worked as a writer and actress. Born in Prague on 16 October 1854, Kautsky was the first of four children in a German Czech family. His father was a "nationally oriented" Czech, as he later wrote; his mother's parents were Austrian, and in addition to her native German she spoke Czech.[10] Kautsky's schooling introduced him to three different worldviews: the Calvinism of a private tutor, Catholicism at a seminary in Melk, and "modern" humanism at the Academic Gymnasium in Vienna. His family moved to the Austrian capital in 1863, after his father found a permanent position as a painter at the Imperial Burgtheater, lifting his "family of intellectuals," Kautsky wrote, from "impoverished Bohème" into "solid prosperity."[11]

Victor Adler and Jean Jaurès—the final pair of our group of protagonists—were unique among them because they broke with their families' intellectual leanings by embracing social democracy, albeit relatively late in life. Adler was born in Prague on 24 June 1854. Like Kautsky, he first grew up in Prague and then moved to Vienna. His father was a cloth merchant from a Jewish Moravian family who worked his way up to considerable prosperity as a stock- and real-estate broker in Vienna. In 1884 Adler and his own two sons converted to Catholicism—partly out of religious conviction and partly out of a practical desire to assimilate.[12] Adler was the oldest of five children, all raised in a "patriarchal" and "spartan" manner. His wife later wrote that the "austerity of his childhood" and early encounters with everyday antisemitism made a deep impression on him.[13] Perhaps this contributed to his stutter, which was cured at a specialized clinic when he was nineteen. His family's wealth allowed him to receive a first-rate secondary and university education. He studied medicine in Vienna at the same time as Sigmund Freud and became a doctor. The young Adler was inspired by German nationalism, adopting his parents' national-conservative outlook before gradually embracing more socially critical positions. After his father's death in 1886, Adler used his inheritance to establish *Gleichheit* (Equality), the first Social Democratic Party newspaper in the Habsburg Empire.

Jaurès's biography resembles Adler's in two respects. Jaurès, too, came to socialism late (at the age of thirty-one), and his choice upset some family members. Like Plekhanov, he grew up in the countryside and was well acquainted with rural life. He was the first of two sons, born on 3 September 1859 in Castres, a small town in the *département* of Tarn in southern France. Both of his parents came from well-situated families, and in the 1860s they acquired a farm on the outskirts of town. His father, who has been described as gentle and cheerful, exchanged his modest income as a merchant for a career in agriculture, one that was no less arduous. His mother passed down her Catholicism and faith in human goodness. Jaurès's childhood was shaped by his family's privileged social background as well as its persistent financial difficulties. An outstanding student, he attended the Collège de Castres with the aid of a scholarship and gained a reputation for loving "to learn as much as to eat," as his biographer put it.[14]

He completed his secondary schooling at the top of his class and with additional financial support attended the elite Parisian École Normale Superieure, where Émile Durkheim and Henri Bergson were among his schoolmates.

These biographical sketches show that none of the protagonists fits the stereotype of the professional revolutionary, someone who burns all personal bridges and plunges into the working-class struggle as a "bourgeois radical"[15] or "bourgeois deserter," as Robert Michels put it.[16] The attributes of radicalism and breaking with the past are usually quite vague, not necessarily corresponding with how Marxists saw themselves. Karl Marx himself liked to use the word "radical." Referring to the term's Latin origins (*radix*, meaning "root"), he applied it to both thought and action, without separating the two categories. The following passage in the *Critique of Hegel's Philosophy of Law* was paradigmatic for this understanding, and it simultaneously became a central point of reference for all students of Marx:

> The weapon of criticism certainly cannot replace the criticism of weapons; material force must be overthrown by material force; but theory, too, becomes a material force once it seizes the masses. Theory is capable of seizing the masses once it demonstrates *ad hominem*, and it demonstrates *ad hominem* once it becomes radical. To be radical is to grasp matters at the root. But for man the root is man himself.[17]

Marx pulled philosophy down from the theoretical heavens so it could play a practical historical role. For Marx, thought was always a form of taking action. In his critique of philosophy without humans at the center, the boundary between theory and practice dissolved itself dialectically, as if on its own. To be "radical" meant reimagining humans as godlike—as the point of departure and terminus of social critique. This view was essential to how Marxist intellectuals understood themselves, and it justified the transformation of Marx's name into an analytical and programmatic concept: Marxism.

Even so, none of the protagonists in this study broke absolutely with their own past by rejecting family, friends, acquaintances, or a "bourgeois" lifestyle. It would be misleading, for example, to say,

as one scholar does, that Adler "distanced" himself from the "bourgeois world."[18] His family's life was upended for some time by his
social democratic engagement; house searches, arrests, and financial
shortfalls became part of their everyday life. And yet by 1905, at the
latest, when Adler was elected to Parliament, they were (once again)
accepted among the respectable bourgeoisie. Emma Adler wrote in
her memoir that her husband was treated with "reverence and respect," and he was a government minister when he died in 1918.[19]

Even the four who most closely approached the image of the professional revolutionary—Guesde, Plekhanov, Lenin, and Luxemburg—
upheld connections to their relatives and previous lives, despite time in
prison or exile. After Luxemburg's arrest in 1906, her family in Warsaw
lobbied for her release and posted bail against her will.[20] Guesde's
father, whose livelihood as a private school teacher required an un-
sullied reputation, appealed personally to French president Adolphe
Thiers to pardon his hot-headed but "patriotic" son, who had fled
the country after the defeat of the Paris Commune.[21] And when
Luxemburg, Lenin, Plekhanov—and Adler, for that matter—were not
in prison, they (like the others) maintained a bourgeois lifestyle on
the lower fringes of the middle class, which can be explained only by
their upbringing.

Of course, their revolutionary careers hardly followed the usual
patterns of (lower) bourgeois life, as they themselves would have
readily conceded. To this extent, it is true that they "sacrificed their
conventional place in society" to join the social democratic movement. However, they saw this as a logical step, not as a "sacrifice."[22]
Most made this decision before gaining a foothold in the professions
for which they had trained—attorney (Lenin), engineer (Plekhanov),
bank employee (Bernstein), or clerk (Guesde). They went underground or into exile to escape arrest for their political activism. They
defy assignment within a specific economic class, as the lens of "class"
is itself problematic; it creates analytical categories that are much
more rigid than historical reality. By reversing this lens and viewing
the protagonists' paths of socialization and politicization from the

perspective of lived experience, we can see that tropes such as "class desertion" and "broken existence" do not capture the essence of their coming of age.

Moreover, the protagonists themselves did not see Marxist engagement as a radical break with their own past, nor can we coax this interpretation from their personal writings. Instead, their embrace of the emerging workers' movement followed a specific biographical logic. The decision to become politically involved (which was undertaken with great solemnity and self-confidence), to make contact with workers' and revolutionary circles, and to abandon a relatively ordered life path, did not happen abruptly. Rather, they came to this decision gradually, through an increasingly critical view of social relations. In fact, Eric Hobsbawm's thesis—that revolutionary engagement is grounded in lived experience—frequently held true. They became revolutionaries because they came to believe that their subjective expectations for their own lives, which were relatively independent of objective social conditions, could not be fulfilled without their own engagement on behalf of a fundamentally different society. As a matter of fact, Hobsbawm's thesis and related observations about Marxism's founding generation have been confirmed by sociopsychological research on the motivations for political engagement.[23]

The men and woman in this book saw social democracy not as an escape from their own history or class but rather as the only step toward adulthood that seemed reasonable, even essential, given the conditions they observed. Even when their parents' loyalty to the status quo hindered their own socialist engagement, heated discussions at the dinner table did not break family ties. Guesde was born Jules Bazile, but he took his mother's maiden name at the age of twenty-one, after leaving the Prefecture of the Seine, so as not to endanger his father's professional reputation or disturb the family peace.[24] Jaurès's in-laws frowned upon his election to the National Assembly as a socialist. An aunt on his mother's side accused him of becoming a socialist for financial reasons, so his apparently demanding wife Louise could live comfortably[25]—but even here, we can hardly speak of a break with his past.

Among them all, Adler had to overcome the greatest family resistance to his socially critical ideas, and it is evident how fiercely political disputes upset the patriarchal order of his family. In a letter to his friend Engelbert Pernerstorfer, the nineteen-year-old Adler described a scene that transpired at his family's kitchen table in the spring of 1871, following the outbreak of demonstrations in Paris:

> The topic of conversation was the Commune. In no way do I agree with the movement, but I had to defend it against the objections and labels that my father applied—murderers, thieves, ruffians, etc. But because in these kinds of debates it's clear from the start that paternal authority triumphs, this is how it goes, round and round, in the familiar circle. And if that doesn't help, the roar: "brute, ignoramus, etc." Finally, the regret that I've lost all morals and sense of justice, that I don't understand the difference between mine and yours, and all of a sudden there's a ruffian and thief right here at the table.[26]

This unyielding attitude discouraged Adler from actively engaging on behalf of social democracy while his father was still alive. He loved him nevertheless. In 1896 Adler wrote to Kautsky that his father's death had left a great void: "My old man never entirely understood what I wanted, but insofar as he understood me, he was against it, and so we were eternally at odds. But I miss him even so."[27]

Things were similar in the Bernstein household. The father disapproved of his son's embrace of social democracy in the early 1870s, "not out of any class allegiance" but because of the movement's attacks on the *Berliner Volks-Zeitung*, the liberal democratic newspaper that featured the writing of Bernstein's uncle Aaron. The conflict between father and son was thus not particularly dire. "As fierce as my father could be, he was hardly vindictive" and would "move an especially good piece of meat from his plate to mine, or he gave other such signals of fatherly love."[28] The father's criticism, however, did not go further than well-intentioned admonitions or words of advice—as when the twenty-two-year-old Bernstein, freshly involved with the

Social Democratic Party of Germany (SPD) in Berlin, set out to agitate for the cause in outlying areas. His father warned that the locals did not want to hear from him and would "go after him with rods and sticks."[29] Bernstein's family tolerated his political activism as long as it was limited to holidays and weekends and did not disrupt his work as a bank clerk at S. & L. Rothschild. He could bring party comrades home with him only when his father was away.

Bernstein's example shows especially clearly how the life of a "bourgeois radical" could fit within the bourgeois world. This self-described "non-proletarian"[30] worked for the Rothschilds for seven years (1871–78), and he agitated for the SPD in the same period without any difficulties: "The income that I earned as a bank employee put me . . . in the happy position of being able to pursue my party activism without recompense. I devoted my entire soul to it. I spent almost my entire free time exercising my political conscience, whether in party assemblies and committee meetings, or agitating for the cause in a wide radius around Berlin."[31]

The Kautsky family also tolerated their son's socialist engagement. Kautsky's father was "tremendously annoyed" that his son's activism brought a "neverending" stream of social democrats in and out of the family home, as the twenty-two-year-old Kautsky wrote to his mother in July 1877. However, the father did not forbid this activity, which was not without some risk in Vienna at that time.[32] When Kautsky joined the Social Democratic Workers' Party in Austria (SDAPÖ) in 1875, the father did initiate a serious conversation and advised him to reconsider. But in the end, he could not, or would not, stop his son from taking this "fateful step." Similar to Guesde, Kautsky decided to use a pseudonym in the party press so as not to compromise his father's reputation or that of his studio. Five years passed before Kautsky worked as a journalist under his real name.[33]

This book compares nine biographies from four very different countries. Those who joined the social democratic movement as engaged citizens (Bernstein in Germany, Jaurès in France, and Kautsky in Austria), often writing for the party press, encountered state repression but were not automatically persecuted as dangerous subversives. The same was true for Guesde and Adler, who worked for republican or nationalist causes. The situation was different for Luxemburg, Plekhanov, Struve, and Lenin, who lived in the extremely repressive tsarist state. The early workers' movement in the Russian Empire recruited from the ranks of former populists, Narodniks, and terrorists, who largely believed that solving the Social Question meant toppling tsarist rule.[34] Bourgeois or class culture was much less defined in the tsarist empire—a fact that led Luxemburg to observe from afar, shortly after the turn of the century, that Russia's socialist intelligentsia had "a much less well-defined class character" and was "to a far greater extent declassed, in the precise sense of the word," compared to their western European counterparts.[35] Thus, any discussion of "bourgeois deserters" or "bourgeois radicals" who broke radically with their class is even less apt within the Russian-Polish context. Such labels imply a degree of bourgeois rootedness (or alienation) that was not evident in the biographies I present here.

Rather than speaking of an escape from their past, we can compare the protagonists to those "marginal men"—merchants, artisans, and free tradesmen—whom the historian Lynn Hunt has identified as urban activists during the French Revolution. They, too, were (overwhelmingly) men, "outsiders" or "peripheral" personalities who were not fully part of the mainstream, if not necessarily isolated or prone to violence. They were not bound by ties to traditional institutions. Because of their family origins, relative marginality, mobility, and networking, they were willing and able to question long-held "political customs and commonplaces of the past."[36]

Following the sociological insights of Karl Mannheim, we can describe the careers of our nine main figures as "relatively uncommitted," since they began their political lives in a kind of "middle-of-the-road position." They came from different social milieus, and it was largely through education—according to Mannheim, *the* medium of the "modern mind"—that they came together as an "intellectual generation" (in the words of Hans Jaeger). When their turn toward Marx was complete, they understood Marxism as the quintessence of a learned, or "scientific," socialism. Following Mannheim further, they were not "suspended in a vacuum" above the other classes; rather, from their position of relative uncommitment they chose to identify with a class "to which they originally did not belong." Their social habitat—the expanding European social democratic network—was at once local and global, national and transnational, rooted and detached. At best, they cultivated a special sensitivity for social conflict and worked "to make this mediation a living one, and to connect political decisions with a prior total orientation." At worst, their relative distance from the process of production—which is to say, from how actual workers lived and worked—led to mutual mistrust and ideological fanaticism. In order to compensate "for the lack of a more fundamental integration into a class," Mannheim argues, some intellectuals slid into radicalism.[37]

The lives of these nine individuals are characterized more by continuities than ruptures—an observation that is closely related to the question of family background. What role did family traditions, values, and beliefs—bequeathed from grandparents, parents, or siblings—play in shaping the young protagonists' political and ideological convictions? The protagonists set off on their journeys with a biographically predetermined store of knowledge, a kind of imaginary backpack that enduringly shaped their political coming of age.[38] This intellectual (or intellectual-historical) endowment had a far-reaching effect on their individual development—beyond intellectual and religious beliefs, educational opportunities, or suggested readings. Some families even encouraged their children to engage with the socialist ideas that were becoming more widely known. However, the protagonists' turn toward Marx usually occurred in a second step, independent of their family's political orientation—through self-determined study, through correspondence or dialogue with like-minded comrades, through travel, or even by visiting the "master" himself in London.

The socially critical, humanist leanings of three of their mothers are especially noteworthy. Kautsky's mother, Minna, published several novels and stories that openly promoted socialist ideas. Jaurès's Catholic mother raised her son as a devout Christian, although she later showed considerable tolerance when he renounced religion as a young man.[39] Maria Plekhanova has been described as a kind, good-natured woman, who instilled in her first-born son a sense of justice and empathy for the suffering of others.[40] In Kautsky's case, his maternal grandfather also played an important role. Correspondence from 1869 to 1874 shows how the grandfather engaged his teenage grandson in a warm, open conversation about God and the world. Finally, Lenin directly experienced the reality and existential consequences of social revolutionary engagement through his brother, Alexander. Recent research has confirmed that Alexander's imprisonment and execution left a lasting impression on his younger brother.[41]

I will take a closer look at the effects of this relationship in the pages ahead. With an eye to the other protagonists, previously neglected personal writings can provide new insights. Some families had no discernable political leanings (as with Luxemburg, Struve, and Bernstein); in other cases (Jaurès, Guesde, and Plekhanov), our knowledge is limited due to a scarcity of relevant sources. The tendencies of the Kautsky, Adler, and Ulyanov families, by contrast, are very well documented.

Socially critical influences are most evident in Kautsky's early years, through his mother and her family. Minna Kautsky was the daughter of Anton Jaich, a theatrical scenery painter in Prague who nurtured his daughter's dramatic and literary ambitions from an early age.[42] Her sporadic stage career was cut short by a lung ailment. By 1862, when Kautsky was eight, she had devoted herself entirely to writing. Her stories provide some insight into how Kautsky's family perceived working-class life. Minna described working people with reverence and a hint of paternalistic affection, and she sought to represent their lifeworld and "proletarian" identity authentically. She wrote about the rules of survival that she had heard from "poor people." The hero of her first successful story, "A Proletarian Child," is the metal-worker Franz Denk. He falls in love with the proletarian girl Marie ("Mietz"), who has been exploited by the system and by her own father. Minna conveyed the proletarian lifeworld with dialogue such as the following: "We workers are a family and have the same kind of stomachs; bread . . . will have to satisfy us until we have won the meat to accompany it" and "Health is the most precious possession for poor people like us, Mietz; as soon as we start to lose it, we're done for."[43] Her stories were among the first examples of socialist *Tendenzliteratur* (literature that was committed to a cause). Her works were praised by some for their political engagement; Marx called one of her novels the "most remarkable story of the present."[44] Others (including, intriguingly, Engels) saw them as all too transparent propaganda; he made the friendly recommendation that she read Balzac to hone her own social criticism.[45]

Minna also contributed to the popular *Austrian Workers' Calendar*, which had informed and entertained Austrian workers since 1875; her son once explained to her that its audience was the average worker, the "poor devil who doesn't get anything else to read all year."[46] Kautsky had written several unpublished novels himself, and he wrote that his mother's "poetic talent" towered over his own. At the same time—not only in his memoirs but also in his early letters—he stylized himself as well-versed in the "proletarian world," suggesting that his mother had found her way to it through him. It is "indeed unfortunate," the twenty-four-year-old wrote to her from Zurich in February 1880, "that you don't come into contact with the circles for whom you write, so you can't see the impression made by your work."[47] Two months earlier, Kautsky had moved to Zurich to assume his first paid position, as Karl Höchberg's private secretary. Curiously, in March 1880 he wrote to his parents that he "didn't get together with workers at all," nor did he feel the need to, "because I have so many intelligent, like-minded comrades here."[48]

There is no indication in Kautsky's letters that he carefully observed or intensively engaged with the "proletarian world." He wrote about workers only in conjunction with lectures and party meetings, where he was surprised that the attendees were not the "malingerers" described in "bourgeois reporting." Instead, the proceedings were usually "calm, sober" and "strictly parliamentary."[49] In letters that sometimes read like treatises, he described workers as a "class." He railed against the lack of "common spirit" among unemployed academics (the "proletariat of the intelligentsia"), in contrast to the solidarity of the workers, who—whether hard-working, clever, not so clever, or unemployed—all understood that they could improve their situation only by standing together.[50] Given these rather unsophisticated remarks about workers and their lifeworld, his later observations about his relationship to his mother in his memoir seem somewhat insincere: "My mother, 17 years older than I, was naturally far more experienced and knowledgeable about the world. But it was I who introduced her to the proletarian world."[51]

Kautsky's youthful contacts in the proletarian world, however they transpired, were undoubtedly the subject of intense political discussions at home. His surviving correspondence is full of political commentary on current events. These letters show that Kautsky (who joined the SDAPÖ at the age of twenty) soon came to see himself as an experienced politico, ready and able to explain the party platform whenever he was asked. He also edited and critiqued his mother's manuscripts and suggested suitable outlets for their publication.

Kautsky's maternal grandfather must have been similarly influential; they began corresponding when he was thirteen years old. Kautsky recalled in his memoir, "[M]y uncles and aunts rollicked about with me; my grandfather quenched my thirst for knowledge."[52] The surviving correspondence shows that Anton Jaich was no proponent of socialist ideas but a tenderhearted, devout grandfather who took an interest in his grandson's development and regularly offered advice and encouragement. Their warm relationship is evident, for example, in an 1875 letter, in which the twenty-one-year-old reported enthusiastically about his discovery of Charles Darwin, recommending that his grandfather read *The Descent of Man*, which had been available in German since 1871:

> Dearest grandfather!
> If, one day in heaven, reading Darwin's works counts against me as a sin, hopefully I'll be forgiven for giving them to you to read, too, since you're already hopelessly lost to the holy church, whose embrace you'll always flee to. With this comforting thought, I'm sending you the first installments of *The Descent of Man*. Although you may be familiar with excerpts of the work, it contains such a wealth of stimulating details that I hope it will seem new and interesting to you. I'm quite enthusiastic about it.[53]

Shouldn't Darwin be compared to Aristotle? Kautsky asked. Like Lassalle, Feuerbach, Haeckel, and Schopenhauer—the other great thinkers of the day—didn't Darwin show that these times were not completely devoid of "great men"? One year later, Kautsky published his own interpretation of Darwin, his first long article, which appeared in the series "Darwin and Socialism" in the Viennese journal *Gleichheit*.[54] In it, Kautsky argued that socialism was the only political program that sought to establish the "social instincts" of the animal world—togetherness, solidarity, and cooperation—as principles of humanity, thereby rendering deadly, competitive struggle obsolete. For the rest of his life Kautsky stood by this dubious interpretation of Darwin, which counted on the "goodness" of socialized humans and the "derivation of morality from social instincts."[55]

The young man had limited success impressing his grandfather with his reading. Jaich wondered where Kautsky found time to study "all these works" and recommended the church fathers instead: "The natural sciences and works of new philosophers are works of the devil and lead (it's said) straight to hell, so think this over well."[56] Nevertheless, he agreed to read Darwin and "send it back in good condition as quickly as possible." Jaich commented extensively on Kautsky's reflections about joining the social democratic cause, and he warned about the voluntaristic, radical thinking that seemed to animate his grandson's letters and future plans. Jaich ended the aforementioned letter with a

warning not to get "caught up too rashly in the Charybdis of politics."
"The way to the light," he added, "is long, thorny, and arduous, and it
can be reached only with patience and stamina, because otherwise the
majority, those who are weak, are left behind."[57]

This advice had a tempering effect on the young Kautsky, as he initially limited his political engagement to what was legal and possible at
the time. He took care not to hurt his own reputation or his family's.
His romantic-revolutionary novel manuscripts, which he wrote (and
his grandfather read) through the mid-1870s, attest to a brash faith in
"communism" as the ultimate goal of humanity. The Paris Commune
was a frequent backdrop for his stories of star-crossed lovers and mis-
taken identities; one couple, crying "Long live freedom!," perish in a
hail of monarchists' bullets, while another flee to England.[58]

The grandfather thought he recognized one of the heroes, Leon
Gagneur ("winner" in French), as Kautsky's alter ego; the character
was not a "communist" but a "democrat" and a "noble soul."[59] Jaich
"fully agreed" with the protagonist's views, insofar as "they were based
upon the noblest humanity." He abhorred "absolutism" as much as his
grandson did, but he also believed that goodness could be achieved
only gradually, without haste or duress: "Absolutism is the fruit of
patriarchal life, which enshrines injustice through fear and violence,
and mocks human dignity. It has become untenable for the future,
no doubt about that, but the laws of organization will not tolerate
a leap forward; what communism wants to achieve in one blow can
be attained only gradually, by advancing the common good."[60] Thus,
both generations agreed that the social injustices of the current system
had become untenable. The grandfather's critique was no less radical
than the grandson's; their disagreement was about ways and means.
Years later, Kautsky asserted in his autobiography that his family home
was a "quite unpolitical house of artists"; no one was "blind or indifferent to the intensity of political life," but all "thinking and striving"
were geared toward art.[61] The correspondence indicates, however, that
adults who were important to Kautsky supported and reinforced his
socially critical thinking as a young man.

Although a source base comparable to the Kautsky family archive does not exist for the other figures, two other mothers evidently assumed a formative role in the lives of their sons. Jaurès's mother, Adélaïde, has been described as a graceful, smart, and strong-willed Catholic woman. Her husband's lack of professional success was a source of frustration, and so she dedicated herself all the more intently to the upbringing and education of their two sons. Her piety must have had a lasting influence on Jean. Although his own worldview eventually shifted away from Catholicism, he could thank his mother for the lifelong spiritual sensitivity that channeled his lost faith in God as an adult into hope for a socialist paradise on earth.[62] Adélaïde gratefully accepted every offer from relatives and teachers to further the education of her offspring, and she urged her sons to attend the best schools.[63] Her liberal mind (her grandfather was a professor of philosophy who adored Voltaire, and her parents were described as extremely tolerant) ensured that the two boys enjoyed a loving, carefree childhood.[64] Jaurès's biographers have emphasized his affinity for rural living, his deep love of nature, and his understanding of agricultural workers' dependence on the whims of weather and the natural rhythm of the seasons.

Unfortunately, no family letters or other personal writings that describe Jaurès's family home have survived. His earliest known correspondence—with teachers, patrons, and close friends—is from 1876.[65] The letters clearly reflect the importance of his early education, as seen in the seventeen-year-old's note of thanks to the director of the school in Paris where he had been granted admission:

> Monsieur . . . I don't have the words to acknowledge your benevolence: Please know, however, that my gratitude corresponds to the greatness of your deed, and that this deed is doubly valuable to me: It allows me to continue my studies, so that the student whom you have accepted can express his gratitude with more than words. Monsieur Deltour [Jaurès's history teacher, to whom he later dedicated his dissertation] promised that I will thank you for your benevolence with my hard work and success. As for myself, I do not dare to promise more than my best intentions. The rest is up to the gods of fate, who bestow

their lasting favor upon no one. On behalf of my father and mother, I thank you again.

Your sincere and grateful student, Jean Jaurès.[66]

The crucial role of schooling in Jaurès's upbringing was echoed in the other families who raised some of the most important founders of Marxism. Only in the Plekhanov home, however, do we see the same mixture of a mother's emotional and intellectual support.

Biographies of Plekhanov stubbornly insist that his "first teacher of revolution was undoubtedly his mother."[67] This is certainly overstated, since Maria was no revolutionary. All his life Plekhanov proudly boasted that his mother was distantly related to Vissarion G. Belinsky, a leading early figure of radical criticism in Russia. In 1918 Plekhanov was even buried next to this supposed distant relative in St. Petersburg's Volkovskoe Cemetery. No reliable evidence, however, proves a family connection. We know that Belinsky was one of Plekhanov's favorite authors and that Plekhanov called him the "sharpest mind" among Russian writers.[68] Belinsky's portrait hung next to images of Engels, Goethe, Chernyshevsky, and Voltaire in his study; Marx was conspicuously absent.

This imagined family heritage notwithstanding, Maria Plekhanova's altruism did influence her son. Her former serfs considered her a benevolent, good-natured woman. As a young daughter in an impoverished noble family, she was apparently mistreated by her stepmother, an experience cited by many Plekhanov biographers as formative to her empathy with the woes of others. Despite her family situation, with the aid of a scholarship she attended the Smolny Institute, a school for aristocratic girls in St. Petersburg. Restrictions on women's learning kept her from pursuing a higher education, so she subsequently worked as a governess and tutor. After marrying Valentin Plekhanov, a widower, she taught his seven children, and eventually her own. She doted on Georgi, her first-born, reading to him often and teaching him to read at a young age.[69]

Plekhanov's biographers suggest that his passion for justice was awakened and nurtured by his mother. In other cases, however, such encouragement could have the opposite effect. Schiller was revered in the Luxemburg household, particularly by Rosa's mother Line, who introduced the young Rosa to Schiller's love for freedom.[70] Yet as an adult Rosa Luxemburg came to despise him—certainly a reaction not only to the German Social Democrats' appropriation of Schiller as the popular voice of the "rebellious inclinations of the working classes" but also to years of maternal inculcation.[71]

Line Luxemburg's enthusiasm for Schiller aside, the mothers of the young protagonists mainly fostered their children's empathetic and critical interest in the world. The fathers, meanwhile, sought to uphold the existing order, which they directly or indirectly served. Their investment in the status quo, which arose from their professional commitments—as civil servant (Struve), army officer (Plekhanov), school inspector (Lenin), or entrepreneur (Adler, Luxemburg)—is not surprising in and of itself. Most bourgeois women of the era did not work outside the home.[72] The fathers, moreover, were often ethnic or social *arrivistes*. Some were second-generation immigrants: Struve's father had German roots; Adler's, Silesian Galician; and Kautsky's, Czech. The fathers of Struve, Lenin, Adler, Luxemburg, and Jaurès were all ambitious, self-made men—another parallel to Hunt's revolutionaries of 1789. They often transferred their ambitions to their children—especially the desire for integration within the educated bourgeoisie or non-Jewish/Russian mainstream society—and sought to give them the best possible education.

Adler's father, Salomon Markus Adler, doubly embodied these ambitions. He came from a family of modest means, became a successful merchant, converted late in life to Christianity, and sought to attain cultural and social respectability for his family within the Viennese bourgeoisie. This ambition permeated all that he did. He was nevertheless bound by his heritage. His daughter-in-law Emma Adler described Salomon as a "handsome man" with "a powerful forehead [that] attested to his great intellectual gifts." She also wrote that his "large, stately figure was hunched over, even in his youth; he believed that this trait was inherited from his forefathers, from the poor Jews who were not allowed to settle down and had to carry their worldly goods or wares on their backs from place to place."[73] In contrast to Victor's father, Emma further recounted, his mother, Johanna, was more interested in the "hereafter than [in] the here and now." She hated Rousseau because, while he gave parenting advice, he left his own children in a foundling home. And she despised Heinrich Heine because of his "venereal disease," which befell only "indecent people," as she put it. Victor's authoritarian father sometimes turned to corporal punishment, though he was receptive to Rousseau's ideas and prioritized his children's education.[74] Victor's younger brother Heinrich described their father as a stern and "spartan" but devoted parent: "His children were to partake in all of the intellectual joys, to study all of the disciplines—in brief, they were to achieve everything that was kept from him and made him suffer. He found joy and consolation in their accomplishments."[75] Pernerstorfer, Victor's schoolmate and sometime political comrade, believed that his friend's father's methods of upbringing exhibited "the common characteristic of his race": "high esteem and regard for knowledge" and the desire "to open all gates of education" for his sons.[76] These sentiments— which may have been particularly pronounced in Jewish families, though by no means unique to them—were incidentally also shared by Luxemburg's father, an enthusiastic supporter of the Polish school system. He moved from rural Zamość to Warsaw, in part, to enhance his children's educational prospects.[77]

Few of Adler's own reminiscences about his father have been preserved. Paternal rigidity notwithstanding, the letters he received from his parents in the late 1870s and early 1880s attest to an affectionate and relatively open relationship.[78] Anecdotes from other sources suggest that traditional state and family hierarchies were strictly upheld in the Adler household, but that Victor sometimes found ways to subvert them. On the occasion of Crown Prince Rudolf's wedding in Vienna in 1883, a fierce argument erupted over whether Victor (who was already married) would commemorate the day as expected, by illuminating the windows of his home; he prevailed in the end, and the windows stayed dark.[79] Around the same time, Salomon Adler signaled that he approved of his son's ambition to become a state-approved factory inspector. When the son—who in the meantime had completed his medical studies—was under consideration for this post, the Interior Ministry made clear that, if offered the job, he would need to refrain from "all political activity." Victor refused to accept these terms, and so Salomon sent in "the reserves": a relative tasked with extracting a promise of political abstinence from his son. In response, Victor reprimanded the emissary "like a schoolboy" and threw him out of the house.[80] Although Victor could generally count on his father's support for his social engagement, this support was strictly contingent upon his pursuit of a respectable career (such as medicine, or Imperial service as a factory inspector).

The fathers who were teachers had a much more direct pedagogical influence: Guesde's father worked as a private school teacher, and Lenin's father was a school inspector. Guesde grew up in the middle of Paris, in a family of modest means. His father, François Joseph Bazile, taught at a small private school in Passy, a poorer and newly annexed district of the metropolis. As a result, according to his biographer, Guesde "did not have to bow his head to the leveling discipline of public schools" and instead enjoyed a liberal, Catholic-influenced upbringing and became one of his father's best students.[81] Ossip Zetkin, who knew him in the 1880s, later wrote that Guesde grew up in the "devout, quiet middle." However, his notes and schoolwork (now held at the International Institute for Social History [IISH] in Amsterdam) attest to the critical and enlightened—although hardly revolutionary—spirit of his father's instruction. Challenging the political order would not have occurred to Bazile, a dutiful *citoyen*. Yet this was exactly what his son had in mind. In his early twenties, Guesde gave up his position as a clerk to become a radical republican journalist. In 1871 he was sentenced to six months in prison for his passionate defense of the Paris Commune, prompting him to flee to exile in Switzerland. Two years later Bazile wrote to President Thiers, the man who was responsible for the Commune's bloody suppression in May 1871, asking that his twenty-seven-year-old son might be allowed to return to France. In the name of a "family in mourning," from which three sons "had fought bravely against the Prussians," Bazile requested forgiveness for a young patriot who came from an "honorable" home. Admittedly, in the heat of the moment Guesde had forgotten all "prudence" toward his fatherland, which was under siege by the Germans, but he had merely condemned the bloodshed during the Commune as a "war between brothers." Upon his return, he would surely dedicate "his life and his pen to the defense and glory" of his fatherland. "I, his father," Bazile concluded, "assure you that he has a generous heart, open, honest, and loyal."[82] The father's appeal for mercy was denied. Guesde's honorable home was thus a site of ambivalent loyalty to the French political system.

The reformist period of the 1860s played a prominent role in the childhood and youth of the three Russian protagonists of this story. The rising bourgeoisie hoped that Tsar Alexander II's plans for reform might gradually overcome the country's autocratic structures and backward mindset. Struve's father, Bernhard, the son of German Danish immigrants, was a hardworking civil servant. He held high-ranking positions under the Siberian governor N. N. Muraviev, and he himself later served as the provincial governor of Perm. Nevertheless, his career was troubled. Struve's biographer Richard Pipes has characterized Bernhard as one of the many "'unlucky' Germans" (a category coined by Dostoyevsky) who sought their fortunes in tsarist Russia with only mixed success. A corruption scandal (which did not directly involve Bernhard but occurred under his lax watch) led to his early retirement in 1871. Supported by a state pension, he accepted work at a publishing house and wrote his own books on the side: a biography of Muraviev, articles about the emancipation of the peasants (a reform he supported with "religious adulation and admiration"), and a memoir of his years in Siberia.[83] His youngest son, Peter, born in 1870, thus grew up in a pensioner's home. The patriotic and Slavophile impulses of Peter's youth and childhood, which he emphasized in his own memoirs, must have been encouraged by his father. Peter's feelings toward the revolutionary movement verged on "hatred," as he put it, since the assassination of Alexander II in March 1881 touched off a period of reaction that strangled the reformist spirit of the 1860s.[84]

Lenin's father, Ilya Ulyanov, like Guesde's father, supported enlightened ideals and dutiful service to the existing order. Biographer Robert Service has described the importance of educational and political idealism within the Ulyanov home, and how closely this was associated with mobility into the respectable provincial elite.[85] The Ulyanovs were less concerned about rising within old Russian hierarchies and much more about bolstering reforms that had been introduced since 1861. However, the social foothold that Ulyanov worked to achieve in Simbirsk (until his sudden death in 1886) was always precarious, not only because he and his family were perceived as newcomers but also, and especially, because of the revolutionary activities of his oldest son, Alexander. Alexander's role in the assassination attempt of 1887 of Alexander III, followed by his imprisonment and execution, effectively ended his parents' social ascent. His political engagement was seen as a devastating lapse, raising questions not only about his upbringing—which was oriented around knowledge, hard work, ambition, and discipline—but also about the head of the family's achievement as a school inspector. And so, from the time he was sixteen years old, Lenin's family was excluded from the social life of their town.[86]

The revolutionary engagement of Alexander Ulyanov, and its significance for Lenin's life path, has only recently received the scholarly attention it deserves. Alexander suffered under the strictures of the Russian school system—first as a schoolboy, then even more so as a university student in the natural sciences in St. Petersburg after 1883.[87] He did have "to bow his head," as one of Guesde's biographers put it, to the rigid discipline of Russian schools, and he responded to the harassment and restrictions with defiance and increasingly radical criticism of the tsarist regime. Unlike his father, Alexander no longer believed that the Russian state could be improved through reform. Rather, in the dispute between moderate revolutionaries and those who were prepared to use violence (including a twenty-something Plekhanov, who had already emigrated), Alexander turned to the side of terror by the mid-1880s. After his group attempted to assassinate the tsar on 1 March 1887 (the sixth anniversary of the murder of Alexander II), he assumed more culpability in the courtroom than was actually necessary. Instead of showing remorse, he expressed his revolutionary views, which censors otherwise prevented from reaching the public.

Alexander was acquainted with Marx's work. Having translated some pieces into Russian himself, he belonged to the first generation of Marx readers in Russia. Lenin admired his brother, who was four years his senior, although because of their different temperaments they were not especially close. As a teenager, he was well aware of his older brother's revolutionary pursuits and even inherited a trunk full of Alexander's subversive books. However, this did not mean that Lenin was already a Marxist revolutionary by the time he finished school. Philip Pomper, Alexander's biographer, has interpreted Lenin's career as a campaign of revenge for his brother's murder,[88] but Service emphasizes that Lenin was impressed less by the substance of his brother's engagement and more by his rigor, decisiveness, and bravado. A family tutor recalled that Lenin was in shock after his brother's execution and that he attempted to console his family, who were searching for answers, by assuring them that Alexander "couldn't act in any other way." Lenin's politicization may have started with learning about the cause for which his brother had sacrificed his life. His cognitive and emotional steadiness recalled his brother's rigid defiance: his secondary school examinations began on 5 May 1887, three days after Alexander was hanged, and he completed four weeks of exams without interruption, receiving the highest grade in all ten subjects.[89]

In none of the other protagonists' biographies are the poles of loyalty and subversion so paradigmatically defined. The social engagement of Lenin's father, and that of his brother, could not be more different. No firsthand testimony from the period immediately after

1886–87 suggests how Lenin responded to this, or how he assessed their significance to the rest of his life. Conspicuously unpolitical letters to his mother after 1893 (certainly attributable to fear of censorship) contain few memories of his childhood or youth; he never mentions the dramatic events surrounding his school examinations.[90] And so we can merely take note of this ambiguous legacy. Perhaps it was a combination of paternal virtues—discipline, hard work, intellectual curiosity—and his brother's passionate, rigorous commitment that can explain Lenin's rise to the pinnacle of power in Russia.

If Lenin's path to becoming a professional revolutionary (and particularly his tenacious eloquence in ideological, political, and military disputes) might be explained by the ambivalent influences of his family legacy, Valentin Plekhanov's methods of military discipline might be the source of his son's authoritarianism, unapproachability, and arrogance. Georgi was respected and feared for these qualities within the socialist movement. His father, a noble officer who had served in the Crimean War, belonged to tsarist Russia's struggling elites. As a landowner, he was beset by constant economic difficulties; complicated inheritance disputes and poor management had shrunk the family estate steadily since the early nineteenth century. The 1856 defeat of the tsar's army in the Crimean War had been especially bitter,[91] but Valentin could at least claim a role in suppressing the Polish uprising of 1863. He left military service soon thereafter, to attend to the precarious state of his family estate. Before his second marriage, he was a widower who provided for seven children on his own. He could be strict, prone to anger and violence, and he did not want his children to rely on servants. He tied five-year-old Georgi, the first child from his second marriage, to a spirited horse and told him to hold on tight. (The boy was said to have passed this and other "tests of courage" without complaint.) Plekhanov's biographers suggest that his father's browbeating hardened him; his "devoted service," as one biographer put it, to the revolutionary movement more than matched his father's commitment to discipline and order.[92]

Military drill seems to have impressed Plekhanov. By the time he was ten, he wanted to attend the military academy in Voronezh, where, despite his father's initial resistance, he remained for eleven years. The father does not seem to have inspired his son intellectually. Rather, it was the mother who encouraged his development. Plekhanov later stylized his military education as the rugged backstory and logical prelude to his revolutionary engagement, without referring to his father, who had served the tsar. As he drilled with his fellow students at the academy, weapon in hand, he dreamed of one day going "into combat for the Russian people."[93]

What sense can we make of these observations about family influences, childhood, and youth? What experiences did the protagonists of this story share, and what fundamental differences distinguished them? How did they reflect on their origins and family influences? And was there a common path of socialization or generational experience that encouraged their turn to Marx?

Only three of the protagonists—Bernstein, Kautsky, and Struve—published memoirs. They described their origins with an exceptionally well-defined sense of the historical setting in which they grew up; their Marxist training was readily apparent. All three placed their births in a historical context that aligned with their respective (ex-)Marxist self-image. Bernstein attributed his modest scholarly ambitions to his family's lower-class status in Berlin: "The conditions in which I grew up as a child and young boy, and also my years as a teenager, were not especially favorable for becoming a scholar."[94] Kautsky, who was born in mid-nineteenth-century Prague, established at the outset of his autobiography in 1921, "The state where I was born no longer exists,"[95] offering a laconic summation of his life-long need for a definitive, big-picture view. The narrative of his five-hundred-page memoir, which he wrote in the 1930s, encompassed two hundred years of family history. Kautsky justified its broad scope with this very need for intellectual and, indeed, ideological coherence. Just as he had spent his life "investigating the facts," as he put it, he had always felt a "compulsion" to merge these facts, including those in his own biography, "into the overall context of my theory, without contradictions."[96]

Struve situated his origins in the turbulence of Russia in the last third of the nineteenth century. Unlike Kautsky, he emphasized the fluctuations in his own intellectual development between Slavophilism, Marxism, and liberalism. The 1880s, "a period of political reaction which followed on the regicidal act of 1 (13) March, 1881, and the utter defeat of the movement known as 'The People's Will,'" shaped the political awareness of his generation with its "patriotic impulses" colored by "Slavophile sympathies," all verging on that aforementioned "hatred for the revolutionary movement."[97]

These three autobiographical portraits show how strongly the Marxist worldview still shaped these men's self-perceptions late in life, though two of them had since become prominent revisionists. Bernstein never renounced Marx entirely, but in his middle years he fundamentally questioned Marx's doctrines and the German Social Democratic Party's positions that derived from them. At the age of thirty, Struve declared himself no longer a Marxist, "on the ground of all my economic studies and all my life experience."[98] These flashbacks demonstrate a tendency toward self-stylization that informs many autobiographies: Bernstein, the simple man; Kautsky, the universal thinker; Struve, the steadfast liberal. Each echoes the pathos of the young Engels, quoted at the beginning of this chapter, aware of his mission as a child of the nineteenth century.

Beyond these self-portraits, some notable similarities in all of the protagonists' upbringings stand out. Each one of their families revealed an affinity for learning and literature, a well-developed sense of curiosity about the world at large, and an interest in both everyday and received knowledge about current affairs. It was frequently the mothers who shaped their children's worldview, while fathers tended to supervise or even provide the children's formal education. The parents' attention to schooling gave all of the protagonists an extraordinarily good start in life, at a time when rates of illiteracy were around 20 percent (Prussia), 40 to 45 percent (France and Austria), and 90 to 95 percent (Russia). Even in western Europe, only around 1.5 percent of young people received a higher education.[99] The authoritarianism of the era influenced all of their biographies, in a variety of ways. Stefan Berger has observed that Otto von Bismarck's antisocialist measures enduringly influenced an entire generation of German Social Democrats.[100] The same can be said of the respective national experiences of the other protagonists: the persecution of the Communards in 1870s France, Habsburg rule in Austria (scorned by Adler as "despotism tempered by incompetence"),[101] and the rollback of reforms under Tsar Alexander III. Finally, six of nine figures in this book came from an immigrant and/or Jewish family, and so they shared, at least for a time, a comparatively marginal social status.

The Jewish heritage of Adler, Bernstein, and Luxemburg deserves special attention, as scholars of socialism and the history of "leftist" engagement have deemed this background particularly relevant. It is widely accepted that the Jewish historical experience predisposed this group for critical, even revolutionary engagement.[102] In fact, some nineteenth-century Jews did become prototypes of a new kind of European intellectualism, driven by emancipation, disengagement from Judaism, and orientation toward the secular world. In the absence of a collective (especially national) framework, they were literally "rebels without a cause." Heine, Marx, and Luxemburg, all Jews, were ostensibly filled with some measure of self-dislike and paradigmatically embodied the revolutionary energies of their era with their radical ideas.[103] Alongside much older stereotypes of Jews as usurers or capitalists, the pairing of Jew and socialist (or "revolutionary") gained momentum at the end of the nineteenth century, not only among antisemites.[104] Today it is undisputed that the history of modern revolutionary thought is a meaningful part of Jewish history, especially the Jewish history of emancipation—and conversely, that the "age of ideologies," as Klaus von Beyme framed it, would have been quite different without the contribution of Jewish intellectuals, ideologues, and revolutionaries.

The writings of two protagonists highlight this connection. At the beginning of his social democratic engagement, Adler called himself a "quite useful colporteur of foreign ideas"—which is to say, socialist ideas. "We Jews are practically predestined for colportage," he wrote in one of his first letters to Kautsky in 1886.[105] His choice of words is significant, as they point to Adler's entanglement with a culture that he not only viewed critically but had just rejected with his conversion to Christianity. A popular encyclopedia of the time defined "colportage" as "peddling wares," especially printed matter. Many poorer Jews were stereotyped as peddlers. Thus, Adler was humbly identifying himself here as a Jew—as an ideological "peddler" and willing "soldier" for social democracy.[106] By claiming an apparent weakness as his strength, his self-description may have also been a subtle defense against a common antisemitic stereotype. For we know from the writings of his wife, Emma, that Adler often felt out of place because of his heritage. While attending school and university, "his Jewishness depressed him," she reported. "He felt no connection to committed Jews; he felt like a German, and he sought German education and knowledge."[107] The adult Adler converted to the Protestant faith, as he wanted his children to assimilate fully—against the explicit will of his wife—so they would be protected against the discrimination that he had experienced in his youth.

Bernstein abandoned Judaism at the age of twenty-seven, but he referred to his Jewish heritage over the course of his life with much greater self-assurance. The idea of the Jew as intermediary and communicator appears in his work. His first long text about Judaism, "On the Duties of Jews in the World War," from 1917, describes Jews as "born pacifists" and "mediators of nations"; their centuries without a homeland had fostered their awareness of what connected and separated people across borders.[108] The humanist core of this outlook was also embedded in Bernstein's most pointed self-description. During the Reichstag debate of 20 June 1913, over whether Jews could participate in military service, he responded to antisemitic attacks in the chamber by saying, "First of all I am human, a German, and then I come from the Jews."[109] He repeatedly emphasized how little attention he paid to "religious differences and those of ancestry" in everyday affairs; all that mattered to him was "pure humanity." He cherished the hope that "as the Jewish Question assumed more intense forms," the Socialist International would prove "the redemptive power" that would "some day bring the Jewish Question to rest." For Bernstein, the capacity of socialism to transcend borders and nations was, not least, a "Jewish utopia."[110]

Luxemburg, by contrast, was disinterested in all things Jewish. She had little patience for either the "Jewish Question" or the "Woman Question." Even so, her biographers insist that these identities were highly relevant to her development. The historian Robert S. Wistrich has speculated about the impression that the Warsaw pogrom of Christmas 1881 must have left on ten-year-old Rosa, asserting—with no particular evidence—that it was "a deeply repressed but profoundly significant if unacknowledged event in Luxemburg's life."[111] Her biographer J. P. Nettl depicts the Luxemburg family as highly assimilated, though also suggests that the generally precarious position of Jews—the "most vulnerable" minority in the Polish part of the tsarist empire—must have inspired her later engagement.[112] In fact, social tensions in the empire did increase following Tsar Alexander II's murder in 1881, and minorities bore the brunt of it. And then there was the Polish nationalist movement, which Luxemburg bitterly opposed her entire life. Thus, her third minority status, as a Pole, had a similarly demobilizing effect.

In her 1966 review of Nettl's biography, Hannah Arendt praises the author for discovering "the Polish-Jewish 'peer group'" that was formative to her political engagement. Arendt even goes so far as to argue that the "ethical code of this peer group would be nearly incomprehensible" without tight-knit Jewish families such as the Luxemburgs. The Jewish minority experience generated a unique family cohesion, an atmosphere of "mutual respect and unconditional trust, a universal humanity and a genuine, almost naïve contempt for social and ethnic distinctions." Herein lay the roots of what Arendt called Luxemburg's "rare self-confidence."[113] The example of Luxemburg suggests that the experience of marginalization and a humanist sense of mission may be related—even if Luxemburg herself did not identify as a Jew, nor did she want to be identified as such. Some authors have noted that her sense of humor was "typically Jewish" and that she sometimes repeated Jewish sayings. However, in other instances her attitude toward Jews and Jewish worlds of experience ranged from cool to hostile.[114] She fought passionately for the liberation of the working class but expressed mere disdain for antisemites and no open sympathy for the victims of their attacks; she viewed the antisemitic pogroms in tsarist Russia as no more than a diversion, or "lightning rod," that ultimately served the ruling classes and distracted from the real issues.[115]

The ambivalent elements of Luxemburg's personality and biography—similar in their way to those of Adler—suggest that the Jewish experience is a distinct context that deserves attention. At the same time, we should be wary of deterministic arguments that uncritically and retrospectively associate certain characteristics (self-assuredness, courage, a sense of justice) or ideals (humanism, equality, solidarity) with a particular life experience. Our group of young and aspiring Marxist intellectuals provides an excellent opportunity to probe certain assumptions. It is striking, for example, that *all* of the protagonists had unshakeable confidence in themselves and in their chance of success and a well-defined sense of their position in history. This observation both demands further explanation and, as I'll argue, is critical to understanding their engagement. It was precisely the connection between theory and practice in Marx's work that spoke to the protagonists' convictions that their own thoughts and actions could change the course of history. These convictions cannot be explained without considering individual psychology and primary socialization, what developmental psychologists like Erik Erikson call an "internal locus of control."[116] Those who have it believe that the key to shaping their own and the world's destiny lies overwhelmingly with themselves—and not with another person, force, or event. Historians, of course, cannot question their protagonists directly and should not resort to armchair psychologizing. Yet historical sources, particularly the protagonists' own writings, provide us with the basis for an informed, qualitative analysis of their self-images and motivations. Some of them, like Adler and Kautsky, experienced nagging self-doubt and uncertainty as young adults, as their letters and diaries reveal. These were ephemeral expressions, however, of basically stable, well-grounded personalities who believed in their own potential—part of the usual emotions that fuel what Erikson called a "healthy" search for identity between "growth and crises."[117]

By not giving in to teleological, circular reasoning, or to the pathos of their own testimonials, a portrait of Marxism's founding generation begins to take shape. What emerges is a group of extraordinarily self-assured, versatile, well-educated, and determined personalities whose intellectual and practical interventions in the course of history gave form and meaning to their lives. This is not to say that their personal development inevitably led to Marxism. Rather, this group biography seeks to identify the reciprocal affinities between the individual personalities and the ideas in Marx's texts. From the time they started out, it was their sometimes synchronous, sometimes asynchronous—but always intertwined—reading and interpretation of Marx's texts that defined them. The formative generational experience lay less in comparable socialization through similar kinds of collective experiences and more in the shared experience of reading and politicization—interrelated processes by which they transformed into a specific "voluntary elite,"[118] as Lutz Niethammer called it. This history of the intellectual and emotional appropriation of Marx, connected but not orchestrated, cannot be fully understood without paying careful attention to each individual biography. The transition from the family home to school, from primary to secondary education, involved the canonical transfer of knowledge, reading for school and for pleasure, and first attempts at making sense of the world. The evidence from these transitions, encompassing the initial chapters of the protagonists' political coming of age, suggests that their politicization began at a remarkably early age.

2

Adolescence and Its Discontents

Emerging Worldviews

The reproach that the natural sciences separate us from God may be true for some individuals; in general, however, it is unfounded. On the contrary, the rigorous investigation of nature leads us to God, giving the wise man who sees the interrelationship of God's creations astonishing insights into the workings of divine providence. This investigation elevates the superficial deification of nature to the height of a worldview, so that all creation seems to attest to the wisdom and love of God, thereby placing the sharpest weapons against superstition, as against disbelief, in our hands. Using them is a demand of our time that cannot be spurned.

—Father Emerich Gabely (Victor Adler's mathematics teacher), 1864

One of the most important cultural processes in nineteenth-century Europe was the rapid spread of literacy.[1] With varying speeds, Europe's monarchs and governments came to accept that educating broad segments of the population was a duty of the state. "The state became a 'school state, and the society, a 'school society,'" as historian Jürgen Osterhammel writes.[2] The rise of state schooling began in Prussia and soon became a worldwide trend. Educating the "masses" became a necessary measure of modernization that promoted industrialization while simultaneously upholding the sociopolitical status quo. Mass schooling was a project that sought to join the latest scientific and scholarly advances with a still theocentric world order, yet it ultimately transformed intellectual and social relations of power. The first tremors of these seminal changes could be felt before they actually took effect. Dr. Emerich Gabely, philosopher and Catholic priest, was Victor Adler's mathematics teacher during his first year at the Gymnasium zu den Schotten, then the most prestigious school for boys in Vienna. In the school's 1864 annual report, Gabely presented his views on nature and the effects of weather. The report was to inform students, parents, and interested members of the public about school events, curricula, and the teachers' intellectual endeavors. Gabely began his contribution by explaining the elite secondary school's philosophy of education. His remarks can be understood as a reassuring, even pugnacious response to already palpable uncertainties. Investigating the laws of nature could only lead to God, Gabely assured; in fact, these laws affirmed the truth of "divine providence." Wise men who investigated nature forged the "sharpest weapons" in the battle against "disbelief." Gabely was firmly convinced that attaining "the height of a worldview" demanded loyalty to God. His scholastic affirmation clearly rejected all secular approaches toward nature, which at the time had become increasingly popular as the sign of a new era.

A rich source base allows us to reconstruct the protagonists' schooling in considerable detail. Heretofore neglected documents such as lecture notes, essays, and other schoolwork still exist for Adler, Kautsky, and Guesde. University-level writing by Adler, Kautsky, Jaurès, and Luxemburg has also been preserved. The relevance of these sources does not lie in any supposed foreshadowing of the protagonists' later convictions; rather, they provide an opportunity to retrace the protagonists' intellectual (and emotional) coming of age—what they learned about the world as children and young adults—*before* their turn toward "scientific socialism." A closer understanding of this appropriation does not in itself provide sufficient explanations, but it is an important precondition for understanding their later intellectual and political engagement.

The protagonists' experiences at school carry enormous explanatory potential. The fifteen-year-old Adler, for example, was once asked to write an essay on the statement "When one sees everything at once, one sees nothing." His response echoed his mathematics teacher's scholasticism, while introducing facets of his own worldview. Adler began his smart essay (to be discussed more in the following pages) with a cheeky observation: "Whoever sees everything at once, sees nothing—thoroughly, that is. Of course he sees, but he doesn't understand."[3] In 1884, as a grown man, he expressed similar skepticism about the comprehensibility of (social) reality in the following words: "Gathering experience is not the same as observing, and the material for an answer is not the answer itself."[4] This example might serve to illustrate that—beyond lived experience, coincidence, and the spirit of the times—we must also consider individual personalities and character traits. Their traces can be found along the protagonists' individual paths of socialization. In some cases, we can engage only in an *external* consideration of psychological factors, by studying autobiographical narratives. In other cases, valuable sources such as diaries, notes, and academic writing offer a glimpse into the *internal* histories of the protagonists' coming of age.

All of the protagonists except Guesde, who was schooled by his father, had to "bow their heads" at state or parochial schools.[5] Many learned to read and write at home and did not begin their formal schooling until they were seven, eight, or even ten years old. Biographers have described Plekhanov's, Jaurès's, and Bernstein's school experiences as positive, while Luxemburg's was extremely negative. Most of the protagonists seem to have been outstanding students; school records for Lenin, Luxemburg, Jaurès, and Guesde reliably document their achievement. In general, all of the protagonists received good, or even outstanding, educations. Three received professional training (Guesde as a trade apprentice, Bernstein as a banker, Plekhanov as a mining engineer), and the other six earned higher

degrees. They studied law (Lenin, Struve), medicine (Adler), economics (Kautsky, Struve, Luxemburg), history (Kautsky, Luxemburg),
philosophy (Kautsky, Jaurès), and the natural sciences (Struve).

Each spoke or read at least four languages. Nearly all of the
protagonists learned Latin, Greek, German, and French in school; many
also knew English and Russian. Lenin spoke Russian, German, and
French, and he could also read English and a little Italian. Luxemburg
spoke Polish, Russian, German, and French fluently, and she had a
good working knowledge of Italian and English. Kautsky's mother
tongue was Czech; he also knew German and French. Plekhanov
read five languages. Furthermore, in the best tradition of the educated bourgeoisie, all shared a love of literature and were impressively
well-read. They either had to read or wanted to read works of literature in their original language. Jaurès spoke German fluently; he
later learned English to read Shakespeare and Hume, and he traveled
to Spain to learn Spanish.[6] Multilingualism was an everyday part of
their childhoods. As adults, many of the protagonists deepened and
expanded their linguistic abilities. Multilingualism was both precondition and expression of their later cosmopolitan lifestyle, which any
doctrinaire notion of "internationalism" cannot adequately describe.[7]
Plekhanov, the eternal exile, had a personal library that epitomized
this multilingual, transnational lifestyle; by the end of his life, his personal library included books in sixteen different languages.[8]

Except for Guesde, who was taught privately by his father in order
to save money, all of the protagonists attended primary and secondary
school. The Bernsteins, who were also not wealthy, saved money so
that their son Eduard could attend a private boys' school in Berlin.
When he was thirteen, he passed an admission test that allowed him
to enroll in the city's prestigious Friedrich-Werdersches Gymnasium.
In his childhood reminiscences, recorded in 1924–25, Bernstein
described himself as an average, sickly student ("no shining light"),
who nevertheless had "a good head for abstract thinking," a gift for
languages, and a very good memory. With some amusement, the
seventy-something Bernstein recalled the tough discipline (including

corporal punishment) that he had endured in Prussian schools, but he nevertheless retained overwhelmingly positive memories of the conscientious, "esteemed teachers" who had kept him in line. Because of his relative laziness, he left school around Easter in 1866 without earning a diploma. For a few months, he became "something of a street kid," until he started his bank apprenticeship that October.[9]

Bernstein's extensive childhood reminiscences, together with Kautsky's *Erinnerungen und Erörterungen*, are the most detailed autobiographical sources about schooling, complementing the authors' earlier personal writings, which offer an "internal" history of the same experience. Self-stylized assertions of intellectual (dis)continuity have undoubtedly shaped these autobiographical accounts, which suggest how two aging Marxists connected their idealized life paths back to their own schooling. Bernstein accomplished this with considerable restraint. Above all, he pointed to the inflammatory effect of history lessons that depicted "catastrophes" like the French Revolution from the perspective of the absolutist state, but he did not assert that this was the origin of his revolutionary idealism. Kautsky's detailed recollections of his childhood and youth, by contrast, were far more narcissistic. He unironically depicted himself as an avid bookworm and know-it-all who sought to make sense of the world; he portrayed himself as always studying his teachers' lessons about the world closely, so that he could then reject them as nonsensical, obsolete, or dangerous.

Kautsky received the most eclectic education of all the protagonists, attending a bizarre succession of institutions as a child and teenager. Between the ages of eight and ten, he was taught by a Calvinist tutor at his parents' home in Prague. He then spent two difficult years at a Catholic seminary in the Austrian town of Melk, and finally he attended a traditional, liberal academic Gymnasium in Vienna, which fostered creative talents such as drawing.[10] His exposure to different ways of looking at the world, and their corresponding images of society and humankind, fostered his early—and ultimately lifelong—search for *the one* worldview that could explain everything coherently.

Without considering this eclectic education, his all-encompassing turn toward the "school" of Marxism cannot be fully understood.

Luxemburg's biographers largely assume—although she herself never stated—that her experiences in a Polish school system constrained by Russification must have set her on the "path of struggle,"[11] a path that led "toward open struggle against all existing authorities."[12] She, too, started school quite late, when she was eight years old. It is not altogether clear whether she first attended the coeducational First Gymnasium in Warsaw before switching to the Second Girl's Gymnasium when she was ten.[13] Both schools were intended for well-to-do Russians. Poles and Jews were generally excluded, but Luxemburg—similar to Jaurès—gained admittance on the basis of her outstanding achievement.[14] She graduated with "excellent" marks in fifteen subjects and "good" marks in four.

Luxemburg was already active in Warsaw's revolutionary underground by 1884–85 and had ties to one of the earliest socialist associations in Poland. The Social Revolutionary Party, or "Proletariat," represented a mixture of western Marxism and Russian Narodnik doctrine inspired by Plekhanov. Since the *Manifesto of the Communist Party* was one of the association's programmatic bases, we can assume that by the time she was a teenager she was already familiar with Marx's core ideas. Her final school years were already shaped by the activism that engaged her practically and theoretically for the rest of her life. She observed some of the realities of underground terrorism, including the arrests, trials, and executions of activists in 1883–84, when she was just thirteen years old, and the murder of "traitors" in the party's own ranks, which (at least in retrospect) she supported.[15] Luxemburg herself never explicitly spoke or wrote about any of this. Her 1897 article about the beginnings of the Polish workers' movement in no way suggests that she had been personally involved. A single exception might be her admiring description of revolutionaries who escaped the waves of arrests in the 1890s by suicide ("journeying to a better place"). She summarized these brutal experiences with one dry sentence: "Prison and premature death were already part of the Polish socialists' trade."[16]

On the one hand, this absence of personal reflection corresponds to her general autobiographical reticence; in her later writings, she rarely mentioned experiences from her childhood or youth. On the other hand, this absence might indicate that she was less intensely involved in the early workers' movement than her biographers have asserted, and that her "path from a rebellious attitude in school to revolutionary socialism" was hardly "prescribed by fate."[17] What we can say for sure, based upon the thin sourcing, is that, even as a young girl, Luxemburg harbored a fascination for risk and danger. She was drawn to adventure and adventurers, and she was convinced that living authentically also meant living dangerously. It seems plausible that the pressure to speak only Russian in school (although Polish was also a subject of instruction) and "narrow-minded measures of repression"[18] in the name of the tsar might have turned her teachers into natural enemies. But there is no evidence that Luxemburg began to combat the injustices of the world while she was still in school, as nearly all of her biographers claim.

Rather, she seems to have been driven chiefly by obstreperousness and a desire to rebel against authority (outside her family). This is supported by her teacher's final evaluation and by the one poem that remains from this period, a send-up of the German kaiser and his "wily fox Bismarck." She should have received her school's gold medal for academic achievement, but she was denied this honor at graduation because of "her oppositional attitude toward authority." She is said to have written the poem in 1884, on the occasion of the second meeting between Wilhelm II (accompanied by Chancellor Otto von Bismarck), Alexander III, and Franz Joseph I, which took place in Warsaw. The meeting was supposed to shore up the troubled "Three Emperors' League," which had been established in 1872. It is unclear whether Luxemburg wrote the poem in Polish (her mother tongue) or German, since her German was still rough when she studied in

Zurich a few years later. This translation is based on the German text
(as recorded by Henriette Roland Holst):

> At last we shall see you, mighty man of the West,
> Should you come to the Saxon Garden, that is,
> Since I don't frequent your courts.
> Your noble relationships mean nothing at all to me.
> But I would like to know what you chatter about.
> You're supposed to know "our" emperor well.
>
> I'm still a foolish lamb when it comes to politics,
> So I don't even want to talk that much with you.
> There's just one thing, dear Wilhelm, I'd like to say:
> Tell your wily fox Bismarck,
> For the sake of Europe, Emperor of the West,
> That he shouldn't ruin his peacemaking pants.[19]

Luxemburg's relatively insubordinate school career was unique
among the protagonists. Lenin was once reprimanded by his father
for making fun of his French teacher—the only example of defiance that his biographers have found.[20] For the biographies of Struve,
Plekhanov, Jaurès, and Adler, no such anecdotes are known—although
they might well exist. In general, the four youths fulfilled their school
requirements in a disciplined way. Lenin and Jaurès, like Luxemburg,
were outstanding students.

Lenin attended the Simbirsk Classical Gymnasium from the age of
nine; he finished school at seventeen, at the top of his class. The curriculum included Russian and Classical languages, writing, mathematics,
geography, and religion. Older students also learned history, German,
and French. Greek and Latin constituted half of the instructional time in
years six to eight. The Ministry of Education in St. Petersburg believed
that Classical values and teachings would promote loyalty toward
the Romanov dynasty. Russian literature was taught only sparingly;
students were required to memorize dozens of poems. Nevertheless,
with his parents' encouragement, Lenin read the era's great novels by
Pushkin, Gogol, and Turgenev, although school authorities considered
these works subversive. Before he discovered Russian literature, his

favorite book was *Uncle Tom's Cabin* by Harriet Beecher Stowe. The young Plekhanov also devoured critical literature, thanks to a liberal teacher at his military academy, but Lenin's headmaster Kerensky was much more restrictive. He sought to "insulate" students from contemporary influences, including the natural sciences, and emphasized discipline, religious morals, and corporal punishment instead.

This strict regime did not hinder Lenin's achievement, as he was disciplined and ambitious by nature. He was considered something of a loner. If provoked by other students, the stocky young man fought back physically. Biographer Robert Service suggests that Lenin's schooling toughened him, introducing him early on to the repressiveness and brutality, but also the small-mindedness, of state authority. Stefan Plaggenborg has described Lenin's revolutionary personality as distinctively "modern," characterized by a direct, unskeptical, and pragmatic way of thinking. The roots of Lenin's modernity thus may lie not only in family upbringing or "western" Marxism, but also in his rigorous school experience.[21] Even Lenin's contemporaries noticed that his later arguments as an attorney were sometimes written in the style of a show trial, as stigmatizing indictments. Hence, the style of thinking and learning that Lenin acquired at school and university was no less important than the curriculum itself.

As we know, Lenin passed his final school exams with flying colors, even though these took place during the scandal surrounding his brother and the assassination attempt on the tsar. Lenin seems to have emerged from school as a tenacious young man, with the best possible preparation for his further intellectual and professional development. Had Alexander Ulyanov not brought disrepute upon the entire family as a terrorist, the adult Lenin would have automatically risen into the nobility, following in his father's footsteps. Despite this setback, an adequate civil career was still possible for Lenin in 1887. After completing his studies, he practiced law in Kazan and then in St. Petersburg. Soon he made his first contacts in the revolutionary underground and tangled for the first time with the tsarist police state.

Struve was the same age as Lenin, but his school career was less consistent because of his father's professional struggles. Struve's formal education began during his family's three years in Stuttgart, where he started primary school at the age of nine. He learned to speak German fluently, although little else is known about him at this time. In 1882 the family moved to St. Petersburg, where he attended the Third Gymnasium, considered the city's best secondary school.[22] Drawing upon Struve's eloquent autobiographical sketch, Richard Pipes writes that the young man burned with "moral and intellectual fire," always in "inner dialogue" with himself. Struve thus appears as a disciple of Immanuel Kant, who famously said that "thinking is speaking with oneself."[23] According to Struve's recollections, written fifty years later, he was a committed liberal and advocate of freedom by the age of fifteen, long before he had ever heard the word "socialism."[24] His self-described intellectual socialization was oriented around formative readings (Aksakov, Saltykov-Shchedrin, and Dostoyevsky) and conversations with his family about political events. He hardly mentioned school. His acquisition of knowledge, in the broadest sense, was apparently self-evident. He emphasized that his worldview was grounded on the study of facts and his own observations, not just "bookish influences."[25] Learning came easily to him. As a teenager he already read scholarly journals and newspapers, participated in the intellectual life of St. Petersburg, attended public dissertation defenses and the funerals of important thinkers, and pored through his brother's university notes.[26]

There is no doubt that these reminiscences are highly stylized. Even so, it is important to acknowledge the intellectual and cultural climate of the time. Struve grew up literally at the center of his country's debates about the essence, fate, and future of the Russian people and state.[27] By reading newspapers and conversing with others, by attending lectures about Shakespeare in St. Petersburg's literary clubs, he participated much more directly than either Lenin or Plekhanov in the Russian intelligentsia's search for a "national soul." Struve did not see himself and his family as part of a "narrow" revolutionary intelligentsia but rather as members of "ordinary educated society, which was already fairly developed."[28] In fact, this is an apt description. As a provincial governor, and in the course of his work for a St. Petersburg publishing house, his father frequently entertained prominent guests—including Alexandre Dumas (in 1866, before Struve was born) and Ivan Aksakov (in 1882, to the delight of the twelve-year-old and his mother).[29]

Years later, Struve reminisced about these gatherings in his family home, and about important cultural (and thus, in Russia, also political) events like the dedication of the Pushkin monument in 1880 and the funerals of Dostoyevsky and Saltykov-Shchedrin in 1881 and 1889, respectively. His youthful experiences indicate the extraordinary breadth and depth of his education, largely outside his formal schooling. While we should be skeptical of the ideal-typical biography of an (ultimately) steadfast liberal that he himself and, among others, his most eminent biographer Pipes have composed, these experiences undoubtedly fostered his development into a critical and engaged observer of his time.

Struve began his university studies in zoology in 1889. He switched to law in 1890, and in 1894 he published a book on Russia's economic development that attracted considerable attention.[30] During these years, Struve's institutional education was not decisive. Instead, his worldview took shape elsewhere: in his landlady's intellectual circle, on the pages of newspapers, on travels to Germany and Switzerland, and in a discussion group that he formed to study the works of Marx and other socialists that he brought back from these trips.

Plekhanov, the third Russian protagonist, had already spent ten years in exile by 1890, and his writings were among the subversive classics that Struve's reading group "greedily swallowed."[31] Against the will of his father, Plekhanov had enrolled in the Voronezh military academy in 1866, when he was ten years old. The reforms of War Minister Dimitri A. Miliutin in the 1860s allowed a liberal breeze to waft through this boys' school. Plekhanov especially profited from the relatively progressive philosophy of two teachers: the historian Mikhail

F. de-Pulé and educational theorist Nikolai F. Bunakov. Plekhanov was a very good student in religion, French, geography, and history, although he was weaker in the natural sciences. Bunakov was an advocate of Pestalozzi's and Diesterweg's educational reforms; he was involved in national education policy and wrote his own textbooks. He believed that students learned by listening and by repeating facts, and that the role of the teacher was to help students understand their own intellectual capabilities.[32]

The educational program of these two teachers departed radically from the authoritarian methods of Plekhanov's father. Despite only average grades, Plekhanov thrived at school. His passion for reading and writing, and eventually his brilliant rhetorical talent, can be attributed to his schooling and good relationship with these few controversial teachers. Leo Tolstoy engaged closely with Bunakov's principles and criticized them sharply in his own pedagogical texts, arguing that teachers should not merely reinforce what students already knew. He sought a broader discussion about "what to teach and how" and a greater understanding of the (Russian) "masses" and their traditional ways of learning.[33] Tolstoy was well ahead of his time with this enlightened criticism. Still, the "German ideas" that Bunakov and other Russian reformers had espoused since the 1860s were at the time considered thoroughly progressive—and they were, to a certain extent. Bunakov's faith in the productive power of hard work and discipline, coupled with his encouragement of self-sufficiency and personal interests, was evident in the praise that his famous student Plekhanov later bestowed: "[Bunakov] instilled in me a love of literature, and he taught me to speak and write correctly, definitely, clearly, and simply."[34] It was presumably Bunakov who introduced the young Plekhanov to great works of contemporary Russian literature by Belinsky, Chernyshevsky, and Dobroliubov.[35]

Despite his interest in literature and poor marks for discipline, the seventeen-year-old Plekhanov decided to continue his military education at the academy in St. Petersburg. When asked, however, whether as a soldier he would serve the tsar or the Russian people, he felt conflicted, and he withdrew from the academy after one semester. The military education that he did complete enduringly shaped his personality. The spartan upbringing by his father, a former military officer, was also formative. Contemporaries described Plekhanov as a cool, disciplined, and hardworking thinker, condescending toward others and vituperative toward his opponents. His father, school, and military drill all played a role in shaping his character. His perceptive talents were informed not only by reading but also by his everyday experiences and encounters with others.

Like most of the other protagonists, Plekhanov as a teenager was already convinced of his own abilities. He felt a certain superiority, and he believed that his preoccupation and dissatisfaction with social conditions was self-evident. Like the others, upon leaving school he felt ready and determined to have his say—an existential attitude of protest that Albert Camus has described in terms of "rebellion." According to Camus, rebellion is founded on "the confused conviction of an absolute right which, in the rebel's mind, is more precisely the impression that he 'has the right'" not only to defend himself but also to make demands.[36] The protagonists' personal writings suggest that by the time they finished school, at the latest, they were convinced that the world was theirs for the taking. Their young lives were characterized by a more or less diffuse state of anguish, by the (stereo)typical adolescent need be true to *one* cause, and by a sometimes joyful and ambitious, sometimes joyless and strained dedication to the bourgeois ideal of self-improvement.[37]

This is illustrated by autobiographical anecdotes and the protagonists' personal writings. Plekhanov, for example, recalled an episode that illustrates the connection between his personal ideals and broader social and political questions, foreshadowing his eventual decision to break off his military career. During a drill in his last year at the academy, a fellow student grasped the barrel of his gun and whispered to Plekhanov, "Oh, if I could only take this weapon and go into combat for the Russian people!" Plekhanov later recalled, "[T]hese words, spoken furtively within a few paces of a strict military official, were deeply engraved on my memory."[38] A second example is Kautsky's report to his mother about his school graduation ceremony in July 1871. The sixteen-year-old scorned the speeches of loyalty to the kaiser and the pledges made by the "youth of our dynasty." In an act of open rebellion, most students left the hall before the end of the national anthem—although Kautsky did not reveal to his mother whether he himself was among the rebels.[39]

It is difficult to say whether the silent protest in such anecdotes surpassed the usual rebelliousness of young adults. Youth became a topic of scholarly inquiry at the end of the nineteenth century, and this life stage simultaneously became instrumentalized as a "myth" or "political slogan." As a result of social changes that accompanied industrialization, young adults across Europe were increasingly seen as a potentially vulnerable or else rebellious group.[40] Thomas Nipperdey has suggested that the emotional culture of the German-language youth movement was an exceptional phenomenon. He nevertheless points to aspects of everyday life that were shared by "bourgeois youth relieved of work" (a group which, broadly speaking, included all of the protagonists) across Europe: turning toward abstract reality in response to the decline of traditional (rural and family) community; "growing reflexiveness" and emotional fragility; idealization of role models outside home and school; and a "tendency toward the absolute," expressed in devotion to *one* cause, *one* friend, and *one* composer, poet, or philosopher.[41]

The school-age Jaurès and Adler developed a subtler form of this heartfelt desire to have a say. Alongside Luxemburg and Lenin, Jaurès was the third highly gifted student. Scholarships financed his entire secondary and higher education. After a few years at a small private school run by a priest, he transferred to the Collège de Castres with his first scholarship in 1869. He remained for seven years, earning recognition from teachers and students for his outstanding achievement. He was remembered as a gifted speaker, a curious and friendly bookworm. Hardly any of his own writings from this period survive. The few descriptions of him emphasize his remarkable talents and introverted character. A typical recollection describes Jaurès as a "little boy of nine, fair, plump, lively, and bright [who] had a passion for school; he loved to learn as much as to eat, and he digested the fundamentals of Latin as easily as roast goose."[42]

Jaurès felt most at home in the countryside, and he is the only school-age protagonist whose interest in the world was largely directed inward. He especially loved ancient literature, philosophy, and history, and he remained an unpolitical young man well into his university career. The eleven-year-old Jaurès apparently took no note of the Franco-Prussian War or Paris Commune—events that Kautsky, Adler, Guesde, and Bernstein recalled (from various perspectives) as significant to their childhood. Jaurès was said to have felt mild patriotic sympathy for France's defeat, but he had no recollection of the popular uprising in Paris.[43] This apparent lack of interest in the world was, of course, normal for a child. Kautsky's and Bernstein's (contemporary) remarks about the events of 1870–71 were unusual, and Adler and Guesde observed, or personally experienced, the war and Commune as young adults.

In the meantime, religious and philosophical questions commanded Jaurès's attention. Both in primary school and at the Collège in Castres, he was taught by open-minded, liberal teachers who introduced him to the history of religion and fundamental moral questions of human existence in an undogmatic way.[44] He won his school's top prizes for achievement in religion class.[45] His doctoral thesis, "The Reality of the Sensible World," was the culmination of years of reflection, begun while he was still a schoolboy, about metaphysical and evolutionary views of the world.[46] Neither the deep faith of his mother nor his well-intentioned Catholic schooling bound Jaurès to Christianity. In 1876 he transferred first to the Lycée Sainte-Barbe, and shortly thereafter to the renowned Lycée Louis-le-Grand in Paris, where he studied for two more years. He gradually lost his faith in God, but not his religious ideals—or, as he himself put it, his faith in the "great spirit," the truth and preciousness of creation, and the power of "great religious feelings."[47]

The migraine headaches that plagued Jaurès for the rest of his life began around this time, as he immersed himself in his studies and expanded his worldview in Paris. He missed the countryside and began to write poetry.[48] His first known poem is from February 1878. Written in the style of a ballad, it depicts the experiences of a *guignol*, a traditional French marionette character, who moves from the countryside to the city. Adopting the shifting perspective of *le guignol provincial* and *le guignol parisien*, the nineteen-year-old poet showed that he was at once a light-hearted and serious, witty and eloquent, thinker. He conveyed distinctions between "good" and "bad," "then" and "now" with vivid precision.[49] This is a selection from the poem's thirty-four stanzas:

The Country Guignol and the Parisian Guignol[50]

If, good sirs, we could create a philosophy
I would develop a deep system:
The thing is, it's not a detail in life,
Not a fact, that brings home its lesson.

An example to illuminate my thinking.
Please you, it involves one tale in two scenes.
And because I'm the one telling the story
Naturally I get to be its hero.

In the first scene, I am in the Corbières,
In a little village with grayish houses
Where in August warm baths with waters reputed to be healing
Give new life to three hundred souls.
[…]
But to ward off a little the boredom that devours us all,
We have a Guignol, truly original,
From his ancient heritage recalled once again,
Polichinelle, speaking in a Provencale patois.
[…]
Now en route for the capital
We follow a different story,
Prepare yourselves for the École Normale
And with it the Parisian Guignol.
[…]

Here is my second scene, near the little theatre
With its bright flags, where I open my eyes.
Good heavens! This Guignol is not like that poor plaster one!
He is more distinguished-looking, and in Parisian style!
[. . .]
With this one everything is new. The old Polichinelle
Formerly so chatty and now so mute,
Who could but dance at the end of a string
And show off the gold in his costume to the public.
[. . .]
Now in his place is one whose vulgar tone
Makes mockery of everything, of his father and the law;
And has nothing to show other than ordinary jokes
That reflect that often banal Parisian wit.

Philosophizing and writing poetry was as much a part of the nineteen-year-old Jaurès's everyday milieu as studying diligently. He lived at his Parisian lycée with a group of fellow students who, with their own gifts and talents, sought admission to the École Normale Superieure: "Some [of the students] here prefer literature; some, history; and others, philosophy. We talk about our lessons, our ideas, our passions, our discoveries, our system (yes, 19-year-olds nowadays have a system)," he wrote in February 1878 to Jean Julien, a friend back home. Jaurès participated enthusiastically in "political, literary, cultural life, which always has an echo in the Parisian schools; on free Sundays, we wander through galleries, museums, we stream into theaters, matinees, and soirees."[51] At the same time, this exciting metropolitan world overwhelmed and exhausted him; he complained that the multitude of distractions created an "unhealthy irritation" in his brain. He memorably marked the caesura of his move to this jarring new world with the lyrical figure of the *guignol parisien*.[52]

Parisian life was not merely a distraction, however. Jaurès's academic achievements opened the door to the École Normale Superieure. In the early summer of 1878, he participated in a public speaking competition called the *concours général*, which was part of his final exams. Jaurès selected an anecdote from the sixteenth century for his speech: the destitute scholar Jacques Amyot received a generous grant from the king to support his translation of ancient Greek texts. Although the king's motive was unknown, the young Jaurès invented a story that attributed the king's beneficence to the intervention of a local bishop. In Jaurès's telling, the bishop delivered an impassioned speech about the scholar's extraordinary talents and financial need, simultaneously underscoring the contemporary significance of Classical texts and the value of scholarship in general. The king was duly persuaded and became Amyot's benefactor.[53]

Jaurès won first prize with a speech that undoubtedly reflected aspects of his own biography. He had been "discovered" by his history teacher Nicolas-Félix Deltour, to whom he later dedicated his dissertation. Jaurès's entire education was publicly funded. He understood this support not as charity but rather as an investment in the *citoyen* and national welfare. The importance of state schooling became one of Jaurès's lifelong convictions. He not only believed that all children had the right to a decent public education; he also considered learning a patriotic duty. So his speech about the bishop and destitute scholar was an early sign of his fundamentally affirmative relationship to state authority. This was a significant departure from the subversive and critical lessons that the others—especially Luxemburg, Lenin, and Plekhanov—drew from their own schooling. Jaurès saw his education as a continuous process of self-improvement, and he believed, *mutatis mutandis*, that state and society developed through a similar process of learning, rethinking, and reform, which eventually led to fundamental social change. He sometimes described these changes as revolutionary, although he understood "revolution" as a wide-ranging process, not necessarily as violent upheaval. We should be cautious, however, with such assumptions about the roots of his evolutionary thinking. Jaurès was by no means thoroughly politicized when he began to study philosophy at the École Normale in 1878.

Adler is the last of the students in this group. Like Jaurès, he came to Marxism relatively late. While Jaurès arrived at Marx through philosophy, Adler's path led through nationalism. Scholars have heretofore paid remarkably little attention to Adler's childhood, youth, and education, hardly exploring the rich testimonials from this period. According to his wife's narrative, Adler learned only the basics in his strict family home before he started school at the age of ten in 1863. His father had "high esteem and regard for knowledge" and sought "to open all gates of education" for his sons,[54] but at first the family had little money for books or cultural activities. Adler's parents initially acquired popular editions of classic literature on credit from traveling salesmen. Excursions were sometimes canceled at the last minute, to teach the children that life was no walk in the park. The paint set they received from an aunt was a precious, rare gift.[55]

As the scion of a family of growing means, between 1863 and 1870 Adler attended the prestigious Gymnasium zu den Schotten in Vienna. Its annual report was the source of the treatise on the relationship between science and God's creation, cited at the beginning of this chapter. Like Bernstein and Luxemburg, Adler was in a minority at his school. In his first year, there were seven "Israelites" among the 340 schoolboys. As a "paying" student, he also belonged to a (larger) minority: the annual report listed 185 "free" students, 53 scholarship recipients, and 155 "paying" students.[56]

When he was thirteen, Adler befriended Engelbert Pernerstorfer, a fellow student two years his senior; they later bonded over politics as well. Pernerstorfer not only admired his friend but also wrote one of the few realistic reminiscences about Adler's school years. This is how Pernerstorfer described their experiences at the Gymnasium:

> A cohesive, vibrant, and lived spirit of community prevailed in our class. We were not an easy people to govern. We banded together firmly against our professors. . . . So how did Victor Adler behave in school? Let it merely be said: He was no angel. As intellectually active as he was, and as much as he liked to exercise his intellect, he frequently responded to teachers' demands with gentle but staunch resistance. . . . But he still made good progress, rose from class to class, and earned recognition. . . . No one would have expected that the boy Victor Adler would become an outstanding speaker. Above all, a speech impediment stood in his way. It was not an outright stutter, but his tongue had some difficulty with certain consonants or consonant combinations, especially at

the beginning of words. This impediment compelled him early on to concentrate on his thoughts and speech. Instead of using a word that tripped up his tongue because of its opening sound, he attempted to help himself by substituting another with the same meaning—an intellectual exercise that was no doubt beneficial.[57]

The boys developed a lively interest in literature outside school. Before long, between six and ten of their fellow students gathered on Sundays at the Adlers' country house. His mother fed them, and his father saw that they were left undisturbed. They were free to dedicate themselves, in a "healthy and voracious" way, to their "own creations" and "good German literature."[58] The boys established a literary club and occasionally organized "musical-declamatory academies"—cultural evenings that might feature recitations of Ludwig Uhland's poetry, performances of Sarastro's aria "In diesen heil'gen Hallen" from *The Magic Flute* or short pieces by Schubert and Mendelssohn, or readings of Adelbert von Chamisso's *Prophecies of Nostradamus for the Year 2000*.[59] These gatherings were infused with revolutionary pathos and the nationalism they imbibed at school, typical of the zeitgeist among bourgeois youths.[60] The literary club became more political as the boys moved from Gymnasium to university. In 1870 they reinvented the club as the Association for Clarifying and Establishing Our Views on the Social Question. Adler's engagement and his intellectual contributions to the association, to be discussed in detail below, provide the prehistory of his later social democratic engagement.[61]

Much of Pernerstorfer's portrait appears to be accurate. Adler was not an outstanding student, but he harbored a lively interest in the literary and social questions of the day. Rather than shaming or unsettling him, his speech impediment seemed to strengthen his will and sharpen his tongue. Being forced to grapple with language and his own self-expression must have fostered his later formidable talent for speech and debate. Pernerstorfer's description of Adler's "staunch resistance" against his teachers, however, is surely exaggerated. Although his conduct was initially deemed "unsatisfactory," his later grades ranged from "commendable" to "very commendable." At least according to his school records, he was not a rebel. After an initial reprimand, his grades for diligence and attentiveness were "adequate," "sufficient," or "commendable."[62]

The school essays that Adler was assigned to write in the fifth grade and after are particularly noteworthy; essay topics are listed in the school's annual reports. He wrote about the laws of history, human fortune, and questions of justice—although they do not necessarily reflect Adler's *actual* thoughts, as schoolwork had to meet certain expectations and adhere to the accepted boundaries of discourse. Essay topics included the elaboration of proverbs, maxims, and quotations by great thinkers; critical summaries of literary works; translations; and other kinds of descriptive assignments. This is a selection from 1866–67:

Fifth grade.
A useless life is an early death. Explain the sentence and relate to the requirements for students at the beginning of the school year.
How should a student demonstrate his love of country [*Vaterlandsliebe*]?
The winter evening. A description.
"Whoever sees everything, sees nothing." Explain this sentence and illustrate with real-life examples.

Seventh grade.
Good books are the best company.
Drawing upon examples from ancient history, show how impiety and depravity ruin states and peoples.
Explain the fate of Orestes before he is saved, according to Goethe's *Iphigenia.*
Whoever does not go forward, falls back.

Eighth grade.
On the value of money.
On Schiller's words: If you cannot please everyone with your deeds and your art, do right by a few; to please many is bad.

On the impact of external circumstances on the intellectual
formation of man.[63]

For all of its authoritarian and parochial tendencies, this list shows
a broad spectrum of efforts to form character and communicate
values. The Gymnasium zu den Schotten was run entirely by priests.
Fundamental questions about coexistence and reflections about
human nature were as important to the school's curriculum as the
study of literature and language, as was the cultivation of loyal subjects
who were pious, patriotic, and historically aware. This mixture of
motivations allowed for a broad education that was not entirely free of
dogma, but not strictly confined by it, either. Neither the teachers nor
the system, state nor kaiser, were the enemy; *Vaterlandsliebe* was among
the dogmas that the boys genuinely embraced. Not coincidentally,
Adler and Pernerstorfer began their later political careers among the
nationalist supporters of Georg von Schönerer, and Adler did not join
the Austrian Social Democratic Party until his early thirties.

The only truly rebellious act (that we know of) from Adler's school
days was his protest against an imaginative student initiative to elect
class leaders according to Roman example. Pernerstorfer led the initiative, which was apparently inspired by the students' history lessons.
The three Jewish students in the class were supposed to elect their
own "tribune," a provision that thirteen-year-old Victor protested
with the following flier:

> Colleagues!
> Today the class received a diktat that the three Jews should elect their
> own "tribune." A diktat, because the decision wasn't made by the class,
> but simply announced by Pernerstorfer as law. He said that it "had to"
> happen, but I would certainly like to hear the reasons why it "had
> to." I am convinced that had Pernerstorfer thought more carefully, he
> would not have done this. Because I believe that he is bright enough
> to see his colleagues not as Jews and Christians, but rather as colleagues.
> But instead it looks as if he views the Jews as a special corporation.
> The outward appearance of his gesture does seem very tolerant. But
> we don't want toleration—or, in German, *Duldung*! If there is a dif-
> ference between Jewish and Christian colleagues, then elect a Jewish

and a Christian tribune! ~~Do the Jews have different interests than the Christians in this matter?~~ If not, then the Jews have a privilege [*Vorrecht*]. What happens then to the equality of all colleagues? If so, then go ahead and build a Jewish ghetto in our school, and block the Jews from the Christians with a wall!

A Jew who wants justice [*Recht*] but not privilege.

Victor Adler.[64]

After the festivities surrounding Adler's sixtieth birthday in 1912, the anecdote became a miracle story that was told again and again. Adler was by this point the undisputed hero of Austrian social democracy, and the flier from the hand of his thirteen-year-old self became a kind of "relic."[65] A critical analysis of this indeed remarkable document, however, has not been undertaken. Likewise, no one has noted that its second half is not entirely logical, or, at least, is imprecisely formulated. Adler probably meant that the Jews would enjoy a special privilege if they could elect their own tribune, despite having the same interests as Christians. However, if one presumed that Christians and Jews were different and thus had different interests, this would amount to the usual discrimination against Jews and one could "go ahead and build a Jewish ghetto."

In other respects, too, previous interpretations have not considered the content of this document carefully enough. Beyond the young author's rejection of any kind of special status for the Jews, and the absolute desire for assimilation that was embedded in his protest, this text is much more than Adler's "first confrontation with the Jewish problem"; it reveals far more than his "lifelong effort at assimilation and rejection of such German 'tolerance,'"[66] and it does not merely document his unease with his own heritage.[67] Above all, the text shows an instinctive sense of justice that is not corrupted by Adler's own interests, as well as a readiness to seek alternatives and expedients. His words demonstrate empathy for the viewpoint of others, a willingness to understand their perspective and offer friendly criticism. Instead of dressing down Pernerstorfer (whom he had not yet closely befriended) as an antisemite hiding behind philosemitism, Adler proceeds from the assumption that Pernerstorfer truly meant well but had not thought carefully enough about the consequences and actual meaning of his suggestion. Finally, the text attests to the formidable self-assurance (shared by the other protagonists) that allowed a thirteen-year-old stutterer, who was hardly at the top of his class, to formulate and present such a courageous argument before his fellow students. Adler, too, was a quick-witted teenager who was interested in the complex interpersonal and political questions of his time.

"We were for freedom," Pernerstorfer recalled about his last years at the Gymnasium with Adler. "We were intoxicated by the French Revolution."[68] In mid-nineteenth-century Prussia, Friedrich Engels identified with the hero Siegfried and admired almost-revolutionary poets like Karl Immermann; in his appeal to the "sons of the century," Engels articulated the pathos of youth. In 1860s Vienna, the boys at the Gymnasium zu den Schotten were similarly enthusiastic about their "poets of freedom," especially Ferdinand Freiligrath. Freiligrath provided the poetic backdrop for the socialist-inspired revolutions of 1848—and for the next act in the German national drama, which exploded into the Austro-Prussian War in 1866, leading to bitter defeat for the Habsburg Monarchy. Freiligrath was forced to emigrate in 1849, and he subsequently became a London businessman who wrote poetry on the side. When a fundraising campaign for Freiligrath's return to Germany was initiated in 1868, Adler and his fellow students in Vienna participated eagerly. After their headmaster banned the initiative, the boys continued their work in secret under the motto "Freili grad!" (a pun on the poet's name, also meaning "sure enough" or "more than ever"!).[69] Adler's archival papers include a "revolutionary song" inspired by Freiligrath that was dedicated to Adler by a friend. It imitates the style and text of Freiligrath's revolutionary songs, lauding the "new, all-out" revolution instead of the "old" 1848:

Arise! Arise! A song that we know well!
Arise, arise. A song clear as a bell.
Sing it out as the start of revolution!
To the new revolution!

The new one whose swords and lances will break the very
   last chain—
Don't sing to the old, or to the half-way!
For us, just the new, just the new, just all-out revolution!
The new rebellion. All-out rebellion.
March! March! March! March!
If to death, if to death!
And the flag we wave is red. . . .[70]

The carefree, almost playful, references to "revolution" recall the term's popularity and diverse usage at this time. It was everywhere in political discourse. Responding to the first workers' demonstrations in Vienna, the Austrian interior minister complained, "[W]hat you are starting is revolution."[71] Adler and his friends had gotten to know the idea of "revolution" and its various connotations early on. Revolution sounded exotic and utopian, but it was also a historical event with concrete significance for the present. And it had a Romantic flair. Rhyming "death" with "red" (in German, *Tod* and *roth*) was part of the repertoire of bourgeois youth culture. Composing insurrectionary verses was not necessarily the first step toward joining the revolutionary workers' movement, but it underscores the highly charged political climate, stretched between the poles of extreme reaction and revolution, all over Europe.

The poem from Adler's friend raises another point that is essential for understanding the initial appeal of Marx's ideas—namely, that Marxism also drew upon the Romantic tradition. Leszek Kolakowski identifies Romanticism as one of Marxism's three motifs, alongside a "Faustian-Promethean" motif and the motif of the "rationalist, determinist Enlightenment." From this perspective, Marx's theory of alienation and his belief in a future "in which no middle term intervened between the individual and the community" can be seen as an extension of the Romantic criticism of liberal philosophy. Marx countered the retrospective utopia of conservative Romantics with a prospective utopia of human emancipation.[72] Rüdiger Safranski, in his study of Romanticism as a "German affair," also points to the roots of Marx's thinking in German philosophy (the "holy family"). Romantic elements can thus be found not only on the right of the political spectrum but also on the left; they can at least partially explain the attractive power of the great ideologies they inspired.[73]

The potentially sinister connection between literary Romanticism and romanticized—or romanticizing—politics is a recurrent characteristic of the developing worldviews of the first Marxists. A glance at their literary heroes shows how familiar they were with the Romantic movement. Works by Heine, Schlegel, Uhland, Chamisso, Wagner, de Staël, Hugo, Pushkin, Gogol, and Mickiewicz make frequent appearances in their early writings. Of course, a hallmark of Romanticism is that neither its essence nor its adherents can be neatly classified or defined. The aforementioned poets and artists have been associated not only with Romanticism but also with movements such as Realism (Chamisso, Gogol) and Classicism (Pushkin).

Thinking about the political temperament of the first Marxist intellectuals—and the "intellectual climate"[74] of their engagement—leads us to consider the extent of the relationship between Romanticism and radicalism. "Orthodox" or "radical" Marxists (Luxemburg, Kautsky, Guesde, but not Lenin) had a well-defined sense of the Romantic and an affinity for "romanticizing." The poet Novalis, who formatively influenced the genre, explained "romanticizing" in this way: "In lending a higher sense to something commonplace, a mysterious appearance to something usual, an unknown value to something known, an infinite appearance to something finite, I romanticize it."[75] These thought patterns permeated (not just) early Marxism. Marxists regarded the misery of those who were exploited with empathetic distance. "The proletariat" was a concrete, but also transcendent, historical force; history and its patterns were a cipher to be solved by humans; and the socialist society of the future would be the eternal, final stage of humanity. More than a few early Marxists lent complex historical processes a "magical" dimension, as when Luxemburg summarized Polish industrialization (the topic of her dissertation in economics): "As though by the waving of a magic wand, the whole of Poland's life, interior and exterior, changed in short order to the point of becoming unrecognizable." In this eulogy for her favorite poet Mickiewicz, Romantic premodernity and capitalist modernity, powerful opposites, collided with fateful consequences.[76] In sum, all three elements of Novalis's "romanticizing" approach to the world—idealization, mystification, and prophecy—can be found in the Marxist worldview.

Developmental psychologists describe the transition from childhood to youth—from primary socialization at home to secondary socialization at school—as a process of awakening. This awakening is accompanied by the development of ego identity and social roles, as well as an expanding horizon of interests and a broader outlook on the world. Sooner or later, a child in this life stage experiences disenchantment for the first time. She learns that the words spoken by parents to console young children—"Everything's going to be all right"—are not true: nothing in the world is all right, or at least many things are not.[77] This loss of basic trust is part of healthy child development; ideally, it leads to the self-confidence to explore the outside world. A sense of conscience, autonomy, industry (feeling useful), initiative, and identity all develop in this process.[78] Discovering the social world beyond the family home, which usually occurs through the prism of school, serves as a kind of initiation to young adulthood.

Beyond a child's natural curiosity, school "feeds" this discovery with ideas, tasks, norms, and intellectual orientation. Children occupy themselves with questions that have been deemed relevant by the state. This compulsory occupation has left us with some striking historical sources, which show not only what and how the protagonists learned but also how they wrote within a prescribed framework (and perhaps even what they thought). Socialization at school allows us to reconstruct the symbolic repertoire that the protagonists drew from as students, the experiences and discursive practices that shaped them, and the horizon of expectations that began to orient their lives. This was particularly evident in their affection for revolutionary Romanticism, and in their understanding of history.

The "Age of Revolution," which had shaped the decades between 1789 and 1848, cast long shadows—political, social, and semantic.[79] From the perspective of conceptual history, Reinhart Koselleck describes the dynamic, "modern" energy that infused the concept of revolution following the French Revolution. On the one hand, "revolution" was a descriptive term for upheavals already experienced, a "title that legitimated change." On the other, it was a forward-looking concept that placed "salvation" within a "politically attainable and historically feasible future."[80] This dual meaning was reflected in the young protagonists' writings in a variety of ways. Given the prominence that revolutionary history and ideas assumed at the time, it seems that politicization was an almost natural process in their lives.

Thinking about society as a whole, beyond their own lifeworlds, was a self-evident pastime for the protagonists, beyond their work at school. Past and future revolutions assumed special significance in their thoughts. The revolutionary poetry preserved among Adler's papers, which was recited or sung at literary evenings, suggests not only that "revolution" was a familiar concept to youth but that it was broadly understood as something positive.[81] This observation is reinforced by Bernstein's recollections of his history teacher Löffler's "counter-revolutionary history lessons": "The bottom line of his lessons about the course of the [French] revolution was a warning about radical opposition." In order to illustrate the destructive energies of every revolutionary act, Löffler apparently turned to the poetic wisdom of Friedrich Schiller. In his 1799 poem "The Song of the Bell," Schiller warns against the ostensibly beneficial "heavenly torch of Light" (which is to say, the Enlightenment): in the hands of the "ever blinded," the torch lights the way for the "bad" and displaces all that is "sacred." Rather than enlightening the blind, "it guides him not, it can but kindle / Whole states in flames and ruin blent."[82] Nevertheless, Bernstein and his classmates were unimpressed by the "old man's pious solemnity." Hearkening back to the memory of 1848, they believed that a "new revolution" was now within reach.

It is an open question whether or not fourteen-year-old Bernstein was able to assess the explosive potential of the constitutional conflict between Chancellor Bismarck and the Prussian legislature. However, because his uncle Aaron David Bernstein was a leading journalist for the liberal *Berliner VolksZeitung*, Eduard was quite familiar with members of the "radical press" who had not been taught "properly" (as his teacher Löffler put it). The "anti-government tone" of conversations overheard daily piqued the revolutionary fantasies of young Bernstein and his classmates, with the exception of a police officer's son. The boys imagined "revolution" not only as a recurrent historical phenomenon but as a once-in-a-lifetime adventure. In his memoir, Bernstein accordingly portrayed the drive to rebel as a typical boyish virtue. Traces of this revolutionary Romanticism also shaped his political thinking through his years in Zurich, although the older Bernstein later distanced himself emphatically from these ideas.[83] After decades of debate about the movement's "end goal," however, Bernstein did not address this significant personal transformation in his 1926 memoir. He apparently forgave himself his earlier obsession with revolution as a transitory sin of youth.

Kautsky's revolutionary pathos is easier to reconstruct. Literature, love, and politics were the three pillars of his youthful identity. By the end of his school years, he had written his first novels and political treatises and drawn revolutionary heroes with pencil and charcoal. As a young man, he shifted between genres effortlessly, as the internal conversation in his diary shows. "Writing [fiction] is going nowhere, let's throw ourselves into politics," the eighteen-year-old wrote on a warm summer day in 1873.[84] The diary fragments in Kautsky's archival papers suggest that political affairs preoccupied him just as intensely as his liaisons with Laura, Rosa, or Emma. His interests in politics and early socialist engagement were inseparable from his overall emotional state, as he himself noted in a treatise on the ideal constitution, which he worked on for weeks: "If I can't find happiness in love, then I want to find it in hate, hate against tyrants. Now, let's continue with the draft of the constitution."[85]

Kautsky's diary contains all of Eric Hobsbawm's ingredients for an authentic revolutionary: general discontent with the world, desire to rebel, and personal dissatisfaction tied to a sense of alienation with the fate of humankind. Kautsky wanted to "fight society all the time; it's what disgusted me from the start and may also make me unhappy." Questions of sexuality and moral expectations apparently lurked behind these sentiments. "Since I've known Laura," Kautsky wrote, "I hate society twice as much as before. . . . Why shouldn't I hate it, this state of unnatural ossification? What is natural is called indecent, but shamelessly unnatural behavior is called propriety [Anstand]. . . . When can I be alone again with my Laura? With my Laura?"[86] This probably refers to a sexual relationship that should have led to marriage, according to the customs of the time. Kautsky's parents, however, were opposed to the match. Laura's feelings grew deeper, and she even asked for his photograph. Kautsky increasingly saw her as a burden, and he began to keep his distance. He soon downplayed their relationship in his diary; she was pretty if not "brilliant, but she can't help this." He pondered whether lying was an acceptable means of ending the relationship: "Does the end justify the means? Not in general, but doing something that hurts no one, but works for me, surely isn't bad, is it?" Perhaps he could usher in a "romantic end" by inventing a "moving story"—having to emigrate to America, for example, to escape military service. This kind of justification, he reasoned, would surely please his girlfriend more, and be more acceptable, than a "boring" story of growing apart.[87]

There is little here that foreshadows the sober guardian of Marxist orthodoxy that Kautsky later became. Instead, we see a creative, passionate, and quite arrogant young man who was reveling in pathos in his last months at school, who was channeling his romantic and existential woes into texts, drawings, and stories, and who grew convinced that he would ultimately lead a life of privation as a committed revolutionary. Kautsky turned his past lovers into characters in his novels, carefully documenting their physical appearance in his diary "for later." His "disgust" toward society was rooted at least in part in the complex relations between the sexes that was prescribed by bour-geois life. Adler's diary captures similar moods and experiences. His writings, too, are characterized by a mixture of youthful romance and worldly reflection.

Kautsky wrote his first political texts during this period of searching. He invented, for example, an ideal voting system ("communist, radical") within an ideal constitution. Even in these very first efforts, he strove for intellectual coherence. Before he had even formed an opinion about specific political issues, the eighteen-year-old anticipated objections that his ideas were "hazy and unclear" with the "structure of a constitution."[88] Read together, these texts offer an idiosyncratic mélange of romantic woe and worldly discontent, resignation and rebellion, powerlessness and determination. Revolution, which Kautsky sometimes imagined as an "explosion" or "thunderstorm," was a long-awaited calamity that would bring salvation; it repeatedly tore through history and could not be stopped.[89] In September 1874 Kautsky wrote a letter to an imaginary girlfriend, explaining why revolution would bring the redemption that God had refused. Having been comforted by faith in God, having placed their hopes in prayer for thousands of years, humans would soon recognize that it was not God but rather the liberating act of revolution that would bring an end to their suffering. This was the scenario he awaited:

> The people who are devastated and enslaved, full of rage over their misfortune, they will turn against those who are responsible, murder the tyrants, call all to freedom; revolution will burn across Europe, everything will be upended, the old will be cast aside to make way for the new. Woe then to the propertied, who will face the frenzied rage of the enslaved people; the guilty and the innocent will be destroyed; finally, there will be vengeance for [the enslaved] having been left to crudity and barbarism until now. . . . You laugh about this prophecy? You wouldn't be the first; time and again, I've been declared a fool. Nevertheless, I know this is coming. . . . When the black clouds approach and when the wind storm suddenly rises . . . when lightning flashes in the distance, doesn't this mean a thunderstorm is coming? The

wind can drive it away, but soon it returns all the more ferociously. Still, however terrible it might be, it is useful and necessary.[90]

Kautsky's thoughts about the "rage of the enslaved" and the futility of placing hope in the divine clearly converged here with his personal feelings of alienation and inferiority; he felt that adults were laughing at him and took him for a "fool." Nature metaphors such as the rising thunderstorm were typical of an age that was both fond of metaphor and increasingly politicized. Moreover, he loved drawing expansive landscapes; a surviving sketchbook is filled with his detailed pencil drawings. Revolution as a force of nature—or "natural law," as Kautsky later called it—was not only a personal leitmotif but one of the most important themes in modern political discourse.[91]

The idea of revolution was inseparable from the Social Question, another recurrent theme in Kautsky's personal writings that reflected the discourse of his era. His thoughts on the topic were still quite scattered. On the one hand, he believed that there was no satisfactory solution to the Social Question—least of all by way of elections, such as the curial voting system that was introduced in Austria-Hungary in 1873 and strongly favored the wealthy. Instead, he asserted that revolution was "unavoidable" and that it could be predicted "with almost mathematical certainty." On the other hand, he did consider possible paths of reform. In October 1873, for example, he wrote that a solution might lie in a combination of equality, freedom, and better education, complemented by a "strict prohibition on idleness, also for the wealthy." If workers became "capitalists" through codetermination in nationalized industries, then something "tremendous" would be attained "since the revolutions will end when there is no longer a proletariat."[92]

These first political ideas were infused with Kautsky's belief that every revolution was preferable to the status quo and that its only thinkable outcome was improvement. To him, revolution was the only legitimate means for achieving a sacred end. Kautsky composed his second political text in February 1874, shortly before his final exams.

Written in the style of a legal defense, the text collected his thoughts "about the justification of socialist ideas." One year before he joined the party himself, he sympathized openly with the Social Democrats. "They want to overturn society," he affirmed. "Indeed, that is what we want, but only to replace it with another, better society (which can hardly be worse than the current one)."[93] The young Kautsky's defense had certain limits: should the Social Democrats strive to "destroy the family (the only thing that brings happiness)," he would oppose the party vigorously. In the first place, however, this was not their intent, and second, such an undertaking was quite impossible because "family is not merely conventional, but a relationship deeply rooted in nature." Here the influence of Kautsky's affectionate upbringing is clearly discernable. Later in life he continued to place great value on domestic harmony and family ties—even though his first marriage ended in divorce. The teenage Kautsky took care that his draft constitution upheld conventional bourgeois values: the popularly elected president had to be at least thirty years old, with an "irreproachable past."[94]

Kautsky's early political texts were characterized by self-assurance and optimism for change but also by the dark expectation that he was fated to lead a lonely, restless life. In 1873 he noted that he would never marry because a wife would pose "too great an obstacle" to his plans for reform. Persecuted for his political convictions, he would "die a lonely, forsaken old man—perhaps in prison—or even earlier on the barricades, or before a military tribunal as a high traitor." Elsewhere he wrote, "It's determined by fate. I'll never sit in my family circle, next to my wife, surrounded by thriving children—I'll never experience that. Behind prison walls, struggling against depravity, fleeing from the henchmen of tyrants—I'll lead a joyless existence, perhaps until, on a barricade, a bullet pierces my heart."[95]

Kautsky's sketches—doodles in his school notebooks and more elaborate drawings in his sketchbook—show how vividly he experienced these ideas.[96] Drawing, a pastime that his school certainly encouraged, underscores the Romantic underpinnings of his youthful engagement. His heroes have long, flowing hair, and they wear splendid garments and robes; they ride wild horses across vast natural landscapes. The intricate drawings may foreshadow elements of Kautsky's narrow-mindedness and obsession with details, qualities for which he was soon known all over Europe.

Donna Anita.   *Don Martial.*

From Karl Kautsky's sketchbooks, around 1872–73
Credit: International Institute of Social History, Amsterdam (Karl Kautsky papers)

Just as Kautsky recorded in his diary his thoughts about a future constitution, the young Guesde wrote treatises about the organization of state and society. Under the direction of his father, a private school teacher who also taught his own son, Guesde wrote about absolutism, war, slavery, and the caste system. Ossip Zetkin, who lived in Paris in the 1870s and maintained close ties with Guesde, later reported that the fourteen-year-old had helped his father instruct younger students; his strongest subjects were Classical languages and mathematics. He completed the *baccalauréat* by the age of sixteen. The political and social questions addressed in his (difficult to decipher) *notes de lectures* from 1860–70[97] suggest he received a socially critical, liberal education. This observation corresponds to his early reading material by Sand, Kant, Balzac, Hugo, and Michelet. From the time of his youth, Guesde often cited one of his favorite verses from Hugo's *Châtiments* (Castigations), a nearly seven-thousand-line takedown of Louis Napoléon's 1852 coup d'état. These lines certainly reflect some of his hostility toward the (man-made) conditions that fueled his lifelong political engagement: "Hunt him down in a savage rout / And let the insects drive him out / Since men are too afraid!"[98]

The roots of Guesde's socially critical thought can be found in the years of his father's instruction. Among other topics, the young man's notes addressed the role of women, sharply criticizing systematic discrimination against them,[99] also covering questions of governance and the role of the military ("a danger to the well-being and freedom of every nation," only seemingly invulnerable, like the ancient Achilles). Guesde further considered the nature of war. Its only purpose, he wrote, was to turn people into soldiers to "extinguish" other people— according to a "law of destruction," in the name of a divine mission. All states engaged in such legitimization, and each war's outcome was rooted in its declared ideology and intentions.[100] Guesde wondered what could possibly be "honorable" about sending innocent people to war, to "shed innocent blood" for a supposedly higher purpose. Under closer examination, it was inexplicable to him why "military glory" had always been (and still was) valued so highly. History had left behind a world drowning in innocent blood; as if following a universal law, wars were waged under the pretense of eradicating all that was bad, "until the death of death."[101] On these pages, the fifteen-year-old Guesde was already interrogating the relationship between war and power, between war as fate (divine providence) and war as a means of pursuing worldly interests: "War is divine through the protection of the powerful,"[102] although its consequences "absolutely contradict all human reason." This "terrible riddle" of human history could be understood only by recognizing that "the hand of God" was nowhere so influential as in questions of war and peace. Guesde followed these observations with a historical discussion about the

divine right of kings and the relationship between sacred and secular authority. Royal families invoked divine providence because they
knew that their power would otherwise crumble; they differed from
other humans only "as a tree" differs from "a bush." The association
with "priesthood" (*sacerdoce*) was the basis for all their power, although
Guesde understood this as a mutual dependency: "If one retreats, the
other will suffer."[103]

Parts of this critique are supported in great detail; it is no mere
expression of youthful outrage. Guesde incorporated Voltaire's critique of the historical "alliance between priesthood and empire,"
as well as Jacques Bénigne Bossuet's seventeenth-century *Discours
sur l'histoire universelle*, known to historiographers as one of the last
comprehensive efforts to explain human history as the realization of
God's will.[104] For Guesde, Bossuet's convictions that God's authority
was "immortal" and that the state would exist "forever" explained
why all peoples in history sought "to give their laws divine authority
[*rigueur divine*]."[105]

The young Adler had to engage at greater length, and much more
explicitly, with the increasingly dire social conditions in the Habsburg
Empire since the upheavals of 1848. As an eighteen-year-old student,
he received the opportunity to develop an almost socialist, if still pre-
Marxist, argument with a school assignment that asked him to discuss "the bright and dark sides of many people living together in big
cities."[106] Adler began his essay by noting the inextricable and potentially adversarial relationship between individual "human interests"
and the "interests of the whole." In principle, he contended, interest
"binds and divides, builds communities and then dissolves them." He
emphasized the primacy of the common good, a position that was
surely in line with his headmaster's teachings, by praising "the individual who can subordinate his special interest to serving the interest of the whole." His reflections on city life as both a blessing and
a curse foreshadow the socially critical and public health–oriented
texts that he later wrote as a doctor and aspiring factory inspector.
The young Adler saw urbanization as a form of association- and

community-building among certain groups of people with common interests. He viewed advocacy for separate interests as the "reason why the common good emerges." Because interests change, however, and because the pursuit of certain interests could be an advantage to some and a disadvantage to others, urban community-building was a process of winners and losers. Precisely in big cities, the resulting "bright" and "dark" sides were glaringly apparent. Adler saw the positive aspects of urbanization in "material prosperity," access to education and culture, and a "broad field for benevolent engagement." As negative aspects, he noted the great disparities in living conditions and the sanitary problems that arose from many people living together in a tight space. For the individual, big cities often posed a health risk: "[s]tatistical tables on the incidence of disease and mortality" offered ample supporting evidence. Nevertheless, science had already made significant progress in combating these unfavorable conditions. In the eyes of this eighteen-year-old, the advantages of urbanization were not outweighed by "this evil," which society had worked hard to alleviate; "Wanting to abolish the big cities on this account has never occurred to anyone."[107]

Adler's interest in social issues, medicine, and public health was already apparent in this essay. Upon completing his schooling, he engaged intensively with these fields in his medical studies and later as a Marxist politician. Even more significant, however, is the third "dark" aspect Adler named in his German essay, alongside inequality and health risks: the "concentration of capital." Just as this concentration would have been unimaginable without the formation of cities as sites of concentrated commerce, the control of capital in the hands of a few was "very harmful" to the "cultural development of humanity":

> As a consequence, they [the few] make the satisfaction of everyone else's interests dependent upon their own. And so they exercise a kind of dominion that is even more pernicious than that of the nobility, because it is not grounded upon imagined privileges. The other consequence of the concentration of capital is the emergence of the proletariat, and all of the questions that together comprise the social question, which awaits future resolution.[108]

Adler was already familiar with the catchwords and challenges of the young socialist movement, even if in this essay he saw the looming conflict between "capital" and "proletariat" as more of a challenge for the future, not the present. The term "proletariat" stands out most starkly. Corresponding to the spirit of the times, he used it in an analytical/sociological sense, as well as a "practical revolutionary term."[109] Thus, his school essays already incorporated key issues of contemporary political journalism. By the 1860s, in fact, the theses of Ferdinand Lassalle and Marx were being disseminated ever more widely in the Habsburg Empire. Early Viennese working-class newspapers such as *Arbeiterblatt* published excerpts from the *Manifesto* and *Capital* for the first time in 1868.[110] The works Adler read with his literary club raised his awareness of the Social Question. This issue was important enough to the young men in Adler and Pernerstorfer's circle that they continued their Association for Clarifying and Establishing Our Views on the Social Question as university students.[111] One of Adler's first presentations to the association dealt with recent works by the economics professor Hermann Schulze-Delitzsch and the German labor leader Lassalle. Lassalle's critique of Schulze-Delitzsch's "bourgeois" theses referred to Marx's "epochal" *Critique of Political Economy* from 1859, so we can presume that by his first year at the university, at the latest, Adler had encountered Marx's ideas.[112]

Some of the protagonists' schoolwork allows us to reconstruct their early interest in society and politics and also to make a few assumptions as to the origins of their distinctive styles of thinking. Beyond their interest in certain ideas, there were striking differences in their styles and methods of argumentation. The young Adler, for example, was asked by his teachers not only to articulate his personal convictions but also to describe his expectations of life and to reflect on his own behavior and the behavior of others. Once he was even asked to consider different ways of perceiving the world. In the spring of 1867, the fifteen-year-old Adler wrote his essay on the prompt "When one sees everything at once, one sees nothing . . . (Explain and illustrate with examples)." Drawing upon the example of a walk in the woods, he argued that perception is a subjective process. It can be rationally directed and necessarily depends on the standpoint and perspective of the observer:

> Whoever sees everything at once, sees nothing—thoroughly, that is. Of course he sees, but he doesn't understand. He looks, but he is not aware of what he has seen. And when someone goes to the forest and admires the wisdom of nature, and then goes home and observes a grain of pollen through a microscope, he acquires a steadier grasp of the workings of nature than when he previously marveled at an entire forest.[113]

These lines demonstrate an astonishingly mature sense of the relevance of perspective, and the need to acknowledge this subjective relativity of perception.

While the young Adler developed a knack for careful deliberation that would later distinguish his political thought and actions as party leader, the teenage Kautsky already saw himself as a rigorous, systematic thinker with an eye on the big picture. Kautsky cultivated this persona in his private diary and as a student with journalistic ambitions. Shortly before he completed school, in 1872, he cofounded the student newspaper *Minerva*, named after the goddess of artistry and handicrafts. The first issue has been preserved in his archival papers. Its editors announced on the front page, "We, who come from your midst, are beginning an enterprise that will initially encounter many small animosities, but later, with your support, it will bloom. We'll stay the course." The lead article, authored by Kautsky, was titled "Three Thousand Years Ago: A Great Historical-Political, Aristocratic-Monarchical Novel by Me." On an archaeological expedition to Assyria, the novel's narrator unearths the "entire library of the royal Assyrian university," including the "priceless" king's chronicle: "Now a translation of part of the priceless document will see the light of day. It was only for the good of humanity that I undertook this effort, because I would not have needed to translate it for myself."[114]

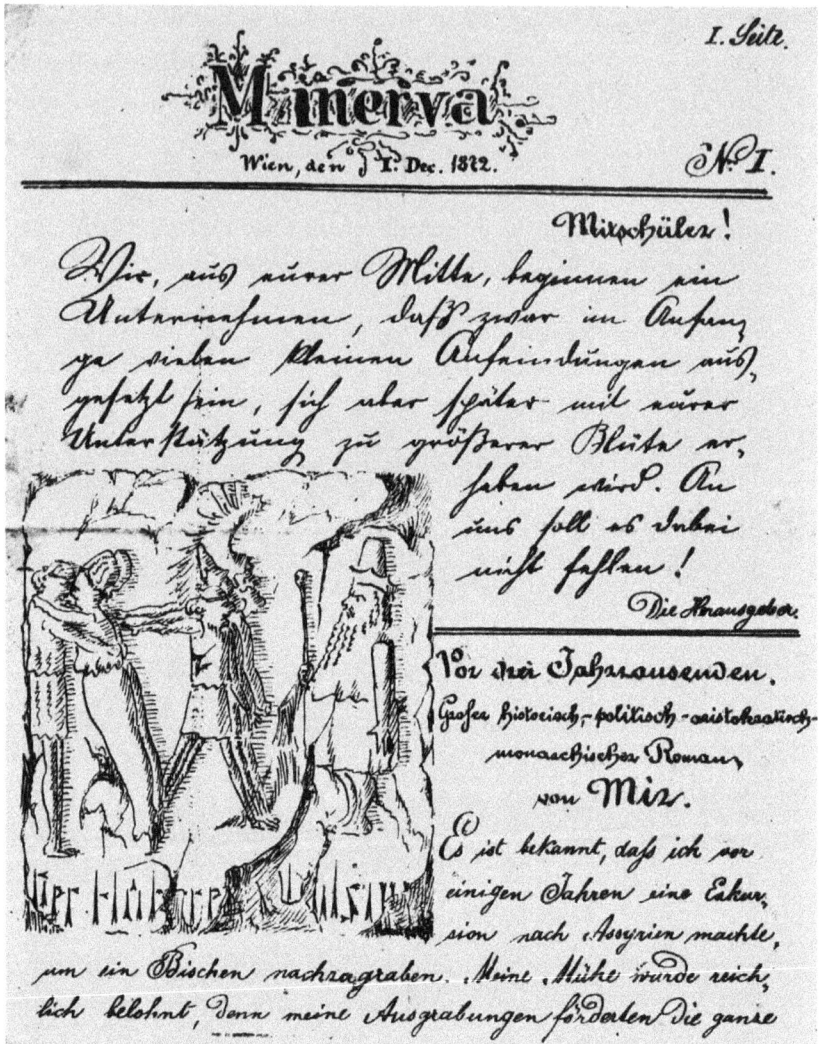

Front page of the first edition of the student newspaper *Minerva*, edited by
Kautsky, 1 December 1872
Credit: International Institute of Social History, Amsterdam (Karl Kautsky
papers)

Creative, inspired by the culture of ancient scholars, and full of its
lead editor's confidence in his own intellectual potential, this student
publication foreshadowed the *actual* service of "translation" for (proletarian) humanity that Kautsky would ultimately perform fourteen

years later. His *Economic Doctrines of Karl Marx*, first published in 1887, became the first popular overview of Marx's doctrines and a standard of the German working-class movement.[115] Thus, as a student journalist and imagined Mesopotamia expert, the young Kautsky had already undertaken his first effort to render a "masterpiece" perfectly.

In addition to concern for the Social Question and fascination with the idea of revolution, the protagonists' early writings also reveal their convictions in the significance of history. As Koselleck has shown, the eighteenth century brought a fundamental transformation of historical thinking. For the previous two thousand years, history (*Historie*) had been understood as a collection of stories that had served as "life's teacher" (*magistra vitae*); it was a "school" that had offered its students timeless lessons from the past. The Enlightenment ushered in a new understanding of history (*Geschichte*) as a series of distinct events that comprised a greater whole, or "epic unity," and nineteenth-century philosophers and professional historians began to narrate it as such. "History" itself became a subject of study; it acquired direction, power, agency, and its own internal laws.[116]

History lost its ability to teach, but now it could be made. Humans could shape the course of events because the future was open. Before long, historians and other scholars who studied the "laws" of the past were believed to have special insight into what was happening in the present and what might happen in the future. Historical knowledge acquired explosive—and thus "modern"—potential as an all-purpose political foil. The lessons of history, according to Koselleck, reentered political life "via the back door of programs of action legitimated in terms of historical philosophy," and "the first revolutionary teachers seeking to apply such lessons" included Mazzini, Proudhon, and Marx.[117] By way of its politicization, thus, history was reaffirmed as *magistra vitae*.

This changed conception of history was manifest in the protagonists' schooling, particularly in the German- and French-speaking parts of Europe. In some cases, we know what history books the protagonists actually read. In other cases, their surviving schoolwork contains observations about history in general, or about the origins, progression, and consequences of specific historical events. Under his father's tutelage, Guesde read Bossuet's *Discours sur l'histoire universelle*, the "classic" from 1681. Guesde's notes suggest that the then nearly two-hundred-year-old book was likely assigned as an exercise in critical reading, as a means of illustrating the development from a teleological, God-centered historiography toward more universal and humanist approaches.[118] Guesde also read works by Jules Michelet,[119] who first identified "the people" (*le peuple*) as an actor in (political) history, celebrating the French Revolution for its role in birthing republicanism and democratic nationalism. Michelet's passionate historicist narratives of freedom addressed its national audience in an entirely new way—searching for, but also forging, identity.[120]

Jaurès's religion teacher gave him a copy of Bossuet's standard history as a reward for good achievement,[121] but other aspects of Jaurès's schooling were less pious. He read ancient works and was influenced by progressive teachers who passed on three ideals: rationalism, belief in progress, and republicanism.[122] As an adult, Jaurès's view of history was shaped by Hegel and Fichte as well as Marx, and he consistently strove to harmonize "idealist" and "materialist" conceptions of history. Around 1894 he participated in a public discussion with Paul Lafargue (a medical doctor and socialist who was also Marx's son-in-law) and Parisian students in the Latin Quarter. On this occasion Jaurès articulated his historical aspirations in his distinctively pragmatic and synthesizing way: "One can explain all historical events and phenomena simply through economic development, but one can simultaneously look for their impetus in humanity's longstanding, sustained yearning for a higher form of existence."[123] This was the defining goal of Jaurès's lifelong occupation with questions of human perception in his philosophical and historical studies. He believed that humans had progressed rationally from "darkness," or a state of "sleep," to the "clear" insight that they themselves ultimately "controlled the course of things."[124] He understood history as both the fate and the creation of humans; emancipatory socialism tamed the former tendency while empowering the latter.[125]

Little is known about Plekhanov's teacher de-Pulé, so it is difficult to generalize about his instruction in history. De-Pulé was not only a teacher; he also worked as a literary critic and journalist. He advocated for a liberal, bourgeois Russia and the integration of its Jewish minority,[126] and he published the work of Ivan S. Nikitin. Nikitin's poetry depicted scenes of nature and the daily life and tribulations of the Russian people, and Nikitin himself was an advocate for literary education in his hometown, Voronezh. It is fair to assume that Plekhanov came into contact with enlightened ideals and progressive conceptions of history at school. Later in life, he, like Jaurès, sought to contribute to public debate about the laws and course and history with his own ambitious historical and philosophical works.

We know more about the histories read by Luxemburg and Kautsky. As young teenagers, both read books by English historians. By her own account, Luxemburg's "first 'serious' book" was Sir John Lubbock's *The Origin of Civilisation and the Primitive Condition of Man*, which first appeared in German in 1875.[127] Lubbock was a disciple of Darwin, whose theories he sought to support with archaeological evidence. He studied "the mental and social condition of savages" in different parts of the world in order to reconstruct the "primitive" state of humanity. The novelty of his argument was that, as a result of natural selection, human communities had diversified culturally as well as in their biological capacity to utilize culture. According to Rudolf Virchow, who wrote the preface to the German edition, Lubbock concluded that "humans originally existed in a condition of extreme barbarism; by their own power, multiple races succeeded in uplifting themselves to a higher state of culture."[128] Lubbock's theses attracted attention well beyond England. Luxemburg later recalled that as a girl she had read the book "with ardent zeal," even recommending it to Antoni, the caretaker with "an interest in arts and letters" who swept the courtyard of her family's apartment building. However, he returned the book two days later, explaining that it was "worth nothing." "As for me," she wrote in a letter to Kautsky's wife (and her own good friend) Luise in 1904, "it took a few years for me to realize how right Antoni was."[129] As a well-read economist and Marxist, she developed reservations about the book that ultimately resembled those of Marx himself. She could not have known about Marx's critique of the book, which was not published until 1972, but her trained Marxist historical eye brought her to the same objections about the presentist orientation of Lubbock's work.[130]

Kautsky completed his Gymnasium education with the top marks in history and philosophy. After years of struggling academically, he found his academic footing as an upper-level student. He especially enjoyed his history classes with a certain Dr. Ludwig Blume, who tried "to elevate the history that he presented above the bleak monotony of names and numbers, and to include at least some cultural history, for which we were grateful."[131] Blume apparently drew upon works of history that went beyond the standard Gymnasium textbook by Wilhelm Pütz, *An Overview of Geography and History in the Ancient, Medieval, and Modern Eras.* Kautsky's surviving writings from school include an 1871 essay on the Middle Ages, which cited the English politician and Enlightenment philosopher Henry St. John, First Viscount Bolingbroke, and discussed the nature and purpose of historical writing. The sixteen-year-old Kautsky noted that the intent of history was "to convey facts in writing," regardless of whether its subject was the "human race," "human associations," or indeed all humanity. Its objective was to convey a "picture," which imprinted the "entirety of the facts" in the reader's mind "in chronological order." Even so, such a "picture of facts is never quite complete," as it is "blurred" by two factors: human "selfishness" and the "pull of our time," by which Kautsky meant the inherent bias of all works of history and their inevitable anchoring within a particular place and time. With some distance, however, one could reconstruct history by depicting religious, political, or military events with the aid of "examples," which were detached from the "needs of the moment."

In fact, he repeated one of Lord Bolingbroke's fundamental lessons from his well-known *Letters on the Study of History* (1752): "I think, that history is philosophy teaching by examples."[132] This "old topos" (in Koselleck's words) of history as life's teacher tied the present and future directly to the past; studying history was thus associated with a broader search for truth and meaning. Bolingbroke believed that history's power to teach lay in the "force of example," "which appeals not to our understanding alone, but to our passions likewise"; these two poles make "the whole man of a piece."[133]

Kautsky appears to have followed these words enthusiastically; they encouraged a lifelong historical gaze that he proudly adopted at every possible turn. His interest in history extended from his school days into the final years of his life. In his memoir, he claimed a "talent for history" and an "inclination to investigate, and thus to comprehend, all familiar phenomena in their state of becoming."[134] One could understand the present only by studying the past—"of human society, but also of nature." Kautsky believed that history offered answers to the questions that individuals posed about themselves and their place in the world.[135] In light of his historical and philosophical education, it is no surprise that he became particularly impressed by the bold historical theses of Marx and Engels. Their "historical materialism" was related to historicism, even though they constantly argued against it. Marx and Engels claimed to have sussed out history's laws, and thus its future direction.[136] "Via the back door," as Koselleck put it, Marxism cleverly brought the lessons of history into the present.[137]

Finally, a glance at an essay by Kautsky's history teacher (written in 1874, Kautsky's final year at the Gymnasium) points to the general importance of his early instruction in history for his entire subsequent intellectual career. Ludwig Blume authored the featured essay in the school's annual report, "The Ideal of the Hero and the Woman in Homer: With Attention to German Antiquity," about ancient Greek and Germanic conceptions of "heroism," based on Blume's reading of the works of Homer. Kautsky's own efforts at epic storytelling around this time may have been inspired by his teacher's writing.

There is no doubt that the essay contains a tenet that Kautsky himself later repeated—namely, that history and the natural sciences taught, as Blume put it, "respect for what has become" (*Achtung vor dem Gewordenen*). The sentiment resembles Jaurès's historically informed conservatism, which was likewise fostered by an influential teacher: all that exists today can and should be investigated historically, because "both [history and the natural sciences] want to recognize, understand, before they judge."[138]

And so this chapter ends as it began, with the scholarly musings of a teacher who influenced the historical thinking and interests of a boy who later became a leading theorist of Marxism. As the editor of the *Neue Zeit*, Kautsky later gave the emerging "Marxist School" its intellectual framework. Even without approaching the sources in this chapter teleologically, the protagonists' socialization at home and school shows the extent to which their biographies were shaped by an early, subjective, profound, and sustained interest in their social environment. The canonical and dogmatic education that they received at mostly state-run schools was not as stifling as it may first appear from today's perspective. Diverse curricula, deliberate character-building, and extensive reading were often accompanied by critical encouragement from parents and individual teachers, who especially—but not only—encouraged their young charges to view the real world through the lens of literature. This is the subject of the next chapter.

Even though romantic and rebellious sentiments suffuse many of the ego documents examined in this chapter, we should not exaggerate their significance as harbingers of revolutionary engagement in adulthood. Nevertheless, their virulence in this context shows that these nine, even as adolescents, approached *their* reality with remarkable interest, sensitivity, and openness toward the world. The best-documented examples (Kautsky, Guesde, Adler) illustrate how grappling with ideas at school prefigured their later styles of thinking and ways of apprehending the world. All of the protagonists developed a more or less diffuse sense of discontent, which surpassed the usual degree of adolescent angst.[139] The earnestness and occasional outrage of their notes, sketches, and poetry underscore their fundamental receptiveness to the "Romantic furor"[140] of their times. This same furor had, since the 1850s, also inspired a certain Herr Marx to call out the questions of the day and promise to solve them.

3

Beating the Drum

Literary Influences

Beat the drum and don't be afraid,
And kiss the pretty peddler girl!
This is the ultimate wisdom,
This is the books' most precious pearl.
Drum the people out of their sleep,
Drum reveille with youthful aplomb,
And drumming march ahead of all,
This is the ultimate wisdom.
This is the Hegelian philosophy,
This is the books' most secret seed!
I have grasped it because I am bright,
And because I am a good tambour indeed.

—Heinrich Heine, "Doctrine" (1844)

Upon completing their secondary schooling, nearly all of the
protagonists pursued a university education, and thus they belonged to a tiny minority in each of their respective countries. The
proportion of secondary students in western Europe who went on
to study at a university around 1870 was under 1 percent.[1] All of the
protagonists pursued higher education, with the exception of Guesde
and Bernstein; having struggled to pay for their secondary schooling,
attending university was out of the question. Five of the protagonists

earned higher degrees: Adler, in medicine; Jaurès, in philosophy; Luxemburg, in economics; Lenin and Struve, in law. Although they completed their studies in quite different national and cultural contexts, they shared a common experience that transcended state borders. Academic life was similar at the universities in Vienna, Zurich, Paris, and St. Petersburg, in that each of these sites enjoyed a certain intellectual autonomy that was otherwise exceptional in their respective societies. Most of the protagonists found their way to Marx at the same time, and often in the same way, that they acquired higher knowledge and new modes of thinking.

This chapter reconstructs the young protagonists' experiences as readers of literature and philosophy, a process in which university life often assumed a key role. Reading and academic training are central, interrelated means of secondary socialization, shaping young adults' identity formation, their search for meaning, and perceptions of their immediate lifeworlds and wider social reality. Literature and science provide a conduit for, and also form, new emotions and interests. An integrated look at what the protagonists read and studied shows that their emerging political and intellectual engagement was driven by (political) passion and suffused with pathos. This pathos was fed by the interplay of emotion and reason, literature and science. In this chapter, therefore, I consider the works of philosophy and fiction that captured the hearts and minds of all nine protagonists, including the nonacademics. The protagonists' intellectual turn toward Marx (which is the subject of Part II) generally began during these formative years of reading and study, and it was closely tied to their literary interests and youthful search for meaning. This turn was not straightforward, as we will see, although it usually evolved in a steady and internally coherent way. Its roots lay in the years of academic study and eclectic reading that are the subject of this chapter. As the poet Heine mused, books can indeed "drum" their readers to action.[2]

Luxemburg once described literature as society's "finely vibrating social consciousness," noting that authors could articulate "wincingly painful empathy" and offer uniquely "sharpened" insight into social conditions.[3] Indeed, literature makes an impression. Still, it would be misguided for us to seek a common thread in the protagonists' wide-ranging reading material or to attempt to derive their later intellectual positions from their youthful reading experiences. Understanding the role that certain books played in an intellectual biography requires deep biographical excavation and a correspondingly dense source base. In isolated cases, one might be able to demonstrate a far-reaching, lifelong connection to certain authors or literary figures—as Tristram Hunt, for example, has shown with respect to Engels's reverence for the mythical hero Siegfried.[4]

We should begin with the literature that was typical of the time. The protagonists avidly consumed classics by Kant, Voltaire, Goethe, Pushkin, Nietzsche, and Darwin. Their familiarity with these works, which they frequently cited, attests to their solid anchoring within a specific cultural milieu that was shared by the educated bourgeoisie of eastern and western Europe. Literary heroes like Schiller, Freiligrath, Chernyshevsky, Mickiewicz, Sand, and Hugo had additional significance that was tied to their national heritage. The oldest, Guesde, consistently cited four authors: Kant, Hugo, Proudhon (before the experience of the Commune), and Chernyshevsky, whose *What Is to Be Done?* he discovered in Swiss exile and even translated.[5] In an 1878 illustration of his study, portraits of his political *saintes icônes*[6] Ferdinand Lassalle, Henri de Saint-Simon, and Robert Owen are pinned to the wall.[7] Guesde himself ordered his intellectual biography around two classics and one revolutionary reading experience: Hugo's *Les Châtiments* made him a republican, Kant's *Critique of Pure Reason* made him an atheist, and the Commune made him a socialist.[8] We have already seen the influence of Hugo's incendiary verses on Guesde, who saw Hugo's critique of absolutism as a call to action for the "men [who] are too afraid," who had acquiesced to this rule.

Bernstein's family home was exceptional for this group, in that it had no bookshelves full of classics. According to his own recollections, the worn, secondhand editions that his parents could afford did not spark his desire to read. The first serious works that he read outside of school were likely the political economy texts that made the rounds among Berlin's Social Democrats in the 1870s: Lassalle, Schulze-Delitzsch, and Dühring. Thomas More's *Utopia* played a role in his young adulthood, albeit in a decidedly unpolitical way. It inspired the name of a tavern discussion circle, an "idealistic association that stood above all day-to-day bickering," that he established with friends and fellow students in 1871. The young men had not read More's work but "only heard that he depicted a communal paradise."[9] Beyond this vague utopia, no one harbored "any political or socialist goals."[10]

The works of Schiller did have special meaning for Bernstein from childhood on. He cited Schiller frequently, and as an old man he wrote a sentimental piece about Schiller's influence on "young souls"—a text that speaks not only to his youthful reverence for Schiller but to his adult ambivalence toward Schiller's Wallenstein portrait in the aftermath of the fight of his own life, the revisionism debate. As a fifteen-year-old student, Bernstein was especially moved by the pro-logue to the first part of the Wallenstein trilogy, *Wallenstein's Camp*, and, by his own account, was never able to read it without "his eyes welling up."[11] Still, to him this was "no pathetic declamation, tempered for delicate constitutions," but a serious character study of the age of the Thirty Years War. At the end of the eighteenth century, Schiller wistfully recalled the hard-fought peace settlement that ended "thirty wretched years of war"; the French Revolution had since rendered it obsolete. Bernstein found Wallenstein's personal fate even more tragic. Wallenstein is found guilty of treason and brutally murdered in the third part of the trilogy. Bernstein considered this fate a "true tragedy," and through Schiller's eyes he regarded the fallen general with em-pathy and understanding. Perhaps he secretly related Schiller's ded-ication to Wallenstein to his own political (after)life: "Observed by partisan love and hate, his profile / Remains uncertain in the gaze of History."[12]

The young Adler was influenced particularly by Goethe, Schopenhauer, and Nietzsche, if we are to believe the account of his wife. Even as party leader, Emma recalled, he read Shakespeare or Dostoevsky late into the night to "restore his energies" after a long day.[13] At home, in school, and with his literary club, the young Adler read widely and deeply—especially German-language literature, philosophy, and economics. Over and above his enthusiasm for Wagner, we know that as a student he read Plato, Rousseau, Mill, Gervinus, Immermann, Nietzsche, and Schopenhauer. The guiding themes of his young adulthood were "Nietzsche's pessimism and cynicism, Schopenhauer's subjectivism, and Wagner's aesthetic religion."[14] Adler's letters to Pernerstorfer reveal a fascination not only with certain themes and great thinkers but also with the "madness" and "assurance of victory" that these men brought to literature and philosophy. Adler was so moved by his reading that he was sometimes overcome by "real dizziness" and felt his skull would "burst."[15] At the age of twenty, he felt this enthusiasm for an unpublished book by a now-forgotten Polish Jewish writer, Josef Ehrlich. Ehrlich was an impoverished friend in Vienna who shared his reverence for Nietzsche, and both Adler and Pernerstorfer sought to provide him with financial and moral support. In this sense, literature was a "real," sensate experience for Adler, and he was deeply impressed that someone like Ehrlich felt called, whatever the cost, to dramatize his views for the world.

Portraits of Voltaire, Goethe, Belinsky, Chernyshevsky, and Engels adorned the walls of Plekhanov's study in Geneva. The selection of thinkers reflected Plekhanov's literary and philosophical orientation between humanism, Enlightenment, and social criticism; to this we might also add the spirit of his antihero, Hegel. Aside from Plekhanov's own writings on the history of social thought and his routine quotations from the work and correspondence of Belinsky, there is almost no autobiographical material that provides deeper insight into his experiences as a reader. He sometimes identified Chernyshevsky and Marx as his two "favorite authors," and he pointed to Chernyshevsky's novels as "a major event in my literary life."[16] The arrangement of his portrait gallery is perhaps the most personal evidence of his relationship to philosophy and literature. Upon closer scrutiny, one might even interpret this arrangement allegorically. Plekhanov saw Russian literature as a material response to the challenge of German idealism, which he, like Marx and Engels, criticized radically. Hegel had not pursued the "real, internal causes of the historical movement of humanity"; instead of "considering the real causes of social phenomena," he sought the origins of historical development in abstract ideas.[17] Plekhanov shared Engels's critical reverence for Hegel as "a man of tremendous and truly genial intelligence." Marx and Engels had "corrected" Hegel's fundamental error in theory, he believed, and Russian literature put the correction into practice. Authors such as Belinsky and Chernyshevsky had "yielded to the insistence of reality" by depicting a Russia that was shaped by slavery, despotism, and censorship—a reality "so infamous that Hegel himself would have never recognised it" as such.[18]

Nevertheless, the adult Plekhanov, who lived through the revolutionary failures of the 1870s, deemed the social criticism of Russian revolutionary literature, with its focus on real life as a response to Hegel's misguided idealism, as theoretically "insolvent." Only Marx's "discovery" of historical laws that "turned Hegel's philosophy upside down" brought Russian social criticism into "the general channel of scientific thought." According to Plekhanov, Marx's materialism saved Russian social criticism from theoretical bankruptcy. "A firm objective *basis* for the negation of Russian reality"—that is, for solving the Social Question in Russia—"was found *in that reality itself.*"[19] Plekhanov saw himself as Russian social democracy's most important thinker, who would help transform social criticism in Russia into a "social science." For Plekhanov (as for Kautsky, Luxemburg, and Lenin), literature revealed and reinforced the necessity for action. Like other emerging Marxists, he felt personally responsible for answering this call to action with his own "scientific" scholarship.

The intellectual biography of Jaurès shows how narrow the distance between abstract philosophy and social reality could be. The academic and extracurricular readings that the student of philosophy devoured as his daily bread can hardly be separated by genre. He, too, came under the spell of German philosophy. In 1891 Jaurès wrote his second dissertation (*thèse complémentaire*), "On the Origins of German Socialism," thereby becoming the first "doctor of socialism" in France. Initially written in Latin, his work reached a broader audience when it was published in French by the *Revue Socialiste* in 1892. The editor remarked that the time had come to establish a chair in the study of socialism at the Sorbonne.[20] Over the course of his studies, Jaurès acquired an intimate knowledge of important philosophical works—and so it seems almost irrelevant to wonder about his "favorite books." Since his youth, Jaurès had been known as an almost obsessive reader, commentator, and author of literary and philosophical texts. He chose German philosophy as a special focus because of its inseparable connection between the abstract and the concrete, the ideal and the real. Drawing upon the example of socialism, he wanted to investigate how philosophy assumed a "warlike exterior," took arms, and threw itself into "political combat" by finally considering not only the workings of heaven but also those on earth: "Just as Socrates brought philosophy down from heaven, socialist philosophy brought justice to earth."[21] The enthusiasm of these opening sentences in his *thèse complémentaire* is the result of long years of reading experience.

The young Jaurès was an introvert whose studies were largely detached from the outside world. Reading, rather than investigating the world around him, was what eventually sparked his interest in the realities of his time. His boyhood heroes were the ancient philosophers. Since primary school, he had been closest to his philosophy teachers and those who knew ancient literature. They discussed philosophical questions on walks, and Jaurès memorized long passages of ancient poetry.[22] The recollections of his contemporaries and a few surviving letters mention ancient and Enlightenment works that especially preoccupied the young Jaurès. These included old and new classics such as Thucydides's rendering of Pericles's orations and Schiller's *Wilhelm Tell*.[23] For Jaurès, history and geography were the cornerstones of a well-rounded education. Only when he began to study in Paris did the allures and risks of the present come more sharply into focus.

Jaurès seems to have resembled an awed student as he read. Even after he distanced himself from the Catholic faith of his youth, he continued to appreciate the Bible as a core text of the human quest for meaning and justice.[24] He was a critical reader of history, including contemporary works by Ernest Renan and Fustel de Coulanges on the history of religion and church institutions, as well as Bossuet's divinely oriented historical philosophy. Despite their contradictions, Jaurès saw these works not as opposites but as intellectual beacons along the path toward human enlightenment. He later combined these readings effortlessly with the world of socialist ideas. His view of history was "materialist with Marx and mystical with Michelet," as he himself provocatively asserted in the introduction to his edited collection about the history of socialism in France.[25]

My introduction to the literary "favorites" of Guesde, Bernstein, Adler, Plekhanov, and Jaurès has drawn upon the comparatively thin sourcing available in each case. I draw upon more comprehensive evidence from the literary worlds of Kautsky, Lenin, Struve, and Luxemburg, examining aspects of their reading that more or less directly inspired their political engagement. These four protagonists saw literature as a guide and companion on the road to adulthood, and they routinely cited particular heroes and motifs. Well beyond offering inspiration in the narrower sense, a few books indeed taught them how to "drum," as Heine described.

Kautsky considered himself a precocious reader. By the age of eight, he was already studying thick reference works on world history, and he consumed "everything there was to read that I could find in my family home."[26] Through his mother's work as a writer, he came into contact with socialist literature at an early age. Reading Sand's novel *The Sin of Monsieur Antoine* at the age of seventeen was a turning point that ended his "fretful wavering over socialism." Around this time, he began writing his own novels as a means of self-expression. Sand's literary treatment of her theme—industrial exploitation and the destruction of humans and nature—fed the young Kautsky's sense of outrage. Her proposed solution gave him a point of identification,

which he later described at length, and not without some vanity, in
his memoirs: the wealthy Marquis de Boisguilbault, who was too old
to realize his humanitarian goals himself, bequeaths his fortune to the
socialist student Emile. In his memoir, the eighty-year-old Kautsky
cited the passage in which the marquis gives Emile his great commission: "You need knowledge of social science, and that is the result of
long-continued labor to which you will apply yourself with the aid of
the forces which your generation, not mine, will develop more or less
successfully, as God wills."[27] The marquis thereby hands Emile "the
instruments" to put his "opinions in practice," but also warns him,
"[T]hat does not mean that you have the ability as yet." To acquire
this ability, Emile will need "social science."[28] The marquis has faith in
Emile's intelligence "because it has its source in the heart. May God
give you genius, Emile, and may He give it to the men of your time!
For the genius of one man is almost nothing."[29]

Kautsky's reading of Sand marked the beginning of his "scientific" quest to solve the Social Question. Kautsky likely identified
with Emile and took the marquis's commission as his own. Both the
stylized narrative in Kautsky's memoir and his years of intellectual
labor after reading Sand's novel suggest that this literary identification
had a momentous effect on his development. Sand showed Kautsky
that the "search for one redemptive formula was quite foolish, and that
fully realized socialism would not spring from the minds of socialists
all at once. Embracing this science—insofar as it already existed—and
working on its further development became my highest goal from
this point on."[30] Kautsky failed to mention in his memoir that he had,
in fact, nurtured many different professional ambitions over the years
and that—as his diary and letters show—he had often been plagued
by great self-doubt. Nevertheless, the heart of this testimonial accu-
rately describes the beginning of his socialist turn. Kautsky saw himself as the practitioner of a new science, and he effectively became a
co-creator of Marxism on a quest to enlighten the people of his time.
Establishing Marxist doctrine as a "social science" became the project
of his life.

Lenin was sixteen years younger than Kautsky, so his potential reading material automatically included the first "classics" of an emerging Marxism—that is, not only Marx and Engels but also Plekhanov and Kautsky. His literary interests were relatively limited. In his early twenties he read from a canon that he cultivated hermetically thereafter. Later in life, he rarely read anything new outside of political economics and tactics. Since his brother Alexander's execution, he increasingly viewed the world through the periscope of his canon—like a "revolutionary in a submarine," according to Stefan Plaggenborg.[31] By his mid-twenties, he had little interest in the theories or philosophies of anyone other than the aforenamed founders of his worldview and thus remained "stranded within a small snippet of nineteenth-century intellectual life."[32] The work of Darwin was a lone exception. Lenin's mindset thus matched the characterization of a dyed-in-the-wool revolutionary in his favorite Russian novel, Chernyshevsky's *What Is to Be Done?* (1863). This is how one of the book's protagonists describes his philosophy of reading:

> There are only a few fundamental works on every subject. All the rest merely repeat, dilute, and distort what's more fully and clearly stated in these few fundamental works. One need read only those; anything else is a terrible waste of time. Take Russian literature, for example. I would say, "I'll read Gogol first of all." In thousands of other stories I can see, by reading only five or so lines on five different pages, that I'll find nothing but a corruption of Gogol. Why should I read them? . . . I read only original works, and only enough to grasp their originality. . . . Every book I read spares me from having to read hundreds of others.[33]

We do not know whether Lenin selected his own reading material in such a precisely utilitarian way. It seems likely that Plaggenborg's submarine metaphor is only partially apt. Later in life, Lenin had a strong inclination to glorify or condemn certain books, and the scene in *What Is to Be Done?* certainly approaches his understanding of literature and science. Nevertheless, his horizon of reading material was broader than either this scene or the periscope thesis suggests.

Lenin's reverence for Chernyshevsky's *What Is to Be Done?* merits closer attention, as biographers have long considered the novel formative to his identity, not least because he adapted the title for his own work in 1902. Robert Service writes that "it is a good bet" that Lenin identified with the novel's main character.[34] And yet one woman and three men have leading roles in the book—four "new persons" who know exactly what to do: what is "necessary," as Rakhmetov, the "extraordinary man," repeatedly affirms. The awkwardly constructed novel features the author's ongoing dialogue with both the reader and his characters. Chernyshevsky thus avoids and even defies conventional literary style. The heart of the story is about building a utopian future in the present: Vera Pavlovna escapes her repressive family home by entering into a platonic marriage with the medical student Dimitry Lopukhov; she founds a successful sewing cooperative and, in the end, becomes a doctor. It is tempting to draw parallels between Lenin's own childless and open marriage to Nadezhda Krupskaya and the novel's depiction of the ideal marriage as a companionable partnership of equals. Pavlovna's apparently asexual spouse Lopukhov feigns suicide so that she and his friend, Alexander Kirsanov, another "new man," can experience true love. Pavlovna's sewing cooperative embodies the successful collectivization of labor, consumption, and leisure; it is presented as the realization of a simple truth that is not yet widely understood: that humans are egotistical and constantly seek their own advantage, but as soon as they recognize that they are better off cooperating with one another, a just society becomes possible. Chernyshevsky's magic formula is solidarity through egoism, not altruism—the realization that every cooperative gesture is also self-serving.

These unsentimental ethics, which Chernyshevsky expressly conceived as a counterpoint to "idealism,"[35] fit easily with what many biographers have come to write about Lenin's personality. His engagement was based on a "dislike for sentimentality in politics."[36] He was goal-oriented, not altruistic; driven by reason, not emotion; he recognized pain and suffering, but only with respect to their "usefulness" in a given situation—as with the 1892–93 famine that played an important role in the early history of Russian Marxism.[37] Chernyshevsky's novel is full of reflections about the relationship between men and women, between theory and practice, and between reasonable desires (all poor people want to be wealthy) and unreasonable "fantasies" (all women want to be men). The affinity between many of these reflections and Lenin's own thinking is striking—or, put another way: this book apparently made a deep impression. Giving his most important political text the same title (published under the name "N. Lenin" in 1902) is only the most obvious sign. One can turn to nearly any page in the novel and find a theoretical dispute that contains core elements of Lenin's "cold," "prosaic" approach to the world. Dimitri Lopukhov (one of three possible figures of identification for Lenin), for example, tells Vera Pavlovna that all human behavior is driven by self-interest. She responds:

> "Let's assume that you're right—yes, you are right. All actions, as far as I can see, can be explained by advantage. But isn't that theory rather cold?"
>
> "Theory is supposed to be cold. The mind is supposed to make judgments about things coldly."
>
> "But it's merciless."
>
> "It shows no mercy toward fantasies that are empty and harmful."
>
> "But it's prosaic."
>
> "Poetic form isn't appropriate for science."
>
> "So this theory, whose validity I have no choice but to accept, condemns people to a cold, pitiless, prosaic life?"
>
> "No, Vera Pavlovna. The theory is cold, but it teaches man how to procure warmth. A match is cold, as is the side of the matchbox against which it's struck, as is the wood—but together they produce the fire that cooks our food and heats our bodies. This theory is pitiless, but by following it, people will cease to be pitiful objects of idle compassion. A lancet isn't supposed to bend, or else we'd have to pity the patient, who'd be no better off for our pity. The theory is prosaic, but it reveals the genuine motives of life; poetry resides in the truth of life."[38]

This passage illustrates why Lenin felt drawn to Chernyshevsky not only on a rational level but emotionally as well.[39] He shared Chernyshevsky's sober dogma toward improving the world. His conviction that "idle" sympathy would not ease suffering is apparent in a letter he wrote to his mother from Siberian exile in September 1897; the twenty-seven-year-old Lenin complained that his younger brother Dmitri, a medical student, wanted to help peasants who had contracted the plague.[40] Lenin also imitated his role model Chernyshevsky in the tone and style of his writing. While Chernyshevsky's protagonists repeated that they had to do what was "necessary," Lenin's own *What Is to Be Done?*, written at the height of the revisionism debate, divided the history of Russian social democracy into three periods of varying success. He ended his text with a blunt appeal: "By way of summing up what has been expounded above, we may meet the question, What is to be done? with the brief reply: Put an End to the Third Period."[41]

The undisputed influence of Chernyshevsky notwithstanding, Lenin's interest in literature cannot be reduced to a hidebound socialist canon. With the help of memoirs written by members of Lenin's family, Service has reconstructed the diverse literary influences that shaped him as a child and young adult, leading Service to suspect that the adult revolutionary even had a "secret intellectual life."[42] Lenin's outwardly narrow interest in revolutionary tactics and methods was apparently inspired by his early reading of Chernyshevsky, but he simultaneously read authors as diverse as Stowe, London, Nietzsche, Clausewitz, and Machiavelli.

Indeed, in her memoirs, Krupskaya portrays a man who worked, read, and thought without ceasing. Her highly stylized recollections were part of a "quasi-religious myth"[43] that she worked to establish after Lenin's death. Although we should approach Krupskaya's text with great caution—keeping in mind its intended audience, the Russian "working class"[44]—her detailed description of Lenin's literary interests supports the thesis of a double intellectual life. If we believe that, after his brother's execution, the young Lenin developed a "physical aversion to the lifeworld of 'educated society,'"[45] a circumspect relationship to the bourgeois classics seems altogether plausible. According to Krupskaya, Lenin had admired not only Chernyshevsky but also Turgenev and Pisarev since his youth. In Siberian exile he read Hegel, Pushkin, Nekrasov, Lermontov, Goethe's *Faust*, and Heine's poetry. In Paris, he was said to have immersed himself, like Guesde, in Hugo's *Les Châtiments*. During the First World War, he was fascinated by *Le Feu*, Barbusse's personal novel about the horrors of the trenches on the Western Front. In his final months, he wanted to hear Saltykov-Shchedrin and Gorky. And two days before his death, he asked his wife to read him London's short story "Love of Life," about a gold prospector who staggers through the North American wilderness and barely escapes starvation.[46]

All of these works have something to say about Lenin's relationship to literature and its "usefulness." Beyond how these works affected him emotionally, which is difficult to reconstruct, he appreciated them for two reasons, beginning with their function as authentic reflections of social reality. Lenin was impressed by Turgenev's depictions of rural life, Stowe's depiction of slavery in *Uncle Tom's Cabin*, and Chekov's portrait of an Okhrana prison, which reminded Lenin of his own experiences in detention and even made him physically sick.[47] Second, Lenin read—particularly Chernyshevsky's *What Is to Be Done?*—as a guide and call to action. That he read these books at all is testament to his upbringing in a cultural environment that supported "national, political and social freedom."[48]

Even so, Lenin showed no trace of sentimentality toward literary themes; he saw sentimentality in literature as a manipulation of social reality. The best example of this is his caustic analysis of the work of Tolstoy, which he published in tandem with Plekhanov after the Revolution of 1905. His criticism shows how thoroughly—and how thoroughly grounded in *one* perspective—Lenin read great works of literature. He approached Tolstoy's work through the aforementioned lens of literature as a supposedly "correct" reflection of reality: "To identify the great artist with the revolution which he [Tolstoy] has obviously failed to understand . . . may at first sight seem strange," since "a mirror which does not reflect things correctly could hardly be called a mirror." Lenin nevertheless justified his preoccupation with the widely revered Tolstoy with this grudging admission: "If we have before us a really great artist, he must have reflected in his work at least some of the essential aspects of the revolution."[49]

Russian socialists were thus challenged to formulate a political response to the most popular and engaged Russian writer at the beginning of the twentieth century. They regarded Tolstoy's mantra of nonviolent resistance as a dangerous trend, which sought to "augment" Marx with Tolstoy's "generosity."[50] In Lenin's view, Tolstoy's work and engagement reflected "the contradictory conditions of Russian life in the last third of the nineteenth century." Tolstoy might "episodically" describe the liberation of the peasants—which was accompanied by capitalist rules that brought different, not less, social misery—but only Marxist socialists could grasp and combat this misery systematically. After the failed Revolution of 1905, Lenin spoke for these socialists when he asserted that Tolstoy's writing had fed "the immature dreaming, the political inexperience, the revolutionary flabbiness" that had prevented the Russian masses from boldly seizing power. Instead, they had "put on the yoke again—quite in the vein of Leo Tolstoy!"[51] This kind of literature was completely unsuitable as a guide to revolutionary action—and thus, for Lenin, it had little value.

To a certain extent Struve agreed with Lenin's critique of Tolstoy, even after he and Lenin had parted ways around 1900. Struve had already abandoned Marxist socialism before the Revolution of 1905, but he, too, honored Tolstoy as a "colossal presence in Russian literature" and recognized the fundamental contradiction in how Tolstoy and the Marxists sought to change the world. Struve respected Tolstoy's radical pacifism and agreed with his rejection of "social revolution," as such a process merely replaced one kind of violence with another.[52] Unlike Lenin, Struve did not criticize Tolstoy's supposed dogma of acquiescence. Instead, he focused his critique on Tolstoy's thesis that society could not be reformed externally but only through the "moral," "internal reform" of each individual. Struve believed that a combination of social and individual interests was essential to the creation of a just order under "democratic socialism."[53]

Struve was Lenin's contemporary in multiple respects. Born in the same year, both grew up in families that greatly supported their education and intellectual curiosity. Both cherished their years as university students in the metropolis of St. Petersburg, where they embraced Marxist doctrine and became cofounders of the Russian Social Democratic Party in the 1890s. Reading Pushkin, Aksakov, Saltykov-Shchedrin, and Dostoyevsky was second nature in Struve's family home, which was a politically and socially open-minded, if not always peaceful, place. Books were important enough to Struve that he organized his own biography around readings that had been especially meaningful to him. Unlike Lenin, he described the emotional effect of books as a sensual experience: "I did not merely take in their ideas and their utterances, I lived them through in the strict sense of a profound sympathetic experience, verging on agitation and possession. And these things never go for nothing, especially when one is young, when one's soul is fresh and plastic."[54]

An early, key example of a sensual literary experience was his "discovery" of Pushkin through Dostoyevsky's memorial address, delivered at the unveiling of the Pushkin monument in Moscow in June 1880. Struve had just turned ten years old. He must have learned about the tumultuous event through the newspaper or in conversations at home. Dostoyevsky praised the great writer as the voice of the Russian people, touching off waves of thunderous applause. Shortly after that memorable day, Dostoyevsky wrote to his wife that some members of the audience had responded with "wails of ecstasy" and even lost consciousness.[55] It was the tone of Dostoyevsky's speech, above all, that triggered passionate affirmation as well as sharp criticism. He ardently declared the national poet, who had passed away in 1837, to be the prophet of a Russian "universal humanity" that aspired to unite all peoples.[56]

For the young Struve, this speech was an intellectual wake-up call. The "discovery and disclosure of Pushkin by the prophetic utterances of Dostoevsky" represented "the first strong, purely spiritual, purely cultural experience, upheaval, and revelation" of his childhood.[57] As

an adult Marxist, however, this metaphysical revelation provided no
release from the many dilemmas of the tsarist empire. To the contrary,
Struve saw the mystical enshrouding of the "Russian soul" as part of
the problem. Nevertheless, his recollection of this speech underscores
his deep grounding in the Slavophile discourse, which he never really outgrew, and which he returned to after distancing himself from
Marxism.

Struve's parents revered Dostoyevsky: "My mother was one of . . .
Dostoevsky's contemporaries; for them, around 1880, he became life's
teacher, a worldly spiritual father, what the French call a *directeur de
conscience*."[58] Once she even received a letter from her hero, which
was treated by the family like a holy relic. The sight of Dostoyevsky's
handwriting and signature was indelibly etched in Struve's childhood memory, and his father's tales of the author's "grand burial in
Petersburg" were just as unforgettable. According to Struve's later
recollections, Dostoyevsky's literary worlds, the ambivalent characters
and the complexity of their fates, continued to fascinate him for the
rest of his life. He drew on Dostoyevsky's panoramas of human experience to make sense of his own biography. In a 1931 speech about
Dostoyevsky as a "great sinner," he made explicit reference to his own
life: via his mother, he recalled, he had learned from Dostoyevsky that
good and evil were not mutually exclusive because human nature was
complex. Humans could be both saints and sinners, as Luther had once
preached. Struve saw the question of a just society as correspondingly
complex. As a young man, he believed that he had found the answer
in Marxism. However, he ultimately renounced this worldview, not
least because of its simplistic notions about human nature.[59]

Reverence for Pushkin and Dostoyevsky thus ran deep in Struve's
family and was reinforced by his own reading—a narrative that
corresponds to his own self-characterization as a child patriot. As
an adult, Struve demonstratively sought to distance himself from his
youthful pathos, at least with respect to his socialist years. He later
emphasized that he had never been an "emotional" social democrat
but rather one of "conviction." Although he had felt "passion" and

"love" for "freedom" and Russia, "it was simply by way of reasoning" that he became "an adept of Socialism."[60]

Struve's second literary hero, Ivan Aksakov, was likewise revered by his entire family. Here, too, his parents' reading habits and openness to discussion—Aksakov's journal *Rus* and especially its criticism of tsarist domestic and foreign policy—exerted a formative influence. His 1924 eulogy for Aksakov includes reminiscences of his own childhood. Read together, Struve's autobiographical texts suggest that he may have oriented his own biography toward Aksakov's, whose fusion of morality and materialism, of intellectual and practical engagement on behalf of the Russian people, were qualities that Struve liked to see in himself.[61] The renowned writer grew increasingly critical of the policies of Tsar Alexander III after 1885, asserting that "genuine" patriotism meant loyalty to the Russian people, and not to the monarchy. The Struves followed his antiroyalist turn, and the fifteen-year-old became a liberal nationalist. In a prominent article in *Rus* on 6 December 1885, Aksakov responded to a formal reprimand from the Interior Ministry that he was a traitor because of his "unpatriotic" criticism of the regime.[62] Struve later described this text as another key event that he—and along with him, an entire generation of young Russians—experienced in a profoundly moving way.[63] Aksakov's public affirmation of "genuine" patriotism "acted as the warm or even hot breeze in which my own love of freedom finally matured."[64]

Struve's third hero was the writer and journalist Mikhail Saltykov-Shchedrin, who had long influenced Russian public discourse.[65] As a young man, Struve read and reread Saltykov-Shchedrin's satires, stories, articles, and letters. He was particularly impressed by the writer's "invective against the stagnating, deadening public reaction of the eighties, pervaded not so much with anger as with ironic sorrow and secret anguish."[66] Despair over the state of Russia after the assassination of 1881, the subsequent wave of repression, and the kowtowing of the intelligentsia were central motifs of Struve's intellectual development. He admired Saltykov-Shchedrin's courageous engagement as a public intellectual and his unsparing, satirical criticism of obeisance. Not unlike Lenin's criticism of the pacifist Tolstoy, Saltykov-Shchedrin's late satires of the 1880s pilloried the supposed cowardice of the Russian people and the impotence of their leaders.[67] We can safely assume that for Luxemburg, too, literature was both an intellectual and even a sensual experience. Her biographer J. P. Nettl notes that "she was the type of person who would always want to fill out her knowledge of history and science with the perceptions of fiction."[68] Her idol was Adam Mickiewicz, the father of Polish Romanticism, whose idealism she shared and passionately admired. Among friends, she referred to the poet by his first name only.[69] Mickiewicz had a wide audience all over Europe in the nineteenth century. His poetry articulated a "visceral and at the same time ethically provocative attachment to a cause," speaking with "unusual power on behalf of a people that dared resist the brutal might of reactionary empires."[70] His importance for the history of Polish literature has often been likened to Goethe's influence in German-speaking Europe. Luxemburg herself rejected this comparison, which was already common during her lifetime, by asserting that Mickiewicz should not be compared at all, not even to Homer.[71] Genuine masters were unique. For Luxemburg, the young Mickiewicz was a prophet of national freedom, shaped by Napoleon's fight against Prussia and Russia and subsequent hopes for reestablishing an independent Polish state. On the occasion of his one hundredth birthday in 1898, Luxemburg celebrated him as a Polish adept of German Romanticism; this movement had inspired the turn toward history and idealized a Polish nation that had not existed as a state since 1795. "Whole constellations of glittering young talent" had emanated from this inspiration, and "the most brilliant star of this dawn twilight, the mighty genius of Adam Mickiewicz, arose in the firmament of Polish literature."[72]

Luxemburg frequently cited the 1820 poem "Ode to Youth," a key text in her Mickiewicz canon. The poem's imagery and references to Goethe's "Prometheus" recalled the Icarus legend, calling upon the youth to soar "above a dead world" and the "nations of skeletons," toward "the heavenly land of illusion," full of wonder and hope for renewal. The youth—"mighty in union, in exaltation wise"—understand that "the nectar of life is only sweet . . . when it is shared with others."[73] In her personal translation of the poem from the Polish, Luxemburg described its quintessence as a call to a "whole generation to unite all its forces and 'lift this mouldering world off its hinges' to steer it into new courses."[74] She occasionally used this image in her speeches—as, for example, in a lecture from April 1910: "Our own mission, the historic calling of the proletariat, is to lift the entire bourgeois state off its hinges, with all of its bourgeois parliamentary splendor, and to realize socialism."[75]

While Mickiewicz largely emboldened his readers to look at present conditions and imagine a better future, Luxemburg read these verses (which struck her like "hammer-blows") as a call for revolutionary action—indeed, for lifting the world off its hinges. There was nothing sentimental about her reverence for the Romantic poet or her own penchant for romanticization. Although she accepted that looking to the past was a meaningful undertaking for some Romantics, the political realist in her chose the opposite path; instead of seeking refuge in the past, she sought to take the present by storm. Thus, Luxemburg's relationship to Mickiewicz was ambivalent—emotionally warm, yet intellectually cool. The "nightingale of Polish nationalism" had ultimately devoted himself to a cause—the national idea—that history had rendered dead on arrival. Luxemburg had little appetite for the efforts of the emerging workers' movement to paint the naive and utopian elements of Mickiewicz's thought as socialist. For her, the "true cause" was transnational. The "enlightened" Polish proletariat had the right, even the prerogative, to claim Mickiewicz's work as part of their cultural heritage and to hold up his heroism as a model of engagement for a higher cause. Yet truly appropriating Mickiewicz meant overcoming his naive political Romanticism. Just as Marx had placed German philosophy at the feet of the German "proletariat," she declared the Polish "working class" the sole legitimate "heir of Romantic poetry."[76]

Luxemburg had an intimate relationship with literature, despite—
or perhaps because of—her persistence in emphasizing its connection to "reality." She expressed this connection most clearly in the
introduction to her German translation of Vladimir Korolenko's
History of My Contemporary, which she completed in prison in mid-
1918. The text is a celebration of Russian literature; her impassioned
gaze explains why she did not regard the great Tolstoy with the
same disdain as did Lenin and Struve, although she, too, considered
his "ascetic and moralizing tendency" reactionary.[77] This text about
Korolenko underscores Luxemburg's generally instrumental understanding of literature: without a political worldview, literature is essentially meaningless. Conversely, literature that is "anchored" in an
"established great worldview" is literally powerful enough to spark
revolution. Only the "vibrating social consciousness" of a "poetic
personality," she asserted, can fully grasp the psychology, mystery,
and complexity of reality, "capturing it in powerful works." In the
best case, as with Korolenko, literature could even pave the way for
a "new historic 'violence,'" which in 1917 Russia "was to lift its beneficent arm"—the arm of labor and the fight for liberty.[78] And so,
six months before her death, she celebrated the Russian Revolution
as a political *and* literary achievement. She routinely cited the first
and last lines of her favorite works and poems in letters, speeches,
and other texts. Literary witticisms often seasoned her remarks,
as when she ironically commented on a windfall ("more loot for
us") with the well-known line from Schiller's "Ode to Joy": "Seid
umschlungen, Millionen!" (Be embraced, millions!).[79] Schiller's
"millions," of course, were a reference not to money but to the
brotherhood of man.

A handful of texts, including Mickiewicz's "Ode to Youth," played a
particularly prominent, symbolic role in Luxemburg's biography. Like
many socialists and liberals in the second half of the nineteenth century, she revered the works of the Swiss writer Conrad Ferdinand
Meyer, notwithstanding his post-1871 turn toward anti-French chau-
vinism.[80] Meyer published his epic poem *Hutten's Last Days* in the

fall of 1871, after Germany's victory over France. The title character's poetic "confession" embodied the era's "revolutionary mentality at its most romantic."[81] Luxemburg even considered these verses for her own epitaph, although she eventually rejected them as too over-wrought. She wrote to a friend that she would prefer the onomat-opoetic *zwi-zwi* of a titmouse on her grave, a choice that suggests a relationship with nature no less intense.[82]

Luxemburg was fond of quoting long excerpts of Hutten's regretful "confession" to her friends—as in 1904, when she sought to illustrate her mood after her defeat at the Amsterdam congress of the Second International. Frustrated but unbroken, she would continue to carry the torch of "orthodox 'radicalism.'" In a letter to her friend Henriette Roland Holst, she repeated the following verses from *Hutten's Last Days* in order to underscore her resolve:

> Here, now, I'm walking over my grave—
> Hark, Hutten, won't you make your confession?
>
> It's a Christian custom. I'll beat my breast.
> Who is a person and not conscious of guilt?
>
> I regret having recognized my duty all too late!
> I regret that my heart burned too weakly!
>
> I regret that I didn't enter my feuds—
> With sharper blows and bolder deeds!
>
> I regret the hour I wore no armor!
> I regret the day I struck no wound!
>
> I regret—strewing ashes on my head—
> That I didn't believe more firmly in victory!
>
> I regret that I was banished only once!
> I regret that I often knew human fear!
>
> I regret—I'll confess contritely—
> That I have not always been Hutten!

Luxemburg interpreted this epic poem, like Mickiewicz's "Ode," as a call to battle, and she even used the same metaphor to describe its effect on her: "Is this not written with brazen hammer blows?"[83] In the same letter, from December 1904, she complained elaborately about what she saw as the lethargy of the German Social Democrats. The SPD was counting on its growing membership numbers to take power "automatically," not grasping that "for a revolutionary movement not to go forward means—to fall back." "Quantity must be transformed into quality," Luxemburg insisted, so the "masses" could become a revolutionary force. This did not mean merely "'going into the streets' or any kind of artificial adventurism." Rather, "our entire work must be given a different, deeper tone," and "consciousness of our own strength must be raised."[84] The letter shows, yet again, Luxemburg's strong faith in her own abilities—evident, not least, in the drive to push herself (and the movement) ever further. Ulrich von Hutten's confession (as imagined by Meyer) seemed to affirm her self-empowered thinking, and she interpreted Hutten's half-hearted empowerment as a missed opportunity.

From the vantage point of the late nineteenth century, the humanist and militant reformer Hutten was no longer a tragic hero, but a victor of history. His unconditional, powerful engagement was famously embodied by his motto, "I dared!" Luxemburg sympathized with Hutten's radicalism—although, as she herself noted, her connection to him was more "psychological" than "logical." (In the end, he fought "only" for a revolution in faith, not for universal social change.)[85] Meyer's Hutten was particularly appealing to Luxemburg because he was both a writer who fought and a fighter who wrote. He not only used language as a metaphorical weapon; he fought with real weapons:

> I *am* a wordsmith! That's what I call myself!
> In the fire of my anger I forged
> Armor and weapons as needed
> And truly, my swords cut deep![86]

Luxemburg's relationship to language was similarly instrumental; she was extraordinarily confident in her own ability to wield it effectively.[87] She eclectically drew upon the most trenchant verses of literary forefathers who had once tried out the role of political intellectual (a role she herself had been practicing since her youth): Heine, Ludwig Börne, and of course Meyer. Their literary engagement could not have been more different. Heine was a political poet whose rhetoric of action was limited to using the mind as a weapon—the "reflexive power of thought," as Jürgen Habermas once put it. He was revolutionary in the Hegelian sense but could hardly be considered a revolutionary socialist. (Thus, only in post-1945 Germany did he acquire a certain following as an intellectual role model.)[88] Luxemburg nevertheless perceived a similar attitude in the works of all three poets, seeing them as drummers of mobilization. It was typical, therefore, that she turned to the first lines of Heine's poem "Doctrine" (quoted at the beginning of this chapter) in order to urge a wavering comrade not to be discouraged by internal party squabbling: "Just don't think about leaving! Stay right where you are and recite Heine's verse: 'Beat the drum and don't be afraid. . . !'"[89]

Luxemburg's relationship to language figured prominently in her search for role models. Although now and then she quoted a witticism by Heine, it was his adversary Börne whom she anointed as her third hero—a literary influence that has received comparatively little attention among her many biographers. In contrast to Meyer, Luxemburg complained, no one in Germany—or at least, in the SPD—read "my dear Börne" (anymore). Social Democratic publications like *Vorwärts* and the *Neue Zeit* did, however, pay tribute to this "noble man" and "free-spirited cosmopolitan."[90] Börne's notorious, bitingly satirical commentaries on current events served as a model for Luxemburg, in both style and substance. She was impressed by his irreverence toward authority figures of all kinds, including the Germans' "fearful consuls," Goethe and Schiller, whom he pilloried in his "Third Letter" of October 1831:

And these are the consuls the German people [*Volk*] elected! Goethe—
who is more fearful than a mouse, who burrows into the ground upon
the slightest noise, giving up air, light, freedom, indeed the entire spectrum of life, longed for even by stones that are dead, just so he can
nibble on a stolen scrap of bacon in his hole, undisturbed—and Schiller,
at once noble but spineless, hiding from tyranny behind a cloudy mist,
pleading in vain for help from the gods above, so blinded by the sun that
he no longer sees the earth, forgetting the people he wanted to save.
And so—without leader, guardian, advocate, or protector—the hapless
country will become a prize of kings, and the people will become a
laughingstock.[91]

Luxemburg notably defended Goethe against Börne's criticism,
describing the two adversaries as great, if incompatible, characters.
Börne, whom Luxemburg appreciated for his broad perspective,
commented on the decline of his fatherland like a "Roman republican.""But the whole light-hearted world of appearances," Luxemburg
observed, "existing beyond state boundaries and civic responsibilities,
beyond good and evil—that was closed off to him." She saw Börne
as Robespierre, and Goethe as Danton, representing "the primordial,
eternal opposition of a 'Christian' ascetic nature toward a 'Hellenic'
sybaritic one" (although Börne, as she certainly knew, was born into
a Jewish family).[92]

This character sketch says more about Luxemburg than about her
two literary heroes. The artistic, nature-loving, sybaritic side of her
personality, which is still admired today, is also the most difficult to
explain with respect to her political engagement. Her personal letters,
sketches, and poems—and the hagiographic portrayals of her love for
plants, insects, and titmice outside her prison window—have tended
to obscure the radical core of her political personality. (Scholarship
of anticommunist provenance is a significant exception.) The ability
to countenance, even to practice art and politics, gentleness and acer-
bity, side by side was not only a talent that she ascribed to Börne;
in a certain sense, this "split personality" was surely her most important quality. The Dutch writer and communist Henriette Roland
Holst was one of few contemporaries who recognized her "divided

nature"; Roland Holst's portrait of Luxemburg captures this back-and-forth between affection and distance.[93] Perhaps, however, we can reframe this duality as a coherent character trait by considering, for example, Luxemburg's deployment of animal and nature metaphors in political battle. She once summarized her critique of Bernstein's revisionism thus: "Forgotten *Kathedersozialisten* who buried themselves, long dead and rotting away because of their long, pointless speeches; 'subjectivists'; Stammler's fickle 'social ideal,' which, like a frisky butterfly, can never be caught ('the end goal is nothing to me, the movement—the act of catching—everything')—all this was suddenly revived in the theories of Bernstein and his followers."[94] Here she misappropriated the simple beauty of nature to disparage her political opponents.

In contrast to Börne's critique of Goethe, Luxemburg mostly shared his critique of Schiller. Luxemburg's childhood and youth—not unlike that of her later rival Bernstein—was formatively influenced by her mother's "cultic" admiration for Schiller's works.[95] Luxemburg did not, however, develop similar reverence. Her distaste for Schiller was a reaction not only to overexposure at home but to his veneration within the SPD, most notably by men such as Kautsky and Franz Mehring, who stylized him as a bourgeois master storyteller who was "close to the people," in touch with the "rebellious tendencies of the working classes."[96] Only after revisiting Schiller's work, including his histories, later in life did Luxemburg come to develop her own appreciation for the writer.[97] She reviewed Mehring's Schiller biography, part of a wave of commemorative literature that marked the one hundredth anniversary of his death, for the *Neue Zeit* in 1905. Although Mehring was in fact a vocal critic of Schiller's glorification by the party, Luxemburg still criticized his portrait of Schiller's *life*—in a very subtle way: she cloaked her critique in generous praise. According to Luxemburg, Mehring brought German workers closer to the "sublime beauty" of Schiller's work and encouraged their reflection by suggesting that the revolutionary aspects of Schiller's writings were not the result of a genuinely materialist, socially critical worldview, but rather the author's search for literary material. After all, Luxemburg wrote, "Schiller was above all a true *dramatist* on a grand scale"; his entire work was characterized by "the flight from social misery into the sovereign world of art." This explained the "petit-bourgeois" misinterpretation of Schiller's "revolutionary idealism," "which sees a 'revolution' in *every* protest against the existing laws, that is to say in the external appearance of protest, irrespective of its inner tendency, its social content." In fact, Schiller's "inner tendency" was clearly antirevolutionary; the "great French Revolution" repelled him, precisely because it was a revolution.[98]

Despite Luxemburg's critique of Schiller's stylization as a revolutionary—which, to her mind, did not correspond with a Marxist worldview—she still thanked Mehring in a personal letter for the "enjoyment" that "your Schiller provided; you convinced me to love him."[99] Although literature and politics were inseparable, Luxemburg counted Schiller's works among the "grandfather novels" of the outgoing, "decadent" century. According to the grown daughter's Marx-informed analysis, Mother Luxemburg had read Schiller in a conventional bourgeois manner, unaware that his "merely" sentimental and humanist works constituted an ultimately ineffective protest against the existing order.[100]

Luxemburg thus agreed with Börne's sharp critique of Schiller as a poet in the artistic heavens who was out of touch with the world. His scorn for Goethe in no way dampened her enthusiasm for Börne. As she wrote to her Zurich friends Robert and Mathilde Seidel shortly after moving to Berlin in 1898, she always returned to Börne's *Letters from Paris* for rhetorical inspiration, for its welcome contrast to the "so wooden, so stereotyped" language of her party's publications. She liked to borrow Börne's metaphors precisely because of their antidotal effect—as when she described the arguments of the revisionists in Bernstein's circle as "hollow nuts." She felt like Börne, who compared reading "the texts of his semi-official opponents" to "cracking hollow nuts"; he cracked them with "honest effort" and with a certain anticipation, but in the end all that remained in his mouth was the "repulsive taste—of worms." She felt the same way, Luxemburg wrote in another polemic against the revisionists in 1899, when she read the "countless texts, pamphlets, and articles about the 'crisis in Marxism' that have literally been raining down in the past months, like nuts in a strong wind."[101]

Time and again, Börne's texts thus helped to (re)vitalize her personal engagement, the passion and commitment that the *one* cause demanded:

> I believe that every time, every day, with every article, you have to live and feel through the whole matter again; then fresh words, which speak from and to the heart, can also be found for the old and familiar. But you get so used to a truth that you rattle off the deepest and greatest things like a paternoster. I am determined, when writing, never to forget my enthusiasm for what I've written or my introspection. That's exactly why I read old Börne from time to time; he faithfully reminds me of my oath.[102]

These lines provide insight into the overall temperature of Luxemburg's engagement, her need to live and feel truthfully, and her sworn devotion to the cause. Börne's inspiration not only stabilized her unusually strong faith in her own potential; it also lifted her spirits and reinvigorated her devotion. As Heine rhapsodized in his poem, books can indeed drum people awake.

PART II

Politicization

Paths to Marxism I: London, Paris, Zurich, Vienna (1878–88)

> O mighty knowledge, fill our league
> With all your fortitude,
> Show your invincibility
> In our important work!
> You are our shield, our armor,
> The sharp point of our swords,
> That, by our hand, false idols
> Of the day are overpowered.
>
> —Festive hymn of the Workers' Educational Association in Vienna, 1873,
> composed by Joseph and Andreas Scheu, Schweizerisches
> Sozialarchiv Zürich, Schweizerischer Arbeitersänger-Verband,
> Ar 58.31.10, 1

In April 1887 Kautsky reported to his friend Ede Bernstein that the editors of the *Austrian Workers' Calendar* in Brünn wanted to publish a group portrait of the "representatives of scientific socialism":

Engels in the middle, surrounded by the others. So there's also an Austrian in the group, they insist on including me. In such a situation, I think being coy is as ridiculous as pushing oneself to the fore. But they asked me (here I was eating bread and butter [referring to a grease spot on the page]) whom else I would recommend. Now I need some good advice. Naturally Lafargue, Bebel, Liebknecht. But who else? Having me in the group complicates things because, if we want to go with equal status, we'll actually have to include countless others: Stiebeling, Douai, Bax, Aveling, Nieuwenhuis, G. Deville, Guesde, and plenty of Germans—not to mention the deceased. . . .

I think, however, one can avoid the quandary by defining scientific socialism as Marxism, limiting the field to consistent [*konsequent*] Marxists, and selecting only those who are interested in the Austrians in some way. . . . I ask, therefore, that you send your picture and biography, as soon as you receive the request from Brünn. . . .

Moreover, I have to admit that I find the whole thing awkward, and most awkward of all, that I'm supposed to participate in the selection. Perhaps I'll reconsider and decline, and I'll just send them my photograph because they're asking so clearly for it, and I'll let the editors of the "Workers' Calendar" take responsibility for their choices. In any case, I ask you to share your thoughts.[1]

After weeks passed without a reply from Bernstein, Luise Kautsky asked Bernstein's wife, Regina, to pursue the matter further; postscripts by spouses were quite common in the Kautsky-Bernstein correspondence. In May 1887 Regina wrote to Luise, "Ede says to tell your husband that he should send them his own picture and decline to give advice. He thinks that without singling out special groups—Reichstag delegates, "martyrs," etc.—there's no reasonable way to draw a line with the masses of barnyard fowl gadding about the movement. In the end, the question of individual worth is a matter of personal opinion."[2]

The 1887 conversation between Kautsky, Bernstein, and their wives shows how closely the project of Marxism was tied to the personalities and personal relationships of its "epigones."[3] Kautsky believed that the group portrait should present an established "school"[4] of "consistent" Marxists, living or dead, thereby offering canonical orientation to the Austrian movement. Bernstein, on the other hand, warned that any selection would ultimately be a subjective judgment. Bernstein was not yet concerned by what Kautsky already saw as political necessity—although Kautsky did feel a certain unease about claiming this authority. At this moment in time, the two friends were in exile—Kautsky in London, and Bernstein in Zurich. They had studied the works of Marx and Engels together in Zurich between 1880 and 1885, publishing their first related texts soon thereafter. They collaborated closely on a German translation of Marx's *Misère de la Philosophie* (1885). Bernstein wrote the first volume in the "Social Democratic Library" series, *Social and Private Property* (1883), and Kautsky wrote *The Economic Doctrines of Karl Marx* (1887), a summary of Marx's *Capital*. The students were well on their way to becoming teachers themselves.

The following reconstruction of the protagonists' readings of Marx is part of the creation story of Marxism—a vast political project, which Engels could never have accomplished on his own after Marx's death in 1883. Participants in the conflict between Marx, Lassalle, and Bakunin had used the term "Marxist" since the 1850s, but usually to mean an authoritarian style of politics and leadership rather than Marx's ideas.[5] Only as Marx's works became more widely read in the 1870s and 1880s did the term accrue ideological meaning and political heft. Even in 1887, as Kautsky's letter to Bernstein shows, there was uncertainty about how to present the emerging Marxist canon to the wider world. Building ideological (self-)assurance was an extensive learning process, which also involved writing the first texts *about* Marx's works. For Kautsky and others, this process of learning was a virtue born of necessity. "As long as Marxism is not taught in schools and we have to approach it autodidactically, each of us will find our way only through trial and error," Kautsky wrote in 1886.[6] His learning experience was typical of many emerging Marxists.

By investigating how each of the protagonists came to terms with Marx's works, we can analyze how one of the most influential modern political worldviews emerged and spread. Why did Marxism provide the strongest ideological foundation for the continental workers' movements? The historian Hans-Ulrich Wehler has observed that, in the last third of the nineteenth century, the German Social Democratic Party (SPD) increasingly formulated "all its problems and aims in its struggle for emancipation in the language of Marxism," a phenomenon (not unique to Germany) that deserves closer explanation.[7] More recently, Thomas Welskopp has argued that Bismarck's exclusionary policies robbed the movement of a realistic "option for revolution," and so a heightened need for utopia arose by the mid-1870s,

as expressed in numerous texts about socialism as a vision for the future, by authors such as Johann Most and August Bebel. This "utopian
production" increasingly adopted Marx's vocabulary and exploited his
rhetorical potential.[8] In seeking to identify reasons for the emergence
and spread of Marxism, we should not underestimate its explanatory
power, at all levels of the movement, by the late 1870s. The first generation of Marxist intellectuals effectively brought Marx's ideas to the
organized workers' movements by interpreting and popularizing his
work. The original texts by Marx and Engels had limited resonance
among workers, who more often read texts by Kautsky or Plekhanov.[9]

John P. Nettl remarks in his Luxemburg biography that late-
nineteenth-century socialists differed from earlier revolutionaries in
their emphasis on "a period of study." In fact, socialism's entrance on the
stage of European political ideas transformed the key qualifications for
becoming a revolutionary: theory and canonical knowledge increasingly took precedence over practice and the courage to fight. Science
became the most important weapon, and the supposed synthesis of
theory and practice was both the point of departure and the ultimate
goal of Marxist socialism.[10] The history of Marxism's founding must be
understood in the context of industrialization and the expanding authority of science (*Verwissenschaftlichung*). Marxism was both precursor
and product of the *Verwissenschaftlichung* of society and the ensuing
"interference of science and politics" that set in around 1880.[11]

In Marxism, "science" simultaneously functioned as both paradigm
and pathos, intellectual framework and emotional anchor. Most of our
nine protagonists came to theory from practice. Already politically and
socially engaged, they then began to read the groundbreaking texts that
were circulating among a critical, left-leaning European public.[12] At the
start of the 1870s, the available corpus of work by Marx and Engels was
still extremely thin. It grew significantly by the end of the decade, thanks
to new editions, translations, syntheses, and Engels's own late work.[13]

In general, it is surprising how little we know about the protagonists'
first encounters with Marx (which is to say, with works written by
Marx and Engels). Just as Marx's writing is unthinkable without
Engels, without Engels's own work there would be no Marxism. Most

of the protagonists' biographers rely on a mixture of autobiographical statements, well-worn legends, and repeated suppositions about
the protagonists' first encounters with *Capital* and the *Manifesto of the
Communist Party*, but they do not actually reconstruct their subjects'
reading experiences.

If we look collectively at the protagonists' youthful encounters with
Marx and when these occurred, the picture that emerges is quite varied.
However, the emotional and intellectual impacts of these encounters
were astonishingly consistent. The protagonists did not read Marx; they
discovered him. There was even a typical "Marx experience."[14] Studying
Marx's texts did not mean reading them only once; it meant embarking
upon a process of learning that never really ended. This insight is in no
way diminished by acknowledging that this generation's defining experience was the repression of the socialist movement—and not, in fact,
reading Marx.[15] Both experiences can be understood as complementary
conditions. The protagonists' repressive reality prefigured their reading
of Marx, and, conversely, Marx's theses structured their perceptions of
state persecution. Getting to the bottom of this relationship demands
attention not only to the protagonists' personal writings and early
published work but also to the circumstances of their lives. Texts that
sought to popularize Marx (including Kautsky's *Economic Doctrines of
Karl Marx*, Luxemburg's *Introduction to Political Economy*, and Plekhanov's
Socialism and Political Struggle) often contain the authors' relatively unfiltered impressions. Their personal enthusiasm shines through when their
intent in writing was to win over readers. Marx's significance for the
protagonists and their worldview should not be reduced to the potential of his vague political beliefs.[16] Rather, we should view Marx's work
as a package of incendiary ideas—an extraordinarily compelling analysis of the present and an avant-garde, and ostensibly scientific, manual
for improving the world.

My own analysis of the protagonists' reading experiences is divided
into two periods. The first encompasses the long 1880s, as Marx's
ideas gained a foothold in France, Germany, and Austria, and is illustrated by the experiences of Guesde, Jaurès, Bernstein, Kautsky, and
Adler. This period begins in 1878, when Guesde first wrote to Marx

about the ideological direction of the socialists in France. It ends with the Hainfeld congress in 1889, when—thanks to Adler's reception of Marx—the Austrian Social Democratic Party (SDAPÖ) unified under a clearly Marxist banner. The second period encompasses the long 1890s, when Plekhanov, Struve, Lenin, and Luxemburg brought the new "doctrine" of Marxism into the Russian and Polish workers' movements. This period begins with Plekhanov's widely read polemic against the Narodniks, *Our Differences*, which was published in 1885. Plekhanov characterized capitalism as a historical necessity and a revolutionary challenge; it could be mastered only by a working class that was organized and schooled in Marxism. The second period ends in 1903, with the thirty-three-year-old Lenin's no less influential *What Is to Be Done?*—a practical guide, containing ideas well beyond Marx, for mastering the very challenge that Plekhanov outlined.

4

Translating Marx

Guesde and Jaurès

Jules Guesde around 1906
Credit: International Institute of
Social History, Amsterdam
(F. Calmel papers)

Jean Jaurès around 1904
Credit: International Institute of
Social History, Amsterdam
(Nadar papers)

❝In appearance he looked like a prophet who had stepped out of the Old Testament. His frame was thin and tall; his hair, black and long, falling back almost to the nape of his neck; his thin, pale face, framed in a full, flowing beard, giving him the air of a mystic. Having uttered the first few sentences, his incurable stage fright vanished and his words flowed on uninterruptedly in a clear, metallic voice which at times grew sharp but which more often sounded like the rhythmic beats of a hammer. When he came to the finale of his speech, in which he showed that a collectivist society would result in a life of happiness and plenty, he rose to his full height with his long hands raised while his audience sat transfixed, seeing visions of a new world.[1]❞

This talented speaker was the French journalist Jules Guesde. He had fled to exile in Switzerland as a republican in 1871, and he returned to Paris as an anarchist five years later. He contacted Marx around 1878. By adopting Marx's teachings, Guesde laid the foundation for the spread of Marxism among France's fractured socialists. He also granted Marx the personal satisfaction of seeing his ideas return to the country where, more than three decades earlier, he had first formulated them as a young exile.[2] This description of Guesde reflects the key characteristics of most other surviving firsthand accounts, which depict an outwardly imposing yet frail figure, with a breathtaking political temperament and gift for public speaking. Some eyewitnesses described these traits as demonic and aggressive—as, for example, *Le Figaro* journalist Gabriel Terrail, who (under the pseudonym Mermeix) published one of the first accounts of the founding of the French Workers' Party (Parti Ouvrier Français, or POF) in 1886.[3] He saw nothing magical about Guesde's personality. Instead, he was struck by the passionate hatred that Guesde's engagement seemed to inspire: "When Monsieur Guesde speaks—even about trivial matters—his lips move as if burning with anger. His mouth is fierce. When he walks, he's quite stiff; his arms and legs move fitfully. You have to see Monsieur Jules Guesde on the podium. The flow of his words is sometimes much too fast, but full of rage! His clear voice, which carries far, is terribly raspy."[4] Beyond the bizarre rhetorical effect of

Guesde's voice, Terrail noted his predilection for "stiff, caustic dialectics" and vitriolic irony: Guesde often spoke as if "society had committed an appalling crime against him that morning." His speeches were the "epitome of social grievance and resentment."[5]

Guesde had an unquestionably stalwart political temperament. Separating the form and substance of his engagement is impossible; both elements informed his development from republican refugee of the Paris Commune to Marxist chief strategist of the French workers' movement. Like Adler, Guesde was a practical theoretician, not a "student" of Marxism. He did not seek to deepen and expand Marxism with his own contributions, but was the pragmatic "soldier of an idea."[6] For this reason, the relevant literature rarely counts him among Marxist theorists. As a journalist, exile, and (ex-)convict, Guesde read an eclectic selection of political and economic books in multiple languages. After a long intellectual journey, in 1880 he finally landed in Marx's London study, where he, Engels, Marx, and Marx's son-in-law Paul Lafargue composed the original party program for the POF.

The pragmatic decision to unite the French movement under Marx's variation of socialism (or, as Marx himself called it, "our element")[7] in no way contradicted Guesde's political radicalism. Guesde was a revolutionary well before he discovered revolutionary Marxism. As a local journalist in 1870–71, he was persecuted for enthusiastically chronicling the collapse of the monarchy and the birth of the Third Republic. He described the evolution of his own worldview as an intellectual journey with three key waystations: "Kant made me an atheist; Hugo, a republican; and the Paris Commune, a socialist."[8] He was already thirty years old when he began to engage seriously with Marx's texts in 1874—at first, through the work of Italian political economists, which he got to know in exile. Upon returning to Paris in 1876, this engagement was reinforced by his contacts with Marx's cosmopolitan confidant Carl Hirsch, the Belgian doctor César de Paepe, and Marx's first translator in France, Gabriel Deville. Guesde's experiences as a reader were unsystematic but very intense. If his political temperament was simmering in a pot that was already filled to the brim with his ideals and experiences, Marx provided a perfectly fitting lid. Guesde thereby not only initiated the spread of Marxism in France but contributed significantly to the genesis of Marxism itself.[9]

After completing his education under his father's tutelage, followed by several years of studying on his own, Guesde worked as a translator for the Ministry of the Interior in the Parisian Prefecture of the Seine under Georges-Eugène Baron Haussman.[10] Little is known about these years before he became a journalist. Previous biographies have not focused on Guesde's political coming of age before his anarchist period.[11] Scholars have overlooked a handwritten autobiographical sketch at the IISH in Amsterdam, as well as the handwritten texts "Das Capital," "On Darwin," "Happiness," and "Thesis—Antithesis—Synthesis," written between 1872 and 1876. There is also a notebook of poems from 1888.[12] These texts show Guesde's evolution from hot-blooded anarchist—who saw the abolition of private property as a liberating cure-all and universal suffrage as a bourgeois construct that would merely maintain the status quo[13]—to the organizationally savvy founder of a political party, schooled in the social sciences and armed with propaganda.

In his first years of exile, Guesde was preoccupied with the defeat of the Paris Commune. His published works from this time are despondent over the brutal suppression of the Parisian "proletariat," and the republicanism for which it had fought. He already referred to socialism as the "contemporary order." Despite—or perhaps because of—the defeat of 1871, the working class had become increasingly aware of its needs and rights. The goal of its struggle was social and political freedom, "complete equality of opportunity for everyone"; Guesde believed it was continuing the work of the French Revolution.[14]

In Geneva (his first station in exile, during 1871–72), Guesde came to terms with the Parisian "massacre" by joining the Section of Revolutionary Socialist Propaganda and Action, an association of activists who had fled from France, and an anarchist group of western

Swiss watchmakers, the Jura Federation.[15] His poor health notwithstanding, Guesde soon became the group's leader and played a significant role in Bakunin's (eventually) successful campaign against Marx's dominance in the First International.[16] Short on money, Guesde moved to Rome in 1872, where he supported himself as a journalist and French teacher. He learned Italian and connected with local workers' organizations, running afoul of the Italian police because of his continued ties to the First International. He read works of political economy and became a true anarchist, denouncing voting rights as a scam, the state as a warden, and private property as theft.[17] Guesde took Bakunin's side in the conflict over the direction of the First International, and he criticized Marx's authoritarian style of leadership. In an April 1873 open letter, he protested that "Marxists" had co-opted the spirit of the International. His text had a palpable anti-Prussian undertone, which, years later, would return to haunt the spread of Marx's ideas in France, as French workers had to be persuaded that their salvation lay in the hands of two Germans.[18] Even committed Marxists took pains to show that socialism was *also* a French idea.[19] The Second International was persistently challenged by the loyalties and sensibilities of its members, who felt bound to the idea of the nation—political sentiments that ultimately led to its downfall in 1914.

Long before this development, however, Guesde's journalism in exile dealt with the living and working conditions of Italian workers and peasants. He criticized the division of the "great human family into the propertied and propertyless," denounced the living conditions of simple, hardworking people in Lombardy, and he began to see an indirect but proportional relationship between profit and misery.[20] In 1873 Guesde moved to Milan, where he married Mathilde Constantin, the daughter of a Napoleonic soldier who had stayed in Italy. They had one child and lived in relative poverty until 1875.[21] His personal life was not easy. He was often sick and went through periods of extreme exhaustion and despondency, and in such moments, he compared the existential ups and downs of his life with the ebb and flow of the tides in nature. In one of these moments of exhaustion, he began to write poetry that grappled with the personal cost of his political engagement:

> But when will I be reborn?
> Man, where are my tides
> Restoring my strength and will?
> Who knows whether I will ever in the struggles to come,
> Fight again the good fight, *Humanité?*[22]

We can assume that Guesde encountered Marx's theses in his Italian readings by 1872 or 1873, although their influence was not yet evident in his own social criticism. In 1877 he published an open letter, in Italian, to the Catholic senator Fedele Lampertico.[23] A bourgeois political economist and critic of Marx, Lampertico advocated for "organic" social reform inspired by Christian ideals, presuming that states could enhance overall prosperity by redistributing resources. Lampertico's optimism fundamentally contradicted Guesde's own political convictions.[24] His open letter not yet a formal political program but an impassioned plea for radical change. Guesde's point of departure was the appalling reality of social conditions, which he presented to the senator in the style of a legal argument:

> If, for a moment, you leave your post as professor and senator and take a look around, what will you see in Italy, England, Germany, and everywhere else? Millions of people, stooped over ceaselessly, without control over the soil that claims most of their time, their sweat, their entire lives (especially in the Roman countryside, the Tuscan Maremma, the rice fields of Lombardy, etc.). But do they own this soil, which they cultivated over centuries, from generation to generation—which has practically become their own creation? No. And who does own it? A small number of people who do nothing, who know it only through an intermediary—profit. So the determining characteristic of ownership, "genuine ownership," is property without labor—and on the other side, labor without property. . . . Even today, who largely cultivates the earth? The propertyless, who have nothing to gain from the harvest, working the land only to feed themselves—or more accurately stated, not to starve.[25]

Guesde supported his argument with statistics about wages and "serious physiological studies" about the limits of endurance for a grown man. An agricultural worker needed the daily equivalent of one kilogram of meat and one and a half kilograms of bread, but "today's farmer cannot even fill his stomach with potatoes or polenta."[26]

This example shows that Guesde was not yet concerned with the modern industrial proletariat; his focus was primarily on rural poverty and work. He had not yet come to a class analysis of economic conditions, but he criticized the fundamental injustice of the still strongly agrarian societies that he knew from his own experience. He was outraged by the luxurious lifestyles of the rich and the insufficient financial and educational opportunities for the poor: "The small number who have managed to attend primary schools that are not completely free of charge learn nothing more than what is needed at that moment to maximize the profits of property owners—the capitalists who exploit them."[27]

Parallel to his eclectic readings in political economy, Guesde worked on a French translation of Chernyshevsky's novel *What Is to Be Done?* Guesde described the novel, which strongly influenced Lenin, as the "true Gospel of the new generations."[28] Guesde also engaged intensely with Darwin's *On the Origin of Species.* In his surviving notes from 1875, Guesde seems much more critical of Darwin's theories than the other protagonists.[29] He was particularly offended that Darwin went beyond zoology, his field of expertise, and sought to extend his deterministic theses to human sociology. The existential competition (*concurrence vitale*) of the animal world did not have to affect humans negatively, Guesde argued, but could instead serve as an agent of progress.[30] Guesde's first programmatic text, his *Essai de Catéchisme Socialiste* (1875), did not yet bear Marx's intellectual signature; it was controversial even among socialists because of its aggressive language.[31] In this "catechism," Guesde summed up his ambivalence toward Darwin with an aphorism that drew upon Ludwig Feuerbach's criticism of religion and a tradition that extended back to Greek antiquity: "Animal animali lupus," but "homo homini deus" (Animals are wolves to one another, but man is the god of man).[32]

Guesde's rejection of Darwinist determinism was initially driven by hope. When he first engaged intensely with Darwin in 1875, Marxist determinism—with its ostensibly scientific outlook and faith in the future—was still undeveloped. Guesde was a "materialist" but not yet a "dialectician."[33] He reflected on subjective and objective happiness and on the limits imposed by the material world on the individual pursuit of happiness. He understood freedom as the opportunity to act on one's own accord, "with muscles and intelligence."[34] Guesde is often associated with a tendency (later reinforced by Marx) to see people as "abstract individuals," as beings detached from "social context and the process of production."[35] But this generalization does not do justice to his simple affection for other people. He continued to articulate this affection publicly and privately, even after his turn toward Marx, as demonstrated by this 1888 draft of a poem about death:

> O Death, I have understood you and that is why I love you!
> I love you for your scythe, which makes room for tomorrow,
> Killing today, I love you, O Death, in the end,
> As a condition of life itself.
> [. . .]
> But I hate what is within you, death, the jolts
> Inflicted in a world gone wrong. It is the grave dug
> before its time. The wolves at the door:
> Misery, hunger, backbreaking labor.[36]

Guesde's reorientation toward Marx was first evident around 1875, one year before he returned to Paris. He had begun to engage more systematically with methods and theories that supported a socialist critique of society, as seen not only in his notes on *Capital* and Darwin's theories but in an 1875 treatise, "Thesis—Antithesis—Synthesis." Guesde attempted to explain the Italian debate about universal suffrage as a historically logical, dialectical process. The somewhat confusing treatise shows his engagement with new explanatory models and his early adoption of Marxist terminology.[37] By the end of his exile, he had acquired some practice in dialectical argumentation.

Guesde's year in Brussels before he returned to France also played a formative role in his path toward Marxism. In Brussels he met César de Paepe, a politically engaged doctor with anarchist leanings, who sought to integrate anarchist and Marxist ideas. Alongside Carl Hirsch and José Mesa (whom Guesde met in Paris in 1876), this learned "man with a heart"[38] did the most to nudge Guesde toward Marx. Guesde deepened his canonical knowledge in conversations with de Paepe and by reading the texts that de Paepe suggested. In Brussels Guesde also had his first encounters with the industrial proletariat.[39] Few substantial sources survive from this time, so the extent of these meetings and their influence on Guesde's thinking remain unclear.

We know just as little about the circle of young intellectuals whose gatherings at the café Soufflet attracted Guesde upon his return to Paris at the end of 1876. Street cafés like the Soufflet in the Latin Quarter served as gathering points and headquarters for planning workers' congresses (which were still illegal). The cultivated sociability in these cafés was "both context and pretext" for disseminating Marx's ideas to the working class.[40] Here Guesde met the students and intellectuals who had developed into the "officer corps of the socialist workers' army" by the end of the 1870s—a contemporary description that was wholly in tune with the Guesdists' militaristic metaphors.[41] Among the members of this group was Gabriel Deville, who worked with Marx to create the first—and soon very influential—popular rendering of *Capital* in French. Other café patrons included Mesa, "a sympathetic Spanish socialist, and the learned German socialist Carl Hirsch, an ardent supporter of Marx and Lassalle." According to their comrade and later rival Benoît Malon, these two men directed Guesde's attention toward the systematic historical and economic thinking of Marx and Engels.[42] As a result, Guesde gradually—and increasingly publicly—distanced himself from the anarchist critique of his years in Swiss exile, when he had virulently attacked Marx as an authoritarian "chairman" and London "proconsul."[43]

As with many of the other protagonists, Guesde's actual reception of Marx transpired over the course of his work as a newspaper editor. In 1877 he founded *L'Égalité*, which sought to provide a single voice for the heterogeneous Parisian workers.[44] *L'Égalité* touted its "republican character, because the republic is the highest stage of a state's political development, and only it can make way for economic and social revolution." Even so, the newspaper's foremost identity was "socialist" because its "direct goal" was "economic revolution." *L'Égalité* would thus prepare the way for a great party, which, at the right moment, would use force "in the service of justice."[45]

Founding a French workers' party was an ambitious undertaking. The Parisian and entire French economy was agrarian, dominated by artisanal and small-scale production until the early twentieth century. Industry and thus the potential "industrial proletariat" long played a marginal role.[46] There was no organized workers' movement in the immediate aftermath of the military defeat against Prussia, the Paris Commune, and the economic crisis of 1873. Blanquists, anarchists, Communards, and all kinds of cooperatively oriented socialists gathered at the Parisian street cafés without any uniform organization.[47]

And so there was a vacuum to fill. Guesde's interpretation and propagation of Marx's doctrines in *L'Égalité* created the preconditions for an umbrella organization to unite the tens of thousands of French workers who already belonged to various brotherhoods, cooperatives, or benevolent funds. The process of founding this organization began with *L'Égalité*, but it proceeded at a "snail's pace."[48] To succeed, Guesde needed Marx—or, more precisely, Marx's "apocalyptic vision of the class war."[49] Guesde did not have to study Marx or think *about* him; instead, Guesde thought *with* him.

What did Guesde learn from Marx, and which elements did he bring to his own political practice (which, at the time, was mostly agitation)? How did he successfully found a movement, Guesdism, that provided "a powerful alternative to liberalism" and enduringly changed the French political landscape?[50] Guesde particularly valued three aspects of Marx's thought: the appeal to human reason (emancipation), acceptance of social reality (being), and the promise of scientifically grounded insight (consciousness).

Guesde integrated these modes of thinking, which augured the emancipatory merging of being and consciousness, within his journalism in a disciplined way. He saw his task as enlightening and raising the awareness of propertyless workers, who would at last fight for self-representation. Past experience had shown that property owners pursued only their own interests. "The law of human nature" was "neither surrender nor heroism," he wrote in a commentary about the Parisian workers' congress of 1876. All previous self-declared workers' representatives had sacrificed the interests of the whole— and especially the interests of the "working class"—for their "personal needs." It was astonishing that the workers, "the victims of these conditions," had not already opened their eyes to this injustice.[51] Self-representation was thus a belated but important expression of "healthy human reason." Guesde did not acknowledge that his idealized portrait had little to do with reality, as many of the party leaders did not actually come from the working class.

This argumentation suggests that Guesde believed more in agitation than in self-emancipation. In order to make his commonsense argumentation politically feasible, he needed an expert teacher who could corroborate the late awakening of healthy human reason with realistic, scientific truth. Marx's ideas fit the bill nicely, as we can see by the text that introduced them to a French audience. Deville's abridged translation of Marx's *Capital* made this work accessible not only to Guesde but to hundreds of thousands of French workers. Seven editions were printed between 1883 and 1948. In the book's preface, Deville announced that Marx's work—which was grounded in reality and based upon science—held the key to the success of the modern workers' movement. Idealists had previously sought to make "realities correspond to their fictive ideals of absolute justice." Marx, by contrast, did not proceed from a "more or less subjective perspective."

Instead, he meticulously examined the facts, systematized his findings, and drew a conclusion that, at last, provided a "scientific explanation of the historical development of humanity."[52]

Deville thus wholly agreed with Engels's assertion of "the development of socialism from utopia to science." Like Engels's 1882 pamphlet, which was published in English as *Socialism: Utopian and Scientific,* Deville's *Le Capital* became a bestseller. In the 1890s, a copy cost three and a half francs, or half of a French worker's daily wages.[53] This accessible introduction to Marx's theories was also pivotal to Guesde's own reception of Marx—and in a quite practical way, as he and Deville had met regularly in cafés and newspaper offices since 1876. Guesde witnessed the book's creation firsthand. Although Guesde (unlike the other eight Marxists) saw himself as a journalist and professional revolutionary but not as a scholar, he, too, was persuaded by Deville's emphasis on science—that is, by the propagandistic potential of having established a scientific foundation for socialism.

Marx's "doctrine" was useful to Guesde because of its power to persuade and mobilize—even though he only partially understood it and could explain it only simplistically. Theoretical reductionism and rhetorical fundamentalism were the most important ingredients in the Marxism that the Guesdists brought to French politics, which is why Guesdism is sometimes described as "vulgar" Marxism.[54] Guesde and his supporters read Marx's texts as a scientifically grounded indictment of social conditions. They armed themselves with the "weapon" of science in their battle against the current order. In an 1878 speech, Guesde explained that the worker who exists merely to work, "like a locomotive or a horse, cannot live any other way." He is bound by "the limits of his usefulness to the few who, with capital, have monopolized the means to live."[55] Marx's analysis of capitalism—which ultimately reduced people to their "productive force," like the capitalists he criticized—gave Guesde the tools to channel his social outrage into a political program.[56]

In 1879 Marx reached out personally to the enterprising editor-in-chief of *L'Égalité.* In a letter that has not been preserved, he

congratulated Guesde on founding the newspaper and simultaneously pardoned him for his earlier anarchist escapades.[57] Shortly before, Guesde had been arrested for planning a workers' congress, and
in a public trial he was sentenced to six months in prison and ordered to pay a fine of two hundred francs.[58] He spent half of his sentence in the hospital because of his poor health. The effects of the
public trial were explosive, and it is often described as the moment
in which the POF was born.[59] Guesde had eloquently, but unsuccessfully, defended himself and his thirty-eight codefendants, and the
Parisian workers celebrated him as a new hero of the movement.
Petitions were written in his support, and donations collected to
cover his court costs and to publish the speech he had made in his
self-defense.[60] A pamphlet that he wrote in prison ("Programme et
adresse des socialistes révolutionnaires français"), which called for the
founding of a socialist party, contributed to Guesde's growing renown.
He prophesied a "1789 of the workers," which would burst the "bourgeois legalism that encircles us like an iron ring." It was signed by 541
workers, including many in the textile and leather industries, as well
as some artisans and miners.[61]

Amid these events, Guesde must have been terribly pleased by
Marx's generous letter. Guesde's response to "très cher citoyen" shows
that his reorientation was not based on theoretical or intellectual fe-
alty but on a specific principle of political organization. Criticizing
the Italian anarchist and firebrand Carlo Cafiero's "senseless" tactics
of rebellion, Guesde assured Marx that, as a "revolutionary" like Marx
himself, he believed in the "use of force to solve the social question in
a collectivist or communist way":

> Like you I am convinced that before thinking of action, one must set up
> a party, a *conscious* army, by means of continuous propaganda.
>   Finally, like you I do not believe that the simple destruction of what
> exists will be enough to build what we want, and I think that for a more
> or less considerable period the impulse, the direction should come from
> above, from those who are "better informed."
>   It is in these conditions that, since my return, I have been busy set-
> ting up this "independent and militant workers' party" which you so

rightly declare to be "of the highest importance" in view of the events which are being prepared.[62]

Guesde affirmatively quoted from Marx's letter (which has not been preserved), and thereby sought acceptance, as Marx's equal, within his inner circle, among those who looked down "from above" and were "better informed." A break with French socialist tradition was imperative, Guesde continued. The proletariat had to be "delivered from the dupery of bourgeois Radicalism and . . . persuaded that its emancipation can only be achieved through struggle." On the one hand, the new party's leaders had "to free our workers from the moorings which have held them in radical, or bourgeois-Jacobin waters." On the other, they had to explain why the well-intentioned solutions of the bourgeoisie would remain ineffective. It was regrettable that "our workers' France" had grown accustomed to "seeing salvation only in the collectivization of all immobile and mobile capital. This, the program of the International? Nonsense! At best, it's the Proudhonists' program." Happily, "our workers"—which is to say, Guesde's supporters—were the most intelligent, and they would no longer follow Proudhon's "cooperative jokes." The break with his own ideological past and the disciplined organization of those who were "better informed" was Guesde's two-pronged "plan." He ended his letter with the following remark: "If I were not so ill—and so poor—I would announce my next visit to you, so much would I like to have a long talk with you. But I do not dispose of myself either physically—or pecuniarily. And I must limit myself to sending you all my thanks and assuring you of my complete devotion. To you and to the Revolution."[63]

In the ongoing dispute between the supporters of cooperative and anarchist solutions to the Social Question, Guesde became the first prominent French socialist to opt for the establishment of a party that could organize, enlighten, and lead the working masses as a better-informed, intellectual vanguard.[64] Like Marx, he was convinced that building "a party, a *conscious* army, by means of continuous propaganda" was essential to gaining long-term political influence.[65]

Here Guesde clearly parted ways with other French socialists (such as Malon and Paul Brousse), who favored either revolutionary/anarchist or cooperative tactics and who either rejected party and parliamentary activism altogether or else approached it skeptically. In their circles, the term "Marxism" was still synonymous with the absolutist, authoritarian (and Prussian) style of leadership which had brought Marx notoriety since the founding of the First International in 1864. It was certainly not a forward-looking, intellectual foundation for the unified proletarian struggle.[66] Guesde—whom Marx had personally praised for his conversion to "*le socialisme moderne scientifique*, i.e. the *German* variety"[67]—was thus considered by many opponents to be "Marx's mouthpiece," as the well-informed Bernstein reported to Engels in the fall of 1881. Intriguingly, Bernstein further noted that Guesde not only tolerated but actually encouraged this association "for easily comprehensible reasons." Guesde hoped to attract some reflected glory from the growing radiance around Marx's name—a legitimate desire, according to Bernstein, given the struggle for leadership within the French workers' movement.[68]

Despite widespread skepticism about a "German" takeover of the movement, Guesde's agitation for an effective and tightly organized workers' collectivism paid off. The demand for completely nationalizing the means of production spread "like an oil spot" among Parisian workers' organizations, and the efficacy of older guild-based models of self-administration and self-determination was soon widely questioned. By the end of the 1870s, the Parisian police reported that one-third of the city's fifteen thousand organized workers could be considered "collectivists."[69] With the resignation of President Patrice de MacMahon and the election of Jules Grévy in early 1879, the devastated republic recovered from the upheavals of the Paris Commune, and both chambers of the National Assembly at last found some stability after eight years of provisional government.[70] The fragmented socialist movement also profited from the onset of this period of liberalization in public life. Guesde helped to plan the movement's pioneering congress in Marseille in October

1879, although he was unable to participate himself because he was ill. The delegates addressed ten "questions," beginning with the Woman Question; the seventh concerned property. Guesde's confidant Jean Lombard delivered a long speech about the need for collectivization and gained approval for an array of demands, including "collectivization of land, the instruments of labor, social redistribution of unsalable raw materials that belong to all . . . [f]ormation of a workers' party to be organized by trade chambers and workers' commissions for social concerns, consumption, and production."[71] The success of Guesde's collectivists at the Marseille congress (albeit without specific reference to Marx)[72] shows that a degree of momentum had been reached that greatly facilitated the spread of Marx and Engels's theses.

The two "Londoners" observed this dynamic attentively, betting on Guesde's rhetorical and motivational gifts—if not his knowledge of theory—in order to anchor their ideas permanently within the French workers' movement. In the aftermath of the Marseille congress, in January 1880 Malon's newly founded *Revue Socialiste* published contributions by Guesde, Kautsky, and de Paepe, and Lafargue's three-part translation of Engels's *AntiDühring*. The socialist scene profited from the overall political thaw—not least from the general amnesty that was granted to Communards in July 1880. Guesde's *L'Égalité*, which was banned in 1878, resumed publication and dedicated itself explicitly to propagating Marxist ideas and works.[73] The correspondence between Marx and Guesde marked the beginning of a mutually advantageous personal relationship. The political significance of this relationship was underscored by Guesde's collaboration with Marx and Engels on the draft of a party program in the spring of 1880. (The circumstances of his trip to London have been described in very different ways in the historical literature.)[74] Guesde was hardly an unknown quantity in London. Even before his correspondence with Marx, Hirsch and Lafargue had already come to appreciate the smart but hot-headed activist with a gift for public speaking. Even more important for Marx and Engels, "Guesde's pamphlets and articles . . . are the best to have appeared in the French language, and he is, moreover, one of the best speakers

in Paris. Also, we have always found him forthcoming and reliable."[75]
Marx praised *L'Égalité* as "the first 'French' workers' paper in the true
sense of the term," thanks to Guesde "having come over to us."[76] The
correspondence between Engels and the young Bernstein—who had
just established the *Sozialdemokrat* in Zurich and was closely following
French developments—underscores these sympathies. Engels's discussion of Guesde's character and his value to the movement illustrates
the loosely symbiotic and trusting relationship that connected the
"Londoners" with their counterparts in France. Moreover, the discussion gently caricatured the entire Parisian socialist establishment.
Engels was extremely confident that Marx's ideas would take off rapidly, bolstered by the connection with Guesde:

> Lastly Guesde. In matters of theory this man is by far the most lucid
> thinker amongst the Parisians, and one of the few who takes no ex-
> ception at all to the German origins of present-day socialism. *Hinc illae
> lacrimae.* Which is why the gentlemen of the *Prolétaire* are letting it be
> known that he is merely Marx's mouthpiece, a rumour which, with
> lugubrious mien, Malon and Brousse carry further afield. Outside that
> clique no one dreams of such a thing. . . . That he is domineering may
> well be true. Every one of us is domineering in the sense that he would
> like to see his views predominate. If Guesde seeks to do this by direct
> and Malon by tortuous means, it says much for Guesde's character and
> for the superiority of Malon's worldly wisdom—especially in dealing
> with people like the Parisians who obstinately dig their heels in if you
> try to dictate to them but are only too delighted to let you lead them
> by the nose. . . . Guesde's failings are of quite a different kind. First, the
> Parisian superstition that the word revolution is something one must
> continually bandy about. And secondly, boundless impatience. He is
> suffering from a nervous complaint, believes he has not much longer
> to live [at the age of thirty-six] and is absolutely determined to see
> something worthwhile happen before he goes. That, and his morbid
> excitability, provide the explanation for his exaggerated and sometimes
> destructive thirst for action.[77]

What exactly Engels meant by "nervous complaint" is unclear;
in the nineteenth century the term was an all-purpose label for
various mental and psychosomatic ailments.[78] Guesde apparently

suffered from severe pneumonia during his second prison sentence in 1879–80.[79] In fact, his poor health was so storied that it had even become part of his ascetic revolutionary image, influencing his political work—as Engels described—in ways that could be beneficial but also "destructive." Guesde apparently insisted less on classical revolutionary values than on constancy and loyalty toward former compatriots. The "Londoners" viewed these traits with a mixture of respect and amusement, as when Engels attributed Malon's rise at *L'Égalité* to the fact that Guesde "thought, in typically French fashion, that as a writer one had to have a *working man* beside one,"[80] or that, all political differences aside, Guesde "still has something of a soft spot—of a *personal* nature—for his erstwhile anarchist brothers."[81] All this notwithstanding, Marx and Engels valued Guesde, and they especially respected his headstrong demeanor. In October 1881, at the peak of the criticism leveled against Guesde that he was nothing more than "Marx's mouthpiece," Engels wrote to Bernstein that they communicated with Guesde only irregularly: "Every now and again Marx, like myself, has transmitted advice to Guesde via Lafargue, but it has hardly even been taken."[82]

A foremost example was Engels's recollection of the aforementioned debate about the party program, which took place in his London apartment in the summer of 1880. Guesde had taken their advice while stubbornly clinging to his own ideas—especially the demand for a legally fixed minimum wage, which he saw as central to his propaganda. Although Marx regarded this demand as "foolishness," and Guesde theoretically agreed that the abolition of wage labor was the actual solution, Guesde nevertheless insisted, to Marx's irritation, on doling out "these sops" to the French workers.[83] All this notwithstanding—and in contrast to the debate over the German Social Democrats' Gotha program five years earlier, in which Marx's criticism went unheard—both Marx and Engels substantially influenced the content and tone of the first French program. Guesde gratefully accepted most of Marx's suggested phrasing, especially for the preamble (*considérants*), because of the simple and powerful messaging. Engels proudly summarized Marx's accomplishment:

> The worker is free only when he is the owner of his instruments of labour—this may assume either individual or collective form—the individual form of ownership is being daily and increasingly superseded by economic developments, hence, all that remains is that of communal ownership, etc.—a masterpiece of cogent reasoning, calculated to explain things to the masses in a few words; I have seldom seen its like and, even in this concise version, found it astonishing.[84]

From Engels's theoretical perspective as well as Guesde's strategic one, the preamble's striking element was its bold embrace of capitalism and technical progress, which, by Marx's logic, created the necessary preconditions for collectivizing the means of production. Because the individual worker in a modern economy could no longer produce increasingly complex goods with increasingly complex machines *on his own*, collective production necessitated collective ownership of the means of production, in both a material and an intellectual sense. Collectivization could "only spring from the revolutionary action of the producing class—or proletariat—organised into an independent political party."[85]

   This argumentation injected a completely new kind of energy into French socialism, which had thus far been shaped by Proudhonian and other cooperative approaches that were oriented toward workplace and professional activism rather than party strategy. Guesde recognized this potential and channeled it into a minimalist program for participation in future elections, seeking thereby to maximize voting rights as a "means of organization and struggle." According to Marx's preamble draft that Guesde accepted word for word, universal suffrage was transformed from an "instrument of deception" into an "instrument of emancipation." At the same time, this text gave the socialist movement in France "a new revolutionary dimension" by declaring a tightly organized proletarian party to be the precondition for "revolutionary action of the producing class."[86] The Guesdists wanted to radically change the political culture and political system of a fundamentally "anti-Marxist country," which was dominated by an apparently "ineradicable, petty bourgeois socialism."[87]

The injection of an organizational principle that had not arisen organically within the French workers' movement has often been taken as the reason for Guesdism's limited success in France.[88] In fact, this principle was based on the assumption of steadily increasing industrial mass production, which hardly corresponded to economic realities at that time. As late as 1906, 60 percent of French workers were engaged in home-based production or worked for companies with fewer than ten employees.[89] Industrial development in France and Russia was similar, in that everyday conditions for workers (and their supposed "class character") lagged behind Marxist notions of capitalism. In this context, Marxist analysis became pure speculation.

And so Guesde's strategy was not terribly successful. He earned only 493 of 10,868 votes in his first run for office in the Roubaix region in 1881. The reformers and trade unionists in Brousse's circle continued to expand their influence in Paris, while the Guesdists had only marginal success and began to concentrate on the industrial proletariat in a few large cities (Lyon, Roanne, Lille, Roubaix), participating actively in strikes. The party program draft from London was ultimately rejected; at the Saint-Étienne congress of 1882, the eighty-six delegates who supported Brousse outnumbered the twenty-six Guesdists. Conflict between the two groups had less to do with ideological substance—the reformers around Brousse largely shared Marx's analysis and critique of capitalism—and more with questions of internal party democracy and organization.[90] The Guesdists' demonstrative exit from the Saint-Étienne congress hall and establishment of their own party, the POF, marked the beginning of Guesde's "special path" within French socialism. The division acquired greater ideological and personal intensity with the involvement of Jaurès at the end of the 1880s, and the split's consequences would continue to occupy the French Left well into the 1930s.

Marx and Engels were in no way pleased with this development. They frowned upon Guesde's and Lafargue's revolutionary phraseology. Their unartful authoritarian tactics, verbal threats against political opponents, altercations in newsrooms, and emphasis on short-term propaganda over the support of a well-organized party inspired Marx's well-known comment "Ce qu'il y a de certain, c'est que moi je ne suis pas Marxiste" (If anything is certain, it is that I myself am not a Marxist)—by which he meant, not *this* kind of Marxist.[91] In short, the first French "proletarian" party experienced severe birth pains, and the POF did not attain real political influence until the 1890s. Even so, Guesde's adaptation of Marxist principles and rhetoric between 1878 and 1882 enhanced Marx's prestige enormously within the French workers' movement; Marx had become a political factor. Texts by Marx and Engels found their way into the socialist canon in France. Marx's theses, theorems, and formulas gradually became part of the overall discourse around socialism and trade unions—although their influence was weaker than in Germany's SPD.[92]

Engels observed these developments with considerable satisfaction in October 1881. Because of Marx's "theoretical and practical achievements," the "best people" from the workers' movements of many European countries—particularly Germany, France, and Russia—now turned to him in confidence, and "they generally find that his advice is the best." His "peculiar influence . . . an influence of the utmost importance to the movement" was due to the fact that he did not impose his opinions; "rather it is these people who come to him of their own accord."[93] From Engels's perspective as a tireless, polyglot, and in-demand correspondent, Marxism appeared to be a political movement that was just getting started. Its beginnings in France were largely attributable to Guesde's embrace of Marxist doctrines—not as a student but as a *confrère*. Guesde seems not to have completely grasped Marx's philosophy or economics, but as a politician he understood how to put Marx's ideas into practice—a practice in which goals and program were identical.[94] The Social Question could be resolved only when the proletariat had come to power. Guesde's revolutionary, uncompromising political temperament became an ideal conduit for Marx. One of Guesde's followers summed up the fortuitous connection between uncompromising doctrine and uncompromising personality in a remarkable eulogy from 1908:

> The future founder of the French Workers' Party had always hated every half-measure with the depth of his soul. His worst opponents had to admit that he was a man of unrelenting character. . . . Clarity, logical consistency, holding firm to the end—these qualities stayed with Jules Guesde throughout his entire life. These character traits, which he developed to the highest degree, prepared extremely fertile ground for the reception of Marx's doctrine—the doctrine of systematic, complete, unmutilated, and undiluted proletarian socialism.[95]

At the height of his own political influence in 1904, Jaurès asserted that the class struggle–obsessed Guesde had merely taken from Marx the "most extreme and simplest formula" of "expropriating the expropriators."[96] Four years earlier, during the *grand débat* in Lille, over whether socialists should participate in bourgeois governments, Guesde accused the cooperation-fixated Jaurès of betraying Marx and socialism: rather than working to "conquer state authority through socialism," Jaurès had himself been conquered by the bourgeoisie. Guesde, the rehabilitated Communard, took an additional swipe at Jaurès's biography. Jaurès, who was fourteen years younger, had not experienced the Paris Commune and so did not realize that he was tying the proletariat to "the tail of the imprisoning bourgeoisie, which had the shooting bourgeoisie of 1871 behind it."[97]

The decades-long feud between the two uncontested leaders of the French workers' movement between 1880 and 1914 is generally recounted as a debate over theory and tactics.[98] We should not forget, however, how the personal, almost "brotherly" aspects of this spat have structured the historiography about the beginnings of Marxism in France. The early German translation of the proceedings of Guesde and Jaurès's *grand débat* was, in fact, published under the title *Zum Bruderzwist in Frankreich* (On the fraternal strife in France). The gaunt, radical ascetic Guesde espoused an ostensibly orthodox Marxism, which refuted the ostensibly moderate Marxism of his nemesis, the stout and bookish philosophy professor Jaurès. To borrow the categories that Max Weber would formulate around twenty years later in his lecture "Politics as a Vocation," Guesde was the prototypical politician of "conviction," while Jaurès was alternately praised or scorned for his ethic of "responsibility." And yet, for all their differences, both men drew critically from French socialist tradition, both possessed an extraordinary gift for public speaking, and—not least—both turned to Marx relatively late, when they were already in their thirties.

Neither Guesde nor Jaurès were one of Marx's students (although Guesde considered himself Marx's colleague, or *confrère*). "It is, of course, impossible to count Jaurès among Marx's disciples," his biographer Madeleine Rebérioux has firmly stated.[99] Even so, Jaurès's socialism is inconceivable without Marx. Historical overviews of Marxism consider Jaurès a major philosophical influence, and other biographers describe him as a Marxist, albeit a critical and idiosyncratic one.[100] Jaurès's religious nature is considered at least as important to understanding his personality and political worldview. More recent studies, in particular, have interpreted his Marxism as religious socialism. His idiosyncratic political philosophy understood socialism as a "true" religion—the basis for a good society in the here and now.[101] The religious undertones in his thought can be attributed to a liberal education that was not rigidly bound by confession. Not coincidentally, the philosophical leitmotif of his political understanding strongly recalls the deeply conservative motto of his religion teacher at the Collège in Castres, Abbé Martial Bouisset: *Conservez les choses du passé en faveur de l'avenir*—Protect the past for the future.[102]

This insight grounded Jaurès's evolutionary understanding of revolution and his resolute opposition to all forms of political radicalism. He was not a revolutionary who took inspiration from Marx; rather, he was driven by "what Marx so splendidly called *revolutionary evolution*."[103] Although Marx himself never actually used the term, the incoherence of his theory of revolution allowed Jaurès to define "evolutionism" as a program of revolutionary ends, not means.[104] "Fraternal strife" over methods aside, Jaurès responded to his critics at the famous debate in Lille, where he underscored the importance of unity among French socialists, "through the Enlightenment, through conviction, through organization; everything that allows us to participate in the works of reform, and to achieve the work of revolution, fundamental change, through reforms. Because I am no 'moderate,' I'm a revolutionary like you."[105]

Marx had long played no role whatsoever for Jaurès. During his academic training, followed by his years as a teacher of philosophy at the lycée in Albi (1880–82) and the University of Toulouse (1882–86), he gradually worked through the nineteenth-century canon of philosophical and socialist literature, but he had little interest in socialist activism himself. He later remarked that, in 1886, when he first represented the *département* of Tarn in the National Assembly, he "did not know that there were Socialist groups in France and a whole agitation of propaganda and fervour of sectarian rivalry, from Guesde to Malon."[106] By this point, Guesde had already served for six years as the leader of the POF. The party's influence was growing, particularly in industrial cities; it quintupled its ranks from two thousand to ten thousand members between 1889 and 1893.[107]

Another clear sign of Jaurès's relative distance from Marx in these years is the fact that Marx's name does not appear even once in Jaurès's published texts and correspondence until 1889. However, according to Jaurès's autobiographical account, by the beginning of his university studies he "had either discovered or tried to discover the whole of Socialism from Fichte to Marx."[108] It is not entirely clear which texts of Marx he read; he did not read *Capital* until he was thirty, when he returned to his professorship in Toulouse after losing his bid for reelection as republican deputy to the National Assembly.[109] He must have been familiar with the few, but very important, texts by Marx that had already been published when he was a student: *Critique of Hegel's Philosophy of Law* (1844), *The Holy Family* (1845), *The Poverty of Philosophy* (1847), and *The Civil War in France* (1871). At some point, he had certainly read the *Manifesto of the Communist Party*, although any reference to it remained conspicuously absent in his own speeches and writings. He later regarded the *Manifesto* as a "mystical," "outdated," but still significant document of its time, as we will see in the pages ahead.[110]

In the 1880s and 1890s, Jaurès recognized important elements of his own worldview in Marx's early writings and in Marx's fundamental critique of the capitalist system in *Capital,* especially questions about the meaning of human existence and the ambivalent role of religion as an expression of a basic human need. Marx had not only condemned religion as "the opium of the people"; he also saw it as "the sigh of the oppressed creature, the heart of a heartless world." Religion was a response to the "complete loss of humanity" in modern society, which was oriented around earning wages. He interpreted the drive for self-liberation as an inevitable movement toward the real utopia of "universal human emancipation."[111] Jaurès also agreed with Marx's thesis about human "self-estrangement." Marx's political economy gave Jaurès empirical evidence that this self-estrangement was intensifying under capitalism to intolerable heights and that it would not stop until the system was abolished.[112] And even though Marx sharply criticized the French socialists— especially Proudhon, who also drew upon Hegel—Jaurès saw a certain congruence between German and French socialism: as the two main "intellectual sources" that flowed together in contemporary socialism, together they united to form a "single socialism" that would prepare the way for the "victory of humanity."[113] Jaurès maintained this integrative view of the heterogeneous reservoir of European socialist ideas all his life, as underscored by the title page of the first volume in his edited series, the *Histoire Socialiste,* from 1901. Marx is the only non-French philosopher who adorns the evergreen bough of knowledge. The metaphor (which draws upon Christian symbolism) embodies Jaurès's eclectic, life-affirming, and quasi-religious socialist ideal. Marx and Engels's unrelenting criticism of the utopian French socialists who share the branch is completely negated by the illustration.[114]

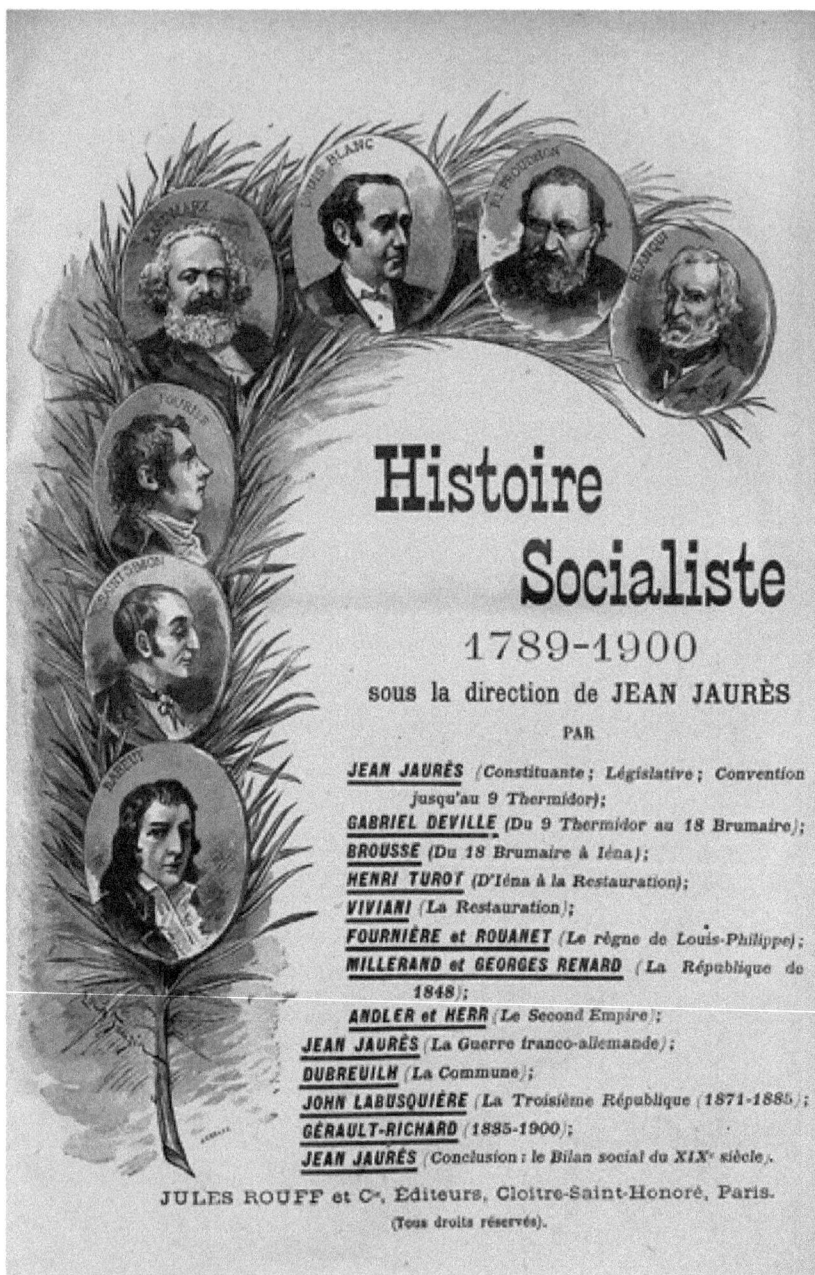

Histoire
Socialiste
1789-1900

sous la direction de JEAN JAURÈS

PAR

JEAN JAURÈS *(Constituante ; Législative ; Convention jusqu'au 9 Thermidor)*;
GABRIEL DEVILLE *(Du 9 Thermidor au 18 Brumaire)*;
BROUSSE *(Du 18 Brumaire à Iéna)*;
HENRI TUROT *(D'Iéna à la Restauration)*;
VIVIANI *(La Restauration)*;
FOURNIÈRE et ROUANET *(Le règne de Louis-Philippe)*;
MILLERAND et GEORGES RENARD *(La République de 1848)*;
ANDLER et HERR *(Le Second Empire)*;
JEAN JAURÈS *(La Guerre franco-allemande)*;
DUBREUILH *(La Commune)*;
JOHN LABUSQUIÈRE *(La Troisième République (1871-1885)*;
GÉRAULT-RICHARD *(1885-1900)*;
JEAN JAURÈS *(Conclusion : le Bilan social du XIXᵉ siècle)*.

JULES ROUFF et Cⁱᵉ, Éditeurs, Cloître-Saint-Honoré, Paris.

(Tous droits réservés).

Title page of the first volume of the *Histoire socialiste*, 1901
Credit: Title page from Jean Jaurès, *Histoire socialiste: 1789–1900: Constituante et législative*, vol. 1

Integrative eclecticism also guided Jaurès's interactions with political opponents. His political understanding was always oriented toward compromise, as illustrated by a scene that played out between him and Luxemburg at the International Socialist Congress in Amsterdam in 1904. Luxemburg criticized Jaurès, as she regularly did, for his cooperative stance toward the bourgeois parties. However, in Amsterdam she was not only a delegate but also an interpreter. After she condemned all cooperation with the bourgeoisie in her own speech, she was supposed to interpret for Jaurès, who was next on the program. He began his remarks with this disarming observation: "And yet, within a few minutes, you will see the citizen Rosa Luxemburg translating me into German; you will thus see how there CAN be useful co-operation despite conflict."[115]

Distinguishing himself starkly from Guesde both intellectually and personally, Jaurès celebrated Marx, not as the herald of a higher truth but as *one* of many philosophical masters. Jaurès wrote his second dissertation, "On the Origins of German Socialism," at the University of Toulouse after his first term in the National Assembly. He argued that Marx's dialectical materialism showed that the conventional vocabulary of political economy was not based on eternally valid categories such as labor, capital, or wages. Like all areas of life, economics was "deeply permeated by the dialectic."[116] The past flowed into the future—quite in the spirit of Abbé Bouisset's motto. Nothing was eternal "except the law of the dialectic itself." Jaurès concluded his observations on the significance of Marx's philosophy by noting that the flow of progress had brought "general unrest," heralding socialism's imminent approach.[117]

Jaurès wrote these words after four years of parliamentary experience as a center-left republican.[118] Having lost his bid for reelection in 1889, he returned to his professorship in philosophy at Toulouse. Only a few years before, at the beginning of his teaching career in Albi, he had explained philosophical problems in his lectures without any references to the pressing questions of the day. "Philosophy investigates the true, real essence of things as much as their innermost, hidden being," he had begun his introductory lecture. He came no closer to social problems of the present.[119] Upon his return to Toulouse, by contrast, he was a highly politicized professor—as is evident, not least, by the exegesis of Marx in his second dissertation. He stayed up to date with current events as a reader and, after 1890, also as a municipal councilman. Jaurès wrote regularly for *La Dépêche de Toulouse* about education, religion, and various aspects of the Social Question, with special attention to the living and working conditions of local miners, glass workers, and peasants. And when serious labor disputes erupted at the mines of Carmaux (northeast of Toulouse) in 1892, Professor Jaurès got personally involved. In August a miner who had been elected mayor was fired from his job, and his outraged coworkers stormed the home of the company's director. Because the miner had been denied sufficient time off to exercise his elected position, Jaurès argued that the principle of universal suffrage had been violated. He lobbied more openly than ever for republicanism and socialism as the two equal cornerstones of his political worldview.[120]

These experiences formatively influenced his thinking, actions, and self-image—as illustrated by the metaphor that he adopted from this point forward, in order to defend his engagement on behalf of the Republic (not least, in the Dreyfus and Millerand affairs) against the attacks of radical Guesdists: "When a miner who is loosening one block of coal after another with his pickaxe suddenly notices that the gallery and supports are wobbling and the ceiling is sagging, he sets down his axe for a moment and shores up the supports. Does that mean that he stopped working and abandoned his strong tools? No, to the contrary, he secured the progress and success of his labor."[121] For Jaurès, the class struggle (the "pickaxe") was subordinate to the preservation of the democratic order (the "gallery"). Without the proper "supports," the incremental elimination of injustices in the old order (loosening "blocks of coal") could destroy an entire society by collapsing the "ceiling." Jaurès's embrace of the workers' movement during the strike in Carmaux merged his own center-left republicanism of the 1880s with the POF agenda of the 1890s. He joined the party's list of regional candidates and was elected to office in 1893.

Marx's theses played an increasingly important role in Jaurès's political engagement. He made his first public reference to Marx (and—as usual—Lassalle) in a February 1890 article for *La Dépêche* about the German Social Democrats' recent electoral victory. Here, too, Jaurès took an integrative view of the German and French socialist movements. Before expanding upon the lessons of the SPD's success, he noted that the French republic had positively influenced the development of the German socialist movement. Likewise, the French could learn from the Germans' discipline and endurance by studying the German masters, Marx and Lassalle. French socialists could do "their idea" the greatest service by knowing it well. After all, German socialism was "no vague coalition of dissatisfaction and appetite [*coalition vague de mécontentements et d'appétits*]. It represents a doctrine, an idea, and this idea is spreading among the masses. What makes this new German democracy so powerful is the precision of its fundamental ideas."[122] Deeply impressed by the Germans' accomplishments, Jaurès implored the French socialists—who, ten years after their party's founding, still had no uniform organization or program—to learn from their neighbors' intellectual stringency and propagandistic efficiency.

Jaurès was fascinated by the methodical precision of SPD politics, which were schooled in Marxist thought. He praised *Capital* as a "powerful algebraic work" (*livre vigoureux et algébrique*), and he particularly recommended the chapters about surplus value and the relationship between surplus value, wages, and profit. He agreed with Marx's assessment that a growing and increasingly self-aware industrial proletariat had emerged as a "decisive force" in human history, although it was childish to "think that all that is now necessary is a decree, a *Fiat lux*, of the proletariat to make the Socialist world rise up forthwith." On the other hand, it was short-sighted to deny "the irresistible power of evolution which condemns the unjust ascendancy of the middle class and the whole class system to extinction."[123] Jaurès, too, became convinced that Marx had discovered the laws of history. This fascination with inevitability permeated his remarks on Marx's theory like a mantra. Jaurès had to justify his stance as a Marxist for the first time during the campaign of 1893, and he defended his political engagement—now openly legitimated by Marx—with corresponding fervor: when asked if he agreed entirely with all of Marx's ideas, he responded in *La Depêche*:

> Yes, in so far as Marx is a collectivist. . . . I find most admirable and true his analysis of the nature of value and of the growth of capital by incessant exploitation of the worker. He has also shown in a striking manner that capitalism prepares its own destruction by the very excess of its development. . . . Finally he has demonstrated most forcibly that it is useless to rely on the spontaneous devotion, on the union and grouping together of all the interested people, that is to say, on the privileged class; only the proletariat can be relied on. With all that I agree. Those truths I accept.[124]

These assumptions informed Jaurès's political activism for the rest of his life. He believed that the theory of value united Proudhon and Marx. He revered the Frenchman for having recognized the "theory of value as the cornerstone of socialism"[125] and the German for having worked through all of its ramifications: "Marx has shown that the value of a product is created only by the labor that is involved in making it, and the profit of capital merely draws from the value of labor." The "tremendous fortune" to be made by exploiting the force of labor comes "from the flesh and blood of the proletariat."[126] The cunning of capitalism was that the modern laws of the marketplace ensured that this process was both efficient and opaque. For Jaurès, Marx's theory of value revealed the internal logic of a bitter human reality. Its victims were not only the exploited workers but also the capitalist exploiters; the latter were so thoroughly embedded within the matrix of the economic system that they themselves could not see that, as employers, they were necessarily exploiters. Even the capitalist was deceived by the increase in capital that came from the surplus value created by human labor. This process occurred, Jaurès wrote, "as

Marx says, 'behind his back.'" The capitalist did not even notice that he was robbing his workers because he paid them wages set by the market, which he believed were fair. He could not see that he was only one part of a "gigantic" community of exploitation. And because "the spoils are divided among capitalists according to set rules, they forget that these are spoils."[127]

Jaurès's discussion of seemingly secret or mysterious laws was partly derived from *Capital*. Marx expressed this idea in a variety of contexts, as when he spoke of the "invisible threads" that bound slaves to their masters. He used the same metaphor to describe the credit system, which "by unseen threads . . . draws the disposable money, scattered in larger or smaller masses over the surface of society, into the hands of individual or associated capitalists. It is the specific machine for the centralisation of capitals." And Marx asserted that the true relationship between employer and employee remained invisible when the power of labor was transformed into wages and prices—in other words, when labor was transformed into profit. Labor only appeared to be valued and remunerated in a rational way. In reality, this was the "mystification" of an economic model that was based on ruthless exploitation.[128] Marx (and, by extension, Jaurès) used the idea of a market acting "behind the backs" of its actors to illustrate complicated and consequential relationships without fully explaining them. Hegel's "cunning of reason" (*List der Vernunft*) was among his sources of inspiration—although Marx replaced Hegel's mystical "world spirit" (*Weltgeist*) with a materialist "market spirit" (*Marktgeist*).

Beyond its programmatic depiction of reality, this mode of thinking reveals a deep-seated mistrust in social relationships (and their knowability) and a mystical (i.e., Romantic) conception of the underlying rules of human coexistence. Jaurès appreciated Marx's vivid metaphors, although he did not share Marx's social mistrust or tendency toward mystification. While embracing Marx's narrative about the lack of transparency in capitalist economic relations, Jaurès thought that the "mystical" elements of Marx and Engels's texts (particularly the *Communist Manifesto*) were "misguided."[129]

Passages from Jaurès's treatise on the theory of surplus value show why he believed that Marx's analyses of the market were so significant. Jaurès believed that Marx had identified the fundamental laws that governed modern production and the distribution of goods. Because these laws permeated human existence in the age of industrialization, they were of great philosophical importance. Jaurès was impressed by the "totality" of Marx's engagement for socialism as a "global philosophy and political weapon."[130] Marx's work had such great intellectual and political influence because he had systematically combined philosophy, history, economics, and sociology in an unprecedented way, undertaking the most persuasive attempt yet "to find, in the realm of 'ideas,' a practical model for our life on earth."[131]

Like the other eight protagonists, Jaurès was fascinated by the Marxist method and confident in its ability to penetrate reality, and thus to solve the immense social problems of the day. By "precisely observing and investigating actual conditions [*Dinge selbst*]," Marx had revealed the "actual progression of economics and history." Jaurès understood the epistemological hubris of this undertaking, and he immediately anticipated its critics. In his dissertation on German socialism, he argued that, although the "economic dialectic of socialism" seemed to arise from "metaphysics and an *a priori* position," it had actually been achieved "*a posteriori*." At least as a young man, he was convinced that Marxism made no a priori assumptions about reality and that it was the ideal type of a materialist worldview.[132] He believed that Marx was the ideal practical philosopher—someone who had made a powerful, empirical contribution to the socialist ideal in the era of the "factual gaze."[133] Jaurès saw Marx as both an heir of humanist tradition and a herald of the historic "victory of humanity." There was certainly anger and outrage in his critique of capitalism, but—unlike Lenin, Luxemburg, or Guesde—Jaurès did not treat the capitalist class as inherently evil. Instead, he saw a group of individuals who had been molded by economic rules. Because of their position within an increasingly complex economic order, they were unable to reflect upon the consequences of their actions. Jaurès was enough of a socialist to denigrate these developments, but he was enough of a humanist to empathize with the affected individuals. He recognized both the endemic suffering of the "proletarians" and the systemic pressure on employers to turn a profit.

Jaurès did not merely adapt Marx's theses as the basis for political action at the beginning of the 1890s. As a student of intellectual history, he also historicized Marxism (although he did *not* identify it as such; he felt bound only to *one* universal "ism": socialism), and he developed his cautious critique of Marxism from this historicizing perspective. Even so, his critical texts reveal the same enduring fascination that characterized the political worldview of all the protagonists—including the other "flexible" (or, some would say, apostate) Marxists, Bernstein and Struve. Jaurès had studied intellectual history, and he had learned to see the merging of philosophy and social criticism since the Enlightenment as a historical process.

One of Jaurès's most thorough reflections on his relationship to Marx can be found in a letter to Charles Péguy, who was preparing to publish a collection of Jaurès's texts in 1901. Jaurès credited Marx, in a very abstract way, for uniting the workers' movement and the socialist idea—separate historical phenomena that had meandered aimlessly in the first half of the nineteenth century. Marx had shown the proletariat struggling in vain "against the oppressive power of capital" that "the communist form of ownership" would be the "conclusion and consummation of its efforts."[134] Before Marx, socialism had not known that "its living realization, its concrete historical power" was based in the workers' movement. After Marx, socialism and proletariat were inseparable; in fact, this may have been his one accomplishment that was beyond all dispute.

Marx had been dead less than twenty years, but Jaurès situated him firmly in the nineteenth century. Marx's entire worldview had coalesced in the shadow of the French Revolution and the revolts of 1848, as the working class had gradually advanced from its role as powerless observer to weak bit player. This was the only way Jaurès could explain Marx's "convoluted" theory of revolution, in which an immature social group would obtain political power by waiting for a "favorable opportunity" to push through "proletarian revolution" as a kind of surprise attack, on the heels of a "victorious bourgeois revolution." Marx gleefully bet that he could "outwit" the history of the bourgeoisie, speculating that a historically immature class could engage in a "parasitic revolution" by acquiring the "signals and means of its own movement" from the very opponents it sought to overthrow. As Jaurès saw it, the plan was steeped in Marx's "sarcastic irony" and his enthusiasm for intellectual games. Long before these games became a historical reality in 1917, Jaurès suspected that such a "strange undertaking" could succeed only through "revolution in permanence." Jaurès situated the *Manifesto of the Communist Party* in the "period of utopia" and declared that its theory of revolution was "entirely outmoded, in any sense of the word." He understood the *Manifesto* as a reflection of certain social conditions, as a document from less civilized times. He explained, with great emphasis, why Marx and Engels had insisted upon the misguided theory of increasing misery—not least because this way of thinking corresponded with his own religious predisposition. Only the force of economic developments and their social consequences—and Marx's Hegelian training—could explain why Marx needed a "wholly impoverished and pauperized proletariat for his dialectical construction of history." Because the stakes were nothing less than the "idea of humanity itself," Marx had to develop the story of a completely disenfranchised and "pauperized proletariat," so that "pure humanity, eternal in justice as in misery," could ultimately shine through. Jaurès posed the great question: How could one pretend to understand Marx without descending into the "dialectical primal earth, the deep springs of his reasoning"?

Jaurès found this primal earth in the *Critique of Hegel's Philosophy of Law*, which (fore)saw the "positive possibility of German emancipation" in the formation of a "proletariat" and its social liberation. By styling the proletariat as a "modern savior," Marx essentially crafted a vision of *human* emancipation.[135] In order to convey the urgency and enormity of this task, he had to present proletarian suffering as "universal suffering," which could be eased only by forming "an estate that is the dissolution of all estates, a sphere of society having a universal character because of its universal suffering." The old society and all of its spheres would dissolve with the formation of this special class. The "complete loss of humanity" would be followed by the "total redemption of humanity," Marx had prophesied in his *Critique*.[136] For Jaurès, this passage contained the essence of Marx's story of redemption.

Leszek Kolakowski has aptly summarized Marx's idea of emancipation—a description that illuminates Jaurès's enduring fascination with Marx's work, despite his criticism of the historical figure. According to Kolakowski, Marx presupposed that "there can be a perfect identity between collective and individual interests, and that private, 'egoistic' motives can be eliminated in favour of a sense of absolute community with the 'whole.' Marx held that a society from which all sources of conflict, aggression, and evil have been thus extirpated was not only thinkable, but was historically imminent."[137] Jaurès held firm to this communist ideal, and (especially) in the controversy over Bernstein's revisionism, he firmly rejected any effort to renounce an end goal. Even though, by the end of the nineteenth century, Marx's (and Engels's) core texts could seem outmoded, misguided, or mystical; even though they exaggerated the deepening misery of the proletariat and overestimated its power to ignite revolution; and even though Engels's book *The Condition of the Working Class in England* had been "almost completely refuted by history"—the meaning and purpose of their intellectual engagement remained as valid as ever for Jaurès. Strengthened by the "methodical and legal organization of [their] own forces and the law of democracy and universal suffrage," the workers could count on the gradual introduction of "the communist order . . . in our society."[138] This hope was the product of a very western European gaze. Jaurès was familiar with the lingering remnants of German absolutism, but he had little experience with conditions in tsarist Russia or

the world of the eastern European socialists, whose affinity for violence and "half-mystical expectations for a redemptive catastrophe"
he strongly opposed.[139]

There was one more element that enduringly connected Jaurès
with Marx and Engels. Beyond his fascination with their systematic
approach, disciplined empiricism, and idealistic social criticism, Jaurès
considered Marx and Engels to be committed republicans. Inspired
by Engels's published remarks on the draft of the SPD program of
1890, Jaurès recalled that the republic was *the* "political form of socialism." Engels's critique of the draft's (to his mind) absurd notions
about present-day society "developing towards socialism" showed that
Marx's renowned friend—and thus the master himself—in no way
considered the democratic republic a purely bourgeois form of government, as some "supposed Marx experts" asserted. Being loyal to
"Marx's true thoughts" meant defending the Republic in times of
crisis—certainly a reference to Jaurès's own position in the Dreyfus
and Millerand affairs, which some critics had stigmatized as a be-
trayal of working-class interests. Here it must be emphasized that
Jaurès read—or perhaps co-opted—Marx and Engels in a very idiosyncratic way. Jaurès highlighted Engels's criticism of the party program for not demanding a democratic republic, which Engels had
described as "the main political aim" of social democracy and "even
the specific form for the dictatorship of the proletariat."[140] Imprecise
contemporary definitions of "democracy" and "dictatorship" notwithstanding, neither Engels nor Jaurès apparently recognized the inherent contradictions of this position.[141]

Jaurès co-opted Marx in two different ways. First, he presented
Marx to himself and the world as an evolutionary thinker, ascribing
"irresistible power" to the idea of "revolutionary evolution." This
"splendid" motto, which ostensibly came from Marx, appears nowhere in his work—although it was easy enough for Jaurès to derive
it from Marx's deterministic theory of history and society.[142] Second,
Jaurès declared Marx to be a committed republican—a claim that has
fueled lively debates among generations of Marxologists ever since.

The consensus today is that Marx's political theory was one of revolution, not republican democracy.[143] Nevertheless, Jaurès confidently navigated toward Marx's least disruptive elements. Jaurès held fast to his assertion that Marx's attitude was fundamentally democratic, with the possible exception of the period after the failed revolution of 1848.

Jaurès largely ignored the despotic aspects of Marx's political thought—not least because Marx had applied the ancient concept of dictatorship only sparingly in his work. (The modern notion of dictatorship emerged only later in the nineteenth century.) When Marx did use the term, he did not explain what it meant. Kolakowski has shown how little Marx's and Lenin's conceptions of democracy have in common: Marx "not only did not question the principles of representative democracy but regarded them as a necessary part of popular rule"; in speaking of the "dictatorship of the proletariat," he sought to emphasize "the class content of the power system and not, as Lenin did, the liquidation of democratic institutions."[144] Jaurès and Lenin thus represent two possible, but extremely different, versions of a political program that was based on Marx.

When Jaurès did occasionally grapple with the authoritarian aspects of Marx's thought—evident, for example, in the *Manifesto of the Communist Party*—he relativized them by emphasizing their historical context. He accepted these aspects as a side effect of the awakening spirit of class struggle, which tended to glorify violence and mystify the actions that were available to the expanding ranks of the disenfranchised in an increasingly unstable social order. With a historian's love for analogy, Jaurès placed the *Manifesto* on par with the Declaration of the Rights of Man of 1793. Both were "life-affirming documents" that commanded "respect for life"—the "actual essence of communism," according to Jaurès.[145] Marx played a key role in this analogy since, without his "discovery" of the proletariat, the ideals of 1789–93 would have remained an unattainable utopia. The *Manifesto* gave shape to this utopia and made it seem possible. Jaurès rejected Marx and Engels's specific prescription for how the proletariat would fulfill its historical role, but he believed that the general historical tendency and underlying principles diagnosed in the *Manifesto* were beyond dispute. This imprecise mixture of determinism and voluntarism allowed Jaurès to find politically flexible, tactical solutions. He envisioned a thoroughly republican working class, which would advance the cause of socialism by democratic means. Or, to borrow a telling metaphor from Jaurès himself, which echoes his deep connection to the countryside: by sowing the seeds of communism in capitalist soil, a good society could be reaped.[146]

5

Star Students

Bernstein and Kautsky

Eduard Bernstein around 1882
Credit: International Institute of
Social History, Amsterdam
(Jean Gut papers)

Karl Kautsky around 1874
Credit: International Institute of
Social History, Amsterdam
(Kautsky papers)

In contrast to France, where a conflict between two charismatic leaders pulled Marxism in different directions, an unusual friendship made Marx the defining figure of the German workers' movement. Bernstein and Kautsky, a study in opposites, met in Zurich around 1880, at the respective ages of thirty and twenty-six. Together with Engels, they laid the intellectual and programmatic foundations for the "Marxification" of the German social democratic movement. At first, Bernstein and Kautsky studied together. They discussed the writings of Marx and Engels on mountain hikes around Zurich and felt closely connected in their search for a definitive worldview. As the years passed, however, Bernstein had trouble relating to Kautsky's compulsion for theoretical consistency. He had never shared Kautsky's obsession with theory, and he lacked the intellectual self-assurance and stamina for charting such expansive theoretical waters. Seen in this light, the eventual breakup of this remarkable friendship over the so-called revisionism debate was no surprise.

And yet, in his first two decades of work for the social democratic movement, the great revisionist Bernstein was undisputedly among the most loyal and influential supporters of Marx and Engels's revolutionary theses. Biographers usually depict his path from Marxism to revisionism without closely analyzing his worldview between 1879 and 1896, the year when his "moulting" (*Mauserung*) into a revisionist began.[1] As a result, Bernstein's entire biography tends to be told as the story of a lifelong moderate who was ground down by internal party fighting—quite in line with his own self-characterization as a tragic Wallenstein. Into his mid-thirties, however, Bernstein was a passionate advocate of an outlook that was grounded in class struggle, full of hope for revolution and the collapse of the capitalist system. "Infected" by Marx, he was, in his own way, as intensely involved in the creation of Marxism as Engels and Kautsky.[2]

The young Bernstein had been active in Berlin's social democratic movement for years before his introduction to the Marxist worldview. Having come from a family of modest means, he led a double life as a young adult. While working as a bank apprentice, he participated in workers' associations, collections for strike funds, and charitable initiatives to assist Berlin's homeless families; he also distributed fliers, agitated in outlying areas, and spent evenings at taverns that sometimes turned into brawls (less with the police than with his own people). He later wrote about these years in a staid account of the history of the Berlin workers' movement; the book rarely, but unambiguously, mentions his active participation in the movement from the beginning of 1872.[3] His depictions of party life in Berlin drew from a variety of contemporary textual and visual sources: fliers, petitions, facsimiles of newspaper articles, "bourgeois" caricatures of ostensibly dangerous or recalcitrant workers, "proletarian" poems and illustrations of everyday life in the slums. These sources reflected political engagement that was not yet structured by a dominant worldview.[4]

Bernstein's activism began in an era of increasingly frequent, ever larger strikes (1869–73), which showed that workers' readiness to defend themselves collectively had in no way abated despite the disorder and division within the labor movement, and also its persecution, since 1848.[5] German foreign policy was dominated by the Franco-Prussian War and the Paris Commune. Bernstein was impressed that two social democratic delegates in the North German Reichstag, Wilhelm Liebknecht and August Bebel, had criticized the hard Prussian military line against France in 1870–71, abstaining from the vote to approve war credits. Meeting Ignaz Auer and Bebel in person at a speech in Berlin inspired the twenty-two-year-old Bernstein to join the Social Democratic Workers' Party (SDAP), also known as the Eisenachers, in 1872.[6] He plunged into party work, which involved meetings in taverns (three evenings a week by 1873) and what he called "agitation." He later recalled that the "handful of Eisenachers were an officer corps without soldiers: almost every member was a speaker." Their goal, according to Bernstein, was social justice.[7]

He continued his education informally in his free time. After his employer, the Rothschild banking house, switched to English business hours in 1874, he had time to attend evening lectures at the University of Berlin: Tuesdays and Wednesdays, political economist

Eugen Dühring on "The Past and Present of Socialism" and "The Materialism in Philosophy and Natural History"; Thursdays, Adolph Wagner on "The Social and Worker Question." He got to know the field of political economy quite well, providing this overview of the current discussions in his first (surviving) letter to Liebknecht:

> [Wagner] is the well-known *Kathedersocialist*; for a newcomer, he speaks quite radically, but anyone in the know immediately notices his softer stance, which often lurks in insignificant remarks. Dühring is otherwise right down our line in his lectures. . . . He differs from Marx in that he doesn't derive political oppression from economic [oppression], but argues for the inverse. In his view, the germ of our current socialist movement is not the development of industry, but instead the French Revolution.[8]

The letter does not reveal how Bernstein felt about this distinction, but at the time he probably did not perceive an unbridgeable divide between Marx and Dühring. Both thinkers claimed to have developed an original, "purely scientific system," which could explain the past and present and also design a better future. Dühring's personal arrogance drove his attacks on the "terrible abuse of the term science" by people such as "Herr Marx" in the "low manner of Jews" in his *Critical History of National Economy and Socialism* (1871), which spurred the biting response from "Hegel's spinsters" (*Hegeljungfern*) Marx and Engels in *AntiDühring*.[9]

In the mid-1870s, shortly before this public spat, Bernstein underscored his sympathy for the Eisenachers (who were oriented more toward Marx) by referring to them as "us." He nevertheless appreciated Dühring's version of the materialist critique of society—not least because it offered a bridge between nonacademic social democrats (like himself) and the university milieu.[10] Dühring's Wednesday lectures accorded materialism the standing it deserved, Bernstein continued in his report to Liebknecht. Dühring could prove that "precisely because of materialism, a nobler—and in the best sense, moral—worldview could be established and put into practice."[11] As an evening student and independent learner, the twentysomething Bernstein was looking for a worldview to support his already well-developed party engagement. He had no problem accepting both Marx and Dühring—for the time being. Bernstein did not reject Dühring until he had personally experienced the political economist's "abnormally narrow horizon" and hatred for Jews on several occasions, and the "Londoners" began their public campaign against Dühring's theses in 1876.[12]

Bernstein knew the main tenets of Marx's writings and admired his political commentary and analysis. He was particularly impressed by Marx's application of his social and revolutionary theory and his thesis of the historical role of the "working class" to the concrete example of the Paris Commune in *The Civil War in France* (1871).[13] In addition to this canonical text of "scientific socialism," Bernstein was familiar with Engels's drastic account, *The Condition of the Working Class in England* (1845). He read Marx's *Critique of Political Economy* (1859) and *The Poverty of Philosophy* (1847) only in Zurich after 1881.[14] Bernstein had been involved with programmatic questions since 1874, the year that he first met Liebknecht in Berlin, and he served as a delegate to the Social Democratic program commission at the Gotha conference in 1875.[15] The Gotha program was supposed to unify the fractious German social democrats, and Liebknecht himself defended its provisional character by noting that socialism was not only a political party but also a science. Social democracy would continue to develop and advance, Liebknecht argued, and so the intellectual work was never complete. Missing elements could be added later, and "reactionary" passages could be retracted.[16] Marx's sharp (and later renowned) critique of the program went largely unheard in Gotha. The party discussed it openly only in the context of the next programmatic debate, at the Erfurt conference in 1891.

Just as Bernstein's personal acquaintance with Bebel and Liebknecht brought him closer to the practical movement after 1874, his correspondence with Engels fostered his "Marxist" attitude after 1879. *Avant la lettre*—and almost contemporaneously with Kautsky—Bernstein began to speak of "Marxism" (in quotation marks) in his letters.[17]

He simultaneously rethought the "noble" and "moral" motives that had shaped his years in Berlin. Rational and scientific insight, not moral outrage, made socialism the only worthwhile vision of the future. Engels was empathetic, smart, attentive, and kind; he became a loyal mentor to almost anyone who earned his trust. He wrote the young Bernstein candid, loquacious letters that contained just what Bernstein needed: reassurance, encouragement, praise, suggestions for reading, personal contacts, news from the Marx household, and unfailingly constructive criticism.

Bernstein decided to leave Berlin in 1878. Two attempts on the life of the kaiser in May and June 1878 made an already oppressive situation for the Social Democrats unbearable, and legal party work became impossible under what became known as Anti-Socialist Laws. Despite Bismarck's campaign against the SPD, which resembled a "witch hunt," Bernstein's employer had no intention of firing him; in fact, that very summer he was offered a raise. It was Bernstein who decided that Karl Höchberg's job offer in the social democratic press was more appealing, and so in 1879, alongside Georg von Vollmar, he became a founding editor of *Der Sozialdemokrat*, the newspaper for German social democrats abroad.

The "Londoners" swiftly recognized that Bernstein was a quick study and well-suited to steering party propaganda in the direction they desired. The correspondence between Engels and Bernstein reveals, on the one hand, a savvy and experienced teacher. Just as the socialist movement was utterly demoralized, Engels gave the young editor countless stylistic and substantive suggestions, drawing upon his own experience with the *Rheinische Zeitung* and *Neue Rheinische Zeitung* in the 1840s, and tirelessly explaining how Marx should be understood. On the other hand, the correspondence reveals a "modest, but self-assured and tenacious"[18] student who was a rising star of the socialist movement. Bernstein listened attentively and became increasingly confident in his own judgment and opinions. Within two years, he had increased the circulation of the weekly journal to seven thousand—a considerable achievement, if one considers that the three most influential social democratic daily newspapers in Germany, before they were banned in 1878, had around forty-five thousand subscribers in all.[19]

Bernstein's letters to Engels about this work, which he began to write in 1879, allow us to reconstruct his early, revolutionary Marxism. Coming from Berlin, Bernstein was well-versed in the practical risks and opportunities of social democratic engagement on the street, in working-class neighborhoods and factories. In dialogue with Engels (by letter) and Kautsky (in person), his diffuse motivations became a fixed worldview. He skillfully mediated, on the one hand, between Marx and Engels and "our people" in Germany and, on the other, between the generations (as when he suggested that Engels should write about his participation in the Baden campaign of 1849, which was unfamiliar to younger socialists).[20] Engels gave the young editor practical suggestions and advised that sarcasm, contempt, and mockery were the most effective weapons against reactionary opponents. Engels warned that treading softly and acquiescing to the Anti-Socialist Laws' destruction of party structures were signs of weakness, as were "revolutionary tittle-tattle" and the inflationary use of "high-flown rhetoric" and "forceful expressions."[21] And together, the two men reflected on materialist answers to questions as wide-ranging as whether the Christian halo had evolved from the profane cow's horn crown of Isis—because, after all, "everything has a natural cause."[22]

Engels explained to Bernstein that, in the end, socialism was not the "logical outcome of any idea or principle such as justice, etc., but the ideal product of a material-economic process, of the social process of production at a given stage."[23] Both men agreed that "modern society" was "bankrupt," a message the *Sozialdemokrat* could help to spread.[24] Bernstein believed that Germany, Austria, and Russia would soon no longer exist, and that socialism was "in the air"; it was the only form of social organization that could usher in the inevitable revolution, because the SPD was, by this point, the only remaining force that was genuinely revolutionary.[25] All internal quarreling notwithstanding, Bernstein was convinced that the movement, which

represented the "modern working masses," remained united and disciplined: "Once things get going in Germany, I think the full meaning
of the word 'revolutionary army' will prove true."[26] Both men scorned
the idea that the Anti-Socialist Laws could be repealed through the
parliamentary process, as the "possibilists" of the party expected—"no,
only revolution" could obliterate these laws.[27]

And so by the early 1880s, Bernstein (now more than thirty years
old) espoused the very "attentism" that he later criticized so sharply.
Hoping and waiting for a violent upheaval, he was in a constant state
of alert so he could seize the initiative at the right moment. These
unmet expectations may have contributed to the state of exhaustion
that he repeatedly described in his letters—or even to the nervous
breakdown he suffered in London, his second station in exile. He felt
abandoned and complained that he had lost touch with colleagues
in Germany, since many no longer had a permanent residence there;
he missed "interactions with people who could provide intellectual
stimulation," aside from "the workers . . . who at least provided a
particular kind of inspiration."[28] He was often angered by those in
the party who no longer believed "in the possibility of a proletarian
revolution" and who "abhorred" the very thought of it. As the editor of an official party newspaper, he hated the stylistic and rhetorical boundaries that were imposed by more moderate comrades, the
"utopians of 'gradual development.'" Seeking to keep the movement's
fighting spirit alive, he published fiery articles in the *Sozialdemokrat*
under telling pseudonyms: "Leo" (king of the animals) and "Vitellius"
(a Roman emperor who was respected for his bold language, despite
his reputation as a drunkard).[29] Bernstein adopted correspondingly
bold metaphors to convey his own thwarted desire for revolution,
explaining to Engels that the "official" party line crippled him "at
every opportunity"; he was like a "convict" staring down the barrel
of a gun.[30]

Internal party conflicts were only one front in the political
journalist's daily struggle. Bernstein also worried that "bourgeois social insurance policies"[31] could take the wind out of the movement's

sails. Bismarck introduced these policies in the early 1880s to "do-mesticate" the workers socially and politically—or, in the impe-rial chancellor's own words, "to stamp on this communist ant-hill with domestic legislation."[32] Bernstein urged Engels to criticize this "socialisme bismarquien" in the German edition of *Socialism: Utopian and Scientific*.[33] In November 1882 Bernstein and his coeditor Vollmar announced that they were launching a campaign to update the party program, dismissing the idea of producer cooperatives and calling for a standard workday as an essential political goal.

Engels's response—which Bernstein ultimately accepted—was un-sparing. He warned that such a campaign would make sense only if the proposed changes were undisputed, but the party was "bound hand and foot" because questions involving mandates and decision-making procedures were enormously difficult to resolve. Finally, Engels questioned how Bernstein's life in exile had affected his state of mind: "The greatest danger to any political émigrés lies in the urge to be up and doing; something has really got to happen; something has really got to be done! . . . Might you and Vollmar be suffering from the urge to be up and doing? If so beware—of yourselves."[34] A few months earlier, Engels had discussed the role of exile quite differently (although his premises were similar), suggesting harassment under the Anti-Socialist Laws could explain the moderate views of the movement's leaders in Germany: "For the thousands instantly ruined thereby, it is a personal disaster not to have been placed in an imme-diately revolutionary situation, i.e. exile. Otherwise not a few who are now bemoaning their fate would have gone over to Most's [anarchist] camp or at any rate found the *Sozialdemokrat* far too moderate."[35]

This stance of awaiting revolution, which Engels described so am-bivalently, was apparently Bernstein's natural state of being. His en-gagement in the SPD was self-evident because "we [are] not only a party of the oppressed, but also a party . . . of the exploited." This was the source of "our 'right,'" which was also "our 'strength.'" The worst consequence of the Anti-Socialist Laws was that "our people" had lost confidence in the party. For Bernstein, the social democratic project needed "no justification."[36] In fact, many other social democrats shared this attitude, which was more enduring than recent studies of the party's early history suggest. Further, the party comrades who had fled Germany were no longer solely or primarily motivated by the memory of 1848. It is not hard to imagine Bernstein holed up in his Zurich newspaper office, "fist clenched in his pocket . . . hoping for a renewed 'let's go' at any moment"—thus reflecting the collective stance of waiting and constant alertness that Thomas Welskopp has described as a "popular revolutionary undercurrent."[37]

Bernstein's reference to the "right" of the SPD—which is to say, the justification of its ideas and demands—suggests that he was convinced that the strength of the movement came from being on the right side of history. His conviction was rooted more in faith that modern history was developing toward socialism (based on his firsthand experiences with the Berlin workers' movement in the 1870s) and less in his admiration of socialism as a scientific discovery or achievement. For Bernstein, practice came first—and then came the stringent, "illusionless" theory that explained why this sensible practice would necessarily prevail.[38] Even as an old man, Bernstein historicized Marx as a thinker and politician, and he always emphasized Marx's political practice rather than idealizing him. Marx had not created the workers' movement, but he gave it direction and a "solid scientific foundation"; he gave the workers "faith in themselves," an "expanded intellectual horizon," and an "unshakeable awareness of the victory of their cause."[39] These emotional certitudes had played a significant role in the young Bernstein's own transformation into a Marxist.

And so Bernstein's first programmatic text did not discuss what socialism was, or even whether it was possible, but only how it could be realized. The slender volume *Social and Private Property: A Contribution toward Explaining the Socialist Program* became the first installment of the "Social Democratic Library" series, which was published in Zurich under the motto "The Best of What's Good," beginning in 1885. Drawing upon the workers' party program that Guesde and Lafargue had composed with Marx and Engels in London in 1880, Bernstein sought to dispel the ostensible "depravity" of socialism as a trick of bourgeois propaganda, recasting it as a social program that could appeal to a broad majority. He cited the classic sentences from *Capital*, in which "the knell of capitalist private property" sounds at the moment when the conflict between the means of production, concentrated into ever fewer hands, and the masses, toiling ever harder, bursts the "capitalist shell," and the "expropriators are expropriated." Bernstein explained that nothing in these sentences was "as unheard-of as our opponents love to assert." Merely mentioning the "terrible word" "expropriation" makes the "respectable burgher leap up in horror, as if one wanted to burn down the roof over his head."[40]

Bernstein wanted to show that expropriation would not bring violence, plunder, or the "worst injustice"—but, instead, that it was just and essential. By "returning all means of production to collective ownership," expropriation would restore the natural state of human society, as revealed by recent prehistorical research.[41] A majority merely needed to be convinced that this was an automatic process of modernity, explosive *and* evolutionary, which would transpire to the long-term benefit of the many people who currently owned no property, and to the short-term detriment of the few who did. Capitalists, broadly stated, did not run their own enterprises; instead, they exploited not only manual laborers (*Handarbeiter*) but also the intellectual workers (*Kopfarbeiter*) who oversaw production. This explained why the transition to an economy without capitalists would proceed with little friction.[42]

Bernstein understood the concept of expropriation as the quintessence of Marx's *Capital*, and his intense engagement with the term (which was not in the Gotha program) marked his turn toward a Marxist understanding of socialism. His passionate support for the process of collective expropriation, which he saw as justified and essential, stayed with him long beyond his time in Zurich. Even in 1919, after the November Revolution in Germany, he unsuccessfully attempted to portray socialization as a realistic political process.[43] Bernstein— who had left the Jewish community in his mid-twenties—saw the necessity of expropriation as a matter of faith, as illustrated by a short text that he wrote to his wife, Regina, in a personal album in 1889. Regina was fully integrated in his political engagement; politics were an essential part of their personal relationship. Bernstein dedicated the album to her, his "loyal comrade," and he referred to the final sentences of *Social and Private Property* as his "social and political confession of faith":[44]

> Seizure of the means of production by an organized society is no longer a utopian ideal of the future; it has become an *essential imperative* for the further development of society, the only means of counteracting the complete pauperization of the working class. In order for this to succeed, the working class in whose interest this lies must come to political power. Brute force is not sufficient for coming to political power; rather, one must also know exactly what one wants and aspires to. . . . In the womb of bourgeois capitalist society, the seeds of a new, socialist society have developed. The hour is drawing ever closer, because the ripened fruit is pushing to burst the capitalist shell, to obtain the air and light it needs to develop further, healthy and strong. The necessary act of midwifery is called: Expropriating the expropriators.[45]

This pathos, which was simultaneously voluntaristic and deterministic, characterized many texts of the first generation. Bernstein's primary fascination was not the supposedly scientific underpinnings of the Marxist worldview. He saw Marx more as a patriarch, a "teacher and fighter in practice," whose call to battle had given the movement intellectual and (especially) emotional support. By this point in time—Bernstein was almost forty—he was absolutely certain that "healthy and strong" development toward socialism would have to be violent. Violence was an essential factor, if not sufficient in itself. It had to be premised on a clear vision of the goals to be achieved; only purposeful violence could help "birth" a new society from the old. This goal-oriented thinking, and the accompanying focus on enlightening the "masses," is what Bernstein later "revised" in the 1890s. What soon became known as "revisionism" was encapsulated in his famous remark that the way forward, the movement, was everything to him, while the end goal was nothing.[46]

Many biographers have described Bernstein's political transformation (which Bebel called "moulting") without offering a
conclusive explanation—in no small part because Bernstein's revolutionary Marxism, which he espoused through the early 1890s,
has received too little attention.[47] And yet, upon closer scrutiny,
the break in Bernstein's worldview around 1896 was actually quite
drastic. Neither the "English glasses" so often cited by his opponents
and biographers, nor the bourgeois reform socialism of his Fabian
friends in London—influences that Bernstein himself consistently
sought to downplay—can sufficiently explain this break. Bernstein's
first biographer, Peter Gay, identifies the "sources" of Bernstein's revisionism (Marx, Engels, Lassalle, Dühring, Fabier) without precisely
analyzing how Bernstein received them, or how this reception may
have changed over time.

Gay largely draws from Bernstein's memoirs and other sources
from the second half of his life, which explain these influences only
in retrospect. Writing years later, Francis L. Carsten emphasizes the
peace Bernstein found upon settling in London, after years of political hyperactivity. Troubled that, as a seasoned Marxist, he had not yet
written a stand-alone book, in London Bernstein concentrated on
his journalism, followed Marx's example by studying at the British
Museum, and produced a complete edition of Lassalle's works. His first
"flirtation" (Engels) with the Fabian reform socialists dates to 1892—
the same year of his nervous breakdown, the immediate causes of
which remain unknown. Thomas Meyer suggests that Bernstein first
grappled more intensely with theoretical questions and confronted
the "internal contradictions of Marx's theory" when he wrote for the
Neue Zeit in London.

Bernstein himself discussed his intellectual development only briefly
in his written recollections, describing his transformation as an inevitable process of rethinking, which was based upon the "adjustment of
assumptions in favor of facts."[48] All of these accounts mostly neglect
such factors as exhaustion, homesickness, or growing older, which
might explain his suddenly pointed commentary on SPD tactics and

his emphasis on the idea of a political homeland. His contemporaries repeatedly raised these concerns in their letters to and about him.[49] He responded candidly to the criticism of his disappointed comrades that he had demonstrated tactical ignorance. And so, in March 1899, he responded to Adler: "You in the struggle have different needs, and also different eyes, than someone who, by the whims of fate, is damned to eternal observation." He was forced to direct his attention toward what he could see, and not toward the day-to-day needs of a geographically distant party.[50]

All this notwithstanding—and even in the second, revisionist half of his life—Bernstein held firm to Marxist socialism as an "immanent confession of faith."[51] Through all of Bernstein's intellectual revisions, he continued to understand Marxism as a perspective, not a truth, as "an insight, not a recipe."[52] His latching onto a Marxist point of view was based on an idealistic need for meaning, not a rational drive for knowledge. Ever since he was a young man, Bernstein had deemed such an "emotional standpoint" legitimate, even if he had long sought to minimize it by expanding his own knowledge and view of the world.[53] Despite Engels's whispers in his ear during those years in Zurich, Bernstein was fascinated by socialism as a "principle," not as an "ideal product."

"In a sense, we socialists are all autodidacts," wrote the elder Kautsky, reflecting back on how his "intellectual generation" had learned about Marxism. Not a single "university professorship in the science of socialism" had been created by the bourgeois state. Some young people were lucky enough to have received reading suggestions or guidance from party comrades, but others (like himself) had to find their own way.[54] Kautsky sought to recount his winding path toward Marxism by crafting his memoir in the style of a Bildungsroman. He traced his intellectual growth from being an instinctual, inquisitive atheist who embraced an "ethical-aesthetic emotional socialism"[55] to a fully developed Marxist schooled in materialism. He did not so much discover Marx and Engels in his mid-twenties as he found that these "titans" confirmed his own views:

I became a resolute socialist in 1873. But if Jacob had to serve for seven years in order to marry his beloved Rachel, then I had to serve the cause of socialism for seven more years before achieving completely Marxist views. . . . On my own, I would have never advanced toward a materialist conception of history. This was only possible under the leadership of Marx and Engels. But at least my own conception of history did not block the way. I did not have to overcome it completely, but only modify and deepen it, in order to arrive at a materialist conception.[56]

Kautsky's memoir is rich in biblical allusions, and, like Lenin, he cloaked these as romantic metaphors (Marxism as a lover to be conquered). His account suggests when he first read classic texts: *Capital* and the *Manifesto* in 1875, Engels's *Anti-Dühring* in 1877–78, and the *Critique of Political Economy* after 1880. And yet, despite his extensive recollections and numerous personal texts, his experiences as a reader are difficult to reconstruct. He must have gotten to know some titles in the emerging canon as a schoolboy, because he dates the beginning of his "ascent toward socialism" to 1871, when he was seventeen. Four years later, however, he did not include Marx or Engels in a list of intriguing titles and authors that he compiled for his grandfather.[57] Kautsky later recalled that he first read *Capital* "only" in 1875, the year he began his higher education and joined the SDAPÖ, and he got to know the *Manifesto of the Communist Party* later still.[58] Here Kautsky's own recollections may not be entirely accurate, because in 1874 he paraphrased the final lines of the *Manifesto* in one of his unpublished early writings, "about the justification of socialist ideas": "Gentlemen . . . consider that hunger and desperation are the midwives of the freedom you hate so much; abundance and prosperity, its gravediggers. The most dangerous enemy is one who has nothing to lose, everything to win."[59]

Getting to know Marx's magnum opus was a laborious process that Kautsky undertook on his own. Reading *Capital* had astonishingly little to do with his academic studies in history, law, and philosophy, which he commenced that same year. If we can believe his own recollections, he already knew that "fancying" socialism was not enough; instead, he sought to establish it scientifically. In line with his own interests and talents, he believed this could be done only historically, and so he enrolled in lectures in history. He simultaneously got involved in Vienna's loosely organized social democratic circles, which, to his surprise, included few other academics. (Adler had the same experience a few years later.) His extracurricular interests apparently did not interfere with his studies, which he completed in 1879. The university certified that "the candidate's academic behavior wholly corresponded to the legal requirements."[60]

Kautsky's recollections suggest that the workers who rallied around the contraband newspaper *Gleichheit* were impressed by his intellectual prowess—which could not yet have been well developed in these years of arduous study. He "immersed" himself in the "Bible of socialism," as *Capital* was known at the time, shortly after getting to know the Viennese social democrats around Johann Schwarzinger in early 1875.[61] He did not understand the work right away, and so his revelation that the Social Question was less about morals than about the mode of production must have evolved more slowly than he later depicted. His first articles in the socialist press did not mention Marx. His articles began to appear under the pseudonym "Symmachos" (an invention of the *Volksstaat* editors) in 1875, although he had signed his first manuscript "Prommachus"; he wanted to act as a spearhead (*Vorkämpfer*), but he was instead assigned the role of fellow combatant (*Mitkämpfer*). Symmachos's terminology and style of argumentation did not yet reflect the refined dialectics that distinguished Marx's devotees.[62]

In fact, during these years of unsatisfying academic study and his first party contacts, Kautsky spent much more time applying Darwin's ideas to the social sciences and making verbose world-historical pronouncements. One of his 1877 articles cited a certain "Carl Marx" and erroneously dated the first edition of *Capital* to 1859 (instead of 1867).[63] His 1879 contribution to the *Workers' Calendar* on the "modern proletariat" did not so much as mention its singular role as the driver of history, as asserted by Marx. At this point in time, Kautsky still understood the Social Question as "how one could transform the proletariat from a class that merely works, to one that enjoys; from a class that is oppressed, to one with equal rights."[64] His concern was what could be done for the workers—and not how, through class struggle and awareness, they could seize control of their own fates, as Marx demanded and prophesied.

Even Engels bemoaned the insufficient Marxism of Kautsky's early socialist texts, unaware, of course, that these were the rough early work of his soon-to-be most important epigone:

> It would seem to be impossible for our people—some of them, at least—to confine their articles to what they have really understood. In proof I cite the endless columns of theoretical-socialist matter by K-Z, Symmachos et al. who, with their economic blunders and false perspectives and ignorance of socialist literature, furnish the means best calculated to destroy completely the superiority hitherto enjoyed by the German movement in the field of theory.[65]

This was, of course, the opposite of what the twenty-one-year-old Kautsky hoped to accomplish with his articles. For the time being, however, he read and cited economists, historians, and (especially) natural scientists in a pre-Marxist way. He was enthusiastic about Darwin's theories and (mis)applied them to socialism all his life.[66] As a student in the late 1870s, he explained Darwin's social scientific relevance in articles that appeared in *Volksstaat*, *Vorwärts*, and the *Austrian Workers' Calendar*. He argued that human beings—the most highly developed animal—possessed a "communal instinct" so deep-seated that they engaged cooperatively in the struggle for existence.[67]

Kautsky thought intensely about the realization of individual interests and redistribution of property in a free, communist society. Within this context, his precarious professional existence is important to keep in mind. Before going to work for Höchberg in Zurich in 1880, he was perpetually starting new careers. He dabbled in theater, creative writing, journalism, and science, tormented for years over how to earn a living. But there was one thing he knew for sure: he was an intellectual worker. And so he wrote long treatises about how the future state could harmonize intellectual and manual labor, and how enough people might be recruited for the less pleasant manual tasks.[68] Intellectual workers could, of course, be required to perform at least two hours of manual labor per day, but, according to Kautsky, this would not cover society's need for consumable goods. Similarly inspired by his personal circumstances, he championed the idea that only in socialism could the arts develop freely.[69] The twentysomething Kautsky's observations were permeated by the conviction that the material determined the ideal, and that only fair—which, to Kautsky, meant "socialized"—relations of ownership could guarantee a fair society. In the eyes of Marx and Engels, the young Kautsky was a classic utopian who was completely oblivious to the actual "laws" of social development.

Within just a few years, however, Kautsky developed from a student into a young master at breathtaking speed. While visiting Paris in 1880, he met several socialists close to Malon and Guesde, all "infected by Marx," including a not yet famous Plekhanov, and he reported back to his mother, "Truly, Marxism keeps gaining ground."[70] His personal relationship with Engels between 1880 and 1894 led to his role as the administrator of Marx's and Engels's papers and facilitated his acceptance within the inner circle of founding fathers.

Kautsky first met Marx and Engels in person in 1881. He wrote extensively to his mother about Marx's daughters, who unfortunately were already married,[71] but he ultimately established closer ties with Engels, who recognized the young man's potential—and impressive tolerance for alcohol. Marx, on the other hand, described Kautsky as "an exceptionally good chap, but a born pedant and hairsplitter in whose hands complex questions are not made simple, but simple ones complex." Further, "he's a mediocrity, narrow in outlook, overwise (only 26 years old), a know-all, hard-working after a fashion, much concerned with statistics out of which, however, he makes little sense. I unload him onto *amigo* Engels as much as I can."[72]

This personal constellation, established at their first meeting, helps to explain why Engels, rather than Marx himself, became Kautsky's mentor. Kautsky's ascent was closely intertwined with Engels's late work and the founding of the *Neue Zeit*. Engels's texts—from *Anti-Dühring* and *Socialism: Utopian and Scientific* to his prefaces to new editions of Marx's works and correspondence—were milestones in Kautsky's education in materialism.[73] Kautsky later wrote to Engels that *Anti-Dühring* had done more than any other book to enhance his "understanding of Marxism." Although Marx's *Capital* was "more powerful," it was "only through *Anti-Dühring* that we learned to understand and read *Capital* correctly." And so Kautsky concluded his own most important work, *The Economic Doctrines of Karl Marx*, not with a core idea from Marx's magnum opus but with a quote from Engels, that the socialization of production in communism was "humanity's leap from the kingdom of necessity to the kingdom of freedom."[74]

A much older Kautsky later described his repeated readings of *Capital* as a years-long process of coming to terms with Marxism. Here we can take Kautsky at his word, as he acquired the Marxist worldview as a method of understanding the world as a whole. His search for a "historical theory, for the principle that drove the historical process forward," is what led him to Marx and Engels.[75] Kautsky's actual reading of Marx becomes easier to reconstruct in the *Neue Zeit* (beginning in 1883) and his slender volume *The Economic Doctrines of Karl Marx* (1887). He developed his thoughts on Marx in close dialogue with Bernstein.[76] Sometimes the two went swimming together or relaxed outdoors, "a text by Marx at our side," or otherwise worked collaboratively, "interpreting Marx."[77]

Over the course of his studies with Bernstein, Kautsky became one of a small elite. As his self-confidence steadily increased, he sought to become an "intellectual leader of the party."[78] His contact with Engels encouraged him to work toward becoming a party theoretician. But first, in 1881, he abruptly lost financing for his intellectual undertakings in Zurich, when his benefactor and employer, Höchberg, lost his entire fortune in a bank collapse.[79] He was forced to reconsider his professional future, and he returned to Vienna for a few months in 1882. Over the next year, he and his former schoolmate, Heinrich Braun, in collaboration with Bebel and Liebknecht, "hatched" the idea for a "great project": a scientific journal to propagate Marxism, to be called the *Neue Zeit*. The new journal would not "tootle about reform" but would "stand completely on Marxist ground."[80] Critical, informative, and multifaceted, the *Neue Zeit* would refrain from all "utopianism."[81]

Kautsky obsessed for months over the location that would be best suited for him to protect and expand his newfound authority. Carefully weighing his personal and internal party prospects, he decided to move to London in 1885. His ruminations, which are documented in the many letters he wrote to his family, reveal, on the one hand, a quite arrogant young man. On the other hand, this correspondence reveals an emerging Marxist community that was already well-networked—and thinking transnationally, at least within Europe. In August 1884 Kautsky wrote to his father about his future plans:

> What can London offer me? Nowhere but London could I engage in such research for a history of socialism, because not only the British Museum, but also the private library of Engels and Marx, are at my disposal—as well as the experience of the former, who is himself a living history of socialism. In addition, everything that comes from London receives much more attention than what comes from Vienna. . . . One other thing to consider. Next to Lafargue, who lives in Paris, and perhaps also Plekhanov in Geneva, I'm the preeminent representative of the Marxist school today—aside from Engels, of course. If I lived in London, I would be the natural successor of Engels and Marx, the editor of their papers. That is a truly commanding scholarly position [*Stellung in der Wissenschaft*], because everywhere today—with the possible exception of a few uninformed Viennese journalists—Marx and Engels are considered first-rate scientific authorities. As the editor of their papers—Engels is already very old—some of their glory will be reflected on me, and then I, too, can make a truly outstanding scientific

achievement. I can attain a scholarly position like few others in our century.[82]

Kautsky outgrew the role of student relatively quickly in these years. With the establishment of the *Neue Zeit* and his decision to move to London soon thereafter, he could at last devote himself to the project for which he felt most suited: going beyond Marx to propagate Marxism as a science. "Our camp" had to advance beyond the often "amateurish . . . regurgitation" of Marx, he editorialized in the first issue of the *Neue Zeit*. There was a need for "independent, truly scientific studies": "We want to popularize knowledge, enlighten the workers in such a way that we can explain the science to them at all times, so that it is always up-to-date." Pointing to Fichte as a source of inspiration, the young editor-in-chief emphasized that this was nothing less than a national mission.[83] Kautsky had at last found his role. As a child of the bourgeoisie, he complained about the chaotic, fractious, insufficiently trained—and yet urgently needed—Austrian social democratic movement: "We are culturally very, very far behind."[84] Nevertheless, he claimed the movement as his own. With the word "we," he staked his position among the working class. Rather than burning bridges to his past, he built new ones to connect the bourgeois and working-class worlds.

Kautsky came to see his background and eclectic education as an asset that could help the movement gain momentum and prestige. He was practically intoxicated by a Marxist founding spirit during these months. "The demand for Marx and your writings was never greater," he wrote to Engels in November 1882, just a few days before the publication of the first issue of the *Neue Zeit*, and yet "the supply was never scarcer than now."[85] Kautsky was right: the years between Marx's and Engels's deaths (1883–95) became the "golden age" of Marxism. His first words to his readers were accordingly self-assured: "We are not introducing ourselves with an apology, as is customary among journalists. We're here, and our actions should prove our right to exist."[86]

The *Neue Zeit* was justifying not only its own but also Kautsky's existence; he led the journal with great dedication until 1918. Unequivocally engaged—at last—as a partisan writer in the Marxist sense, as a "midwife of truth,"[87] Kautsky had found a way to earn a living that fully exploited his talents. In his April 1883 eulogy for Marx, Kautsky described his own rise as coauthor of the Marxist project in the following way:

> The authority of the genius lies in *perception* [*Erkenntnis*]. The higher you climb, the greater the genius appears to you, the more you understand, the more willingly you bow to him. This is not timid submission to church authority; this is not grudging subordination to the corporal's stick; this is joyful, self-aware recognition of the greatness that the human spirit can attain. It is grounded not in servility, but in self-esteem.[88]

Latching onto a Marxist perspective was more than settling on a worldview, and it was more than the end of a journey for "a bourgeois intellectual driven by moral duty and social idealism, who turned toward the idea of socialism and took the side of the workers."[89] Latching onto this perspective allowed Kautsky to pursue his diffuse ambitions and to cultivate a paradoxical self-image as a "consistent" Marxist who nevertheless continued to search and to study.

Kautsky's and Bernstein's reading of *Capital* in Zurich inspired what soon became the most important Marxist journal in German-speaking Europe. However, this was just the beginning of Kautsky's engagement with *Capital*. In 1885, from his exile in London, he wrote to Bernstein that he was working through *Capital* for the fourth time, gaining new understanding with every reading.[90] In the meantime, he had come to see the acceptance of Marx's thought system as an all-or-nothing proposition, which demanded a radical posture against the status quo: "Marx's system is so tightly interlocking that one must either accept all of its theoretical consequences or cast all of them aside. . . . Anyone who stands on the ground of the Communist Manifesto has cut the tablecloth between himself and the ruling classes; he can return to them only as a renegade."[91]

Kautsky's absolute conviction fueled his relentless engagement, and he soon became a master of party communications. In addition to his work with the *Neue Zeit*, he sought to propagate the Marxist worldview with a popular text. His 1887 book, *The Economic Doctrines of Karl Marx*, was "presented in a generally comprehensible way and elucidated by Karl Kautsky," according to its German subtitle. Originally conceived as a collaboration with Bernstein, the volume ultimately contained only one chapter section by his coauthor and appeared under Kautsky's name alone—not least because Bernstein was wanted by the German police.[92] Kautsky introduced himself as a member of Marx's "school" (*Angehöriger der Marx'schen Schule*) along-side, and as defined by, Engels. He lauded Marx for having discovered the "laws of motion" of capitalist production and for dismantling the theories of bourgeois "vulgar economists."[93] By viewing the history of society dialectically, through a materialist lens, revolutionary scientific socialism was no mere call for benevolence, but the logical end point of history. It could explain even the most insignificant social phenomena and "deduce" future developments accordingly.[94]

The Economic Doctrines of Karl Marx concisely summarized Marx's theses about the emergence of modern relations of production. Kautsky adopted a tone that gently guided the reader ("Let us return to our silk weaver"; "Let us follow the capitalist in his workplace"), provided examples from familiar settings (in the workshop, peasant's cottage, etc.), and explained how labor was transformed into a commodity. Adler was among those critics who thought that Kautsky's attempt at popularization missed the mark; he wrote that Kautsky was unable to disguise his "condescension toward the common, unedu-cated people."[95] Nevertheless, Kautsky's book was an honest effort to explain the social function of every commodity through its exchange or surplus value, its accordingly superficial "fetishistic character," and its seemingly unlimited potential for exploitation. Kautsky packed Marx's observations into readily comprehensible theses, such as that "the value of commodities is not a relation of things, but represents a relation of men to each other concealed in a material shell."[96] In contrast to simple commodity production—in which the producer consumes what he makes, and labor and property belong together—capitalist production destroyed this relationship by distributing increasingly elaborate means of production among a few private owners. The propertyless masses produced; the few property owners profited. This situation "necessarily" gave rise to social distortions and could be alleviated only by socializing the means of production. The "truth" of Marx's analysis arose not from the moral necessity of ending the modern misery of industrial production but from the "objective" insight into the logic of this development. Marx's socialism was a rational, not an ethical, doctrine. It drew its evidence, and thus its validity, from the power of allegedly objective social facts:

> Marx was the first thinker who revealed the fetishistic character of the commodity, who recognised capital not as a thing, but as *a relationship between things, and as a historical category*. He was the first who investigated the laws of movement and of the development of capital. And he was the first who deduced the aims of the present-day social movement as a necessary consequence from the anterior historical development, instead of excogitating them out of his inner consciousness as the dictates of some "eternal justice." . . . With this, however, a new epoch opens for mankind. Anarchical commodity production is replaced by the deliberate systematic organisation of social production, and an end is made of the domination of the producers by the product. Man, who has become to an ever increasing extent the master of natural forces, will thereby become the master of social development.[97]

This passage from Kautsky's conclusion points to the power of the Marxist worldview as a modern, epoch-defining vision, which was ultimately about the fulfillment of progress under complete and exclusive human control. The Marxist worldview referred to what is, demanding the clear-eyed perception and description of what was "real." This postulate of reality characterized all of the epigones' efforts to further develop Marx's doctrines. Kautsky himself conceded the "mere relative value" of knowledge, but he negated this principle just as readily as did Luxemburg (in the years ahead) by insisting upon the absolute validity of the dialectical method of knowing, so that analysis became the byproduct of an almost automatic thought process.

Dialectical materialism itself was not an absolute worldview but a particular "method of investigating the infinite world," he explained in his memoirs. Marx had "materialistically overturned" Hegel's dialectic, thereby describing "the form of the development of real things in nature and human society . . . without preconceived idealistic vagaries."[98]

This kind of social analysis—and the sociopolitical program derived from it—directed and structured Kautsky's search for a comprehensive worldview, enabling him to think "uniformly" and "consistently."[99] Ingrid Gilcher-Holtey has aptly summarized Kautsky's dogmatizing efforts for intellectual consistency, noting that he sought to determine the goal of the political workers' movement "on the basis of theoretical insight into actual circumstances."[100] Without this insight, Kautsky believed, the movement was doomed to lapse into utopianism or opportunism. The close connection between theory and practice defined this political engagement, initially fascinating Bernstein's practical mind as much as Kautsky's theoretical one. There were, however, many ways to interpret an increasingly complex social reality—an observation that irritated Bernstein as much as Kautsky denied it. Just a few years after their Zurich idyll, it was this difference that broke their friendship.

6

Theory and Practice

Adler's Belated Marxism

Victor Adler around 1880
Credit: International Institute of
Social History, Amsterdam

In 1888, two years after aligning openly with the social democratic movement, Adler wrote with his distinctive blend of irony and earnestness that he was a "defector from the class of monopolists to the cause of the people." The thirty-three-year-old Viennese doctor had surmounted numerous obstacles on his road to Marxism: a nouveau riche and bourgeois Jewish heritage, a well-meaning but strict and conservative father, a speech impediment and depressive temperament, and the antisemitic and antibourgeois prejudices of political comrades. He was an introvert who also sought intimacy. He could lose himself not only in philosophy and contemplation but also in the brutal social realities that he confronted firsthand as a practicing doctor and aspiring factory inspector.

Since he was a teenager, Adler had felt connected to the social democratic idea. Although his biographers have tended to interpret his early intellectual musings as more nationalist than socialist, these were shaped by the Social Question from the very beginning. Despite his participation in the nationally minded Arminia fraternity and Georg von Schönerer's German nationalist movement (which was strongly oriented toward the working class) and his celebration of the victory over Napoleon III and MacMahon in the 1870s, his letters to friends like Engelbert Pernerstorfer and Anna Wertheim show that his early politicization was defined by a strong social empathy.[1] Adler's passion as a student was "red," although as Prussia and France went to war in the summer of 1870, he remarked, "I must be black-red-gold [for a small German (*kleindeutsch*) solution to the question of national unification], but red, the one red—with my lifeblood, I'd like to color all the flags red."[2]

Adler had already lived a full life before his election as chairman of the unified Austrian Social Democratic Workers' Party in 1888. Fraternities, drinking sprees, and reading groups in philosophy and politics shaped his years as a university student (1870–76). He simultaneously dealt with the challenges of a tumultuous love life: a scandal involving an ex-girlfriend who threatened suicide and attacked him with acid; another girlfriend's unwanted pregnancy (and subsequent abortion, discreetly financed by his father); and a relationship with a pianist twelve years his senior, who accompanied him to the premiere of Wagner's Ring Cycle in Bayreuth in 1876.[3] His life appeared to settle down only after he earned his diploma. In 1878 he married the beautiful, artistic, and often depressive Emma Braun, who did not believe that her husband's colorful lifestyle was driven by meaningful sociopolitical engagement. According to Emma, the heads of Adler and his friends were filled with nothing but "alcohol, nicotine, and hollow phrases in speech and writing." She denigrated his "failed career" (referring either to social democracy or his medical practice for impoverished patients), convinced that it would lead the family to ruin.[4]

Similar to Kautsky, the young Adler grappled with tribulations both worldly and romantic, and with a search for political and personal meaning. Emma Adler's candid recollections and his own correspondence suggest that his social engagement was punctuated by doubt and phases of melancholy. Uncertainty about his professional prospects mixed with a vague but fateful sense of mission, particularly in the pre-Marxist years of his teens and twenties. The twenty-four-year-old wooed the aforementioned pianist with a poem by Hieronymus Lorm, "After One Hundred Years: To a Woman."[5] As befitting a true late Romantic—who was influenced by Schopenhauer, Nikolaus Lenau's Weltschmerz, and the sobering experience of 1848—this lament over unrequited love was steeped in the pathos of the transience and futility of the human condition. Fragments from Adler's diary that survived from these years suggest how strongly this poetry moved him. One entry from September 1872 reads, "I'm looking for a mode that will justify or allow my existence—My inward state is: distraction, chaos, having savored everything, knowledge, will—that is, if one means conscious will—My ego is self-centered like everyone else's. Upon reflection, compassion [Mitleid] heightened to suffering for the world [Weltleid]—Weltschmerz—a concept so abstract, it becomes ludicrous, because it repels, or rather, ignores the individual."[6] These lines reveal an extraordinarily empathetic, pensive young man who sought direction and purpose for his universal compassion. He questioned—and was practically repulsed by—his suffering for the world, a feeling that was both real and fantastic, concrete and abstract. An eclectic list of interests and role models, which he jotted down around the same time, suggests points of reference for his brooding: "Medicine—social question—poetry—epistemology—Kant, Wagner, Darwin." And, of course, Schopenhauer. Before going to sleep at night, Adler read his *Essays and Aphorisms* (1851), from which he drew sentiments such as "There is no doubt that life is given us, not to be enjoyed, but to be overcome—to be gotten over."[7]

Adler began to study chemistry at the University of Vienna in the fall of 1870, switching to medicine with an emphasis in psychiatry in 1872. During his final year at the Gymnasium, he had earned merely a "satisfactory" grade in the natural sciences, but his work in introductory philosophy had been deemed "excellent," and he had expressed interest in philosophy as a career. The summer before he commenced his university studies, he fretted that, like Hercules, he stood "at the crossroads between party and truth."[8]

Adler ultimately pursued philosophy only as an avocation, participating in the Viennese Workers' Educational Association, the Association for Clarifying and Establishing Our Views on the Social Question, the Reading Society of Viennese German Students, and the Political Association for Truth in Vienna (an ephemeral group of social democrats and intellectuals working to support the unification of the Viennese socialist movement). After years of socially critical reading and organizing, Adler and Pernerstorfer founded the German National Association (which later became Schönerer's party) only in 1879. Disgusted by the party's antisemitic turn, they parted ways with the German nationalists no later than 1883 (the year of Marx's death and Kautsky's establishment of the *Neue Zeit*). Although scholars have often asserted otherwise, Adler and Pernerstorfer sought neither "revenge on bourgeois society" nor an ersatz religion to substitute for Judaism. Rather, they were frustrated that the German nationalists always subordinated social policy to other political priorities.[9]

Although Adler's evolution from medical doctor who served the poor to social democratic party leader was in no way inevitable, his biography illustrates the appeal of Marx's worldview even—or particularly—to a young intellectual who was theoretically rather adrift. The fact that a dispirited medical doctor found his steadiest foothold in the intellectual framework of a politically washed-up social philosopher speaks to the power of this framework's ability, or claim, to make sense of reality. For Adler, Marx literally captured the mood on the street. Marx made sense of the new kinds of social relations that had arisen through industrialization, and he had invented or reinterpreted concepts ("laws") that depicted the accompanying individual and social experiences—sometimes with "ingenious" brevity, as in the *Manifesto of the Communist Party*. Marx may not have dreamed up something "new," but he had illuminated the new social reality of the capitalist age like no one before him. He was a "seer." In Marx, the working class had found their "master," who "articulated their misery, dignified their struggle," and assured them of victory.[10]

Although a wealth of Adler's personal writings have survived, it is surprisingly difficult to determine when and how he first read Marx. Most of Adler's biographers are silent on this point. His own recollections suggest that he had read the first volume of *Capital* multiple times since his days as a medical student. He read the posthumously published volumes 2 and 3 in the 1890s—using his time in prison productively, like a true Marxist. Before beginning his sentence in the spring of 1895, he asked for Engels's advice in approaching the two volumes, which he had resolved to read behind bars. After three months' detention in the Viennese district of Rudolfheim, Adler wrote to Engels in London about his experience with the entire *Capital*:

> I've worked through all of Capital II and III, and reread almost the entire Volume I and the "Critique" [of Hegel's Philosophy of Law]. I'll admit that, especially in II, I sometimes ran out of air, but III paid off generously. Part III gave me the feeling of exhilaration like the view from a mountain peak that was arduous to climb, where you suddenly see where you went and why. As to the danger that you suspected, that

loneliness was making me crazy, I have to tell you that the impression of *transcendence* outweighed everything else.[11]

Marx himself, Adler continued, felt this way as he wrote, and he had found "truly victorious" language for it. The third part of the third volume, which also inspired Kautsky, was about the "the law of the tendency of the rate of profit to fall," and it essentially repeated the theses of the *Manifesto of the Communist Party*. After decades of systematic study, Marx argued here that capitalism was doomed to fail: "that it has its barrier, that it is relative, that it is not an absolute, but only a historical mode of production corresponding to a definite limited epoch in the development of the material conditions of production."[12] Adler wondered who would popularize and historicize volumes 2 and 3, since Engels himself was overburdened—and, as it happened, would die only weeks after this exchange. Was Kautsky, with his condescension for the "common, uneducated people," again the only candidate?[13]

These reflections and exchanges about reading were part of the extremely warm and trusting relationship that Adler enjoyed with Engels. Engels repeatedly sent Adler significant sums of money, which supported both the Viennese party organization and the Adlers as a family; the expense of treating Emma's "nervous" disorder left them in constant financial straits. In the fall of 1893 and July 1894, for example, at Bebel's behest, Engels sent Adler one thousand marks—a sum that was approximately three times the annual income of the average Viennese worker.[14] Marxism in its founding era was an all-encompassing engagement; the personal and political were inextricably linked—not only in an abstract or ideological way but also as a matter of lived experience.

Adler's knowledge of the works of Marx and Engels was probably superficial, at best, when he began his university studies in the fall of 1870—when the literary association founded by his school friends renamed itself the Association for Clarifying and Establishing Our Views on the Social Question. Marx does not appear on a list of the association's books, which included pertinent titles by Lassalle (all "owned by Victor Adler"), Mill, and Smith.[15] The group did receive *Gleichheit* (equality) and the *Volksstimme* (people's voice), which had published excerpts of Marx's works since 1869.[16] The Reading Society of Viennese German Students maintained a library that held mostly literary fiction, although it did possess a number of works by Lassalle and other political economists (but none by Marx) around 1874. Into his mid-twenties, therefore, Adler may have read only the *Manifesto of the Communist Party*—which he fondly cited, even later in life, because of its mobilizing message.[17]

And so Adler's path to Marx began outside Vienna's existing social democratic circles, as the well-intentioned extracurricular pursuit of a critical, sensitive, and solidly middle-class medical student. In the early 1880s, after a few years of practical experience as a doctor, he began to look for an opportunity to receive "truly sociopolitical training"—without breaking with his father, who would not have tolerated his son's political conversion (at least, this is what Adler believed). Not coincidentally, his search coincided with the beginnings of Austrian social policy. Between 1879 and 1893, the government of Minister-President Eduard Graf Taaffe introduced a slew of labor and trade reforms and new legislation that resembled Bismarck's social reforms in Germany, although not directly inspired by them.[18] The revision of the Trade Law (1883), followed by new social legislation (accident insurance in 1887, health insurance in 1888), created an acute demand for experts in this new political field.

Adler seized this opportunity, and, at the age of thirty-two, he applied for a position as a factory inspector with the Ministry of Trade. One year earlier, with travel funds supplied by his father, he had engaged in a months-long factory inspection tour in Germany, England, and Switzerland, seeking to enhance his qualifications for the newly formed inspectorate. He carried not only an official letter (*Offene Ordre*) from the trade minister to the consulates of these three countries but also a letter of introduction to Marx and Engels, arranged by Kautsky—who was, in the meantime, well-connected. (Kautsky described Adler as "an eager, like-minded comrade, completely in-dependent and doesn't need the work; he's interested in factory in-spection merely to help us and for the opportunity to collect valuable material.")[19] And so Adler set out with intentions that were at once subversive and loyal to the government.

The outcome of this journey, which Adler reflected upon in let-ters and thoroughly documented in a report to the Ministry, had, at best, an indirect influence on the new legislation.[20] Most interesting in the context of this book is his own explanation for applying to the inspectorate; he mailed his report to the Viennese authorities from London in August 1883.[21] Hoping to present himself as a suitable can-didate for the newly created position, he emphasized both his per-sonal and his professional qualities. In all of his previous endeavors, he had been motivated by a "serious and deep interest . . . in the situation of the working classes"; he had made their "uplift" the "highest and holiest task" of his life. As a doctor, he had gained "insight into the inner life and needs of these classes." In his medical practice for the poor, he was compelled "to study the social causes of workers' illnesses and the means to remedy them—social hygiene as a guide for social policy." In order to determine which means were necessary and ap-propriate to deploy, he had familiarized himself with the "production process in its individual stages," which was the primary motivation for his trip to the three countries.

The core passage of his letter reveals a self-assured, goal-oriented applicant who was simultaneously eager to learn. He believed that he had found the royal road to solving the Social Question—without a social democratic party, without reference to Marx's theories, and without any revolutionary expectations. He outlined the characteris-tics of the ideal candidate (which, of course, he personified):

> The ideal factory inspector would have to be a doctor and technician—an all-purpose technician, social policymaker [*Socialpolitiker*], and public administrator—but, most of all, an energetic man with a heart for the cause. As a doctor and hygienist, he should be able to assess the condition

of industrial workers and its causes; as a technician, he should be able to use production technology to identify where and how known hazards . . . can be prevented; as a social policymaker, he should know the scope for providing relief within the existing economic order in every single case, he should know how to protect the interests of the workers without endangering those of industry; as a public administrator, he should know his role as a specialized organ within the organism he is there to help.[22]

Even though (or perhaps because) he so eloquently described his suitability for the position, the Trade Ministry turned him down—a decision that Adler himself had anticipated. He was too young, the authorities explained, and, for this job, his work as a doctor was more of a drawback; perhaps he could apply for a different position in the future.[23]

Viewed in the context of Adler's Marx reception, his unsuccessful effort to become a social policymaker for the existing regime apparently gave him the final push he needed to move toward practical social democracy and "revolutionary" Marxism. Just as Marx and Engels had decried supposedly utopian humanitarianism and "professorial socialism" (*Kathedersozialismus*) in their texts, by the summer of 1884 Adler had quite personally lost patience with reform efforts that merely alleviated the state's guilty conscience. He shared this frustration with all of the protagonists. They believed that Marxism had maneuvered socialism out of the corner of social criticism and the ideological defensive onto the expansive playing field of social policy and the ideological offensive—turning a cry for help into a program for action, utopianism into realism, and the Social Question into its solution. This orientation toward the present further explains why Marxism spread so rapidly after 1880. It fueled not only a deterministic "attentism" but also a voluntaristic presentism.

Adler was not alone in his impatience and exhaustion with gradualist social reform, which bourgeois interests overtly supported as a "preventive measure" (per Bismarck) against the threat of revolution.[24] He—and to his mind, all workers—were tired of relying on the goodwill of the well-to-do, a sentiment he conveyed in his formal remarks at a memorial celebration for Marx in 1893. After a workers' choir performed the Scheu brothers' festive hymn about knowledge as a weapon (quoted at the beginning of Part II), Adler vividly described this loss of patience: "Marx ripped the concept of 'humanity' into *classes* and exposed 'general human kindness' as a conflict of class interests. He unmasked the bourgeoisie's goodwill toward workers, the equalizing justice of the state, and today, underneath the friendliest mask, the proletariat can easily recognize the class state as an organ of the exploiting class (applause)."[25]

When Adler reflected back on his own intellectual development, he always mentioned Engels. Adler welcomed Engels's terse rhetoric as a contrast to Marx's often long-winded, obsessively detailed, and circuitous writing style. Engels knew, like few others, how to write "compactly"; Adler felt he almost learned "too quickly" (*überhaps*) when reading Engels's work.[26] Not coincidentally, Adler's first published reference to the London duo involved a work by Engels. Adler published a review on the topic of occupational sickness in the second issue of the *Neue Zeit*.[27] The book under review (Moritz Popper's *Lehrbuch der Arbeiterkrankheiten und Gewerbehygiene*, published in 1882) gave Adler an opportunity to discuss issues related to factory workers' health. He identified three closely interrelated "enemies of workers' health: social misery, overwork, and harmful activity." He cited everyday examples from the experience of Austrian workers, and he contrasted the average life expectancy of printers and miners in Prague (thirty to thirty-two years) with that of the city's general population (forty-six years). He noted that the degree of damage wrought by toxins ("lead colic; mercury poisoning; phosphorus workers' facial burns; coal, iron, silicon, cotton, and tobacco lung, etc.") depended on workers' standard of living; "well-nourished" people were less affected than the "chronically hungry," who "were employed in this way 12, 15, or even 18 hours a day or night."

Referring to numerous studies about various branches of work—including Engels's *Condition of the Working Class in England*—Adler sought to reframe work-related ailments as a social issue. These had to be understood as an affliction and responsibility of all society, not as the "effect of a single cause, the type of work." Accordingly, tuberculosis was not an occupational sickness but the logical consequence of malnutrition—as demonstrated by the example of female lace workers in the Ore Mountains, who subsisted on a diet of potatoes and chicory.

The review reflected Adler's great impatience with self-help and private charity, which were both unreliable and vastly overrated. As befitting a graduate of the esteemed Viennese Gymnasium zu den Schotten, Adler concluded his review with a prophecy cloaked in literary metaphor: a universal right to health would soon be considered a public good—not least because typhus, a "powerful *memento mori*," was appearing "more and more, like Banquo's ghost, in the midst of the most splendid residences."[28]

Adler's first reference to Marx can be found in his report to the Trade Ministry about his factory inspection tour. In this context he did not cite the theses of a revolutionary social philosopher, but rather the views of an established economist, who had himself studied the legal and material history of factory inspection and labor protection in England since the early nineteenth century. Adler's reference to the chapter on "machinery and modern industry" in the first volume of *Capital* concerned the well-substantiated argument that labor conditions in larger factories were not truly regulated until the introduction of relatively independent—and thus "effective"— state inspectors in 1833.[29] Here, too, Marx was relentless in his obsession with details. In a tone that swung between outrage and sarcasm, he illustrated the consequences of unregulated employment in the proto-capitalist factories of England, Ireland, and Scotland. His discussion of silk mills that employed schoolchildren under the age of eleven was a notable example. According to the manufacturers, child labor was necessary because of "the delicate texture of the fabric in which they were employed, requiring a lightness of touch, only to be acquired by the early introduction to these factories." For this silk production "out of the blood of little children," Marx wrote, "children were slaughtered out-and-out for the sake of their delicate fingers, as in Southern Russia the horned cattle for the sake of their hide and tallow."[30]

Marx based his account on government documents and newspaper reports, judicial files, statistics, medical expertise, and the eyewitness accounts of individual employees—in brief, the very sources that informed Adler's socialism. If one or another civil servant in the Viennese Trade Ministry had actually taken the time to study the literature that Adler had cited in order to prepare the new inspectorate in Austria as thoroughly as possible, he would have been struck by the social inequities of an unfettered capitalist economy; he also would have confronted powerful contempt for capital and manufacturers, with their "thousand-year empire of free trade" and "vampire thirst for the living blood of labour." With growing unease, this civil servant would have read Adler's own, at least indirect, references to the seizure of power by Austria's awakening working class. According to Marx, limits on working hours (which, in the meantime, were enforced in many English factories) were "not at all the products of Parliamentary fancy" but had instead "developed gradually out of circumstances as natural laws of the modern mode of production": "Their formulation, official recognition, and proclamation by the State were the result of a long struggle of classes."[31] These would have been disturbing prospects for a government official. Perhaps Adler's application was rejected precisely because his report was so thorough and—in multiple respects—alarming.

Just a few months later, Adler took a decisive step toward promoting the idea of continuous class struggle in the Habsburg Empire. After his father's death, having at last become "master of his own path,"[32] he invested nearly half of his inheritance in establishing the weekly newspaper *Gleichheit*. This project consumed most of his money, time, and energy for decades to come, and it energized the Austrian workers' movement in an enduring way.[33] A first, sample issue was published in December 1886. The journal provided a forum for the

socially engaged doctor, who held no public office, to put his decidedly oppositional theoretical and professional views into political
practice. As we have seen, Adler had long joked with like-minded
colleagues about his lack of theoretical inspiration, casting himself as a
mere "colporteur of foreign ideas."[34] Now he put this talent to work,
building a new political party.

Having since become better acquainted with the political situation
in Vienna, he saw the diversity of its socialist camp—from the "'radical' as homo novus" to the bourgeois "soldier in the soc.-dem. camp"
like himself—not as a drawback but as "material for building a new
party."[35] And, in fact, Adler was the right man for the job. The fractious
Viennese workers' movement, semi-organized around the journal
Wahrheit (truth), was ripe for coordination by a talented colporteur
and networker with bourgeois and academic sensibilities who was
primed for political engagement after his own efforts to reform state
behavior in a socially responsible way had come to naught. Adler eagerly familiarized himself with the Viennese party organization in the
spring and summer of 1886, and he was shocked by the "absolute lack
of talent and discipline . . . but especially the lack of self-assurance"
in the social democratic ranks. He found it shameful "how my very
cautious entrance, certainly not seeking to impress, was received," and
how great the "degree of influence [was] that I achieved in just a few
weeks," he wrote candidly to Kautsky in August 1886.[36]

These weeks simultaneously marked Adler's coming out as a
Marxist. The lead editorial in the sample issue of *Gleichheit* was infused
with the terminology of the materialist analysis of capitalism, class
struggle dialectics, and Marx's predictions about the organization and
concentration of "proletarian" power. "Introducing the workers to a
weapon they have long and sorely lacked in Vienna, in the struggle
for their rights and the truth they recognize, irrespective of factional
differences—this is our endeavor's open intent and only goal," the
first page declared under the headline "Workers!" Further aspirations
included "propagating and deepening class awareness" and "openly
organizing as a political party." The working class would bear the
"world-historical task" of supporting the "coming social order." Until

then, fighting for adequate and effective worker protection laws was essential "to defend against the physical degeneration that the prevailing economic system had imposed upon the working class."[37]

How did Adler understand Marxism? Twenty years after the death of its namesake, Adler responded to the query "What does Karl Marx mean to us?" by pointing to Schopenhauer, the hero of his youth—and by emphatically contradicting the elder philosopher's words. Schopenhauer, after all, had written that "only a brief celebration of victory is allowed between the two long periods during which [a new truth] is condemned as paradoxical, or disparaged as trivial." By contrast, Adler believed, Marx's "truth" was enduring; it would not "grow old and rust. Because these are not mere platitudes; instead, the best of what he gave us are methods of recognizing historical, economic, and political relations." If socialism had long been only a "cry of distress, a call for help, a complaint," it was now the "purposeful politics" of an enlightened working class.[38]

Adler also recognized that Marx had to be historicized, and that many aspects of his work were ephemeral. For not only had the bold thinker "recognized a historical process in its essence," but he was "also a child of his time, subject to every error in assessing the importance and duration of contemporary events." Even so, his work remained equivalent to Darwin's doctrine of "organic life as development [*Werdegang*]." Marx had dispelled the "superstition of an eternal order of ownership and economic relations, showing that this was historically dependent on the development of the mode of production." Adler was fascinated by Marx's historical and philosophical daring and his understanding of history as a process that followed Hegelian conceptions of movement. Sovereignty and property rights were not fixed, as Adler had once learned at the Gymnasium zu den Schotten. For all the criticism of his "many" miscalculations, it was Marx's great service—testament to his "unparalleled diligence"—to have derived "capitalism's law of motion" from a "plethora of facts."[39]

Adler's critical devotion to Marx shines through in the letters and texts that he wrote during the revisionism debate. Whatever theoretical revisions might be necessary, Adler argued, Marx remained an

indispensable compass for social democratic practice. Adler wrote to
Bernstein that his "subjectivist" critique was a "painful surprise" and
that he had done the party a great disservice.[40] Adler condemned
Bernstein's intervention as the product of incorrect ideological criticism, tactical ignorance, and deficient political instincts. Adler was
annoyed by the timing of Bernstein's essay collection, *Evolutionary
Socialism: A Criticism and Affirmation*, which was published in the
spring of 1899, in the midst of debates about the SPD's participation
in Prussian state elections. The pragmatic Adler scolded Bernstein:

> Now the Germans truly have other concerns than having their defects
> recounted to them. . . . Mark my words, the workers may read your
> book, it won't affect them directly, but it certainly will through the me-
> dium of precisely those literary types you despise—I and all the young
> voices in the party will pounce on this. Karl [Kautsky] is quite right:
> "None of the young people have read Marx, but they've all overcome
> him,"[41] and you're helping them. . . .
>
> I'm mostly annoyed by the tactical side—the theoretical [side] is re-
> mote to me, work that out with Karl. You construct a concept of "rev-
> olution" that no one has anymore, except for a few old policemen, and
> then you emphatically state we're not "revolutionary," we're a reform
> party. . . . You portray us as a sheep in wolf's clothing, and you want to
> steal our hide! These are things that could only occur to you in your
> isolation—whims that will pass, I'm sure about that.[42]

More often, however, Adler took critiques of Marx's theories coolly,
and he did not see them as in any way diminishing the master's allure.
After all, Marx's theories were a mutable superstructure that, viewed as
a whole, "only illuminated the movement's path, without prescribing its
tracks."[43] Adler was enchanted by the idea of illumination, an incandes-
cent worldview in which it was "impossible to determine what in us
arose from him [Marx]." Underneath this sentimental exterior, however,
lay an enlightened and rational core. As Hannah Arendt later noted, Marx
and Engels had introduced their promise of progress and prosperity to the
world through their momentous politicization of the "quest for bread."[44]

In the end, Adler's Marxism was an utterly practical worldview—
an outer skin (or "hide") that cloaked his political thought and action, that he was ready and willing to adjust for political expediency.

He accused the "ideologue" Bernstein and "fanatic" comrades such as Plekhanov, Alexander Parvus, and Luxemburg of being unable to relativize their positions. With a generous dose of irony and the imagery of a scientist, Adler wrote that the "overall state" of social democracy was not "as dangerously brittle as a Bologna flask that crumbles into dust when marred by the slightest scratch; it is not a construct of dogmas held together by literal faith that falters when doubt rattles individual tenets."[45] Rather (and here Adler's argument precisely matched Kautsky's), Marxism was a "method of insight," a "living, organic system of insights achieved," the security of which was not assured by their "inviolability" but instead by "constant critique." Thus, Adler, like Kautsky, acquired a very specific perspective from Marx's doctrines, which henceforth filtered and structured his view of social reality and human relations.

For the calmly independent Adler, who embraced even Marx's weaknesses, the rigidity he saw—even in Bernstein's revisionism—was a consequence of the "heated class struggle" in which they were all soldiers. If, during the heat of battle, one engaged in fundamental discussions about what was supposed to be true, then "we risk bringing along our soldiers' habits . . . which will tarnish the impartiality of our philosophy in an alarming way."[46] In the end, Adler considered his critics' loss of impartiality and growing rigidity—whether in the guise of "doubting shittiness" (*Zweifelsscheißerei*) on the right or delusional fanaticism on the left—to be a question of "character" or political temperament.[47] His "overheated" comrades, meanwhile, interpreted his plea for a certain intellectual levity as evidence of insufficient ideological fortitude.

Under Adler's leadership, *Gleichheit* sought to propagate Marxism without "doubting shittiness" or "fanaticism." Beyond this ideological goal, the weekly newspaper also took aim against the "physical degeneration" of the exploited—a second field of activism that clearly bore Adler's fingerprints. By merging Marxist theory with the sociopolitical interests he had acquired as a doctor, Adler fashioned a coherent political worldview that was saturated in real-world experience. The very first issue of *Gleichheit* was an empirically saturated *and* ideologically framed panorama of news, features, and commentary; it clearly illustrated the "degenerating effects" of the current order and the workers' right to self-preservation. The spectrum of topics included the unemployed workers ("white slaves") who cleared snow from Viennese tram lines for starvation wages, the unfair labor practices of manufacturers who employed women and children at night, the German Anti-Socialist Laws, and the "ghastliest living conditions" in Vienna. Reader competitions were especially popular, with riddles such as "Should the social question be solved by taxation or public debt?," "How can the social question be solved best and most cost-effectively?," and "Has there really been no new textbook in political economy since Meidinger?"—a question that was certainly intended to inspire Marx's *Capital* as an answer.

The most prominent example of the newspaper's social criticism was a series of articles by Adler himself on the working and living conditions of Viennese brick workers. As we will see in Part III, this series actually led to legislative reform.[48] The criticism in *Gleichheit* was precisely directed toward lifting the "wretched self-awareness" that Adler had found so surprising upon his introduction to the Viennese social democratic movement. The fact that, over the next three years, a "renegade" like Adler succeeded in uniting the Austrian social democratic movement within a single party demonstrates the viable link between his own socially critical practice as a medical professional and Marx's professionalized social criticism. What's more, Adler successfully rallied the Austrians around the strictest Marxist program anywhere in Europe at that time.[49]

Gleichheit initiated, oversaw, and structured this process until the newspaper was banned in 1889. (Its work then continued as the *Arbeiter-Zeitung*). *Gleichheit* earned accordingly high praise from Engels, Kautsky, and Bernstein—the inner circle of Marx's epigones. Kautsky wrote to Adler at the end of 1886:

> I'm very pleased by Gleichheit, and so is Engels. I have no objections whatsoever to its stance. The sample issue was a bit doctrinaire for a workers' paper, but the issue from 25 Dec. is much livelier and more contemporary. The commentaries will have great appeal. I'm really missing a feature article about a current topic; on the other hand, the

number of academic articles (including my own [about socialism in Russia and America, in the first issue]) could be reduced significantly. The workers don't like to read long articles. Above all, they're interested in an overview.[50]

The last page of the sample issue of *Gleichheit* featured an advertisement for the latest *Austrian Workers' Calendar*—the subject of Kautsky's and Bernstein's agonizing at the beginning of the previous chapter. The advertisement promised an "outstanding agitational tract" with an "artistic cover." The calendar's touted contents included scholarly articles that were comprehensible and enlightening to workers, as well as stories, socially relevant poems, practical advice, and a sociopolitical retrospective. The advertisement further noted that the *Austrian Workers' Calendar* was banned in Germany.

The cover of the next year's calendar—which was, indeed, quite elaborate—celebrated the icons of a rising Marxism, as represented by the social democratic parties: Marx, Lassalle, a benevolent Libertas, possibly Galileo Galilei (the father of modern science), and the toppled pillars of absolute monarchy ("L'État, c'est moi"). The bust in the lower right-hand corner bears a resemblance not only to Galileo but also to Zeus, the god of gods. If indeed this figure is Zeus, then the ruler of the heavens is positioned below the teachers of Marxism—brought down to earth, one might say, and surrounded by the scientific instruments that promise mastery of the world. The traces of destruction or collapse symbolize a radical upheaval. We might nevertheless interpret the decision to depict a peaceful Libertas carrying the torch of progress—instead of the bare-breasted fighter Marianne, as in Eugène Delacroix's commemoration of the July Revolution of 1830—as a fitting allegory of the politics of Austrian Marxism since the early 1880s. By leafing through the pages of this calendar over the course of 1888, readers would have gotten to know the minds and principles of a political movement that, under Adler's leadership, may have preached revolution in theory but acted evolutionary in practice.

Finally, the cover of the *Workers' Calendar* shows that its editors decided against a group portrait of the "representatives of scientific socialism," possibly because of the difficulties of selection that Kautsky had raised. Instead, they opted for an iconographic cover with Marx and Lassalle representing the movement's lowest common denominator in German-speaking Europe. An interior illustration featured all of the Social Democratic delegates in the Reichstag, the imperial parliament in Berlin. Instead of a canon of the movement's "consistent Marxists," the calendar showcased its elected representatives.[51]

Austrian Workers' Calendar (1887)
Credit: *Marx-Engels Gesamtausgabe*, I/31, 485

Paths to Marxism II: Geneva, Warsaw, St. Petersburg (1885–1903)

Study, propagandize, organize.
—Wilhelm Liebknecht, cited in Lenin, *What the "Friends of the People" Are* (1894)

As Adler was preparing the way for a unified social democratic movement in the Habsburg Empire, the American explorer George Kennan (a distant cousin of the well-known historian and diplomat George F. Kennan) returned from a months-long tour through Russia.[1] Similar to Adler, Kennan was on a constant quest for empirical truth. After the assassination of Tsar Alexander II in 1881 had directed the world's attention toward the Russian revolutionary movement, Kennan sought to get to know and understand the political terra incognita of the tsarist empire—at first, with no subversive intent. Rather, Kennan wanted "to ascertain how the Government treats its enemies." His detailed report documented the tsarist penal system and drew the following conclusions from his encounters with political prisoners in Siberian exile: "The two things that are most exasperating to a liberal and warm-hearted young Russian are, first, official lawlessness [*próizvól*] in the sphere of personal rights, and second, the suffering brought by such lawlessness upon near relatives and dear friends."[2] The severity and capriciousness of criminal persecution ("better to punish ten innocent persons than to allow one criminal to escape") had created an atmosphere in which rebellion and terrorism were the last means of defense against an inhumane state.[3] This context was essential to understanding revolutionaries who were increasingly willing to use violence—and the comparison with western European autocracies like the Habsburg Empire showed that they had been left with few other alternatives:

> A government that acts in this way sows dragons' teeth and has no right to complain of the harvest. The so-called "propagandists" of 1870–74 [the Narodniks] did not resort to violence in any form, and did not even make a practice of resisting arrest, until after the Government had begun to exile them to Siberia for life with ten or twelve years of penal servitude, for offenses that were being punished at the very same time in Austria with only a few days—or at most a few weeks—of personal detention. It was not terrorism that necessitated administrative exile in Russia; it was merciless severity and banishment without due process of law that provoked terrorism.[4]

Questions about the origins and essence of Russian revolutionary tradition have occupied generations of historians, who to this day debate whether, or to what extent, *one* branch of this revolutionism in the moment of its historical triumph—Bolshevism in October 1917—was a child of the despotic system it toppled.[5] The history of political ideas in Russia is unusually difficult to separate from the country's social and cultural history, and so the failure of democratic forces in the "Red October" has been firmly linked to Russian political culture and social history.[6] In no other European state was the combination of absolutism, serfdom, and an agrarian economy so deep-seated or enduring. As backward as many aspects of life under tsarism were, a "powerful state machinery"[7] effectively suppressed all oppositional criticism through policing and censorship. This regime "created a society in which there was scarcely any middle term between servility and rebellion," as Kolakowski observes at the beginning of his remarks about Russian Marxism. Well into the nineteenth century, "freedom was conceived only as anarchy, as the absence of law, since law presented itself in scarcely any other form than as the arbitrary will of a despotic ruler."[8]

We should consider Russian Marxism within this context, as one variation in the history of Russian socialism. Marxism in Russia—unlike in Germany, France, or Austria—was not just an alternative design for resolving the Social Question within an autocratic framework; it was a project of self-defense against an autocracy built on extreme social misery. And so we must consider the specific appeal of Marx and Engels's texts for Russian social revolutionaries within the context of late tsarism. From a multiply marginalized position—exiled, imprisoned, censored, isolated—this small, quarrelsome group successfully asserted Marxism, with its pithy theses and extraordinarily mobilizing rhetoric as the dominant arm of the Russian workers' movement, following its institutionalization in western Europe.[9]

As Kennan's travelogue noted, being a full-time critic of the government in Russia necessarily meant living underground. Anyone who engaged in antitsarist opposition, overstepping the police state's narrow boundaries of permitted ("legal") discourse, became a pariah—and also avant-garde. This is not to suggest that a one-sided and monocausal path led directly from Alexander Ulyanov's confrontation with tsarist authority at the gallows to the "scientific" worldview and putschism of his brother Vladimir.[10] Rather, many intellectuals on the Russian left, including Plekhanov and Struve, experienced an interplay between oppression and engagement, a mutually reinforcing dynamic of radicalization, at decisive turning points—when confronted, for example, with the question of violence or internal party opposition. Other activists escaped this dynamic of radicalization through imprisonment or exile. Still others, including Lenin and Luxemburg, driven by boundless faith in their own agency, plunged into this dynamic headfirst.

7

The Social Question as a Political Question

Plekhanov's Turn toward Marx

Plekhanov around 1880
Credit: International Institute of Social
History, Amsterdam

❝ My dear Plekhanov, First of all, please spare me 'mentor'—my
name is simply Engels," the elder man wrote to the exile and "father" of Russian Marxism in Geneva in May 1894.[1] By the time forty-
year-old Plekhanov received these first lines from Engels, he had, by
his own account, already twenty years of experience as a "revolutionary from the 'intelligentsia.'" After supporting the Narodniks for
years, he had drifted away from the movement and found his mooring
in Marxist doctrine. He had become Russia's best-known student of
Marx, an accomplishment that Engels respectfully acknowledged.[2] In
the Russian revolutionary scene of the 1880s and 1890s, identifying
oneself as a "student" was enough to show one's Marxist sympathies
while remaining safe from censorship. This indicated not only a very
specific system for making sense of the world but also a self-image as a
"servant" and an "instrument" of a "necessary" historical movement.[3]

By the time of this surprisingly late first contact with Marx's "loyal
friend," Plekhanov had already led an extraordinarily eventful life.
Like Guesde and Bernstein, he underwent an intensely political, but
pre-Marxist, socialization. He got to know the various currents of the
Russian underground, from terrorism to social democracy, and he
made his first contacts with urban workers in the mid-1870s. During
these years he lived out of wedlock with a much older woman. He
eventually married someone else, but for some time he effectively
lived as if he had two wives. He fathered four children, two of whom
died at a young age. In his mid-twenties, he slept with a revolver
under his pillow and trained with a dagger and brass knuckles. He
stood out among other revolutionaries with his neatly trimmed, dark-
red beard and proper, elegant clothing that served as a kind of cam-
ouflage, saving him from arrest more than once. He fled Russia for
the first time in 1876. After returning briefly, he left for good in 1880,
at the age of twenty-four, following a failed assassination plot against
Tsar Alexander II. He did not return to Russia until 1917.[4]

Like several of the other protagonists, Plekhanov's young adulthood
(before his flight to Geneva and turn toward Marx) has received little
scholarly attention, although his most thorough biographer, Samuel

H. Baron, docs emphasize that the years between 1875 and 1880, when he shared the "hopes and frustration" of the Narodniks, set the stage for his later "conversion" to Marxism.[5] Plekhanov presented himself to the exile community in Switzerland as the savvy veteran of a failed movement, the tsar's eventual murder notwithstanding. And, in fact, he had acquired firsthand experience with the possibilities, limits, and risks of revolutionary practice. He had participated in demonstrations and factory strikes, helped to plan assassinations, and witnessed the public castigation, exile, and execution of like-minded comrades.

Unlike Kautsky, Lenin, and Luxemburg, however, Plekhanov did not engage with Marx's doctrines or local opposition groups during his first semester as a student. We must count him—along with Guesde, Bernstein, Jaurès, and Adler—as one of this study's late bloomers; he was politicized well before he turned to Marxism. Upon enrolling at the Mining Institute in St. Petersburg in 1874, he initially abstained entirely from politics—even though the social revolutionary movement was attracting a massive following at this time.[6] In the summer of 1874, hundreds of student Narodniks ("populists")—inspired by pioneers as diverse as Peter A. Kropotkin and the Nechayev disciple Alexander V. Dolgushin—descended upon central and southern Russian villages and called upon the peasants to revolt, hoping to spark enthusiasm for what was supposed to be the peasants' historical role in constructing a more socially just society.[7] Plekhanov, on the other hand, studied so diligently in the 1874–75 school year that he won an academic scholarship. Only in 1875 did he begin participating in oppositional activities—producing fliers, speaking at factories, and holding meetings (also in his home), so that he was expelled for repeated absences at the end of his second year.[8]

In the ideological warfare between the nihilists under the influence of Mikhail A. Bakunin, Pyotr A. Tkachev, and Sergei G. Nechaev, who sometimes engaged in acts of terror, and the propagandistically engaged Lavrists (named for Pyotr L. Lavrov), Plekhanov initially sided with the Narodniks, who, like Bakunin, believed that the rural population was naturally inclined toward revolution. Following the arrest of hundreds of students across the countryside in 1874, Plekhanov got to know the few remaining Narodniks who—as the name *narodnichestvo* indicated—had gone "to the people." His initiation into St. Petersburg's underground movement occurred just as Russian revolutionaries were shifting their utopian focus from peasants and rural villages toward heretofore neglected urban workers. Plekhanov's friend Pavel B. Axelrod later recalled that, at first, no one wanted to see "people outside of the peasantry" and that workers were considered a "lower genus of 'people.'"[9] But after the mid-1870s, the St. Petersburg intelligentsia encountered more and more educated and politicized urban factory workers who had developed from allegedly backward peasants (the "gray man from the countryside" [*seryi derevenskii chelovek*], in Plekhanov's words).[10] Plekhanov wrote only a few lines about these experiences, describing his personal encounters as an experience of awakening:

> The first worker revolutionary whom I was destined to meet was a certain Mitrofanov, who later died of consumption in prison. I got to know him in Petersburg at the end of 1875. Like all students—the revolutionaries of the time—I was of course a great Narodnik, although for me—and the other revolutionaries, too—the term was very murky and undefined. I loved "the people" but did not know them well—or, better stated, I knew absolutely nothing about them, even though I grew up in the countryside. When I first met Mitrofanov, I immediately recognized him a worker—which is to say, that he was one of "the people." My soul was moved by mixed feelings of sympathy and a certain uneasiness, as if for some reason I owed him something.[11]

Generations of Russian intellectuals, irrespective of their background or education, shared Plekhanov's mixed feelings. A (guilty) social conscience was central to their political engagement. Articulating this condition was at least as important as the emotions themselves, as the extensive scholarly literature shows.[12] We should consider these encounters, and their significance to Plekhanov's political socialization, in the context of his earlier experiences with the rural population. In contrast to the peasants who worked his parents' estate and responded to unwelcome decisions by burning and pillaging, urban factory workers who were eager to learn and organize must have seemed like far more promising political allies.

We have only thirdhand information on the turmoil that involved around one hundred serfs on his parents' estate in Gudalovka in 1873. According to these accounts, the seventeen-year-old Plekhanov behaved just as hot-headedly and "irrationally" as the rebellious serfs. When a merchant outbid local peasants for the Plekhanovs' land, Georgi threatened to burn down the merchant's property (and then turn himself over to the police) if his mother sold to the merchant instead of "our peasants." The mother gave in to her son, but some of the peasants nevertheless set fire to the manor house in order to prevent the sale; at the last moment, the same peasants saved the family's furniture from the flames. These fierce conflicts must have left a deep impression on the young Plekhanov, although he did not discuss them at the time or later in life.[13]

After returning from his first exile three years later, Plekhanov unsuccessfully sought a position as a village schoolteacher in the vicinity of Saratov. He wanted to work among the rural population as one of their own—to be a subversive influence as well as to educate. Although he wisely disguised his intentions, his application was unsuccessful. Until he fled Russia for good in 1880, Plekhanov's sympathies lay with the *derevenshchiki* (country workers), opponents of the terrorist faction who traveled across the countryside to live among the people and gain their trust. Little is known about these experiences. Plekhanov mentioned the arduous undertaking only in the broadest terms in an autobiographical text.[14] Years later, as a mature Marxist, he was principally averse, or even hostile, to the Russian peasantry. Like the young Lenin, he fundamentally doubted their aptitude for socialist reform, let alone revolution.[15]

And so coincidences, missed opportunities, and early political disappointments all contributed to Plekhanov's turn toward urban workers. After 1875, when he informed his family that he had committed to the life of a professional revolutionary, he quickly rose to influence within the emerging Zemlya i Volya (Land and Liberty) movement because of his intellectual and oratory talents. He sheltered the well-regarded Axelrod, four years his senior, in his Petersburg apartment in the winter of 1875—an act that brought him, a revolutionary newcomer, into the movement's inner circle. Plekhanov became increasingly involved in agitation and other work for the revolutionary underground, which responded to the failed Narodnik movement of 1874, and its reliance on the power of words, by turning instead to "propaganda of the deed."[16] He was well-regarded and soon received sobriquets like "Orator" and "Eagle."[17]

On 6 December 1876, when Plekhanov was barely twenty years old, he delivered a spontaneous, fiery speech in defense of the imprisoned Narodniks at a demonstration of around two hundred students and workers on St. Petersburg's Kazan Square. He invoked the fate of Chernyshevsky, who had been similarly incarcerated (since 1863) for the "crime" of uplifting the people. The factory workers at the square found Plekhanov's performance pretentious, and the few demonstrators soon clashed with the police. The chaotic proceedings were later criticized by the revolutionaries themselves, with Lavrov privately commenting, "What lunacy!"[18]

Plekhanov later suggested that the workers had initiated the incident and persisted under difficult circumstances; he did not mention himself or his speech, although he self-critically interpreted the fiasco as a lesson in the life of a young movement and its equally young supporters. The Kazan demonstration showed, he later wrote, that "we will always stand alone when we allow our revolutionary activities to be guided only by passion for abstract agitation, and not oriented toward the urgent needs of the surrounding world that drives our agitation."[19] And so his first political debacle, on the wintry Kazan Square of 1876, typified the persistently fraught communications between workers and intellectuals, which would occupy (not just) Plekhanov for the rest of his life.

Like Guesde and Bernstein, the young Plekhanov was a driven, but still inquisitive, proponent of the kinds of action that dissidents favored for addressing the Social Question: popular enlighten-ment and mobilization at the grassroots level. He was convinced that a revolutionary movement could succeed only as a majority movement of the people. Individual strikes, uprisings, and terrorist attacks might intensify a situation but could never topple the system without massive support. Russian radicals split between Bakunin and Lavrov quarreled over appropriate means—terror or agitation—and, even more fiercely, over the actual goal of social revolutionary engagement. The ideological, strategic, and tactical premises of this debate fundamentally changed with the gradual introduction of Marx's ideas.

Plekhanov's reading of Marx around 1875 seems to have disciplined and subdued his political development, connecting his self-image as a revolutionary (originally inspired by Chernyshevsky) with Marxism to form a monistic, materialist philosophy. The young Plekhanov's decision to become an engineer instead of a military officer (as his father had intended, and his brothers did) had less to do with the un-easiness that recalled his first, "fateful" meeting with the "worker rev-olutionary" Mitrofanov. Instead, this decision may have reflected the utilitarian zeitgeist that Chernyshevsky had articulated so effectively in his socially critical, technophile work.[20] Plekhanov was an early reader of *What Is to Be Done?*, a "cult book" among young Russians,[21] and he wrote about it on multiple occasions over the course of his life.[22] The novel's version of socialism pointed him toward technical education (at first, quite untouched by revolutionary sentiments), allowing him to find an autonomous role in Russian society and to support social revolution in a variety of ways.

For the first time in Russian literature, the envisaged proletarian community in *What Is to Be Done?* accorded technology—that is, its maximal command and exploitation—a prominent place in the vision of a future socialist order. Although not intended as such by Chernyshevsky, this vision smoothed the way for the acceptance of capitalism as a necessary step on the road to socialism. Plekhanov broke with his former allies, the Narodnik followers of Lavrov, by taking up this cause in the 1880s. And, not least, Plekhanov supported Chernyshevsky's ideas about free and equal partnerships between men and women—a position that aligned with his own untraditional relationships and a reason for his enthusiasm for Chernyshevsky that should not be underestimated.[23]

As an enlightened, progressively oriented (noble) young man—who, like other non-firstborn sons, had no claim to an inheritance—Plekhanov's choice of career was quite practical. His only hope of building a future for himself was as a free professional—a social group that had steadily grown since the reforms of Tsar Alexander II. Plekhanov himself reflected frequently on this relatively "unattached" (in Karl Mannheim's sense of the word) existence, which disregarded or transcended social rank and status. In one of his works about Chernyshevsky, Plekhanov proposed that a new group of "people from different ranks" (*raznochintsy*) had in the 1860s begun to draw not only from civil servants, newly prosperous landowners, and the technical intelligentsia, but also from supporters of the revolutionary opposition. Plekhanov explicitly counted his hero Chernyshevsky as a member of this group—and, implicitly, himself, a "child of impoverished landed nobility."[24]

So how did a motivated and favorably disposed *raznochinets* find his way to Marx's ideas? Anyone in St. Petersburg seeking the Russian edition of *Capital* in 1875 could have found the book in select locations. It was available, alongside works by Lassalle, in the small, clandestine library of the Narodniks.[25] In 1872 state censors had banned all works by Marx and Engels, with one exception: *Capital*. The officially stated reason for this exception was that the "difficult, inaccessible, strictly scientific work" contained "a colossal mass of abstruse, somewhat obscure politico-economic argumentation," and so it would certainly be read by few people, and understood by even fewer.[26]

Three thousand copies of the first edition were printed in 1872, and nine hundred were sold in the first few weeks. The book received brief but favorable reviews. Before long, *Capital* was regarded as *the* handbook on western European capitalism, and its author the rising star of continental economics. Beyond its theoretical concepts and prophetic theses, *Capital* was most often used to compare social realities, since the misery of the Russian workers seemed not far behind that of their English counterparts. The book became one of the most important—and simultaneously controversial—reference points in the debate about whether capitalism, because of its modernizing power, was a desirable stage on Russia's path to socialism, or whether it ought to be feared for the misery it wrought.

After an initial flurry of attention upon the book's publication, interest faded in the years thereafter. To the Narodniks, the capitalist misery described in *Capital* still seemed "light years"[27] away from the misery they had fought against in their journey "to the people." A second, brief wave of interest in Marx commenced in 1877, following the disappointments and arrests that Plekhanov had experienced firsthand. It would be another twenty years before Marxism gained a solid foothold in Russia—not least due to Plekhanov's *Development of the Monist View of History*, which he published in 1894 under the pseudonym Beltov, an aristocratic noble in the work of Alexander Herzen. The septuagenarian Engels praised the book as "a step forward," and it was long considered one of the best syntheses of Marxism in the Russian language. It marked forty-year-old Plekhanov's breakthrough as the foremost Russian Marxist.[28]

The road to this summit was long. Both Kolakowski and Baron describe Plekhanov's appropriation of Marx's thought world as a "conversion,"[29] a term that stylizes a process of learning into a transformational experience, which did not occur, thereby obscuring the continuities in Plekhanov's political thought. His early writings and few autobiographical remarks suggest that—for all his hubris—he remained open, curious, and eager to learn. He responded to the circumstances he encountered and the persons he met in order to sound out the possibilities and means of an effective political movement. Among Petersburg factory workers, he apparently saw himself as a (visionary) king in a land of one-eyed men. His condescension and dismay about illiterate "gray men" moving by the thousands from rural Russia into the cities in search of work was accompanied by a sense of awe at their willingness and capacity to learn, which, in truly opportune moments, could lead to communication on equal terms and genuine understanding.[30]

Plekhanov began to read *Capital* on his own around 1875. At the same time, he studied the works of men who were already familiar with Marx, such as *Historical Letters* by the moderate Lavrov, who was close to Marx and later inherited the Russian works in his library. Plekhanov also read economic studies by the Kievan professor Nikolai Ziber, "a fanatic proponent of Marxism" who believed that Russian peasants would have to be "cooked up in the industrial boiler" in order to become proletarian.[31] A third intermediary was the student Ivan F. Fesenko, who organized a St. Petersburg circle that read and discussed *Capital* in the mid-1870s. Plekhanov's first exposure to Marx's magnum opus is said to have come through this circle.[32]

By the end of 1878, when Plekhanov wrote his first long article for Zemlya i Volya, "The Law of Economic Development in Society and the Problems of Socialism in Russia," he was already well-versed in Marx's doctrine. In this article Plekhanov aimed to show "the extent to which it is useful and necessary to make Marx's work the point of departure for our own program." Marx had established a scientific basis for socialism by discovering the developmental laws of human society. These laws not only applied to western capitalism, the focus of Marx's analysis, but were universally valid. The development of human society could not be forced in a particular direction; one could merely influence this development within the pathways predetermined by natural laws. Further, *Capital* taught "how life reveals even the necessary social changes in a country, how the mode of production prepares the minds of the masses for the introduction of socialism," thereby molding their historical significance and the power to effect change. And Marx's work showed, he added (with an eye to his own unsuccessful years of agitation), "when, in what form, and to what extent socialist propaganda can be viewed as a waste of productive energy." To underscore this statement, Plekhanov quoted directly from the preface to the first edition of *Capital*—specifically, Marx's explanation that "the ultimate aim of this work" is "to lay bare the economic law of motion of modern society." Anyone who did not know, or ignored, this law of motion was effectively agitating against history—and doomed to fail.[33]

On the other hand, Plekhanov pointed to the relative flexibility of this apparently closed thought system. History was not a "monotonous, mechanical process," and Marx did not seek to press humanity into a "Procrustean bed" of "universal law." Unlike Malthus, Marx applied "abstract laws" only to the plant and nonhuman animal world, regarding human society as a much more complicated phenomenon. Indeed, there were no "universal laws of social dynamics"; there were "processes that were interwoven differently in different societies, and that could lead to completely different developments—just as the law of gravitation can make a planet's orbit elliptical in one case, and parabolic in another." Marx's theory was static and flexible; it offered intellectual orientation and inspiration; it could support an argument and leave room for debate.[34]

Elsewhere in this remarkable text, Plekhanov expressed the desirability of capitalism in Russia, and he weighed the chances for social revolution in a centuries-old (a)political culture that was rooted in agriculture, poverty, and illiteracy. Marx's paradigm of a relatively fixed course of development framed Plekhanov's speculations to the extent that these were resolutely oriented toward the west, and also toward the future. Years before leaving Russia, Plekhanov bluntly held up a mirror to his like-minded comrades. His first substantial publication introduced a new program—a new strategic direction inspired by Marx, and accompanying tactical suggestions.

Especially relevant within this context are Plekhanov's remarks on the role of urban workers. His comments, which were largely informed by personal experience, reveal the first traces of his lifelong optimism regarding workers' independent agency.[35] "Life itself," according to Plekhanov, compelled the revolutionaries to take up the question of urban labor, after years of agitating exclusively among the rural population. For too long, Russian radicals had denied the factory workers' capacity and willingness to learn. Recent strikes revealed the potential for mobilizing urban workers; official Petersburg statistics registered more than three hundred labor conflicts between 1870 and 1879.[36] "Where were our socialists in these moments? What role did they play? Practically none!"[37] The Northern Union of Russian Workers was a first important effort at organizing and bridging the divide between the revolutionary intelligentsia and a "small, self-educated *élite*" of politicized workers.[38] Such new forms of organization embodied a shared learning process that was grounded on "mutual respect." To the astonishment of the intelligentsia, political freedom began to assume an increasingly important role as a precondition for social revolution.

In the end, Plekhanov argued, urban workers were the revolutionaries' natural allies; they embodied the Russian people since they, too, were the sons of peasants. For years, in fact, textile workers who had moved from the country to the city still lived, dressed, and amused themselves according to peasant folkways. Their discussion of communal interests, and even their daily alcohol consumption, reflected unchanged patterns of rural culture. Plekhanov himself described the gradual transformation of the "gray man" as a political awakening—an experience that could bring greater opportunities for self-determination, but also emotional and intellectual estrangement with rural family members.[39] Once the serial revolts long awaited by the Narodniks at last erupted across the countryside, Plekhanov expected that urbanized peasants would call for "revolution in the city" and ensnarl government forces in urban chaos. A shared peasant heritage would fuel a chain reaction, leading to the success of a general revolution. In order to tap this potential, socialist propaganda had to be firmly anchored in reality, in "facts" and "truths" from the workers' lifeworld. Concrete examples from everyday life mattered more than abstract revolutionary logic. After centuries of exploitation and social marginalization, workers had to be shown that they could count on allies who took their needs and interests seriously.[40]

At the end of this text—which began with Marx's western European doctrines and then systematically considered their portability to tsarist Russia—Plekhanov (like Kennan) recalled the comparatively harsh start conditions for the Russian social revolutionary movement and its correspondingly defensive stance. No thinking person could call the workers' movement unprincipled because it was compelled to "answer violence with violence. . . . When the terroristic government and slave-driving factory owners treat every attempt by the workers to improve their situation as a punishable offense, and when the government does not even stop the execution of children involved in strikes," then it was hardly surprising that this "white terror" would at some point "turn red."[41]

This first long article by Plekhanov reveals far more than "clear evidence of Marxian influence," as Baron has observed.[42] On the metalevel of historical materialism, it already attests to an intellectual position that is clearly and rigorously oriented toward Marx—and on the level of everyday opposition, to an insistence on orienting theory toward practice. Time would soon show, however, that these ideas could not be realized in Russia's foreseeable future.

Plekhanov opposed the Narodniks' "red terror" but remained a proponent of rural agitation. These differences of opinion culminated in 1879, with the organizational division between the People's Will (Narodnaya Volya), later responsible for the murder of Tsar Alexander II, and the populist splinter group the Black Redistribution (Chernyi Peredel), which Plekhanov struggled to lead in the last months before his exile. He published a newspaper by the same name with a few trusted colleagues, including Lev Deutsch and Vera Zasulich. The three later continued this work during their exile in Geneva. Plekhanov gloomily summarized these last years in Russia: "Each of us [exiles] had brought along experiences from Russia, acquired over years of revolutionary agitation, and the more or less clear awareness that these experiences sharply contradicted the populists' theory. This awareness was extremely agonizing. . . . Each of us sensed the urgent need to put our revolutionary ideas in order."[43]

Plekhanov never again had the proximity to revolutionary practice that was evident in his articles between 1876 and 1879. He arrived in Geneva at the beginning of January 1880—at first, without his partner Rosaliia Markovnia Bograd and their first baby, who died shortly after Bograd departed for Geneva. Plekhanov's decision to leave Russia was largely driven by his fear of arrest and his frustration with advocates of terror who had become increasingly influential. A third reason—often stylized by scholars as an ideological crisis[44]— was the bleak political outlook for understanding and changing the hypercomplex problems of contemporary Russian society by laboriously stitching together (older) Russian ideas with (newer) ideas from western Europe.

And so, for Plekhanov, exile was an exit. It was not the continuation of revolutionary struggle by other means, but a conscious turn away from practice—although certainly not a "retirement."[45] Intellectual work suited him. He studied, wrote, and debated with passion, and at least once before leaving Russia he seriously considered returning to his studies in engineering. His thirst for knowledge seemed like a remedy for the disappointments of everyday politics—and a life dedicated to scholarship, his only viable career path.[46] And so in January 1880 he sought to reinvent himself as a professional intellectual in picturesque Geneva, where he could live much more freely than in the tsarist police state, although existential worries, both material and ideal, plagued him for years. Bograd had trouble continuing her medical studies in Geneva, so she could not support the family as planned. They lived on odd jobs, monetary gifts, and small loans, changing apartments frequently because they could not pay the rent. As Plekhanov sarcastically remarked in a letter to Lavrov, their mountain of debt was higher than the Russian state's. They spent several months in Paris and stayed temporarily with Guesde, whose existence was just as bleak. Bograd is said to have cared for Guesde's sick wife, Mathilde. In Paris, too, her plans to complete her medical examinations were foiled by the intervention of tsarist authorities, who pointed to her relationship with a wanted revolutionary. The

Plekhanovs returned to Geneva with little to show for themselves at the end of 1881.[47]

Exile was a new way of life that demanded justification. Marx himself is said to have scornfully compared the Black Redistribution activists (who "voluntarily" exited Russia's revolutionary stage) with the brave terrorists "whose heads are at stake": the Redistributionists (Peredeltsi) wanted to found a party to propagandize in Russia—but they went to Geneva instead! The authenticity of Marx's remark is questionable, as it comes to us from a 1912 memoir that was written by a Russian visitor. The anecdote nevertheless reflects a sentiment that was common to European socialists in many times and places. Exile can build solidarity and communities of fate, but it can also create an inescapable compulsion for self-justification.[48]

Although we can only speculate whether such political gossip ever found its way back to Plekhanov, there is no doubt that he had to prove himself to the movement in an entirely new way. With no other meaningful recourse, he had to rely on the power of his words. While according his former allies their due respect, he now aimed to annihilate his opponents' arguments and to make a decisive contribution to "our revolutionary literature." Plekhanov's rhetorical radicalization resembled that of Marx himself, whose biography had taken a similarly polemical turn in 1842, when he, too, was in his mid-twenties. Plekhanov cleverly defended Marx's (and thus, his own) sharp tongue, arguing that it was not a sign of "irrepressible contentiousness, which allegedly stemmed from his cantankerous nature," but was instead driven "by the social significance of the idea he defended."[49] We might further speculate that the more powerless the two men felt, the more violent their language became.

Plekhanov's extensive literary output in exile suggests a second phase in his appropriation of Marx. A distinguishing feature of his mature Marxism was that his enthusiasm for Marx's work was never a purely positive, or offensive, intellectual engagement; it was also a defensive struggle, closely tied to the movement's ups and downs. Defensiveness shaped his memorialization of Marx, whom he praised as "the most outstanding man" of his century, as a "saint" who "forged the mighty spiritual weapon" that armed an "international army of industrial workers." Marx taught them how their "day-to-day struggle" could be united "in a coherent whole" with "revolutionary struggle against the existing economic system." Plekhanov's Marx was also unsentimental. Marx's "scientific socialism . . . decisively exposed the basic contradictions of capitalist society and ruthlessly show[ed] up the naive futility of all plans of social reform—sometimes most ingenious and always well-intentioned—advanced by utopian socialists." The "present-day proletarian" renounced these illusions and embraced the new scientific theory, learning to be "revolutionary both logically and emotionally."[50]

In 1880s Geneva, Plekhanov immersed himself in the emerging Marx-Engels canon, and he contributed significantly to its influence (in Russia) with his own translation of the *Manifesto*. Marxist intellectuals in other countries came to know and respect his work, which brought him greater prestige. Practical benefits came in the form of publishing opportunities, as when Kautsky engaged him to write for the *Neue Zeit* as a Russian voice of "international Marxism."[51] Plekhanov's standing within the multinational Marxist community grew quickly. After visiting Plekhanov in Geneva in 1886, Bernstein was struck by his intellectual savvy and commitment, writing to Kautsky:

> I can't help it; the man impresses again and again. Of all the Russians I have gotten to know, he is the only one who has not merely read "Capital," but also worked through it. He interpellated me about a point in the theory of value, and it was truly a pleasure to debate with him. He is desperate to get together once with Engels, and if he could afford it, he would have already made the pilgrimage to London long ago. I think Engels will like him, too.[52]

Beyond Plekhanov's newfound prestige there was an emotional aspect to his cooperation with the western European Marxists. He saw this circle as his one remaining homeland, and he looked especially to the German Social Democrats, whom he revered as the "avant-garde of the socialist proletariat." Working with them made exile bearable.[53]

Among Plekhanov's new reading material in Geneva was a series of articles by Engels, "On Social Relations in Russia," which ran in *Der Volksstaat* in 1874–75. Engels analyzed Russian social conditions and predicted that "revolution is surely approaching," to be delayed only by "a successful war" for the tsar or "a premature attempt at insurrection" undertaken by naive terrorists. Plekhanov read these articles avidly; like most Russian revolutionaries, he hung on every word that came from the pens of the London masters.[54] From this point on, his "intellectual gaze" was pointed "in one direction": toward "social democratic theory, that is, of Marxism," as he later stated. He and his friends in exile were extraordinarily moved by the abundance of reading material that was available in Geneva:

> Anyone who did not live through that time can hardly imagine how fervently we dove into social democratic literature. . . . Personally, I can say that reading the "Manifesto of the Communist Party" represents an epoch in my life. I was enthralled by the "Manifesto" and immediately decided to translate it into Russian. . . . Marx's theory led us, like Ariadne's thread, out of the labyrinth of contradictions that had ensnared our thought, thanks to the influence of Bakunin. By the light of this theory, it seemed wholly comprehensible that revolutionary propaganda received an incomparably more sympathetic reception from the proletariat than from the peasantry.[55]

Although Plekhanov's introduction to the *Manifesto of the Communist Party* had likely occurred at an earlier time, his 1881–82 reading and translation was in fact a transformative experience. The metaphors of light and Ariadne's thread (also used by Luxemburg and Adler) point to the ordering power of Marx's idea of class struggle and his dialectically trained perspective. Plekhanov was persuaded by Marx's theory because it "harmonized" his experiences, revealing itself to him as a "harmonic whole."[56] Marx's faith in the proletariat affirmed Plekhanov's own experiences and restored his depleted optimism. The perspective of class struggle made up for the lost hope that peasants would overturn the system and emancipate themselves. From this point forward, Plekhanov saw politics and economics, political rights and social conditions, as inextricably linked. Moreover, his physical distance from the Russian underground made the abstraction of rebellious Russians into revolutionary "subjects" seem increasingly plausible. The very name of the Emancipation of Labor group, which he cofounded in Geneva in 1883, did not distinguish between rural and urban workers; the group sought not to liberate workers but rather work itself.

The *Manifesto* gave Plekhanov clear, comprehensive answers to many unresolved questions of his time. He read the *Manifesto* as the foundational text of a "new epoch of relentless criticism of the present relationship between labor and capital, [an epoch] in which socialism is scientifically grounded and rejects all utopias."[57] Marx and Engels had shown that "wherever there are classes, class struggle is unavoidable. Wherever there is class struggle, the efforts of each struggling class to obtain complete victory and unfettered dominance over its opponent is necessary and natural."[58] Further, the materialist theory of history and society, which derived "the social relations of people" from economic conditions, brought "clarity and consistency" to the tangle of social phenomena. Marx and Engels had found the "basic principle" that united all of these complex phenomena into a single "harmonic whole."[59]

A transparent logic of social development offered certitudes that had, to this point, been missing among the Russian opposition, which was bitterly divided and caught in a hopeless struggle against tsarist autocracy. Although these new certitudes were disconnected from the social lifeworld of Russian peasants, they came very close to the lifeworld of an east–west socialist discursive community.[60] This new communal— and community-building—engagement was based on increasingly canonical terminology that structured individual perceptions of reality and "coordinated" these perceptions with concepts shared across languages. Conversely, these inventions—which were later elevated to "basic concepts in history"—identified and gave meaning to discrete historical experiences, such as the rise of an urban workforce (the "proletariat") in a new kind of economic system ("capitalism").[61] These concepts were, in the words of Reinhart Koselleck, both "causal factors" and "indicators of historical change." On the one hand, they delineated intellectual positions in the "semantic struggle" to interpret the present; on the other, they invigorated political programs that aimed to shape the future.[62] And so, to Engels and others, Plekhanov defended the Geneva group's semantic decision to establish a Russian social democratic party by arguing that the words "social democracy" and "social democrats" had practical significance. They promoted a feeling of working-class solidarity across national borders and an auspicious, shared perspective.[63]

The *Manifesto* not only conveyed "necessary" and "natural" certitudes about the orientation of human history around class struggle; it also modernized and politicized Plekhanov's social engagement. He came to believe that only a political struggle, geared toward organizing and mobilizing social majorities, could succeed. And so he primarily emphasized the *Manifesto*'s *political* achievement. Like no other text before it, the *Manifesto* showed that the "meaning of politics" lay in "class struggle" and that the power of the state depended on the ruling classes (which is to say, their interrelationship). And so Plekhanov insistently identified Marxism as "*contemporary materialism,* at present the highest stage in the development of that *view upon the world.*"[64]

Marx and Engels's insistence on the principle that "every class struggle is a political struggle" in the first chapter of the *Manifesto* was—positively viewed—a call for emancipation through political participation. It marked an important, if also contentious, chapter in the history of democratization in the nineteenth century.[65] According to Eric Hobsbawm, the core idea of the *Manifesto* was that historical change was the result of "social praxis, through collective action." Further, "the commitment to *politics* is what historically distinguished Marxian socialism from the anarchists, and from the successors of those socialists whose rejection of all political action the *Manifesto* specifically condemns." It not only proclaimed "what history shows us will happen" but also—long before Lenin—"what must be done."[66] The apodictic determination of the social as a *political* question belongs to the standard repertoire, even today, of activists who identify as "Marxist."[67] Plekhanov underscored this dictum ("Every class struggle is a political struggle") in the introduction to his translation of the *Manifesto* in 1882, and, naming Marx as its sole author, he made this the epigraph of his first political work, *Socialism and the Political Struggle*, in 1883. Lenin later used these words routinely, usually without attribution.[68]

By the early 1880s, Plekhanov had become known as the "father of Russian Marxism" (per Baron), precisely because Marx and Engels's politicization of the "quest for bread" had transformed the Russian socialist movement. His commitment was not only intellectually and practically grounded but had an emotional side as well. As an agnostic—he considered Marxism "Spinozism disencumbered of its theological pendant"—Plekhanov celebrated this "new doctrine" as a "new Gospel," and himself as its disciple.[69] According to Kolakowski, Plekhanov no longer "wrote as a man seeking for the solution of a theoretical problem, but as an adept defending an established doctrine."[70]

As Plekhanov grew older and more famous, he fought back vigorously against the accusations of ideological narrow-mindedness that his stance inevitably provoked. He did not entirely succeed, as he himself may have come to see. If his early texts were written in a mode of polemical defense, his later ones lost this verve and were increasingly rote. Marx's assertion that all aspects of human existence were material in origin was in no way "one-sided" economic determinism but rather showed his "striving towards monism," Plekhanov wrote about the "fundamental problems of Marxism" in 1908. Of course, human relations could not be explained monocausally—and yet, "in the final analysis," material conditions were decisive. According to Plekhanov's dictum, "*the variety of 'factors'* in no way disturbs the *unity of the fundamental cause.*"[71] The course of history was set, but dialectical thinking showed that those who grasped this development could still influence it. For Plekhanov, natural evolution and political revolution, continuity and change, were two sides of one coin. Those who, like Marx, understood the course of history could approach the Social Question as something to be mastered and solved.

This view of the world was irresistibly edifying. Although exile had crippled Plekhanov politically, he still had cause to celebrate. "What healthy optimism breathes in the words that mankind always sets itself only tasks that it can solve," he wrote (quoting Marx), completely overlooking the undialectical spirit of this sentence. No, what resonated for Plekhanov was the (self-)certainty that he invoked and reflected—that "calm and courageous faith in the achievement of the 'ultimate aim.'" Plekhanov's worldview, like Lenin's, united his two philosophical heroes Marx and Chernyshevsky. Plekhanov concluded his remarks on the fundamental problems of Marxism with Chernyshevsky's credo: "Come what may, we shall win."[72]

Appropriating this thought world thus promised empowering, emancipatory insight into supposedly real—not divine or juridical, but natural—laws. The role of the individual was not that of a passive actor, carried away by the tides of history. Rather, by understanding these tides' direction, he could "freely" participate in their movement. According to this idiosyncratic notion of freedom, individuals learned to master history by understanding imperatives, thereby becoming ever more "free." Plekhanov developed this idea in his 1894 book, *The Role of the Individual in History*.[73] Inspired by the Scottish historian Thomas Carlyle's scholarship on heroism, particularly *On Heroes and Hero Worship and the Heroic in History* (1846), Plekhanov described the "beginner," or "great man," who "sees *further* than others, and desires things *more strongly* than others." It is hard not to see this figure as a portrait of his teacher Marx, and as his own self-ideal: "He solves the scientific problems brought up by the preceding process of intellectual development of society; he points to the new social needs . . . he takes the initiative in satisfying these needs." He is a "hero," but not "in the sense that he can stop, or change, the natural course of things, but in the sense that his activities are the conscious and free expression of this inevitable and unconscious course."[74] His work ends with "the final triumph of mind over necessity, of reason over the blindness of law," thereby leading to an age in which humans have learned to steer and tame those processes "over which they formerly had no power."[75]

This paradoxical theory of historical agency—part avant-garde leadership, part instrumentalism—characterized the self-image of every Marxist. The ability to guide history "freely" could be exercised only politically, and this, in turn, led back to Plekhanov's whole-hearted embrace of Marxism as a "modern," and decidedly western, political science. His much-cited appeal in *Socialism and Political Struggle* called upon the disillusioned Narodniks to stop demonizing the state as a reactionary means of power, and instead to reimagine and use it as a *proletarian* means of power. In the context of Russian socialism, this was Plekhanov's most innovative argument and the grounds for establishing a political party. His entire argument, which persistently referred to "life itself," relied on an unshakable faith in the capacity of the workers to learn and practice democracy. Nevertheless, realizing their full potential and becoming self-aware would require the intellectual leadership of the intelligentsia—that is, people like Plekhanov—fighting on their side.[76]

This was the voice of Lenin's teacher—the first Russian so-cial democrat who committed fully to the "abstract scheme" of Marxism.[77] Plekhanov's faith in the genuine participation of workers contained the seeds of the alliance between Lenin and Struve, as well as their falling-out. Both men sought to institutionalize Plekhanov's exile Marxism of the 1890s with a political program in Russia. Their falling-out had to do with the blessing and curse of a "capitalist revo-lution" (Engels) in Russia, but also with an effective social democratic response. Above all, it had to do with the appropriate balance between party organization and worker participation—that is, with power.

8

The Social Question as a Question of Power

Struve and Lenin

Peter Struve, 1890
Credit: Richard Pipes, private
archive

Vladimir Lenin, around 1891
Credit: International Institute of
Social History, Amsterdam

❝ ❝ The old 'friend of the people' has gone his way / And in his stead, von Struve now holds sway."[1] This popular epigram reflected the long absence of Plekhanov and his "friends of the people" in St. Petersburg in the mid-1890s. For all that they had accomplished with their writing in Geneva, they were far from establishing Marxism as a political program in Russia—as German, French, and Austrian social democrats had done around 1890. From the perspective of the Russian Marxists, the 1880s were a depressingly ineffective "decade of isolation";[2] the attempt to assassinate Tsar Alexander III in these years had merely led to heightened repression. However, in the 1890s a second generation of Russian Marxists emerged, appropriating the Genevan ideas with self-assured detachment and pushing them further. Struve and Lenin were members of this generation. Their intellectual development and political rise can be narrated in tandem, as the story of two like-minded, and yet opposing, students of Marx.[3]

All four of our protagonists who were born in the tsarist empire stood on the "periphery of European socialism." Highly aware of this marginal status, they appropriated Marxism as the "ripest fruit of European philosophical and social scientific thought," as Dietrich Geyer aptly describes. The Marx-Engels corpus, newly elevated to the status of an "ism," offered both "science and world-view," and identifying as a student of Marx meant participating in this cutting-edge discourse.[4] The three contemporaries Struve, Lenin, and Luxemburg first read this corpus through the eyes and texts of their elders: Plekhanov, Pavel Axelrod, and Vera Zasulich.[5] In the end, however, these native teachers played only a subordinate role. Although Struve later wrote that he had "greedily swallowed their writings"— and that Plekhanov's work, in particular, had exuded great "charm"— he was not the only one who came to feel that their arguments were "too doctrinal and simplist."[6] Struve, Lenin, and Luxemburg turned early to the German-language originals, which were composed in the far-off west. Unlike the older protagonists (Guesde, Bernstein, Adler, and Plekhanov), this younger trio steered directly toward a specific discursive community. They completed this maneuver largely, if not exclusively, in the context of relatively structured academic studies—like the two other younger protagonists, Kautsky and Jaurès.

Struve began his university studies in 1889. At first (like Luxemburg) he studied zoology, but after his first year he switched to law. Around half of all students in St. Petersburg were studying law at this time. University admission requirements for nonnoble applicants had been tightened after the failed plot to assassinate Alexander III on 1 March 1887. Lenin's brother, Alexander Ulyanov, was one of the student conspirators hanged for this plot. Despite heightened police surveillance, the reformist spirit of the 1860s continued to shape university curricula until the more definitive rollback after the first Russian Revolution of 1905.[7] Decades later, Struve self-critically recalled how little he had been touched by academic life. As a student, he had unfortunately "taken less from the university than it could give. . . . [P]olitical interests often took much time while simultaneously narrowing my intellectual horizon." He claimed to have had a "superior," or even "dismissive," attitude toward science whenever it seemed irrelevant to political issues.[8] His contacts in the revolutionary student milieu and relative detachment from his academic studies notwithstanding, Struve gained a reputation as a bookworm and as an extraordinarily talented, eloquent speaker.[9] He spoke about socialism in barely legal reading circles and "cited endlessly from the . . . masses of books he had read. The printed word, it seemed, was his world."[10]

Similar to Luxemburg and Jaurès, Struve got to know the discipline of political economy in part through his academic studies. In St. Petersburg, of course, works of "scientific socialism" were not part of the regular curriculum—although these were already being taught in Zurich, where Luxemburg was studying at this time. Instead, Struve read and discussed these works alongside his formal studies, among a small circle of interested students. This is how he got to know Alexander N. Potresov, who became a close friend and supported him financially.[11]

Struve's personal life as a student was quite unusual. His father's death in 1889 was rumored to be a suicide, and he apparently had no more contact with his "neurotic" mother before her own death in 1905. As a university student, Struve lived practically rent-free with the family of a classmate, whose mother, Alexandra Kalmykova, initially introduced him as her adopted son. She was his lover through the mid-1890s. She owned a small bookstore, and—even more important—a hectograph, which Struve used to copy his texts free of charge.[12] He was often sick and summered in western Europe (in Geneva, Graz, Stuttgart, Berlin) or at a spa in southern Russia. Alongside his studies he worked as a librarian, and he earned extra money with his first published articles, mostly reviews of Russian and English economic literature in specialized German journals like the *Sozialpolitisches Centralblatt* (Social Political Gazette) and the *Archiv für Soziale Gesetzgebung und Statistik* (Archive for Social Legislation and Statistics). Pipes has described him a passionate, often erratic but hardworking bookworm, who was brimming with plans and ideas. He constantly started new projects but rarely finished them.[13]

Struve composed several autobiographical texts in the 1930s, but it is still not easy to reconstruct his reading of Marx—especially since he distorted individual aspects of his biography after the fact. Two of his most emphatic assertions later in life were that he had become a social democrat "by way of reasoning," not "passion," and that he had turned away from Marxism not "through any bookish influences" but because of "life experience." These statements reflect the older Struve's profound need for distance, and their degree of conviction is certainly misleading.[14]

Struve did not see himself as an ideologue, whipped up by pamphlets and dreams of revolution, but instead as a sober, solution-oriented analyst of the "fundamental problems" of contemporary Russia: economic and social backwardness and a "burning" lack of prosperity and freedom.[15] In a narrower sense, Struve saw Marxism as the scientific discovery and analysis of capitalism, including its economic laws and accompanying social conflicts. For Struve, Marx offered (at least, for some time) the only economic and sociological doctrine that was appropriately current, but not a philosophical system that offered meaning. Struve emphasized Marxism's groundbreaking economic and scholarly significance and praised its "unsentimental approach to social phenomena," although he later denied its persuasive power.[16] Especially later in life, Struve emphasized that his entire political passion had always been directed toward liberalism and freedom: "Socialism was an abstract and remote ideal, while the struggle for civil and political liberties was a vital task."[17]

Things looked different in the early 1890s. At the time, he certainly considered Marxism a "complete philosophical and sociological worldview."[18] He was impressed by Marx's "philosophical style of construction" and the "brilliantly" idiosyncratic "physiognomy" of his writing style. As an admirer of the neo-Kantians and positivists, he had learned to appreciate a theory for what it explained, and not what it didn't. His veneration of Marx had a strong aesthetic component, as when he praised Marx as a "first-rate writer" with an "original" style. Even in the post-Marxist phase of his life, he never relativized this praise. In two essays from 1933–34, he placed Marx on a pedestal alongside Richard Wagner (who "fatefully" died the same year as Marx), and he celebrated both men as Germany's greatest—if altogether different—intellectual "state builders."[19] This steadfast admiration meant that Struve, even as an ex-Marxist, could acknowledge the contradictions in Marx's "doctrine" without relativizing its revolutionary influence on philosophy, economics, and other social sciences.

Struve's aesthetic approach had palpable consequences for his understanding of Marx. He was the only protagonist who did not primarily celebrate Marx as an inventor or discoverer, but insistently pointed to the rich (bourgeois) heritage that informed Marx's work, including the theory of value. In his preface to the new Russian edition of *Capital* in 1899, Struve wrote that "Marx's great originality and tremendous scholarly achievement lies in the *conscious proclamation and execution*" of his views—which is to say, Marx's coupling of historical and sociological analysis with political objectives and practice.[20] For Struve, the significance of Marx's work lay not in its content but in its *claim* to understand, and thereby overcome, an entire economic system, as well as in the *style* in which this claim was presented.

A broad explanation for Struve's admiration of Marxism is embedded within his remarks about the Kiev economics professor Nikolai Ziber, who also taught Plekhanov:

> He was no longer alive when I came to be a "Marxist," and I did not know him personally. He was a pure scholar who, as far as I know, never believed in the social revolution achieved by political methods as prophesied and set forth by Karl Marx in the "Communist Manifesto" and later; he was a Marxist only in the sense of adhering to Marx's economic theory and his historical and sociological conceptions.[21]

Struve, too, saw himself as a pure scholar. His engagement focused more on studying reality, and less on changing it; it was grounded on conviction, not passion.

Struve's matter-of-fact view of his own enthusiasm for Marx obscures the emotional side of his commitment (which is not hard to understand, given Marxism's transformation into power-hungry Leninism in the early twentieth century). And yet—independent of, and in contrast to, Luxemburg, Lenin, and Kautsky—Struve did not understand scholarly engagement as the translation of scientific "truths" into practical politics, and certainly not into social revolution, which he scorned as a flight of fancy.[22] Instead, he wanted to lead politics (and the state) toward the insights that he had acquired in his studies. He thought of himself as a voice of "Russian public thought," which was "strenuously and painfully trying to work out a solution" to the main problems of national life.[23]

Struve's strong and consistent focus on macroeconomic questions is remarkable. He was always driven more by questions of political and economic modernization and by the effects of a backward rural economy that functioned largely without money, and less by the actual conditions in which peasants lived and worked. Hunger, for example, was among Russia's most urgent problems in the 1890s; Struve's early writings depict it as a grave, but always abstract, side effect of a dysfunctional economic system.[24]

This impression is confirmed by Struve's first writings on the internal migration of destitute peasants and the famine of 1891–92, and by his later autobiographical remarks.[25] In this context we should also consider Struve's very private admission in a letter to his friend Potresov, who had accused him of ending his long relationship with Alexandra Kalmykova in a cowardly and hurtful way. Struve justified his indecision toward his unhappy lover with the following confession: "I am not only a person with a weak will (I will readily confess this) but I am also particularly powerless when confronted with the suffering of others. The suffering of others, especially involving persons close to me, drains me of the last ounce of . . . will power."[26] Kalmykova had apparently also acted as a surrogate mother in Struve's life, which complicated their separation, while Struve's birth mother seems to have been emotionally distant, with little connection to her son. His confession suggests that his lifelong emphasis on objectivity may also have been a means of protecting himself from the emotional consequences of empathy.

Other constellations in Struve's family had a more positive influence on his life. These included the deep German roots on his father's side of the family and a tradition of progressive thinking that was oriented toward the west and the natural sciences, lending the Struve family the aura of a scholarly dynasty. Struve was already well-traveled as a child, and as an adult he continued to have the means to explore the western world. In his memoirs he portrayed himself as an admirer of western Europe, fascinated by materialism and modernity. He enthusiastically reported on his first long journey as a young adult: an 1890 trip to Berlin, Stuttgart, and Geneva (although he did not look up Plekhanov). Despite his ostensibly limited financial resources, in Switzerland he purchased "a whole library of important Social-Democratic publications."[27] Ten years later, he wrote, "[T]he richness and intensity of material culture, and the astonishing, almost abject adaptability of Western man to it, made on me a tremendous and indelible impression." Well beyond his positive childhood memories of Stuttgart, Struve loved European culture "like the sun, like warmth and clean air; decaying carcasses and gray heads I cannot bear. *Und damit Basta!*"[28]

Struve's contrast between western and Russian realities—between sophisticated Europeans on the one hand, and starving Russian peasants on the other—betrayed his deep-seated intellectual and sensual aversion to the "gray" backwardness of Russia and its "decaying carcasses." According to his biographer Pipes, he was ill at ease with "common people" and unsure how to speak with them.[29] And he privately criticized "the smell of carrion exuded by our progressive literature."[30] In light of the wretched social conditions in working-class neighborhoods of many European cities and in rural Russia and France, it is striking that only Luxemburg and (indirectly) Lenin are also known to have expressed their remove and disgust in this way. As we will see more thoroughly in Part III, the other protagonists, especially Jaurès and Adler, tended to respond with empathy or indignation.[31]

Struve's first published articles were shaped by his ambivalence toward the social misery that, even in wealthy St. Petersburg, was omnipresent; by his family's affinity for political liberalism and the positivist-rational natural sciences; and, finally, by his intellectual and emotional ties to western Europe. He bucked family tradition by following his own interests, changing his course of study to law in 1890, and he then got to know the international field of political economy alongside, rather than as part of, his formal studies. His first published articles, which appeared in German and Russian beginning in 1891, were reviews of works in political economy. He wrote these articles during the famine of 1891–92, which had truly "epochal" significance in the history of Russia.[32] Struve later contrasted this event with his reading of *Capital*, a remarkable effort to relativize the book's relevance for his own development: "As far as I am personally concerned, the hunger of 1891–92 made much more of a Marxist out of me than the reading of Marx's *Capital*."[33] In any event, he did not experience the famine in Russia firsthand. Instead, he sought treatment for severe pneumonia at a spa in Graz, where he also attended the lectures of sociologist and Darwin disciple Ludwig Gumplowicz during the summer semester of 1892. He returned to Russia in the fall of 1892, but not to the university. Instead, he worked as a librarian in the Ministry of Finance, which facilitated his access to state statistics and reports.[34]

Struve's first article about the "migration question in Russia" appeared in the *Sozialpolitisches Centralblatt*, which was edited by Heinrich Braun, in the summer of 1892. From Graz, he described the intolerable living conditions of the Russian peasants as a result of failed harvests. He left no doubt that these conditions were symptoms of capitalism's unstoppable advance into Russia. In order to escape starvation, tens of thousands had decided to "migrate internally." Struve criticized the Russian authorities' attempts to regulate this movement, through forced resettlement or otherwise, as insufficient and ineffective. "Expulsion" would not cure hunger; rather, it was "in the power of the state to alleviate these birth pangs of the capitalist economic order for Russia."[35]

Here—as in the two dozen articles he published through 1895, and in his first book, *Critical Remarks on the Question of Russia's Economic Development* (1894)—Struve developed a perspective that subtly followed Marx and that (like Marx) deliberately mixed analysis and prediction. He saw the Russian state of emergency as a consequence of the decline of "irrational" farming practices. In the transition to a "more rational," capitalist agriculture that was based on sound economic principles, the situation would initially deteriorate, until the emerging peasant "reserve army" turned into "proletarians." Given the impoverishment of the peasants, the "transition to rational cultivation could only occur very gradually," and it would be accompanied by a "temporary decline in agriculture" and a "kind of devastation." No wonder that these prospects drove the peasants "from their homelands with elemental force," creating a "rural reserve army" that relied on begging and seasonal migration. Not only was the human misery "immeasurable," but there were lurking social dangers, such as taxation shortfalls and public health risks, when "entire troops" of itinerants overran and infected the rest of the country.[36]

Struve's analysis clearly reflected his reading of Marx. Marx had routinely spoken of "a mass of human material ready for exploitation," which was both the cause and the effect of the capitalist mode of production—the "condition of existence" and "lever of capitalistic accumulation," as he wrote in *Capital*. The innovative concept of the "reserve army" flowed directly from Marx's "logical and conceptual framework."[37] Like Marx, Struve saw the social costs and dangers that accompanied ever more efficient production in advanced capitalism, particularly the "great masses of men" (as Marx said) who were always disposable. Struve transferred Marx's analysis to Russia, where comparable upheavals were not merely the consequence of a completely dysfunctional agricultural system but also the harbingers ("birth pangs") of emerging capitalism.

This view distinguished Struve from most other Russian economists, whom he (and soon Lenin) criticized for their reactionary, "populist" convictions in a Russian path toward socialism (the "Slavophile superstition that the Russian peasant is a born socialist").[38] The prominent economist Nikolai Danielson, for example, complained that the introduction of capitalism in Russia had caused "a fundamental break in our economic life," and this had led directly to the famine of 1891.[39] For Struve (and Lenin), the famine was a side effect of an emerging capitalism that was otherwise principally progressive. The populists, however, saw the famine as a symptom of entirely disastrous, statesanctioned development.

Although Struve's first articles often dealt with social misery, hunger, and the hopelessness of rural Russians, he wrote from the bird's-eye perspective of a political economist. He cited statistical analyses and government publications, and he saw social misery more as a macrolevel cost than an individual plight. The young author's foremost concern was the overall future of his country.[40]

The only escape from Russia's economic and social misery, Struve argued, necessarily involved state support for the "positive, productive work of the process of capitalist development." Only when a "rational," "capital-rich and resilient" monetary economy replaced the existing "non-rational," "capital-poor peasant economy" would the Russian people thrive. Formerly "independent producers'" would lead a less miserable, more secure existence as agricultural and industrial workers in a developed economy.[41]

The centrality of Marx's ideas to the young Struve's social criticism and view of the future was evident in his repeated affirmation of Marx's "scheme," or "principle," in his early texts. He proceeded from "Marx's conception of the sociologically and, particularly, *economically primary significance of the moment of production,"* which was also the source of his own "sociopolitical views."[42] The "primary significance of the moment of production" was the essence of what Struve found most important in all of Marx's work: the passage in the preface to the *Contribution to the Critique of Political Economy* (1859) about "social being" determining all consciousness.[43] In this passage Struve saw a theoretically messy but nevertheless persuasive evolutionary theory of revolution. The core of this theory, according to Struve (citing Marx's words in the preface), was that "the process of social, political, and intellectual life in general is determined by the mode of production of material life. At a certain stage of their development, the material productive forces of society come into conflict with the existing relations of production." As a result of these contradictions, sooner or later the entire system must change fundamentally.[44]

In the context of these "realistic" expectations about the development of societies, Struve believed that the advance of a modern, monetary economy and capitalism into Russia was self-evident and historically inevitable. The "proletarianization" of large segments of the peasantry demonstrated this advance especially clearly. At most, this process could merely be delayed, "thereby making it more painful"— a pure waste of energy that would do nothing to stop it. Marx and Engels had simultaneously emphasized, however, that counting on the benevolent power of the state would be foolish. The state was never an "ideal independent power . . . but instead the political expression of existing social relations."[45]

Struve stubbornly deflected challenges to this evolutionary logic from the left. He was an especially sharp critic of Luxemburg's "theory of collapse, which was flimsily constructed on the dialectic."There was, according to Marx, "only one form of social movement"—namely, the accommodation of legal norms to socioeconomic development. Economic phenomena "genetically preceded" the legal norms that sought to regulate them.[46]

By promoting a theory of social revolution that was fixated on collapse, many of Marx's most fervent disciples had lost the organic and evolutionary aspects of his argumentation. At the same time, these disciples assumed that as the economy became increasingly capitalistic, the law (as the codification of "social life") would miraculously develop in the direction of socialism. Struve argued that this viewpoint fundamentally contradicted the core idea of Marx's theory: the mutual dependence of both spheres.[47]

Struve's ambitious, opinionated, and distinctively Marxist reviews of the 1890s reveal a precocious young author who was convinced of the primacy of economics and the power of the state. Within just a few years, he had introduced the most important works of Russian social theory to prominent (German-language) journals of political economy. This double feat of translation was the result of a polyglot, western-oriented reading of the social democratic canon, which had, by this point, enshrined Marx and Engels's analysis of capitalism as the foremost analysis of the present. Struve faithfully presented this analysis as Russia's only path forward into the future, even as he embraced capitalist modernity to an extent that perplexed or even irritated many like-minded comrades. No wonder, as he countered supposed facts with cool one-liners, such as "Our peasants do not produce enough food."[48] And he was equally fond of sweeping, often apodictic conclusions, such as that agriculture ought to be based on private ownership instead of the previous "public-spirited" approach to work. As western development had shown, only individualism could encourage a more effective use of resources, including land—thereby leading to the collectivism that Marx had prophesied. In sum, "[a] powerful peasantry can arise only from the ruins of today's communal property."[49]

This brash optimism also permeated Struve's first Marxist book, *Critical Remarks on the Question of Russia's Economic Development*, which made him famous overnight and soon became known as the "sensational" founding text of second-generation Russian Marxism.[50] The book brought together arguments from his pre-1894 articles as a contribution to political economy, and thereby managed to evade censorship.[51] It was the first Marxist text to be published legally in Russia, establishing Struve's reputation as the founder of "Legal Marxism." Among the influential Russian socialists, his pro-capitalist argumentation was comparable only to that of Lenin. But even Lenin was put off by the degree of Struve's enthusiasm, which culminated in the audacious appeal "Let us admit our lack of culture and enroll in the school of capitalism!"[52]

Struve reaped fame as well as criticism for his first book, which was not uncommonly read as a "paean to capitalism." His collective tarring of all populists as "reactionary" struck Russian socialists of all stripes as presumptuous, unfair, or even "improper."[53] Dissent even came from within the Marxist ranks; Lenin and Plekhanov led the way, targeting Struve's factual argumentation less than his "standpoint"—that is, his style and habitus. Lenin particularly objected to how the excitement around Struve's book had relativized, or even downgraded, Plekhanov's status as the founding father of Russian Marxism. In his idiosyncratic way, Lenin accused Struve of believing in class struggle not as a true "materialist" but as an "objectivist," in a manner that was "too abstract and idealistic." Only a materialist possessed the necessary sense of partisanship and could precisely detect class antagonisms and align his personal standpoint accordingly.[54] Plekhanov launched a similar attack: Struve could not be truly Marxist on account of his "moral qualities"; that is, he had not overcome his bourgeois heritage.[55]

And indeed, we must ask why Struve embraced capitalism and its progressive potential from the very beginning, instead of accepting it as a necessary evil, like Marx or Plekhanov (whom he rarely mentioned as a "mentor"). Even Engels objected to his approach, remarking that "Herr Peter von Struve" had grossly underestimated the magnitude of the social consequences in Russia's transition to capitalism. The curiously optimistic writer, who signed his German texts and correspondence as "Peter von Struve,"[56] compared the social misery in Russia—"an old and politically backward country"—with the relatively benign spread of capitalism in the United States, "a young country that also occupies the highest level of culture and is free of all inhibiting traditions."[57] But in contrast to the United States, as Engels wrote in a letter to Danielson, the "capitalistic revolution" in Russia is "a real social revolution," and this change naturally must be "far more violent, far more incisive, and accompanied by immensely greater sufferings." Struve would nonetheless have agreed with Engels's metaphorical understanding of social revolution as an evolutionary process, and also his confident conclusion: "There is no great historical evil without a compensating historical progress."[58]

Struve seamlessly united his own cultural hopes with Marxism's essential faith in progress. His emphatic analysis of the beginnings of capitalism in Russia deepened his own longing for the liberal civilization and rational cultivation of Russian society, and he saw that capitalism had a "genuinely progressive" effect on economic, political, and cultural "superstructures."[59] In 1896, after completing his education, and at the height of his influence on Russian Marxism, Struve traveled to Germany and wrote a report for the Institute for Public Welfare in Frankfurt, linking the question of Russia's future and social democratic movement to its lack of bourgeois and liberal traditions, and indeed, to culture itself.[60] Possibly fearful of Russian spies, he published the report under the pseudonym P. Inrodzew ("stranger" or "foreigner") and revealed nothing to his western European readers about his own involvement in the workers' movement. He introduced his portrait of the movement with the St. Petersburg strikes of the summer of 1896 and—doubly dissembling—presented *his* Marxism as a cultural movement that arose within capitalism and that would naturally succeed it. Struve had helped to plan the strikes, but he left for Germany before they erupted, having been sent by St. Petersburg's Social Democrats to inform Bebel, Liebknecht, and Paul Singer about the state of affairs.[61]

This was the context for Struve's report, although we do not know whether he actually met the three men. The text of the report reflected his vacillation between antibourgeois social democracy (where he had placed all his hopes) and disappointment about the failures of liberalism (where, despite his upbringing and intellectual leanings, he no longer felt at home). And so this portrait of Russian social democracy reflected its author's doubts and hopes as he sought to harmonize his political engagement with his position "in the middle"[62] between the bourgeoisie and the working class.

The historical weakness of Russian liberalism, according to Struve, created a political and intellectual vacuum that Marxist-oriented social democracy sought to fill. It remained to be seen whether or not this movement could succeed, as two powerful lines of development were about to collide in contemporary Russia: expanding capitalism and a steadily increasing need for "popular enlightenment." As educated citizens, workers would certainly keep challenging the capitalist state—and thus the political system as a whole.

Struve concluded his report with a very personal prophecy, asserting that the emerging popular movement of Marxism would reflect the course of history as it led from capitalism (not merely an economic system but also a cultural movement) to the end of tsarism and the dawn of a more just era. In the end, Struve was "too much of a realist and an idealist at once to believe that the bludgeon of the police, though it may ruin thousands of lives, would also have the power to destroy a movement that is deeply rooted in the country's economic (in the narrower sense of the word) and general cultural development."[63]

As Struve took stock of the Russian social movement and his personal motives for engaging in it, his liberal Marxism—or Marxist liberalism—was in no way "schizophrenic."[64] He saw the civilizing effect of capitalism not just as the remedy for Russia's immense problems; through dialectical logic, it also carried the potential of overcoming capitalism itself. Before rendering itself obsolete, capitalism would bring the cultural progress that was "rooted" in the country, and in people like Struve, to full flower; this progress had already begun to blossom in the social democratic movement. Thus, social democratic politics could and should become the "living heart" of every bourgeois person.[65]

As Struve wrote this report, he had become a key figure in the coalescing Russian social democratic movement. Two years later, in 1898, he was tasked with drafting a manifesto for the newly founded Russian Social Democratic Labor Party (RSDLP) at a secret meeting in Kiev. In the end, however, he did not even travel to Kiev. Soon thereafter, he distanced himself from the manifesto's "drastic" Marxist orientation, even portraying it as a half-baked compromise that was based on a fiction; despite the motto on the party flag ("The Russian working class will liberate Russia"), not a single worker had participated in its conspiratorial founding. Struve, in fact, had been the one to insist upon the word "labor" in the party's name, a choice that was apparently not self-evident for the other founding members.[66]

In the meantime, Struve had traveled widely throughout western Europe, conducting research at the Royal Library in Berlin in 1895 and attending the London congress of the Second International in 1896. He did meet Plekhanov on a second trip to Geneva, although their encounter did not go well. Influential texts by both men had been formative to the decentralized founding of the League of Struggle for the Emancipation of the Working Class. The league's embryonic local groupings temporarily united intelligentsia and workers, preparing the way for the strikes of the 1890s. However, neither Plekhanov nor Struve was directly involved in these groups. Plekhanov lived in exile, and Struve's experiences as a student agitator (engaging in "rather crude and cautious, and yet very dangerous social-democratic propaganda") had not always been positive. His comrade Golubev's "ordinary and 'democratic' fur coat" had been an essential disguise—since "one could not possibly visit the workers in student's uniform" or in a radical's "careless and shabby" dress. Golubev's discovery and arrest also meant the loss of this precious fur coat, and since then Struve had avoided this form of political practice.[67]

While Struve traveled abroad, conflicts between factory workers and owners came to a head in St. Petersburg in the mid-1890s. As a consequence of ongoing industrialization, spontaneous strikes erupted across Russia with unprecedented strength and tenacity. In European Russia alone between 1895 and 1899, the number of workplaces affected by strikes rose from 68 to 215, involving nearly sixty thousand workers. Thirty thousand textile workers went in strike in twenty-one St. Petersburg factories in 1896–97.[68] One of the earliest contemporary analyses of these labor conflicts was Struve's aforementioned secondhand account for western European readers. Some students and workers united under the umbrella of the League of Struggle for the Emancipation of the Working Class, although this did not become a permanent cooperative framework.[69] Factory owners in St. Petersburg responded by shortening the workday from fourteen to eleven and a half hours. This became the maximum legal workday in 1897.[70] A parallel discussion commenced about further legal protections, leading to an array of reforms that, at least on paper, soon corresponded to the advanced standard of worker protection laws in western Europe. Struve wrote several detailed analyses that raised this favorable comparison.[71] It was his last great topic as a committed Marxist.

After renouncing Marxism, Struve stubbornly insisted that he had only supported it out of conviction, not passion (although the two motivations are not mutually exclusive). However, even Struve's later texts, which criticized Marx, were simultaneously filled with admiration. Similar to the other protagonists who sought to popularize Marx's doctrines, Struve took a defensive approach. He introduced his critique with an indisputable premise: every "great and substantive system"—and certainly the "most magnificent construct of the modern social sciences"—will have contradictions and inconsistencies, as Struve conceded in his 1898–99 essay "The Marxist Theory of Social Development," which bore the subtitle "A Critical

Attempt." In his first book, *Critical Remarks*, Struve seemed to anticipate his later misgivings; he excused potential biases in Marx and Engels's "historic-economic materialism" by noting that "this theory will always have to its credit having provided a profoundly scientific, truly *philosophical* explanation of many historic facts of utmost importance." Struve did not believe—as Pipes suggests—that Marxism was "mortal," but instead that it was relative.[72]

By tracking down Marxism's contradictions and biases with "painstaking and critical attention to detail," scholars would advance the "collective science." Here Struve was referring, of course, to himself—and to the question of whether Marx's "logical and conceptual framework" for his theory of social development (bourgeois capital economy, impoverishment of the working masses, formation of a revolutionary proletariat) "meshes easily with the entirety of our experience." Struve suggested that Marx and Engels's epistemological reflection was insufficient. After all, they had sought not only to "establish facts" but also to interpret them; they wanted to divine the sociopolitical future from the "facts of the past and present."[73] Struve's probing approach accommodated his fascination with Marx's thought system, as well as his growing need for critical detachment. *Without* tearing down Marx's framework or fundamentally revising his own worldview, Struve (like Adler) sought to historicize Marx's contribution to social science.

Historicizing Marx meant situating him as a struggling revolutionary of his era. "The psychological pressure to prove the historical imperative of the collectivist economic order compelled the socialist Marx, in the 1840s, to deduce from premises that were quite inadequate,"[74] was Struve's firm but sympathetic assessment in 1895. He was similarly charitable toward Marx and Engels's polemics against the German philosophical establishment, although he cast them as part of this intellectual tradition. Marx and Engels had rigidly asserted their distance from Hegelian philosophy in the 1840s; the great importance of German philosophy to the development of "scientific socialism" was not as clear to them then as it would be later on, when the new worldview had become a "complete and integrated school of thought."[75] Struve had no trouble explaining this "psychologically": an early goal had been to overcome "philosophical idealism," and simultaneously to discredit the many "confused comrades" who dreamed of "true socialism" while insisting upon their "intellectual ties to German philosophy." In this context, it is hardly surprising that Marx and Engels often exaggerated their philosophical distance and polemics against like-minded comrades.

Struve's take was more than a purely economic or scientific assessment. Indeed, his situation of Marxism among the greatest achievements of German intellectual history reveals the enduring fascination that this Herculean "breakthrough" exerted over Struve himself. In the end, he had no interest in debunking an entire theory. It was far too enticing for him—and not just analytically, but emotionally as well. At the turn of the century, he did not believe that criticizing Marxism would shatter its foundations: "The richness and dignity of the individual elements, the ingenuity of their combinations, are a benefit to science—despite this work of demolition." There was much that could still be retrieved from the "ruins." And even Struve the apostate found something in Marxism that was religious, uplifting, even sublime. Moved by "conscious piety," he plied the hammer and chisel of criticism to improve a "splendid towering structure." As a Marxist himself, it was a "matter of the heart" to show that his critique of the master was a constructive, affirmative "work of demolition."[76]

Before Struve embraced revisionism around the turn of the century, he had spent years engaged in the historical and intellectual study of Marx's early thought—which further shows that his commitment to Marxism was hardly dispassionate. He immersed himself in the early socialist press during his months-long stays in Germany in the 1890s, and in Berlin's Royal Library he was thrilled to discover two essays that had been anonymously published by Marx. The master's writing style was unmistakable. In 1895 Struve reported on his discovery in the *Neue Zeit*, presenting the texts—in the manner of a Marxologist—as key documents from the "critical breakthrough period of scientific socialism."[77] The Marx essays—which attacked two representatives of "utopian," or "true," socialism, Karl Grün and Hermann Kriege—documented the inception of an "epochal doctrine."[78] Struve even asserted that he had found the moment in Marx's thought that ushered in the unsentimental age of socialism.[79]

The verve of Struve's critique underscored the tremendous pull of Marx's ideas—not only their bold argumentative content but how Marx literally hurled them into the world. This is how they must have struck (not only) the twenty-five-year-old Struve, as he read the first sentences of the anonymous text in the stately reading room of the Royal Library and began to recognize the young Marx as the author of these lines:

> The sentimental heart that shudders at the sight of the prevailing misery is . . . the liveliest advocate of communism. General human kindness, as preached by early Christianity, is *one* source of the ideas for social reform, which is why some people see it as the realization of communism. It is well known that all earlier, and many more recent, social efforts had a Christian, religious stripe; one preached of wicked reality, of hatred versus the *kingdom of love*. For a start, that was enough. But when experience teaches that, in eighteen hundred years, this love has not become functional, that it has not been able to reshape social relations, to establish its kingdom—it clearly follows that love, which could not conquer hate, does not bring the necessary vigor to social reforms. . . . And so the actual conditions of this world—the harsh contrast in contemporary society between capital and labor, between bourgeoisie and proletariat, present in industrial commerce in their most developed form—[these conditions] are the *other*, more powerful source of the socialist worldview, of the demand for social reforms. These conditions cry out to us: "This can't stay the same, this must change, and we humans must do it ourselves."[80]

The combination of indignation and emancipation lent these lines a persuasive power that enthralled quite different political temperaments. Like Struve, Adler embraced Marx's irresistible promise of change and empowerment, while Guesde, Plekhanov, and Bernstein drew upon the "vigor" of Marx's intellectual order and stringency—the product of "actual conditions." Luxemburg, as we will see, grew just as weary as Kautsky and Jaurès of compassion without consequences. And for Lenin, Struve's antagonist, Marx reflected his own absolute contempt for his social environment. Marx's rhetoric heightened all of the protagonists' already well-developed confidence in their own potential. Given the pressing need to act in the face of such shocking misery, it was easy to derive from Marx the right to have a say.

Nevertheless, for Struve—like Bernstein—Marxism's promise of agency lost much of its persuasive power over time. Struve's 1899 essay on Marxist theory was the last long text that he wrote as a Marxist. Its final paragraph already hinted at the (paradoxical) reasons for his change of heart: "Marx's and Engels's achievement as humans— and much of their historical greatness—came from their identity as utopians and revolutionaries. But they failed—and as men of science, they had to fail—to the extent that they had given themselves the titanic assignment of aligning that which repeatedly strives to be- come one and never succeeds: what is and what should be. However, this scientifically hopeless effort elevated them as men of action."[81] If Marx's role in the field of political economy was "comparable, in a sense, to Kant and Hegel in philosophy," he was simultaneously a "passionate fighter" whose "tendentiousness" precluded him from being accepted as a scholar.[82] After only a few years, Struve came to see Marx's scientific socialism, which was entirely oriented toward revolution, as a hopelessly unscientific endeavor. He debunked Marx's supposedly inductive reasoning as wily and dishonest: "Descriptions and statistics illustrate Marx's position, but never prove it. The wealth of such 'inductive' illustrations should not deceive us with respect to Marx's characteristic method of reasoning," which for Struve lay in the inverse of these illustrations, in abstract-deductive argumentation.

After ten years of intensive study, Struve at last concluded that this method was unscientific, thereby sealing his rejection of Marxism as a method of scholarly inquiry. It could be salvaged only when all of its followers returned to a "realistic" analysis of the present and were willing to abandon the dialectic, which speculated with the social fu- ture and subtly hypertrophied a "social ideal" into ideology.[83] Struve recognized Marxism's relationship to reality as a systematic blurring between what is and what should be. This was his basis for criticizing Marx, the failed genius philosopher, as well as Marx's more dogmatic students, especially Lenin and Luxemburg. They would not, or could not, see—let alone reflect upon—the problematic nature of Marx's appeal to reality.

A central motif of Lenin's Marxism was its distinctive appeal to reality, namely, the claim to bridge the divide between theory and practice. As Marx himself had written in the introduction to his *Critique of Hegel's Philosophy of Law*, "It is not enough for thought to strive for realisation, reality must itself strive towards thought."[84] Wilhelm Liebknecht's motto "Study, propagandize, organize" quoted at the beginning of this section, was used by Lenin in his 1894 treatise, *What the "Friends of the People" Are*. Seeking to capture the quintessence of the social democratic movement, whereby "theoretical and practical work merge into one," Lenin quoted the "veteran Social-Democrat" Liebknecht in German (*Studieren, Propagieren, Organisieren*).[85] However, Lenin's order and choice of words was imprecise; he probably cited Liebknecht only from hearsay. Liebknecht's actual appeal from 1887 was "Agitate, organize, study," and thus did not convey the procedural logic that Lenin's paraphrase suggests.[86] Lenin's version corresponded much more to the logic of his own political coming of age, becoming an autobiographical statement and reflecting the conception of Marxist-oriented social democracy that he had doggedly pursued since 1895. Had Lenin known the precise phrasing of Liebknecht's appeal, he probably would have found it useful but not methodical enough to uplift as the motto of Russia's first social democratic party.

For years, most young socialists understood themselves—like Kautsky—as mentorless students or autodidacts. After a brief and intense phase of initiation, a few felt called not merely to read Marx's work but also to interpret and develop it further, applying it as a manual for practical politics. Lenin was foremost among these young socialists. His introduction to Marx's work came through the trunk of books he inherited from his brother Alexander Ulyanov.[87] An analysis of Alexander's school essays from the early 1880s shows that he had no problem reconciling his family's ethical standards—discipline, diligence, and perfectionism—with the values of a nihilistic and rebellious subculture.[88] After getting to know the radical ideas of Russian social revolutionaries as a schoolboy, as a university student in St. Petersburg he read Marx's theses about the laws of history and economics as a plausible, "rigorously scientific" complement to his views about the necessity of a violent upheaval. According to Philip Pomper, the "feeling of dissatisfaction with the general state of affairs" in his early youth hardened into a "firm conviction about the abnormality of the existing order, and he came to see terror as the only solution.[89] Alexander's small revolutionary library, which his younger brother inherited after his execution, encompassed a selection of contemporary Russian literature (Turgenev, Dostoyevsky), works of science (Darwin, Spencer), and social criticism (Pisarev, Lavrov), including works by Marx and Engels, some of which Alexander had even translated into Russian himself.[90]

Lenin followed his older brother's development attentively, even seeing him as a role model and trying to imitate him. We do not know exactly how and when he began to read Marx. The Soviet edition of Lenin's works states that he studied *Capital* in 1888 and translated the *Manifesto of the Communist Party* the following year.[91] Similarly, Robert Service dates Lenin's first reading of Marx to the period after his return to Kazan, as part of the circle around the student N. I. Fedoseev; the group also read David Ricardo, Darwin, and the histories of Henry Thomas Buckle.[92] Lenin began to study law in Kazan in August 1887, just a few months after his brother's execution (and three years earlier than Struve, who was the same age). By December 1887, Lenin was already involved in student protests that led to the temporary closing of the university and his own expulsion. The Ulyanov family had moved to Kazan because of the disgrace brought by Alexander's participation in the plot to assassinate the tsar. And so the younger son's incendiary behavior created an extraordinarily difficult situation for the entire family, including his school-age siblings. Despite multiple petitions in 1888, Lenin was not readmitted to the university in Kazan. Around the same time, his mother sought a new estate as a permanent residence. In the summer of 1889, she acquired a house in the Samara province, purchased from the holdings of a wealthy philanthropist who had earned his fortune in Siberian gold. The philanthropist happened to be the patron of the writer Gleb I. Uspensky, who had lived in Samara in the 1870s. Uspensky was revered by the Narodniks, although his stories about rural and peasant life were controversial. His realistic but wholly disillusioned descriptions of the peasantry lacked any "superstition" (according to Struve[93]) in their natural inclination toward socialism. Stories like *Manners of Rasteryaeva Street* (1866), *The Power of the Soil* (1882), and *The Impoverishment of the Peasants* (1892) painted a sobering picture of a hopeless, backward, drunken, and brutalized people.[94] After his family moved to the estate at Alakaevka, these stories framed Lenin's encounters with the local peasants, about whom he had little to say, preferring to cite from statistical reports or others' observations. This was already evident in his first treatises, "New Economic Developments in Peasant Life" and "On the So-Called Market Question," both written in 1893 but not published until 1923 and 1937, respectively. Thus, he cited a statistical survey to show that the "peasants themselves" used the word "depeasanting" to describe the growing division of the rural population into a "bourgeoisie" and a "proletariat." And he reported others' observations about "indolence" and "drunkenness" and stories about arson and horse theft. Without more closely supporting his skepticism about these observations, and—at least in the first text—without explicit reference to Marx, Lenin asserted that peasant culture was not, in fact, the root cause of rural distress, which was caused by the dueling economic interests that capitalism brought to the countryside.[95]

The Ulyanov family had their own unpleasant experiences with insubordinate peasants in Alakaevka. Lenin showed no interest in agriculture; he grudgingly offered his services as a teacher in the village instead. Without a suitable manager for the estate, his mother quickly decided to resell the land, and the family used the house only as a summer residence for five more years. In September 1889 the Ulyanovs moved to the provincial capital of Samara. Lenin was not able to continue his formal studies here, either, but he began to translate the *Manifesto of the Communist Party* and "engage[d] in Marxist propaganda among the youth of Samara," according to the vague formulation in the first volume of his *Collected Works*, published by the Institute of Marxism-Leninism in Moscow.[96] After repeated applications, in the spring of 1890 he finally received permission to register as an external student—in other words, to study independently—so that he could take the jurisprudence exams at the university in St. Petersburg.

Thus, Lenin's university career was hardly typical, although after 1890 he did live in St. Petersburg, his point of departure for frequent visits to Moscow and Samara. With few reliable sources, it is difficult to say whether and how he experienced the effects of the great famine in those years. Service presumes that Lenin not only saw these effects with his own eyes, but that his family's conflicts with the local population in Alakaevka even exacerbated the situation for the starving peasants.[97]

The famine became a fixed reference point in Lenin's early writings, from 1893 to the turn of the century. His cool tone, assessment of the catastrophe as a "useful" turning point for social democracy, and his (unsubstantiated) refusal of any assistance—because it would only prop up capitalism—have since become fixtures of every Lenin critique.[98] Already in *What the "Friends of the People" Are* (1894), he fought back against criticism that he had downplayed the famine as a necessary evil in the transition to capitalism, by responding that it was "shameful cowardice to fear to look reality in the face." Reality, however, was very abstract (not only) in this text; Lenin spoke broadly about the "hopeless poverty of the masses" and the "starvation of millions of people."[99] He addressed the topic more thoroughly in his long treatise, *The Development of Capitalism in Russia*, which he wrote in exile between 1896 and 1899. With reference to Engels, he interpreted the famine as evidence of the "home market"—that is, as a side effect of capitalism, and not the result of poor governance in Russia:

> The transformation of the peasantry into a rural proletariat creates a market mainly for articles of consumption, whereas its transformation into a rural bourgeoisie creates a market mainly for means of production. In other words, among the bottom groups of the "peasantry" we observe the transformation of labour-power into a commodity, and in the top ones the transformation of means of production into capital. Both these transformations result in precisely that process of the creation of a home market which theory has established for capitalist countries in general. That is why F. Engels, writing on the famine of 1891, said that it signified *the creation of a home market for capitalism*—a proposition that is unintelligible to the Narodniks, who regard the ruin of the peasantry merely as the decay of "people's production," and not as the transformation of patriarchal into capitalist economy.[100]

Lenin referred to Engels's text in a footnote, sharpening his argumentation and extending it: the famine did not merely signal the development of capitalism, as Engels had suggested, but actively contributed to it, "ruin[ing] masses of peasants and at the same time hasten[ing] the process of the creation of a home market."[101] In fact, the most important cause of the famine was the harsh climate of the previous year, with average winter temperatures of $-30°$ Celsius. Most of the seeds that were planted froze, resulting in a catastrophic harvest the following summer. Half a million people died by the end of 1892.[102]

These events coincided with the beginning of Lenin's professional career. He passed his examinations at the end of 1891, received permission to practice law, and accepted a position in a law office. In St. Petersburg he began to participate in Struve's reading circle, where in 1895 he met and befriended Julius O. Martov, the driving force behind the League of Struggle for the Emancipation of the Working Class. Lenin joined contemporary debates about the Russian economy with his first (surviving) essays from 1893, although these were not published until much later. In 1895 he finally received a passport (which he had sought since he was eighteen). That summer he traveled abroad—to

Berlin, Paris, and Geneva, where he met Liebknecht, Lafargue, and Plekhanov, whom he revered and even "loved."[103] Like Struve, he acquired as many books as he could carry. He returned to St. Petersburg in September 1895, shortly before the strikes that marked his initiation into the world of industrial workers. During these years, Lenin was materially and emotionally well cared for. Thanks to the prosperity of his family, he was able to live like a "middle-class *rentier*."[104]

His first pamphlet "to the workers" was written in this period. Going into unusual detail about the living and working conditions of the Petersburg textile workers, he railed against their drudgery and privations as if they were his own:

> If we all remain indifferent to the fate of the weaving sheds, we shall dig with our own hands a pit into which we, too, shall soon be thrown. Latterly the weavers have been earning, in round figures, 3 rubles 50 kopeks a fortnight, and during the same period families of seven have contrived somehow to live on 5 rubles, and families consisting of husband, wife and child on 2 rubles in all. They have sold the last of their clothes and used up the last coppers they earned by their hellish labour at a time when their benefactors, the Thorntons [the factory owners] were adding millions to the millions they already had. . . .
>
> The pressure has been regularly increased with the most heartless cruelty. . . . Without any explanation, they have started mixing noils [short fibers that are difficult to weave] and clippings with the wool, which slows the job down terribly; delays in getting the warp have increased as though inadvertently; finally, they have begun without ado to introduce short time, and now the pieces have to be five instead of nine schmitz [about 3.5 meters] long, so that the weaver has to fuss around longer and oftener in obtaining and fixing the warps, for which, as is known, not a kopek is paid. . . .
>
> Comrades, don't be blind, don't swallow the employers' bait, stand up for one another more firmly, otherwise it will go badly for all of us this winter. We must all keep a most watchful eye on the employers' manoeuvres aimed at reducing rates, and with all our strength resist every tendency in this direction for it spells ruin for us. . . . Turn a deaf ear to all their pleadings about business being bad: for them it only means less profit on their capital, for us it means starvation and suffering for our families who are deprived of their last crust of stale bread.[105]

This description of the Petersburg textile workers' everyday working and living conditions, which was based on Lenin's own observations, gave unusually concrete expression to Marx's conception of class struggle. Two of Lenin's other texts from this period have similar immediacy: an open letter (on behalf of the League of Struggle for the Emancipation of the Working Class) to the tsarist government, about its response to the Petersburg factory strikes; and the pamphlet "What Are Our Ministers Thinking About?," on the consequences of government repression and the growing "knowledge" of the "working people." These vividly illustrated texts contrast sharply with Lenin's letter to the workers of Petrograd, "On the Famine," of 22 May 1918. The 1918 letter briefly mentions the "extremely harrowing picture" drawn by a comrade in the Putilov Works, but it devotes pages to Lenin's appeal for "a mass 'crusade'" against "the bourgeoisie and the rich generally, including the rural rich, the kulaks." Lenin narrowed the question of hunger to one radical dictum (the "prime, basic and root principle of socialism"): "He who does not work, neither shall he eat."[106]

References to the everyday life of Petersburg factory workers in the pamphlets of the 1890s reflected a young man's impressions that were still quite fresh. Before this point, Lenin had engaged with such "realities" only "theoretically," in long, statistics-based analyses that had garnered little public attention. His later wife, Nadezhda Krupskaya, recalled in her memoirs that Lenin had read *Capital* aloud to workers during this period, discussing it intensely and explaining its significance.[107] He knew that factory schools would teach workers' children to remain submissive forever, unless their parents intervened: "Without knowledge the workers are defenceless, with knowledge they are a force!"[108]

Although we have no concrete evidence of these encounters, we know that Lenin had direct contact with workers who labored physically—not merely intellectually, as propagandists in the proletarian elite—in his Petersburg years between 1890 and 1895. It was *these* workers whom Lenin saw as "Russia's men of the future"—and not the peasants, who were the focus of the Narodniks' "peasant socialism," and whose fates must have seemed distant to him.[109] According to Lenin, only those who had seen the bitter division of the factory cosmos—and society as a whole—into "oppressors" and "paupers" understood the stakes of the fight.

Even when Lenin addressed human misery in his pamphlets, he was motivated not by sympathy for the "working masses" but by a feeling of self-esteem that he conferred on them, and that empowered both sides. Social democrats recognized "the worker as the sole fighter for the socialist system." Political freedom could ease the workers' struggle, Lenin argued in *What the "Friends of the People" Are*—a polemical text aimed not at average workers but at socialists who had allegedly lost their way. The "conciliatory, cowardly, sentimental, and dreamy" Narodniks—these "friends of the people" and "ideologists of the petty bourgeoisie"—completely misunderstood the significance and role of the worker. They turned to him "simply as the one who suffers most from the present system, who has nothing more to lose and who can display the greatest determination in fighting absolutism." But this meant "compelling the worker to drag in the wake of the bourgeois radicals, who refuse to see the antagonism between the bourgeoisie and the proletariat behind the solidarity of the whole 'people' against absolutism."[110] This was Lenin's reproach against Struve—his "twin," as Lenin called him, even in 1900, out of a mixture of awe and contempt.[111] Since 1893, Struve had enjoyed a reputation in Petersburg circles as the sharpest mind among the Russian Marxists. Unlike Lenin (who was the same age), Struve had become a celebrated author, both in Russia and abroad.[112]

Lenin was arrested in early December 1895, four weeks after the publication of his pamphlet for the Petersburg textile workers. In order to arrest as many activists as possible, the Okhrana, the tsarist secret police, had allowed the League of Struggle for the Emancipation of the Working Class to grow. But now, after the attention-grabbing strikes of the fall, the time had come to break up the group. Within weeks, the "elders" (*stariki*) were tracked down, arrested, and sentenced.

Lenin was sentenced to two years in detention, followed by exile in the southern Siberian village of Shushenskoe. In contrast to the experiences of fellow activists such as Martov and Fedoseev (who killed himself), Lenin's living conditions in exile were comparatively mild—and not merely with respect to the weather.[113] He resumed his studies and, while still in detention, wrote a social democratic party program aimed particularly at factory workers. The "exploitation of labor by capital" was at its most extreme in factories, and thus would compel all workers to unite in struggle as the Russian working class. This struggle would be part of the international social democratic movement, and Lenin's proposed party would assist it "by developing the class-consciousness of the workers, by promoting their organisation, and by indicating the aims and objects of the struggle."[114] After his release in 1900, as the ascendant leader of the RSDLP and the Bolsheviks, Lenin put these same principles into practice. By 1895, he had already answered the question "What is to be done?" for himself. Unlike his "twin" Struve, he remained loyal to his draft program for a Marxist party, which he had composed at just twenty-five years old.

And so Lenin's experiences between 1890 and 1895—encompassing his academic studies, early career, and underground activism—came to define his appropriation of Marx.[115] His first known reference to *Capital* appears in a posthumously published essay that was based on his speech to a circle of Petersburg Marxists, a group he had participated in since the early 1890s. The seventy-five-page treatise disputed the economist G. B. Krasin's thesis that Russia was not developing toward capitalism because of the absence of a market. Here Lenin demonstrated an already mature, practiced familiarity with Marx's theses and theorems, which he applied schematically to Russian society. In order to show where Krasin—a like-minded comrade with populist impulses—had erred, one had "to turn straight to Marx." Of course, this also meant citing his personal translation of the master.[116]

Lenin presented his treatise to the Petersburg discussion circle of "elders," who were concerned about macro-level details—that is, about the statistical reality of Russian economic life and the "general

law of development of capitalist society." Of course, they came nowhere close to answering the pivotal question: Did "the one fact of
the masses being impoverished" make capitalism in Russia "something impotent and without foundation, incapable of embracing
the entire production of our country and of becoming the *basis* of
our social economy?"[117] Nevertheless, Lenin's presentation—how he
spoke, formulated his critique, and imparted his economic and intellectual worldview—left a lasting impression on the attendees. To
the "youngsters" (*molodye*), on the other hand, the twenty-five-year-
old Lenin seemed like an old man. Potresov, who was part of Lenin
and Struve's circle of friends, recalled Lenin's "pallid face, the baldness
that covered his whole head except for some sparse hair around his
temples, the thin, reddish little beard, the screwed-up eyes that looked
slyly at people from under his eyebrows, the old and harsh voice."
Lenin has since been perceived as the avant-garde revolutionary par
excellence, but even as a young man he seemed old beyond his years.
Potresov found Lenin's intellectual characteristics even more striking.
In conversation, Lenin already seemed like a "Marxist sectarian" who
had completed "serious Marxist training." He had "strong energy, but
simultaneously something one-sided, insistently simplified, and insistently simplifying the complexities of life."[118]

Struve was also a member of this circle. In his own recollections,
which were colored by his later enmity with Lenin, he depicted him
as a dark personality: astute, well-read, and determined, but also cold,
cruel, brusque, mistrustful, filled with animal hatred, obsessed with
power, and disciplined to the point of self-castigation.[119] For Struve,
Lenin's dedication to Marx could be explained only psychologically.
Lenin's dominant trait was hatred, Struve wrote in 1933:

> The doctrine of the class war, relentless and thoroughgoing, aiming at
> the final destruction and extermination of the enemy, proved congenial
> to Lenin's emotional attitude to surrounding reality. He hated not only
> the existing autocracy (the Tsar) and the bureaucracy, not only the law-
> lessness and arbitrary rule of the police, but also their antipodes—the
> "Liberals" and the "bourgeoisie." That hatred had something repulsive

and terrible in it; for, being rooted in the concrete, I should even say animal, emotions and repulsions, it was at the same time abstract and cold like Lenin's whole being.[120]

These lines were clearly written in the shadow of 1917. Struve's choice of words reflected the violence of the Bolshevik Revolution. Even though the fundamental characteristics of Marx's personality and those of his doctrine may align, and even though Marxist engagement can surely also be explained psychologically, Struve's retrospective portrait is nonetheless quite extreme. Class struggle did figure prominently in Lenin's earliest writings, although not to the extent that Struve suggests. Likewise, hatred was not Lenin's only emotion; he could admire and love just as fervently as he hated, if in much smaller doses. Service has noted that Lenin, the "young heterosexual revolutionary," directed these positive emotions less toward his lover, and later his wife, and more toward a handful of ideological mentors and friends: Marx, Plekhanov, Engels, and Chernyshevsky foremost among them.[121]

Lenin's early writings were less hate-filled than Struve and other contemporaries from the Petersburg years have suggested. Instead, his early work reflected an intellectual fascination with the boldness and modernity of Marxist thought and a compulsion to underscore its scientific relevance and political explosiveness. This work took aim against ideological rivals in the guise of Narodniks and populists—that is, against opponents within the socialist ranks. Marx's argumentation dazzled Lenin with its self-assurance. Its claim to truth and power to effect change energized him and the other protagonists, reinforcing their already well-developed faith in their own potential. The "discovery" of natural laws within human society especially fascinated those protagonists who believed that such laws could exist—and who, in principle, could not imagine a world without them; this was true of Lenin, Kautsky, Plekhanov, and Luxemburg. For these four protagonists, science and politics merged. Analysis and application, diagnosis and therapy, fused into a single worldview (or better: a promise of changing the world) that replaced classical politics and bridged the divide between theory and practice. Erudition was both the precondition and the result of their professional occupation with the material world. This occupation, and the faith in their own competence that the activists derived from it, was at the heart of Marxist politics—although Marx himself practiced politics as a *scholar* and never developed a theory of political action.[122] The first Marxists were more than uninspired epigones, as they sought to expand Marx's legacy creatively, by merging science and political practice, and by shifting their own role as engaged intellectuals toward greater political activism.

Because we have no explanatory testimonials from Lenin himself, we must carefully study his first publications in order to reconstruct his reading of Marx. His written engagement with certain lines of reasoning reveals traces of his experiences as a reader. Lenin's fascination with Marx's theses is evident in his early writings, which were published under various pseudonyms. When speaking of his teachers Marx, Engels, and Plekhanov, Lenin used the imagery of "love" and "human friendship."[123] And precisely because these texts—like so much of Lenin's work—were polemics, not stand-alone essays, they reveal, as if in the heat of battle, the essential elements of this intellectual fascination and emotional bond.

For Lenin, Marx's "stroke of genius" was applying "materialism in sociology," thereby elevating sociology for the first time "to the level of a science." Marx thus developed a "strictly scientific" system, method, or theory (Lenin used these terms as interchangeable synonyms).[124] United in intimate friendship, Marx and Engels "substituted science for dreams," casting aside all that had come before them, and creating a "firm basis for the conception that the development of formations of society is a process of natural history." Engels ultimately put in twenty-five years of intellectual labor to prove Marx's "ingenious" hypothesis.[125]

Marx was certainly comparable to Darwin. By focusing on the relations of production as the "structure of society," Marx had found a way to investigate these relations objectively, as "regular" and "recurrent" social phenomena. The core *thesis* of Marx's investigations—the relationship between being and consciousness—was simultaneously his core *conclusion*: "[t]hat the course of ideas depends on the course of things," as expressed by Lenin in terms that could be grasped by every worker.[126] The underlying reasoning dissolved all distinctions between fact and thesis, analysis and prediction. This reasoning was already evident in the foundational text of scientific socialism, the *Manifesto of the Communist Party*, and it informed all Marxist works thereafter. The *Manifesto* began with an assertion presented as analysis ("The history of all hitherto existing society is the history of class struggles"), and it ended with a prediction presented as fact: "Let the ruling classes tremble at a Communistic revolution. The proletarians have nothing to lose but their chains. They have a world to win."[127]

These lines from the *Manifesto*, like Lenin's first political texts, sought to explain the world in an absolute, ultimate way. The authors' emphasis on "true," "serious," "firm," and "strict" scientific inquiry suggests, on the one hand, a rather murky notion of science. What is "scientific" or not has always been subject to negotiation; the will and ability of a discipline to reflect upon itself—and, in this sense, to subject itself to negotiation—is among the most important ground rules of scientific work.[128] The co-opting of "science" by Marxist social analysis may have been the most effective political idea of social critics on the left in the nineteenth century. It turned Marx's theses into Marxism, and an intellectual worldview into a political truth. "Scientific" status bestowed an aura of respectability, objectivity, and incontestability, allowing Marxism to profit immensely from the "unprecedented cultural authority"[129] that the sciences acquired over the course of the nineteenth century.

On the other hand, early Marxist texts' insistence on descriptors of quality like "strict," "firm," and "true" can also be read as an expression of covert doubt, a preemptive defense against criticism that such universal claims would surely provoke. Lenin's veneration of science was more than the charismatic affectation of a man who preferred action over contemplation, as Hannah Arendt has asserted. Nevertheless, his interest in science was largely instrumental, and Arendt is correct that Marx took science "more seriously" than Lenin did.[130]

Returning to Lenin's reading of Marx, we must recall that these encounters did not occur in an intellectual vacuum, but alongside his reading of other notable works. Lenin likely read Marx's *Capital* around the same time as Chernyshevsky's *What Is to Be Done?*[131] Considering these two books side by side brings Lenin's Marx reception into sharper focus. Lenin's *similarities* with the young Struve simultaneously become more apparent: on the one hand, the native Russian, intuitive utopia of overcoming the tsarist regime; and on the other, the rational, cool, western, scientifically informed study of the epochal, but ephemeral, capitalist system, the precise knowledge and mastery of which would lead to its eventual superseding. (Russian) lifeworld and (western) science might have seemed far apart from one another, but were closely intertwined in these two books. Chernyshevsky spiked his novel with numerous, sometimes veiled references to western thinkers, and he himself had read and corresponded with Marx. Marx's *Capital*, meanwhile, was filled with examples from the everyday life of (especially English) workers. On the basis of these implicit and explicit mutual references, Lenin insisted that Marx, unlike the "abstract" thinkers who preceded him, "showed the whole capitalist social formation to the reader as a living thing—with its everyday aspects."[132]

For Lenin, this was the heart of Marx's thought world. He repeatedly countered accusations of dogmatism by pointing to Marx's ambition to formulate "what is going on before our eyes"—that is, to deal with "real social and economic relations and their actual evolution" by looking reality "straight in the face."[133] Lenin believed that reality could be depicted representationally, and thus its "true" representation promised genuine understanding. His references to the apparently undogmatic description of reality showed not a hint of reflection that its perception and interpretation are highly subjective processes, dependent on many factors. Nor did Lenin recognize that perception and interpretation are mutually dependent, not separate and sequential intellectual processes. Indeed, a source of Lenin's dogmatism was his belief that cognition was nothing more than a straightforward representation of "objective" existence. Further, his persistence in pointing to Marx's "scientific" apprehension of reality justified the rigidity of his own ideas about changing it in practice. Lenin "was never a theorist in the sense of approaching questions in a spirit of intellectual curiosity and the disinterested quest for a solution. All questions, even epistemological ones, were potential instruments of the revolution, and all answers were political acts."[134]

Wholly in line with this practical bent, a goal of Lenin's writing had always been to popularize Marxism as a "doctrine" of and for the workers (he coined the term *Marxpopularisatoren*, or "popularizers of Marx," for himself and his comrades).[135] As such, Lenin created his own metaphors to illustrate and explain the master's work. He compared Marx's intellectual achievement in *Capital* with the (divine?) creation of human beings out of bones, flesh, and blood. Setting out to study "factual material"—which Lenin understood as the "production relations between members of society"—Marx made it possible "to discern how the commodity organisation of social economy develops, how it becomes transformed into capitalist organisation, creating antagonistic classes." This was the "bones," or "skeleton," of *Capital*. Even more important, Marx "did not content himself with this skeleton" by confining himself to conventional economic theory. Rather, "while *explaining* the structure and development of the given formation of society exclusively through production relations, he nevertheless everywhere and incessantly scrutinised the superstructure corresponding to these production relations and clothed the skeleton in flesh and blood." This holistic approach explained the power of Marx's ideas:

> The reason *Capital* has enjoyed such tremendous success is that this book ... showed the whole capitalist social formation to the reader as a living thing—with its everyday aspects, with the actual social manifestation of the class antagonism inherent in production relations, with the

bourgeois political superstructure that protects the rule of the capitalist class, with the bourgeois ideas of liberty, equality and so forth, with the bourgeois family relationships.[136]

In this understanding of Marx, the economy, in the broadest sense, was the framework, or "skeleton," of society. Its flesh and blood were the government and bureaucracy and their accompanying ethics and morals. Marx himself had described market relations as vampiric, and he denounced the blood- (money-)sucking capitalists who used their dead capital to squeeze the living commodity of labor out of human flesh and blood. Lenin himself later spoke of capitalists as "bloodsuckers."[137] This martial language, which "enfleshed" the critique of the capitalist system, was already apparent in Lenin's early writing, as he used the metaphor of the human body to extol Marx's analytical prowess. The "body," of course, was Lenin's own society. Thus, when Lenin equated government with despotism—or when he spoke contemptuously of the well-meaning, "childish" moralists who sought to model a just society on the goodness of human nature—he was clearly distancing himself from the ideals of his parents and the foundations of his own upbringing. The values of liberty and equality that he scorned as an adult had once been embraced in his strict, but intellectually open, family home.[138]

His attitude—which contradicted his close-knit, real-life family ties—was driven by the *emotional* camaraderie he had found in various subversive writings since his brother's execution. The underlying motivation of these writings (as he perceived it) justified and encouraged his own political engagement. Lenin's enduring emotional connection to Marx and Engels came from this feeling of understanding and being understood. A "feeling of hatred" connected him to these two distant "fighters and teachers." Lenin's eulogy for Engels, which he wrote at the age of twenty-five in the fall of 1895, might also be read as a rare personal testimonial. Certain passages even recall Struve's portrait of the young Lenin as a pathologically hate-filled politician in the making:

Marx and Engels, who both knew Russian and read Russian books, took a lively interest in the country, followed the Russian revolutionary movement with sympathy and maintained contact with Russian revolutionaries. They both became socialists after being *democrats*, and the democratic feeling of *hatred* for political despotism was exceedingly strong in them. This direct political feeling, combined with a profound theoretical understanding of the connection between political despotism and economic oppression, and also their rich experiences of life, made Marx and Engels uncommonly responsive *politically*. That is why the heroic struggle of the handful of Russian revolutionaries against the mighty tsarist government evoked a most sympathetic echo in the hearts of these tried revolutionaries.[139]

Here Lenin's choice of words and italicization are important. His engagement *against* the existing order was highly emotional; like Marx and Engels, he "hated" this order as a "democrat"—that is, as an advocate of a form of government that arose from the "masses." A core idea of *What Is to Be Done?*, Lenin's 1902 treatise on the "burning questions of our movement," was that "the Social-Democrat's ideal should not be the trade-union secretary, but *the tribune of the people.*"[140] By contrast, Lenin's engagement *for* the liberation of the oppressed was more rationally motivated, based on his insight into certain "theoretical" relations. The uncommon political "responsiveness" that Lenin assigned to Marx and Engels (and, by extension, to himself) presumably had to do with the well-calculated mixture of "feeling and reason" in their diagnosis and prescription for the future.[141] Marx and Engels's students poured this mixture into a vague but real political program, aided by the notion of class struggle as natural law. And finally, Lenin's italicization of "politically" in the above passage suggests that he had already recognized this potential while he was still in his twenties, long before his first exile as a dangerous dissident.

9

Engagement as Science

Luxemburg

Rosa Luxemburg, 1890
Credit: International Institute of Social History, Amsterdam

Luxemburg's introduction to the works of Marx and Engels must have occurred when she was around eighteen years old, through her contacts in Warsaw's socialist opposition. There is, however, no firm evidence.[1] A rare, if indirect, testimonial is her 1897 essay on "Socialism in Poland," in which she analyzes three strains of the Polish workers' movement since the 1880s. She apparently joined the first group, the Social Revolutionary (or "Proletariat") Party, as a teenager, and so she was already familiar with its conspiratorial methods, including the "committees" and "first- and second-tier agents" who "preached terrorism." In practice, however—and in contrast to the People's Will in St. Petersburg—the party inflicted no great damage. A notable exception was the murder of two "traitors" in their own ranks, which Luxemburg described as an act of "self-defense."[2]

In 1889 she fled to Zurich, to escape impending arrest. Her remarks about the Proletariat Party's programmatic foundations suggest that the *Manifesto of the Communist Party* was known by its members. The group accepted the *Manifesto*'s general argument but acted upon it only in part, concentrating largely on terrorist activities to overthrow tsarism. Party dogmas did include the "opposition of the material interests of the proletariat and the bourgeoisie, the capitalist order as the objective precondition of a socialist revolution [*Umwälzung*], and the historic mission of the working class to enact this revolution." However, the party did not find common cause with the western European workers' movement until 1889, after Luxemburg was already studying in Zurich.[3] Before then, the party had no serious political program. In Luxemburg's retrospective assessment, it was more a movement based on the "theory of the Blanquist coup, grafted onto Marx's doctrine of class struggle." Had she already read the thick volumes of her "masters," she surely would have mentioned this in conjunction with the "masses of pamphlets, brochures, and socialist journals" that the party consumed and produced.[4]

Contrary to frequent assertions, Luxemburg probably began reading *Capital* in a systematic way only in the context of her university studies. For some time, she seems not to have possessed her own copy. Shortly after arriving in Berlin in 1898, after she had earned her doctorate in Zurich, she asked Leo Jogiches to send her the *Neue Zeit* regularly, as well as "books, including, of course, Marx." She borrowed *Capital* from a Berlin library in July 1898.[5] A glance at her dissertation, "The Industrial Development of Poland" (1897–98), shows that she cited the work—the third volume, published in 1894—only once. She mentioned the first volume only in passing, without an exact citation. Although her dissertation advisor Julius Wolf later wrote that Luxemburg "came to me from Poland already as a thorough Marxist," it is difficult to say what he meant by this.[6] Perhaps the professor, who was only eight years her senior, took her generally oppositional attitude as refined expertise. In 1892 Wolf had sharply criticized Marx's "economic theory of evolution" in his own, much-debated book, *Socialism and the Capitalist Social Order*, and he surely articulated this criticism in his lectures. Many years later, in light of Luxemburg's revolutionary career, Wolf referred to his role in her biography as an "academic stirrup-holder."[7] The remark pointed to his own mixed feelings about helping his later so notorious student forge the weapons for revolution.

Wolf's assertion about his most gifted student's precocious Marxism has since been cited by biographers as fact, although there is no reliable evidence for this thesis. Nettl, for example, writes that Luxemburg went to Zurich to get closer to the "final stage of Socialism," to study the capitalist system, and to meet the "distinguished Marxists" among the resident exiles. However, Luxemburg's degree of ideological and political commitment upon her arrival in Zurich seems exaggerated in this narrative. Nettl himself writes that Luxemburg's chief interests were initially zoology and mathematics. She began to study zoology in the winter semester of 1889–90. She switched to political economy only the following year, attending some classes with her partner Jogiches, whom she met in Zurich in 1890. Jogiches assumed a central role in her life for years to come, and so her academic studies and political coming of age must be understood in the context of this relationship. As late as 1896, as she was about complete her studies and move to Germany, as an increasingly influential activist in the Polish and international socialist movement, her own correspondence left no doubt that, given a choice between politics and her romantic relationship, she would certainly choose the latter.[8]

In the early 1890s Luxemburg attended university lectures in statistics, finance, and philosophy, including a course on "socialism in the light of philosophy" that was taught by the Hungarian rabbi and philosopher Ludwig Stein. University records indicate that she also attended Stein's accompanying "philosophical-pedagogical circle" on classic works.[9] Stein's courses were part of the relatively liberal atmosphere at the Zurich university, although she studied with him, unlike her other professors, for only one semester. This was surely because Stein's evolutionary and state-affirming social philosophy made him a "late representative of bourgeois Enlightenment ideals."[10] She probably read Marx in his classes, although we have no firm evidence of this. In 1892 Luxemburg began to study law alongside political economy, henceforth devoting around half of her academic schedule to subjects like fundamental concepts of jurisprudence, state law, international law, contract law, insurance law, "subjective" (civil) law, and public law.

This reorientation was significant, pointing to Luxemburg's growing interest in the political and legal resolution of social questions and recalling the biography of Marx himself (as Luxemburg noted a decade later, without explicitly mentioning this parallel). In her review of a first edition of Marx's early writings and biographical documents, compiled by Franz Mehring in 1902,[11] she stressed that the young Marx had engaged much more intensely with questions of law than with "abstract" philosophical questions. From the very beginning, Marx had "instinctively" reached toward law—"the adjacent, most immediate ideological form of material social life." By the time he was a young student, he had already commenced his "first internal struggles with the philosophical-critical illumination of the entire legal sphere." As a journalist, he became a "practical fighter," always aware of social conditions. Luxemburg saw this as evidence of

Marx's humanist engagement—a controversial position, even in her lifetime. She argued that the "old master" had dedicated his "heart" to the actual living conditions of the people, which were codified in legal texts.[12]

Luxemburg's book review included some very personal takes on the intellectual "forefather." She wrote that Mehring's masterful collection taught its readers "to understand and love Marx" and that it revealed two distinct lines in Marx's development: first, an "ongoing internal crisis, which expressed itself in the search for a resolution to the philosophical conflict between thinking and being, between the material world and the process of thought"; second, an array of intensive contacts with the "practical world" and its "contemporary political and economic issues." Luxemburg believed that Marx's empathy drove his search for philosophical and practical truth—in other words, *his* engagement: "Above all, as Mehring himself says, it was Marx's deep and true sympathy for the 'poor, politically and socially disenfranchised mass,' it was—already in his idealistic phase—'the heart' that drove him to fight and that dictated his partisanship."[13] This empathetic figure had much more to do with Luxemburg's own wishful thinking, and that of many of her contemporaries, than with the historical Marx and his own worldview.[14]

Yet Luxemburg was a Marxist, above all, in her insistence that purely "empirical" complaints about social injustices were not enough to understand and overcome them. For this, one needed the "granite block" of "science." Unlike all the "shallow minds" who (like Bernstein) spent their energies cobbling together a shallow "'empirical' socialism," Marx strove for a "monistic, unified approach toward a physical and intellectual, a moral and material world," she wrote in the context of the revisionism debate. Further, it was clear that "Marx could not have found [this world] until he discovered it for himself."[15]

Luxemburg's deep admiration for Marx (which she shared with Lenin and Kautsky) drew upon the hypostasis of "historical materialism," or "scientific socialism," as a science, and thus as the key to "truth"—and upon the veneration of Marx as its discoverer.

Like Lenin, her understanding of science was astonishingly one-dimensional. She regarded "scientific socialism" as an "unshakeable"[16] science, and thereby disregarded the generally accepted understanding of modern science as "shakable" in principle. She saw Marx not only as the creator and discoverer of this doctrine but also as a searcher and initiate. After all, Ariadne's mythical thread needed someone like Daedalus, who knew the way out of the labyrinth—or like the modern Daedalus, Marx, who knew the way forward to socialism. And Marx knew not only the way, but also who would proceed along it and how. He had discovered the underlying "laws" of human history as well as the group that now held the historical thread:

> Marx has discovered, so to speak, the modern working class as a historical category—that is, as a class with particular historical conditions of existence and laws of motion. Before Marx, a mass of wage laborers existed in the capitalist countries. Led to solidarity by the similarity of their social existence within bourgeois society, seeking a way out of their situation, some looked for a bridge into the promised land of socialism. Marx was the first to lift them up as a *class*, by uniting them in a special historical task: in the task of seizing political power by socialist revolution [*Umwälzung*].[17]

Marx had not only discovered the path "into the promised land of socialism"; he had also identified those who would blaze it. Luxemburg therefore described his work as not only a "first-rate scientific achievement, but also a historical *act*."[18] Her praise pointed to the political tinder—the practically relevant spark—that she had found in Marx's thought world. A postulate was stylized into proven knowledge, and the mission that united wage laborers—seizing political power—forged the identity of an entire "class." Marx and his most loyal epigones felt called to fulfill this mission, which they had defined, for the "class" that they had discovered.

Building upon Benedict Anderson's work on nationalism, one might argue that the discovery of the "working class," through and with Marx, was essentially the invention of a *transnational* tradition.

The narrative of class struggle—which, according to the *Manifesto*, ended with the proletariat "constituting itself as a nation"—was a "cultural product" and thus an ephemeral construct, like every nationalism.[19] This narrative promoted a specific group identity, or "imagined community," that was, by definition, independent of the nation. It lent this community emotional as well as intellectual legitimacy, formed a (socio)political program tailored to the declared interests of the members, and inspired a claim to political power and self-determination that was soon adapted worldwide.

Like Marxism's other cofounders, Luxemburg used vivid language to describe this original creative achievement, particularly in her popular texts. Her lectures on political economy, which she gave at the SPD school in Berlin in 1909–10, celebrated the science that had been developed by Marx and his "joint creator" Engels as the "unshakeable" foundation of the workers' movement, precisely because it did not limit itself to moral outrage but laid bare the economic laws of "capitalist anarchy."[20] Her conception of socialism was not haphazard; rather, she saw socialism as the "fruit" of capitalism, and therefore a "historical necessity." Social democracy was the "theories of Marx and Engels become flesh."

As a young university student, at the latest, Luxemburg knew and was fascinated by Marx's works. Away from her Polish homeland—at first in Zurich, and after 1893 in Paris—she became more involved in political practice. She edited the exile newspaper *Sprawa Robotnicza* (The Workers' Cause), made a controversial appearance without a real mandate at the congress of the Second International in Zurich, and subsequently cofounded the Social Democracy of the Kingdom of Poland (SDKP) Party in September 1893. She routinely quoted and commented on the socialist movements' canonical texts. Her earliest surviving letters, from her time in Paris, reveal an academic breaking into practical politics. She was initially quite cautious about applying the theoretical weapons she had forged in Zurich to her advocacy as a journalist on behalf of Polish workers. She spent longer periods in Paris after 1892, working in the city's libraries and networking with

Polish émigrés. Paris made a powerful impression. She complained re-peatedly about the noise, which "deafened" her day and night, but she was impressed by the city's attractions. "I saw the Trocadero, the Arc de Triomphe, the Eiffel Tower, and the Grand Opera. I'm deafened by the noise. And how many beautiful women there are here! Really, all of them are beautiful, or at least they seem to be," she wrote to Jogiches on the day of her arrival, 11 March 1894.[21]

Jogiches had sent her to Paris for a newspaper project: sharpening and reorienting the content of the monthly journal *Sprawa Robotnicza* toward the international class struggle. The newspaper had been published by Polish emigrants, including Luxemburg's acquaintance from Warsaw, Adam Warszawski, since 1893 (the Zurich congress of the Second International). It primarily aligned itself against the Polish Socialist Party (PPS), which advocated for the restoration of the Polish state and was supported by influential men like Plekhanov.[22] In September the small editors' clique of the *Sprawa Robotnicza* founded a new party, conceived as the direct successor to the Proletariat Party, which had broken down after 1889. At Luxemburg's suggestion, the new party was called the Social Democracy of the Kingdom of Poland, a geographical reference to the pre-1772 kingdom, thereby marking Poland's subsequent partitions as a nonissue. The twenty-three-year-old student became a prominent voice in the new party, which represented a minority position within the Polish émigré movement.

According to Nettl, Luxemburg quickly gained a reputation as the brazen, even ferocious "bogey-woman of Polish Socialism."[23] Her first political appearance, at the Zurich congress, revealed her mis-sionary zeal. As the speaker for a minority faction that opposed the nationally oriented socialists of the PPS, she claimed to represent nothing less than the views of the Polish socialist proletariat,[24] and she was ruthless in asserting her positions. Nettl's characterization of Luxemburg as a Joan of Arc–like figure at this congress is nevertheless problematic. He does not question the legitimacy of the mandate she claimed for her *Sprawa* group, even though, until 1900, the SDKP es-sentially functioned as a "head without a body." Indeed, this episode offers early evidence against Nettl's subtle and influential thesis, that Luxemburg always sought influence over power, as this distinction makes sense only in retrospect. In practice, Luxemburg's lifelong ambition for political power was fruitless until the beginning of 1918. Her political role was therefore limited to her tremendous intellectual influence—first in the Polish, and then the German social democratic movements.[25]

Luxemburg's Parisian articles about the "workers' cause" were the product of her intense correspondence with Jogiches, which—when read between the lines—also reveals her considerable emotional dependence on him. Jogiches's affection was tied to her intellectual creativity and productivity, a circumstance that she addressed head on: "Of course you will pardon me, won't you, that I'm now only writing to you about our cause? . . . I am entirely yours, I dream about you in every free moment, I smile at you in my thoughts. When, when will I embrace you at last? But I *don't want to rush anything*, I want to earn this moment with my work."[26] This remarkable collaboration between the editor-in-chief in Zurich and his Parisian correspondent produced numerous articles that have neither been published in English or German translation nor fully considered by Luxemburg scholars.[27]

Only a few copies of *Sprawa Robotnicza* survive, from the years 1893 through 1896. Luxemburg wrote for the newspaper under the pseudonym R. Kruszyńska, which may be a derivation of the verb *kruszyć* (to crush or crumble), suggesting a woman who would strike a blow for others.[28] The articles written under her aegis were a mixture of reports about social conditions and historical or political essays. These included articles about the 1 May workers' holiday (declared by the Second International in 1889), debates surrounding a shorter workday, and current events. Socialism was depicted as the era's great hope, and capitalism as its great evil. In the June 1896 issue, Luxemburg commented on the St. Petersburg strikes. This "powerfully significant" chain of events underscored the value of such "conflicts" for training the movement's intellectual leaders. The strikes had shown what an important role "our comrades, the Russian socialists" played, how much these experiences contributed to the "enlightenment of the working masses," and "how much easier it is to approach agitated souls, to disseminate agitational literature, [and] how much easier the socialist idea reaches the masses." The chore (literally, "ant work") of organizing had to continue—a call that she herself followed in 1898, with her tours to Silesia for the German SPD. Her choice of metaphor suggests, however, that she may already have realized the difficulty of translating her "idea" into practice.[29] Marx's name and aura were part of these articles, although references to his "achievement" remained very broad. These references were intended to uplift and inspire, as in Luxemburg's April 1895 response to the question "What is socialism?":

> My God! they will cry. Is it even possible that such a wonderful order can become reality? Socialism sounds like a tale from "One Thousand and One Nights." After many years of study, the scholar Karl Marx has determined that socialism seems to be necessary on Earth. It's clear that the sun shines. It's also clear that the Earth revolves around the sun. And it's just as clear that socialism will prevail. . . . Karl Marx has not only proven this. He has likewise shown which path we should choose in order to reach socialism.[30]

In these years, as Luxemburg simultaneously worked on her dissertation, it seemed especially important to prove Marxism's touted connection to reality in order to rouse the "masses" from their "indifference."[31] In the context of her work for *Sprawa Robotnicza*, she sought out authentic correspondence by Polish workers in an effort to fill a March 1895 special issue with "workers' scribbles" (*Geschreibe der Arbeiter*), as she called them. Working with these texts was an important but burdensome undertaking, since their content, orthography, and style presented an editorial challenge. Luxemburg's approach to this challenge illuminates her distinctive approach to the world, which oscillated between realism and romanticism. *Her* illustrations of social reality had to reflect "life and truth," as she reported to Jogiches, and so the workers' issue texts had to be reproduced as authentically as possible. She chose not to rely on her own observations and encounters in the working-class neighborhoods of Paris or Zurich (quite like Lenin, who contemporaneously sought "*raw* material from Russia" for his newspaper work in Geneva).[32] Instead, she turned to correspondence from her distant homeland and its journalistic utilization:

> It has to do with how the workers' scribbles [*Geschreibe der Arbeiter*] should be edited. I've . . . decided only to improve the orthography, and the style in the most blatant spots, and also, wherever possible, to insert program points inconspicuously. As a sample, I'm sending you a letter (from among the worst), so you don't create a scandal later on. If one edits everything so that the unique character of its level of development, its manner of thinking and style remains intact, the result will be an issue that makes an impression on the entire world, like that letter for Engels in the *Condition of the Working Class*. It will cause a sensation everywhere. On the other hand, if we edit it intellectually, we'll rob it of its integral character—then the articles will be neither ours nor the workers'. I'd like to give the issue a completely original character that breathes life and truth. In the editor's introduction I will emphasize this comes from the "broader working masses."[33]

The end result, which was published as the "workers' issue" in March 1895, succeeded—in Luxemburg's eyes—precisely because she had preserved as much of the workers' texts as possible, standing her ground against Jogiches. The issue featured vivid, detailed reports about the working conditions in various factories in Warsaw and Łódź; about comparable dynamics in conflicts between workers, foremen, and employers at many sites; about fourteen- to sixteen-hour workdays; child labor; poor hygiene; catastrophic safety standards; and insufficient work breaks. The reports identified specific companies by name, contrasting the workers' "exploitation" with detailed descriptions of the few owners' extravagant "palaces."[34] In March 1895 Luxemburg wrote to Jogiches that this issue of *Sprawa Robotnicza* "from the workers' hand"[35] would provide enduring propaganda, showing the close ties of the editors and the young SDKP party to the "genuine" world of the "working masses":

I completely agree with you that the issue should express the workers' programmatic development, otherwise we gain nothing. But you didn't consider that it would be quite ridiculous and contrived to impute programmatic-agitational views to *every* article. I arranged the issue so it genuinely reflects the working masses as they are in reality. Out of twelve articles, two large ones are *exclusively* programmatic-agitational; the general content includes a few naive complaints and thoughts from the widest masses. In other [articles], views are scattered here and there, sometimes about the government, sometimes about inspection, sometimes about socialism, sometimes about the unions—in a few dashed-off opinions. Finally, the feature from Łódź looks back at the change in program and the movement's transformation from one of the "Proletariat" to Social Democracy. Together with the poems, the introduction, and the conclusion—from the editors—the issue certainly makes a tremendous impression. It has plenty of devastating facts from the life of the workers. All of the articles breathe life, truth, and sincerity. . . . Between the content and our connections, the issue will certainly make a colossal impression on the intelligentsia, and for the workers, it will certainly be one of the best agitation issues with lasting value. . . .

You have the air of an intellectual, there's no doubt about it. If your hand had been involved, there would certainly have been "your caricature" of know-it-all-workers, who—instead of eating, sleeping, speaking—would only have "agitated." In any case, you might have changed your opinion while editing.[36]

Luxemburg's effort to distance herself from "the air of an intellectual" at the end of this letter points to her increasingly confident self-image as an active politician. Since completing her studies, she had worked to place herself "at the forefront" of the "desperate economic struggle" breaking forth from the "miserable material situation of the Polish workers" in order to rouse these "indifferent masses," to give them "a unified plan, an organization," and to pursue this struggle in a "purposeful" way.[37]

Following these glimpses into the beginnings of Luxemburg's journey from journalism to party work—what Max Weber described as the "political fate" of many social democrats[38]—we must likewise examine her reception of Marx in the context of her dissertation and academic studies, which occurred at the opposite pole of her life between Paris and Zurich. A subtle mixture of ideological positioning and scholarly analysis characterized not only her dissertation, which was meticulously edited by Jogiches for publication,[39] but also her final exams. In the preface to her dissertation, she notably established the relevance of her topic by referencing the economic competition from Russia that threatened western Europe. The "mighty Empire of the North" had assumed an increasingly important role in European politics. The case of Poland as one of "the most important and most advanced industrial regions of the Russian empire" perfectly illustrated the political dimension of political economy. She wanted to show that the fiercely debated Polish question could be resolved only by recognizing that "the material development of society" holds "the key to its political development." Contemporary historians and other specialists agreed that Luxemburg's dissertation provided an empirically rich, important scholarly contribution to the analysis of this development—although, as she herself warned in the preface, she occasionally took "the liberty of doing some direct finger pointing of a political nature."[40]

In fact, Luxemburg's political temperament and already well-developed ideological resolve occasionally shone through, and not just in her dissertation. In her final examination in political economy (taken in the spring of 1897), she boldly introduced her discussion of Marx's theory of wages with the remark "[H]ere, like so many other areas of political economy, the real critique was first given by Marx." Thanks to his dialectical method, he had proven that in capitalism there was no fixed law of wages, but instead a flexible one, which accommodated the conditions and needs of production.[41] Capitalist production for the unlimited world market (the core idea of her later critique of imperialism, *The Accumulation of Capital*)[42] could grow and grow, and there would always be enough "capital and arms (in both senses)"—that is, enough money, working hands, and starving workers—to perpetuate this expansive system. She was so carried away by the end of the exam that the graders admonished her for "polemics"—especially for passages that sounded more like a political

tirade than an academic treatise: "The contemporary law of wages—
Marx cries—is worse than "iron"—it is elastic! Its name today is neither "wage fund," nor another special law, but instead—the entire
contemporary economy, instead—capitalism itself!"[43]

Luxemburg's teachers tolerated the ideological fury that shone
through in her academic work only because her intellectual achievement and knowledge of political economy were so impressive.
One grader remarked that political economy must be a "memory-
strengthening science" since it enabled Luxemburg to recall the exact
years that literary masterpieces first appeared: "Nearly a dozen of
these figures in an extemporaneous essay!"[44] The twenty-six-year-old
Luxemburg's scholarly achievement further shows how fundamentally her views were, by this point, influenced by Marxist principles.
In the introduction to her essay, she wrote:

> In political economic critique, as with all social scientific questions,
> two kinds of critique are possible. First, one can critique the content of
> a given theory in its own right, exposing its inconsistencies, its logical
> shortcomings. Second, one can view the object of criticism in histor-
> ical relation to those social facts that gave rise to the theory in question.
> In this case, the theory's objective material basis must be discovered
> and then considered not on its own terms, from a logical-theoretical
> standpoint, but instead from a material-historical one. The first crit-
> ical method judges absolutely, as a juror: as "guilty" or "not guilty"
> (or "true" or "false"). The second [method] considers the relativity of
> truth—namely, historically conditioned truth; it does not judge the
> theory, but only shows that the theory may be outmoded.[45]

This understanding of the "relativity" of the emerging social sciences foreshadows Luxemburg's stance toward Marx and his orthodox defenders in her main work, *The Accumulation of Capital* (1913).
Seeking to build upon Marx's premises about the behavior of capital,
she was criticized by orthodox Marxists for insufficient reverence toward the master. ("We believe," she summed up in her examination,
"that there is no more effective rebuttal [of criticism] than one that
explains in which social relation a doctrine was 'reasonable'"—and
thus, in which other ones it is 'nonsense.'")[46] Marx had always looked

for the "real," "sober," and "objective" facts within "social reality," and so during her studies, she came to see him as an exemplary relativizer of truth. Paradoxically, and precisely because of this relativizing insight, Marx could also be regarded as an absolutist of truth, as the founder of the "true" science of the laws of human history.

Similar to Lenin, Luxemburg did not accept that the description of reality was subjective, regardless of the statistics that informed this description. Her reverence for Marx's "discovery" of the link between being and consciousness had no more epistemological consequences for her than for Lenin. She approached the world and formulated her arguments as if there were only one possible perspective on "social relations"—or only one "prism" for viewing them, to borrow one of her metaphors. The following passage, from her review of Kautsky's edited first volume of Marx's *Theories of Surplus Value*, is a prime example:

> Marx does not treat the concept of "productive labour" as an etymological definition but as a historical category. . . . A *social relation* lies hidden behind the concept of "productive labour" as well as behind the concept of capital. Seen through the prism of that concept, capitalist society *emerges before us as if on the palm of our hands, in the clearest colors and contours*, in all the *objective madness* of its laws and in all the subjective perversity of its ideas; a society in which the innermost, the specific purpose of human labour, as it was given from God and nature, is the enrichment of others; a society in which exploitation is the norm, whereas labour for the worker's own good is regarded as an abnormality, a superfluity which serves no purpose; a society in which the ever-growing mass of people only fall under the concept of "productive workers" to the extent that they produce their own social slavery.[47]

Luxemburg considered the relativizing of historical insight (that is, the acknowledgment of relative "truths") as one of Marx's most valuable intellectual achievements. For this reason, however, she simultaneously revered him as the founder of a higher, "unshakeable" truth. In her examination she assured Professor Gustav Vogt that statistics could be interpreted in more than one way, but in the same breath she "indirectly" derived the validity of Marxist theorems by referring to "social phenomena that can only be explained by the *presumption* of advancing proletarianization."[48] This so-called dialectical method was openly constructed on "ingenious *hunches* at the great connections of the capitalist economy, on *intuitions.*" As a trained political economist, Luxemburg considered the "higher vantage point" of the socialist as he surveyed "the *limits* of the bourgeois economy form" to be "masterful and rigorously scientific."[49]

And so hypotheses turned into facts, or—as Plekhanov once stated—an idealistic worm became an omniscient god.[50] This intellectual operation from a "higher vantage point"—a position that Guesde, Kautsky, Plekhanov, and Lenin likewise claimed—corresponded with Marx and Engels's potent mixture of analysis and prediction in the *Manifesto of the Communist Party*. With their assertion at the end of the manifesto's first section, the two masters seemed to step out of history: "The development of Modern Industry, therefore, cuts from under its feet the very foundation on which the bourgeoisie produces and appropriates products. What the bourgeoisie, therefore, produces, above all, is its own grave-diggers. Its fall and the victory of the proletariat are equally inevitable."[51]

Luxemburg, like the other protagonists, developed a relatively early appreciation for the *Manifesto of the Communist Party*. However, the pamphlet's resonance among the post-1848 generations is still debated today. Hobsbawm has called it "the most influential single piece of political writing" since the *Declaration of the Rights of Man and Citizen* of 1789. This was certainly true in Marxism's founding years—not least because the text was perceived by some as a threat and by others as avant-garde. And yet, in contrast to Hobsbawm's assessment, closer analyses of the *Manifesto*'s reception history have shown that before 1870 it circulated only among a few veterans of the 1848 revolutions. Only in the last third of the nineteenth century did social democratic movements embrace it as a "cherished but somewhat dusty birth certificate of revolutionary socialism" and as "an early and abiding symbol of the political and intellectual independence of the working class," as Gareth Stedman Jones writes.[52] The pamphlet's "apocalyptic scenario" gained attention only after the (world) revolutionary events of 1917, losing its political and symbolic significance upon the collapse of the Soviet Union. Other scholars dispute whether its influence ever extended beyond the circle of organized workers, a few socially engaged bourgeois intellectuals, or the year 1917.[53] Among the protagonists in this book, however, the experience of reading the *Manifesto* overwhelmingly assumed a key role as the earliest intellectual exposure to the thought world of socialism. This exposure often resembled a rite of passage—true for Luxemburg, as well as for Guesde, Kautsky, Adler, Plekhanov, and Lenin.

Capital, by contrast, demanded years of study, and the protagonists sought to popularize it with their own writing. With *Capital*, Marx made his name as a scholar, "discoverer," and founder of an increasingly influential political movement. The heart of this movement was the idea of a collective historical actor that had emerged alongside capitalism. Marxist theory and terminology enabled the simultaneously empirical and predictive analysis of capitalist "anarchy" and the unfettered industrial market, promising not merely future salvation but a means to understand the present. This analysis involved class struggle as the motor of history, development governed by natural laws, a singular collective actor, and dissection of the capitalist "mode of production" with the assistance of memorable, and sometimes innovative, concepts and theories (surplus value, rate of profit, reserve army, commodity fetishism, invisible market laws). These ideas disciplined and structured the protagonists' earlier political engagement, which tended to have an anarchist, state socialist, or nationalist hue. Marxism gave their engagement rigor, direction, and support.

The chapters in Part II have traced the long birth of a political worldview. It was initiated by Marx and Engels in the 1840s, gradually gained a foothold in many European countries, and found political influence in the 1880s through the intellectual engagement of a handful of students who appropriated and publicized their teachers' doctrines. This worldview's mothers and (many more) fathers saw it as a "modern," "scientific" undertaking with far-reaching social and political consequences, which they considered inevitable.[54] They simultaneously understood it as a project of popular enlightenment—disseminating and publicizing (or, according to Kautsky, "translating") the insights of "scientific socialism" among the working "masses," whom they considered politically unaware, and considering how these insights might be usefully and practically implemented.

The individual protagonists' appropriation of Marx, usually through the *Manifesto* and *Capital*, occurred in the context of their first political experiences. I therefore describe it neither as a conversion nor as the outcome of a firm decision, but as a long and emotional process—a kind of tertiary socialization.[55] First-generation Marxism should not be understood as a "secular faith," in which true believers "voluntarily submit their actions to an absolutely defined cause."[56] Studying Marx was no act of submission, but was instead a hard-fought, radically secular, and sobering experience of illumination. Early Marxism promised enlightenment, not salvation. The early appeal of the Marx-Engels canon had more to do with its contemporary relevance and grounding in the present, and less with a hazy vision of the socialist future.

Leszek Kolakowski, who was a Marxist himself before he became a critical historian of Marxism, expressed this sentiment in a very personal interview: "It is true: Marxism attracted me—like so many people—through its having appeared to offer a rational yet unsentimental vision of history in which all was explained. Everything—only seemingly, of course—appeared understandable; not only was the past explained, but the future became transparent as well."[57] For the circle of intellectuals who established the Marxist school, the fascination with the enlightened promise of understanding the world—past, present, and future—cannot be emphasized strongly enough. Marx promised that knowledge was power. "Mighty knowledge" augured the liberating destruction of the existing order, not only for the Viennese worker singers of 1873 but for generations of socialists thereafter.

PART III

Engagement

On Misery, or the First Commandment: The Radical Study of Reality

I am asking you what you value more: the slow way, consisting of the writing of social novels and bureaucratic attempts to come to decisions on paper about human destiny for the next thousand years, while despotism swallows up the roasted morsels of meat which would fly into your mouths by themselves and which you are not allowing your mouths to catch; or do you hold to a quick solution, whatever it may consist of, but which will untie people's hands once and for all and will give mankind the freedom to build its own society, and that in fact, not on paper. . . . What makes you happier: a tortoise-like procession in the swamp, or crossing the swamp under full sail?

—Dostoyevsky, *Demons* (1871/72)

The first commandment of Marxism was the "radical" study of reality. As Marx asserted in his *Critique of Hegel's Philosophy of Law*, it was time for humans to move to the center of political philosophy. Theory had to demonstrate its views "*ad hominem*" and "grasp matters at the root"; the root for man was "man himself."[1]

"The essence of man," Marx stated in *The German Ideology*, "is not an abstraction inhering in isolated individuals. Rather, in its actuality, it is the ensemble of social relations."[2] Marx's call for philosophy as practice—which Engels later understood as a call to study "the whole of history" anew[3]—was a grand social scientific program that came to exert tremendous influence over political philosophy and practice, well beyond Marxism. All nine protagonists felt committed to this program, as my reconstruction of their readings on the previous pages has shown. In Part III, I turn to the protagonists' efforts to meet this factual and empirical challenge in their personal and other writings.

As I proposed at the outset, Marxism can be understood as *one* answer to the Social Question—even if Marx himself dismissed contemporary discourse around this question as sentimental nonsense. In his remarks on the Gotha program of the Socialist Workers Party of Germany (Sozialistische Arbeiterpartei Deutschlands), Marx criticized the naivete of Lassallean faith in reforms and "state aid" during the transition to socialism, even accusing Lassalle of reducing "class struggle" to a "newspaper scribbler's phrase": "*solving the social question.*"[4] Engels dismissed Lassalle's views just as firmly in a letter of protest to August Bebel. Engels, ever the theoretician, fumed about the Marxist ignorance of his German comrades who were engaged in practical politics: "As though in our case there were still a social question that remained unsolved in theory!"[5] His criticism was an expression of the ostentatiously unsentimental gaze that promised, at long last, an objective understanding of social conditions. This gaze exerted particular appeal among Marx and Engels's epigones.

The promise of sober, clear-eyed wisdom impressed all of the protagonists, even when their own engagement was also driven by feelings such as empathy or solidarity. Such empathy was not necessarily limited to the socialist "clientele," as Ute Frevert has shown in her work on the role of emotions in modern European history. Marxism's founding generation was not governed by a friend-or-foe mentality that precluded empathy with capitalists. Indeed, early Marxists felt a sense of obligation toward the thousands of master craftsmen—the "small masters" of the capitalist system—as Thomas Welkopp has shown with respect to Germany. My own analysis of the protagonists' readings of Marx shows that the shift away from well-intentioned bourgeois philanthropy toward politicized solidarity with workers can be understood as the (liberating) consequence of deep frustration—particularly in the case of moderates such as Adler, Bernstein, and Jaurès. Similarly, Frevert has considered how the move away from "wasted" empathy toward calls for justice affected the workers' movement since the French Revolution. In the long run, the political idea of class struggle seems to have destroyed the moral idea of universal solidarity.[6]

The conceptual and discursive history of the Social Question helps to illuminate these developments. The expression first appeared in France in the first third of the nineteenth century, and it was brought into German by Heinrich Heine. The Social Question identified problems that were associated with "accelerated industrialization," including the protection of industrial workers from life's unpredictable extremes.[7] Public discussions of pauperism and the Social Question reached an early peak around 1848. By the 1870s, the Social Question had become a standard fixture in philosophical and sociopolitical discourse that was inextricably linked to the emergence and political rise of the workers' movement. As late as 1905, the entry for "Social Question" in *Meyers Konversationslexikon* (a widely read German encyclopedia) referred readers to "Workers' Question" and opened with an explanation of the word "worker." By this encyclopedia's definition, a worker was a person who "expended energy to produce value"; to this extent, the Social Question was actually a "Wage Laborers' Question." It was one social problem among many—if also the most serious one, which explained and justified the synonymous usage of Workers' Question and Social Question. Its resolution involved society as a whole, and so it was eminently political.

Because the politicization of social concerns occurred simultaneously in many European countries (and thus was a thoroughly "transnational" phenomenon),[8] the Social Question became much more than a "newspaper scribbler's phrase." Indeed, it was a concept that actually *created* an experience—what Reinhart Koselleck has called an *Erfahrungsstiftungsbegriff*. Unlike other "-isms" and terms of working-class struggle that flourished around the same time—"proletariat," "class struggle," "International," and so forth—the Social Question was a "receptive" concept that illuminated a real historical experience. It held the intent and threat of a fundamental transformation, or an "opening to the future."[9] The concept's politically explosive potential was recognized (not only) by advocates of social reform, and—long before Frevert's critique of social justice movements—it emboldened intellectuals to make demands. This was the context for Hannah Arendt's disapproval of the politicization of the "quest for bread" since 1789, which Marx had driven to an extreme. Arendt worried that economic demands would dilute core Enlightenment principles: democracy, freedom, and human rights. And so, she argued, the belief that bread would bring freedom was a "fatal mistake," revealing how little Marxism was actually concerned about political freedom.[10]

Arendt's objections were not new, her rhetorical flourish notwithstanding. Observers around the turn of the twentieth century raised similar concerns. In 1899 the prominent Parisian critic and journalist from *Le Temps*, Francisque Sarcey, complained that the Social Question could no longer be avoided, even at the theater: "My ears are stuffed with politics all day long . . . and when I go to the theater in the evenings, once again I have to hear long treatises about the relationship between workers and owners."[11] Even critics in the social democratic press grew weary of plays so intensely partisan that they sacrificed not only the "truth of life" but also "art itself." Works such as Gerhart Hauptmann's *The Weavers* did, however, prove that art and social engagement were not mutually exclusive.[12]

In fact, the private premiere of Hauptmann's drama, which took place in Berlin in 1892, suggested the motif of misery to the artist Käthe Kollwitz, inspiring her remark that she always viewed misery with a mixture of "horror and love."[13] Her comment is paradigmatic for how the protagonists of this study saw and wrote about human misery. Many of their responses were characterized by this same dis-arming mixture of pathos and candor in the face of collective suf-fering and collective rebellion. Accordingly, these responses ranged from profound empathy to blatant revulsion.

Kollwitz's art was political, but not politicized; she worked to avoid the appearance of any tendentiousness, let alone agitation. Her work was defined more by empathy than "genuine revolt," and it was pre-cisely this "ambivalence of 'horror and love'" that saved much of her art from becoming propaganda.[14] This emotional ambivalence can be explained, in part, by the absence of a third element in Kollwitz's gaze toward reality: the outrage that all of our Marxists expressed in various ways. Outrage lent their engagement an enduring political dimension. Outrage is not a short-lived emotion but a passion that enduringly reinforces certain "emotional dispositions" and mobilizes them politically, as Oliver W. Lembcke and Florian Weber describe in their reflections on the relationship between emotion and revolu-tion.[15] According to Lembcke and Weber, passion does not necessarily muddle perception and reason, but it "corrupts" these faculties by making them serve a purpose that is ostensibly universal: eliminating the grounds for outrage. This fateful tendency shows us *one* way that emphatic horror sometimes turns into fascination—as evident partic-ularly in Luxemburg's relationship to misery and violence.

The socially engaged art of Kollwitz can help us situate Marxist discourse within the social, aesthetic, and literary "discovery of misery"[16] at the end of the nineteenth century.[17] Further, Kollwitz's genre-defining efforts to depict social realities in the visual arts raise concerns that are also significant to our nine Marxists' reflections: "This 'hunt' for reality and its authentic portrayal necessarily involves technical, economic, and ideological considerations, as well as inten-tional distortions. Anyone who turned toward 'real' misery and sought to show it moved in this complex and contradictory web. Depending on the weight of these considerations, those who were portrayed disappeared behind their portraits, and the reality of their portrayers became that much more visible."[18]

Teasing out the fine difference between the misery that was portrayed and the portrayer's own reality is as important as identifying the considerations and distortions that informed the portraits themselves. In effect, we are dealing not with images *of* misery (*Bilder des Elends*) but images *created from* misery (*Bilder vom Elend*), as Kollwitz herself identified her early works in the journal *Simplicissimus*. Kollwitz's use of the preposition "from" foregrounds the role and presence of *her* reality in the drawings.[19] Further, the context and purpose of all depictions of reality—particularly textual ones—are highly significant. Unlike works of visual art, the protagonists' correspondence, diaries, and other personal writings were not immediately intended for public consumption. In the following pages, I analyze such private texts alongside published works and speeches. Comparing private and public texts provides further insight into the protagonists' worlds of experience, their ways of approaching the world, and their (often subliminal) intellectual and emotional dispositions.

By emphasizing the study of reality, Marxism became a social science. Realism gave the Marxist worldview its aura and long-term potential for ideological mobilization. This potential was not exhausted until the second half of the twentieth century, when the declaration of "actually existing socialism" exposed the failed utopia. Marxism united some of the late nineteenth century's most important intellectual historical developments—including the "discovery of misery," the *Verwissenschaftlichung* of social relations, and the factual gaze. With all this mind, in the following pages I analyze the protagonists' own remarks about the living and working conditions of workers. Drawing upon examples that address the Social Question in a variety of ways, I illuminate the social-historical context of the emergence of Marxism.

Beyond the well-studied question of how intellectuals and "bourgeois radicals" (mis)understood workers and constructed them as "proletarians,"[20] my focus here is on the specific content of these depictions. I am less concerned with the "working class" as a part-real, part-imagined clientele, and more with how the conditions of their existence were portrayed. Improving these conditions was a cause that all of the protagonists rallied behind.[21] I do not restrict my focus to industrial wage labor but also include agricultural work and "labor market" prostitution. This geographic and historical journey leads to metropolitan London and Paris, factories in Vienna and St. Petersburg, and rural communities in southern France. I consider the various forms of the protagonists' engagement, which ranged from agitation, labor conflicts, and parliamentary reforms, to the first Russian Revolution of 1905–6. Stepan Trofimovich Verkhovensky, Dostoyevsky's protagonist in *Demons*, describes this as a spectrum between the slow, marshy path of writing and the path of the "quick solution, whatever it may consist of . . . which will untie people's hands once and for all"—a spectrum, in other words, between engaged observation and actual intervention in political affairs.

10

Miserable Lives

The Everyday World of Proletarians and Peasants

The protagonists' lifeworlds have played an important role in the first two parts of this book. By retracing their paths of socialization, we have seen that only four of the young protagonists—Guesde, Bernstein, Jaurès, and Plekhanov—had close childhood contacts with the "common" people of Paris or Berlin, southern France or central Russia. In the context of their later politicization, by contrast, all of the protagonists had various encounters with the "exploited" and disadvantaged, whose interests they sought to represent and promote. The propertyless majority of society—Lassalle's "eighty-nine percent"—largely survived on wage or day labor, or else on alms or public assistance.[1] The framing of the *Communist Manifesto* meant that self-identified Marxists focused overwhelmingly on the former group, dismissing the latter as "social scum" (*verfaulte Lumpenproletarier*), and declaring the "property question"—not the "poverty question"—to be the movement's central issue.[2]

Beyond everyday, coincidental, or passing encounters, the protagonists' exposure to the living and working conditions of wage laborers usually did not occur on its own. Their early social democratic engagement was often limited to the "party milieu"[3]—newspaper

offices, taverns, or gatherings of organized workers. Encounters beyond this milieu were rare—which is to say, in the terminology of
the sociologist Alfred Schütz, that it was rare for them to step away
consciously from their own social world (*Umwelt*) and circle of peers
into the less familiar world of contemporaries (*Mitwelt*). Thus, in
these two different worlds, the protagonists observed and acted with
different "conceptual perspectives" and "degrees of intimacy."[4] Their
surviving references to the working-class *Mitwelt* are often incidental;
investigative tours like Adler's were the exception, not the rule. The
protagonists more often entered the everyday world of the lower
classes for various professional reasons (broadly defined)—Bernstein,
Jaurès, and Luxemburg to agitate for their respective parties; Guesde,
Lenin, and Plekhanov to plan strikes and demonstrations in Paris or
St. Petersburg. Adler's proximity to working-class misery was exceptional; as a doctor for the poor, he gained intimate access to
Viennese living conditions long before his Social Democratic party
career.

Kautsky and Struve had the least contact with the lower classes.
Struve came across as clumsy, or even speechless, when conversing
with workers; he had little to say about any of his encounters with
them.[5] In his work he mostly referred to statistical and scholarly literature or to contemporary political journalism. He was interested in the
workers' lifeworld, but his discussion of it was always abstract. His own
assertion that he drew inspiration and information less from books
than from life itself is hardly supported by his own writings. Kautsky's
epistolary remarks about his encounters with workers at lectures and
demonstrations in Zurich or London reveal his long-standing discomfort around the "poor devils" and the "masses."[6] He styled himself
an "intellectual leader of the party" while he was still a young scholar.
French workers reminded him of "children—amiable, naive, entirely
governed by their emotions," and he distinguished between the "quiet
and respectable . . . actually working proletarians" and the "depraved
Lumpenproletariat."[7] As Kautsky later described in his memoir, the
worker for whom *he* wrote and engaged was the "proletarian who

participates actively in the class struggles of his time, who was educated in and by them; who has learned to think independently, to
break away from the traditions of his forefathers; who reads the newspaper regularly and attends public meetings, gleaning from them a
certain mass of general public education and knowledge about the
state of the world."[8] Kautsky was interested in a theoretical ideal type,
not "man himself," as demanded (more emphatically than literally)
by a reality-obsessed Marx. And when Kautsky criticized colleagues
for being "out of touch"—as with Bernstein during the revisionism
debate in 1905, or the Genevan émigrés around Plekhanov—he was
invariably referring to party structures and attitudes, not the everyday
life of workers.[9]

The connection that Adler—and to a certain extent, Luxemburg—
felt and articulated was altogether different. Both Adler and Luxemburg
tended to romanticize their personal writings, whereby Adler's view
of his environment was much more realistic. In the midst of a personal crisis at the end of 1891—Emma Adler was again suffering from
depression, and the couple was deeply in debt—he described his existential dependency on the "earthy smell of proletarians." Persecution,
imprisonment, and battles with political opponents were "nothing"
compared to the tedious disputes ("ignorance, pettiness, brutality")
within his own camp. "Forgive me for being so sentimental," he wrote
to Engels, "but I always get this way when I've been out of touch for
some time with the workers, with the masses. Compared to the giant
Antaeus, I'm wholly lacking, but what I share with him is feeling
mighty and powerful when I detect the earthy smell of proletarians
around me, while I fold up like a pocketknife when I'm alone."[10]
Behind Adler's evocation of a physical connection to "proletarians"
lay genuine interest and engagement in their experiential world. This
was the source of his great popularity, capacity for integration, and
charismatic presence—all of which elevated him, even within his lifetime, to the status of a working-class savior, as illustrated by a postcard printed by the Viennese brick workers in honor of his sixtieth
birthday.

Postcard in honor of Victor Adler's sixtieth birthday; the two images compare
the status of the brick worker in 1887 and 1912.
Credit: Verein für Geschichte der ArbeiterInnenbewegung, Vienna

Luxemburg made an entirely different impression. The charismatic aura of the melancholy fighter is a largely posthumous
invention—surely one consequence of her cruel death. Many of her
contemporaries viewed her as a compelling but polarizing personality.
Although she was a Polish émigrée, her spoken German was soon
outstanding, and she once wrote that she felt as comfortable on a
speaker's podium as in her own bedroom.[11] Her descriptions of social
realities varied widely, according to context and audience. Her public
statements—beginning with the Polish-language articles in *Sprawa
Robotnicza*, which accompanied the "workers' scribbles" (described in
Part II)—were highly stylized appeals that sought maximum rhetorical effect. The fate of the exploited was a bottomless source of inspiration for her arguments.

Most of her speeches and writings had to do with intellectual and
economic history, with foreign, trade, or military policy, or with party

strategy and tactics. Her discussion of "circumstances" or "conditions" was usually confined to social statistics and macroeconomic data. She conveyed their dramatic impact with rhetorical flair, but her depictions often remained abstract and broadly drawn. She believed that "facts and numbers speak a language of life" and that they released "devastating screams of misery, exploitation, and subjugation."[12] After all, according to Marx, human labor was "nothing but *money*."[13]

In her personal letters and conversations, by contrast, Luxemburg seemed radically open to new impressions, even to the point of overstimulation. She valued the immediacy of an experience and promptly committing it to paper. She was easily carried away by impressions from the "outside world," and she reveled in her own stories. She nevertheless demonstrated striking ambivalence toward the suffering of others and a certain distaste for unsavory circumstances— evidence of conditional empathy. She often felt repulsed by the "crush of humanity," by "filth" or noise on the street—sometimes wanting even "to shut myself off completely from the outside world, to board myself up." And while Adler declared that the "masses" revitalized him, Luxemburg felt drained or even "insulted" by their intrusions: "I don't know if the problem is that I'm made of such poor stuff that I absorb too readily from the surrounding atmosphere," she wrote to her friend Robert Seidel in Zurich in June 1898, "but I cannot remain one day longer in the crush of humanity without my own spiritual level declining at least one notch. And it actually doesn't depend so much on the kind of people I'm interacting with; the interaction itself is the thing, the contact with the outside world that rubs off and erases my own edges and sharp lines—but of course that's only for the moment."[14]

The ambivalence of Luxemburg's approach toward reality should not be confused with Kollwitz's feeling of being torn between "love and horror." Kollwitz never articulated revulsion in her pictures, while Luxemburg was unafraid of a mass revolt (to the contrary—this is what she longed for). Rather, the private Luxemburg observed social misery from a paradoxical perspective of distant empathy. Her remark to Seidel in August 1902—"I am most humane when I don't see anyone"—aptly expressed her need for distance.[15] This is especially evident in letters that recount new impressions, as in the summer of 1898, when the twenty-eight-year-old Luxemburg returned to her Polish homeland after a long absence. It was her first trip as an unofficial agent for the SPD in Silesia. She wrote to Leo Jogiches from one of her waystations:

> About personal matters, there's so much I could write (just think!— so many new impressions!) that I don't know where I should begin, and most important, I don't have a moment's peace. The surroundings here have made the strongest and most emphatic impression: cornfields, meadows, woods, broad expanses, and Polish speech and Polish peasants all around. You have no idea how happy it all makes me. I feel as though I've been born anew, as though I have the ground under my feet again. I can't get enough of listening to them speak, and I can't breathe in enough of the air here! Yesterday I had to wait for about an hour for the last train to Leschnitz [Polish name, Lesnica]. I crept around there in the fields of grain a little, and picked cornflowers and poppies. For my complete happiness there was lacking only "one." . . . Meadows with cows, being watched over by a five-year-old barefoot child, and our [favorite] pine forests! And our peasants, emaciated, unwashed, but a magnificent race! In Kandrzin I saw three families, two peasant families and one Jewish family, who were going to America! What poverty! It almost brought me to tears, but at the same time I was so happy to see them I couldn't keep my eyes off them.[16]

Here Luxemburg's nostalgia for her homeland combined with her observations of the needy, who filled her sentimental portrait almost as a natural part of the scenery—at once concrete and nebulous, sympathetic and pathetic, realistic and romantic. In December 1899 she described another visit to Silesia ("semi-Asia") in similar terms: the miners, black with coal dust, who had walked two hours to hear her speak at a meeting were "humorous and touching at the same time." The "very nice," "naive" comrades had received her warmly, and she was moved by their attention. Ever the alert activist, Luxemburg also learned that these "people with strong feelings" were especially approachable over a glass of beer.[17]

Luxemburg's loyal and perceptive friend Henriette Roland Holst interpreted her ambivalent empathy as an expression of her "strong need to idealize life." Luxemburg even poeticized suffering: "However ruthlessly her keen reason dissected the elements of reality, her poetic disposition—moved, in its quiet chamber, by yearning and expectation, adulation and adoration—blithely kept weaving the golden fabric that allowed a part of this reality to glisten in unreal beauty. This was a dichotomy in her nature that she never entirely overcame."[18] The discourse of (German) inwardness is apparent not only in Roland Holst's description but in the temperament she described.

Luxemburg shared these thoughts only in her private correspondence, and—even here—relatively seldom. Occasionally, however, she published highly subjective accounts of actual events in the party press, stylizing these narratives to an extreme that was astonishing and otherwise unknown to many contemporaries. One example is the story of Wilhelm Histermann, a thirty-eight-year-old Berlin salesman who was going blind and who killed himself and his two daughters on 26 April 1899. There is no indication that Luxemburg knew anything more about him than what she had read in a fifteen-line newspaper article. And yet she (anonymously) published her own version of the story in the *Leipziger Volkszeitung* on 4 May 1899, transforming the murder-suicide into a vivid, much-embellished fable of "gasping and sputtering big city life": A "fading human life trembled in terrible agony" behind a "thin wall," struggling with "spiritual and physical loneliness" and dying helplessly. Utterly captive within society, he exercised his humanity and chose the "boundless" freedom of death. Bourgeois "society" was unconcerned about this tragedy until it was too late—dutifully "taking possession of the corpses, recording the dramatic conclusion of three lives," and simultaneously cloaking them in a "veil of invisibility." This society had "burst" all bonds between people, compelling them to take their own lives and murder [their] children." And as for "ourselves, every day with a bored glance, don't we fly over the 'miscellaneous news' on the next-to-last page of our daily newspaper, this great garbage bin, into which of the refuse of bourgeois society ... is unloaded daily?"[19]

Luxemburg paired her empathy—heightened here to the point of fiction—for "a human life" in a "monstrous" bourgeois society ("inhumane, deaf, blind") with her "jaded," disgusted callousness toward the social "garbage" of her day. Moved and repelled at once, she proposed total solidarity with the "millions of victims" of this system. Her authentic but embellished depiction was sensational and effective, and it quickly established her reputation as an uncompromising defender of the "common" man. Her rhetorical brilliance impressed even her opponents, as there were few others who could report on current events at the same intellectual and verbal level. Further, her gender and Jewish Polish heritage lent her an "exotic" aura that she made no effort to conceal; to the contrary, she played it up in just these kinds of texts.

Her article's introduction and conclusion drew upon the somber, woeful world of eastern European legend, demonstrating the extent to which her imagination and empathy—and thus, her way of appropriating the world—remained rooted in her homeland. She introduced her story of contemporary hopelessness with a Polish proverb ("Before the sun rises, the dew will ruin our eyes"), and she concluded with the eerie Slavic legend of Viy, the iron man, who rose from the depths of the earth, whose iron eyelids dangled to his feet. His gaze alone, the story went, could destroy evil spirits that roamed the earth's surface—invisible, supernatural forces that "defiled and killed and drank human blood." In Luxemburg's account of the impoverished Berlin family, the desperate father symbolized the "man of the iron muscles, the iron hammer, the iron wheel—*the man of labor*." Although in reality he had died, in Luxemburg's telling he rose from the "dark underground, into which society had banned him," onto the "sunny earthen surface," and Luxemburg herself raised his iron eyelids, allowing him to "*see* and extend his iron hand, so that the invisible evil spirits, which had plagued humanity for millennia, sank powerless to the ground."[20]

These scenes of rural misery and urban desperation reflected the subjective sensibilities of their illustrator much more than the actual families, whose fates became manifestations of universal gloom. Those who were portrayed disappeared behind their portrayer.[21] While Adler—who was metaphorically refreshed by the "earthy smell of proletarians"—had engaged for years with the real conditions in which the lower classes lived and worked, Luxemburg's engagement with misery was limited to romanticized (or even fictionalized) outrage over individual fates, apparently selected at whim. Concrete social experiences could be reflected with various degrees of abstraction, and Adler and Luxemburg embodied the two extremes in an ideal-typical way.

How much we know about the childhood, youth, and everyday experiences of the first Marxist intellectuals depends not only on the diversity of these experiences and the available documentation but also on the protagonists' own need to explain their motivations— to themselves and others, or else for posterity. Bernstein, Kautsky, Plekhanov, and Struve wrote relatively detailed memoirs or other autobiographical texts, while Lenin, Luxemburg, Jaurès, Guesde, and Adler spoke sparingly, even reluctantly, about their childhood and youth—sometimes incidentally, in letters (Lenin and Luxemburg) or as anecdotes in speeches (Jaurès and Adler). In all cases, the protagonists' social and family background determined the intensity of their contacts to "average" people.

Accordingly, these contacts were closest for the young Bernstein and Guesde, who grew up in lower-middle-class households in Berlin and Paris, playing with workers' children in their neighborhoods and recalling similar experiences. As an old man, Bernstein adopted the voice of a lifelong social democrat who had remained true to his ideals when he recalled the "sentimental" singing outside the window of his childhood home; it was an "echo of the sentiments . . . troubles, and woes" of the "poorer classes," who, like all afflicted peoples, accompanied their everyday routines with mournful songs in a minor key. Further, he recalled that as a seventeen-year-old, he had watched working women in Zurich carry bricks up a mountain, witnessing how "each time that they emptied their load, they sashayed gracefully down the mountain in serpentine lines, singing in an evidently joyful mood."[22] Bernstein excelled as a mediator between social milieus. As a young man, he was readily accepted into the culture of local workers' associations in Berlin; his "sincere—that is, unreserved engagement" was perceived as such and respected, not least because of his familiarity with working-class life.[23]

Interacting with the "average" residents of Berlin and its outlying areas was a formative part of Bernstein's young adulthood. In the years of his double life as a social democrat and bank clerk, he often drank with workers and joined their Sunday excursions. His writings from the 1880s and 1890s are sprinkled with everyday anecdotes that reflect a genuine and detailed interest in working-class lifeworlds. He was familiar with workers' social routines, and he instinctively addressed them as "comrades" or used the informal "you." Later, during his exile in London, he reflected on the predicament of working men who understood the necessity of striking but also worried about supporting their families. And he recounted his conversations with these men without a hint of condescension:

> On the eve of the great English engineers' strike of 1897/98, one of the participating engineers—a married worker—explained to me that he was not at all enthusiastic about the strike. He had a good position, had just gotten settled in a small house with a garden, and having to give it all up now would be disastrous for him. When I responded that it was uncertain whether or not he would have to move, he replied: "Once blood has flowed, there will be real war." Meaning that any kind of a strike would necessarily lead to a very bitter and drawn-out struggle. Despite such a pessimistic view . . . once the strike became a reality, the man fought along loyally until the end.[24]

We have no similarly detailed descriptions of Guesde's encounters with workers, although he, too, came from a family of modest means. His speeches and articles about the Social Question consistently took aim against the same infuriating truths about the ongoing class war;

like Luxemburg, he wrote with a mixture of rhetorical force and an obsessive love for statistical detail. As we have already seen, even before his turn toward Marxism in the mid-1870s, Guesde favored colorful language and often repeated the same metaphors and quotes: the Social Question was like the sun; anyone who didn't see it was blind. The world was divided into workers without property, and property without work. Class struggle was not a Darwinian struggle for survival; people could end the capitalist struggle of "each against all."[25] Even the "perfected, *automated* machines" that increasingly competed "with the worker for his *place in life*," rationalizing it away, could ultimately be transformed into forces of good, into "'gods' for the worker."[26] Like Luxemburg, Guesde was fond of peppering his arguments with statistics—although this demonstrative precision ultimately served a version of reality that was highly abstract.[27] And unlike Bernstein, he rarely used personal anecdotes to support his standpoint or illustrate his outrage.

The other protagonists' correspondence and written work contain almost no significant conversations with individual workers. The few exceptions are largely in Jaurès's and Adler's papers. Kautsky and Luxemburg mentioned, in passing, everyday encounters related to party work, as when Luxemburg inquired about printers' wages in order to negotiate a lower price for producing a brochure.[28] Thus, the study of social reality was rarely a dialogue with the persons who occupied it, but more often was a monologue about them. Indeed, this corresponds with Thomas Welskopp's observations about the artisanal class pride that shaped the early social democratic movement: "One did not communicate *with* subordinates, but rather *about* them, as a person of higher social standing. The symbolically outstretched hand toward the 'Lumpenproletarier' intentionally kept them at a distance."[29]

Bernstein, on the other hand, did recognize and note the relevance of Sunday church attendance and the persistence of artisanal traditions.[30] He was interested in how workers spent their free time, and the personal consequences of state repression. From Zurich, for example, he explained to his friend Kautsky about the spiral of violence that occurred in clashes with the police, and he reported to Engels about his sobering conversations with newly politicized workers.[31] In his disputes with rivals within the party, he always emphasized the importance of "face-to-face meetings." And after the outbreak of the revisionism debate, he pointed to the growing support for his theses not merely in the "'salon' and study" but also in the "workshop and proletarian tavern."[32]

In contrast to Bernstein, Kautsky's childhood memories centered around the artistic and intellectual aura of his family home. References to the wider world beyond his "family of intellectuals" were rare and often patronizing. He described his summer vacations in the Bohemian countryside as an opportunity to "get to know the agrarian question." As a boy, he found the "lifestyle of the peasants . . . very simple and monotonous," although "there were also some wealthy peasants who lived in luxury." In general, however, "small farming" prevailed: "It was poor, but did not degenerate into dirty or hopeless poverty. I encountered great cleanliness and gaiety everywhere."[33] Kautsky initially knew even less about urban workers. When he joined the Viennese social democrats in the early 1870s, he had yet to get to know the "proletarian psyche . . . proletarian striving and aspirations."[34] We have already seen how rarely he mentioned actual workers in his letters. These contacts must have been so unusual for him that he described them in close detail. In a letter to his mother, he recounted his "exhilarating" discussion with a "poor tailor" about the weaknesses of one of her novels. Significantly, Kautsky used "poor" not to describe the tailor's living conditions but rather his difficulties understanding the end of Minna's novel.[35]

The proximity to the workers that Kautsky (over)emphasized in his letters and written recollections did not correspond to his actual knowledge about "proletarians." Instead, he saw "theoretical study" as the key to understanding reality. Although "many a Philistine" might look upon scientific socialism "as a purposeless building of castles in the air," Kautsky wrote in *The Road to Power* in 1909, it "is in reality the result of the deepest study, and consequently is based upon the most careful consideration of reality."[36] Kautsky's attitude underscored his need for abstraction. He fretted constantly that his closed theory would be destroyed by "empiricism and eclecticism" or, in the case of Bernstein, by "plain skepticism."[37]

Unlike Kautsky, who justified his expertise in the "agrarian question" with his summer vacations in the countryside, Jaurès grew up among peasants—an experience that informed his own, far-reaching conclusions on a very different level. Drawing upon childhood memories, he believed that he knew and understood how peasants lived and thought. This sense of familiarity fed his idiosyncratic emancipatory optimism. In content and substance, Jaurès's writings about the French peasantry from the 1880s and 1890s most closely resembled Adler's texts about workers. As we have already seen, Jaurès had a lifelong, heartfelt affection for country life. The academically trained philosopher was described by his contemporaries, without condescension, as a "cultivated peasant" who had been shaped by the impressions of his childhood and youth.[38] This was a highly significant affinity, given the strong agrarian influence on French economic life—particularly since the agricultural program of Jaurès's Marxist rival, Guesde, and his French Workers' Party, was so incoherent and detached from actual conditions in the countryside. As Robert Stuart has shown, the POF initially banked on "revolutionary hope," "polemical efficacy," and the schematic rhetoric of class struggle, instead of what they denounced as "sociological realism." However, the Guesdists' strategy actually impeded the spread of socialist ideas among the rural population.[39] In 1892 the POF finally passed a new agricultural program at its Marseille congress, using the results of a survey and other means to develop a more effective approach toward the needs and demands of the rural population. The following year, Jaurès stood for election with the party.[40]

Jaurès's thoughts on how collectivized agriculture might be practically introduced, to allow familial as well as communal ownership of land, helped the party gain acceptance in the countryside after the mid-1890s. It tripled its share of the vote to 5 percent between 1889 and 1893.[41] Jaurès believed that it was pointless to hope for the development of a strong proletarian movement in areas with few proletarians, such as the Albi plateau or the vineyards around Gaillac in his home region. He also pointed to Marx's remark (relayed by Engels) that revolution would be cheapest if the "big landowners could simply be bought out." And so, based on the latest scientific and technical advances, he pleaded for the gradual transformation of landownership into national, communal, or cooperative property, True to his revolutionary evolutionism, Jaurès foresaw an "almost unconscious" development that was nonetheless revolutionary. Small landowners, who had previously feared socialist expropriation, would learn "to unite their love of the soil, their old fanatism for property, with concern for technical progress," and they would ultimately grow into collectivism.[42] The Guesdists notably supported this reformist program, and thus played their part in the eruption of a years-long debate around the agrarian question—which would occupy not only French politics but also German social democracy and the Second International into the early twentieth century.[43]

Similar to Adler, Jaurès connected his intellectual reflections with (often sensual) memories of peasant life, thereby drawing conclusions for his political thought. In an article about the "peasant mentality," published shortly after his failed bid for reelection to the National Assembly at the end of 1889, Jaurès wrote about "real peasants" and the need to promote "individual thinking" in "rural democracy." He thereby revisited his life's theme, the central role of education for personal and social well-being:

> The political and moral education of the peasants is of great importance. Its success depends on loving the peasants and knowing them well. The peasant is a serious human being. He has to work hard, save, and be wary. He does not waste his intellect on follies and trifles; he uses his mind not as a toy, but a tool. He is not a heckler or a fantast;

he knows nothing about what they call flimflam in the cities. I'm speaking about real peasants, the ones who have grown up with their fields, who plow and sow. . . . This sober peasant spirit means . . . taking pleasure in the most insignificant joke. One example: It's the wine harvest, and in the vineyards many men and women are making wine; the sound of bells comes down the hill and through the sun-drenched air. A peasant woman says with a knowing expression: "Someone over there is hanging himself"—namely, the bell ringer on his rope. It's an old and tired joke, but everyone takes pleasure in it; they retell it, too, and find it to their liking. This is why the bright minds in the village have such success among the peasants. Once these untried, profoundly earnest souls have been animated, they can converse about the smallest thing. . . . It's our task, bit by bit, to bring independent thinking into rural democracy.[44]

This passage highlights Jaurès's apparent familiarity with rural life and his respect for peasant culture, songs, and idioms (which demonstrated "poetic sensibility," despite having little to say about the "beauty of nature"). Further, it illustrates how Jaurès, based on his experiences growing up, was sure that he could both enlighten and direct "the" peasants toward political emancipation. These generalized and paternalistic assessments about the peasant character reveal as least as much about the soul of the "portrayer" as those who were portrayed. Even so, Jaurès's remarks attest to a sophisticated interest in the particular— an intellectually distanced, yet humane empathy that sought to grasp the essence of the peasantry as a lived experience. In the same text about the mentality of the peasants, Jaurès wrote that he "knew old men" who returned from work and lay on the dark earth (under which they would soon disappear), speaking about death with a kind of awed resignation: "'Everything will be over soon,' they said, 'and no one comes back from there.'" Jaurès concluded that many peasants' ideas about life and death apparently conflicted with those of the church: "The peasant holds in his consciousness, without knowing it, two opposing ideas." Yet no conflict arose for the peasant because "he doesn't reflect enough; [the two ideas] are simply contrary." On the one hand, the peasant believed in the church's vision of the hereafter.

On the other hand, "because his whole existence consists of arduous manual labor and a struggle with the earth, he cannot imagine, or even feel, what part of himself should live on in another kind of existence; seen from this perspective, it seems that the earth, once it covers him, will also completely possess him."[45]

In contrast to Jaures's reflections, which were informed by personal experience, we can only speculate about the connection between upbringing and political thought in Plekanov's writings about the peasantry. As we have seen, the dissolution of his parents' estate was hardly a pleasant experience for him. He may have been as close as Jaurès to rural lifeworlds, but he sought no deeper understanding of them, nor did he recall them nostalgically. Nevertheless, his early writings about the peasantry were empathetic and reflective, and he grasped the hopeless situation that Russian social democrats encountered in the countryside. He composed his first programmatic text, *Socialism and the Political Struggle*, in 1881–82, while he was in exile but still close to his experiences with "rural agitation" in Russia. He addressed "our peasantry" in the final pages of the text, pleading for a realistic assessment of the prospects of winning them over to socialism. Even if Plekhanov did not believe that the peasants would first have to become "landless proletarians," their village communities "disintegrating under the influence of capitalism," he felt that the socialists' influence would necessarily remain limited in rural Russia and that "the opposition which they will inevitably encounter" should not be underestimated. On account of the peasants' living conditions, their lack of freedom and education, they were "less responsive" to the movement initiated by the intelligentsia:

> [The rural population] has greater difficulty in mastering the socialist teachings, because its living conditions are too much unlike the conditions which gave birth to those teachings. And besides, the peasantry is now going through a difficult, critical period. The previous "ancestral" foundations of its economy are crumbling . . . the new forms of labour and life are only in the process of formation, and this creative process is more intensive in the industrial centres. Like water

which washes away the soil in one place and forms new sediments and deposits in others, the process of Russian social development is creating new social formations by destroying the age-old forms of the peasants' relation to the land and to one another.[46]

These reflections departed significantly from Jaurès's attitude toward the "earnest souls" of the peasants in southern France. Plekhanov's discussion of the Russian village communities' precarious situation only indirectly conveyed his familiarity with the peasants' relationship "to the earth and one another," which Jaurès so emphatically described. Plekhanov's depictions of reality were entirely subordinate to whichever political strategy seemed best suited to bringing socialism to the rural population. The disappointing experiences of the Narodniks in the 1870s overtook his own memories of the Russian peasants' miserable living and working conditions. The image of naturally shifting social relations underscored the intellectual filtering of his own life experiences. Everything came down to the prediction of social revolution, a self-fulfilling prophecy—carefully packaged as analysis—that went hand in hand with socialist agitation. The new "sediments," "deposits," and "social formations," Plekhanov believed, "contain the embryo of a new social movement which alone can end the exploitation of Russia's working population." The industrial workers, "who are more developed and have higher requirements and a broader outlook than the peasantry," could be won over first. The new movement could then proceed flexibly and gain a foothold "among the people" over time.[47]

Less than a decade later, far removed from the political and social realities of this prophesied development, Plekhanov bitterly wrote of the peasants' degeneration into *Lumpenproletarier* (he favored the German term) or "barefoot gangs" (a Russian idiom). Mass migration from the Russian countryside had exposed the much-touted "power of the land" as a myth—truly no sign of a "splendid village idyll," as he wrote in an 1890 article for the *Neue Zeit*. Similar to Luxemburg, he embellished his abstract portrait with lurid salvos of words, painting the "crisis of the people" as a "lament" and "song of starvation" and drawing upon real-world examples only for rhetorical effect. Many peasants no longer returned to their villages after their seasonal quest for work, "neither in the winter, nor in the summer. In the spring they look for work, but in the winter . . . yes, what do they do in the winter?—They meander in various urban hideouts, spending the night in shelters." The following spring, anyone not fortunate enough to be able to sell his labor must "beg in Christ's name."[48]

In Lenin's case, a scarcity of sources complicates our ability to reconstruct a similar development. The aforementioned political pamphlets, which Lenin composed during the Petersburg strikes of the mid-1890s, are evidence of a once closer relationship that grew more detached, even before his exile. As with Plekhanov, Lenin's family was skeptical, if not outright hostile, toward the local peasants, and Lenin himself had no interest in managing an estate. When Lenin was a young boy, he was apparently rescued from a bog by a worker—but apart from this episode, we do not know anything about his experiences with the rural population. We do know that he had little practical knowledge about his countrymen's everyday lives.[49] The supposedly natural affinity with workers that was ascribed to Lenin during his lifetime can be traced back, at least in part, to Nadezhda Krupskaya's ease in dealing with ordinary folk. As a night school teacher in St. Petersburg, she engaged with workers directly. The compelling descriptions of human misery in her memoir, including a reprinted account by Maxim Gorky, provide a marked contrast to the few authentic depictions we have from her husband.[50]

Lenin's cool, even pitiless demeanor is broadly acknowledged today. As we saw in Part II, Lenin spoke with noticeable warmth only about close teachers or like-minded comrades. He was a high-achieving student who sought to extend the emancipatory project of the educated bourgeoisie to all ranks of Russian society; his parents had encouraged this project at home with deeply humanist intentions. And so Lenin obsessively read, studied, and analyzed, and he used the narrowly circumscribed freedoms of student life to join conspiratorial circles in Kazan and St. Petersburg. Toward the end of his studies, he began to take action by spreading his ideas about Russian conditions. For this, he was pursued by the police, arrested, and sent to Siberian exile. From this point forward, he was condemned to the role of distant agitator, in both political and family matters. Even in private correspondence with his family, he kept his personal remarks brief. As we saw in Part I, the twenty-seven-year-old Lenin wrote to his mother from detention in September 1897 about his brother Mitya (Dmitri), a medical student who aspired to treat plague victims: "Why is Mitya thinking of going where there is plague? If he is so anxious to travel and practice medicine I am ready to suggest a place at some resettlement centre. In Eastern Siberia, for instance. . . . All jokes aside, however, I really am surprised at his 'plague' plans; I hope there will not be any plague, and that he will not have to go there."[51]

Such a strong reaction is rare in Lenin's published letters to his family, which were usually quite matter-of-fact. The letter simultaneously reflects Lenin's view that one could alleviate misery without getting too close to it. The same cool realism was evident in Lenin's political correspondence, as in a letter to a comrade in Russia, written eight years later, about his newspaper work. Lenin reported that his new journal badly needed "*raw* material from Russia," that is, "articles on questions of Russian life," "correspondence of diverse length about everything," and "interesting passages and quotations from local Russian and special Russian publications." He added, "We shall be able to work it up from a literary angle and make use of it ourselves."[52] Here, too, Lenin's perceptions of Russian reality were indirect, acquired from and mediated by others. His actual interest was in politically exploiting the "raw material," not in the raw material itself.

II

Miserable Labor

The Proletarian World of Work

The first-generation Marxists led extraordinarily mobile lives. Travel and residence abroad, voluntary or otherwise, were part of all the protagonists' biographies. This mobility was reflected in their descriptions of travel, especially during their stays in large cities like Berlin, Paris, and London, arenas of the emerging "proletarian" world of work. Their fascination with the metropolis as a great hub of accelerated modernity often mixed with feelings of overstimulation and disgust about big-city noise and filth. On Kautsky's first visit to Paris, in 1881, he perceived the city as a large Vienna, and he had trouble imagining a productive life amid so many overwhelming distractions. He raved about London's beautiful parks and "pretty students," but otherwise saw only "cheerless" streets full of "architectural monstrosities."[1]

Jaurès had lived and attended school in Paris since 1876, but by his own account, he became more aware of the wider world only toward the end of his university studies. His few surviving letters from this period hardly mention big-city life, except that he was frequently plagued by migraines, exhaustion, and homesickness. Jaurès did recount his first conversation with "real" workers, which took place on his homebound train after he had visited the World Exhibition in Paris. Unlike the peasants he knew at home, "ces braves gens" were enthusiastic about the ideals and "drama" of the great revolutions, and he was impressed by their political passion and amusing "curiosité."[2] Jaurès later asserted that his early years in Paris were formative to his life. Goldberg writes that Jaurès was shocked and depressed by "the utter loneliness of men and women thrown together in that vast city." Jaurès himself recalled seeing "thousands upon thousands of people, passing each other without the slightest sign of recognition, each one completely isolated from all the rest." He asked himself "how they could accept it, how such an unjust social order could endure." These flashbacks (which recall Engels's description in *The Condition of the Working Class in England* of the "brutal indifference" and "unfeeling isolation" of life in London) also suggest an older politician's rhetorical gift for embellishing his mature worldview with hazy memories of the mass, anonymous misery of the Paris of his youth. Jaurès saw these workers as both the agents and the victims of a social system that, in his youth, he had neither wanted to—nor could have—revolted against.[3]

Luxemburg's letters and other private writings contained concrete, often romanticized observations about her urban experiences, while her public remarks remained more abstract. Life in the metropolis tended to repulse and disturb more than it fascinated her. She initially "hated" Berlin, and she found corners of it "proletarian," loud, stinking, and dirty. She felt the same way about Paris. After a walk through the city, she felt sick from exhaustion, and for two hours she lay "there powerless, white like a corpse, cold like ice."[4] These letters did not describe the misery she had observed, but—with the appropriate statistical underpinning, in line with the ideological and strategic needs of the party—that misery eventually found its way into her sociopolitical reporting. In one of her "economic and sociopolitical overviews" for the *Sächsische Arbeiterzeitung* in 1899, she suggested that the Parisian underclass (which she estimated at 10 percent of the city's two million inhabitants) was not a "support" but a "hindrance" to the workers' movement. The massive misery that defined Paris and every other modern metropolis was, as a "social *symptom*, a death sentence for the capitalist economy." An order in which millions of workers were abandoned to "complete pauperization" was an "abnormality, a madness," and incompatible with the "continued existence of society."[5]

Like the other exiles in this study, Luxemburg relied on the reports of others for information about her homeland. Her depiction of urban workers' misery during yet another famine in the tsarist empire, published in the *Leipziger Volkszeitung* in 1898, drew upon Russian newspaper accounts; these eyewitnesses had lifted the "veil of secrecy" from the "terrible" picture of "desperate privation." Luxemburg cited one source who had visited a working-class neighborhood in a "small city in the hunger zone." He had met half-naked, sick, and starving small children, who were wasting away on cold stone floors in miserable huts filled with "stink, smoke, and the stench of extreme misery"; those who could stand went begging or cooked soup from oak leaves and branches. Luxemburg cited this scene as the "symptom" of an emerging order that, through untold numbers of individual deaths, already carried the death of the system within itself. The capitalist government of the tsar sought new sources of income through major investments like the railway network because the once most important source—the peasantry—had finally begun to collapse. While the government's helpless, belated response to the famine demonstrated "every bewildering virtue of bureaucracy," "the peasants were falling like flies from hunger and sickness."[6]

At the same time, cities offered immense material and cultural riches. Struve and Lenin, who both traveled to Berlin as young men in the 1890s, reported only on the advantages of big-city life. Struve admired modern, adaptable westerners and their material prosperity; backwardness and misery were Russian problems.[7] In August 1895 Lenin (like Luxemburg three years later) enjoyed Berlin's "splendid" Tiergarten neighborhood; he swam daily in the Spree River, and he traversed the city easily by "urban railway." After the ban against Gerhart Hauptmann's *The Weavers* was lifted in October 1893 (the play's powerful message had rallied even the conservative press against censorship), Lenin attended a performance at the German Theater in the summer of 1895.[8] He focused primarily on his poor German-language skills, writing to his mother that he "could not catch all the phrases," even though he had read the "whole play" the night before. By day Lenin worked in Berlin's Royal Library (as had Struve in the summer of 1891), and in the evening he "wandered around," observing the "amusements and pastimes of the people."[9]

Lenin's stays in Paris unfolded similarly—in 1895, following a stop in "splendid" Switzerland, and in 1900, for the World Exhibition. He wrote home about his first visit in June 1895, in a letter that was unusually descriptive (by his own standards). Paris was

> a huge city, spread out a good deal, so that the suburbs (where I spend most of my time) give you no idea of the centre. It makes a very pleasant impression—broad, light streets, many boulevards, and lots of greenery; the people are quite unrestrained in their manners—at first it comes as rather a surprise after one had been accustomed to the sedateness and primness of St. Petersburg.[10]

His remark is a good reminder of how the protagonists' previous life experiences influenced their perceptions of the European metropolises. Luxemburg came to Paris and Berlin by way of orderly Switzerland; Kautsky came from Vienna and (later) Zurich; and Jaurès hailed from the southern French countryside. Bernstein was steeped in working-class life in Berlin before he moved to Zurich and London. Plekhanov, Struve, and Lenin knew only the restrictive "primness" of the tsarist empire before they set foot in western Europe. Adler was the well-traveled son of well-to-do parents; as an adult, he was the only protagonist who toured European industrial centers with a sociopolitical agenda.

Finding out something realistic about the everyday life of workers cost time and money; it also took intellectual and (not least) physical exertion. The classic text from the age of industrialization, Engels's *The Condition of the Working Class in England: From Personal Observation and Authentic Sources*, showed this determination more strongly than most. "After roaming the streets of the capital a day or two," Engels wrote, making headway with difficulty through the human turmoil and the endless lines of vehicles, after visiting the slums of the metropolis, one realises for the first time that these Londoners have been forced to sacrifice the best qualities of their human nature, to bring to pass all the marvels of civilisation which crowd their city. . . . The very turmoil of the streets has something repulsive, something against which human nature rebels.

In London, Engels saw himself as witness to "the dissolution of mankind into monads, of which each one has a separate principle, the world of atoms, is here carried out to its utmost extreme. . . . [T]he social war, the war of each against all, is here openly declared." He saw himself as a kind of war correspondent, reporting for a German audience on his front-line experiences in the most industrialized country in the capitalist world. He dedicated his polemic to the "working men" of England, who had become the first fighters in this "bloodiest war."[11]

In contrast to the brash Engels—who was, moreover, a battle-tested veteran of 1848—four decades later Adler engaged with the realities of capitalist production as an aspiring factory inspector. From July to October 1883, the thirty-one-year-old Adler traveled through England, Germany, and Switzerland on behalf of the Austrian Ministry of Trade. Anticipating the establishment of a new factory inspectorate in the Habsburg Empire, Adler reported on similar institutions and bolstered his credentials for this new office. He reported soberly on his visits and conversations, avoiding the pathos of a "misery tourist." Party bigwigs like Bebel and Engels emphatically supported Adler's undertaking; they had plenty of agitators but, as of yet, no allies in the state administrations. This is precisely where reliable people would be needed after the seizure of power, Engels is said to have remarked.[12]

As we saw in Part II, Adler's application was rejected. Nevertheless, his tour allowed him to get to know four closely interrelated, but often opposing, perspectives: that of the factory owners, the factory and workshop employees, and the state inspectors and civil servants, as well as the broader perspective of social policy. Adler subsequently built upon these experiences as Austria's Social Democratic Party leader and as the editor of the Viennese newspapers *Gleichheit* and (later) the *ArbeiterZeitung*. He went undercover to report on the scandalous living and working conditions of Viennese brick workers in 1888–89, and he participated in various fact-finding commissions for the imperial Parliament. Beginning in 1901 he served as a delegate in the Lower Austrian diet, and beginning in 1905 as a delegate in the imperial Parliament, focusing on worker protections, housing, public health, municipal waste disposal, and hospital construction.[13]

In 1884 Adler published the results of his factory inspection tour of England, Germany, and Switzerland in *Conrads Jahrbüchern für Nationalökonomie und Statistik*, and—under the pseudonym Dr. Fritz Tischler—he subsequently incorporated this work in essays that appeared in *Deutsche Worte*, a monthly journal edited by Pernerstorfer.[14] In these texts Adler analyzed the "organization, professional activity, and efficacy of the corresponding state institutions from [his] own perspective," considering employees' living and working conditions alongside the interests of factory owners and the procedures of individual inspectors. He recalled that, in all three countries, reform debates around worker protections had been sparked by child labor. In Germany and Switzerland, compulsory schooling had made the problem more manageable by reframing it in terms of state interest, and German and Swiss schools had become a "powerful ally of factory regulation."[15] In England, by contrast, factory owners were assigned responsibility for the schooling of children (known as "half-timers") in their employ. More or less independent factory doctors assessed the children's age and capacity for work. Adler described the consequences of this practice as follows:

> If one no longer finds (at least in the factories made accessible to me) the terrible conditions depicted by the Children Employment Commission into the 1860s, it is sad enough to see these "half-timers" who are permitted to work 4 1/2 hours a day, or nine hours three times a week. Having fallen behind in their physical development, they are almost all smaller than their birth certificates suggest, while their limp

features, tired eyes, and waxy yellow skin give their faces a sad, old character. If you see them leaving the factory in the afternoons, beginning a journey home that often takes hours, then you will understand that the results of half-day instruction, to which the employer is held by law, are so insufficient.[16]

Adult factory workers were better off. In general, labor protection in England was well developed and, for the time being, also accepted by employers. Factory owners had "come to see that they could survive with a nine-hour workday," and they had reconciled themselves to most provisions, or at least learned "to grin and bear them."[17] Adler contrasted these findings with conditions in smaller, "cottage" workshops—for example, in London's East End—where employers themselves were often poor artisans on the brink of survival. They often saw workplace regulations as an "imposition" and "incomprehensibly sentimental." They usually went no further than hanging up the guidelines in workrooms, although many employees—and some workshop owners—could not read.[18]

In contrast to England, inspection practice in Germany was decentralized, and thus very uneven. The law was "fragmented in a mass of ministerial decrees, government and police ordinances," and not uniformly implemented, even within the same branches of industry. Pointing to mirror factories that processed mercury in Berlin and Bavaria, Adler outlined the consequences of this inconsistency for owners (who viewed strict controls as a competitive disadvantage), as well as for their employees' living and working conditions. The conditions in barely regulated Bavarian mirror factories were especially unsettling:

I visited four of these. . . . Because factory managers stayed away from the worksites on Saturdays, I could speak with the workers undisturbed. I received the stereotypical answer from eight "masters": "All of us will get sick; some sooner, some later; we just work as long as we can." It's the same for the women who help the masters, and I met one who was in the late stages of pregnancy. No restrictions whatsoever on working hours; no rooms for washing, eating, or changing clothes. Overcoats were exchanged for [work] smocks, but these were left hanging in the workroom. How much mercury the workers must have carried home on their boots alone can be assessed by observing the floor, which has a positively metallic glow, even paved with asphalt. After staying for just a few minutes, you can taste the metal in your mouth. Several supervisors later assured me that laundry is done carefully at home; anyone who knows the habits of workers will find that improbable.[19]

Adler knew workers' everyday routines—how they lived, how they ate and washed, and what they did with their refuse.[20] After observing the practices of this factory in Fürth, he concluded that its conditions were unsustainable. He underscored the imperative of labor protection and hygiene, even from the perspective of factory owners (following Engels, who suggested that the "liberal bourgeoisie" could be defeated "by casting their own words in their teeth").[21] As a counterexample, Adler pointed to a strictly regulated Berlin competitor, even empathizing with his displeasure:

> The factory owner spoke openly about his, it seems to me, justified grudge about "the unequal and unjust treatment," but he admitted that he was actually not as disadvantaged as it might have first appeared. He previously had to exchange his people all the time, because one after another got sick, while in the last two years there had been no case of poisoning, and he had trained capable people.[22]

Adler composed his report for the Trade Ministry from the perspective of sociopolitical reason and the common good, and he concluded it with a measured summary. In assessing the advantages and disadvantages of English and German inspection practice, he emphasized how strongly implementation depended on the personality and motivation of individual inspectors, on local administrative structures, and on the uniformity of procedures. The more consistent and even-handed the controls, the less these could be evaded by "owners as a class." He praised Switzerland's young inspection practice, which was easily surveyed (on account of the relatively small industrial sector) and which combined the advantages of the other two countries. Beyond his own observations, Adler reviewed inspectors' reports and statistics from each of the three countries. For the

Austrian inspectorate, he recommended a thorough procedure that effectively reflected *and* synthesized the various case studies. All involved parties could learn from "the smallest and most inconspicuous" details. Of decisive influence, finally, was the personality of each inspector—and particularly the inspector's ability to cooperate with the workers, whom Adler himself believed he knew especially well. Workers in Austria, unlike those in England, had not fought for labor protections themselves, and they were less educated than Swiss workers. It was to be expected, therefore, that they would come to recognize the sense and usefulness of workplace regulation only over time. Adler's clearly self-referential conclusion: "And so—particularly with respect to the workers—knowledge of human nature, intellectual superiority, discretion, and tact are essential to implementing the law with rigor, but also with equity."[23]

Only a few years later, Adler—as a Social Democratic Party leader, editor, and member of Parliament—renounced his multiperspective approach to the common good. After the dispute surrounding the Viennese brick factories in the early 1890s (and others like it), he lost his faith in the government's will for reform, and he doubted whether the police and other authorities would accept, let alone fulfill, their state-mandated welfare obligations in the foreseeable future. The industrialization of Vienna and its outlying areas had proceeded rapidly since 1857, when Kaiser Franz Joseph had ordered the demolition of Vienna's city walls and fortifications, making way for the construction of the Ringstrasse and dozens of magnificent buildings. Between 1840 and 1870, the population had more than doubled, from 440,000 to 900,000 residents, and factories, railway lines, and the Danube canal sprang up around the city. The fast-growing financial and banking sector created immense opportunities for speculation and investment, and industrial production and workers' settlements clustered on the city's outskirts.[24]

Thousands of workers who labored in the clay pits on the city's south side lived on the grounds of the Wienerberg brick factory, which was founded in 1869. Their living and working conditions were notorious as the worst in Vienna. Local workers avoided "going to the brick ovens" whenever possible, and so mostly Czech and Bohemian "foreign workers" were employed at the factory. Their wages were lower than the minimum for survival (as calculated by workers' education associations), and they were not even paid in gulden, but in scrip that could be used only at company stores.[25] Practically speaking, this was compulsory labor. Based on his own research and what he learned from worker informants, Adler published a series of anonymous exposés in *Gleichheit* at the beginning of December 1888. His description of the factory's unlawful practices created a tremendous stir among Viennese readers: employees were treated like "slaves," with no freedom of movement; they were paid only indirectly; and they lived by the dozens in "workers' houses" that were monitored by factory security guards. The police opened an investigation—not of the factory but of the *Gleichheit* informants—and, in cooperation with the management, arrested Adler's contacts and searched the workers' residences for the offending issue of *Gleichheit*. In one of the articles, Adler reported on a woman who gave birth in a crowded bedroom, under terrible circumstances, "in the presence [of] 50 half-naked, dirty men." The woman and her husband were easy to identify in the report, and they were "chased away" by the factory management.[26]

But Adler could certainly point to successes, too. Factory inspections, which had been required by law since the mid-1880s, were gradually implemented. After the first visit from a state inspector, conducted just days after the initial exposé, the Wienerberg brick workers were henceforth paid in cash, as *Gleichheit* reported on 5 December 1888. In the same issue, Adler warned that inspections would need to continue into the future, and he called on the workers to organize, "to assert what had already been achieved."[27]

It was surely no coincidence that the articles appeared just before the Hainfeld congress, which unified the Austrian Social Democratic Party and called for labor protections at the year's end. The articles guaranteed that party unification gained momentum and attracted the greatest possible attention among workers. At the Hainfeld congress, just weeks after the eruption of the brick worker scandal, Adler described social misery as the necessary point of departure for a unified Austrian social democratic movement. Both crises were the end result of an "entire social process." There could be no more illusions about the efficacy of "bourgeois ideals." Only the power of the proletarian movement, which had been "discovered" by Marx, would lead to socialism. At last, the Austrian workers had outgrown their childish ways.[28] From this point forward, Adler increasingly described social misery as a systemic failure, and the suffering majority as a structurally marginalized "class," which—as a self-conscious "proletariat"—necessarily opposed the existing order, the police state, censorship of the press, unfree elections, and social exploitation. Thus, in the debate around fighting tuberculosis, he no longer limited his focus to details about hygiene or residential infrastructure but instead warned that "the fabric that torments the people, like the Shirt of Nessus, is not only woven from the weft, but the warp. The bacilli are the weft, but the infection is the warp; this is social misery in all its forms." In short, the question of tuberculosis was a "question of class."[29] On his factory inspection tour, Adler had shown understanding for business interests and state supervisory bodies' limited room for maneuver. After the 1880s, however, he no longer expressed this view publicly—not only because competitive pressures had enabled the conditions at the Wienerberg brick factory but also because his own voice had become increasingly partisan, as the highest representative of the "proletarians" (as he now usually identified workers).[30]

Adler took a similarly decisive stand a few years later, in the debate around banning white phosphorus in the matchstick industry. This was a relatively small industry, with around five thousand workers in the entire Habsburg Empire—but in Vienna alone, around one hundred of them died from phosphorus poisoning between 1895 and 1904, comprising more than half of all poisonings on record in the Viennese hospitals. During an emergency session of Parliament in July 1908, Adler quoted from a doctor's records:

Pale, with a distended lower part of their face, they stood apart from the [other patients], for whom they were an object of disgust. They could not distract themselves in conversation because their speech was difficult to understand, and they could be seen occupying themselves spitting out the pus that flooded their mouth, wiping away the streams of pus that dirtied their neck, shoulders, and shirt. (Movement.) Perhaps such a picture has ruined some of your appetites—I do not know whether you have already dined or not. But I bring this up—not to affect your nerves, but your will—and to prepare you that, when faced with such things, one can't be content with a feeble effort or with a written excuse. I would like to say that, with hygiene, one must really do something decisive, something effective.[31]

His party therefore demanded not only tighter regulation, but a ban on processing phosphorus. Over the years, Adler learned that enacting effective state reforms was a gradual process. After his December 1888 exposé about the conditions in Wienerberg, there were only small improvements until inspections were regularized. Structural changes came only in 1895, after a strike of ten thousand brick workers turned violent. Only after the regional governor intervened *against* the factory management and compelled negotiations did the parties agree on higher wages, an eleven-hour workday, and Sundays off.[32] Through it all, Adler was and remained a confirmed reformer. He considered the real "revolutionary work" to be the "work of political organization and the work of introducing reforms in order to situate the proletariat somewhat better." He accepted violence only as an act of defense; as a means of offense, it was "unreasonable."[33]

Adler's role in the Viennese labor struggles of the 1880s and 1890s was comparable to Jaurès's experiences with the miners' strike in Carmaux in 1892, even though Jaurès was just at the beginning of his "partisan" engagement. After these sometimes violent, but ultimately successful, disputes over miners' rights of participation and representation, Jaurès adopted similar tactics in his open engagement for a socialist republic. Both Adler and Jaurès became full-throated parliamentarians. Their constructive role in the context of labor conflicts, strikes, and the legislative process was unique among the early Marxists.

Bernstein served in the German Reichstag from 1902 to 1907, 1912 to 1918, and 1920 to 1928, but even he assessed his parliamentary contribution as relatively negligible.[34] Guesde sat in the French National Assembly from 1893 to 1898 and 1906 to 1922, but his service as a delegate has hardly been studied—not least because it marked a clear caesura in his biography as a revolutionary "apostle."[35] Guesde moved to the executive branch in 1914, embodying the collapse of the Second International by accepting a post in Prime Minister René Viviani's Ministry of War. With respect to the other protagonists, Russia had neither a parliament nor institutionalized party politics before 1905. Holding elected office or other posts was difficult in exile. Most of the protagonists expressly channeled their political ambitions into extraparliamentary work; at least Luxemburg and Kautsky might have aspired to political office, but they limited their engagement to an "intellectual mandate."

Lenin, Plekhanov, and Struve wrote about protecting factory workers at a considerable remove from their subjects, basing their work on government documents, newspaper reports, and scholarly publications in the social sciences.[36] For Kautsky and Luxemburg, the workplace and capitalist labor relations comprised the main arena of Social Democratic politics, evident in the protracted debate over the "mass strike" as a means of political engagement.[37] In April 1889, during the strike of Vienna's horse-drawn streetcar drivers, Kautsky remarked to Engels, "I'm writing in haste; my thoughts are more on the street than at my desk." The comment reveals an idiosyncratic, theoretical interest in "actual relations," as Kautsky did not discuss actual events on the Viennese streets in this letter or any others, in the weeks before or after.[38] Guesde, too, was interested in labor conflicts, such as the strike in Decazeville (1886), primarily as a means of winning over "soldiers" for the revolution—and not in the cumbersome negotiation and representation of workers' everyday interests. The Guesdists' electoral success was correspondingly meager in these years.[39]

Perceptions of contemporary conflicts and grievances depend on many factors, even among highly politicized persons. Kautsky's notable lack of interest in the struggles of Viennese workers in the spring of 1889—despite his assertion to the contrary—can be attributed in part to a serious crisis in his marriage in the months before. His behavior toward his first wife, Luise, caused great consternation among his close circle of family and friends (which included party leaders). He returned to Vienna from London in the fall of 1888, seeking to monitor Adler, the "rising star" of Austrian social democracy. On behalf of the party, Kautsky was concerned that Adler was being "driven too much by his environment" and that Adler saw "doing right by everyone" as a "triumph of diplomacy."[40] Kautsky's correspondence with Bernstein shows that he did not notice—or at least did not mention—the reporting and turmoil around the Viennese brick factories in the winter of 1888–89. Instead, Kautsky's letters to Bernstein and Engels in this period revolved around his estranged wife Luise, his affair with another woman (who, seeking greater security than Kautsky could provide, ultimately left him for his brother Hans), and a failed attempt to reconcile with Luise in the spring of 1889. Bernstein's letters to Kautsky, who was shunned within the party for his actions, are a testament of great friendship and loyalty.[41] Bernstein walked a tightrope between explaining and defending Kautsky's actions to a furious Engels and a disappointed Bebel and, in so doing, placed himself at the receiving end of Engels's rancor for weeks. Although Kautsky's biological family quickly supported his desire for a divorce, the affair cost him his "second," socialist family, and he wrote that "only Eduard" understood his actions. "No longer a member of the family, whose presence was always welcome," Kautsky never again felt as comfortable in the Engels home.[42]

Kautsky nevertheless took quite seriously the vetting of Adler's character in the interests of the party, and his letters show that he kept up his editorial work, marital crisis notwithstanding. He gave Adler his highest praise in an April 1889 letter to Engels: "At every opportunity, his conduct was splendid."[43] Which opportunities Kautsky meant (aside from Adler's successful organization of the Hainfeld party congress) are as murky as Kautsky's views on the labor conflicts involving the brick workers and the horse-drawn streetcar drivers, which also occurred around this time. A schematic need for classification and abstraction framed Kautsky's praise for Adler. Rather than evaluating Adler's engagement for the Social Question according to his involvement with pertinent social problems, Kautsky assessed the authenticity of Adler's habitus and identity as a "class warrior." The contrast to Adler's (and Jaurès's) own self-image, their engagement with reality, and their view of workers and others could not be greater—as evident in the following passage from the *Neue Zeit* honoring Adler's sixtieth birthday, in which Kautsky recalled his first encounter with Adler in 1881:

> I got to know and appreciate Adler as a smart, knowledgeable man, who approached our cause with the greatest sympathy, and with whom I happily conversed. But I made no effort to draw him closer to us. Anyone who comes to us from bourgeois circles is acceptable to our party only when his passion for socialism is so great that he overcomes all obstacles. Anyone who must be *drawn* to us from the bourgeois camp will generally remain an extremely unreliable comrade. For bourgeois intellectuals, who have all of the literature for and against socialism at their disposal, the matter of propaganda is altogether different than for poor proletarians, who can receive the light of knowledge [*das Licht der Erkenntnis*] only by socialist agitation.[44]

The workers received a message, but every bourgeois—on account of his educational privilege—had to recognize the core of this message by himself in order to be considered (like Kautsky) a reliable "comrade." Although Adler had not only counted "knowledge of human nature" and "tact," but also "intellectual superiority," among the preconditions for his social democratic engagement, he nevertheless understood this project as a dialogue on a level playing field. By contrast, Kautsky's intellectual work (*Kopfarbeit*) for the cause of "manual laborers" (*Handarbeiter*) was a hierarchical project, in which he monologically transmitted insights that he had acquired on his own. He thereby resembled Luxemburg and Lenin more than he could have liked, and more than he himself was probably aware.

A final example from Bernstein and Kautsky's unpublished correspondence shows that merely diagnosing an experiential and intellectual gulf between party intellectuals, on the one hand, and the party rank and file, or "proletarians," on the other, is not enough to understand the dynamics that were at play here. Further, the two friends' exchange about the sexual exploitation of young girls by men from London's upper crust points to the importance of journalism as a source of information. And perhaps most significant, this example shows how the protagonists viewed and evaluated misery through a Marxist prism, and how bourgeois and Marxist ideals became intermingled. In the summer of 1885, these two editors-in-chief exchanged letters that, for weeks, dealt almost exclusively with newspaper coverage of a child prostitution scandal. The letters reveal a surprisingly indifferent Bernstein and a surprisingly animated Kautsky. Their letters show us not only how the two men intellectually and experientially formed their perceptions of reality, but also that these perceptions did not unambiguously conform to a single "sense of reality" (in Isaiah Berlin's sense). Finally, the correspondence shows how intensely one might engage with the Social Question and its dramatic consequences, even if entirely from a desk.

In July 1885 Kautsky wrote to Bernstein in Zurich about an article in London's *Pall Mall Gazette*:

> Dear old boy!
> I've just read the *Pall Mall Gazette* from 7 July, which, as you have certainly heard, brings an array of sensational revelations with respect to prostitution. . . . There's fundamentally nothing new in what's said; everyone knows how victims are led to prostitution. The only sensational thing is *that* it was said publicly at all. I want to share just one passage with you; maybe you can use it in the paper.[45]

The source of the sensation was a four-part series, "The Maiden Tribute of Modern Babylon," by London journalist and editor William T. Stead. In 1885 Stead had researched the city's prostitution scene by posing as a client for four weeks, a ruse that subsequently resulted in his own arrest. The exposé quickly became an international sensation, and today it is recognized as a milestone in the history of tabloid journalism.[46] Engels wrote to Kautsky, "Stead is a thoroughly mad sort of chap, albeit a brilliant businessman. . . . [W]henever there's a chance of creating a sensation, he ruthlessly seizes on it."[47] Citing the second article in the series, Kautsky wrote to Bernstein about how thirteen- to fifteen-year-old female virgins were procured for "wealthy lechers," adding in a footnote, "They don't have a brothel, but come right to the home." Kautsky explained that the business was governed by "supply" and "demand" and that a growing number of "vamped virgins" had recently disrupted the market by deceiving clients about their inexperience.

Kautsky quoted the article's interview with a "procuress" at some length:

> We do not know anything about vamped virgins. Nor, with so many genuine maids to be had for the taking, do I think it worth while to manufacture virgins. I should say the market was looking up and the demand increasing. Prices may perhaps have fallen, but that is because our customers give larger orders. For instance, Dr.——, one of my friends, who used to take a maid a week at £10, now takes three a fortnight at from £5, to £7 each.

In his own words, Kautsky concluded that her "horrid" profession was lower than that of an executioner:

> The revolutionary bourgeoisie denounced the stag park of Louis XV; now every comfortable bourgeois has his own stag park. Sexual pleasure no longer satisfies them if it is not accompanied by the horror and wailing of an assaulted child. The *Pall Mall Gazette* provides an array of evidence. The victims . . . are lured to the gentlemen under deceptive pretenses; the more [these men] take pleasure in them, the greater the victims' fright, the louder their helpless cries.
>
> The same old phenomenon repeats itself; the more degraded the woman, the more she becomes a mere apparatus for copulation [*Begattungsapparat*], and the more lascivious and aggravated the man, the greater his desire for virginity. In Turkish harems as in the London

houses of procurers, the human commodity is examined for her "maid-enhood," to see whether she is worth the money or not, and doctors in London certify the virginity of the victims on demand, in order to protect the gentlemen from "deception." Nevertheless—thank God the lessons of free love are still unknown in England, the authority of the church is not yet undermined, the party of revolutionaries still weak; and so morality is not endangered, except by articles like these in the *Pall Mall Gazette*.[48]

Kautsky's dismay is evident in every line of his letter. He followed up with Bernstein the very next day, upon receiving the conclusion of the "story" on loan. (The edition had sold out immediately.)[49] In ago-nizing detail, Kautsky again quoted the "procuresses" about the actual course of the rapes (the "real seduction"): it "very often came to pass that 2 procuresses had to keep holding down the girl while the gen-tleman violated her."[50]

Kautsky, like the majority of the public at that time, responded to this brew of social criticism and voyeuristic sensationalism with a mix-ture of horror and fascination. Judith K. Walkowitz has impressively described the "electrified" atmosphere of a scandal-hungry public in London, showing how Stead's investigation, and its legal and judicial consequences, fundamentally changed the discourse about the sexual identity of both women and men. In fact, the *Pall Mall* story was im-mensely overdrawn. The proportion of child prostitutes in London was far lower than the articles suggested. Moreover, the depiction of girls as victims was accompanied by their subtler identification as seductresses, carriers of sexually transmitted disease, and symbols of immorality.[51] The introduction to the German edition of the "Maiden Tribute" articles (more than 1.5 million copies were sold worldwide in multiple translations) pointed German readers to the apparent ambiv-alence of the female subjects' fates. Stead's investigation had not only denounced this crime "without reservation," but had also warned po-tential victims to uphold their "virtue" and "innocence."[52] Kautsky wryly expressed the same sentiment in a follow-up note to Bernstein, recounting his comment to the surprised news dealer from whom he had purchased ten copies of the *Pall Mall Gazette*: "I'm sending them as a warning to a girls' boarding school in Switzerland."[53]

Kautsky's Marxist worldview simultaneously shaped his assessment of the scandal, which he understood as the outgrowth of a thoroughly corrupted "comfortable, bourgeois" order. The sexual exploitation of girls was "fundamentally nothing new." The newspaper was reporting "only the facts; we can easily recognize what caused them."[54] While Kautsky could comprehend the demand for "love for sale," given the "difficulty of satisfying sexual urges within and outside of marriage," this did not explain the "lust for assaulting adolescent virgins." The causes for this lay elsewhere: "Nowhere else but England have hardship and misery compelled so many people to sell themselves; nowhere else are so many means for buying people amassed in so few hands. The proletariat is servile and depraved, the bourgeoisie smug and presumptuous, and so they crown their dominance and elevate the defiling of defenseless proletarian children to a sport for their 'heroic sons,' to an institution of capitalism."[55] Prostitution was a systemic issue for Kautsky, like tuberculosis for Adler. And so Kautsky entirely ignored its long history, reaching back to antiquity. Anticapitalism overwhelmed all other potential motives for a critique of prostitution. Kautsky's interpretation thus prefigured the argument that prostitution was a transnational problem of capitalist modernity, "the most international institution of social life," as Luxemburg later put it.[56]

Here Kautsky was hardly alone. The depiction of prostitution and wage labor as two sides of one coin—with prostitution as the consequence of poorly paid labor—was widespread among English Marxists and trade unionists. This attitude was particularly pronounced in response to the "Maiden Tribute" articles. "Children, girls and women are daily bought and sold in London, just as underpaid factory girls and shopwomen are constantly driven to vice by sheer want," an editorial in the social democratic newspaper *Justice* announced one week after the publication of the first Stead article. The miserable state of working-class daughters was well known, the editorial argued: that they earned so little, even when working regularly, that they were driven to prostitution. The newspaper had not previously published these details because "the causes for this infamy are economical and can only be removed by a complete overthrow of the existing society."[57]

Discourse that compared or directly linked prostitution and wage labor had a tradition. Engels's identification of the factory as a "harem" in *The Condition of the Working Class in England*—with employers exploiting the labor of women and girls by day, and their bodies by night—reinforced this critique with an image that was both shocking and memorable. In Engels's portrayal, the role of the victim mixed with references to a generally "immoral" and "unchaste" environment, which was a predictable consequence of the "centralization of people" in factories. Although Engels cited numerous studies, he offered no attribution for his assertion that factory owners, appealing to *jus primae noctis*, systematically assaulted female employees.[58] By situating this abuse in a world of endless exploitation, Engels (like Kautsky and the newspaper *Justice*) effectively tamed his own consternation. Kautsky ended his second long letter to Bernstein on this topic by noting that he had almost written his own newspaper article about it, "but it is only fleeting, it lacks acuity, make of it what you will." He expected that Bernstein's *Sozialdemokrat* would "utilize" the misery of London's involuntary child prostitutes, which had become a larger "story."

"Thank you very much for your letters about the *Pall Mall* circus. I used these for an article, but I can't say that I succeeded." These two sentences are all we have from Bernstein about Kautsky's extensive reporting. After weeks of silence, Kautsky complained, "No word! Is that the gratitude for the *Pall Mall*?" Perhaps there is a personal explanation for Bernstein's reticence. His later memoir contains an anecdote about his encounter, when he was eighteen years old, with a "public girl" on Berlin's Friedrichstrasse.[59] He framed the experience, not unlike Stead in London, by describing the institution of street prostitution in 1870s Berlin: Friedrich Wilhelm IV's ban on brothels had given rise to street prostitution that was nothing but "slavery": "The worst brothel could not be more dire. . . . In particular, as I later had opportunity to discover, so-called free prostitution did not place the affected female persons in a position to feel even somewhat free." Every few minutes on his way home from work, Bernstein was approached by "one of these females selling herself." Among the young men his age who were financed by knowing fathers, it was accepted practice "to find release from time to time by carrying out, technically stated, the act of sexual intercourse." Bernstein ascribed this "general custom" exclusively to the bourgeoisie. (His own family existed on the bourgeoisie's lower fringes.) Among his contemporaries, paying for sex outside of marriage was wholly accepted, as long as one followed "certain formal rules." Because he felt increasingly ashamed about his sexual inexperience, "one day" he did go along with a "public girl," whose "appearance and demeanor" was "certainly not unpleasant." This "visit," however, was a "great aesthetic disappointment."[60] Perhaps this experience explains Bernstein's tight-lipped reaction to Kautsky's scandalous reports from London. It was unusual for Bernstein to have no comment on Kautsky's agitated musings, and he said nothing to his friend about his youthful encounter with a prostitute.

In the previous pages, I have investigated numerous variations of the protagonists' engaged gaze—an overwhelmingly distant, but nonetheless durable, preoccupation with contemporary social conditions. In order to generalize about the different ways of observing and depicting—and thereby "sedimenting"—lived experience, we might arrange the protagonists' testimonials, speeches, and other writings along an imaginary spectrum. On one end, we could place interpretations of the world that are more concrete, reflecting a detailed interest in social reality in all its complexity, and on the other, interpretations that ponder reality in more generalized and abstract ways.[61] In the spirit of Isaiah Berlin's critical writings on the history of ideas and ideologies, we might say that each of these interpretations reflects a more or less defined "sense of reality." According to Berlin, a "sense of reality" allows us "to detect the relationships of actual things and persons"; it attests to an "acquaintance with particulars." All theory, by contrast, "deals with attributes and idealised entities—with the general."[62] Although the dichotomy between reality-based "empathy" and abstract theorization may not be as absolute as Berlin's model implies, systematizing the protagonists' approaches to reality is nevertheless helpful. Their depictions shifted along a spectrum between the particular and the general, with both tendencies converging at times.

As we have seen, the surviving sources are often few and far between. However, even passing anecdotes can be instructive, as the examples from Luxemburg's and Lenin's correspondence show. Moreover, we can draw distinctions between the protagonists' childhood and more mature years, and between mundane, everyday experiences and intentional encounters. In this way, a panorama of very different life paths emerges. These paths' shared foundation was the socially critical engagement that the protagonists understood as their life's purpose, which was substantially—but by no means exclusively—inspired by Marx. Finally, the rarer but more extensive depictions of reality—such as Adler's comparative factory investigations or Kautsky's and Bernstein's correspondence about child prostitution in London—show that the protagonists' political worldviews and their interpretations of social misery were interrelated and even mutually reinforcing.

Nevertheless, it would be misplaced to categorize these findings schematically as either close to or distant from reality—or, in the words of Berlin, as either "understanding" or "blind." Whether as an abstract, personally detached occupation with the Social Question (in the case of Kautsky or Lenin) or as an apparently emotional, romanticized approach (Luxemburg or Guesde), all of protagonists shared a persistent "emotional disposition"[63]—a perceptive and *subjectively* rational passion that is essential to long-term political engagement.

On Revolution, or the
Second Commandment:
Philosophy as Practice

When I was a student, I was struck by the fact that during that
period we were in a profoundly Marxist atmosphere where the
problem of the link between theory and practice was absolutely
at the center of all theoretical discussions.

—Michel Foucault, "Interview with Christian
Panier and Pierre Watté" (1981)

There is no doubt that all nine protagonists understood their
own thinking as "interventionist."[1] And yet they went well
beyond what Ingrid Gilcher-Holtey (building upon the work of
Bertolt Brecht and Pierre Bourdieu) has described as "interventionist
thinking." The protagonists' primary sphere of action was not the
world of arts and letters; their primary goal was not merely to shape
public opinion in a nonpartisan, socially critical way. Rather, their
intent was to formulate political programs and to participate in the
"real" transformation of political and social practice—an ambition
that was wholly independent of the offices or functions they held

within party or parliamentary structures. To describe Marx's early epigones as intellectuals who only temporarily assumed the roles of "pioneers" and "mediators of interpretive, perceptive, and classifying schemata,"[2] or, more generally, as "producers and mediators of ideas and worldviews,"[3] would obscure a significant part of their own self-image and belief in their own efficacy.

Even so, in her study of "interventionist thinking," Gilcher-Holtey (following Michel Foucault) also refers to the type of the "Marxist intellectual." With an emphasis on self-image and patterns of behavior, she has developed a list of criteria that applies particularly well to first-generation Marxists and their specific political engagement: they wanted to serve as "mediators of consciousness" based on their understanding of social development; they sought to "organize, steer, and lead" the "struggle for emancipation"; and their audience was the "revolutionary subject."[4]

Without considering the category of experience, however, intellectual history can hardly provide satisfying insights about the origins of a (political) worldview and the dynamics of political activism. And so, in this final section, I bring the history of experience to the analysis of Marxism as political *engagement*. In so doing, I seek to liberate Marxism from its historiographical niche existence and integrate this long and intensely contested subject into general political history. The concept of engagement is particularly well suited to achieve this goal. It not only helps us to grasp the specifics of political action in the spirit and name of Marxism, but it allows us to systematically explore the movement's unique programmatic approach to "reality" as its most influential—and most problematic—ambition.

Engagement is an emphatic concept, frequently used by activists to describe their work on behalf of political, social, or environmental causes. Engagement has also been used to describe a certain approach toward art: Sartre was known for "engaged literature," and Brecht, for "engaged theater." After 1945, the term was primarily associated with a particular kind of intellectual criticism that sought to transcend the usual ideological fronts; Raymond Aron's self-description as an "engaged," or "committed," observer (*spectateur engagé*) is the paradigmatic example.[5] The transitive French verb *engager* originally meant "to take into service." The word moved into other languages in the seventeenth century, with its distinctive emphasis evolving over time. The predicate adjective *engagé* appeared in the mid-nineteenth century; to be "engaged" could mean "bound" or "secured" (by a contract or promise to marry), as well as "involved" or "directly affected." Since the early twentieth century, "engagement" has come to include internal commitment to a cause; the German reflexive verb *sich engagieren* (literally, "to engage oneself") aptly expresses this idea. Its most important roots are in French existentialism. Sartre described *engagement* as "the process of accepting responsibility for the political consequences of one's actions" (even though his concept is sometimes rendered in English as "commitment"). In existentialist thought, accepting responsibility required "*committing* oneself entirely and allowing oneself to *immerse* fully in a situation, but also to *remain* committed to the chosen path."[6] This specific meaning of engagement—driven by exertion, dedication, and persistence—contains the essence of political action in the "age of ideologies" (Klaus von Beyme).[7] Remarkably, in the most extreme realizations of such absolute commitment of thought and action in the first half of the twentieth century, the militant warriors of social revolution on the communist left and the radical engineers of a homogenized "people's community" (*Volksgemeinschaft*) on the far right developed an unsettling resemblance.[8]

One of the few attempts to define engagement (or "involvement") as an analytical concept is Norbert Elias's 1956 essay "Problems of Involvement and Detachment."Without explicitly referencing the discourse of existential philosophy, Elias situated his reflections within the theory and historiography of knowledge, specifically the emergence of the humanities and social sciences. At the heart of his explorations was the fundamental dilemma of social scientists, who—as social beings themselves, and thus laden with indelible motives, interests, and loyalties—seek to investigate their own social nature. According to Elias, such an endeavor can make sense only when grounded upon a balance between involvement and detachment.[9] Elias wrote that "ordered group life depends on the interplay in people's thoughts and actions of impulses in both directions, those that involve and those that detach keeping each other in check." The greatest challenge of the social sciences—and indeed, all social criticism—was to distinguish carefully between what "was" and what "should be." He doubted that the social sciences could ever grasp and discipline themselves as fully as had the natural sciences with respect to the natural world. Writing in the aftermath of two world wars and the Holocaust, Elias drew upon the painful lessons of the mid-twentieth century: when intellectuals and scholars become extremely "engaged," the delicate equilibrium between "involvement" and "detachment" can be easily disrupted, unleashing terrible destruction.

To rein in this possibility, and to promote reasonably ordered coexistence and social scientific study, Elias developed a dynamic conception of engagement. By defining a spectrum between involvement and detachment, he also offered important insights into the engagement of Marxist intellectuals. According to Elias, only children and the mentally ill could be radically engaged, succumbing unreservedly to their feelings in the here and now. And only the mentally ill could be absolutely detached, emotionally removed from everything happening around them.[10] Elias used the following analogy to explain the spectrum between these poles:

> A philosopher once said, "If Paul speaks of Peter he tells us more about Paul than about Peter." One can say, by way of comment, that in speaking of Peter he is always telling us something about himself as well as about Peter. One would call his approach "involved" as long as his own characteristics, the characteristics of the perceiver, overshadow those of the perceived. If Paul's propositions begin to tell more about Peter than about himself the balance begins to turn in favour of detachment.[11]

This analogy returns us to a central issue from the previous chapter: the relationship between a portrait and its creator, between perception and the perceiver. My analysis of the protagonists' "involved" gaze has shown that their perceptions of reality, and thus

their depictions of human misery, depended strongly on how abstract and self-referential (or conversely, how concrete and externally
oriented) these interactions were. Their efforts to address the Social
Question were distinguished predominantly by motives that were
highly subjective—or, in Elias's words, by motives that were more
"involved" than "detached."[12] Selflessness was *not* one of their defining characteristics.

We should not, however, confuse emotional coolness (as in the work
of Lenin, Kautsky, and Luxemburg) with detachment in Elias's sense
of the word, which he has associated with a reflective "autonomy
of thinking." We might describe the attitude of these protagonists as
"pseudo-detached." Saliently (although not exclusively) in Marxism,
specific modes of thinking like abstraction—or appropriating the
premises, models, concepts, and methods of the natural sciences—
are used to circumvent "difficulties which spring from [the social
scientists'] dilemma, without facing it; in many cases, it creates a façade
of detachment masking a highly involved approach."[13]

Despite different methods of perception and strategies of action,
the first Marxist intellectuals viewed themselves and their own ability
to make a difference in a similar way. Over the course of their turn
toward Marxism, the protagonists came to define themselves according to this engagement, which was based on exertion, dedication,
and persistence. They developed a "sustained political passion" that
grew out of their enduring cognitive and emotional occupation with
social conditions—an occupation that transcended their own lived
experience.[14]

And so Marxist intellectuals did not practice criticism as a "profession";[15] instead, they followed a calling. They did not play a role,
but devoted their whole existence to realizing a political program.
Their political activism (frequently described as "commitment," "dedication," or service to a "cause") was not based on the generally inquisitive, autonomous, and socially critical thought of an "all-around
intellectual," but on an ultimately hermetic, unabashedly partisan, and
radically critical worldview.[16] Their engagement was not confined to

speaking their minds or to placing hope in the "power of words." Instead, they directed their talents toward participating in the transformation of society as concretely as possible; indeed, their engagement was based on the *expectation* of such opportunities to shape and engage in "practice." They saw themselves not merely as advocates but as activists for a cause.

In this respect, the contrast between the "old" Marxist intellectuals of the Second International and the "young" revolutionary intellectuals of the New Left is not as sharp as it might first appear. The "elders" did see themselves as the enlightened, intellectual vanguard of the proletariat, but they did not argue and agitate for its interests as outsiders. Rather, they felt—and often were—more closely integrated in proletarian organizational structures and the dissident milieu than one might conclude from their later status as "party intellectuals." Most did not move from theory into practice, engaging in a one-way transformation from advocates into activists. Instead, after their early ventures into socialist circles, associations, and illegal groups, they moved from practice to theory (understood as the self-directed, "scientific" study of socialism). The conventional distinction between theory and practice—"political theorists vs. practical politicians," as Kautsky put it—continues to shape our view of Marxist social democracy even today. However, upon closer observation, this distinction can be misleading, obscuring significant aspects of early Marxist engagement.[17]

The previous chapters have shown that the protagonists' difficulties with studying "reality" had at least two layers. The difficulties began with Marx's Promethean commission to study history and society as they "really" were, and henceforth accompanied every effort to change reality through very different strategies of action and intervention. This spectrum of action ranged from studying the socialist canon, popularizing Marx and Engels's texts, and more or less concretely describing the state of the many poor (the "eighty-nine percent"), to agitating and organizing legal and illegal party work. The litmus test of this engagement was actual revolution—a rare and long-anticipated (but, once it actually happened, deeply unsettling) climax in the lives of the first generation. And so, in this final section, I examine the interplay between revolutionary expectations and experiences, turning to the one revolutionary event in twentieth-century Europe that all of the protagonists shared: the first Russian Revolution of 1905–6.

12

Revolutionary Expectations

❝ My dearest, it's very lovely here. Every day two or three persons are bayoneted by the soldiers in the city. Arrests are increasing daily, but other than that everything is quite cheerful."[1] In January 1906, shortly after arriving in Warsaw, Luxemburg sent these lines to Karl and Luise Kautsky in Berlin. Since protests had erupted one year earlier—in St. Petersburg on 22 January 1905 and in Warsaw five days later—Luxemburg had attempted to make sense of these events from where she stood in Berlin. She wrote feature articles and political reports for *Vorwärts*, hoping to reinvigorate the revolutionary events that had stalled in Russia—getting the "cursed cart [*verfluchte Karre*]" rolling once more, or at least pushing it "out of the mud."[2]

Luxemburg's reaction to the events in Russia and Poland in 1905 illustrates the mixture of voluntarism and idealism, of action and reaction, that characterized the modern conception of revolution. A revolution was not only a historical process that was relatively disconnected from the actions of any one person; it could simultaneously change and expand individual experience to an unprecedented degree, regardless of whether one participated in revolutionary events directly or observed them from afar. This subjective side of revolutionary history—the perceptions, expectations, and emotions of those who experienced it—has only recently become the focus of scholarship on revolutions and social movements.[3]

Yet the complex interplay between revolutionary expectations and experiences in the period before 1918 has often played only a marginal role in the (nonbiographical) literature on Marxist "theorists." This oversight is surely one consequence of the long-standing divide, especially among German-speaking scholars, between the historical study of Marxism and that of workers' movements.[4] Marx's first students imagined and theorized about revolution for years before one actually occurred.[5] They used "revolution" to describe an event as well as a process. Revolution was an inevitable (future) historical occurrence, and it would more or less clearly adhere to Marx and Engels's (less than coherent) analyses and predictions, made between the 1840s and 1880s in their texts about the French Revolution, the revolutions of 1848, and the Paris Commune. These texts, which fluctuated between historical analysis and political commentary, revolved around the role that the proletariat would play, vis-à-vis the other "classes," in the dialectical development of human society from capitalism to socialism. They presumed that the proletariat, a class "having a universal character because of its universal suffering," would emancipate not only itself but all of humanity.[6] Leszek Kolakowski has stressed that "the idea of the proletariat's special mission as a class which cannot liberate itself without thereby liberating society as a whole"—an idea first formulated by Marx in the *Critique of Hegel's Philosophy of Law*—was "a philosophical deduction rather than a product of observation."[7]

Marx's original idea of a "truly human"[8] revolution—endemic to capitalism, but embodied and executed by a collective proletarian actor—was *not* a response to specific political events; rather, it was the result of philosophical contemplation and critique. Thus, Marx, Engels, and (later) the epigones continuously revised their expectations in response to the actual "class struggles" of the following decades, particularly in England, France, and Germany. Engels himself wrote self-critical introductions to new editions of Marx's texts.[9] In essence, the "golden age" of Marxism is the history of these revisions.

Beyond the idea of a working-class "mission," Marx and Engels remained famously vague about the means and methods of (proletarian) revolution. In *The Class Struggles in France 1848–1850* (1850), Marx developed the abstract "formula" that Engels subsequently lauded as the quintessence of "modern workers' socialism."[10] Rescuing the "right to work" from (ostensibly) hypocritical bourgeois discourse, Marx turned this principle into the linchpin of a liberation movement. The formula pointed the way forward in theory, while remaining silent about practice: "Behind the right to work stands the power over capital; behind the power over capital, the appropriation of the means of production, their subjection to the associated working class and, therefore, the abolition of wage labour, of capital and of their mutual relations."[11]

Beyond these foundational assumptions, we can identify three core thoughts in Marxist revolutionary theory. First, revolution was linked to the crisis-ridden social and economic relations that intensified continuously in the capitalist era. Second, an ever larger proportion of the population would become aware of this development, and thus an "overwhelming majority" of the population would work to accelerate the historical movement toward socialism. Third, this movement would succeed only when the first of these revolutions (which Marx and Engels had long believed would occur in England) touched off a worldwide chain reaction.

Although this list of "objective conditions" spoke more to an evolutionary than a voluntaristic understanding of revolution, Marx and Engels firmly believed that a radical upheaval of property and power relations through a socialist revolution could occur only over the course of these developments.[12] They understood revolution as a process that was both natural and man-made—not "a violation of history" but "a fulfilment of its innate tendency." The idea that history was at once overwhelming and a means to overwhelm could be integrated into all kinds of political programs, as opportunities arose. Emblematic in this regard was Kautsky's careful formulation from 1894, that the SPD was a "revolutionary" party but not a "revolution-making" one.[13]

The Marxist vision of a proletarian socialist revolution thus contains the essential elements of the broader, modern conception of revolution. Reinhart Koselleck has shown that this broader conception includes the ambivalent meaning of "history" as a site of action and context (or fate), and that its structuring of events is similarly ambivalent. "Revolution" thus reflects two different realms of experience. On the one hand, the term encompasses concrete events, "the violent episodes of unrest in an uprising that can escalate to civil war"; on the other, it concerns a "long-term process of structural transformation that extends from the past into the future." The term unites "diagnostic and predictive elements," and it can be prosaic or emphatic. It can bundle together historical experiences as a "collective singular," or it can motivate individual actions as a "term of legitimation." Particularly in its Marxist incarnation, as a complementary concept to "evolution," the term exerted tremendous allure. As Koselleck has emphasized, Marx made the most of this "multilayered" concept of revolution and its dynamic spectrum of meaning. By treating "evolution" and "revolution" as complements, not opposites, Marx gave the modern concept of revolution its specifically mobilizing character. His dialectic linked history to the present and future in an idiosyncratic way.[14]

Our protagonists' understanding of revolution was correspondingly versatile and complex. As we have already seen, the romantic ideas of their youth arose from the collective imagination of a revolution-obsessed era. Their individual interpretations of Marx evolved over years of reading and over the course of their politicization in local workers' movements—evidence of the tremendous intellectual and emotional pull of Marx's ideas as a design for politics. Further, these ideas promised a realistic means of political participation and a plausible path to power. Philosophy informed practice in this political worldview—through the central role of the "working class," the discovery of a collective actor as the driver of history, and the call to organize as a party and (wherever possible) come to power through the electoral process. The relative vagueness of strategy and tactics in Marxist politics corresponded to the ambivalence of its revolutionary idea. And so, in diverse and surprisingly enduring ways, Marxism became a kind of blueprint, adaptable in wide-ranging contexts and by many different people, as a worldview, a social science, and a political design.

Seeking to generalize about the first Marxist intellectuals' ideas of revolution, we might distinguish—as Kautsky himself did in *The Social Revolution* in 1902, drawing upon Marx's *Critique of Political Economy*—between a "complete transformation of outmoded forms of human interaction" on the one hand, and a narrower "political revolution" (the conquest of political or state power) on the other. Kautsky understood political revolution as a kind of "elementary event" at the end of a social revolution.[15] At a particular stage of historical development, the proletariat, which was steadily learning and organizing, would mount a political revolution, thereby "growing into" the (social) revolution along its road to power.[16] This position, which was soon characterized as "centrist," had at least as many critics as pragmatic supporters in the Second International before 1914.[17] Kautsky considered the question of violence mostly irrelevant, at least in western Europe, because "every juridical and political measure is a violent measure." He believed that future revolutions in western Europe would probably lead to protracted "civil wars"—meaning cultural struggles without bloody carnage. In Russia, by contrast, "armed insurrections" and "barricade fighting" would likely unleash "sudden outrage against authority."[18] Kautsky's expectations were representative of the European social democratic mainstream at that time. And in fact, Kautsky foresaw the (spontaneous) militancy of a possible Russian popular uprising, which initially failed in 1905–6. When the Bolsheviks' organized militancy finally succeeded in the fall of 1917, the Second International's long-held conception of a gradual "revolution by the book"[19] was shattered once and for all.

Revolutionary scenarios were highly dependent on frame of reference—not only on the theoretical level, as with Kautsky (who, like most European social democrats, were distant observers of conditions in Russia), but also with respect to real-world decisions. As mature Marxists, Bernstein, Guesde, Struve, Jaurès, and Adler all came to share Kautsky's dialectical conception of revolution as an evolutionary—but in some cases, "accelerated"—process of development.[20] Bernstein and Guesde, in particular, deradicalized their original views; they had once hoped to overturn all existing relations, "expropriating the expropriators" with an "intentional army" of proletarians in an explosive class struggle.[21] They had once regarded expropriation and socialization as a defensive act, which sought to revoke and atone for the capitalists' initial expropriation of workers' material and spiritual well-being. Over time, however, both men came to recognize the limits of agitation, the efficacy of parliaments and trade unions, and the "adaptability and flexibility" of capitalism[22]—even when, as "collectivists," they still argued for restitution in the spirit of the *Communist Manifesto*. At the beginning of the revisionism debate, Bernstein suggested that it was "quite utopian" to believe that a social transformation that was linked to the spread of capitalism, driving toward its end, would necessarily begin with a "catastrophe," leading overnight to the emergence of a socialist economic order.[23]

Likewise, already in 1890, Guesde relativized his earlier call for "expropriating" property owners through a violent "political revolution," noting that he meant "political or government-ordered expropriation of the capitalist class, which anticipates and enables economic expropriation."[24] He did not explain how "legally" revoking some citizens' property and voting rights might be executed in practice. He nevertheless insisted that elections were not the only path for the proletariat to come to power. The "revolutionary deed"—a singular act of violence, or *coup de force*—was equally valid, he wrote in a 1907 article about the relationship between *légalité* and *révolution*. The two concepts necessarily complemented one another, as France's political history showed: "Neither haphazard nor constant gunfire . . . without preparation," ending in "completely useless bloodbaths," amounted to a revolution. Rather, revolutionary violence had to serve the cause of justice. A revolution could be realized with gunfire, but also by voting and organizing. And even if the ballot box had not yet rendered guns completely superfluous, by 1879 Guesde had come to acknowledge the revolutionary potential of the vote. Since the ends defined the means, distinguishing between legal and illegal means of class struggle was "particularly idiotic." If the means served revolution, they were— of course—revolutionary means.[25]

In contrast to Guesde, Jaurès as a young philosophy professor had already begun to historicize the "utterly" obsolete, "parasitic" revolutionary theory of the *Communist Manifesto*, which "grafted" proletarian onto bourgeois revolution.[26] According to Jaurès, Marx and Engels had formulated their ideas in a position of weakness, spuriously "rushing the course of events" in 1847–48. And so, a half-century later, Jaurès developed an alternative program of mature "revolution by its own force." By 1901 he saw a much stronger proletariat, with "its own organization and its own power." In trade unions, cooperatives, and parliaments, the proletariat was methodically preparing its own revolution, "or better stated: it is methodically beginning [this revolution] by the gradual and legal conquest of the power of production and the power of the state."[27] Jaurès upheld Marx's evolutionary determinism, but he rejected all revolutionary "attentism" (Dieter Groh's term).[28]

Adler espoused a similarly "methodical" approach. He considered the Austrian socialists, like the Germans, to be "revolutionary," but he saw no cause for speeches repudiating "all parliamentarism." On behalf of his political party, the SDAPÖ, he argued that parliamentarism, voting rights, and worker protections were "only a means to an end, a good means to revolutionize minds and to win over the poor, who are supposed to execute this revolution."[29] Adler proposed that the nineteenth century was an epoch of "world revolution," which was proceeding on two different levels. On an "unconscious, mechanical" level, "economic revolution" was advancing inexorably. On a "conscious" level, meanwhile, the proletariat was coming to terms with its "world-historical meaning" by "revolutionizing minds" and learning to embrace the goal of this emerging consciousness—ushering the current social order "to its grave" and becoming "the bearer of a new social order."[30] For Adler, the means and methods of this burial lay in the work of parliaments and trade unions.

Struve's main contribution to Marxist revolutionary theory was his historicizing criticism, and he, too, rejected the idea of revolutionary liberation erupting from social catastrophe. He dismissed the "inevitable" transition from capitalism to socialism as a "highly illogical notion" of party leftists, along with their faith in "social miracles."[31] Despite his skeptical perspective, his work was firmly anchored in Marxist discourse. In his 1899 essay about the "Marxist theory of social development," he dismissed as theoretical nonsense the idea that social transformation could occur only through revolution. A political revolution "that is supposed to serve as a tool of social transformation already presupposes this entire transformation, according to the main assumption of the materialist view of history."[32] In the face of such logical contortions, Struve felt obliged to defend the "teacher" against his students who had drifted into dogmatism. In his introduction to the new edition of the Russian translation of *Capital*, which was also published in 1899, he complained that those who assumed Marx's "system" was without contradiction diminished not only the "power and meaning" of this "deep and substantive" work but also the "wealth and profundity" of its author's motives.[33] As a Marxist, Struve had always feared that radical rhetoric could intensify the real revolutionary potential in Russian society—in other words, the danger of civil war. He placed his hope in the rationality of a fading capitalist order and its capacity for reform. Given the backwardness of the tsarist empire, the modernizing effects of capitalism still held great social promise.

Struve's countryman Plekhanov, by contrast, saw revolution as a dialectical process in apocalyptic stages. These stages naturally followed the development of the capitalist system, creating the necessary conditions for a bourgeois, and then proletarian, revolution. This development could not be halted or forced, nor could any stage be bypassed. Revolution would not come to Russia through elections and democratization, as the western European Marxists hoped, but rather through a "political catastrophe" set into motion by the workers. Embodying the intellectual approach that Struve had criticized as faith in miracles, Plekhanov's concept of revolution was based on an unalterable plan: "*Economic evolution* leads as sure as fate to *political revolution* and this latter, in turn, will be the cause of important changes in the economic structure of society. The mode of *production* slowly and gradually assumes a social character. The mode of *appropriation* of the products corresponding to it will be the result of forcible revolution."[34]

Plekhanov's maneuvering between catastrophic and gradual stages of development suggests that he, like Lenin and Luxemburg, did not trust that an evolutionary dialectic would "grow into" revolution. Despite the genuinely transnational intellectual horizons of all three protagonists, their revolutionary ideas were grounded in a political context that was altogether different from Kautsky's. Neither did they share Struve's stubbornly western orientation, which was the source of his no less "miraculous" optimism. After the disappointed hopes of 1905, at the latest, any fundamental transformation of tsarist Russia was conceivable only as the consequence of violent upheavals.

Although Lenin and Luxemburg were increasingly at odds over questions of internal party organization, each believed in their own ability to accelerate and direct revolution. Once a revolutionary moment arrived, they would give their all to seize and prolong it. For Lenin and Luxemburg, revolution was not a means to an end, but an end in itself.[35] Their voluntarism enhanced their revolutionary expectations. More than other students of Marx's social and revolutionary theories, they believed that individual or collective interventions could influence the course of history. In January 1905, shortly before St. Petersburg's Bloody Sunday, Lenin wrote, "[I]t is not without reason that a revolution is said to be a successful revolt, and a revolt is an unsuccessful revolution."[36] A professionalized revolutionary elite of intellectuals could turn a revolt into a successful revolution. Intellectuals were "good at solving problems 'in principle,' good at drawing up plans, good at reasoning about the need for action," preparing the way so that workers could "transform drab theory into living reality."[37]

Luxemburg saw revolution as a force of nature that had to be tamed, and she frequently adopted metaphors that expressed this idea. Like Lenin, she believed in jumping on the train of history in order to steer and accelerate it—and in fact, at the end of December 1905 (like Lenin, twelve years later in a sealed train car) she smuggled herself into Warsaw on a train full of soldiers. However, she envisioned a very different role for still inexperienced workers than the one assigned by Lenin. Luxemburg believed that the "masses" would (initially) fulfill their historic mission by learning in vivo, without hierarchical leadership or organization. In a 1904 article about "organizational questions of Russian social democracy," she emphatically criticized Lenin's dogmatic, "subjectivist" idea of "an omniscient and ever-present Central Committee" that was controlled by intellectuals. Such an institution would infantilize the developing workers' movement in Russia, stopping "the pulse of a healthy living organism," and thereby pitting means against end. She argued that Lenin's vision was informed by the psychological effects of tsarist rule: "The ego, crushed and mangled by Russian autocracy, wreaks its revenge by placing itself, in its own system of thought, on the throne and declaring itself all-powerful, as a committee of conspirators in the name of a non-existent 'Narodnaya Volya.'"[38] In Luxemburg's view, a social democratic party had to respond smoothly and flexibly to events. The true role of "the working class's own movement" was alongside, not in advance of, the workers, and in this way the movement would determine the "necessary increase in revolutionary momentum."[39]

Luxemburg never formulated a coherent theory of revolution on paper, and so we must glean her thoughts on revolution from various articles and essays. Helga Grebing argues that Luxemburg understood revolution as the "conquest of political power by the proletariat," pointing to Luxemburg's 1899 treatise *Social Reform or Revolution*. Since 1905 Luxemburg had described revolution as an uprising that was initiated and borne from below by the "masses." Her biographer J. P. Nettl does not attempt to reconstruct her revolutionary theory, but he observes that she saw revolution not as a fixed concept but rather as "a state of mind."[40] And, in fact, this perspective may come closest to her understanding of revolution. While Luxemburg theoretically understood revolution as the dialectical outcome of capitalism's inevitable demise, she simultaneously yearned for the apocalyptic eruptions of revolutionary action. Convinced that "the working class was revolutionary by nature,"[41] she envisioned these eruptions as spontaneous "explosions"—as "elemental forces that are at work in the depths of modern society," or as "lightning storms" suddenly condensing "with elemental force."[42] Sitting at her desk in the well-to-do neighborhood of Friedenau on Berlin's west side, she also extended these metaphors to the actors who experienced the events firsthand. In 1905 she described the "accidental leaders" whom the revolutionary chaos "brought to the surface": "As in all tremendous outbreaks of revolution, the glowing lava at first heaves up over the rim of the crater all sorts of slag or gross sediment from the depths." In a short time, however, "a powerful, healthy, and well-developed nucleus of purely proletarian class consciousness" would coalesce; "the word" would become "flesh" and complete the revolution in "the spirit of Marx."[43] Her language was an expression of political discourse since the French Revolution. The classic metaphor for revolution was the earthquake,[44] a natural phenomenon that unleashed "elemental forces," which Luxemburg (strongly fascinated and somewhat repulsed) used to describe the first Russian Revolution.

Naturalistic metaphors united extremely different political temperaments and ideological positions. Like Luxemburg, Bernstein drew upon natural phenomena to explain the paradoxical, evolutionary-eruptive course of revolutionary events. He made a first interpretive effort in April 1905, recalling that a revolution's outcome was difficult to predict. Revolution was like a tree that sprang from the "womb" of the nation, in a "state of heightened physical and intellectual growth" that allowed all kinds of "shoots" to emerge from the earth—brainstorms that quickly faded or that were "suppressed, strangled by [the forces of] reaction," as well as ideas (like those of

1789) that developed slowly but steadily, proving over time to be more "fertile" and "sustainable" than the "shoots" that sprang up in 1848.[45]

References to human biology—namely, procreation—were even more popular. One of the most frequently quoted passages in *Capital* comes from Marx's preface to the first edition: while a society could not forgo "the successive phases of its normal development," it could "shorten and lessen the birth-pangs."[46] Marxists gladly invoked the metaphor of childbirth in various texts and contexts. In his sociopolitical "confession of faith" from 1885, a young (and still revolutionary) Bernstein called expropriation an "act of midwifery," in which the "ripened fruit" of socialism would burst its "capitalist shell."[47] Kautsky also worked midwifery into one of his early, unpublished texts about socialist ideas. He warned the "lords" of society that "hunger and desperation are the midwives of the freedom you hate so much."[48] Thirty years later, in *The Social Revolution*, Kautsky used the "analogy between birth and revolution" to show that the natural and historical phenomena were basically alike.[49]

Luxemburg adopted dialectical metaphors associated with birth and death in various contexts. In 1903, on the twentieth anniversary of Marx's death, she described his doctrine as the "child of bourgeois society," whose birth "had cost the mother's life."[50] Shortly before her own death, at the founding conference of the Communist Party of Germany, she described the declaration of a socialist republic on 9 November 1918 as the "birth cry" (*Geburtsschrei*) of revolution.[51] Lenin likewise turned to such metaphors routinely, as in his description of the St. Petersburg protests in January 1905: on Bloody Sunday "the old Russia and the new" collided "with startling force," showing "the death agony of the peasants' age-old faith in 'Our Father the Tsar,' and the birth of a revolutionary people, the urban proletariat."[52]

In an 1889 pamphlet Plekhanov recalled that Marx's historical thought belonged to an era in which social violence was regularly compared (not merely in revolutionary or oppositional circles) to the act of giving birth: "Forcible revolutions, 'torrents of blood,' scaffolds and executions, gunpowder and dynamite—these are distressing 'phenomena.' But what can we do about them, since they are inevitable? Force has always been the midwife at the birth of a new society. That is what Marx said, and he was not the only one to think so."[53] These historical upheavals would bring freedom to some, Plekhanov asserted—but destruction to others.

By assigning both creative and destructive energy to political processes, Marxist intellectuals underscored the existential importance of these processes (and of their own role therein). Such imagery was not only used intensively within Marxist discourse but also reflected the zeitgeist of an era that was principally open and widely accustomed to violence. Fundamental, heretofore unknown social changes were both the cause and the effect of popular mobilization and political participation. To most contemporaries, these changes were conceivable only as the result of violent processes.[54]

Iring Fetscher has succinctly summarized the three most important theories of revolution among Marxists before 1914: Kautsky's "pseudo-revolutionary parliamentarism" (espoused also by Bernstein, Adler, and Jaurès), Luxemburg's "democratic revolutionism" (also represented by Plekhanov and Guesde), and Lenin's distinctive "elite revolutionism."[55] These disparate theories, all (claiming to be) grounded in Marx, suggest that the metaphor of revolution drew its power from an extremely heterogeneous capacity to lend meaning, to build community, and also to mobilize. Revolutionary theory ranged between projecting long-term structural transformation and predicting imminent political regime change.[56]

The "revisionism debate" at the turn of the century dramatically exposed the tensions and contradictions in these ideas of political transformation. Marxist intellectuals perceived this debate not as a mere internal party dispute but as a broader crisis of meaning. Beyond undermining the revolutionary standpoint of the party, the revisionist criticisms leveled by Georg von Vollmar, Bernstein, Max Schippel, and others refuted some of Marx's central assumptions, including his theories of increasing misery and collapse. The debate so demoralized and shook the foundations of this intellectual community that longtime comrades parted ways; the falling-out between Kautsky and Bernstein is the foremost example.[57]

Even Lenin, who hardly counted on friendships, related this unsettling experience in *What Is to Be Done?* in 1902. Taking aim at Bernstein, he recalled the solidarity that had characterized the movement to this point:

> We are marching in a compact group along a precipitous and difficult path, firmly holding each other by the hand. We are surrounded on all sides by enemies, and we have to advance almost constantly under their fire. We have combined, by a freely adopted decision, for the purpose of fighting the enemy, and not of retreating into the neighbouring marsh, the inhabitants of which, from the very outset, have reproached us with having separated ourselves into an exclusive group and with having chosen the path of struggle instead of the path of conciliation. And now some among us begin to cry out: Let us go into the marsh! And when we begin to shame them, they retort: What backward people you are! Are you not ashamed to deny us the liberty to invite you to take a better road! Oh, yes, gentlemen! You are free not only to invite us, but to go yourselves wherever you will, even into the marsh. In fact, we think that the marsh is your proper place, and we are prepared to render *you* every assistance to get there. Only let go of our hands, don't clutch at us and don't besmirch the grand word freedom, for we too are "free" to go where we please, free to fight not only against the marsh, but also against those who are turning towards the marsh![58]

Although Lenin (not coincidentally) expressed this threat in the language of political exile, he did not fundamentally challenge the Marxist discursive community. The members of Bernstein's camp continued to insist that they were Marxist revisionists, which caused not only Kautsky to tear out his hair.[59] Bernstein wanted to stay in the "house of Marx." For some time, the heads of this household (like Bebel and Kautsky) expected him to leave of his own accord—but they never expelled him against his will.[60] All participants in this family feud looked to Marx and Engels as their guides. Undaunted, they continued to act as members of a "joint enterprise."[61] As contentious and indirect as their conversation became, it did not really fall apart until 1914. Nevertheless, this group of intellectuals never succeeded in establishing a culture of differentiation and multiperspectivity within its own relatively clear and coherent discursive space. They could agree neither about the desirability or prospects of revolution in different national contexts nor about the principal benefits and practical limits of parliamentary opposition. Instead, in 1901, Lenin framed the transnational strife, the endless quarreling between the orthodox and revisionist members of the Marxist "family," as genuine progress: "The English Fabians, the French Ministerialists, the German Bernsteinians, and the Russian Critics—all belong to the same family . . . and together take up arms. . . . In this first really international battle with socialist opportunism, international revolutionary Social-Democracy will perhaps become sufficiently strengthened to put an end to the political reaction that has long reigned in Europe."[62] Favored reproaches within the larger socialist family—about "English glasses" or hypertheoretical "Russian émigré Marxism"—were essentially biographical arguments. Rather than attempting to turn multiperspectivity into something intellectually or politically productive, many socialists preferred to denigrate others' experiences in exile, or they dismissed them out of hand.[63]

Remarkably, all of the protagonists except Adler and Jaurès had at some point lived in exile, and so they understood the personal consequences of a forced change of perspective. In 1900, the Parisian congress of the Second International passed a resolution that allowed national parties to adopt their own tactics. Three years later, the SPD overwhelmingly distanced itself from Bernstein's theses at its own conference in Dresden. At the 1904 congress of the Second International in Amsterdam, opponents of the flexible political style known as "opportunism" or "possibilism" likewise prevailed.[64] As we will see, the Russian events of 1905 compelled socialists everywhere to consider national contexts more closely and to weigh political means such as general strikes and petition marches more carefully before adopting them elsewhere. Nevertheless, at the programmatic level, where these battles were primarily fought until 1905, day-to-day political debate about "revising Marxism" seemed only to entrench and aggravate the existing conflicts.

13

Revolution at Last?

Dress Rehearsal in St. Petersburg, 1905–6

At the beginning of 1905, for the first time in more than thirty years, a real opportunity for revolutionary action opened up in Europe: the first Russian Revolution, which Lenin later called a "dress rehearsal."[1] With the eruption of violence in St. Petersburg in January 1905, the theoretical and metaphorical scenarios of a future revolution suddenly confronted a new reality. On Sunday, 22 January 1905, government forces violently dissolved a peaceful demonstration of 150,000 Petersburg residents, killing at least 130 people and injuring 1,000 more. Strikes and protests spread across the country. For the next eighteen months, the gigantic tsarist empire teetered on the brink of civil war. After the uprising had spread to hundreds of towns and villages, the tsarist regime gradually reasserted control in a "war of terror" against the population. Between October 1905 and April 1906 alone, an estimated fifteen thousand persons were executed, and another forty-five thousand punished with deportation or exile.[2] In response, antitsarist rebels murdered more than one thousand upper-level civil servants and other government employees between February 1905 and April 1906.[3]

The first general strike in Russian history took place in October 1905, compelling Tsar Nicholas II to issue the October Manifesto, promising reforms and a parliamentary assembly. But upon the outbreak of another uprising in Moscow in December, fears of renewed destabilization gained the upper hand, and the tsar violently put down the unrest. And so the revolution was stopped in the streets, but a new political order had already been put into motion. After the first, semi-free elections in March 1906, the first State Duma convened in April, but the tsar disagreed with its plans for land reform and dissolved the assembly in July. By this date, at the latest, the revolution had failed.

Irrespective of their differences in opinion, all of the protagonists—with the notable exception of Struve, who had already moved to the liberal camp—were transnationally linked through the network of the Second International and felt immediately connected to the events in Russia. They were familiar with the slow progress and struggles of the Russian social democratic movement, although usually at a far remove. *Not* responding to developments in the tsarist empire would have been unthinkable. Bebel described these long-distance ties in the *Neue Zeit* in 1905: "[The] revolutionary burrowing at last bore fruit, hopeless though it had seemed to many who observed it with interest and empathy. The propagated ideas took root. And once the given hour arrived, the world experienced the most surprising spectacle: Russia, once culturally disparaged, finds itself in a state of revolution."[4]

So how did Marx's epigones respond to this revolutionary situation twenty-two years after the master's death, and ten years after his compatriot Engels had passed? Because the unrest involved their political homeland, Lenin, Plekhanov, Luxemburg, and Struve immediately confronted the question of personal engagement—whether they would move beyond articles, lectures, and party meetings and get involved on site. The other five protagonists were, by this point, so far removed from the role of professional revolutionaries that the question did not even arise. Lenin headed to St. Petersburg late in the summer of 1905, and Luxemburg went to Warsaw in December—and so even they were distant observers of the eruption and first months of revolution. Because Struve had already renounced Marxism, he returned to St. Petersburg (after stops in Stuttgart and Paris) as a liberal journalist in October 1905. Days later, he joined the Central Committee of the liberal Constitutional Democratic Party (also known as the

Kadets), although he himself could not run for a seat in the first Duma because of his earlier residence abroad.[5] Beginning in early 1906, he participated regularly in party meetings, following the turbulent developments in and around the first Russian Parliament up close and with growing consternation. Plekhanov, by contrast, remained in Geneva, and not only because of his health—a decision that he and many of his compatriots had to defend from this point on. In this chapter, I consider Plekhanov's commentaries on Russian events from Geneva and (later) Italy alongside the work of Kautsky, Bernstein, Adler, Guesde, and Jaurès, and I compare all of their perspectives to the revolutionary experiences of the three active participants.

Kautsky returned to Germany from England in 1890. He first moved to Stuttgart, before finally settling in Berlin in 1897. As the editor-in-chief of the *Neue Zeit*, he shaped the commentary pages of one of the most important social democratic journals. According to his first article about the Petersburg "bloodbath," Kautsky, "like every socialist," was outraged by the "bestialities" of the "treacherous bloodhounds on the Neva," and he denounced tsarism as a barbaric enemy of the "civilized world."[6] He simultaneously welcomed these events not only as the fulfillment of long-held hopes but as a historically inevitable milestone that had been achieved under extraordinarily difficult conditions. Russia's great achievement was combining "the deepest theoretical insight" with the social democrats' "selfless dedication," thereby triumphing over "hopelessness" and the "urge for adventure" (which Kautsky understood as the means of terror). "Inexhaustible fervor and quiet, goal-oriented labor" had smoothed the way. In twenty years of "arduous and sacrificial labor," Russian social democrats had organized the actual powerhouse of this movement, the industrial proletariat. It would be disastrous to believe (or to persuade the European proletariat) that the liberal bourgeoisie was a genuine ally in the struggle to liberate its historical successor; the liberal bourgeoisie, despite its "democratic airs," opposed tsarist violence for quite different reasons. Without delving deeply into different national contexts, Kautsky broadly compared "1848" with "1905" (even though, in Russia, there had been no "1848"), and he suggested that a process of disillusionment and dissociation had at last come to an end: the working class no longer needed (nor desired) an alliance with the bourgeoisie. While in the mid-nineteenth-century the bourgeoisie had "not quite outgrown its revolutionary phase," in 1905 it had achieved everything that it needed and "thus became conservative."[7]

Strikingly absent in Kautsky's article was any explicit reference to the revolutionary theory of the *Communist Manifesto* or other Marxist canonical texts. Instead, he turned to bold and sweeping analogies to make sense of current events: the Russian Revolution was a semi-proletarian revolution, which appeared bourgeois only in its first "effects." If the revolution succeeded in toppling the tsar, reactionary forces from the west could be expected to band together against the "revolution in the east"—just as eastern reactionary forces at the end of the eighteenth century had fought against the "revolution in the west." But if the European proletariat mastered this "gigantic mission" with "strength, acumen, and self-sacrifice," it would be a "powerful leap forward in conquering an all-new world."[8] At the moment, however, there was little that outsiders could do to contribute to the success of the Russian Revolution. At most, western socialists could help by raising money and public awareness.

Two issues later, Kautsky returned to Russian events on the pages of the *Neue Zeit*, this time taking the role of the peasants as the point of departure for his theoretical reflections. The uprising appeared to be spreading from the towns to the countryside, and correspondents in Russia had reported that the tsarist government was planning a systematic campaign to incite the peasantry against the supposedly treasonous intelligentsia (meaning social democrats, Jews, and *zemstvo* delegates). These reports were also discussed in Germany, even the SPD newspaper *Vorwärts* stoking "fear of an uprising of the dark masses."[9] Kautsky sought to dispel these fears, and he explained how the role of the Russian social democrats, who largely recruited from student circles, had changed significantly since the unsuccessful days of the Narodniks. Unlike the privileged, pompous elites at German universities, Russian students came from modest means and were "more receptive to proletarian sensibilities." Thus, Kautsky argued, it was wrong to speak of a natural antagonism between peasants and intelligentsia—a reasoning that also appealed to Lenin, who, writing from Geneva, praised its "practical" validity.[10] And so Kautsky confidently answered the question of the peasantry's influence on the revolution: "Far from endangering the cause of revolution, peasant outrage must support it."[11]

This confidence notwithstanding, Kautsky attempted to account for social realities, as he saw them, in his theoretical perspectives on revolution. Beyond acknowledging broadly compatible motives, socialists had not yet resolved their position on the peasants. Meanwhile, their favored historical actor, the "industrial proletariat," was still too weak. And so Kautsky conceded that the existing peasant economy could not simply become "a permanent part of the framework of socialist production." Particularly in Russia, the transition from underdeveloped capitalism to highly developed socialism would have to be completely rethought. Kautsky's reflections on the special situation in Russia brought him back to the distinction between social and political revolutions. Russian development was so far removed from the premises that socialists had discussed for years that Kautsky did not have to question their theoretical validity:

> What is at stake in Russia today is not, for the time being, a question of *social* revolution; it is not the conquest of political power by one of society's lower classes as part of the movement toward a *new* mode of production. It is, instead, a question of *political* revolution—removing political obstacles that hinder the free functioning of the existing [capitalist] mode of production. The historic role of the industrial socialist proletariat in this [political] revolution is not laying the foundations of a socialist society, but instead promoting the interests of democracy more boldly, more "radically," than all other classes—for the time being, still on the foundations of today's society.[12]

At stake in Russia, according to Kautsky, was a bourgeois–democratic revolution, supported by the proletariat; this revolution was not yet about introducing socialism but about the "free" development of democratic and capitalist structures. Thus, he was compelled to reconcile Marxist revolutionary theory with quite idiosyncratic events in Russia. He was aware that Russia deviated sharply from the scheme of socialist revolution that Marx and Engels had devised. In turn-of-the-century Russia, there was little distinctively bourgeois property that had been created by capitalist endeavors—although in the *Manifesto* Marx and Engels had declared "the inevitably impending dissolution of modern bourgeois property" an essential precondition for proletarian revolution.[13] Further, Kautsky must have known that Marx had advised Vera Zasulich that the analysis in *Capital* applied only to western Europe. In 1881 Marx had written to Zasulich about his "special study" of the Russian *obshchina*, in which he had concluded that "this commune is the fulcrum of social regeneration in Russia."[14] One year later, in the preface to the second Russian edition of the *Communist Manifesto*, Marx and Engels had further specified that the significance of a Russian revolution would lie only in its global context—namely, in its function as a "signal for a proletarian revolution in the West"; the two revolutions would have to "complement each other." They only vaguely discussed the social order that would come *after* a successful revolt in backward Russia, which did not actually fit into their revolutionary scheme; if the revolutionary spark passed from Russia to western Europe, then the "common ownership of land," as practiced by the Russian *obshchina*, "may serve as the starting point for communist development."[15]

Beyond his initial euphoria (he described "Bloody Sunday" as a "powerful leap" forward), Kautsky did not yet discuss how events in Russia might affect the wider world. Adler, Bernstein, and Struve expressly feared the scenario of world revolution, and Jaurès considered the idea of a "domino effect" to be obsolete. Only Luxemburg, Lenin, and Guesde hoped for the chain reaction once envisioned by Marx, and they came to see the general strike—which had been impressively tested in St. Petersburg and Moscow—as one of the best means of triggering it. In the end, Marx and Engels's twenty-five-year-old remarks about Russia's revolutionary prospects were vague enough to encourage all kinds of hopes and endless "tea leaf reading."[16] This was true not only for Kautsky, and not only in the context of 1905.

Instead of hoping that the revolutionary spark would leap to their own countries, Kautsky and many other western European comrades fixated on the deepening divisions within Russian Marxism. Russian liberals and even some socialists increasingly doubted "the battle-readiness of the Russian proletariat." This concerned even the "former social democrat" Struve, Kautsky reported in November 1905.[17] And yet, only a few weeks earlier, Bebel had enthusiastically written to Adler that the proletariat was acting "splendidly." One could only hope that "it will come to an end and soon," Adler responded with a hint of self-criticism (and no desire whatsoever for world revolution): "In other countries, after all, the proletariat is advancing not because of, but *despite*, its leaders."[18] The social democratic press began to report that Russian society (or its autocratic inertia) was breaking— concerns for which Kautsky, contemplating events at his desk, had no empathy whatsoever. Shortly after the mutiny of the Russian Black Sea Fleet in June 1905, Kautsky remarked contemptuously on a letter in *Vorwärts* by the newspaper's St. Petersburg correspondent, who "whined about the 'chaos,'" exuding "pessimism" and exhaustion." The correspondent ended his "entire unbelievable jeremiad" with a sentiment that Kautsky apparently deemed absurd: that "wherever order, law, and gainful employment" did not exist, every political "hope" would die.[19]

Kautsky was heartened by the elections for the first Duma in the spring of 1906, and he renewed his efforts to generalize about Russian developments. He now espoused an entirely new revolutionary theory, moving beyond commentary on current events to offer sweeping predictions. He proposed that the first Duma neither concluded the revolution nor introduced "an epoch of peaceful evolution," but instead had become the point of departure for a now "centralized revolution." It had become increasingly evident that the parties in the

Duma could not "reconcile or overcome" the contradictions that had emerged. And so the Duma would have to "heighten the revolutionary temperature, increase revolutionary consciousness." Newly represented peasants and proletarians would demand the expropriation of private property, worker protections and the eight-hour workday, freedom of assembly and the press, and direct and equal suffrage. They would prod the Duma forward, declare national bankruptcy, dissolve the standing army, and order "far-reaching confiscations," until they "crippled and ultimately swept away" their opponents. The Duma had introduced a "new and more dangerous stage of revolution," becoming its center. The results of a "centralized revolution" would be "even more irresistible than the glorious achievements of October."[20] These prophecies soon proved overly ambitious, as the tsar dissolved the Duma just seventy-two days after it first convened. It did not implement a single reform, let alone the centralized revolution imagined by Kautsky.

Bernstein responded to events in Russia much more cautiously. The debate around reform or revolution, which he had touched off in the 1890s, had upended his personal and political existence. Since his break with Kautsky and the SPD's formal renunciation of his revisionist theses at the Dresden party conference in 1903, Bernstein had largely resigned himself to the role of a sidelined renegade.[21] Looking back at the controversy, he later conceded with some "embarrassment" that he had underestimated the "spiritual significance" of his criticism for the party. The meaning of the word "revolutionary" had played a central role in this controversy, and Bernstein's admission reflected its ambivalence—not merely with respect to ideology but also to the psychology of the movement. Bernstein reflected in 1924 that although the label "revolutionary," in its usual sense, had not really applied to German social democracy, for workers in the SPD it had been an "uplifting symbol": "It marked the line that distinguished the party they esteemed from all other parties; it demonstrated [the party's] distinctive worldview." His own critique, he conceded, seems not to have questioned "a matter of reason" but rather one of "feeling."[22]

Bernstein had already arrived at these conclusions during the controversy itself,[23] which smoothed the way for his continued party affiliation and even enabled his fresh start as an elected official. Two years after returning to Germany, he was offered the chance to run for the newly vacant district of Breslau-West. Between 1903 and 1912, he led a comparatively quiet party existence as a Reichstag delegate and specialist in taxation and finance. Cured by this prehistory of any desire to predict the course of events, he responded with cautious enthusiasm to Russian developments in the winter of 1905. "Russia is in revolution, there's no possible doubt about it," he wrote in the *Sozialistische Monatshefte* in April 1905, adding that "it would be presumptuous to want to predict the course of this revolution."[24] Quite unlike Kautsky, Bernstein sought historical comparisons to define the character of the Russian Revolution. He recapitulated the course of the English and French revolutions in the seventeenth and eighteenth centuries, as well as the revolutions of 1848, although at the end of his article he hardly did more than repeat his opening thesis. If the "materialist view of history, or whatever one wants to call Marx's historical doctrine," was worth anything—indeed, he wrote pointedly, if "this evolutionary, organic view of history had any value whatsoever"—then it now had to prove itself as a "means of prediction." Based on earlier conditions in Russia, Bernstein concluded, this revolution could only be "bourgeois-liberal-democratic."[25] Measured by the outcome of the revolution, by Bernstein's reasoning, Marx's theory proved worthless.

Bernstein was somewhat more decisive in formulating his thoughts on the peasantry, whom he generally regarded as a "highly unreliable political factor." Because of their hunger for land, they were the most revolutionary—but also the most unpredictable—social force. History had repeatedly shown that "wherever peasants had drawn all they could . . . from the tree of revolution, they always dropped off again, like leeches from a patient's body."[26] This analogy (which recalls his earlier tree metaphor) reveals something of Bernstein's deep skepticism toward the potentially destructive power of "the masses." He continued to grapple with this skepticism in protracted debates about the mass strike as a tactic of social democratic politics, a discussion that only intensified after the 1905 Revolution.[27] Although the events in Russia played almost no role in his autobiographical texts and barely informed his contributions to the mass strike debate, the question of violence, directly related to the problem of revolution, continued to occupy him intensely. In the 1920s, his opposition to the violent "revolutionary romanticism" of Luxemburg's mass strike scenarios led him to reject Bolshevism categorically. He understood Bolshevism as a Marxist mutation of "Blanquism," which he had denounced as a stain on the socialist movement since the turn of the century. Marxism encapsulated the socialists' eternal struggle between "building up" and "tearing down." While discrediting the putsch as a political tactic, Marxism continued "to overestimate the creative power of revolutionary violence for the socialist reconfiguration of modern society."[28]

Kautsky believed that Bernstein's decidedly pacifist convictions were an underlying reason for his friend's distancing from "orthodox" Marxism. It was in the fall of 1897, Kautsky wrote to Adler at the peak of his public dispute with Bernstein, that he was first struck by "Ede's animosity against every revolutionary movement." The occasion was Bernstein's review of the Italian anthropologist Scipio Sighele's study *La folla delinquente*, which was published in German in 1897. Bernstein had contrasted the dangers of mass uprisings with the "almost mythical faith in the nameless masses" among some social democrats: "The mob, the assembled crowd, the 'people on the street' is to this extent a power that can be everything—revolutionary and reactionary, heroic and cowardly, human and bestial, but, in the majority of cases, tends more to destroy than to create. . . . We should pay them heed, but if we are supposed to idolize them, we might just as well become fire worshippers."[29] The destruction of French revolutionary ideals in the Terror was at the heart of Bernstein's unease with the prospects of Russian revolution in 1905. His unwillingness or inability to conceive of revolutionary violence as "creative" may explain why his remarks on these events seem so muddled and shallow.

Among those protagonists who were geographically or biographically distant from the revolutionary action, none felt its political effects more keenly than Adler. His Social Democratic Workers' Party had become an important political factor in the government crises and nationality conflicts that had shaken the Habsburg Empire since 1895. Paradoxically, according to Steven Beller's thesis, Adler's internationalist party, "because of its own supranationality, became one of the Monarchy's best hopes for survival."[30] In the summer of 1905, as Kaiser Franz Joseph supported the Social Democrats' demand for universal suffrage—primarily to neutralize the centrifugal forces of the multinational state but also with an eye to events in Russia—the party walked a thin line between credibly threatening the government with a general strike and taming its own radical voices.[31] Since the mid-1880s, Adler had navigated his party, largely without violence, through the world of day-to-day politics. He denounced radicalism and rhetorical escalation, and he made sure that his colleagues understood the dire consequences of demonstrations or strikes turning deadly.[32] Except for self-defense, he considered all forms of violence (such as looting and plundering during a strike) to be dangerous, in no way revolutionary, and "simply unreasonable."[33]

In the first decade of the new century, the effect of the revolution in Russia on Austrian politics was not unlike the notorious "specter" described in the *Communist Manifesto*. Adler's party speeches from this era, along with his letters to comrades in Germany, urgently warned against drawing parallels with events in Russia and against too hastily portraying the debate over suffrage as a social democratic triumph. In September 1906 Adler wrote to Bebel that he wished "our party will be neither all too famous, nor shrink all too much," and he asked that the "exemplification of Austria" be avoided "*as much as possible*." Although the voting law had passed "with the help of the Kaiser, the Russian revolution, etc.," it was "*altogether undesirable, even dangerous*" to play up these connections—as had occurred at the SPD's recent conference in Mannheim.[34]

In a speech Adler delivered in Vienna at the end of January 1905, he described the excesses of St. Petersburg's Bloody Sunday as an all-too familiar horror. He had heard dreadful tales from Russia throughout his entire life, but now there was hope for the "beginning of the end of the horror." Adler nevertheless remained as circumspect as Bernstein on the prospects of revolution. In his distinctively concrete fashion, Adler compared the situation in Russia to that in Austria, underscoring the "immense" exertion of an uprising for a people that "stands under the most detestable and abominable pressure." Adler saw the uprising's historical significance as its destruction of faith in the tsar as the "father" of the nation, as well as the general erosion of "devotion to the fatherland" among average Russians. When members of his Viennese audience joked that the entire upset must have been caused by a few thousand well-meaning St. Petersburgers attempting to speak with their father, Adler reminded them that this fatal affection was a "serious, deep, and important concern." For all of the "sacrifices and dedication" of the Austrian Social Democrats, their accomplishments paled in comparison to those of the long-suffering Russian revolutionaries.[35]

In contrast to Kautsky and Bernstein, Adler also considered the revolution's structural causes. On the one hand, "Russian capitalism" sought access to new resources and markets in the war against Japan— but it had failed because the ailing tsarist bureaucracy had undermined the "existential conditions for capitalism" and was thus incapable of implementing capitalist policies. On the other hand, the police, in their "devilish or Jesuit manner," had built up workers' organizations in St. Petersburg, Odessa, and Moscow for purposes of surveillance— but they had not counted on the groups developing into genuine "proletarian organizations." Adler went further than either Kautsky or Bernstein in heralding the protests as signs of a "proletarian revolution," wholly in line with Marxist theory:

> The bearer [*Träger*] of this revolution—and this, yet again, validates our viewpoint—is the industrial proletariat. The social democratic movement has always known: As long as the proletariat is absent, we can

prepare for revolution but not enact it. What hopes were placed in the peasantry, how much was expected from the old communist organizations in the villages, from the terrorists, from the intelligentsia alone! Now here they are, the old peasants, but none the wiser—ripped from the soil, the same primeval peasants, now transplanted as exploited proletarians. Landowners reduced to slaves—and, precisely because of this, uplifted as the bearers of a historical transformation.[36]

Impressed by events, Adler reconsidered long-held convictions such as the notion that the most wretched "proletariat" was also the least revolutionary. Instead, he heralded the industrial proletariat—the steelier descendant of the "gray man" from the Russian countryside—as the standard-bearer of socialist world revolution. This shift in argumentation attested to the flexibility of Marxist revolutionary theory, *despite* numerous false predictions.[37]

Adler worried about the quarrelsome Russian and Polish exiles, who would soon be returning to Russia en masse, sowing discord "in all circles, and affecting the movement in the very worst way," as Bebel reported to him in May 1905, on the word of "a very reliable source." The workers did not understand this "hair splitting," and they departed meetings enraged by the Marxists' regular disruptions.[38] Yet, in these months, Adler also expressed concern about the troubled biographies of particularly battle-worn Russian Marxists. He felt sorry for the "terribly pompous" Plekhanov, whom he respected but disliked for his "absurd pieties [*abgeschmackte Pfaffereien*]."[39] He saw Plekhanov as a "downright tragic figure"—a man undeserving of his fate, even though he had certainly "sinned." Reflecting on Plekhanov's decision not to return to Russia (which I will discuss more thoroughly below), Adler considered the extent of his own revolutionary engagement, including his willingness to die for the cause: "In his place, I couldn't take it, I'd go to Russia and have myself deported or shot—forging weapons all your life, and when the battle finally, finally comes, having to stand aside—it's dreadful!"[40]

The decision to keep his distance did not come easy to Plekhanov. He was in poor health and rightly feared that he would be arrested if he chose to return to Russia, and so he opted against Adler's imagined scenario. Soon after the Genevan newspapers reported on the turmoil in St. Petersburg—and one week later, in Warsaw—Plekhanov wrote that workers and bourgeois revolutionaries of all political persuasions ought to find common cause, just as he had imagined a revolution in stages for more than twenty years. "March separately, strike together!" became his well-known motto, which quickly antagonized the Bolsheviks.[41] Plekhanov believed that constructively toppling tsarism demanded the "proletarianization" of society and the spread of socialist ideas, especially among the liberal bourgeoisie. By contrast, Lenin (and with some reservations, also Adler and Kautsky) focused on an alliance with the peasantry.[42] To the same degree that Plekhanov placed his faith in the bourgeoisie and mistrusted the peasants, Lenin set store by the peasants and mistrusted the bourgeoisie. Lenin criticized Plekhanov for deviating opportunistically from Marx's doctrine of a purely "proletarian" revolution, while Plekhanov believed that his gradualism was wholly in line with the revolutionary theory of Marx and Engels. Still others saw Plekhanov as a thick-headed old man who refused to adapt to new realities and who failed to grasp that the Russian circumstances of 1905 demanded new tactics.[43] The revolution itself was sweeping away "tactical differences with astonishing speed," as Lenin wrote in a conciliatory letter to Plekhanov in October 1905. If Lenin (who was still in Geneva) received a response, it has not survived.[44]

The conflict with Lenin had been smoldering for some time. It finally ignited at the second congress of the Russian Social Democratic Labor Party (RSDLP), held in Brussels and London in 1903, and intensified dramatically in the first year of the revolution. Plekhanov received the priest Georgy Gapon, leader of the St. Petersburg protest march, along with sailors from the mutinous battleship *Potemkin*, at his home in Geneva. He sought to position himself outside the Bolshevik and Menshevik camps, and to this end, in the spring of 1905, he founded his own journal, *Diary of a Social Democrat*, which exclusively featured his own texts.[45] As the year progressed, he began to doubt the revolutionary commitment of the liberals. He nevertheless upheld the vision of a broad social revolution, which reinforced criticisms that he was "insufficiently class conscious."[46] Undaunted by his detractors, he criticized the Moscow uprising of December 1905 as amateurish, and its casualties as senseless.

Having decided for whichever reasons not to return to Russia, Plekhanov characterized himself in private conversations as a tragic "deserter." He had long felt as if he had outlived his usefulness as a "revolutionary from the 'intelligentsia'"; it had been years since he had imagined himself in the role of Chernyshevsky's hero Rakhmetov. Already in 1894, driven by a mixture of uncertainty and calculated optimism, he had written that the revolutionary intellectual "has almost finished playing his part. He no longer has any originality, he is repeating himself, growing shallow. His place must, and will, be taken by revolutionaries from the working class, those true 'children of the people.'"[47] Ten years later, confronted with actual revolution in faraway Russia, Plekhanov openly confronted this state of affairs. From this point forward, he contented himself with the public role of a "man of letters." Lenin, meanwhile, understood how to exploit this change of face, questioning the political judgment of "comrades active chiefly as publicists," and contrasting their views with the insights of the "Party workers of the practical centre [in Russia]"—with whom Lenin clearly identified, although he still lived in Geneva.[48]

As befit a "man of letters," Plekhanov turned his attention to the fine arts. In the spring of 1905, he traveled to the sixth International Art Exhibition in Venice, where he criticized much of the art on display as "one-sided" and "deaf to the aspirations of the working class," capable only of urging "pity." In his review of the exhibition, which was published in *Pravda* and the *Neue Zeit*, he rued its lack of connection to the epoch of "protest" that was currently intensifying on Russia's political stage. He complained about the general lack of ideas in modern bourgeois art, and he interpreted widespread references to the Classical era as longing for the "good old days" without confronting troublesome questions of the present. Plekhanov concluded his review with the prophecy that fundamental change was dawning in the east: "The best of those representatives of the upper classes who have not been able to go over once and for all to the side of the proletariat are capable only of wishing '*good night*' to the unfortunate and oppressed. Thank you, kind sirs! But your clocks are slow: the night is at an end, the '*real day*' is beginning."[49] This new reality began without Plekhanov. In early 1906—as the revolution faltered and new arrests signaled that any possible window for returning to Russia had long since closed—Plekhanov traveled to a spa in Genoa. He increasingly shunned party politics, committing himself wholly to his "third life," as a literary scholar (following his careers as an underground activist and party leader).

Plekhanov's absence from current affairs was striking—not only with respect to the tumultuous events in Russia in 1905–6 but also beforehand, among the many Russian émigrés and their sympathizers in western Europe. Paris, along with Geneva, became a second home for many of the exiles. In Paris at the end of 1904, eight Russian opposition parties (including the Union of Liberation, cofounded by Struve) issued a joint declaration, calling for an end to absolutism and the transition to a constitutional order in Russia. Jaurès highlighted this document, and other work by the Russian socialists in exile, in his role as the editor-in-chief of *L'Humanité*.[50] The joint declaration was printed in socialist newspapers all over Europe and distributed in Russia as an illegal pamphlet. Already in November 1904, a *zemstvo* conference in St. Petersburg—the only popularly elected institution in the tsarist empire—had taken up the call for a constitutional assembly.

Jaurès wrote that this first joint campaign by multiple Russian opposition parties would lead the fight against absolutism until "a democratic regime based on universal suffrage" and the principle of "popular sovereignty" prevailed. He could only speculate why the Genevan Marxists close to the "preeminent" Plekhanov had not attended; it was difficult to assess the "tactics and methods" of another socialist party, especially from a country as far away as Russia. Jaurès, ever the optimist, assumed that this abstinence was only temporary and that all "forces of freedom" in Russia would soon unite to topple the tsar and build a democratic order. This momentous act would be the "greatest event in the history of humanity since the French Revolution."[51]

The evident interest of Jaurès and *L'Humanité* points to the lively, if geographically distant, engagement of many French socialists in the Russian Revolution. Between the end of 1904 and mid-1906, Jaurès published no fewer than forty-five lead articles on the Russian question, and *L'Humanité* sent its own correspondent to St. Petersburg in December 1904. In cooperation with other newspapers (such as the Guesdists' *Le Socialiste*), within just a few months France's political left had collected thirty-four thousand francs in charitable donations,[52] attracted subscribers for Russian émigré journals like Struve's *Osvobozhdenie* (Liberation), and founded a French-Russian friendship circle under the leadership of writer Anatole France.[53] Ongoing differences between reformers and radicals notwithstanding, the French saw events in Russia as a continuation of their own liberation movement—as a baton passing from west to east in an avant-garde revolutionary tradition that had shaped European politics for more than a century. Beyond "1789," the defeat of the Paris Commune in 1871 also figured prominently in French reporting on Russia, particularly in the aftermath of Bloody Sunday. Coincidentally, one of the last well-known heroines of the Commune, Louise Michel, passed away around this time; her funeral in Paris on 22 January, the first day of violence in St. Petersburg, received much attention. The French Revolution nevertheless remained a favored analogy to make sense of Russian events. Contemporary debates about their significance, particularly among the followers of Jaurès and Guesde, show how the narrative of revolutionary tradition gradually shifted from France to Russia in early twentieth-century Europe. By the time the Bolsheviks seized power in the fall of 1917, the Russian Revolution was widely recognized as the "international model revolution."[54]

More directly than other Marxists, Jaurès used his analyses of the Russian situation to draw attention to the drastic consequences of imperialism, particularly in the war against Japan. Victims of imperialism included soldiers on all sides who perished or who were compelled to kill and plunder, as well as workers who were shot to death in St. Petersburg and Armenians who were contemporaneously persecuted or murdered by the "Red Sultan" Abdülhamid.[55] Long before the crisis in St. Petersburg, both *L'Humanité* and *Le Socialiste* had reported intensively on the Russo-Japanese War. The Guesdists described this conflict as a "holy war";[56] the more dire the outcome for Russia, the sooner tsarism would collapse and open up a historic opportunity for proletarian revolution. Jaurès, by contrast, questioned the "usefulness" of a lost war for the proletarian cause: "Today the cause of revolution is tied to the cause of peace."[57] He doubted whether a revolution born in war could bring social peace. Thus, already in 1905, he warned about developments that would transpire in Russia in October 1917, three years after his own murder.

Jaurès opposed recalling Russian government bonds—as Guesdist radicals demanded, in protest against the tsar—because the collapse of Russia's already faltering economic system would only heighten the country's misery.[58] In general, Jaurès argued that revolution was to be fostered and celebrated as a step toward freedom. Unlike the Guesdists, he did not hope that a supposed alliance between tsar, capital, and bourgeoisie would force the country into "bankruptcy,"[59] nor did he fear revolution, as did the conservative press. The "death of tsarism" did not have to mean the ruin of a "great people." The Russians had suffered more than anyone under "duplicitous absolutism," and these intolerable conditions had given them the political maturity to take fate by the hand.[60] The Russian proletariat had come to the "battlefield" last, but was now at the forefront of the European struggle. A victory over Russian absolutism would spread across the entire continent, becoming a milestone in the development toward peace, democracy, and justice that had begun in 1789.

The tsar, by contrast, was leading a movement in decline. Invoking the revolutionary evolutionism of Marx and Engels, Jaurès prophesied that the "sinister tactlessness" and brutality of tsarist rule would compromise not only autocratic tradition but also "capitalism as a whole." In his resistance to reform, the tsar had unleashed an unstoppable political force, a "political proletarian revolution, the catalyst for universal social revolution."[61] Jaurès hoped that these conflicts would lead the tsarist empire toward parliamentarism and constitutionalism—which is why he believed (unlike Kautsky, who was always searching for a theory) that the July 1906 dissolution of the first Duma marked the revolution's failure.[62]

Struve had also placed his hopes in this failed development. He and Jaurès were very familiar with one another's work, but they were probably only passing acquaintances. Struve had lived in Paris since the end of 1904, where he was known as a foremost representative of Russian émigré liberalism. In Jaurès's commentaries on the Russian Revolution in *L'Humanité*, he praised Struve as an upstanding constitutionalist, full of "wisdom and courage."[63] As every social democrat in Europe surely knew, Struve had broken with Marxism in 1901, and he had become the voice of Russian liberalism with his journal *Osvobozhdenie*, published first in Stuttgart and then in Paris. This in no way lessened Jaurès's admiration; in fact, the opposite was true. Jaurès saw Struve at the intellectual forefront of a long overdue transition from absolutism to republicanism, toward a "new order of social justice" with ramifications well beyond Russia.[64]

Breaking with the Russian Social Democrats left Struve in turmoil. His autobiographical texts about this period, which he wrote in the 1930s, are steeped in the traumas of the Bolshevik seizure of power in 1917. He complained about the Russian liberals' blindness toward the socialists' virulent, irrational "revolutionism," which fomented "selfish and wild instincts" among "the masses" for political gain: "A fatal organic and indissoluble connexion was revealed between that social-democratic cult of force . . . and that régime of oppression which the Bolshevik Social-Democrats, who have changed their name to

Communists, established in November 1917."[65] He simultaneously criticized the liberals' (and thus his own) unwillingness or inability to build a functional political coalition with the conservatives under Prime Minister Pyotr Stolypin, even after the defeat of autocracy in 1905.[66]

The Red Terror changed Struve's life (he fled to Finland, then Bulgaria, and finally Paris in 1918), and so it may well have overshadowed other, no less formative life experiences during the difficult years of his political reinvention between 1901 and 1906. One such moment was his arrest at a demonstration on St. Petersburg's Kazan Square in March 1901. Struve had just returned from Munich, where he had met with Lenin, Julius O. Martov, and Alexander Potresov, representatives of the Russian Social Democratic newspaper *Iskra*. The men had agreed that Struve would establish his own revisionist publication, but—their differences in opinion notwithstanding—also that he would continue to raise money for the Social Democrats within his liberal circles. Student demonstrations, repression at the universities, and the assassination of the Russian education minister heightened tensions in early March 1901, and on 4 March (also a Sunday) students and members of the St. Petersburg writers' union assembled in protest outside the Kazan Cathedral. The situation escalated quickly. The crowd hurled snowballs and shoes at the approaching Cossacks, who lashed the demonstrators with whips (*nagaiki*). According to a companion, Struve was enraged—less by the Cossacks' ruthless actions in principle than by the fact that he himself had been struck. "What the devil is this? How dare they!" he is said to have shouted. "How dare they strike me on the legs with a nagaika! You understand?—me! me! me!"[67]

Struve's outrage surely did not abate after he and around one thousand other demonstrators were arrested and sentenced to "administrative exile." He elected to spend his one-year sentence in the central Russian town of Tver, a center of the liberal *zemstvo* movement. By the time he successfully fled from this comparatively mild form of exile in 1902, his agreement with Lenin and *Iskra* was obsolete. Upon establishing *Osvobozhdenie* in 1902, and the Union of Liberation one year later, his break with Marxist social democracy and transition to liberalism was complete. Lenin berated Struve as a "Judas," even encouraging his followers to murder him. An aversion to all forms of political violence dominated Struve's worldview from this point forward. He despised how the Social Democrats and Socialist Revolutionaries toyed with the violent tendencies of the "masses," no less than how the tsarist regime brutally responded to even moderate reformers like himself.[68]

From Paris, Struve composed a German-language essay on the revolutionary events of 1905. He understood revolution as a naturally erupting, "intellectual exchange between the revolution of higher, or more educated, classes and the insurrection of lower ones." With "careful tending," revolution could be gradually transformed into a controlled, progressive process. Driven by an "instinctive" will to survive, the masses would engage in an "elementary rebellion against the state," which would then combine with the intelligentsia's deliberate opposition.[69] Struve compared the situation in his homeland to the French Revolution, which had been carried by a strong Third Estate, and also by an "idea of the nation" with a "strong will to political power"—neither of which was present in contemporary Russia. Instead, tsarist autocracy embodied an ambivalent mixture of progress and reaction. The tsar's recent economic reforms aimed to bring Russia from premodernity directly into the "technical prosperity of the twentieth century"—without a medieval era, without a real bourgeoisie, and in spite of the persistent misery and "barbarism of the masses." Meanwhile, an absolute and altogether modern police state blocked the country's political modernization.[70]

Struve asserted that Russia's paradoxical development had led to the "objective necessity for revolution"—but this necessity did not derive from Marx's revolutionary theory and class struggle as the sole force of progress. Instead, it was driven by the beneficent, radical reformism of the aristocratic and bourgeois *zemstvo* movement and Russia's national liberal culture. In no other country were the "educated middle classes" so sociopolitically open-minded. And so, Struve argued, Russia's only hope for a brighter future lay in democratization, rule of law, and becoming a "modern," multiethnic nation. No "socialist miracles" would occur, but an "honestly implemented, democratic constitutional reform" would undoubtedly "inaugurate an era of great social reforms." Even taking "'Marxist' considerations" into account, one could still hope that Russia's "political class struggle" would soften into a culture of "political coalition." Struve envisioned flexible alliances between peasants, industrial workers, and entrepreneurs against the interests of the landed aristocracy (to institute agricultural reform), and between peasants, industrial workers, and the landed aristocracy against entrepreneurs (for worker protection laws).[71] In the future, he hoped, existing class antagonisms could become converging class interests.

Upon his return to Russia at the end of 1905, Struve quickly saw that these hopes were unrealistic. As member of the Kadet Party's Central Committee (but unable to stand for election himself), he was limited to the role of an observer even while serving as an active politician. The tsar's unwillingness to implement substantial agricultural or workplace reforms in cooperation with the Duma, alongside the revolutionary impatience on the left, drained him of all political optimism over the course of 1906. Now more than ever, Struve saw that the practice of "political revolution" had become a dangerous and unacceptable political tool. And so he actively distanced himself from a movement that had, in the meantime, become inseparable from Marx's name. After the dissolution of the second Duma in mid-1907, Struve retreated from party politics once and for all, turning to his work as an increasingly conservative publisher, journalist, and cultural philosopher.

"I see with horror, for God's sake with real horror, that there has been talk about bombs *for more than a year* and yet not a single bomb has been made!"[72] In October 1905, shortly before returning to Russia, Lenin wrote to his Petersburg comrades in the Bolshevik Central Committee. Whereas Struve, who hoped for an end to political violence, returned to St. Petersburg without any friction around the same time, Lenin was immediately placed under surveillance, and from a series of hideouts he assumed a very personal role in escalating the popular rebellion. The violent impatience of his tactical directions suggests that he was racing to engage in the events that had shaped his homeland's politics for more than nine months. He took up his pen almost daily, "to set out certain ideas" and direct his party's leadership, which had relocated to Russia in the spring of 1905. His texts on the first Russian Revolution fill three volumes of his *Collected Works*— more than fifteen hundred pages in all.[73] In his articles, polemics, and internal directives from Geneva, he had complained repeatedly about his status as an observer. However, the actual danger he faced in being arrested on Russian soil shrank considerably over the summer, as the tsarist police state increasingly lost control—overwhelmed by defeat in the war against Japan, protests and strikes, parties and unions, and the breakdown of censorship. Yet Lenin had to be prodded for weeks by his comrades in St. Petersburg before he finally returned to Russia—a striking contrast to the revolutionary impatience he expressed on paper.[74]

In his correspondence, Lenin regretted having to formulate his views "from the hateful 'abroad' of an exile." He self-deprecatingly referred to himself as an "uninformed person," knowing that it was "all but impossible . . . to form a correct opinion" since he not been to St. Petersburg, had never seen the Soviet of Workers' Deputies, and had not "exchanged views with comrades on the spot." Until he could acquaint himself with all these developments—"from something more than 'paper' information"—he reserved the right to revise his opinion.[75] Even so, he already claimed the right to set the course for his party. In fact, managing a revolution from afar was a role that suited him well. He was primarily a strategist and propagandist, not an activist or public speaker. Unlike Leon Trotsky, the rising star of the Mensheviks, Lenin had not yet cultivated the talent of mesmerizing large crowds with his speeches. He was not a "popular tribune," nor did he aspire to become one.[76]

In the few weeks that he spent in Russia in the fall and winter of 1905–6, Lenin was known for whipping the anonymous "masses" into line with his writing and not for fighting on the streets himself with the many newly politicized workers. He was not especially active in the meetings and day-to-day work of the Petersburg Soviet, which essentially controlled the city between mid-October and the end of December. Trotsky, the best-known Marxist, took the lead here, too. Nadezhda Krupskaya later reconstructed these months in Russia almost exclusively from Lenin's articles, but she herself could not recall if he had ever spoken in the Soviet.[77] Lenin was a respected organizer and polemicist, although his ruthless fanaticism and support for anarchist methods (like robbing banks to finance the Bolsheviks) frustrated even seasoned revolutionaries.[78]

Most of the other protagonists emphasized the parallels between 1905 and 1789, and they referred relatively infrequently to Marx's theory of revolution. Lenin, however, pointed repeatedly to the "lessons" of the failed revolts in 1848 and 1871, quoting specific texts by Marx and Engels and calling for "*thorough*" reading—and translating and printing new editions—in the midst of the revolutionary turmoil.[79] He saw Marxism as the "quintessence" of his thought and action, and the "independent, uncompromisingly Marxist party of the revolutionary proletariat" as "the sole pledge of socialism's victory."[80] During these months, Krupskaya reported, Lenin sought out everything that Marx and Engels had ever written about revolutions and insurrections. In preparation for the impending civil war, he also read up on the latest scholarship in military science and the history of war.[81]

Lenin worked throughout the year to develop a flexible extension of Marx's revolutionary "scheme." Although Marx had envisioned that autocracy would first be replaced by "a bourgeois monarchy and then by a petty-bourgeois democratic republic,"[82] in Russia the outlines of this scheme would have to be regarded as fluid. In April 1905 Lenin composed his long treatise introducing the "dictatorship of the proletariat"—an idea he had not drawn from books alone, but formulated in the midst of revolution. The new dictatorship would be provisionally supported by the small "proletarian class" and the "millions of urban and rural poor whose conditions of existence are petty-bourgeois."[83]

For Lenin, flexibility in realizing Marx's scheme in Russia meant acknowledging that the Russian bourgeoisie was more tightly bound to the tsar than had been either the French bourgeoisie in 1789 and 1871 or the German bourgeoisie in 1848, to their respective monarchies. Thus, Russian workers had to embrace the "immense petty-bourgeois, peasant stratum" as allies, in order to transform a half-hearted bourgeois revolution (which was further impeded by Menshevik *khvostists*, or "tail-enders") into one that was truly "revolutionary democratic." Until the Social Democrats had established a "revolutionary democratic dictatorship of the proletariat and the peasantry," successfully defending it against enemies, any transition to socialism would be inconceivable. Marx and Engels's scheme could be realized only by forgoing the phase of bourgeois democracy, in which the proletariat would ostensibly mature into the strongest "class."[84]

Lenin issued this fundamental criticism of the irresolute, pro-liberal Mensheviks just before the RSDLP's third party congress, which was held by the Bolsheviks alone in London in April 1905. The heart of Lenin's criticism contained the program for a European revolution that would shape an entire century. Standing on "the shoulders of a number of revolutionary generations," Lenin styled himself, in opposition to *khvostist* politicians (so called because they "dragged at the tail" of events), as a visionary leader of the avant-garde. Tightly organized revolutionary leadership would ensure the growth of the Russian Revolution into a "movement of many years" and gradually infuse "the European worker, languishing under bourgeois reaction," with a new revolutionary spirit. Lenin believed that this revolutionary upsurge would have "a repercussive effect upon Russia," bringing his small group of Russian Social Democrats to power in a "dizzying whirlwind of events . . . not fearing, but fervently desiring, the revolutionary-democratic dictatorship, fighting for the republic and for complete republican liberties, fighting for substantial economic reforms, in order to create . . . a truly large arena, an arena worthy of the twentieth century, in which to carry on the struggle for socialism." Soon, Lenin wrote, he would no longer proclaim these revolutionary dreams "from the cursed remoteness of Geneva, but at meetings of thousands of workers in the streets of Moscow and St. Petersburg, at the free village meetings of the Russian 'muzhiks' [peasants]."[85]

The many articles and pamphlets that Lenin wrote in Geneva conceal his extremely limited access to information about the revolution for almost its entire first year. His letters to activists and party journalists on site were full of pleas, "for God's sake," to report more thoroughly, more punctually, and more often. In his newly established weekly *Vperyod* (Forward), Lenin relayed vivid details about the civil war–like conditions in St. Petersburg since 9 January 1905 in passages such as the following: "The uprising has begun. Force against force. Street fighting is raging, barricades are being thrown up, rifles are crackling, guns are roaring. Rivers of blood are flowing, the civil war for freedom is blazing up."[86] He took these details from western newspaper reports, rumors in émigré cafés, and one brief meeting with the priest Georgy Gapon in Geneva in mid-January, about which little is known. In a letter to the Bolsheviks' secretariat in St. Petersburg dated 29 January, he complained that no one had attended to "good and thorough correspondence about the 9th of January." The responsible editor had sent just two letters in thirty days, Lenin groused, as if standing in person before the secretary's desk. "What do you say about that? He's gone silent. Not even a sentence for the 'Vperyod.' No word on current affairs, about plans or connections. That is quite impossible, unbelievable, unheard of." Two weeks later, Lenin again complained that "*all* Petersburgers *together* (disgrace and dishonor) did not procure *even one* new Russian connection. . . . It's a scandal, it's the end, it's ruinous!"[87]

He relentlessly reminded the Petersburgers that he urgently needed information directly from Russia: "*fresh facts, fresh impressions, special materials that are inaccessible to the people abroad, and not just arguments,*

not evaluations from the Social-Democratic point of view." In order to keep
these lines of communication open, it was essential to connect "*every*
student circle" and "*every* workers' group" with one of the many
Vperyod addresses abroad. Young Petersburgers, in particular, "should
be roused and filled with zeal; they should, by concrete example, be
taught what is wanted and how necessary it is to utilise every trifle;
they should be made to see how badly needed the *raw* material from
Russia is abroad (we shall be able to work it up from a literary angle
and make use of it ourselves)."[88]

Lenin's months of appeals bore little fruit. His unflagging determination to rise above "phrase mongering" and to establish "intellectual contacts" with the people on site apparently had little effect. He
struggled to determine whether the propaganda had "any resonance
at all, how it is changed by life, and what corrections are necessary," so
that weak "feelings of connection to the party" could be reinforced.[89]
In September 1905 Lenin complained that he, an exiled member of
the RSDLP Central Committee, knew less about events in Russia
than the people at *Iskra* or the General Jewish Workers' Bund.[90]

When Lenin finally arrived in St. Petersburg in early November
1905, the tsar's October Manifesto was already two weeks old and the
revolutionary energy of the workers was almost depleted. Plans for a
third general strike had stalled, along with a campaign by the Soviet
of Workers' Deputies to cripple the state's finances with a coordinated
withdrawal of savings. With a mixture of threats and concessions, by
the end of November the newly appointed prime minister Sergei
Witte had managed to give the tsar some breathing room, thereby
empowering the forces of reaction that, in the long run, almost entirely undermined the small steps toward democratization. While
Struve, at this point, was merely worried about these developments,
Lenin had already denounced them as a reactionary master plan. Only
a war waged by a "people's militia" could tip the "equilibrium of
forces" toward revolution; otherwise the tsar would "skip the revolution" altogether by deceiving the people with an undemocratic
constitution.[91] As Lenin had hoped in January, the revolt had grown

into a revolution, and this could survive only militarily because "revolution is war."[92]

In early December, as more than eighty thousand Moscow workers renewed their strike and around one thousand poorly armed fighters initiated a street war, Lenin headed north and crossed into Finland. He spoke about the political situation at a party gathering and practiced with weapons during the breaks, confident that this uprising was only the beginning of a longer civil war.[93] A few weeks earlier in Geneva, Lenin had urged his comrades to delay the uprising into the spring, if possible, so that soldiers returning from Manchuria could be encouraged to defect. "God knows our Russian revolution is magnificent! . . . The time of the uprising? Who can determine it! . . . No one's asking us, anyhow. Just look at the grand strike now," he went on to write at the end of October, relativizing his earlier directions on the tactics of battle.[94]

The uprising erupted in December, regardless of Lenin's plan. Although it was suppressed in a matter of days, he did not see the seven hundred casualties as a pointless sacrifice: this "new form of action was confronted with gigantic problems which, of course," Lenin wrote, "could not be solved all at once." The defeat had crystallized and clearly laid out the movement's coming tasks. Unlike Plekhanov, who argued against this turn to violence, Lenin insisted, "[W]e should have taken to arms more resolutely, energetically and aggressively; we should have explained to the masses . . . that a fearless and relentless armed fight was necessary."[95]

By the end of 1905, Lenin saw that tsarism could not (yet) be toppled by force and that the fight would have to shift to the first Russian Duma. Seeking to promote his revolutionary program with as many seats in the Duma as possible, he abruptly changed his stance toward the Mensheviks and began to push for a common election campaign. After years of denouncing parliamentarism as a farce, it took some effort to reorient his most loyal followers around orderly parliamentary engagement. Luxemburg had a similar experience in December 1918—but unlike Luxemburg's adherents in the newly established Communist Party of Germany, Lenin's people shifted relatively quickly to support the Duma elections in the winter of 1906.[96] Lenin assumed that the country's general unrest would keep simmering and that the "October-December forms of struggle" would resume within weeks—more tightly organized, led with "more consciousness," and enriched by the experiences of 1905.[97] Like Kautsky—whom Lenin repeatedly cited as an authority, despite his western colleague's Menshevik sympathies[98]—Lenin believed that support from western Europe could revive the revolution.

In early January 1906 Lenin took stock of the first revolutionary year. Because the Russian liberals and wealthy peasants were assiduous forces of counterrevolution, only the "European socialist proletariat" could come to the aid of its Russian counterpart.[99] When this solidarity failed to emerge, Lenin redirected his focus entirely toward Russia, now insisting that the proletariat and "revolutionary peasantry" would have to align against the bourgeoisie, as the latter only sought a "deal with the old authorities." The proletariat should not be fooled by the Kadets' proposed reforms into "laying down arms," Lenin wrote shortly before the meeting of the first Duma, in May 1906. Rather,

> the proletariat must ruthlessly expose the true meaning of this policy, tolerating no ambiguities, no attempts to obscure the political consciousness of the workers and peasants. The proletariat must fully use all the vacillations in the policy of the "powers that be" and of the would-be "sharers of power" to enlarge and strengthen its own class organisation, and to strengthen its contacts with the revolutionary peasantry as the only class that is capable of carrying the liberation movement beyond the Cadet "dam," beyond a Cadet deal with the old authorities.[100]

Maintaining these ties became more difficult for Lenin after the summer of 1906, when he resettled in nearby Finland to evade arrest by Russian authorities. The house in Kuokkala where he and Krupskaya lived until the end of 1907 became a well-known refuge for the Russian underground. A bed on the ground floor, along with some milk and bread, was always waiting for activists who sought refuge during the night. Krupskaya recalled how Lenin immediately turned daily reports from his correspondents in the tsarist empire into articles and pamphlets.[101] Nevertheless, his opportunities for influence rapidly shrank; even in the previous months, his influence as a Bolshevik tactician had been only minimal. Lenin was keenly aware of his political and personal distance from Russia; his short stay in 1905–6 had made this quite clear. While visiting Maxim Gorky on Capri in 1908, Lenin conceded that he knew too little of Russia: "Simbirsk, Kazan, Petersburg and that's about it."[102]

Persistent feelings of powerlessness and isolation may help to explain the virulent fantasies of power—"lessons" from the failed revolution—that Lenin developed in 1906. Citing Marx and Engels, he pleaded in dozens of treatises "that insurrection is an art," with the "desperately bold and irrevocably determined offensive" as its "principal rule." Further, he argued that the "ruthless extermination of civil and military chiefs was our duty during our uprising," and that lack of such ruthlessness was the primary cause of failure in 1905. At the next opportunity, he wanted to make up for the shortcomings of the first Russian Revolution—by recognizing the tsarist forces' "guerrilla warfare and mass terror" as a means of war, by incorporating it "into [our] tactics," and by arming, training, and leading the people, in a regimented way, toward a "great mass struggle." As far as possible, this struggle would need to occur everywhere simultaneously:

> The masses must know that they are entering upon an armed, bloody and desperate struggle. Contempt for death must become widespread among them and will ensure victory. The onslaught on the enemy must be pressed with the greatest vigour; attack, not defence, must be the slogan of the masses. . . . [T]he organisation of the struggle will become mobile and flexible; the wavering elements among the troops will be drawn into active participation. And in this momentous struggle, the party of the class-conscious proletariat must discharge its duty to the full.[103]

This vision of a people's war was premised on a degree of agency that was possessed by neither Lenin nor the Russian Social Democrats nor the Russian population. Although Lenin had not been particularly active in the uprisings, their suppression and the return to the old order was exactly the opposite of what he had sought. Most forms of self-government were crushed, as were the party structures that had just emerged from underground. Lenin was again condemned to exile and paralysis; his vision of "mobile," "flexible," and "energetic" leadership for the Russian masses remained pure fiction.

Realizing that his favored scenario of a revolutionary alliance between workers and peasants had not come to pass, Lenin utterly radicalized his expectations. At once defiant and threatening, he interpreted the end of the 1905–6 Revolution as the end of a "dress rehearsal." Although he did not explicitly adopt this metaphor until 1920, he was obsessed from this point on with the idea of "catching up."[104] His hatred of bourgeois society and its emerging forms of participation and discourse in Russia had only deepened over the past eighteen months. Defeat also fueled his scorn toward the liberals. He publicly taunted "Mr. Struve," who was once his fellow renegade and party cofounder. Unlike Lenin, Struve mourned the failure of the revolution not only as a national but as a very personal drama. Struve's indignation and wounded "noblest feelings," Lenin sneered, was the price that "gentlemen who are trading in the people's freedom, and who serve as brokers during the revolution and as diplomats in a time of war," had to pay for their "haggling" with the tsar.[105] He not only accused Struve's liberals, but also his own Marxists, of insufficient resolve. Whereas the Marxists had temporarily yielded to the overbearing power of the tsarist police state, the liberals had reinvigorated "the old authorities'" with their political naivete.

With good reason, J. P. Nettl has compared Lenin's and Luxemburg's political temperaments—notwithstanding his great sympathy for Luxemburg, which radiates from the pages of his biography. Both Lenin and Luxemburg understood that a "positive revolution" was not merely a destructive subversion of the old order but also a creative act: "Positive revolution requires the fusion of ideology and power."[106] The two protagonists embodied the voluntaristic, subjective dimension of political transformation. Idea and power, theory and practice, were inseparable in their lives. Although few of Lenin's personal writings have survived, we have many more by Luxemburg. This discrepancy notwithstanding, both sets of sources reveal the authors' tremendous confidence in their own ability to make a difference. This confidence supercharged their political activism and encouraged their belief—as in Luxemburg's letter of October 1905, cited at the beginning of this chapter—that they could pull revolution, like a "cart," through history.[107]

Luxemburg's experience and interpretation of the first Russian Revolution is best understood within the context of her own expectations. In her eyes, both poles in the Marxist conception of history—evolution and revolution—appeared to converge harmonically. She questioned the underlying forces of social change—and thus the degree of *her* influence and the opportunities for *her* participation—with a mixture of skeptical materialism and radical individualism. Ever since she had applied Marx's philosophy of history to Polish economic history in her dissertation, she had believed "without a doubt, that an interplay of political and economic factors constantly occurs in social development"—although the economic factor was ultimately decisive. The economic factor was the "driver" (*Triebfeder*) of social life—the dominant, but not the only, "force of development" (*Entwicklungsgewalt*). Even within the most extreme branches of Russian materialism, Luxemburg observed, no one asserted that economic development, "like a self-satisfied locomotive, hurtles down the tracks of history—with politics, ideology, etc. helplessly and passively trailing behind it, like dead boxcars."[108]

Her view of the individual's role in history was less differentiated. Behind her strong sense of self lurked a deep-seated fear that she was wasting her energies, "trailing behind" in a "dead" or "helpless" existence. Alternating fantasies of omnipotence and powerlessness appeared in her correspondence in an unfiltered way. In a letter to the Kautskys from the summer of 1900, she noted that she was overwhelmed by her "own nothingness" when observing forces of nature. Drawing upon naturalistic imagery and an analogy from her Jewish heritage, she explained the motives for her political engagement with unusual vividness:

> I had this same feeling when I saw the Rhine Falls in Switzerland. Their unceasing roar, never abating for a second, going on day and night and outlasting centuries, imbued me with a horrible feeling of annihilation. I got home quite crushed. And even now, whenever I pass there and, from the train window, see the dreadful spectacle, the foam, the white, boiling watery cavern, when I hear the deafening roar, my heart feels strangled, and something inside me says: That is the enemy. You are surprised? Certainly it is the enemy—the enemy of human vanity which has been thinking that it is something and now all of a sudden collapses into being nothing. By the way, there is a similar effect in a philosophy which like [Rabbi] Ben Akiba says of everything that happens: "*It has always been that way*," "Things will turn out all right by themselves," etc.; man with all his ability, his will, his knowledge seems so superfluous.... That is why I hate this sort of philosophy, my dear Charlemagne, and insist that we should rather throw ourselves into the Rhine Falls and go down in them like a nutshell than sagely nod our heads and let them go rushing the way they have rushed in our forefathers' time and will go on rushing after our time.[109]

These were not just empty clichés. Luxemburg was prepared—and not merely in her thoughts—to submit herself and others to all manner of violence, as was particularly evident in her letters and articles in the *Rote Fahne* in the weeks before her murder. More than a few of her companions and biographers subsequently styled her adventurism as courage and her recklessness as ambition.[110] She once half-seriously threatened to "terrorize" her lover until he treated her well.[111] And she confronted her political opponents with a candor that was sometimes shocking. In 1910 the Hamburg trade unionist—and later National Socialist—August Winnig debated the revolutionary leanings of German workers with Luxemburg in her Berlin apartment. Winnig insisted that he would oppose any revolution, but if Luxemburg initiated one nevertheless, "then you'll see me on the other side." To which she responded, "You are marvelously sincere!

But I am too. Sometimes I've already thought: one day I could have comrade Winnig executed!"[112]

She seems to have frequently embroiled herself in such furious exchanges, sometimes reporting on them proudly in her letters. In an October 1905 letter, she recounted a spat with Bebel about the upcoming elections for the Russian Duma. Should a revolution occur in Germany, the party leader "jokingly" threatened to hang leftists like Luxemburg so they would not "spoil the soup" for those on the right. She calmly responded, "You don't know yet who will hang whom."[113] Unlike Plekhanov, Guesde, and Lenin, Luxemburg never trained with a revolver. Yet her "arms and aims" were in no way limited to "those of the spirit, of class consciousness." Although some of her biographers have argued otherwise, her willingness to use force, or to justify it, was never merely defensive.[114]

After her experiences in Warsaw opposition circles as a teenager, and after the rough disputes about Poland's representation in the Second International (which were accompanied by fierce personal attacks), the events of 1905 finally offered thirty-five-year-old Luxemburg her first opportunity to engage actively in a revolution and to make a real difference. The Kingdom of Poland was part of the tsarist empire, but the relationship between the Russian Social Democrats (split between Mensheviks and Bolsheviks) and their Polish counterparts (split between PPS nationalists and Luxemburg's SDKPiL) had been strained since the failed negotiations to integrate the various party organizations in 1903. Like Plekhanov, Struve, and Lenin, Luxemburg struggled with her paradoxical role as an influential party intellectual who was nevertheless marginalized by exile.

After the events of January 1905, she served as the SDKPiL's "post office, letterhead, and contact woman" under the direction of Jogiches, who had lived with her in Berlin since 1902. Although Nettl suggests otherwise, nothing in Luxemburg's correspondence indicates that Jogiches stopped her from traveling to Russian Poland in these months.[115] She did, however, complain about her irregular access to Polish and Russian newspapers, which hampered her "feel" for party matters and the "Polish cause."[116] Nevertheless, beyond vague insinuations that her "writer's" existence was merely the "bloody parody of a political life," she only once (in November 1905) expressed an urge to go east. And this had more to do with escaping the gossip and infighting among the *Vorwärts* editorial staff, which she had just joined, than with a genuine desire to engage in revolutionary "practice" at the side of her lover, who had left for Kraków in February. *Her* practice involved "ceaselessly firing off publications"—writing, packing, and mailing. She eagerly awaited Jogiches's return but was otherwise content with the division of labor: "My peace of mind here *depends on your activity*," she wrote him on 1 November.[117]

Like all of the other protagonists, Luxemburg experienced the first months of the revolution from afar. Jogiches did provide a direct connection to the Polish opposition, but over the course of the year she frequently complained that he did not write enough about his experiences, his local plans, or the arrest of party friends.[118] She supported the German and Polish causes, with shifting emphasis between the two, and she became an influential intermediary between the Russian-Polish and western European social democrats. She was, "by God, now all about Russian revolution," as she wrote to Julius Bruhns in March: "*Meine Ruh' ist hin, mein Herz ist—dort*" (My peace is gone, my heart is—there).[119] Overwhelmed by the unexpected "Russian upheaval," she produced articles, news reports, and commentaries for the *Sächsische ArbeiterZeitung*, *Vorwärts*, and *Neue Zeit*, seeking to establish herself as a lead reporter. In the fall of 1905 she was rewarded with a position on the staff of *Vorwärts* (an achievement she described as "our victory"), and she delivered a key address about the "mass strike" at the SPD conference in Jena.[120] Her well-articulated, if not quite firsthand, expertise on the Russian Revolution helped her finally break into the upper ranks of the SPD.

As an author, correspondent, and logistical coordinator in matters relating to Russian Poland, Luxemburg played an increasingly important role that did not require her immediate presence in Kraków or Warsaw. She sought to portray events immediately and comprehensively: "Great revolutionary events have a certain peculiarity. No matter how much they can be foreseen and expected in broad outline, nevertheless, once they are present in all their complexity, in their specific shape and concrete form, they always confront us with a riddle like that of the sphinx, a lesson the sphinx wants us to grasp, absorb, and learn in every fiber of our being."[121] She worked to synthesize the available information to maximum effect, conveying "trust in our position and victory" through her reading of Polish news reports, and by praising the successes of her party comrades on site. Unlike their Russian counterparts, the Polish social democrats were in command of the latest developments with their "vibrant party life." The SDKPiL showed "incomparably more political initiative and foresight" than the Russian "rabble." ("They can all go to hell, I've had it up to here with them.")[122]

The Polish activists who visited Luxemburg in Berlin also gave her an authentic "feel" for events on site. In mid-May a guest from Warsaw brought along "our flag with bloodstains." Luxemburg developed a migraine headache, but "fortunately," she wrote, the flag did not disturb her writing. A few days later, she brought it to the *Vorwärts* archive. Although she had only intended to show the flag to her comrades, they immediately accepted it as a gift and delivered a "pathetic speech of gratitude." It was too awkward to explain the misunderstanding, so she gave them the flag. And in any event, given her migraine, the flag was better stored in the German party archive than in her linen cabinet.[123]

She was also upset by news of her friend and party comrade Marcin Kasprzak's execution. He was arrested in Warsaw in the summer of 1905, after taking up arms to defend the party's publishing house against the police. During these months she frequently complained about listlessness and insomnia, and she also suffered from pleurisy and a liver ailment. She functioned well under pressure and heightened expectations (as during the September party conference in Jena), complaining only afterward about absolute exhaustion.[124]

Thus, apart from her duties in Berlin and Jogiches's organizational schemes, it seems likely that her health also kept her from traveling to Poland. Her writings from this period fall into two broad categories: interpretive and explanatory texts intended for a German or western European audience, and tactical programmatic texts for Polish readers in the midst of revolution.

Like her adversary Adler, Luxemburg interpreted these events as a "proletarian revolution." In a formal sense, Russia was merely catching up with the legacies of 1848 in western and central Europe. But precisely because the "politically most backward country" was now making its entrance onto the "world stage," a new, "quite particular" type of revolution was emerging.[125] Economic and political protests merged because of the misery of the "working masses." (The rural population played almost no role in Luxemburg's analysis.) And so the fight for socialism in the tsarist empire was more than a purely political struggle.[126] The feeble, reactionary liberalism of "Messrs. Struve & Co.," Luxemburg argued, was as unfit to carry this movement forward as the "loose-jointed and agile stratum of revolutionaries from among the intelligentsia who wavered and swung back and forth at every moment like flexible reeds in the wind, now believing only in the saving action of the bomb and the revolver, engraved with fear-instilling verbiage; now in the blind revolt of the peasants and nothing else; now refusing to believe in anything anymore." Only the social democrats around Plekhanov, Axelrod, and Zasulich, whom others scorned as dogmatists—"that uningratiating, single-minded company, who enjoyed the same respectful dislike in certain circles of the Socialist International as did the French 'Guesdistes'"—had, with the calm assurance of their "scientific, firmly founded worldview," not only predicted the unrest in St. Petersburg but also *paved the way* for it and *brought it about.*" Thanks to Marx's "dogma," they had predicted "with near-mathematical certainty the broad outlines of capitalist development in Russia"; and they had also identified the working class as a collective actor, despite its comparatively brief history. So "the word" became "flesh" on the streets of St. Petersburg; "the spirit of

Marx that struck the first great blow" would soon emerge victorious, "with the necessity of a law of nature."[127]

Marx's "spirit" was decisive for Luxemburg's interpretations of revolution. In 1905 and 1918, this spirit established a direct connection to the era of the *Communist Manifesto* and to the revolutionary movement of that time. After seventy years of "parliamentary skirmishing," Luxemburg wrote in 1905, "a period of elemental mass battles" had finally commenced.[128] Thirteen years later, she announced at the founding conference of the KPD, "We are back with Marx, under his banner." Invoking "true Marxism," she pledged "to transform socialism into truth and deed, and to eradicate capitalism root and branch." This and only this, Luxemburg argued, was what Marx and Engels had sought since 1848.[129]

The great lesson that Luxemburg drew from the first Russian Revolution was that the political potential of these "mass battles" extended beyond Russia. Revolution had come to a country where—according to "pedantic," narrow definitions—the necessary conditions for a general strike were altogether lacking: strong unions, the right to organize, political education, generous strike funds, tested party discipline, weak opponents. And so she formulated her mantra for the future tactics of German social democracy:

> It is not by systematic propaganda for a general strike for its own sake, as a miracle-working form of the proletarian class struggle, and also, on the other hand, it is not by merely engaging in the beehive-type of activity of endless[ly] building new trade union cells, but it is by educating and awakening the masses along the lines of developing their revolutionary understanding—the understanding that in all the most vital political and social questions and decisions they can only rely on themselves, on their own direct action—it is only in this way that we ourselves lay the groundwork for that moment when the workers as a class will be ready, for the sake of their true vital interests, not only to "stop every wheel from turning" but also if necessary to shed their blood fighting in the streets.[130]

Sensing such a moment and leading by "bold initiative" was the foremost task of all truly revolutionary acts.

In contrast to this western-oriented rhetoric of stirring up the masses, Luxemburg drew opposite lessons for Warsaw from the events of 1905. The bloody clashes in the city in January, and in cities like Łodz in May and June 1905, showed that merely possessing enough fighters, arms, and dynamite was not enough to win a revolution. Mobilizing an armed minority was insufficient; revolution could succeed only as a "popular mass movement." The brute-force strategy of the Polish Social Revolutionaries and the PPS under Józef Piłsudski was a "false prescription" that came from a "false diagnosis," thereby endangering the "patient."[131] Luxemburg scorned the PPS's infatuation with guns and the presumption that the "masses" could be summoned at just the right moment, like "extras in the theater," to support the lead actors on stage.[132] Until her departure for Warsaw, she tirelessly promoted a different approach in her Polish articles: consciousness raising, agitating, and organizing.

Luxemburg's correspondence abruptly stops on 6 December 1905, and no other sources tell us who or what moved her to give up her post in Berlin and prepare for her journey. On 28 December she traveled to Illovo in eastern Prussia, where she secretly boarded a troop train. Soon she was sending enthusiastic letters from Warsaw, a city at war. The overall situation was difficult to assess, she wrote, but the party was alert and diligent. In contrast to St. Petersburg, she proudly reported, there was no utter chaos.[133] She was fascinated by the workers' spontaneous solidarity and self-administration in the face of mass unemployment ("*voilà la plaie de la révolution*"—the plague of the revolution), reporting as if she were encountering such activism for the very first time. Her longtime faith in the creative, elemental force of the "masses" at last seemed vindicated by reality, along with her criticism of the SPD for its "domesticated" parliamentarism. Shortly after her arrival, she wrote:

> [A] silent heroism and a feeling of class solidarity among the masses is developing, which I would like to show [as an example] to the Germans. Everywhere the workers are making certain arrangements *on their own initiative* so that, for example, the employed workers regularly take up

a weekly collection for the unemployed. Or where employment has been reduced to four days a week, they arrange things so that no one is left out, but everyone works at least a few hours a day. All this is done so smoothly and self-reliantly that it was only incidentally that information about it was given to the party. In fact the feeling of solidarity and even of brotherhood with the *Russian* workers has developed so strongly that one is involuntarily amazed, even though we ourselves have worked toward that goal.[134]

Other socialists were as surprised as Luxemburg by the Polish workers' spontaneous and efficient organization; under the banner of national resistance against tsarist foreign rule, they created a new political and plural space.[135] This enduring politicization, which was especially evident in the establishment of countless trade unions, was just one of the revolution's consequences. Even more important for Luxemburg, revolution had "deepen[ed] class contradictions and sharpen[ed] and clarif[ied] relationships," which would persist even after the return to "normal conditions." The struggle would only deepen, she suggested in early February 1906. Although the Social Democrats in St. Petersburg had returned underground, her diligent Polish comrades would continue to foster this need for political solidarity, organization, and orientation, which had emerged "*on their own initiative*."[136]

There is no doubt that these few weeks in Warsaw in the winter of 1905–6 affirmed Luxemburg's long-held "belief in the innate revolutionary character of the masses."[137] She integrated what she had experienced into her speeches and writings on the mass strike, and she saw the events as a "veritable gold mine for studying the nature and political importance of the general strike." She understood revolution as a spontaneous process, and social democratic party structures had to adjust accordingly, assuming the role of both servant and leader.[138] Lenin denounced her theory of "organisation-as-process" as "unprincipled," arguing that it "vulgarises and prostitutes Marxism." At best, Kautsky, Bernstein, Adler, and many others criticized Luxemburg's conclusions as strained. At worst, they disparaged her ideas as highly dangerous "revolutionary romanticism."[139]

Luxemburg was arrested only weeks after her arrival in Warsaw, but this hardly dampened her spirits. "On Sunday evening, the 4th [of March], fate caught up with me: I was arrested," she wrote to the Kautskys. "Hopefully, you won't take the matter too much to heart. Long live the R . . . ! [i.e., the Revolution] and everything that comes with it."[140] She maintained at least her outward composure, claiming a "superb" mood during her time in prison. She was proud to have been arrested in Warsaw, "the only oasis in all of Russia where, in spite of storm and stress, the work and the struggle went forward as boldly and merrily as it did." She was not initially recognized in prison, and unlike Jogiches, who was sentenced to eight years in exile, she was released in June with the help of her family.[141] Like Lenin, she spent several weeks in Kuokkala in Finland. The two protagonists met but apparently had little to say; sources offer little information about their meeting.[142] She was "burning with the desire to work—that is, to write," she noted in a letter that summer. She in no way interpreted the end of the revolution as a defeat. Instead, she lived in a "glorious" time, full of "powerful problems" that stimulated thought and inspired passion. She returned to the metaphors of pregnancy and birth to describe the good spirits that accompanied her back to Berlin in September 1906:

> [It] is a fruitful, pregnant time, which gives birth hourly and with every birth emerges even "more pregnant" than before. It does not give birth to dead mice, or to lifeless gnats as in Berlin, but rather to all sorts of enormous things such as: enormous crimes (vide the government), enormous disgraces (vide the Duma), enormous stupidities (vide Plekhanov & Co.), etc. I'm trembling with delight at the thought of drafting a pretty sketch of all these enormities.[143]

Luxemburg saw herself, even in the middle of a revolution, as both an analyst and a visionary. She understood her mission as describing present revolutionary conditions and widening their intellectual horizons—"as though both the revolutionary mind as well as the revolutionary will were capable of infinite expansion under the pressure of events," in the words of her biographer Nettl.[144] The revolution would wither without an interpretation of reality that was constantly pressing forward, holding both the potential of a new reality and the finitude of present conditions. Programmatic thinking and writing were the most important means for Luxemburg's ends. Not only did they have to guide collective political action, supplying appropriate slogans and tactical arguments; they also had to help internalize revolution, intellectually and emotionally, as a state of mind that transcended existing reality.

Kautsky, Bernstein, Jaurès, Guesde, and Adler largely responded to the first and only revolution in Marxism's "golden age" as distant critics and observers; it is surprising how rarely their commentaries referenced the Marxist canon. The self-mobilizing effects of the revolutionary idea had steadily ebbed in the years preceding 1905. For most of the first-generation Marxists, revolution had already lost the aura of a real utopia by the time a space of real revolutionary opportunity opened up in January 1905.

Struve entered this space as a hopeful liberal, at an already unbridgeable remove from the Russian Social Democrats' understanding of political and revolutionary Marxism. His hopes were dashed on all fronts by mid-1906, and he retreated entirely from active politics. Lenin and Luxemburg, on the other hand, solidified their revolutionary expectations over the course of these same months. Both of them gathered experiences of power and powerlessness, which they constantly aligned with their idea of the "spirit of Marx." They found affirmation of their long-held beliefs about the nature of mass movements, collective enemies, and bourgeois reformist politics, and also their mistrust of certain persons (often longtime compatriots). Both drew programmatic and tactical conclusions from the failed revolution that formatively shaped their political future. After a miserable "dress rehearsal," Lenin's revolutionary drama finally got its premiere in October 1917. Luxemburg's failure in the winter of 1918–19 was caused not only by the forces of "counterrevolution" but also by her inability to rally her own followers around a Marxist engagement that swung feverishly between euphoria and pragmatism, between revolution as transformed consciousness and realpolitik.

Conclusion

From Marx to Marxism: Fieldworkers, Bookworms, and Adventurers

> But unfortunately the course of world history does not run according to our wishes.
>
> —Karl Kautsky, *Terrorismus und Kommunismus* (1919)

Many roads led to Marx. His first, loyal disciples devised one of the most influential political worldviews of the modern age. By reading, translating, synthesizing, and writing about Marx's texts, with the dynamic support of an older Engels, the nine protagonists of this book became inventors of Marxism—a school, a worldview, a weapon, a doctrine for explaining the world, and a program for changing it. Their engagement was spurred by the dramatic social, political, and cultural effects of industrialization, which—in the guise of the "Social Question"—had become an urgent concern all across Europe over the course of the nineteenth century. By the 1880s, an ever larger number of European social democrats had come to see themselves as "Marxists"—that is, they committed themselves to the emphatic appeal to reality in Marx's thought, and they embraced the radical study of new social realities as a precondition for "actually" changing the world. Experience and ideology, reality and politics were inseparably fused in their lives from this point forward. They believed that a well-disciplined proletarian party could push capitalism, with its finite lifespan, into an infinite socialist future.

More than 150 years after the publication of the *Manifesto of the Communist Party*, and more than a century after the founding of a "Marxist-Leninist" state in Russia, it is time that we move beyond the well-worn paths of Marxist historiography and the broader historiography of political ideas to shine a new light on the origins, development, and peculiarities of this worldview. From the perspective of experiential history, a focus on the connection between how the first epigones sought to make sense of the world and how they sought to change it, enables us to understand the history of Marxism *also* as the history of a political fascination. Marx—and, as always, Engels—promised insight and emancipation, knowledge and power; they brought the Social Question into the political and programmatic offensive. Their relentless appeal to reality and science, their rhetorical aptitude, and their terminological creativity animated the intellectual curiosity and political imaginations of very different "students" all across Europe. This fascination outlived the "golden age" of Marxism and became a radicalized frame of reference for various political regimes well into the twentieth century—resulting much more often in totalitarian oppression than in more humane societies.

Still, my book has sought to move beyond this teleological view. By reconstructing the protagonists' individual paths to Marx, I have made an unconventional (or, I am tempted to say, "unideological") contribution to the historicization of Marxism, which has proceeded only languidly since the end of the Cold War. Even today, after the demise of state socialism, this discussion continues to be framed by ongoing controversies about the legitimacy of a social critique that identifies as Marxist. Instead, the relationship between finding one's place in the world, formulating a worldview, and practicing politics—in other words, between socialization, politicization, and engagement—has been central to my efforts. I have sought to explore why Marx's texts exerted such a powerful influence over so many different lives and such varied social contexts, to get to the heart of these texts' "seductive force."[1]

A comparative tour through the nine protagonists' individual (although often interconnected) lives—in particular, their transition to young adulthood, their experiences as readers, and their engagement with reality—provides some answers. Their family backgrounds, upbringing, and schooling had a great deal in common. All of the protagonists were raised in mostly warm family homes with an affinity for learning and literature, a well-developed sense of curiosity about the world at large, and great interest in everyday and received knowledge about current affairs. All became accustomed to grappling with the world at an early age—even if most of them were *not* directly affected by the encroaching social misery of their era. Further—this was true for Kautsky, Jaurès, Plekhanov, and (at least in part) Luxemburg—it was more often the mothers who most formatively shaped their worldviews as children, while the fathers tended to supervise or, as with Guesde, even provide a formal education. At a time of widespread illiteracy, when opportunities for higher education were extremely limited, these parents' attention to schooling gave each of the protagonists an extraordinarily good start in life. This was all the more true as the very institution of school in the nineteenth century embodied and enforced these limited opportunities, reinforcing the disciplinary fervor of the authoritarian state.

A comparative biographical perspective allows a remarkable portrait to emerge. It reveals a group of self-assured, well-educated, ambitious, and mobile personalities, whose intellectual and practical interventions in the life of society gave form and meaning to their own lives. All of the protagonists had extraordinary self-confidence and faith in their own potential. They did not see themselves as selfless do-gooders, but instead—fully embracing the pathos of the young Engels—they saw themselves as children of the nineteenth century, with the mission, even the right, to change history. They were a "voluntary elite" who strongly believed in their revolutionary calling—not unlike the political generations of the twentieth century that have received much closer scholarly attention.[2] Generational cohorts who felt called to "make history," with all the constructive and destructive potential this entailed, were not unique to the twentieth century.

This is not to suggest that the protagonists' life paths led inexorably to Marx. Rather, their politicization usually began with early contacts in local workers' or oppositional groups, and it was framed by eclectic readings, often with no connection to Marx. By viewing this politicization comparatively, we can understand the early history of Marxism as an initially very diffuse, polyphonic generational project that was bound to disparate life paths. The decisive aspect for membership was not chronological age but the age of reading. What counted most was familiarity with Marx's texts, communicative proximity to Engels, and inclination and ability to network across state borders with likeminded comrades. Within the context of the First International, the term "Marxist" was originally used as a mostly derogatory description of the "Londoners'" leadership style. Only as Marx's works spread across Europe in the 1870s and 1880s did "Marxist" begin to acquire a more specific meaning. It gradually gained political weight and appeared in debates over national social democratic programs. It was Kautsky and Bernstein, studying the master's works together in their Zurich exile, who made the "breakthrough" to Marxism. Corresponding with Engels while Marx was still alive, they made him the namesake of their envisioned political-intellectual "school."[3]

Reading and appropriating the emerging Marxist canon was a comprehensive, extended learning process for all nine protagonists. Workers, by contrast, rarely read Marx and Engels's founding texts; they turned much more frequently to the first-generation Marxists' popular works and polemics. These included Kautsky's *Economic Doctrines of Karl Marx* (1887), Bernstein and Guesde's *Social and Private Property* (1885), Plekhanov's *Socialism and Political Struggle* (1883), Jaurès and Guesde's *Les Deux Méthodes* (the proceedings of their 1900 debate), Lenin's *What Is to Be Done?* (1902), and Luxemburg's *Introduction to Political Economy* (1909–10). The protagonists spent years studying Marx's ideas before publishing these texts—a painstaking intellectual and emotional learning experience that promised insight into the world and also themselves. Adler spoke of a sublime "feeling of exhilaration" upon reading and rereading *Capital*, "like the view from a mountain peak that was arduous to climb, where you suddenly see where you went and why."[4]

Thus, on the one hand, the first Marxists understood this revelatory engagement as a modern, scientific endeavor, something undertaken from a "higher vantage point" by those who "knew more." On the other hand, they also saw it as a project of popular enlightenment. Translating and disseminating Marxist knowledge among the working masses was an integral component of Marxist politics. Conveying the indisputable value of this worldview was indisputably essential. The first generation of epigones believed that Marx's ideas needed merely to be sparked, that they would necessarily take effect, and that they would inevitably establish the absolute dominance of Marxism: "Every one of us is domineering in the sense that he would like to see his views predominate," Engels once summed up his colleagues' self-assurance and ultimate aspiration.[5] Precisely because of its imprecision, the Marxist political design—not least its fuzzy theoretical views on revolution and social change—proved so flexible and thus applicable to so many contexts across Europe. It was particularly well-suited to channeling and disciplining social democrats' first efforts at organization, which were often overshadowed by infighting about direction and methods.

Despite the prominence of the nine protagonists, surprisingly little is known thus far about their first experiences reading the works of Marx and Engels. Scholars have often relied on isolated autobiographical reminiscences, routinely repeating legends and anecdotes about the protagonists' supposed first encounters with *Capital* or the *Manifesto of the Communist Party*. Although I could not locate any personal copies of these readings, by examining their own writings—especially their popular works and eulogies for Marx and

Engels—I could nevertheless tease out a few explicit and many implicit impressions of what and how they read.

Although they read and wrote about Marx with varying intensity and at various points in time, the emotional and intellectual effects of this experience were nonetheless quite comparable. The protagonists did not just read Marx; they discovered him. The "Marx experience" was evident in all of their biographies. Dietrich Geyer has written that, for Lenin, the experience was like finding an intellectual home. In this book, I have described it as latching onto a particular point of view, and thus as more of a process than an epiphany—a gradual entry into a distinct discursive community.[6] The protagonists' appropriation of Marx's texts and their admission into the Marxist circle (which was always transnational if initially quite small) was accompanied by specific terms and patterns of argumentation, which focused—like "glasses" or a "prism"—on the analysis and interpretation of past and present society.[7] These included concepts like class struggle, reserve army, surplus value, proletariat, commodity fetishism, and the economic law of motion of modern society, as well as a theory of revolution that combined aspects of voluntarism and determinism. Other concepts included the immiseration thesis, the interpretation of social conditions in capitalism as "anarchic," and the description of capitalist market dynamics as a mystical force acting "behind the backs" of human actors. By narrating a history that was driven by class struggle, Marx established a tradition that offered a common identity and instilled an unprecedented degree of sacrificial activism and commitment in a transnational political community—a formidable counternarrative, so to speak, to the nationalist tradition (as described by Benedict Anderson) that had only recently been "invented."

Science played a paradigmatic role in the protagonists' interpretations of Marx, serving both as intellectual framework and emotional anchor. The early history of Marxism was closely bound to the intellectual currents of a science-obsessed age. All nine individuals in this story, regardless of their background, treated the study of Marx's texts as an extended (and often lifelong) process of reading and learning.

Their own syntheses, interpretations, polemics, treatises, eulogies, and reminiscences show how reading and writing about Marx reinforced their own inclinations, experiences, and interests. In some cases, the protagonists learned to express these inclinations for the very first time. For Guesde, this was his postanarchist need for political clarity and discipline; for Jaurès, his search for an emancipatory principle of totality, which Marx's fusion of philosophy and politics seemed to embody uniquely; for Bernstein, his uncertain efforts to establish a scientific basis for his own morality, which was sometimes idealistic and sentimental; for Adler, his bitter impatience as a medical doctor with the bourgeoisie's half-hearted benevolence toward the working class; for Plekhanov, his hope in the transformational and rational capacity of the Russian peasants, when led by members of an intellectual vanguard like himself; for Struve, his trust in the material and cultural promise of capitalist modernity; for Lenin, his hatred of bourgeois society and the naively revolutionary "friends of the people"; and finally for Luxemburg, her thirst for knowledge and drive to act, which was oriented toward a working class that Marx had ingeniously "discovered" and emboldened.

Three motifs played a central role, with varying emphases, in all of the protagonists' readings of Marx. First, Marx was believed to have *discovered* the key to resolving the Social Question on the basis of science. Second, he *enlightened* the workers and the propertyless; he brought a hopelessly idealistic struggle into the political offensive and gave it a realistic perspective on power. And third, Marx *inspired*; he formulated and channeled emotions like no one else before him, and as perhaps no one else (but Engels) could. These three motifs—discovery, enlightenment, and inspiration—mirrored and satisfied three acute political needs in the emerging social democratic movements: education, perspective, and mobilization. For the inventors of Marxism, the appeal of Marx's work had little to do with any utopian promise. Instead, the real historical and analytical underpinnings of Marx's ideas, concepts, and arguments illuminated the "capitalist mode of production" as the matrix of human existence in the *present*—the industrial age. The persuasiveness of Marx and Engels' texts lay in their cool "factual gaze," which was directed toward contemporary society and supposedly never strayed, reflecting the social scientific, positivistic, and broader cultural spirit of the era.

The first generation's appropriation of Marx was neither a conversion experience nor a single decision or act.[8] Instead, Marx's texts and theses offered engaging certitudes about the present, a promise of critical insight into the here and now—not utopian faith in future salvation, but a dialectically informed confidence in the power of (future) facts. His early followers believed that they had found a method of understanding history and society, which seemed vital to overcoming capitalism's appalling social conditions. Thanks to the dialectical method, the first Marxist intellectuals were convinced that an ignorant worm could become an omniscient god and that humans could become their own gods on earth—to recall two analogies from the writings of Plekhanov and Guesde.

The interplay between seeking to understand the world and seeking to change it underscores how contingency, variability, and grounding in a particular lifeworld informed the early development of Marxism. The protagonists' gradual turn toward Marx—which included politicization and, in some cases, radicalization within the movement—did not occur abruptly or impulsively. Instead, as Tânia Puschnerat has shown in her biography of Clara Zetkin, this commitment was a "continuous development," a process of internalization that lasted for years. This dynamic did not arise from a single decision—even though, in retrospect, it could become part of the choreography of a narrated life.[9] And the protagonists' gradually deepening engagement occurred within a specific biographical, intellectual, and emotional context. Surely we cannot fully understand this engagement without considering their lifeworlds.

How did the gradual experiences of reading and politicization inform the protagonists' practical engagement? How did they uphold the two main commandments of Marxism in their daily affairs—studying the world as it "really" was, and then (as politicized philosophers and social scientists) changing it in practice? In order to answer these questions, I have looked past the turn of the twentieth century to investigate the interplay between revolutionary expectations and revolutionary experiences during the Russian Revolution of 1905–6—the first and only revolution within the lifetimes of *all* the protagonists. Their responses to the long awaited—and nevertheless unexpected—first revolution of the twentieth century were more diverse than one might expect, given that all belonged to a discursive community of politically like-minded activists who felt responsible to Marxism. The community frayed, but did not collapse, in the great debates over revisionism and the mass strike.

The Revolution of 1905 compelled all nine individuals to question their long-held ideas about the course of history and their own roles within it. It is striking how rarely they referred to the canon of Marxist theory in their interpretations of events—and how often they did refer to their own national histories or to Russian political and intellectual history. The three active participants drew very different lessons from the spontaneous solidarity of the Warsaw workers (Luxemburg), the bloody suppression of the chaotic Moscow uprising (Lenin), and the parliamentary struggles between a tsarist autocracy incapable of reform and revolution-obsessed social democrats (Struve). Luxemburg, Lenin, and Struve, each in their own way, nevertheless formulated relatively coherent lessons for future action (mass strike, putsch, liberalism) in the context of these experiences. They dedicated the rest of their lives to perfecting these lessons.

Short of intervening in an actual revolution, the protagonists were constantly occupied by day-to-day politics, and—following the first commandment of Marxism—by the permanent study of contemporary social conditions. They were engaged observers of working-class misery. Their tangible experiences show that their perceptions of Lassalle's "eighty-nine percent" cannot be reduced to a dichotomy between their own proximity or distance to reality—that is, to the question of their "sense of reality" (Isaiah Berlin) that I have posed throughout this book. Instead, their individual perceptions of the lifeworlds of the poor, exploited, and disenfranchised shifted between the concrete and the abstract, the realistic and the romantic, the self-centered and the externally oriented. The historical sources rarely suggest a dialogic relationship; the protagonists usually spoke *about,* not *with,* those who were miserable.

For all of the personal variations of the protagonists' engaged gaze, their enduring occupation with social conditions was wholly consistent. Over time, the Marxist worldview began to function more and more like a prism, specifically filtering the protagonists' perceptions and interpretations of these conditions. This is as evident in the exiled Guesde's texts on agricultural labor from the 1870s as in the work of Jaurès, the academic with rural roots, from the 1890s. We can also see it in Plekhanov's reflections from 1880–85, on the difficult transformation of the Russian peasants from "gray men" into class-conscious proletarians, and in Adler's sometimes undercover reports on factory work, worker protections, and "popular hygiene." Correspondence between Kautsky and Bernstein about the sexual exploitation of girls in the London prostitution scene (1886) illustrates the spectrum of possible responses, similar to Lenin's pamphlets for the striking workers in St. Petersburg. Luxemburg's articles about the fates of individual workers—which fluctuated between attention to (fictive) details and ideological abstraction, romanticism and realism—turned the social conditions of her time into gruesome literary fables of capitalist doom. Conversely, real-life experiences could irritate this prism—as was especially evident in Bernstein's and Struve's vexed interactions with English and Russian working conditions and economic development, which seemed to correspond less and less with Marx and Engels's assertions about capitalism in the present and near future.

How might we systematize and generalize about these very heterogeneous interactions with social reality and ways of making sense of the world? Perhaps three typological categories—which derive from the type of interaction and the sources of knowledge involved—are best suited to this task. *Fieldworkers* base their engagement (not exclusively, but primarily) on firsthand experiences. They are on site, in the middle of things; they take note of personal encounters and reflect empathetically; they act as equalizers. They understand Marxism rather as a moral principle than as dogma. Adler, Bernstein, and Jaurès belong in this category. *Adventurers* tend to process the experiences of others; they, too, are on site, but often as activists and agitators. They love being at the heart of a fight, and they accept prison or exile as a legitimate trade-off. They process their own experiences, responding with outrage more than empathy. Luxemburg, Lenin, the young Plekhanov, and Guesde were adventurers. Marxism was their emotional and intellectual home, and they revered it as the ultimate, all-encompassing model for explaining the world. Finally, *bookworms* form their worldview predominantly from secondary sources: government statistics, scientific treatises, and other kinds of reading material. Their workplace is a desk, office, or library; they order the experiences of others in a theoretical structure. They are sober and matter-of-fact, or even cold and calculating. To them, Marxism is a method for understanding the world. If we focus on the primary sources of their social knowledge, the bookworms were (again) Lenin, as well as Kautsky and Struve. These categories are extremely tentative; they can overlap or change, especially over the course of an engaged intellectual's entire biography. Even so, they illuminate the diversity and specificity of ways in which the protagonists sought to make sense of the world and engaged with it. Notably, the "professional revolutionaries" in my group portrait—Luxemburg, Lenin, Guesde, and Plekhanov—were a mixture of adventurers and bookworms; none was a fieldworker.

This group portrait casts a new light on one of the most influential political worldviews, which later expanded into a (state) ideology of the twentieth century. Viewed in this light, Marxism can and should be understood as one form of modern political engagement. I have sought to open up the historiography of Marxism to the broader history of politics and ideas to encourage comparative investigation of the different forms of individual and collective engagement in the "age of ideologies." Since 1789 the mobilization of workers and the general population has often been understood as driven by just a handful of intellectual leaders and programmatic thinkers. Yet, examining the dynamics of (self-)mobilization and participation—and especially the interplay between these two types of historical acts—remains an important historiographical challenge. This is all the more true now that the "end of ideologies" has proven a mirage.

To address these questions with respect to the European political left at the end of the nineteenth century, I have investigated the motivations and experiences of nine historical personalities—about whom, it turns out, there is still much to learn, despite their seemingly familiar status as "usual suspects." By engaging on behalf of the ideas of Marx, these personalities became the inventors of Marxism. They were united by an enduring emotional and cognitive occupation with the social, economic, and political conditions of their time. The degree to which their engagement was internally or externally oriented varied widely. When their occupation became more self-centered or subjective, it could tip into obsession. Those who most strongly and effectively invoked Marx (Luxemburg, Lenin, Guesde) were simultaneously the most ruthless in arguing and engaging in political practice.

Unlike the other six protagonists, this trio lacked any discomfort with the consequences of mobilizing collective forces and emotions. They rarely regarded the "masses" with secret revulsion but devoted their entire political thought and action to reaching and maneuvering them. Although all of the protagonists (except Struve) identified as lifelong Marxists, the members of this trio most closely bound their personal identities to Marxism as a political design and a way of life. Their ostensibly communal engagement was defined by extraordinary egotism, a high degree of self-assurance, and unshakable faith in their own efficacy. The more self-centered their perceptions of reality, the more subjective their engagement, and the more unconditional its means and ends.

Even so, the political thought and action of the remaining six protagonists were hardly characterized by selflessness or simple empathy; they mostly considered these qualities wholly insufficient, or even a hindrance. Instead, their engagement was grounded in a sense of personal mission, which was bound to a clear-eyed, "factual gaze" and a "scientific" drive for knowledge. The epigones thus not only emulated the ideas but also the characters of their worldview's two namesakes—alert, curious, critical, with an emphatic and sober worldliness. The extraordinary political friendship between Marx and Engels thrived on the constant, mutual reinforcement of their world-altering self-assurance. This relationship already possessed the remarkable mixture of self-interest and worldly concern that characterized Marxist political engagement at the end of the nineteenth century and that came to exert tremendous creative and destructive power well into the twentieth century.

Notes

PROLOGUE

1. Hobsbawm, "Intellectuals," 247.
2. On the "Age of Ideologies," see Beyme, *Politische Theorien*.
3. Jaeger, "Generationen," 451–52; Jureit, *Generationenforschung*.
4. Kolakowski, *Main Currents of Marxism*, 2:1.
5. On the influence, or "mandate," of intellectuals, see Nettl, *Luxemburg*, 1:35–36; Gilcher-Holtey, *Eingreifendes Denken*, 22–23.
6. See, most recently, Jones, *Karl Marx*. For an overview of recent scholarship, see Bouvier, "Karl Marx"; for Marx's reception within various disciplines, see Quante and Schweikard, *Marx-Handbuch*. One of the most vicious attacks on Marx and Marxism is Levin, *American Marxism*.
7. For biographical approaches to the history of the workers' movement, see Mittag, *Biographische Ansätze*; Tennstedt, "Arbeiterbewegung." Examples include Sperber, *Karl Marx*; Hunt, *Marx's General*; Schmidt, *August Bebel*; Keßler, *Ruth Fischer*; Shore, *Caviar and Ashes*; Schönhoven and Braun, *Generationen*; Puschnerat, *Clara Zetkin*; Epstein, *The Last Revolutionaries*; Eley, *Forging Democracy*. On the study of social movements, see Rucht, "Zum Stand der Forschung." My work follows the approach of experiential history (*Erfahrungsgeschichte*) that was pioneered by Reinhart Koselleck. A good English-language introduction to this approach is Jureit, "Generation, Generationality, Generational Research."
8. Welskopp, *Das Banner der Brüderlichkeit*, 19. The term "epigone" is from Fleischer, *Der Marxismus in seinem Zeitalter*, 202. On social knowledge, see Berger et al., *Die gesellschaftliche Konstruktion*; Luckmann and Schütz, *Strukturen der Lebenswelt*.
9. Euchner and Grebing, *Klassiker des Sozialismus* and Kolakowski, *Main Currents of Marxism*, vol. 2, informed my selection.
10. See Gilcher-Holtey, *Eingreifendes Denken*, 391, 300ff. My approach emphasizes the role of practice and the protagonists' "interventionist" identity—aspects that are not accentuated as strongly in Thomas

Kroll's definition of post-1945 "communist intellectuals" as "producers and brokers of ideas and ways of viewing the world." See Kroll, *Kommunistische Intellektuelle*, 14.

11. Foucault, "The Political Function," 12.

12. See Morat, "Intellektuelle"; Bering, *Die Epoche der Intellektuellen*; Jung and Müller-Doohm, *Fliegende Fische*; Winock, *Das Jahrhundert der Intellektuellen*; Hertfelder, "Kritik und Mandat"; Gilcher-Holtey, *Eingreifendes Denken*, 9–14; Lepsius, "Kritik als Beruf." With a focus on (German) social democracy, see Alemann et al., *Intellektuelle und Sozialdemokratie*; Bates, *Marxism*; Hübinger, "Intellektuelle und Soziale Frage"; Prochasson, *Les Intellectuels*; Eley, "Intellectuals"; Pierson, *Marxist Intellectuals*; Schelsky, *Die Arbeit tun die anderen*; Hobsbawm, "Intellectuals"; Aron, *The Opium of the Intellectuals*.

13. Hübinger, "Intellektuelle und Soziale Frage."

14. The term nevertheless serves as a viable category of analysis, despite Daniel Morat's argument in "Intellektuelle" to the contrary.

15. Lepsius, "Kritik als Beruf."

16. Elias's thoughts on the fundamental dilemma of the social sciences are relevant here: unlike scientists who study nature, *social* scientists (including Marxists) "face themselves; the 'objects' are also 'subjects.'" See Elias, *Involvement and Detachment*, 12–14; Elias, *Engagement und Distanzierung*, 9–10, 29, 51–52. Elias wrote in both English and German. He first published *Involvement and Detachment* in 1956, significantly altering and expanding the text for the German edition of 1983 (see *Engagement und Distanzierung*, 269–70).

17. Weber and Lembcke, "Emotion und Revolution," 179–80. See also Weber, "Von den klassischen Affektenlehren"; Lembcke and Weber, "Leidenschaft, Affekt und Gefühl."

18. Recent examples include Häberlen and Smith, "Struggling for Feelings"; Häberlen, *Vertrauen und Politik*. On the history of emotions, see Verheyen, "Geschichte der Gefühle"; Aschmann, *Gefühl und Kalkül*. For aspects of emotional history in the study of social movements, see Koller, "Soziale Bewegungen"; Goodwin and Jasper, *Rethinking Social Movements*; Goodwin, Jasper, and Polletta, *Passionate Politics*; Goodwin, Jasper, and Polletta, "The Return of the Repressed."

19. *MECW*, 5:236.

20. Among many critical historical studies, see Davidshofer, *Marxism and the Leninist Revolutionary Model*; Hobsbawm, *How to Change the World*; Bates, *Marxism*; Fleischer, *Der Marxismus in seinem Zeitalter*; Fetscher, *Der Marxismus*; Fetscher, *Karl Marx und der Marxismus*; Lichtheim, *Marxism*;

Anderson, *Considerations on Western Marxism*; Kolakowski, *Main Currents of Marxism*, 3 vols.; Deutscher and Deutscher, *Marxism in Our Time*; Aron and Drachkovitch, *Marxism in the Modern World*.

21. Marx, *Early Political Writings*, 58 and 64 (emphasis in the original).

22. *MECW*, 5:236.

23. Marx, *Early Political Writings*, 64.

24. Engels to Conrad Schmidt (5 August 1890), in *MECW*, 49:8.

25. Marx, *Early Political Writings*, 117.

26. See Knoblauch, *Wissenssoziologie*, 45; Dahrendorf and Henning, "Karl Marx," 68; Henning, *Philosophie nach Marx*, 190–203.

27. Bonß, *Die Einübung des Tatsachenblicks*, 9–28. For context, see Porter, *Karl Pearson*; Brückweh et al., *Engineering Society*; Raphael, "Die Verwissenschaftlichung des Sozialen"; the classic Hughes, *Consciousness and Society*. On the social reform efforts that accompanied these developments, see Grebing and Euchner, *Geschichte der sozialen Ideen*; Ritter, *Soziale Frage*. From a comparative European perspective, see Swaan, *Der sorgende Staat*; Leonards and Randeraad, "Transnational Experts."

28. Bonß, *Die Einübung des Tatsachenblicks*, 23.

29. See Kroll, *Kommunistische Intellektuelle*, 9–10.

30. Berger and Luckmann, *The Social Construction of Reality*, 133.

31. Shore, *Caviar and Ashes*, 6.

32. Dilthey, *Das Wesen der Philosophie*, 49–50, 76–77. For a recent critical approach, see Henning, *Philosophie nach Marx*, 269.

33. Leo, *Der Wille zum Wesen*, 25–26.

34. Fleischer, *Der Marxismus in seinem Zeitalter*, 201–32. Lichtheim, *From Marx to Hegel*, 64, by contrast, historicizes Marxism by describing it as the temporally and geographically distinct "ideology" of the workers' movement. Kolakowski understands it as a variety of socialism, although by this he means "Marxist doctrine," and he clearly distinguishes it from the ideology that certain political parties and movements derived from this teaching. See Kolakowski, *Main Currents of Marxism*, 1:v. Fetscher answers the question "What is Marxism?" most broadly: Marxists are those who seek to "actualize philosophy" under the motto of "changing the world" (*Der Marxismus*, 41).

35. Wehler, *Das Deutsche Kaiserreich*, 88.

36. Hunt, *Marx's General*. The German edition of Hunt's biography is subtitled *The Man Who Invented Marxism* (*Der Mann, der den Marxismus erfand*).

37. Kautsky, "Zum internationalen Kongreß," 578.

38. See, for example, Gleb, "Activist Subjectivities"; Braskén, *The International Workers' Relief*; Schickl, *Universalismus und Partikularismus*; Polexe, *Netzwerke und Freundschaft*. See also Georges Haupt's reflections on a sociology, or social history, of the Second International's leading groups: "International Leading Groups"; and Haupt, "Die sozialistische Bewegung."

39. I thank Alexandra Stelzig, Christian Laret, Kerstin Hein, Magdalena Melonik, and Carolin Kosuch for their assistance with the transcription and translation of selected French, Russian, and Polish sources. My grandmother Marianne Neuber's tireless transcription work allowed me to read the extensive correspondence in the papers of Kautsky, Bernstein, and Adler within a manageable timeframe. I looked for the editions of *Capital* that were owned by Guesde, Jaurès, Adler, Bernstein, Kautsky, and Luxemburg in various archives in Paris, Vienna, Amsterdam, Bonn, and Berlin. For practical reasons I was not able to consult the Russian archives for Lenin and Plekhanov. There are six books, although none by Marx, in the Kautsky collection at the IISH. There are no books in Bernstein's papers at the same institute. Luxemburg's biographer Paul Nettl reported that the Freikorps plundered and destroyed her personal library after her murder; her brother supposedly salvaged parts of the library, but what was saved is unknown. The Jaurès archive in Montreuil contains books with handwritten notes, including a signed copy of Luxemburg's 1913 *The Accumulation of Capital*—but not Marx's *Capital*. The Adler archive in Vienna could provide no further information. The Viennese Chamber of Labor has cataloged more than nine hundred titles from Adler's personal library, although much of it was destroyed by the National Socialists in 1938. *Capital* is not among the surviving titles, but there are copies of Engels's *Socialism: Utopian and Scientific*, Kautsky's *Economic Doctrines of Karl Marx*, and Deville's *Le Capital* (1883) with some underlining on the first twenty pages, presumably by Adler. None of the biographies I consulted mentions physical copies of Marx's work, nor do any ask whether these might still exist.

40. Frölich's memoir was published in 2013 under the title *Politische Autobiografie*. Fewer personal writings from the other protagonists have survived, or else these were not accessible to me for logistical or linguistic reasons.

CHAPTER 1

1. The epigraph is from *MECW*, 2: 168.
2. Bernstein, "Entwicklungsgang eines Sozialisten," 6–7.

3. Gay, *The Dilemma of Democratic Socialism*, 21.

4. Compère-Morel, *Jules Guesde*, 1–2.

5. Baron, *Plekhanov*, 4.

6. Service, *Lenin*, 13–60.

7. Pipes, *Struve*, 6–10.

8. Grebing, "Rosa Luxemburg," 58; Wistrich, "Rosa Luxemburg."

9. Nettl, *Rosa Luxemburg*, 1:50–53; Hirsch, *Rosa Luxemburg*, 8–12. An unpublished biographical portrait by Alexander Stein (Alexander N. Rubinstein), who was an acquaintance of Luxemburg, has been largely overlooked. The manuscript "Rosa Luxemburg and Communism" (1945/46) is held at the IISH, Alexander Stein papers, nos. 125–27.

10. Kautsky, [Self-Portrait], 117.

11. Kautsky, *Erinnerungen und Erörterungen*, 90–107, quotes on 107, 144, 139. Steenson has persuasively debunked Kautsky's efforts to stylize his own family background as proletarian in his memoir. See Steenson, *Karl Kautsky*, 12–13; Gilcher-Holtey, *Das Mandat des Intellektuellen*, 13–15.

12. Mommsen, "Victor Adlers Weg zum Sozialismus," 180–91; Meysels, *Victor Adler*, 23–38, 48–51. Although scholars have asserted otherwise, Victor's wife Emma, who was also born Jewish, did not convert in 1884. See Emma Adler, autobiography, IISH, Victor Adler papers, vol. 4, copy of the unpublished manuscript (1924/25), 181–82.

13. Emma Adler, biography of Victor Adler, unpublished and undated manuscript [1928], IISH, Victor Adler papers, 4:6, 17. See also Wistrich, *Socialism and the Jews*, 232–61.

14. Goldberg, *The Life of Jean Jaurès*, 5–9; Jackson, *Jean Jaurès*, 15–18; Auclair, *La Vie de Jean Jaurès*, 16–17.

15. Welskopp, *Das Banner der Brüderlichkeit*, 175–77.

16. Robert Michels, quoted in Welskopp, "'Arbeiterintellektuelle,'" 43.

17. Marx, *Early Political Writings*, 64 (emphasis in the original).

18. Böck, "Entfernung von der bürgerlichen Welt."

19. Emma Adler, autobiography, IISH, 172.

20. See Luxemburg's letters to the Kautskys (March/April 1906), in Luxemburg, *GB*, 2:249–54.

21. Guesde and Bourgin, "Jules Guesde et sa Famille."

22. Eley, "Intellectuals," 84–85.

23. Zomeren, van Postmes, and Spears, "Toward an Integrative Social Identity Model"; Hobsbawm, "Intellectuals," 247.

24. Willard, "Einführung," 7.

25. Goldberg, *The Life of Jean Jaurès*, 107.

26. Adler to Pernerstorfer (7 April 1871), quoted in Meysels, *Victor Adler*, 25.

27. Adler to Kautsky (7 September 1896), reprinted in Adler, *Briefwechsel mit August Bebel und Karl Kautsky*, 212.

28. Bernstein, *Sozialdemokratische Lehrjahre*, 16.

29. Ibid., 21.

30. Ibid., 15.

31. Bernstein, "Entwicklungsgang eines Sozialisten," 9.

32. Kautsky to his mother Minna Kautsky (2 July 1877), IISH, Kautsky-FA 1552, 1.

33. Kautsky, *Erinnerungen und Erörterungen*, 340–41.

34. See the Russian opposition's history of persecution in Daly, *Autocracy under Siege*.

35. Luxemburg, "Organisationsfragen," part 2, 531. The English translation is from *The Rosa Luxemburg Reader*, 260.

36. Hunt, *Politics, Culture, and Class*, 218.

37. See Mannheim, *Ideologie und Utopie*, 134–43; Mannheim, "The Problem of the Intelligentsia," 105–6. The English translations are from Mannheim, *Ideology and Utopia*, 156–61. See also Jung, *Die Seinsgebundenheit des Denkens*, 250–71. On intellectual generations, see Jaeger, "Generationen," 451–52.

38. On stores of knowledge and social knowledge, see Schütz and Luckmann, *Strukturen der Lebenswelt*, 163–66.

39. Goldberg, *The Life of Jean Jaurès*, 10–11; Auclair, *La Vie de Jean Jaurès*, 16–17.

40. Baron, *Plekhanov*, 6.

41. Pomper, *Lenin's Brother*; Service, *Lenin*; White, *Lenin*.

42. Obermayer-Marnach and Santifaller, *Österreichisches Biographisches Lexikon*, 275–76.

43. Kautsky, "Ein Proletarierkind," part 2, 379; Kautsky, "Ein Proletarierkind," part 3, 391.

44. Michler, "Zwischen Minna Kautsky und Hermann Bahr," 110. On Marx's praise, see Kautsky, "Mein erster Aufenthalt in London," 31.

45. Michler, "Zwischen Minna Kautsky und Hermann Bahr," 100. On Engels's criticism of Minna Kautsky (26 November 1885), see *MEW*, 36:393.

46. Kautsky to Minna Kautsky (30 August 1881), IISH, Kautsky-FA 1553, 1.

47. Kautsky to Minna Kautsky (26 February 1880), IISH, Kautsky-FA 1552, 1.

48. Kautsky to Johann and Minna Kautsky (14 March 1880), IISH, Kautsky-FA 1550, 1.

49. Kautsky, *Erinnerungen und Erörterungen*, 229.

50. Kautsky to Johann and Minna Kautsky (30 December 1882), IISH, Kautsky-FA 1550, 5–6.

51. Kautsky, *Erinnerungen und Erörterungen*, 301.

52. Ibid., 92.

53. Kautsky to Anton Jaich (26 January 1875), IISH, Kautsky-FA 1497, 1.

54. Kautsky, "Darwin und Sozialismus."

55. Kautsky, *Erinnerungen und Erörterungen*, 379–81.

56. Anton Jaich to Karl Kautsky (20 January 1875), IISH, Kautsky-FA 1497, 2.

57. Ibid., 4.

58. The handwritten manuscript is part of Kautsky's papers, in IISH, Kautsky-FA 2163, 1873. See also Kautsky's own summary on 191–93.

59. Anton Jaich to Karl Kautsky (undated, ca. 1873/74), IISH, Kautsky-FA 1497, 2.

60. Ibid., 1–2.

61. Kautsky, *Erinnerungen*, 160.

62. Lévy, "Nouveaux regards."

63. Jackson, *Jean Jaurès*, 16–17; Auclair, *La Vie de Jean Jaurès*, 16.

64. Goldberg, *The Life of Jean Jaurès*, 5.

65. Jaurès, *Œuvres*, 1:30–31.

66. Ibid., 1:35. Jaurès had Nicolas-Félix Deltour to thank for "discovering" him and for the opportunity to attend school in Paris with a scholarship from his hometown of Castres in 1876.

67. Baron, *Plekhanov*, 6–7.

68. Plekhanov, "Notes to Engels' Book," 430.

69. Baron, *Plekhanov*, 6.

70. Nettl, *Rosa Luxemburg*, 1:29; Frölich, *Rosa Luxemburg*, 8–12.

71. Kautsky, "Die Rebellionen in Schillers Dramen," 133.

72. Even in the industrially developed European countries, around three-quarters of all women did not engage in paid labor in the 1890s. See Hobsbawm, *The Age of Empire*, 195.

73. Emma Adler, biography of Victor Adler, IISH, Victor Adler papers, 4:3.

74. All of these details are from ibid., 4:3–9.

75. H. Adler, "Im Elternhaus," 19.

76. Pernerstorfer, "Aus jungen Tagen," 140.

77. Frölich, *Rosa Luxemburg*, 19–20; Nettl, *Rosa Luxemburg*, 1:33.

78. VGA, Vienna, Adler Archive, Familiendokumente I, Salomon Markus Adler, correspondence, M64/T4, 1878, 1884. On the dispute surrounding conversion, see also Emma Adler, autobiography, IISH, 181ff.

79. Emma Adler, autobiography, IISH, 183.
80. This is the recollection of Leopold Braun, who lived in the house as a youth. His father was Heinrich Braun, Emma's brother. See Braun, "Jugenderinnerungen," 60.
81. Rappoport, "Jules Guesde," part 1, 471.
82. Guesde and Bourgin, "Jules Guesde et sa Famille," 73–74.
83. Pipes, Struve, 5–10. Peter's quote is on 10n15.
84. Struve, "My Contacts and Conflicts with Lenin I," 575.
85. Service, Lenin, 23–30.
86. Ibid., 90–91; Pomper, Lenin's Brother, 31–86.
87. Service, Lenin, 52–60.
88. Pomper, Lenin's Brother.
89. Service, Lenin, 60–61.
90. Lenin, Absender, Wl. Uljanow.
91. Jena, Georgi Walentinowitsch Plechanow, 9.
92. Baron, Plekhanov, 5.
93. Ibid., 8.
94. Bernstein, "Entwicklungsgang eines Sozialisten." Also lightly abridged in Bernstein, Sozialdemokratische Lehrjahre, 189–243. For a less polemical but more detailed account, see Bernstein, Von 1850 bis 1872, 4–32.
95. Kautsky, [Self-Portrait], 117.
96. Kautsky, Erinnerungen und Erörterungen, 25.
97. Struve, "My Contacts and Conflicts with Lenin I," 575.
98. Ibid., 577.
99. Gall, Europa auf dem Weg in die Moderne, 21.
100. Berger, "Marxismusrezeption."
101. Adler, ARB, 6:18
102. See, for example, Grebing, "Die linken Intellektuellen," 86; Grebing, "Jüdische Intellektuelle"; Habermas, "Der deutsche Idealismus"; Lichtheim, "Socialism and the Jews," especially 446–47; Wistrich, Revolutionary Jews; Walzer, Exodus and Revolution.
103. Johnson, A History of the Jews, 340, 448.
104. Heid, "'…schreiben mir, dem Juden und Sozialisten,'" 15. On Bernstein's Judaism, see also Wistrich, "Eduard Bernstein and the Jewish Problem."
105. Adler, Briefwechsel mit August Bebel und Karl Kautsky, 15. See also Mommsen, "Victor Adlers Weg zum Sozialismus," 192.
106. Adler, Briefwechsel mit August Bebel und Karl Kautsky, 13.
107. Emma Adler, biography of Victor Adler, IISH, Victor Adler papers, 4:13. See also Wistrich, Socialism and the Jews, 232–61.
108. Quoted in Heid, "'…schreiben mir, dem Juden und Sozialisten,'" 33–34.

109. Ibid., 23.
110. See Bernstein, "Wie ich als Jude in der Diaspora aufwuchs," 86. On "Jewish utopia," see also Heid, "'. . . schreiben mir, dem Juden und Sozialisten,'" 18.
111. Wistrich, "Rosa Luxemburg," 244.
112. Nettl, *Rosa Luxemburg*, 1:43. For the most recent expression of this idea, see Wistrich, "Rosa Luxemburg."
113. Arendt, "Rosa Luxemburg: 1871–1919," 40–41.
114. Nettl, *Rosa Luxemburg*, 1:43; Johnson, *A History of the Jews*, 449; Wistrich, "Rosa Luxemburg," 247ff.
115. Luxemburg, "Einleitung," 30–31. See also Luxemburg, "Antisemitisches Frauenzimmer," *Sächsische ArbeiterZeitung* (18 October 1898), in BA-SAPMO NL 4002/1, p. 79.
116. See Rotter, *Social Learning and Clinical Psychology*; Bandura, *Sozial-kognitive Lerntheorie*; overview in Colquitt, LePine, and Noe, "Toward an Integrative Theory of Training Motivation."
117. Erikson, *Identity and the Life Cycle*, 51.
118. See Niethammer, "Die letzte Gemeinschaft," 21–23. Niethammer criticizes the focus of generational research on youth movements; Mannheim's concept of generations was not geared toward "youth cohorts that ripple across the surface of society in regular waves," but rather toward "voluntary elites within a cohort of shared historical experience" (23).

CHAPTER 2

1. The epigraph is from Gabely, "Ueber Witterungsverhältnisse," 1–2, from the Gymnasium's annual report of 1863–64, eleven-year-old Victor Adler's first year at the school.
2. See Osterhammel, *The Transformation of the World*, 788–98. The quote is on 795.
3. Schulhefte II, 1863–1870, "Schularbeit am 11. April: Wenn man alles auf einmal sieht, sieht man nichts," in VGA, Vienna, Adler Archive, Mappe 5, Tasche 2.
4. Adler, *ARB*, 5:29.
5. Rappoport, "Jules Guesde," part 1, 471.
6. Jackson, *Jean Jaurès*, 154.
7. Here I build upon Georges Haupt's biographical analysis of leading socialists as "international leading groups." Haupt understood the personal and professional networking of leading figures in the European

workers' movement as a kind of lived "internationalism," without underestimating the ideological and propagandistic function of this idea. See Haupt, "International Leading Groups," 98–99. See also Schickl, *Universalismus und Partikularismus.*

8. Baron, *Plekhanov*, 256.
9. Bernstein, *Von 1850 bis 1872*, 80ff., 99–108.
10. Kautsky, *Erinnerungen und Erörterungen*, 97ff.; Akademisches Gymnasium Wien, *JahresBericht*, 60.
11. Frölich, *Rosa Luxemburg*, 20.
12. Roland Holst-van der Schalk, *Rosa Luxemburg*, 11.
13. The details provided by the different biographers are astonishingly different—and yet they cite one another without reference to primary sources. Even Nettl repeatedly cites Roland Holst-van der Schalk and Frölich, neither of whom refers to primary sources. After Luxemburg's murder, Frölich safeguarded her personal papers, although these were lost after 1934, amid the upheavals of the Nazi dictatorship and Frölich's arrest and emigration. See Frölich, *Rosa Luxemburg*, 5. The copy of her final school report, or *Attest*, from the Second Girls' Gymnasium in Warsaw, dated 14 June 1887, indicates that the seventeen-year-old Rosa had completed seven grades. This would mean that she enrolled at the age of ten, as Frölich himself has written. A copy of the school report is among Luxemburg's papers at the Bundesarchiv. See BA-SAPMO NY 4002/1, 1. In *Rosa Luxemburg*, Nettl writes, without attribution, that she enrolled at thirteen, although he reprints this school report on 95.
14. Nettl, *Rosa Luxemburg*, 1:56; Frölich, *Rosa Luxemburg*, 20.
15. Luxemburg, *GW*, 1/1:84. For her and the party, this was a "case of self-defense."
16. Ibid., 1/1:90.
17. Frölich, *Rosa Luxemburg*, 23.
18. Ibid., 20.
19. Roland Holst-van der Schalk, *Rosa Luxemburg*, 11. See also Nettl, *Rosa Luxemburg*, 1:56. The Saxon Garden is Warsaw's oldest public park.
20. Service, *Lenin*, 37ff. The following information about Lenin's education is based on Service's account.
21. Plaggenborg, *Experiment Moderne*, 50–51, 60–61.
22. Pipes, *Struve*, 9.
23. Ibid., 11.
24. Struve, "My Contacts and Conflicts with Lenin I," 576.
25. Ibid., 577ff.
26. Pipes, *Struve*, 13.

27. See the chapter "In Search of the Russian Soul," in Figes, *Natasha's Dance*, 289–354.

28. Struve, "Ivan Aksakov," 515.

29. Pipes, *Struve*, 8, n10; Struve, "Ivan Aksakov," 515–16.

30. Pipes, *Struve*, 11.

31. Struve, "My Contacts and Conflicts with Lenin I," 579–80.

32. Tolstoy, "On Popular Education," 254–55.

33. Ibid., 281–82.

34. Quoted in Baron, *Plekhanov*, 7.

35. Ibid.

36. Camus, *The Rebel*, 13.

37. Erikson, "Youth," 2–3. See also Berger et al., *Die gesellschaftliche Konstruktion*, 155–56.

38. Baron, *Plekhanov*, 8.

39. Kautsky to Minna Kautsky (26 July 1871), IISH, Kautsky-FA 1552, 1.

40. Gillis, *Youth and History*; Koebner, Janz, and Trommler, *Mit uns zieht die neue Zeit*; Roseman, *Generations in Conflict*. On the "political slogan," see Elkar, "Young Germans."

41. Nipperdey, *Arbeitswelt und Bürgergeist*, 116–18.

42. Goldberg, *The Life of Jean Jaurès*, 8–9.

43. Ibid., 10.

44. Lévy, "Nouveaux regards," 14.

45. Ville de Castres, Musée Jaurès, and Poulain, *Exposition*, 58; Soulé, *La Vie de Jaurès*, 19.

46. Jaurès, *De la Réalité du Monde Sensible*. The thesis has not been translated into English. For context and synthesis, see Goldberg, *The Life of Jean Jaurès*, 77–79. Two short excerpts in German are in Jaurès, *RS*, 274–76.

47. Jaurès, "Die nichtkonfessionelle Schule." See also Jaurès, "La Question religieuse" (his core text on religion and socialism); Peillon, *Jean Jaurès* (which identifies socialism as Jaurès's "true religion").

48. Goldberg, *The Life of Jean Jaurès*, 13–14.

49. Jaurès, *Œuvres*, 1:38–42. For more on the poem's history, see Godart, "Un grand parlementaire," 63–64. Godart, who represented Lyon in the National Assembly, got to know Jaurès in 1906.

50. Jaurès, *Œuvres*, 1:38–42. Translation from the original French by Timothy Bent.

51. Jaurès to Jean Julien (24 February 1878), in Jaurès, *Œuvres*, 1:43.

52. See also the interpretation by the poem's publisher in Jaurès, *Œuvres*, 1:40n1.

53. Jaurès, "Discours français pour le concours général," in Jaurès, Œuvres, 1:48–52; Goldberg, The Life of Jean Jaurès, 14.

54. Pernerstorfer, "Aus jungen Tagen," 140.

55. Emma Adler, biography of Victor Adler, IISH, Victor Adler papers, vol. 4.

56. Gymnasium zu den Schotten Wien, Jahresbericht (1864). All of the following statistics are taken from the school's annual reports between 1863 and 1870.

57. Pernerstorfer, "Aus jungen Tagen," 139–41.

58. Ibid., 140.

59. See "Programm der musikalisch-deklamatorischen Akademie abgehalten am 26. Juni 1869," in VGA, Vienna, Adler Archive, Mappe 4, Tasche 3.

60. Nipperdey, Arbeitswelt und Bürgergeist, 116–18; Roseman, Generations in Conflict; Roseman, "Generationen als 'Imagined Communities'"; Gillis, Youth and History.

61. See "Vereinsbuch" (1870), in VGA, Vienna, Adler Archive, Mappe 6, Tasche 10.

62. VGA, Vienna, Adler Archive, Lade 19, Mappe 13.

63. This selection is drawn from the 1867 annual report, covering the 1866–67 school year, when Adler was in fifth grade. "A useless life is an early death" (Ein unnütz' Leben ist ein früher Tod) is from Goethe's Iphigenia in Tauris. "The Winter Evening" ("Der Winterabend") is a poem by Karl Gottfried von Leitner and a lied by Schubert. "Whoever does not go forward, will return" (Wer nicht vorwärts geht, der kommt zurück) is from Goethe's Hermann and Dorothea.

64. See Adler's first "flier," 1865 or 1866, in VGA, Vienna, Adler Archive, Mappe 6, Tasche 5.

65. See Storfer [Engelbert Pernerstorfer], "Victor Adlers erstes Flugblatt," ArbeiterZeitung, 24 June 1912, humorous insert on the occasion of Adler's sixtieth birthday. I refer to the copy in VGA, Vienna, Adler Archive, Mappe 6, Tasche 5, which also holds the original handwritten flier.

66. Wistrich, "Victor Adler," 26. See also Wistrich, Revolutionary Jews from Marx to Trotsky, 99.

67. Braunthal, Victor und Friedrich Adler, 17.

68. Pernerstorfer, "Aus jungen Tagen," 142.

69. Ibid., meaning roughly, "Yes of course!"

70. Hauser, "Frisch auf! Frisch auf! Revolutionslied nach F. Freiligrath, seinem Freunde Victor gewidmet von Hauser, 1870," in VGA, Vienna, Adler Archive, Mappe 4, Tasche 4. See also Freiligrath's poem "Reveille," and its English translation, in Pinkert-Sältzer, German Songs, 44–45.

71. Braunthal, *Victor und Friedrich Adler*, 43.
72. Kolakowski, *Main Currents of Marxism*, 1:408–12. See also Röder, *Utopische Romantik*; Safranski, *Romantik*, 247–49. Loewy identifies "anti-capitalist Romanticism" as a "forgotten source of the socialism of Marx and Engels" in "Romantik," 1153.
73. Safranski, *Romantik*, 13. See also Droz, "Romanticism in Political Thought"; Carl Schmitt's radical criticism in *Politische Romantik*, 227–28.
74. Drawing upon Spinoza, Melvin Lasky describes his study of "intellectual climate" as "less a formal exercise in intellectual history than a kind of meteorological report." Lasky, *Utopia and Revolution*, ix.
75. According to Safranski, *Romantik*, 13, this is still the "best definition of Romanticism." The English translation is from Arctander-O'Brien, *Novalis*, 139.
76. Luxemburg, "Adam Mickiewicz," 1. The English translation is from Luxemburg, *Selected Political and Literary Writings*, 15.
77. Berger et al., *Die gesellschaftliche Konstruktion*, 146.
78. Erikson summarizes these developmental stages: basic trust: "I am what I am given"; autonomy: "I am what I will"; initiative: "I am what I can imagine I will be"; industry: "I am what I learn"; identity: "I am." These stages are followed in adulthood by intimacy/distantiation: "You and I"; and generativity, or parenthood: "I create." Erikson, *Identity and the Life Cycle*, 51–107.
79. Hobsbawm, *The Age of Revolution*.
80. Koselleck, "Revolution," 655.
81. Ibid.
82. Bernstein, *Von 1850 bis 1872*, 95–96. For an early English translation, see Furness, *Schiller's Song of the Bell*, 22–23.
83. See, for example, Bernstein, "Die Menge und das Verbrechen"; Bernstein, "Politischer Massenstreik."
84. Kautsky, diary, IISH, Kautsky-FA 1812.
85. Ibid., 18 July [1873].
86. Ibid., 1 September [1873]. Underlining in the original document.
87. Ibid., 28 December [1873].
88. Ibid.
89. Kautsky, "Einiges über die Berechtigung socialistischer ideen" (February 1874), IISH, Kautsky-FA 2094, 1.
90. Kautsky, diary, 41–42.
91. Koselleck, "Revolution."
92. Karl Kautsky, "Zu den Wahlen" (October 1873), IISH, Kautsky-FA 2095.

93. Kautsky, "Einiges über die Berechtigung socialistischer Ideen" (February 1874), IISH, Kautsky-FA 2094.

94. Kautsky, diary, 15 July [1873].

95. Ibid., entries from 18 July, 24 August, and 1 September [1873].

96. Akademisches Gymnasium Wien, *JahresBericht*, 60. According to this report, drawing exercises in his final school year included "freehand sketches from sample pages, arabesques, animals, heads, and whole figures, as well as landscapes."

97. The originals in Guesde's papers (IISH, Jules Guesde papers, 535-1) are dated 1860–70, which does not seem entirely accurate. If Zetkin's remarks are correct, Guesde completed his schooling in 1861. The same detail ("younger than sixteen years old") is given in Zévaès, *Jules Guesde*, 6.

98. IISH, Jules Guesde papers, 535-1. See the English translation in Hugo, *Selected Poems*, 127.

99. See the English translation in Hugo, *Selected Poems*, 127.

100. Ibid., 306–9.

101. Ibid., 305.

102. Or possibly, "the protection of money/capital."

103. Notes de lectures, IISH, Jules Guesde papers, 535-1, 307, 314–15, 320.

104. Ibid., 319. See also Koselleck, "Geschichte, Geschichten und formale Zeitstrukturen," 141–42.

105. Notes de lectures, IISH, Jules Guesde papers, 535-1, 322.

106. Adler, school essay "Die Licht- und Schattenseiten des Zusammenlebens der vielen Menschen in großen Städten" [ca. 1870], VGA, Vienna, Adler Archive, Schulhefte II, Mappe 5, Tasche 2, 1–2.

107. Ibid.

108. Ibid., 5.

109. Conze, "Proletariat, Pöbel, Pauperismus," 54.

110. Steenson, *After Marx*, 160–85.

111. See the Vereinsbuch (1870), VGA, Vienna, Adler Archive, Mappe 6, Tasche 10, 1.

112. Ibid. The texts in question are Schulze-Delitzsch's *Capitel zu einem deutschen Arbeiterkatechismus: Sechs Vorträge* (1863) and Lassalle's *Herr Bastiat Schulze von Delitzsch, der ökonomische Julian, oder: Capital und Arbeit* (1864). Lassalle praises Marx on 149.

113. Schulhefte II, 1864–70, VGA, Vienna, Adler Archive, Mappe 5, Tasche 2, 1–2.

114. See the student newspaper *Minerva* (1 December 1872), 1–2, IISH, Kautsky-FA 1837.

115. Kautsky, *Karl Marx' ökonomische Lehren*, viii, x.
116. Koselleck, "Historia Magistra Vitae"; Koselleck et al., "Geschichte, Historie."
117. Koselleck, "Historia Magistra Vitae," 64. The English translation is from Koselleck, *Futures Past*, 41. See also Jaeger and Rüsen, *Geschichte des Historismus*, 11–40.
118. Notes de lectures, IISH, Jules Guesde papers, 535-1.
119. Zévaès, *Jules Guesde*, 6.
120. Jaeger and Rüsen, *Geschichte des Historismus*, 78.
121. Lévy, "Nouveaux regards," 14; Ville de Castres, Musée Jaurès, and Poulain, *Exposition*, 58.
122. Goldberg, *The Life of Jean Jaurès*, 11.
123. Jaurès, "Die idealistische Geschichtsauffassung," 552. See also Jaurès, *De la Réalité du Monde Sensible* and *Die Ursprünge des Sozialismus in Deutschland*.
124. Jaurès, "Die idealistische Geschichtsauffassung," 555.
125. Goldberg, *The Life of Jean Jaurès*, 82–84.
126. Dohrn, *Jüdische Eliten im Russischen Reich*, 372.
127. Letter to Luise Kautsky (September 1904), in Luxemburg, *GB*, 2:69. The English translations in this paragraph are from *The Letters of Rosa Luxemburg* (2011), 176–77.
128. Lubbock, *Die Entstehung der Civilisation*, v.
129. Letter to Luise Kautsky (September 1904), in Luxemburg, *GB*, 2:68–69.
130. Marx, *The Ethnological Notebooks*.
131. Kautsky, *Erinnerungen und Erörterungen*, 181.
132. Bolingbroke, "Letters on the Study and Use of History," 323.
133. Ibid., 323–27.
134. Kautsky, *Erinnerungen und Erörterungen*, 175.
135. Jaeger and Rüsen, *Geschichte des Historismus*, 2.
136. Ibid., 164–73.
137. Koselleck, "Historia Magistra Vitae," 64. The English translation is from Koselleck, *Futures Past*, 41.
138. Blume, "Das Ideal des Helden und des Weibes bei Homer," 51.
139. The political scope of youth discontent in the nineteenth century has not been well studied, although it is generally acknowledged that youth rebellions were more prevalent in Germany than elsewhere, and that these experiences can be understood generationally, or at least were generationally imagined. See Roseman, *Generations in Conflict*. Few studies on the secondary socialization of adolescents are based on diaries or schoolwork. See, for example, Dekker, *Egodocuments and History*;

Dekker, *Childhood, Memory, and Autobiography*; as well as the essays in *German History* 28, no. 3 (2010)—a special issue on ego documents—especially Fulbrook and Rublack, "In Relation."

140. Safranski, *Romantik*, 248.

CHAPTER 3

1. Ringer, "Die Zulassung zur Universität," 199–226.
2. On the intellectual, historical, and biographical context of the Young Hegelian Heinrich Heine and his poem "Doctrine" (*Doktrin*), see Rattner and Danzer, *Die Junghegelianer*, 209–11; Habermas, "Heinrich Heine." The English translation of the poem is by Felix Pollak, in Heine, *Poetry and Prose*, 45.
3. Luxemburg, "Einleitung," 11–12.
4. Hunt, *Marx's General*, 34–35.
5. [Guesde], "Jules Guesde chez lui"; S. Bernstein, "Jules Guesde," 31–32.
6. [Guesde], "Jules Guesde chez lui."
7. See the illustration in Willard, *Jules Guesde*, 32–33.
8. [Guesde], "Jules Guesde chez lui."
9. Bernstein, *Sozialdemokratische Lehrjahre*, 198.
10. Bernstein, *Von 1850 bis 1872*, 209.
11. Eduard Bernstein, Friedrich Schillers, des Denkers und Dichters, Einfluß auf junge Seelen [1920s], IISH, NL Bernstein, A 95 (film 3).
12. Ibid., 3 (*Von der Parteien Gunst und Haß verwirrt / Schwankt sein Charakterbild in der Geschichte*). The English translation is by Flora Kimmich. See Schiller, *Wallenstein*.
13. Emma Adler, autobiography, IISH, Victor Adler papers, 4:173.
14. Maderthaner, "Victor Adler und die Religion des Ästhetischen," 109.
15. Letter to Pernerstorfer (3 August 1872), 1, Adler Archive, Engelberg Pernerstorfer II, M138, T1.
16. Baron, *Plekhanov*, 7.
17. Plekhanov, "Notes to Engels' Book," 432.
18. Ibid., 433.
19. Ibid., 434 (emphasis in the original). Here Plekhanov was referring to his three-part essay "Zu Hegels sechzigstem Todestag."
20. Lucien Goldmann, preface, in Jaurès, *Die Ursprünge des Sozialismus in Deutschland*, 104–6.
21. Jaurès, *Die Ursprünge des Sozialismus in Deutschland*, 23.
22. Goldberg, *The Life of Jean Jaurès*, 9–10.

23. Ibid., 11–17. And see the letters in Jaurès, *Œuvres*, 1:36–105, especially 36–37, 65–66, 73–74, and 78ff. Renan and Fustel de Coulanges were both teachers; Fustel de Coulanges had taught at the École Normale Superieure since 1870 and became its rector in 1880, while Jaurès was a student.

24. Goldberg, *The Life of Jean Jaurès*, 78.

25. Jaurès, *La Constituante*, 8.

26. Kautsky, *Erinnerungen und Erörterungen*, 96.

27. Ibid., 188. The English translation is from Sand, *Novels*, 173.

28. Sand, *Novels*, 173.

29. Ibid., 174.

30. Kautsky, *Erinnerungen und Erörterungen*, 188.

31. Plaggenborg, *Experiment Moderne*, 48–66. Plaggenborg, like G. A. Paul, even speaks of a "closed mind."

32. Ibid., 50–51.

33. Chernyshevsky, *What Is to Be Done?*, 282–83.

34. Service, *Lenin*, 65.

35. Saage, *Industrielle Revolution*, 286ff.

36. Service, *Lenin*, 118.

37. Ibid., 87. In *The Development of Capitalism in Russia* (written 1896–99 and published under a pseudonym), Lenin hardly mentioned the famine (see Lenin, *Collected Works*, 3:166, 247, 555). His interest was largely limited to Engels's thesis that the 1891–92 famine revealed the "dissolution of the old communist peasant community" and the establishment of a "home market," and thus should be understood as a side effect of capitalism (Engels, "Die Entwicklung des Sozialismus in Deutschland," 587–99; see the English translation in *MECW*, 27: 247–49). Lenin believed that the Narodniks were wrong to view the people as victims and to draw only "moralizing conclusions." Historian Dietrich Geyer has relativized the Russian Marxists' apparent callousness, arguing that there is no evidence of an explicitly "dismissive reaction to the wave of sympathy" for the peasants' suffering. See Geyer, *Lenin in der russischen Sozialdemokratie*, 41n15.

38. Chernyshevsky, *What Is to Be Done?*, 115–16.

39. Service, *Lenin*, 65.

40. Letter to his mother, M. A. Lenina (17 September 1897) in Lenin, *Collected Works*, 37:102–3.

41. Lenin, *Collected Works*, 5:520.

42. Service, *Lenin*, 203.

43. Ibid., 485.

44. Service was able to view the original manuscript, and he found that even an edition published in the 1980s under Gorbachev was subject to numerous "politically motivated edits" (ibid., 7). I refer here to the first English edition of 1942. On the analysis of Soviet memoirs, see Walker, "On Reading Soviet Memoirs."

45. Geyer, *Lenin in der russischen Sozialdemokratie*, 40.

46. Krupskaya, *Memories of Lenin*, 300.

47. Service, *Lenin*, 43, 51, 79.

48. Ibid., 43.

49. Lenin, "Leo Tolstoy as the Mirror of the Russian Revolution," in *Collected Works*, 15:202.

50. Plechanow, "Karl Marx und Leo Tolstoi," 90.

51. Lenin, "Leo Tolstoy as the Mirror of the Russian Revolution," in *Collected Works*, 15:206, 208. Lenin's argument did, however, help him situate these events in the broader history of the revolutionary movement (as he saw it); the time around 1905 was not yet ripe for revolution.

52. Struve, "Leo Tolstoj," 26–27.

53. Ibid., 24–33.

54. Struve, "My Contacts and Conflicts with Lenin I," 576.

55. Dostoevsky to A. G. Dostoevsky (8 June 1880), in *Dostoevsky: Letters and Reminiscences*, 232–33.

56. See also Dostojewski and Braun, *Rede über Puschkin*.

57. Pipes, *Struve*, 13n22.

58. Struve, "Две речи о Достоевскомъ" [Two speeches about Dostoyevsky], facsimile of an unknown newspaper article dated 10 February 1931, Hoover Archive, Struve papers, box 17, folder 18

59. Ibid., 1–2.

60. Struve, "My Contacts and Conflicts with Lenin I," 576–77.

61. See Struve, "Ivan Aksakov," "My Contacts and Conflicts with Lenin I," and "My Contacts and Conflicts with Lenin II."

62. Pipes, *Struve*, 21–22.

63. Ibid., 22.

64. Struve, "My Contacts and Conflicts with Lenin I," 575.

65. Pipes, *Struve*, 24. As an introduction, see also Foote, *Saltykov Shchedrin's "The Golovlyovs,"* 3–44.

66. Struve, "My Contacts and Conflicts with Lenin I," 576.

67. The satires that Struve emphasizes in his memoirs (*Motley Letters*, 1884–86) have not been translated into English. See the analysis in Draitser, *Techniques of Satire*, 22–24.

68. Nettl, *Rosa Luxemburg*, 1:53.

69. Wistrich, "Rosa Luxemburg," 249–50. See, for example, her letter to Leo Jogiches (3 January 1902), in Luxemburg, *GB*, 1:553.
70. Koropeckyj, *Adam Mickiewicz*, x.
71. Luxemburg, "Adam Mickiewicz," 1. The English translation is from Luxemburg, *Selected Political and Literary Writings*, 15.
72. Luxemburg, "Adam Mickiewicz," 1; Luxemburg, *Selected Political and Literary Writings*, 15.
73. Henze, "Ode an die Jugend." The English translation is from Boswell, *Poland and the Poles*, 217–19. For the poem's context within Polish national culture, see Henze, "Jugendbilder und politische Transformation in Polen," 255–79.
74. Luxemburg, "Adam Mickiewicz," 1; Luxemburg, *Selected Political and Literary Writings*, 14.
75. Luxemburg, *GW*, 2:331.
76. Luxemburg, "Adam Mickiewicz," 1; Luxemburg, *Selected Political and Literary Writings*, 15–16.
77. Luxemburg, "Einleitung," 10.
78. Ibid., 11–12, 35.
79. Luxemburg to Leo Jogiches (30 June 1905), in Luxemburg, *GB*, 2:147.
80. Osborne, *Vom Nutzen der Geschichte*, 50.
81. Nettl, *Rosa Luxemburg*, 1:29.
82. Frölich, memoirs, in IISH, NL Paul Frölich, 13; Frölich, *Luxemburg*, s. 231–32.
83. Roland Holst-van der Schalk, *Rosa Luxemburg*, 217; Luxemburg, *The Letters of Rosa Luxemburg* (2011), 185.
84. Roland Holst-van der Schalk, *Rosa Luxemburg*, 217; Luxemburg, *The Letters of Rosa Luxemburg* (2011), 183–84.
85. Roland Holst-van der Schalk, *Rosa Luxemburg*, 217; Luxemburg, *The Letters of Rosa Luxemburg* (2011), 184.
86. Meyer, "Huttens letzte Tage," 403 (emphasis in the original).
87. See, for example, Luxemburg, *GB*, 1:112–33.
88. Habermas, "Heinrich Heine," 151ff.
89. Letter to Julius Bruhns (14 January 1904), in Luxemburg, *GB*, 2:52.
90. See, for example, Kautsky, "Die Sprache unserer Presse," 2–3; Blos, "Ludwig Börne," parts 1 and 2.
91. Börne, *Mittheilungen*, 15–16.
92. Luxemburg to Mathilde and Robert Seidel (11 August 1898), in Luxemburg, *GB*, 1:182. The English translation is from Luxemburg, *The Letters of Rosa Luxemburg* (2011), 84 (emphasis in the original). Wilhelm Blos, editor of the Social Democratic satire magazine, *Der wahre Jacob*,

compared Börne to an "ancient Roman writer" who wielded the "scourge of a raw satire" against his fatherland's "political and moral decline." See Blos, "Ludwig Börne," part 1, 265.

93. Nettl, *Rosa Luxemburg*, 1:63; Roland Holst-van der Schalk, *Rosa Luxemburg*, 15–16.

94. Luxemburg, *GW*, 1/1:215.

95. Nettl, *Rosa Luxemburg*, 1:29; Frölich, *Rosa Luxemburg*, 19.

96. Kautsky, "Die Rebellionen in Schillers Dramen," 133.

97. During her free time in the fall of 1904, she read volumes 7–9 of his collected works, which she borrowed from Luise Kautsky. See her letter to Luise Kautsky (20 September 1904) in Luxemburg, *GB*, 2:70; also Nettl, *Rosa Luxemburg*, 1:53; Frölich, *Rosa Luxemburg*, 19.

98. Luxemburg, "Rezension Franz Mehring," 164 (emphasis in the original). The English translations are from Luxemburg, *Selected Political and Literary Writings*, 18–19. For Mehring's reaction, see her letter to Leo Jogiches (2 May 1905) in Luxemburg, *GB*, 2:81.

99. Luxemburg to Franz Mehring (2 May 1905) in Luxemburg, *GB*, 2:83.

100. Luxemburg to Kostja Zetkin (4 December 1911) in Luxemburg, *GB*, 2:134–35. On the discourse of decadence around the turn of the century, see Krobb, "'Die Kunst der Väter todtet das Leben der Enkel.'"

101. Luxemburg, *GW*, 1/1:211.

102. Luxemburg, *GB*, 1:153.

PART II

1. Kautsky to Bernstein (20 April 1887), 6–8, IISH, Bernstein papers, RCChIDNI, 204/1-910.

2. Regina Bernstein to Luise Kautsky, ca. May 1887, IISH, Kautsky papers, K.DV 96, 1–2.

3. The term "epigone" is now widely associated with Helmut Fleischer's definition (*Der Marxismus in seinem Zeitalter*, 202), although Kautsky had already used it in a postcard to Bernstein, albeit in the guise of modesty: "The old guard is merging into one, and the epigones can't keep pace." Kautsky to Bernstein (8 December 1886), 2 in IISH, Bernstein papers, RCChIDNI, 204/1-906. In 1899, as he began to distance himself from Marx, Struve criticized the "dogmatism of the epigones." See Struve, "Die Marxsche Theorie der sozialen Entwicklung," 679.

4. Kautsky, *Karl Marx' ökonomische Lehren*, vii.

5. Haupt, "Zur Begriffsgeschichte des Wortpaares 'Marxist' und 'Marxismus,'" 109; Walther, "Marxismus," 940n19.

6. Kautsky to Bernstein (17 July 1886), 2, IISH, Bernstein papers, RCChIDNI, 204/1-888.

7. Wehler, *Das Deutsche Kaiserreich*, 88. The English translation is from Wehler, *The German Empire*, 81. Geoff Eley has discussed this phenomenon at length in *Forging Democracy*, 33–46.
8. Welskopp, *Das Banner der Brüderlichkeit*, 722–24.
9. Berger, "Marxismusrezeption," 193. For a European comparison, see Steenson, *After Marx*. See also Langewiesche and Schönhoven, "Arbeiterbibliotheken und Arbeiterlektüre," 198, about the reading experience of workers in Imperial Germany. Thomas Welskopp discusses the limited influence of Marx's theses on the lived experience of workers before the Anti-Socialist Laws in *Das Banner der Brüderlichkeit*, 67–68.
10. Nettl, *Rosa Luxemburg*, 59.
11. Raphael, "Die Verwissenschaftlichung des Sozialen"; Raphael, "Embedding the Human and Social Sciences in Western Societies."
12. Morina, "Szenen einer marxistischen Familie." See also Joll, *The Second International*, 3–55. There is still no comprehensive study of the practice of the Second International (in the sense of a "social history of international socialism," as proposed by Haupt). See Haupt, *Programm und Wirklichkeit*.
13. Hobsbawm, "The Fortunes of Marx' and Engels' Writings," 328–29.
14. Geyer, *Lenin in der russischen Sozialdemokratie*, 36.
15. Berger, "Marxismusrezeption." Berger discusses social democracy in Germany, but his thesis is relevant to the experiences of the other European socialist movements.
16. Ibid., 202.

CHAPTER 4

1. S. Bernstein, "Jules Guesde," 46.
2. George Lichtheim points to Marx's "grandiose synthesis" of German philosophy, French socialism, and British economics, which was rooted in his own international experience and fused German, French, and English "currents of thought." See Lichtheim, *The Origins of Socialism*, 185–87. On Marx's time in Paris, see Sperber, *Karl Marx*, 117–51; Berlin, *Karl Marx*, 61–88, especially 64–66.
3. Mermeix, *La France Socialiste*, 61–62
4. Ibid., 61.
5. Ibid., 62.
6. Quoted in Stuart, *Marxism at Work*, 25n18. *Idée* was capitalized in the original French text, a weekly column that appeared under the title "Le Parti Ouvrier en France" in the Guesdists' party journal, *Le Socialiste*.
7. Letter to Friedrich Adolph Sorge (5 November 1880), in *MEW*, 34:477.
8. [Guesde], "Jules Guesde chez lui," 1–2.

9. On the history of Marxism in France, see Prochasson, "L'invention du Marxisme Français"; Rebérioux, "Le socialisme Français"; Steenson, *After Marx*; Stuart, *Marxism at Work*; Judt, *Marxism and the French Left*; Derfler, *Paul Lafargue and the Founding of French Marxism*; Lindenberg, *Le Marxisme Introuvable*.

10. Guesde, Papiers autographes, IISH, Alexandre Bracke papers, Ordner IV, 1; Willard, "Einführung," 7.

11. Two works by Willard are an exception, although they contain few references to sources: *Jules Guesde*, 14–20; "Einführung," 7–13.

12. The autobiographical sketch is written in the third-person singular, but it was clearly written by Guesde himself, probably after 1900 at the behest of Alexandre Bracke-Desrousseaux. Bracke was the executor of Guesde's will and the chair of the Friends of Jules Guesde Society, which was founded in 1901. See Willard, *Les Guesdistes*, 683n1; Bracke-Desrousseaux, "Cahier no. 6," 1. Bracke's papers, given to the IISH in the 1950s, include the autobiographical sketch. See IISH, Alexandre Bracke papers, folder IV, Papiers autographes, 2–11. The other texts are in IISH, Jules Guesde papers, 541/1–544/1; the poems (Carnet de poésies) are in 173/2.

13. S. Bernstein, "Jules Guesde," 32.

14. Guesde, *Le Livre Rouge*. See also Guesde, "Republique & Socialisme," *L'Égalité de Marseilles* (10 January 1873). A copy is held at the IISH, Jules Guesde papers, 589/1.

15. Willard, "Einführung," 16–17.

16. See Hunt, *Marx's General*, 250–55; Braunthal, *Geschichte der Internationale*, 190ff. A contemporary account from the perspective of the Swiss anarchists is Guillaume, *L'Internationale*, 232–44.

17. Willard, "Einführung," 20–21.

18. On Guesde's controversial role, see Malon, "Le Collectivisme en France," 998; Dommanget, *L'Introduction du Marxisme en France*, 133–51; Prochasson, "L'invention du Marxisme Français," 431ff.; Kropotkin, *Memoiren eines Revolutionärs*, 480; Steenson, *After Marx*, 124–25. Guesde's open letter is reproduced in Zévaès, *Jules Guesde*, 27; Guillaume, *L'Internationale*, 61–63.

19. Droz, *Der Einfluß der deutschen Sozialdemokratie*, 9.

20. Guesde, *AT*, 99.

21. [Bracke-Desrousseaux], notes biogr. et bibliogr. sur Jules Guesde pour les années 1871/1876, IISH, Jules Guesde papers, 540/1, 7.

22. Jules Guesde, Carnet de poésies [1888], IISH, Jules Guesde papers, 173/2, 2. Translation from the original French by Timothy Bent.

23. This was not published in French until 1914. See Guesde, "De la Propriété," 1n1.

24. For Lampertico's critique of Marx, see Lampertico, *Economia Dei Popoli e Degli Stati*, 256–65; Sensales, "The Catholic Organicism of Fedele Lampertico."

25. Guesde, "De la Propriété," 7, 11–12.

26. Ibid., 17.

27. Ibid., 23.

28. Guesde began to learn Russian in exile, but he could not find a publisher for his translation. The first twenty-five pages of his handwritten translation have been preserved. See S. Bernstein, "Jules Guesde," 32–33n11.

29. There is no pertinent letter or correspondence in Guesde's papers, or in Darwin's papers at Cambridge.

30. Guesde, Du Darwin [1875], IISH, Jules Guesde papers, 544/1, 9–12.

31. L. G., "Rezension Jules Guesde."

32. Guesde, *Essai de Catéchisme Socialiste*, 15–16. See the original phrasing in Feuerbach, *Das Wesen des Christentums*, 408.

33. Willard, "Einführung," 24.

34. Jules Guesde, Bonheur [1875], IISH, Jules Guesde papers, 541/3.

35. Willard, "Einführung," 23; Stuart, *Marxism at Work*, 28–29.

36. Jules Guesde, Carnet de poésies [1888], IISH, Jules Guesde papers, 173/2, 2. Translation from the original French by Timothy Bent.

37. Jules Guesde, Thèse—Antithèse—Synthèse [ca. 1872–76], IISH, Jules Guesde papers, 541/4.

38. Nieuwenhuis, "César de Paepe."

39. S. Bernstein, "Jules Guesde," 33.

40. Haine, *The World of the Paris Café*, 229.

41. Mermeix, *La France Socialiste*, 57.

42. Malon, "Le Collectivisme en France," 998. A similar argument appears in S. Bernstein, "Jules Guesde," 34–35. Ossip Zetkin, who knew Guesde in Paris, dated his thorough study of Marx's works to the period after 1880. See Zetkin, *Charakterköpfe*, 40.

43. Quoted in Guillaume, *L'Internationale*, 63. See also his first public expression of this distance in Guesde, *AT*, 113.

44. Perrot, "Le Premier Journal Marxiste Français," 1–5.

45. Willard, "Einführung," 30–31.
46. Haupt, "Frankreich."
47. Mermeix, *La France Socialiste*, 41ff.; Steenson, *After Marx*, 114–15.
48. Haupt, "Frankreich," 40–49.
49. Stuart, *Marxism at Work*, 28–29, 54.
50. Ibid., 492.
51. Guesde, *AT*, 111–13.
52. Deville, *Le Capital de Karl Marx*, 2–4, 40, 54–55.
53. Hall, "Gabriel Deville," 440. The figure pertains to men's wages in the Département de la Seine; female workers earned only half as much as their male counterparts. See Institut National, *Annuaire Statistique de la France* (1898), 229.
54. Stuart, *Marxism at Work*, 493. Stuart debunks the oft-repeated assertion that Guesde knew *Capital* by heart. See Goldberg, *The Life of Jean Jaurès*, 21n63. On "vulgar" Marxism, see Lindenberg, *Le Marxisme Introuvable*, 75–140.
55. Guesde, *AT*, 122.
56. See Arendt's critique of valuing humans as producers rather than as thinkers or doers, in *Vita activa*, 103–4, 225 (especially n8), 282ff., 379, 414.
57. Zetkin, *Charakterköpfe*, 40.
58. See the details in S. Bernstein, "Jules Guesde," 37–38, and Guesde's own depiction of these events in "Le Collectivisme Devant la 10e Chambre."
59. Willard, "Einführung," 36–37.
60. Guesde, "Le Collectivisme Devant la 10e Chambre."
61. Guesde, *AT*, 136–38; Malon, "Le Collectivisme en France," 1013; S. Bernstein, "Jules Guesde," 38; Willard, "Einführung," 39n49.
62. Guesde, "Lettre à Karl Marx à Londres," 43–46. The English translation is from *MECW*, 45:450–51.
63. Guesde, "Lettre à Karl Marx à Londres," 43–46. See also *MEW*, 34:505; *MECW*, 45:451; S. Bernstein, "Jules Guesde," 40.
64. Moss, *The Origins of the French Labor Movement*, 85.
65. Guesde to Marx (late 1878/early 1879), *MEW*, 34:505n587. It is fully reproduced, in French, in Willard, *La Naissance du Parti Ouvrier Français*, 43–46.
66. Moss, *The Origins of the French Labor Movement*, 76–85, 114–15. On the national animosities between German and French socialists, see Droz, *Der Einfluß der deutschen Sozialdemokratie*.
67. Marx to Friedrich Adolph Sorge (5 November 1880), in *MEW*, 34:475. The English translation is from *MECW*, 46:43 (emphasis in the original).

68. Bernstein to Engels (14 October 1881), in Bernstein and Engels, *Briefwechsel*, 41.

69. Moss, *The Origins of the French Labor Movement*, 88.

70. Tacke, "Von der Zweiten Republik bis zum Ersten Weltkrieg," 337.

71. Congrès ouvrier français, *Séances du Congrès ouvrier socialiste de France*, xvi, 621–40, 813–15.

72. On the significance of the congress, see Blum, *Les Congrès Ouvriers et Socialistes Français*, 31–54; Moss, *The Origins of the French Labor Movement*, 89–94; Adler-Gillies, "Cooperation or Collectivism," 395ff.

73. S. Bernstein, "Jules Guesde," 40–41.

74. See the different versions of this visit in Zetkin, *Charakterköpfe*, 40; Mermeix, *La France Socialiste*, 100ff.; S. Bernstein, "Jules Guesde," 41–42; Moss, *The Origins of the French Labor Movement*, 106–7; Steenson, *After Marx*, 124ff.

75. Engels to Bernstein (25 October 1881), in *MECW*, 46:147–48.

76. Marx to Friedrich Adolph Sorge (5 November 1880), in *MECW*, 46:43 (emphasis in the original).

77. Engels to Bernstein (25 October 1881), in *MECW*, 46:147–48.

78. See, for example, Willard, "Einführung," 38. Samuel Bernstein's otherwise detailed portrait also contains no more specific information.

79. Steenson, *After Marx*, 122.

80. Engels to Bernstein (25 October 1881), in *MECW*, 46:150 (emphasis in the original).

81. Engels to Bernstein (2/3 November 1882), in *MECW*, 46:355 (emphasis in the original).

82. Engels to Bernstein (25 October 1881), in *MECW*, 46:148.

83. Marx to Friedrich Adolph Sorge (5 November 1880), in *MECW*, 46:44. For Guesde's theoretical view of wages, see Guesde, *AT*, 119–23.

84. Engels to Bernstein (25 October 1881), in *MECW*, 46:148.

85. *MECW*, 24:340.

86. Rebérioux, "Le socialisme Français," 154.

87. This was the assessment of the radical Charles Rappoport, who appreciated both Guesde and Jaurès, in his 1907 article "Jules Guesde," part 1, 470.

88. See especially Steenson, *After Marx*, 123ff.; Moss, *The Origins of the French Labor Movement*, 104ff.; Rebérioux, "Le socialisme Français," 142ff.; and most recently, Adler-Gillies, "Cooperation or Collectivism."

89. Haupt, "Frankreich," 58.

90. Moss, *The Origins of the French Labor Movement*, 113–21; Haupt, "Frankreich," 52ff.

91. Engels to Bernstein (2/3 November 1882), in *MECW*, 46:356.
92. Steenson, *After Marx*, 108–22.
93. Engels to Bernstein (25 October 1881), in *MECW*, 46:149.
94. Droz, *Der Einfluß der deutschen Sozialdemokratie*, 8.
95. Rappoport, "Jules Guesde," part 1, 471.
96. Jaurès, *Préface aux Discours Parlementaires*, 86.
97. Jaurès and Guesde, *Zum Bruderzwist in Frankreich*, 26, 24. The English translation is from Gildea, *Children of the Revolution*, 281. Guesde was referring to Jaurès's personal engagement for the rehabilitation of Alfred Dreyfus and to the socialist politician Alexandre Etienne Millerand's acceptance of a ministerial post in Pierre Waldeck-Rousseau's center-left cabinet between 1899 and 1902.
98. For the origins of this narrative, see Rappoport, "Jules Guesde," who does not even refer to Jaurès (the "Possibilist traitor") by name; as well as Kautsky, "Zum Gedächtnis Jean Jaurès"; Braunthal, *Geschichte der Internationale*, 263–66.
99. Rebérioux, "Jean Jaurès et le Marxisme," 233.
100. See Kolakowski, *Main Currents of Marxism*, 2:115–40; Dill and Dill, "Jean Jaurès"; Fetscher, *Der Marxismus*; Prochasson, "L'invention du Marxisme Français," 436ff.; Goldberg, *The Life of Jean Jaurès*, 62–65, 81–84; Jackson, *Jean Jaurès*, 32–37.
101. Peillon, *Jean Jaurès*, 273; Jaurès, *Œuvres*, 2:242.
102. Quoted in Lévy, "Nouveaux regards," 18.
103. Jaurès, "Republik und Socialismus," 57 (emphasis in the original). See also Jaurès and Guesde, *Zum Bruderzwist in Frankreich*, 18; Jackson, *Jean Jaurès*, 68.
104. Ternes, *Karl Marx*, 63, has nicely summarized the opposing perspectives on processes of social change in Marx's theory of revolution: on one hand, a "structural view of historical events" grounded in historical materialism; on the other, a "situational view that remains oriented towards momentary opportunities."
105. Jaurès and Guesde, *Zum Bruderzwist in Frankreich*, 18–19.
106. Quoted in Jackson, *Jean Jaurès*, 28.
107. Droz, *Die sozialistischen Parteien*, 66.
108. Quoted in Jackson, *Jean Jaurès*, 28.
109. Rebérioux, "Jean Jaurès et le Marxisme," 210; Goldberg, *The Life of Jean Jaurès*, 63. Jaurès cited the second (1872) edition of *Capital* in his dissertation, which he wrote in this period. See Jaurès, *Die Ursprünge des Sozialismus in Deutschland*, 94–95.
110. Jaurès, "Einleitung."
111. Marx, *Early Political Writings*, 57, 69.

112. Goldberg, *The Life of Jean Jaurès*, 65. On Marx's critique of Proudhon, see also Jaurès, *RS*, 166–69.

113. Jaurès, *Die Ursprünge des Sozialismus in Deutschland*, 102.

114. See also the reading list that Jaurès sent to a teacher who wanted to learn more about socialism, in Jaurès, *Œuvres*, 2:458ff.

115. Leon, "Flashlights," 1094.

116. Jaurès, *Die Ursprünge des Sozialismus in Deutschland*, 92.

117. Ibid., 93. See also Goldberg, *The Life of Jean Jaurès*, 81–84.

118. Droz, *Die sozialistischen Parteien*, 62.

119. Jaurès, "Cours de Philosophie," 127. The complete lectures are in Jaurès, *Cours de Philosophie.*

120. Goldberg, *The Life of Jean Jaurès*, 97–115. Jaurès's second dissertation, "Les origines du socialisme allemand," was published in 1892. It is published in German as Jaurès, *Die Ursprünge des Sozialismus in Deutschland.*

121. Jaurès, "Republik und Socialismus," 56–57.

122. Jaurès, *Œuvres*, 2:157–58.

123. Ibid., 2:459; Jaurès, *Studies in Socialism*, 22.

124. Quoted in Jackson, *Jean Jaurès*, 36.

125. Jaurès, *Die Ursprünge des Sozialismus in Deutschland*, 69.

126. Jaurès, *RS,* 179.

127. Ibid., 180.

128. *MEW*, 23:59, 121, 485, 599, 655, 562. The English translations are from *MECW*, 35:573, 621–22. See also Muller, *The Mind and the Market*, 65–67; Ternes, *Karl Marx*, 213–14.

129. Jaurès, "Einleitung," 37–43.

130. Rebérioux, "Jean Jaurès et le Marxisme," 209.

131. Jaurès, *Die Ursprünge des Sozialismus in Deutschland*, 23.

132. Ibid., 94–95.

133. Bonß, *Die Einübung des Tatsachenblicks.*

134. Jaurès, "Einleitung," 12–20.

135. Ibid., 37.

136. Marx, *Early Political Writings*, 69.

137. Kolakowski, *Main Currents of Marxism,* 1:131.

138. Jaurès, "Einleitung," 38–42.

139. Ibid., 43–44.

140. Engels, "Zur Kritik des sozialdemokratischen Programmentwurfes 1891"; Jaurès, "Republik und Socialismus," 51ff. The English translations of Engels's critique are from *MECW*, 27:225–27.

141. On the conceptual history of both terms, see Conze, "Demokratie"; Nolte, "Diktatur."

142. Jaurès, "Republik und Socialismus," 57; Jaurès, "Notwendige Rückschau," 82. On the relationship between evolution and revolution in Marx's thought, see Koselleck, "Revolution," 753–56.

143. Schieder, *Karl Marx als Politiker*, 24.

144. Kolakowski, *Main Currents of Marxism*, 1:419.

145. Jaurès, *RS,* 164.

146. Jaurès, "Republik und Socialismus," 55, 58.

CHAPTER 5

1. On Bernstein's "moulting," see Bebel to Bernstein (16 October 1898), in Adler, *Briefwechsel mit August Bebel und Karl Kautsky*, 255–56; Gay, *The Dilemma of Democratic Socialism*, 73. Gay's biography, conceived as a coming-of-age story, characterizes Bernstein's time in Zurich between 1879 and 1888 as "heroic years" of party service (parallel to the SPD's own "heroic era" under the Anti-Socialist Laws) but does not closely examine Bernstein's worldview in those years (see 48–59). Similarly, Carsten merely asserts that Engels's *AntiDühring* "cured" Bernstein of his faith in state and "professorial" socialism (*Kathedersozialismus*), leading him to become a lifelong "student" of Marx; Carstein counts Bernstein among the party's left wing in the early 1880s. See Carsten, *Eduard Bernstein*, 23, 27. Kolakowski accepts Bernstein's own account that *AntiDühring* "converted" him, suggesting that, after 1878, Bernstein became "a zealous exponent of orthodoxy as then understood." See Bernstein, *Sozialdemokratische Lehrjahre*, 71; Kolakowski, *Main Currents of Marxism*, 2:100. With respect to Bernstein's early Marxism, Meyer emphasizes his "hope for the imminent collapse" of the system. See Meyer, "Eduard Bernstein," 203ff.

2. On the Wallenstein motif, see Bernstein to Engels (14 October 1881), in Bernstein and Engels, *Briefwechsel,* 40. The idea of being infected with Marxism comes from Kautsky. See Kautsky to Minna Kautsky (4 July 1880), in IISH, Kautsky-FA 1552–1553, 2.

3. Bernstein, *Geschichte der Berliner Arbeiter-Bewegung*, v, 245, 251.

4. Ibid., 311, 311, 333, 287, 248–49, 264–65.

5. See the overview in Grebing, *Geschichte der deutschen Arbeiterbewegung*, 25–26.

6. Bernstein, *Sozialdemokratische Lehrjahre*, 14–15.

7. Bernstein, *Geschichte der Berliner Arbeiter-Bewegung*, 252–53, 260, 268.

8. Bernstein to Liebknecht (26 November 1874) in Eckert and Langkau, *Wilhelm Liebknecht*, 591.

9. Dühring, *Kritische Geschichte der Nationalökonomie*, v, 562, 566.

10. Bernstein, *Geschichte der Berliner Arbeiter-Bewegung*, 315; Bernstein, *Sozialdemokratische Lehrjahre*, 52–56. On the effects of Dühring's work on National Socialism, see Mosse, *The Crisis of German Ideology*, 131–32.

11. Bernstein to Liebknecht (26 November 1874) in Eckert and Langkau, *Wilhelm Liebknecht*, 592.

12. Bernstein, *Geschichte der Berliner Arbeiter-Bewegung*, 315; Bernstein, *Sozialdemokratische Lehrjahre*, 52–56.

13. Bernstein, *Sozialdemokratische Lehrjahre*, 17; Marx, "Der Bürgerkrieg in Frankreich," especially 71–80, 85–86, 96–101.

14. See Bernstein's letters to Engels from 19 June 1879 and 9 September 1881, in Bernstein and Engels, *Briefwechsel, 8*, 36.

15. Bernstein, *Geschichte der Berliner Arbeiter-Bewegung*, 298–99.

16. Bernstein, *Sozialdemokratische Lehrjahre*, 47.

17. Bernstein to Engels (19 June 1879) and (26 October 1882), in Bernstein and Engels, *Briefwechsel, 7*, 141. Engels also put the word in quotation marks. See Engels to Bernstein (2/3 November 1882), 154. Haupt traces the term (in its meaning at that time) only to Kautsky. See Haupt, "Zur Begriffsgeschichte des Wortpaares 'Marxist' und 'Marxismus,'" 115.

18. Meyer, "Eduard Bernstein," 203.

19. Bernstein to Engels (17 November 1882), in Bernstein and Engels, *Briefwechsel,* 156.

20. Bernstein to Engels (15 September 1882), in Bernstein and Engels, *Briefwechsel,* 129.

21. Engels to Bernstein (26 June 1879, 12 March 1881, and 26 June 1882), in Bernstein and Engels, *Briefwechsel,* 10, 21, 107. The English translations are from *MECW*, 45:363; vol. 46:75, 289.

22. Bernstein to Engels (4 May 1882), in Bernstein and Engels, *Briefwechsel,* 98.

23. Engels to Bernstein (26 June 1879), in Bernstein and Engels, *Briefwechsel,* 9. The English translation is from *MECW*, 45:362.

24. Engels to Bernstein (12 March 1881), in Bernstein and Engels, *Briefwechsel,* 20; *MECW*, 46:74.

25. Bernstein to Engels (14 November 1881), in Bernstein and Engels, *Briefwechsel,* 58.

26. Bernstein to Engels (1 September 1882), in Bernstein and Engels, *Briefwechsel,* 125.

27. Bernstein to Engels (13 November 1882), in Bernstein and Engels, *Briefwechsel,* 128n6, 131–32n17.

28. Bernstein to Engels (14 October 1881 and 4 May 1882), in Bernstein and Engels, *Briefwechsel,* 42, 96–97.

29. See, for example, Leo, "Die schönsten Hoffnungen," *Der Sozialdemokrat, no.* 3 (1882); Leo, "Bekennt Farbe!," *Der Sozialdemokrat, no.* 16 (1882); Bernstein, *Sozialdemokratische Lehrjahre,* 204.

30. Bernstein to Engels (12 January 1882), in Bernstein and Engels, *Briefwechsel,* 66.

31. Ritter and Tenfelde, *Arbeiter im Deutschen Kaiserreich,* 691–702.

32. Quoted in Wehler, *Das Deutsche Kaiserreich,* 88. The English translation is from Wehler, *The German Empire,* 87.

33. Bernstein to Engels (7 July 1882), in Bernstein and Engels, *Briefwechsel,* 114.

34. Bernstein to Engels (1 November 1882) and Engels to Bernstein (4 November 1882), in Bernstein and Engels, *Briefwechsel,* 151, 160. The English translations are from *MECW,* 46:362–63.

35. Engels to Bernstein (25/31 January 1882), in Bernstein and Engels, *Briefwechsel,* 70. The English translations are from *MECW,* 46:187.

36. These remarks, which recall Kautsky's first editorial in the *Neue Zeit,* are from Bernstein's first pamphlet in the "Social Democratic Library" series (*Social and Private Property,* 3). On Bernstein's image of the SPD as the party "in the right," see Bernstein to Engels (12 January 1882), in Bernstein and Engels, *Briefwechsel,* 68.

37. Welskopp, "Generation Bebel," 60. On the SPD during the era of the Anti-Socialist Laws, see Mehring, *Bis zum Erfurter Programm,* 153–327; Kupfer, *Geheime Zirkel und Parteivereine,* 15–36.

38. Bernstein, Guesde, and Lafargue, *Gesellschaftliches und PrivatEigenthum,* 8.

39. See the manuscript for a speech commemorating Karl Marx, given on 5 May 1918, in IISH, Bernstein papers, E 61.

40. Bernstein, Guesde, and Lafargue, *Gesellschaftliches und PrivatEigenthum,* 8–9, 10. See also *MECW,* 35:750.

41. Bernstein, Guesde, and Lafargue, *Gesellschaftliches und PrivatEigenthum,* 3, 8–9, 10. Bernstein wrote the pamphlet's preface, introduction, and conclusion; the rest came from Lafargue and Guesde. On the creation and transmission of the program, see *MEW,* 25:466–86, 802–10.

42. Bernstein, Guesde, and Lafargue, *Gesellschaftliches und PrivatEigenthum,* 14–15.

43. Bernstein, *Die Sozialisierung der Betriebe.*

44. See the typewritten copy of the dedication in IISH, Bernstein papers, A 113.

45. Bernstein, Guesde, and Lafargue, *Gesellschaftliches und PrivatEigenthum,* 31.

46. Bernstein, "Der Kampf der Sozialdemokratie," 556.

47. Bebel to Bernstein (16 October 1898), in Adler, *Briefwechsel mit August Bebel und Karl Kautsky,* 255–56.

48. See Gay, *The Dilemma of Democratic Socialism*, 95–126; Carsten, *Eduard Bernstein*, 46–47, 63; Meyer, "Eduard Bernstein," 206. For Bernstein's own account, see "Entwicklungsgang eines Sozialisten," 22–35. For the context of his friendship with Kautsky, see Morina, "Marx' Prophezeiungen," 100–06.

49. Morina, "Marx' Prophezeiungen," 105–06.

50. Bernstein to Adler (28 March 1899), in Adler, *Briefwechsel mit August Bebel und Karl Kautsky*, 306. For Adler's reproach, see Adler to Bernstein (17 March 1899), 297.

51. Bernstein, "Vorwort," iii–xi.

52. This was a key sentence in a pamphlet written in 1923, the fortieth anniversary of Marx's death, quoted here in Gay, *The Dilemma of Democratic Socialism*, 88.

53. Bernstein to Engels (7 July 1882), in Bernstein and Engels, *Briefwechsel,* 109.

54. Kautsky, "Vorgeschichte meiner Beziehungen zu Engels," 1 (written in 1935). A similar expression of these ideas is in Kautsky to Bernstein (17 July 1886), IISH, Bernstein papers, RCChIDNI, 204/1-888, 2.

55. Kautsky, *Erinnerungen und Erörterungen*, 200.

56. Ibid., 200, 214, 216.

57. Kautsky to Anton Jaich (26 January 1875), IISH, Kautsky-FA 1497.

58. Kautsky, *Erinnerungen und Erörterungen*, 367.

59. Kautsky, "Einiges über die Berechtigung socialistischer Ideen," IISH, Kautsky-FA 2094, 13.

60. "Absolutorium der k. und k. Universität zu Wien," (10 October 1879), IISH, Kautsky-FA 1842.

61. Kautsky, *Erinnerungen und Erörterungen*, 375–76.

62. Important examples include Symmachos [Kautsky], "Die soziale Frage" and "Der Kampf um's Dasein." See also Steenson, *Karl Kautsky*, 33ff.

63. Symmachos [Kautsky], "Der Kampf um's Dasein," 1–2. On Kautsky's early reception of Darwin, see Steenson, "Early Assumptions, Preconceptions and Prejudices."

64. Kautsky, "Das Proletariat," 56.

65. Engels to Bebel (15 October 1875) in *MEW*, 34:162; *MECW*, 45:100. Engels must be referring to Kautsky's article series on "the social question from the standpoint of the intellectual worker," which appeared in *Volksstaat* in 1875.

66. Steinberg, "Karl Kautsky und Eduard Bernstein," 56; Gilcher-Holtey, *Das Mandat des Intellektuellen*, 15ff.; Saage, *Zwischen Darwin und Marx*, 17–59.

67. Symmachos [Kautsky], "Soziale Frage"; Symmachos [Kautsky], "Der Kampf um's Dasein."

68. Symmachos [Kautsky], "Soziale Frage."

69. Kautsky, "Der Luxus im sozialistischen Staate."

70. Kautsky to Minna Kautsky (4 July 1880), in IISH, Kautsky-FA 1552–1553, 2; Kautsky, "Mein erster Aufenthalt in London," 18.

71. Kautsky to Minna Kautsky (3 April 1881), IISH, Kautsky-FA 1553. On his visits to Marx and Engels, see Engels and Kautsky, *Briefwechsel*. Marx's doctrines did not play a major role in his reports to his mother, although he had plenty of opportunities in London to recall them. See Kautsky to Minna Kautsky (26 April 1881), IISH, Kautsky-FA 1553, 1.

72. Marx to Jenny Marx (11 April 1881), in *MECW*, 46:82; Marx to August Bebel (25 August 1881), in *MECW*, 46:137.

73. Kautsky, *Erinnerungen und Erörterungen*, 209–22.

74. Kautsky, *Karl Marx' ökonomische Lehren*, 268. The translated quotation is from *MECW*, 25:270. Although this idea is attributed to Marx and thoroughly developed in the third volume of *Capital*, the volume was assembled by Engels from Marx's papers and first published in 1894. See *MEW*, 20:9, 14, 828. On Kautsky's veneration of Engels, see Kautsky, "Friedrich Engels," 4.

75. Kautsky, [Self-Portrait], 120ff.

76. Morina, "Marx' Prophezeiungen," 97–110.

77. Kautsky to Bernstein (22 December 1885), IISH, Bernstein Papers, RCChIDNI, Fund 204/1-867, 10. I am grateful to Dr. Götz Langkau (IISH) for his typewritten transcripts of the correspondence.

78. This is already how he saw himself by March 1881. See Kautsky to Minna Kautsky (2 March 1881), IISH, Kautsky-FA 1553, 1.

79. Gilcher-Holtey, *Das Mandat des Intellektuellen*, 30–31.

80. Kautsky to Engels (11 October 1882), in Engels and Kautsky, *Briefwechsel*, 64.

81. Kautsky to Engels (23 November 1882), in Engels and Kautsky, *Briefwechsel*, 70.

82. Kautsky to Johann Kautsky (31 August 1884), IISH, Kautsky-FA 1549, 4–5.

83. Kautsky, "An unsere Leser!," 3–4.

84. Kautsky to Engels (11 October 1882), in Engels and Kautsky, *Briefwechsel*, 64.

85. Kautsky to Engels (23 November 1882), in Engels and Kautsky, *Briefwechsel*, 70.

86. Kautsky, "An unsere Leser!," 1.

87. Ibid., 8.

88. Kautsky, "Karl Marx' Tod," 1.

89. Gilcher-Holtey, *Das Mandat des Intellektuellen*, 21.

90. Kautsky to Bernstein (22 December 1885), IISH, Bernstein papers, RCChIDNI, 204/1-867, 7.

91. Ibid., 3.

92. Kautsky, *Karl Marx' ökonomische Lehren*, xiii.

93. Ibid., 58, 267–68. The English translations are from Kautsky, *The Economic Doctrines of Karl Marx*, 1, 246–47.

94. Karl Korsch has criticized this line of thinking for extending well beyond Marx. See Korsch, *Die materialistische Geschichtsauffassung*, 9–12, especially 11n11.

95. Adler to Engels (15 June 1895) in Adler, *ARB*, 1:128–29.

96. Kautsky, *Karl Marx' ökonomische Lehren*, 26. The English translation is from Kautsky, *The Economic Doctrines of Karl Marx*, 22.

97. Kautsky, *Karl Marx' ökonomische Lehren*, 267 (emphasis added). The English translation is from Kautsky, *The Economic Doctrines of Karl Marx*, 247.

98. Kautsky, *Erinnerungen und Erörterungen*, 218–21.

99. Ibid., 437.

100. Gilcher-Holtey, *Das Mandat des Intellektuellen*, 43.

CHAPTER 6

1. Mommsen, by contrast, argues that nationalism was initially Adler's main impulse. See Mommsen, "Victor Adlers Weg zum Sozialismus," 191–92; Steinbach, "Engelbert Pernerstorfer," 276.

2. Adler to Pernerstorfer (mid-August 1870), VA Archive, EP I, M137.

3. Emma Adler, biography of Victor Adler, IISH, Victor Adler Papers, vol. 4.

4. Quoted in Adler to Pernerstorfer (27 July 1893), in VGA, Vienna, Adler Archive EP III, M139, T1, 1. Adler and his wife were at a spa near Linz, where she was receiving treatment.

5. Lorm, *Gedichte*, 22–23.

6. Adler, diary fragment (mid-September 1872), 1, VGA, Vienna, Adler Archive, M6/T6. On the *Weltschmerz* poetic genre, see Braun, *Types of Weltschmerz in German Poetry*.

7. Adler, diary fragment (mid-September 1876), 2, VGA, Vienna, Adler Archive, M6/T6.

8. Katalog der achten Klasse vom Schuljahr 1870, and Protokoll über die Maturitätsprüfung vom Gymnasium zu den Schotten, VGA, Vienna,

Adler Archive, M19, T13. The Gymnasium's annual report indicates that philosophy was Adler's "chosen course of professional study." See VGA, Vienna, Adler Archive, M6, T10, p. 100.

9. Mommsen, "Victor Adlers Weg zum Sozialismus," 181; Steinbach, "Engelbert Pernerstorfer," 278. These authors disagree, for example, with Wistrich, *Revolutionary Jews*, 103–13; Böck, "Entfernung von der bürgerlichen Welt."

10. Adler, *ARB*, 1:149ff.

11. Adler to Engels (15 June 1895), in Adler, *ARB*, 1:128–29 (emphasis in the original). Adler praised Engels's compilation of the two volumes as a tremendous gesture of friendship, which lent coherence and offered "intimate" insight into the work of a one-of-a-kind thinker.

12. *MECW*, 37:258; Berger, *Karl Marx*, 175–76.

13. Adler to Engels (15 June 1895), in Adler, *ARB*, 1:128.

14. Adler to Engels (13 July 1894), in Adler, *ARB*, 1:98–99. Engels called the sum a "few marks" (1:101). One thousand German marks were then equivalent to about six hundred Austro-Hungarian gulden. Adler received an income of twenty-five gulden per week from the party coffers—comparable to a worker's wages, Adler wrote to his brother in June 1890. See Braunthal, *Victor und Friedrich Adler*, 91–93. On Engels's financial situation, see Hunt, *Marx's General*, 261–64. I am grateful to Tim Schanetzky for his help with these calculations.

15. VGA, Vienna, Adler Archive, Vereinsbuch (1870), 4–6. Although Mommsen has asserted otherwise, the *Communist Manifesto* is not in the association's library (today). See Mommsen, "Victor Adlers Weg zum Sozialismus," 181.

16. Steenson, *After Marx*, 162ff.

17. Mommsen, "Victor Adlers Weg zum Sozialismus," 181.

18. Ebert, *Die Anfänge der modernen Sozialpolitik in Österreich* (for the factory inspector law, see especially 163–75); Beller, *Geschichte Österreichs*, 146ff.; Bruckmüller, *Sozialgeschichte Österreichs*, 336. Adler praised these reforms at the Brussels congress of the Second International in 1891, stating that, alongside England and Switzerland, Austria had the "world's best worker protection law." See Adler, *ARB*, 7: 257.

19. Kautsky to Engels (undated), in Adler, *Briefwechsel mit August Bebel und Karl Kautsky*, 7–8.

20. The report is reproduced in Adler, *ARB*, 5:19–66. Ebert's thorough analysis does not mention Adler's application or report. See Ebert, *Die Anfänge der modernen Sozialpolitik in Österreich*, 163–64.

21. The following quotes are from the excerpts that were published in the *ArbeiterZeitung* in 1958. See Fischer, "Victor Adler schreibt ein Gesuch," 9.

22. Ibid.

23. Meysels, *Victor Adler*, 47. Meysels's depiction unfortunately does not explain how Adler's twenty-three-page letter was received at the Trade Ministry. Fischer provides at least a date and file number (8 April 1884, Az. Pr. 25/8/31235). See Fischer, "Victor Adler schreibt ein Gesuch." Even with this information, however, I could not locate the original letter in the Austrian State Archives. On Adler's own doubts, see Adler to Pernerstorfer (7 September 1883), VGA, Vienna, NL Pernerstorfer, Engelbert Pernerstorfer I, M193/T1, 1.

24. See Ritter and Tenfelde, *Arbeiter im Deutschen Kaiserreich*, 697.

25. Adler, *ARB*, 1:61 (emphasis in the original).

26. Adler to Engels (10 October 1892), in Adler, *ARB*, 1:55. This remark contains a bit of veiled criticism, as the colloquial Viennese word *überhaps* means "hasty" or "rash."

27. Adler, "Die Berufskrankheiten der Arbeiter."

28. Ibid., 99.

29. Adler, *ARB*, 5:20. Adler also referred to descriptions in the chapter on "The Working Day." See *MEW*, 23:245–78, 294–315, 391–530.

30. *MEW*, 23:310, n173. The English translations (and original quotation from the English factory owner) are from *MECW*, 35:297–98.

31. *MECW*, 23:253, 271, 298–99; *MECW*, 35:263, 287–88.

32. Adler to Kautsky (21 August 1886), in Adler, *Briefwechsel mit August Bebel und Karl Kautsky*, 13.

33. Steenson, *After Marx*, 173ff.

34. Adler to Kautsky (21 August 1886), in Adler, *Briefwechsel mit August Bebel und Karl Kautsky*, 15. For context, see also Mommsen, "Victor Adlers Weg zum Sozialismus," 192.

35. Adler to Kautsky (21 August 1886), in Adler, *Briefwechsel mit August Bebel und Karl Kautsky*, 13.

36. Ibid. Kautsky's experiences in the mid-1870s, before he left for Zurich, were quite similar.

37. "Arbeiter!," *Gleichheit*, 11 December 1886, 1. Adler served as publisher. Editor-in-chief was Ludwig A. Bretschneider, the "leading voice of Viennese Social Democrats" (according to Brügel, *Geschichte der österreichischen Sozialdemokratie*, 372).

38. Adler, *ARB*, 1:143–49. The translation of Schopenhauer is by E. F. J. Payne in *The World as Will and Representation*, xvii.

39. Adler, *ARB*, 1:149, 144.
40. Adler to Bernstein (17 March 1899), in Adler, *Briefwechsel mit August Bebel und Karl Kautsky*, 297.
41. Kautsky's phrasing is a play on Bernstein's description of his attempts at reform as "overcoming Marxism."
42. Adler to Bernstein (17 March 1899), in Adler, *Briefwechsel mit August Bebel und Karl Kautsky*, 297.
43. Adler, *ARB*, 6:231.
44. Adler, *ARB*, 1:147; 6:230–31. On the politicization of the "quest for bread," see Arendt, *On Revolution*, 53–110.
45. Bernstein to Adler (17 March 1899), in Adler, *Briefwechsel mit August Bebel und Karl Kautsky*, 299; Adler to Kautsky (16 March 1899), 297; Adler, *ARB*, 6:231. A Bologna flask is created by rapidly cooling a bottle's exterior during the glass-making process, so that the exterior becomes extremely strong, while the interior becomes a brittle mosaic. A scratch on the interior can completely shatter the bottle—not merely into shards but into fine grains of glass.
46. Adler, *ARB*, 6:231.
47. Adler to Bernstein (17 March) 1899, in Adler, *Briefwechsel mit August Bebel und Karl Kautsky*, 298; Adler to Kautsky (16 March 1899), 297.
48. On *Gleichheit*, see Brügel, *Geschichte der österreichischen Sozialdemokratie*, 370–75; Miersch, *Die Arbeiterpresse der Jahre 1869 bis 1889*, 173–82; Michler, "Zwischen Minna Kautsky und Hermann Bahr," 114–17. Adler's texts about the brick workers are reprinted in *ARB*, vol. 4.
49. Steenson, *After Marx*, 160–84.
50. Quoted in Adler, *Briefwechsel mit August Bebel und Karl Kautsky*, 26.
51. The early editions of the *Workers' Calendar* are extremely rare and have been archived in the ÖNB without their covers. For this reason, I refer to a reproduction from the *MEGA*. See *MEGA*, 31:485.

PATHS TO MARXISM II: GENEVA, WARSAW, ST. PETERSBURG (1885–1903)

1. The epigraph is cited in German (*Studieren, Propagandieren, Organisieren*) in Lenin, *Collected Works*, 1: 298.
2. Kennan, *Siberia and the Exile System*, vii, 249.
3. Ibid., 248–49.
4. Ibid., 257–58. On the populists' nonviolence ("a collective act of Rousseauism") in the 1870s, see Venturi, *Roots of Revolution*, 469–506; the Rousseauism quote is on 503. On the question of using force, see 499. Populist appeals were issued without violence, although their message clearly encouraged it.

5. See, for example, Holquist, "Violent Russia, Deadly Marxism?" Holquist argues against a binary opposition of "intent" and "context" and instead asks how circumstances and ideology are mutually influencing. Similarly, see Malia, *The Soviet Tragedy*, 51–78. Figes, by contrast, understands the Bolshevik regime as a "distinctively Russian" form of absolute rule and "a mirror-image of the tsarist state." See Figes, *A People's Tragedy*, 811–15. Gerd Koenen's intentionalist argument emphasizes Lenin's brilliant political leadership; in the context of the war, the institutionalization of Bolshevik rule after 1917 was actually "unlikely." See Koenen, *Utopie der Säuberung*, 43–62. On the relationship between the Russian state and people between 1700 and 1917, see Winkler, "Rulers and Ruled."

6. Figes, *A People's Tragedy*, xvi. See also the intellectual historical overview in Hamburg, "Russian Political Thought." For a culturally informed view of Russian political and intellectual history, see Figes, *Natasha's Dance*, xxvii, 72–146, 220–28. Among the most radical (and Marxist) readings of Russian literature as a political act is Luxemburg, "Einleitung."

7. Haumann, *Geschichte Russlands*, 273; Daly, "Police and Revolutionaries."

8. Kolakowski, *Main Currents of Marxism*, 2:306–7.

9. Figes, *A People's Tragedy*, 139–56. See also the comprehensive overview from the Decembrists to the Bolsheviks in Pomper, *The Russian Revolutionary Intelligentsia*. For a focus on the propagation of Marxism, see Haimson, *The Russian Marxists*.

10. On the relationship between Marxism and Leninism, see Wolfe, "Leninism." Upon assuming power in October 1917, one of Lenin's first official acts was supposedly hanging a portrait of Marx in his office in the old Senate building.

CHAPTER 7

1. Engels to Plekhanov (21 May 1894) in *MEW*, 39:247. The English translation is from *MECW*, 50:303.

2. See Plekhanov's references to himself in Plechanow, *N. G. Tschernischewsky*, 123; Plekhanov, "Socialism and Political Struggle," 121; Plekhanov, *The Role of the Individual in History*, 12.

3. Plekhanov, *The Role of the Individual in History*, 12n1.

4. Baron, *Plekhanov*, 13–47.

5. Ibid., viii.

6. Ibid., 15.

7. Axelrod, "Das politische Erwachen der russischen Arbeiter," 37. See also Venturi, *Roots of Revolution*, 469–506; Haimson, *The Russian Marxists*, 13–16; more recently, Daly, *Autocracy under Siege*, 17–19.

8. Baron, *Plekhanov*, 17.

9. Axelrod, "Das politische Erwachen der russischen Arbeiter," 37–38.

10. Plekhanov, Русский рабочий, 131, 137.

11. Ibid., 128. See also Venturi, *Roots of Revolution*, 538.

12. Siljak, *Angel of Vengeance*; Venturi, *Roots of Revolution*; Berlin, *Russian Thinkers*; Billington, *Fire in the Minds of Men*, 386–418; Pomper, *The Russian Revolutionary Intelligentsia*.

13. Baron, *Plekhanov*, 9–10. Baron's depiction is based on a 1923 account by Lev Deutsch.

14. Baron, *Plekhanov*, 20–21; Plekhanov, Русский рабочий, 136 (translated into German by C. M.).

15. Kingston-Mann, "Marxism and Russian Rural Development," 748–51.

16. McKinsey, "The Kazan Square Demonstration," 85. On "propaganda of the deed" and its anarchist origins, see Linse, "'Propaganda der Tat.'"

17. Baron, *Plekhanov*, 27.

18. Quoted in McKinsey, "The Kazan Square Demonstration," 98.

19. Baron, *Plekhanov*, 18; McKinsey, "The Kazan Square Demonstration," 98. Plekhanov's description is from Русский рабочий, 136 (translated into German by C. M.).

20. Baron, *Plekhanov*, 10.

21. Haumann, *Geschichte Russlands*, 273.

22. These were published together in Plechanow, *N. G. Tschernischewsky*.

23. See Plekhanov's very personal appreciation of this stance in ibid., 115–20.

24. Ibid., 18ff.

25. Venturi, *Roots of Revolution*, 482. On Marxism in Russia, see Resis, "Das Kapital Comes to Russia"; Baron, "The First Decade of Russian Marxism"; Haimson, *The Russian Marxists*. On contacts between Marx and the Russian revolutionaries, see Eaton, "Marx and the Russians."

26. Resis, "Das Kapital Comes to Russia," 221–26.

27. Ibid., 235.

28. Engels to Plekhanov (8 February 1895) in *MEW*, 39:405n430. The English translation is from *MECW*, 50:439.

29. Kolakowski, *Main Currents of Marxism*, 2:330; Baron, *Plekhanov*, viii. Haimson also speaks of "conversion" in *The Russian Marxists*, 43.

30. See the anecdotes in Plekhanov, Русский рабочий, 131, 181 (translated into German by C. M.).

31. Kingston-Mann, "Marxism and Russian Rural Development," 735.

32. See the remarks (again, based on Lev Deutsch's memoirs) in Baron, *Plekhanov*, 48–50; Eaton, "Marx and the Russians," 106–10.

33. Plekhanov, Закон экономического, 58ff. (translated into German by C. M.). The English translation of Marx is from *MECW*, 35:10.

34. Plekhanov, Закон экономического, 63.

35. Haimson, *The Russian Marxists*, 33; Mayer, "Plekhanov, Lenin and Working-Class Consciousness." 161.

36. Venturi, *Roots of Revolution*, 509. See also Zelnik, *Labor and Society in Tsarist Russia*; Zelnik, *Workers and Intelligentsia*.

37. Plekhanov, Закон экономического, 68–69.

38. Rabinowitz, *Zur Entwicklung der Arbeiterbewegung in Rußland*, 42. The Union's "program" (published the same month as Plekhanov's article) resembled the Gotha program in many respects. See also Venturi, *Roots of Revolution*, 549–57; the quote is on 539.

39. Plekhanow, Русский рабочий, 137. See also Venturi, *Roots of Revolution*, 510.

40. Plekhanow, Закон экономического, 70–74.

41. Ibid., 75.

42. Baron, *Plekhanov*, 53.

43. Plechanow, "Die Anfänge der sozialdemokratischen Bewegung in Rußland."

44. Jena, *Georgi Walentinowitsch Plechanow*, 34–35; Baron, *Plekhanov*, 56–57; Haimson, *The Russian Marxists*, 42–43.

45. Baron, *Plekhanov*, 59.

46. Ibid., 43. The following remarks also rely on Baron's depiction in 59–77.

47. Ibid., 63–64.

48. Ibid., 67. See also Polexe, *Netzwerke und Freundschaft*.

49. Plekhanov, "Socialism and Political Struggle," 58; Plekhanov, "Karl Marx," 674. On Marx's abrupt transformation, which has not been fully explained, see Sperber, *Karl Marx*, 83.

50. Plekhanov, "Karl Marx," 672–73.

51. Hohberg, "Probleme der Entwicklung," 232–33.

52. Bernstein to Kautsky (30 December 1886), IISH, Kautsky Papers, K DV-76, 7–8.

53. The quote is from Hohberg, "Probleme der Entwicklung," 238.

54. Quoted in *MEW*, 18:567. The English translation is from *MECW*, 24:50. See also Baron, *Plekhanov*, 66.

55. Plechanow, "Die Anfänge der sozialdemokratischen Bewegung in Rußland."

56. Plechanow, "Über die Anfänge der Lehre vom Klassenkampf," 303–4.

57. From Plekhanov's preface to the Russian translation, quoted in Jowtschuk and Kurbatowa, *Georgi Plechanow*, 62–63.

58. From Plekhanov's preface to the second edition of his translation (1900), quoted in Jowtschuk and Kurbatowa, *Georgi Plechanow*, 147.

59. Plechanow, "Über die Anfänge der Lehre vom Klassenkampf," 303–4.

60. Wuthnow, *Communities of Discourse*, 481ff.

61. Marx himself spoke of the "capitalist mode of production." These terms were by no means a socialist invention, but were—and are—used with different meanings and emphases by members of all political camps. See, for example, Conze, "Proletariat, Pöbel, Pauperismus"; Hilger and Hölscher, "Kapital, Kapitalist, Kapitalismus," especially 442–48.

62. Koselleck, "Einleitung," xiv; Koselleck, "Begriffsgeschichte und Sozialgeschichte," 113. The English translations are from Koselleck, "Introduction and Prefaces," 8; Koselleck, "*Begriffsgeschichte* and Social History," 80.

63. Plechanow, "Die Anfänge der sozialdemokratischen Bewegung in Rußland." See also Bartholmes, *Bruder, Bürger, Freund, Genosse*; Morina, "Szenen einer marxistischen Familie."

64. Plechanow, "Über die Anfänge der Lehre vom Klassenkampf," 297; Plekhanov, "Fundamental Problems of Marxism," 117 (emphasis in the original).

65. See Eley, *Forging Democracy*.

66. Hobsbawm, *How to Change the World*, 119–20 (emphasis in the original).

67. See, for example, Marxist historian and journalist Ellen Meiksins Wood, "Politics and the Communist Manifesto" (https://www.solidarity-us.org/node/1151) and political scientist Antonio Negri's remarks about the prospects of "political class struggle" in *Factory of Strategy*, 15–28, especially 21ff.

68. See, for example, Lenin, *Collected Works*, 2:19.

69. Plekhanov, "Fundamental Problems of Marxism," 127; Plekhanov, "Socialism and Political Struggle," 63. On Plekhanov's agnosticism and adaptation of Spinoza, see Plekhanov, "So-called Religious Seekings in Russia," 406–7. He wrote that he was unafraid of death because the radically materialist understanding of an eternal "unity of Nature and man" liberated him from fear.

70. Kolakowski, *Main Currents of Marxism*, 2:344.

71. Plekhanov, "Fundamental Problems of Marxism," 145, 156.

72. Ibid., 182–83.

73. Plekhanov, *The Role of the Individual in History*, 12n1.

74. Ibid., 59–60.

75. Kolakowski, *Main Currents of Marxism*, 2:339; Plekhanov, *The Development of the Monist View of History*, 277.

76. Plekhanov, "Socialism and Political Struggle," 114–21.
77. Lenin, *Collected Works*, 1:193–94. This was the first time that Lenin mentioned Plekhanov (in print), the Emancipation of Labor group in Geneva, and the second influential text that Plekhanov authored in exile, "Our Differences" (1885). Lenin considered "Our Differences" the "first social democratic text" in Russian socialism. He understood "social democracy" as politics based on Marxist theory. On the (intellectual) relationship between Lenin and Plekhanov, see Service, *Lenin*, 132–53.

CHAPTER 8

1. Quoted in Pipes, *Struve*, 100.
2. Baron, *Plekhanov*, 117.
3. Geyer, *Lenin in der russischen Sozialdemokratie*, 1–46.
4. Ibid., 18.
5. Pipes, *Struve*, 209n3.
6. Struve, "My Contacts and Conflicts with Lenin I," 579.
7. On surveillance at the universities (and elsewhere), see Daly, *Autocracy under Siege*, 98–123; as well as the overview in Daly, "Police and Revolutionaries," 645ff.
8. Peter Struve, "Из воспоминаий о С.-Петербургском Университете" (February 1930), Hoover Archive, Struve Papers, box 23, folder 19, 3 (translated into German by A. Stelzig).
9. Pipes, *Struve*, 152.
10. A. F. Meiendorff, "P. B. Struve," Hoover Archive, Struve Papers, box 1, folder 14, 5–7, 23 (translated into German by A. Stelzig).
11. Pipes, *Struve*, 69–70; Struve, "My Contacts and Conflicts with Lenin I," 581.
12. Struve, "My Contacts with Rodichev," 351.
13. Pipes, *Struve*, 25–27, 65ff.
14. Struve, "My Contacts and Conflicts with Lenin I," 577. See also his letter of introduction to Hans Delbrück, publisher of the *Preußische Jahrbücher* (9 July 1902): 7, in which he justifies his turn toward—and away from—Marxism with his own, "quite independent" insights. I am grateful to Richard Pipes for sending me Struve's correspondence with Delbrück.
15. Struve, "My Contacts and Conflicts with Lenin I," 576–78.
16. Kolakowski, *Main Currents of Marxism*, 2:363.
17. Struve, "My Contacts and Conflicts with Lenin I," 577.

18. Struve, *Collected Works*, vol. 1, no. 10:633.

19. Peter Struve, Richard Wagner und Karl Marx [1933], Hoover Archive, Struve Papers, box 21, folder 13; and Peter Struve, "Карль Марксъ и судьбы марксизма," in Hoover Archive, Struve Papers, box 16, folder 15.

20. Struve, "Introduction," xxxi (translated into German by A. Stelzig, emphasis added).

21. Struve, "My Contacts and Conflicts with Lenin I," 579.

22. See, for example, Struve, "Die Marxsche Theorie der sozialen Entwicklung," 672–86, especially 675–66.

23. As in his open letter to the newly crowned Tsar Nicholas II (1895), quoted in Struve, "My Contacts with Rodichev," 352–54.

24. Pipes, *Struve*, 59.

25. Struve, "My Contacts and Conflicts with Lenin I," 578. See also his early articles in *Collected Works*, vol. 1, nos. 2, 3, 7, 9.

26. Quoted in Pipes, *Struve*, 173.

27. Struve, "My Contacts and Conflicts with Lenin I," 578.

28. Quoted in Pipes, *Struve*, 66, 64.

29. Ibid., 74.

30. This remark is from a letter to his friend Potresov in the summer of 1894, shortly after completing the manuscript of his first book, *Critical Remarks*, which left him extremely dissatisfied. See Pipes, *Struve*, 103.

31. For more on this view of poverty, which involved the "mingling of good intentions and blinkered prejudices," see Koven, *Slumming*, 3.

32. Geyer, *Lenin in der russischen Sozialdemokratie*, xiv, Chapter 1. See also Figes, *A People's Tragedy*, 157ff. For a contemporary description of these events, see the "famine articles" in Tolstoï, *The Novels and Other Works of Lyof N. Tolstoï*, 191–295.

33. Quoted in Pipes, *Struve*, 61.

34. Ibid., 76–79.

35. Struve, *Collected Works*, vol. 1, no. 2:346.

36. Ibid., 344–45.

37. Ibid. Marx used the term "reserve army," an otherwise exclusively military term, as a synonym for "surplus population of workers." See *MECW*, 35:623ff. An 1884 article in the *Neue Zeit* was the first to take up the term after Marx, in a thorough analysis of the social plight and costs of these "excess" workers. The article was published anonymously, although the journal's general index from 1905 credits Oscar Eisengarten, Engels's secretary at the time. See Eisengarten, "Englands industrielle Reservearmee." For closer explanation of the term, see

Fetscher, *Grundbegriffe des Marxismus*, 145–47; Berger, *Karl Marx*, 137–45.

38. Struve, *Collected Works*, vol. 1, no. 5:175.
39. Quoted in Pipes, *Struve*, 83.
40. See, for example, Struve, *Collected Works*, vol. 1, no. 2:3.
41. Ibid., vol. 1, no. 3:416–17.
42. Ibid., vol. 1, no. 5:513.
43. *MECW*, 16:469. See also Pipes, *Struve*, 56.
44. Struve, "Die Marxsche Theorie der sozialen Entwicklung," 665–66, 676.
45. Struve, *Collected Works*, vol. 1, no. 5:513, 174.
46. Struve, "Die Marxsche Theorie der sozialen Entwicklung," 672–86. See the similar argumentation in Kautsky, *Sozialreform und soziale Revolution*; Kautsky, *Der Weg zur Macht*. See also Pankoke, *Sociale Bewegung, sociale Frage, sociale Politik*; Kuhn, "Exkurs—christlich-sozial."
47. Struve, "Die Marxsche Theorie der sozialen Entwicklung," 665–66, 676.
48. Struve, "My Contacts and Conflicts with Lenin I," 594.
49. Struve, *Collected Works*, vol. 1, no. 5:514–15.
50. It has not, however, been translated into English. See Geyer, *Lenin in der russischen Sozialdemokratie*, 32. For the original Russian text, see Struve, *Collected Works*, vol. 1, no. 15.
51. Pipes, *Struve*, 52–64.
52. Quoted in ibid., 104. See also Geyer, *Lenin in der russischen Sozialdemokratie*, 33.
53. Pipes, *Struve*, 93–95.
54. Lenin, *Collected Works*, 1:395, 400. See also Geyer, *Lenin in der russischen Sozialdemokratie*, 43; Struve, "My Contacts and Conflicts with Lenin I."
55. Plechanow, "Karl Marx," 676.
56. Pipes, *Struve*, 100n76. Pipes describes this as an insignificant "affectation," but also mentions that Struve's critics used it "to depict him as a German who was indifferent to the plight of the Russian peasants."
57. Struve, *Collected Works*, vol. 1, no. 5:173–74. Engels pointed especially to Struve, *Collected Works*, vol. 1, no. 9:3.
58. Engels to Nikolai F. Danielson (17 October 1893) in *MEW*, 39:149–50. The English translation is from *MECW*, 50:213–15.
59. Struve, "My Contacts and Conflicts with Lenin I," 581.
60. Struve, *Collected Works*, vol. 1, no. 37.
61. Struve, "My Contacts and Conflicts with Lenin II," 72.
62. "Mittellage," in Mannheim, *Ideologie und Utopie*, 127.
63. Struve, *Collected Works*, vol. 1, no. 37:30.

64. Pipes, *Struve*, 221. See also Struve's depiction of his relationship to the Russian liberals in "My Contacts with Rodichev."

65. Struve, *Collected Works*, vol. 1, no. 37:29.

66. Struve, "My Contacts and Conflicts with Lenin II," 75. See also the English translation of the complete text and accompanying commentary in Pipes, *Struve*, 193–96.

67. Struve, "My Contacts and Conflicts with Lenin I," 583. The episode must have occurred in 1890 or 1891. For context, see Daly, *Autocracy under Siege*, 48; Daly, "Police and Revolutionaries," 642ff.

68. Geyer, *Lenin in der russischen Sozialdemokratie*, 59; Rabinowitz, *Zur Entwicklung der Arbeiterbewegung in Rußland*, 74–76; Zelnik, "Russian Workers and Revolution"; Zelnik, *Workers and Intelligentsia*.

69. Zelnik, "Russian Workers and Revolution," 627–29.

70. Daly, "Police and Revolutionaries," 640–41.

71. Struve, *Collected Works*, vol. 1, nos. 11, 16; vol. 3, no. 1. See also Puttkamer, *Fabrikgesetzgebung in Russland vor 1905*; Geyer, *Lenin in der russischen Sozialdemokratie*, 46–72.

72. Quoted in Pipes, *Struve*, 113 (emphasis in the original).

73. Struve, "Die Marxsche Theorie der sozialen Entwicklung," 658ff. (emphasis in the original).

74. Ibid., 662. For Struve, historicizing also meant using "critical analysis" to establish the historical position of Marx's doctrine "within the study of economics"—that is, in relation to the many other theories that were developed before and around the same time as *Capital*. Struve, "Introduction," xxxii (translated into German by A. Stelzig).

75. Struve, "Zwei bisher unbekannte Aufsätze," 53.

76. Struve, "Die Marxsche Theorie der sozialen Entwicklung," 659.

77. He was certainly conscious of how his discovery would be received: "This is not to support Marx philology, but all original documents pertaining to the origins and development of the epochal doctrine should be collected completely." See Struve, "Zwei bisher unbekannte Aufsätze," 4.

78. Ibid., 4, 7.

79. Ibid., 5.

80. Ibid., 7 (emphasis in the original).

81. Struve, "Die Marxsche Theorie der sozialen Entwicklung," 704.

82. Struve, "Карль Марксъ и судьбы марксизма" [Karl Marx and the fate of Marxism, 1934], Hoover Archive, Struve Papers, box 16, folder 15 (translated into German by A. Stelzig).

83. Struve, "Die Marxsche Theorie der sozialen Entwicklung," xxxiv.

84. *MECW*, 3:183.

85. Lenin, *Collected Works*, 1:298. The original title is Что такое »друзья народа« и как они воюют против социалдемократов?

86. Dowe, *"Agitieren, organisieren, studieren!,"* 22. Dowe quotes the saying without attribution.

87. Service, *Lenin*, 56ff., 65, 77–78.

88. Pomper, *Lenin's Brother*, 32–38.

89. Ibid., 44.

90. Service, *Lenin*, 56–57.

91. Lenin, *Collected Works*, 1:540. In *Lenin: Life and Legacy*, 23, Volkogonov writes, without attribution, that "some time on the eve of 1889 . . . he got hold of the first volume of *Capital*." Geyer dates this reading to the years 1887–89 in *Lenin in der russischen Sozialdemokratie*, 41.

92. Service, *Lenin*, 71–72.

93. Struve, *Collected Works*, 1:175.

94. Uspensky and Terpigoriew, *Verlumpung der Bauern*. Later on, Lenin occasionally cited Uspensky to denounce injustice and despotism in the tsarist empire. See, for example, Lenin, *Collected Works*, 4:402.

95. Lenin, *Collected Works*, 1:109n, and 70. "New Economic Developments in Peasant Life" is Lenin's oldest surviving manuscript. It contains a few indirect references to Marx in phrases such as "scientific political economy" (68) and "struggle of economic interests" (72), and a reference to the "market" as "the regulator of social production" (73).

96. Lenin, *Collected Works*, 1:540. His translation of the *Manifesto* has not been preserved.

97. Service, *Lenin*, 87–88.

98. See, for example, the unsubstantiated assertion in Pipes, "The Origins of Bolshevism," 39, 42n55.

99. Lenin, *Collected Works*, 1:195–96. See also Geyer, *Lenin in der russischen Sozialdemokratie*, 41n15.

100. Lenin, *Collected Works*, 3:166, as well as 647n63 (emphasis in the original).

101. Lenin was referring to Engels, "Die Entwicklung des Sozialismus in Deutschland," 587–89. See the English translation in *MECW*, 27:247–49.

102. Figes, *A People's Tragedy*, 157ff. However, it is not true that "even the young Lenin only became converted to the Marxist mainstream in the wake of the famine crisis," as Figes asserts without attribution (162).

103. Service, *Lenin*, 103ff.

104. Ibid., 96.

105. Lenin, *Collected Works*, 2:82–83. For background on the pamphlet's creation, see Krupskaya, *Memories of Lenin*, 285ff.

106. Lenin, *Collected Works*, 2:89–92, 122–27. The letter to the workers of Petrograd is in 27:391–98.
107. Krupskaya, *Memories of Lenin*, 6–7. For context, see Geyer, *Lenin in der russischen Sozialdemokratie*, 47–72.
108. Lenin, *Collected Works*, 2:92.
109. Ibid., 1:299n.
110. Ibid., 1:294n, 296, 332.
111. Ibid., 4:380–82.
112. Lenin had contributed to this attention, discussing Struve's book in his second essay. See ibid., 1:531–32. He praised Struve's insistence on factuality and on the necessity of capitalist economic development in Russia, but he criticized the author's "objective" standpoint, which ignored the importance of class struggle.
113. Service, *Lenin*, 106ff.; Geyer, *Lenin in der russischen Sozialdemokratie*, 66ff.
114. Lenin, *Collected Works*, 2:96. While in exile two years later, he wrote a second programmatic text that led just as directly to the argumentation in *What Is to Be Done?* See Lenin, *Collected Works*, 2:323–51.
115. Pipes, "The Origins of Bolshevism," 35–44.
116. Lenin, *Collected Works*, 1:85.
117. Ibid., 1:79 (emphasis in the original).
118. Potresov, "Lenin," 406–7; Service, *Lenin*, 105.
119. Struve, "My Contacts and Conflicts with Lenin I," 592–93.
120. Ibid., 593.
121. Service, *Lenin*, 103.
122. Schieder, *Karl Marx als Politiker*.
123. Lenin, *Collected Works*, 2:26. On his "passionate attachment" to Plekhanov (and subsequent disappointment), see Service, *Lenin*, 132ff.; Morina, "Szenen einer marxistischen Familie."
124. Lenin, *Collected Works*, 1:139–40.
125. Ibid., 2:20; 1:140–41.
126. Ibid., 1:139–40.
127. *MECW*, 6:482, 519. See also Gareth Stedman Jones's introduction and notes to Marx and Engels, *The Communist Manifesto*.
128. On Marxism as a science, see Carver, "Marx and Marxism."
129. Osterhammel, *The Transformation of the World*, 814.
130. Quoted in Pipes, "The Origins of Bolshevism," 79.
131. Service, *Lenin*, 65.
132. Lenin, *Collected Works*, 1:141.
133. Ibid., 1:190–95. Likewise, Lenin accused the Narodniks of not wanting to observe, "dispassionately and scientifically," the "*real* countryside

and its *real* economics," as depicted in statistics (1:234, emphasis in the original).

134. Kolakowski, *Main Currents of Marxism,* 2:356.

135. Lenin, *Collected Works,* 1:157n.

136. Ibid., 1:141–42 (emphasis in the original).

137. Muller, *The Mind and the Market,* 197.

138. Lenin, *Collected Works,* 1:138.

139. Ibid., 2:26–27. In this context, see also his polemic "Beat—But Not to Death!" (likewise written in 1895), in which he conflated his personal hatred for the police with "popular hatred" (4:402).

140. Ibid., 5:423 (emphasis in the original). On *What Is to Be Done?*, see Haimson, "Lenin's Revolutionary Career Revisited."

141. Haimson speaks of a "marriage of feeling and reason" in *The Russian Marxists,* 26ff.

CHAPTER 9

1. Frölich, *Rosa Luxemburg,* 24; Nettl, *Rosa Luxemburg,* 1:59.

2. Luxemburg, *GW,* 1/1:84.

3. Ibid., 1/1:7.

4. Luxemburg, "Der Sozialismus in Polen," 548–50.

5. See her letters of 31 May, 18 June, 24 June, 3 July, and 12–20 July 1898, in Luxemburg, *GB,* 1:138, 148, 156, 167, 173; Luxemburg, *The Letters of Rosa Luxemburg* (2011), 69. It is also possible that she could not bring part or all of her library to Paris and that the books (including Beethoven) she requested were among her possessions still in Zurich. Nettl, *Rosa Luxemburg,* 1:67–68.

6. Luxemburg, *GW,* 1/1:166n2; Wolf, *Die Volkswirtschaftslehre der Gegenwart,* 200; Nettl, *Rosa Luxemburg,* 1:59–60, 63.

7. Wolf, *Die Volkswirtschaftslehre der Gegenwart,* 216, 220.

8. Luxemburg to Leo Jogiches (30 June 1905), in Luxemburg, *GB,* 2:147. On Jogiches's role in Luxemburg's life, see Nettl, *Rosa Luxemburg,* 1:66ff.

9. For a complete list of her courses, see Stadler-Labhart, *Rosa Luxemburg an der Universität Zürich,* 38–39.

10. Dirsch, *Solidarismus und Sozialethik,* 42. Stein's memoirs do not mention his (later) famous student. See Stein, *Aus dem Leben eines Optimisten,* 39–40.

11. Mehring, *Aus dem literarischen Nachlass.*

12. Luxemburg, *GW,* 1/2:136–39.

13. Ibid., 1/2:135–37.

14. See Isaiah Berlin's classic portrait *Karl Marx*, especially 1–16. The "normative dimension" of Marx's argumentation (Quante, "Die fragile Einheit des Marxschen Denkens," 591) is still debated today, as scholars seek to unearth the ethical foundations of his political philosophy, which ostentatiously challenged (traditional conceptions of) ethics, justice, and morality. In the spirit of E. P. Thompson, van der Linden and Roth recall that "*Capital* discusses the logic of capital, but not capitalism. . . . The 'human experience' is neglected, although this concept expresses a significant aspect" ("Einleitung," 13ff.).

15. Luxemburg, *GW*, 1/2:139.

16. Luxemburg, *Einführung in die Nationalökonomie*, 72.

17. Luxemburg, GW, 1/2:369 (emphasis in the original). In *Social Reform or Revolution*, Luxemburg substituted the metaphor of Ariadne's thread with hieroglyphics: "The secret of Marx's theory of value . . . is—the transitory nature of the capitalist economy. . . . And precisely because, *a priori*, Marx looked at capitalism from the socialist's viewpoint, that is, from the historical viewpoint, he was enabled to decipher the hieroglyphics of capitalist economy . . . [and] give a scientific basis to socialism." Luxemburg, *GW,* 1/1:415–16. The English translation is from Luxemburg, *The Rosa Luxemburg Reader*, 151.

18. Luxemburg, *GW*, 1/2: 468 (emphasis in the original). See also 1/1:414–15.

19. Anderson, *Imagined Communities*, 33.

20. Luxemburg, *Einführung in die Nationalökonomie*, 72–79, 102. This "anarchy" not only brought misery but sowed "anarchist confusion" among the "miserable elements," hobbling the workers' movement like a "brake shoe" (Luxemburg, *GW*, 1/1:329). The description of capitalist society as "anarchist" figures prominently in Marx's *Capital* and Engels's *Socialism: Utopian and Scientific*.

21. Luxemburg to Leo Jogiches (11 March 1894), in Luxemburg, *GB*, 1:15. The English translation is from Luxemburg, *The Letters of Rosa Luxemburg* (2011), 8.

22. Nettl, *Rosa Luxemburg*, 1:70ff.

23. Nettl, *Luxemburg*, I:83.

24. Luxemburg, *GW*, 1/1:5ff.

25. Nettl, *Rosa Luxemburg*, 1:35–36, 73, 83–87.

26. Letter to Leo Jogiches (24 March 1894), in Luxemburg, *GB*, 1:23–24 (emphasis in the original).

27. The collection of Luxemburg's papers in the German Federal Archive includes a typewritten translation of an article about the St. Petersburg

strikes ("The Workers' Movement in Russia, Part 2"), which appeared in the *Sprawa Robotnicza* in 1896. BA NY 4002, 6, 3–7.

28. I am grateful to Magdalena Melonek for her help transcribing and translating the original articles, which are difficult to read, from the SDKPiL holdings at the IISH (IISH Microf./P 428).

29. Luxemburg, "Die Arbeiterbewegung in Russland," Teil 2, *Sprawa Robotnicza* 24 (June 1896), cited from the translation in BA NY 4002, 6, 3–7.

30. [Luxemburg], "Was ist der Sozialismus," *Sprawa Robotnicza* 22 (April 1895) (translated into German by M. Melonek).

31. Luxemburg, *GW*, 1/1:8.

32. Lenin to M. A. Ulyanov (17 September 1897), in Lenin, *Collected Works*, 8:44 (emphasis in the original).

33. Luxemburg to Leo Jogiches (20 March 1895), in Luxemburg, *GB*, 1:52–53. She was referring to Engels's quotation of a letter by a worker from Leeds who was barely able to write. The letter was supposed to illustrate that women's rising participation in the workforce was condemning men to work from home—leading to their "castration," leaving children unprotected, and thus destroying the family. Engels had taken pains to "reproduce" the orthography and dialect in German. See *MECW*, 4:437–39.

34. *Sprawa Robotnicza* 21 (March 1895).

35. Luxemburg to Leo Jogiches (2 April 1895), in Luxemburg, *GB*, 1:71.

36. Luxemburg to Leo Jogiches (28 March 1895), in Luxemburg, *GB*, 1:63–64.

37. The quotes are from her report to the Zurich congress of the Second International in 1893. See Luxemburg, *GW*, 1/1:8.

38. Weber, *Political Writings*, 332.

39. The outlines of this intense editing process can be gleaned from Luxemburg's correspondence with Jogiches. See the letters between June and August 1898 in Luxemburg, *GB*, 1:152–90. Luxemburg sent the book as proof of her expertise to socialist journals and politicians all over Europe, including to Parvus and Jaurès. She later gave a signed copy of her book *The Accumulation of Capital* to Jaurès (information provided on 7 July 2015 by Eric Lafon, Musée de l'Histoire Vivante, Montreuil). See also Stadler-Labhard, *Rosa Luxemburg an der Universität Zürich*, 25–36.

40. Luxemburg, *GW*, 1/1:v–vi. The English translations are from Luxemburg, *CW*, 1:1.

41. "Clausurarbeit" for Professor J. Wolf: "Die Lohnfondstheorie und die Theorie der industriellen Reservearmee," BA-SAPMO NY4002/1, Teilnachlass Luxemburg, 15.

42. See also her prediction at the end of her dissertation that "even in the Russian Empire . . . the days of primitive capitalist accumulation are almost past." Luxemburg, *GW*, 1/1:208. The English translation is from Luxemburg, *CW*, 1:72.

43. "Clausurarbeit" for Professor J. Wolf: "Die Lohnfondstheorie und die Theorie der industriellen Reservearmee," BA-SAPMO NY4002/1, Teilnachlass Luxemburg, 16.

44. Ibid., 19.

45. Ibid., 8–9 (emphasis in the original).

46. See Luxemburg's emphasis on the preliminary character of the second volume of *Capital* in Luxemburg, *Die Akkumulation des Kapitals*, 383–482.

47. Luxemburg, *GW*, 1/2:466. The English translation is from Gaido and Quiroga, "A Forgotten Work by Rosa Luxemburg," 454 (emphasis added).

48. "Clausurarbeit" for Professor J. Wolf: "Die Lohnfondstheorie und die Theorie der industriellen Reservearmee," BA-SAPMO NY4002/1, Teilnachlass Luxemburg, 31.

49. Luxemburg, *GW*, 1/2:469. The English translation is from Gaido and Quiroga, "A Forgotten Work by Rosa Luxemburg," 455–56 (emphasis in the original).

50. Plekhanov, *The Development of the Monist View of History*, 275.

51. *MECW*, 6:496. On the transcendent historical perspective that Marx and Engels inherited from Hegel, see van der Linden, Roth, and Henninger, *Über Marx hinaus*, 18.

52. Jones, "Introduction," in Marx and Engels, *The Communist Manifesto*, 21.

53. Hobsbawm, *How to Change the World*, 102; Marx and Engels, *The Communist Manifesto*, 14–26; Muller, *The Mind and the Market*, 207.

54. Welskopp, *Das Banner der Brüderlichkeit*, 669.

55. Berger et al., *Die gesellschaftliche Konstruktion der Wirklichkeit*, 139–74. On the concept of conversion, see Kroll, *Kommunistische Intellektuelle*, 17–18, 85. Kroll also emphasizes that these conversions were closely linked to the socialization of his protagonists. On Marxism as a faith or political religion, see Tucker, "Marxism"; Aron, *The Opium of the Intellectuals*; Rohrwasser, "Religions- und kirchenähnliche Strukturen."

56. With respect to post 1945 communists, see Kroll, *Kommunistische Intellektuelle*, 10, 17–18, 85.

57. Kolakovsky, "On Marxism, Christianity, and Totalitarianism," 342.

PART III

1. Marx, *Early Political Writings*, 58, 64.
2. Ibid., 117.
3. The quote is from Engels's correspondence with Conrad Schmidt, about publications that were described as "materialist" in Germany. According to Engels, the term was often "a mere cliché with which to label anything and everything without bothering to study it any further." See Engels to Conrad Schmidt (5 August 1890), in *MECW*, 49:8.
4. Marx, "Randglossen zum Programm der deutschen Arbeiterpartei," 395 (emphasis in the original). See also *MECW*, 24:93.
5. Engels to Bebel (18–28 March 1875) in *MEW*, 19:6. The English translation is from *MECW*, 45:63.
6. Frevert, *Emotions in History*, 195–96; Welskopp, *Das Banner der Brüderlichkeit*, 82–97; Koller, "Soziale Bewegungen." For general context, see Hunt, *Inventing Human Rights*; on perspectives for further research, see Plamper, *Geschichte und Gefühl*, 328–32.
7. Fischer, "Der Wandel der sozialen Frage," 104. See also Pankoke, *Sociale Bewegung*; Kocka and Schmidt, *Arbeiterleben und Arbeiterkultur*, 350–66. For social policy in Imperial Germany, see Ritter, *Soziale Frage und Sozialpolitik in Deutschland*.
8. Kocka and Schmidt, *Arbeiterleben und Arbeiterkultur*, 354, 358.
9. Koselleck, "Die Geschichte der Begriffe," 68; Koselleck, "Begriffsgeschichte und Sozialgeschichte," 113.
10. Arendt, *On Revolution*, 53–110. This interpretation has provoked objections. See, for example, Hobsbawm, "Hannah Arendt on Revolution." Hobsbawm criticizes the Hegelian overtones in Arendt's argument that history has been moved by revolutions, not wars, since the nineteenth century.
11. Quoted in Nossig-Prochnik, "Die soziale Frage auf der französischen Bühne," 625.
12. Ibid.
13. Quoted in Winterberg and Winterberg, *Kollwitz*, 127–28, 156. Kollwitz used this phrase in an April 1902 letter. In this context, a contemporary critic's description of Kollwitz's etching *The Carmagnole* (1901) is particularly revealing: Kollwitz "writes the flames of the uprising and the terrifying rule of the masses on the wall, exposes the maiden-turned-hyena of the French Revolution, and—cries with the mothers. Her work is the culminating impulse of that powerful movement, in which

we all—whether welcoming or resisting—are completely and utterly entangled" (156).

14. Ibid., 127f.

15. Lembcke and Weber, "Emotion und Revolution," 179–82; Paris, "Leidenschaft"; Goodwin, Jasper, and Polletta, *Passionate Politics*; Goodwin, Jasper, and Polletta, "The Return of the Repressed." This conception of passion resembles Florian Weber's. See Lembcke and Weber, "Leidenschaft, Affekt und Gefühl."

16. Schwarz, Szeless, and Wögenstein, *Ganz unten*. See also Koven, *Slumming*.

17. Kocka and Schmidt, *Arbeiterleben und Arbeiterkultur*, 350.

18. Schwarz, Szeless, and Wögenstein, "Bilder des Elends in der Großstadt," 11.

19. Vasold, "Die vielen stillen und lauten Tragödien," 140–41.

20. For general context in German-speaking Europe, see Conze, "Proletariat, Pöbel, Pauperismus," 358n53; as well as Welskopp, *Das Banner der Brüderlichkeit*, 60–76; Steinbach, *Ökonomisten, Philanthropen, Humanitäre*, 23ff.; Pierson, *Marxist Intellectuals*; Eley, "Intellectuals and the German Labor Movement"; Neusüß, *Die Kopfgeburten der Arbeiterbewegung*; Schelsky, *Die Arbeit tun die anderen*; Bartholmes, *Bruder, Bürger, Freund, Genosse*. Fetscher's *Grundbegriffe des Marxismus* does not have an entry for "worker," nor for "proletariat"/"proletarian." From the perspective of discourse history, see Colin and Schössler, *Das nennen Sie Arbeit?* On the state of research and perspectives for the future, see van der Linden, Roth, and Henninger, *Über Marx hinaus*; van der Linden, *Workers of the World*, 17–38.

21. On the social history of workers and other nonelites, see Kocka and Schmidt, *Arbeiterleben und Arbeiterkultur*, 37–42. Kocka and Schmidt show how issues related to labor and poverty were long intertwined in the Social Question discourse and only gradually distinguished from one another (104ff., 357).

CHAPTER 10

1. Ibid., 329.

2. *MECW*, 6:494, 519. See also van der Linden and Roth, "Einleitung," 19–20; Henninger, "Armut, Arbeit, Entwicklung."

3. Welskopp, *Das Banner der Brüderlichkeit*, 50. Welskopp describes transcending boundaries between lifeworlds as "mediating milieus" (*Milieuvermittlung*; 158–59).

4. Schütz, *Der sinnhafte Aufbau der sozialen Welt*, 288–89. For the English translation, see Schütz, *The Phenomenology of the Social World*, 142–43.

5. Pipes, *Struve*, 72–73.

6. Kautsky to Minna Jaich Kautsky (30 August 1881), IISH, Kautsky-FA 1553, 1.

7. Kautsky to Minna Jaich Kautsky (3 April 1881), IISH, Kautsky-FA 1553, 7. He frequently repeated the comparison with children, as in a letter to Bernstein (27 June 1886), IISH, Kautsky papers, K DV 204/1-885, 8. In the context of a demonstration in London in September 1885, see Kautsky to Bernstein (27 September 1885), IISH, Kautsky papers, K DV 204/1-861, 2.

8. Kautsky, *Erinnerungen und Erörterungen*, 366. There is a similar, much earlier description in a letter to his brother Hans Kautsky (21 June 1880), IISH, Kautsky-FA 1548, 11.

9. See, for example, Kautsky to Adler (7 March 1899, 21 March 1899, and 20 September 1905), in Adler, *Briefwechsel*, 293–94, 303–4, 461–66. For further examples, see Morina, "Marx' Prophezeiungen"; Gilcher-Holtey, *Das Mandat des Intellektuellen*, 252–67.

10. Adler to Engels (29 December 1891), in Adler, *ARB*, 1:30.

11. This is her own description in a letter to Leo Jogiches (22 May 1898), in Luxemburg, *GB,* 1:124–25.

12. Luxemburg, *GW*, 1/1:592. The English translation is from Luxemburg, *CW*, 1:72.

13. Luxemburg, *GW*, 1/1:415. See other examples in 1/1:57–60, 109ff., 224, 291, 311, 320–21, 328–29.

14. Luxemburg to Robert Seidel (23 June 1898), in Luxemburg, *GB*, 1:152–53. Most of this passage is translated in Luxemburg, *The Letters of Rosa Luxemburg* (2011), 64. Curiously, this translation omits the first half-sentence of this quote.

15. Luxemburg to Robert Seidel (8 August 1902), in Luxemburg, *GB*, 1:642.

16. Luxemburg to Leo Jogiches (9 June 1898), in Luxemburg, *GB*, 1:152–53. The English translation is from Luxemburg, *The Letters of Rosa Luxemburg* (2011), 62–63.

17. Luxemburg to the Kautskys (30 December 1899), in Luxemburg, *GB*, 1:432. The English translation is from Luxemburg, *The Letters of Rosa Luxemburg* (2011), 121–22.

18. Roland Holst-van der Schalk, *Rosa Luxemburg*, 16. See also Flechtheim, *Rosa Luxemburg zur Einführung*, 68.

19. Luxemburg, *GW*, 1/1:467–70.

20. Ibid., 1/1:467 and 470 (emphasis in the original).

21. This was a common phenomenon among contemporaries who "discovered" misery. See Schwarz, Szeless, and Wögenstein, "Bilder des Elends in der Großstadt," 11.

22. Eduard Bernstein, "Was man im Volk vor zwei Menschenaltern sang: Erinnerungen an seelige Sommerabende," [1920s], IISH, Bernstein papers, film 1, no. 53 (RCChIDNI Fonds 204, opis 1, Delo 53). See also Bernstein, *Von 1850 bis 1872*, 44–45.

23. Welskopp, *Das Banner der Brüderlichkeit*, 158–59.

24. Bernstein, *Geschichte der Berliner Arbeiter-Bewegung*, 130ff.

25. Guesde, *Le Problème et la Solution*, 1–2, 7; Guesde, "De la Propriété," 7.

26. Guesde, *AT*, 168 (emphasis in the original).

27. See, for example, Guesde, *Le Problème et la Solution*, 11; Guesde, *AT*, 225.

28. Luxemburg to Leo Jogiches (29 March 1894), in Luxemburg, *GB*, 1:35.

29. Welskopp, *Das Banner der Brüderlichkeit*, 175–77.

30. Bernstein, *Geschichte der Berliner Arbeiter-Bewegung*, 184ff.

31. Bernstein to Kautsky (27 June 1886), IISH, Kautsky papers, K DV-65, 9–15; Bernstein to Friedrich Engels (4 May 1882) in Bernstein and Engels, *Briefwechsel*, 97.

32. Bernstein to Kautsky (30 January 1896) in Schelz-Brandenburg, *Eduard Bernsteins Briefwechsel mit Karl Kautsky*, 61; Bernstein to Adler (28 March 1899), in Adler, *Briefwechsel*, 307.

33. Kautsky, *Erinnerungen und Erörterungen*, 100, 146–47.

34. Ibid., 317, 366.

35. Kautsky to Minna Jaich Kautsky (28 November 1881), IISH, Kautsky-FA 1553, 2.

36. Kautsky, *Der Weg zur Macht*, 19. The English translation is from Kautsky, *The Road to Power*, 22. Gilcher-Holtey in *Das Mandat des Intellektuellen*, 43, has characterized this attitude as the will to "comprehend actual conditions theoretically."

37. Kautsky, "Ein Brief über Bernstein an Plechanoff," 2.

38. Jaurès, *RS*, 205.

39. Stuart, *Marxism at Work*, 396–411.

40. Droz, *Die sozialistischen Parteien*, 58. Neither Willard nor Stuart offers more information about the survey initiative, which is mentioned only by Droz.

41. Ibid., 66.

42. Jaurès, "Die Entwicklung des ländlichen Eigentums," 64–66; Goldberg, *The Life of Jean Jaurès*, 182–87. For Marx's remark, see *MECW*, 27:500.

43. Dornheim, "Sozialdemokratie und Bauern."

44. Jaurès, *RS*, 53–59. This familiarity is also documented in Jaurès, "Die Entwicklung des ländlichen Eigentums"; Jaurès, "Kleine Anfänge."

45. Jaurès, *RS*, 58.

46. Plekhanov, "Socialism and Political Struggle," 120–21.

47. Ibid., 121.

48. Plekhanow, "Die sozialpolitischen Zustände Rußlands im Jahre 1890," 736–37. The great famine broke out in Russia only a few months after this article was published.

49. Service, *Lenin*, 44ff., 76ff.

50. Krupskaya, *Memories of Lenin*, 6ff., 285–95, 301–4.

51. V. Ulyanov to his mother, M.A. Ulyanov (17 September 1897), in Lenin, *Collected Works*, 37:102–3.

52. Lenin to A. A. Bogdanov (10 January 1905) in Lenin, *Collected Works*, 8:44. Lenin was writing about *Vperyod*, which was published weekly by Russian exiles (including Lenin and Lunacharsky) in Geneva between 1904 and 1905, after the *Iskra* project fell apart over a disagreement between Axelrod, Martov, and Malinovsky in 1903.

CHAPTER 11

1. Kautsky to Minna Kautsky (3 April 1881), IISH, Kautsky-FA 1553.

2. Jaurès to Jean Julien (11 January 1879), in Jaurès, *Œuvres*, 1:55–56.

3. Quoted in Goldberg, *The Life of Jean Jaurès*, 17. See also *MECW*, 4:329.

4. Luxemburg to Leo Jogiches (28 March 1895), in Luxemburg, *GB*, 1:60. On Berlin, where she rented her first room ("delightful, quiet") in the "aristocratic" Tiergarten neighborhood, see Luxemburg to Leo Jogiches (16 May 1889), 1:112, 119–20.

5. Luxemburg, *GW*, 1/1:329 (emphasis in the original).

6. Ibid., 1/1:320–21.

7. Pipes, *Struve*, 66, 64.

8. Winterberg and Winterberg, *Kollwitz*, 126.

9. Lenin to M. A. Ulyanova (10 August 1895 and 29 August 1895), in Lenin, *Absender, Wl. Uljanow*, 25–27. The English translations are from Lenin, *Collected Works*, 37:77–78.

10. Lenin to M. A. Ulyanova (20 May 1895, 8 June 1895, and 7 September 1900), in Lenin, *Absender, Wl. Uljanow*, 22–23, 88–89. The English translations are from Lenin, *Collected Works*, 37:73–74.

11. *MECW*, 4:328–29, 297.

12. Adler, *ARB*, 1:vii.

13. Adler belonged to a commission that investigated the living and working conditions of female wage laborers in Vienna. See *Die Arbeits und Lebensverhältnisse der Wiener Lohnarbeiterinnen*.

14. Adler, *ARB*, 5:xiii; 4:108. Here Adler directly referred to Engels's *The Condition of the Working Class in England*.

15. Adler, *ARB*, 5:24.

16. Ibid., 5:47–48.

17. Ibid., 5:xliii.

18. Ibid., 5:46.

19. Ibid., 5:27. In the 1880s, German factory workers worked an average of eleven hours a day, seven days a week. See Ritter and Tenfelde, *Arbeiter im Deutschen Kaiserreich*, 364.

20. Adler discussed these issues in unprecedented detail in both his newspaper articles and parliamentary speeches. See, for example, Adler, *ARB*, 3:67–74, 86–96.

21. *MECW*, 4:304.

22. Adler, *ARB*, 5:21–27, 39.

23. Adler, *ARB*, 5:24, 39.

24. Wondratsch, "Zur sozialen Lage der Arbeitersschaft," 54ff.; Schacherl, "Einleitung."

25. According to this exploitative "truck system," some wages were paid only in the form of commodities (or "trucks").

26. Adler, *ARB*, 4:11–17.

27. Ibid., 4:18.

28. Ibid., 6:51.

29. Ibid., 3:86.

30. Ibid., 4:11–35.

31. Ibid., 3:143–45.

32. Wondratsch, "Zur sozialen Lage der Arbeitersschaft," 63–64; Schacherl, "Einleitung." The Viennese Social Democrats systematically supported the strike. Their years-long engagement provides the context for the birthday postcard from the "grateful brick workers," which is reproduced at the beginning of Part III.

33. See, for example, Adler, *ARB*, 3:93–94; 4:94. Because Adler believed that reform could be revolutionary, he did defend the party's revolutionary *rhetoric* to Bernstein as an indispensable means of mobilization.

34. Bernstein, "Entwicklungsgang eines Sozialisten," 40. Gay devotes few pages to Berlin's parliamentary activity in *The Dilemma of Democratic Socialism*, 331ff.

35. Willard, *Jules Guesde*. Bernstein mentions this aspect of Guesde's political life only in passing in "Jules Guesde," 50ff. Zévaès devotes a chapter to these years, but he largely recapitulates Guesde's campaign, contrasting Guesde's uncompromising, militant rhetoric with Jaurès's more enduring interventions. See Zévaès, *Jules Guesde*, 105–36, 167ff. (especially 133).

36. See Lenin, *Collected Works*, 2:267–315. This text, which Lenin wrote in exile, portrays the legislative process of factory regulation as thoroughly corrupt. See also Struve, *Collected Works*, vol. 1, no. 77; Plekhanov, "Die sozialpolitischen Zustände Rußlands im Jahre 1890." On the history of factory regulation in Russia before 1905, see Puttkamer, *Fabrikgesetzgebung in Russland vor 1905*, 220–54.

37. Documented in Grunenberg, *Die Massenstreikdebatte*.

38. Kautsky to Friedrich Engels (23 April 1889), in Engels and Kautsky, *Briefwechsel*, 242.

39. Droz, *Die sozialistischen Parteien*, 66; Bernstein, "Jules Guesde," 45–47. See also Stuart, *Marxism at Work*, 245–46. Drawing upon primary sources, Stuart paints a less sympathetic image of Guesde than Samuel Bernstein or Guesde's sometime hagiographer Claude Willard.

40. Kautsky to Bernstein (23 August 1888), IISH, Kautsky papers, K C 80, 3.

41. See, for example, Bernstein to Kautsky (13 October 1888), IISH, Kautsky papers, K DV 107, 2–8. See also Engels and Kautsky, *Briefwechsel*, 132–35, 272ff., 304ff., 446.

42. This is Kautsky's retrospective summary from 1935, part of his commentary on his correspondence with Engels. See Engels and Kautsky, *Briefwechsel*, 214.

43. Kautsky to Engels (23 April 1889), in Engels and Kautsky, *Briefwechsel*, 242.

44. Kautsky, "Viktor Adler," 419 (emphasis in the original).

45. Kautsky to Bernstein (8 July 1885), IISH, Bernstein papers, RCChIDNI, 204/1-857, 1.

46. Walkowitz, *City of Dreadful Delight*, 81–82. The series is reprinted in Stead, *The Maiden Tribute of Modern Babylon*, 81–82.

47. Engels to Kautsky (25 October 1891), in *MECW*, 49:274.

48. Kautsky to Bernstein (8 July 1885), IISH, Bernstein papers, RCChIDNI, 204/1-857, 2–4.

49. Kautsky to Bernstein (9 July 1885), IISH, Bernstein papers, RCChIDNI, 204/1-858.

50. Ibid.

51. Walkowitz, *City of Dreadful Delight*, 81–143 (especially 81–85). See also the references on 83n8, as well as Gorham, "The 'Maiden Tribute of Modern Babylon' Re-examined," 371ff.

52. *Der Jungfrauentribut des modernen Babylon*, 3–4. Stead made the same argument in *The Maiden Tribute of Modern Babylon*, 6.

53. Kautsky to Bernstein (10 August 1885), IISH, Bernstein papers, RCChIDNI, 204/1-861.

54. Kautsky to Bernstein (8 July 1885), IISH, Bernstein papers, RCChIDNI, 204/1-857, 4.

55. Ibid.

56. Luxemburg, "Einleitung," 13–14.

57. *Justice,* 11 July 1885, 1, quoted in Gorham, "The 'Maiden Tribute of Modern Babylon' Re-examined," 377.

58. Engels, "Ein gerechter Tageslohn," 373–74. See also *MECW,* 4:441–42. It seems likely, as Tristam Hunt suggests, that Engels heard about such occurrences through Mary Burns's experiences in the factories of Manchester. See Hunt, *Marx's General,* 96.

59. Bernstein, *Von 1850 bis 1872,* 159.

60. Ibid., 157–59.

61. Schütz and Luckmann, *Strukturen der Lebenswelt,* 149.

62. Berlin, *The Sense of Reality,* 35. Berlin's work combined analytical interest with strong normative motives. A staunch liberal, he counted Marx among the forefathers of the totalitarian ideologies he critiqued.

63. Lembcke and Weber, "Emotion und Revolution," 179–82; Berlin, *The Sense of Reality,* 24.

ON REVOLUTION, OR THE SECOND COMMANDMENT: PHILOSOPHY AS PRACTICE

1. In the epigraph, Foucault is referring to Paris in the late 1940s. See Foucault, "Interview," 248.

2. Gilcher-Holtey, *Eingreifendes Denken,* 9.

3. Kroll, *Kommunistische Intellektuelle,* 14.

4. Gilcher-Holtey, *Eingreifendes Denken,* 391.

5. Sartre, "Why Write?," 39; Brecht, "Kleines Organon für das Theater," 667–88; the critique of Brecht's concept of engagement in Adorno, "Engagement," 293–99; Aron, *The Committed Observer.*

6. Heter, "Sartre's Political Philosophy"; Hartmann, "Engagement" (emphasis added).

7. Beyme, *Politische Theorien im Zeitalter der Ideologien,* 17–29.

8. In January 1905 Lenin coined the phrase "Revolution is war." See Lenin, *Collected Works,* 8:107.

9. Elias, *Involvement and Detachment,* 18–19; Elias, *Engagement und Distanzierung,* 29.

10. Elias, *Engagement und Distanzierung,* 9. Elias's thoughts on the "radical engagement" of children and the mentally ill are from the German edition (1983) of his seminal 1956 essay.

11. Elias, *Involvement and Detachment*, 3–4n1; Elias, *Engagement und Distanzierung*, 9–10n1.

12. Elias, *Involvement and Detachment*, 15, 19; Elias, *Engagement und Distanzierung*, 34–35, 57–58.

13. Elias, *Involvement and Detachment*, 15, 19; Elias, *Engagement und Distanzierung*, 34–35, 57–58.

14. Lembcke and Weber, "Emotion und Revolution," 179–80.

15. Lepsius, "Kritik als Beruf."

16. Gilcher-Holtey, *Eingreifendes Denken*, 362, 391.

17. Ibid., 13, 300–301. Kautsky is quoted in Gilcher-Holtey, *Das Mandat des Intellektuellen*, 39.

CHAPTER 12

1. Luxemburg to Karl Kautsky (2 January 1906) in Luxemburg, *GB*, 2:241. The English translation is from Luxemburg, *The Letters of Rosa Luxemburg* (2011), 221.

2. Luxemburg to Leo Jogiches (20 October 1905), in Luxemburg, *GB*, 2:211. The "cart stuck in the mud" (*der Karren steckt im Dreck*) is also in 2:228 (letter from 1 November 1905).

3. See, for example, Gleb, "Activist Subjectivities"; Grimmer, "'Moral Power' and Cultural Revolution"; Figes, *A People's Tragedy*. See also the historiographical overviews in Goodwin and Jasper, *Rethinking Social Movements*; Goodwin, Jasper, and Polletta. *Passionate Politics*; Mittag, *Theoretische Ansätze und Konzepte*.

4. Kramme, "Anmerkungen zur zerbrochenen Einheit." See also Koselleck, "'Erfahrungsraum' und 'Erfahrungshorizont.'"

5. See the compilation of theories from Marx to Trotsky in Fetscher, *Der Marxismus*, 693–790; Lehnert, *Reform und Revolution*.

6. Marx, *Early Political Writings*, 69.

7. Kolakowski, *Main Currents of Marxism*, 1:130. For context on the text's creation, see Sperber, *Karl Marx*, 111–19. Sperber sees little connection between Marx's Parisian experiences and the ideas he formulated in the mid-1840s. He points to some of Marx's first articles on social and economic topics in the *Rheinische Zeitung* (for example, his work on the theft of wood by destitute Rhinelanders, an issue he probably got to know through his father's legal work; 100–101). On Marx's years in Paris, see also Gerber, *Karl Marx in Paris*.

8. Ternes, *Karl Marx*, 38.

9. See, for example, *MEW*, 22:509–27.

10. Ibid., 22:511–12. The English translation is from *MECW*, 27:508.

11. *MEW*, 7:42. *MECW*, 10:78. Here Marx intentionally made a fine semantic distinction between a "right to work" "in the bourgeois sense," which was "an absurdity, a miserable, pious wish," and a "right to work" that implied "power over capital," which could be achieved only by abolishing wage labor.

12. Fetscher, *Der Marxismus*, 693–94.

13. The "innate tendency" quote is from Kolakowski, *Main Currents of Marxism*, 1:127. See also Kautsky, "Ein sozialdemokratischer Katechismus," 368.

14. Koselleck, "Revolution," 653, 735–36, 753ff.

15. Kautsky, *Die soziale Revolution*, 7. A sometimes rough English-language translation, *The Social Revolution*, was likewise published in 1902. See also Groh, *Negative Integration und revolutionärer Attentismus*, 57–80; Fetscher, *Der Marxismus*, 693–790.

16. Kautsky, *Die soziale Revolution*, 53. For the expression "elementary event," see Kautsky, [Self-Portrait], 138. On "growing into" revolution, see Kautsky, *Der Weg zur Macht*; Kautsky, "Ein sozialdemokratischer Katechismus," 368–69.

17. See Van Ree, "German Marxism"; as well as the overviews in Joll, *The Second International*, 77–105; Groh, *Negative Integration und revolutionärer Attentismus*.

18. Kautsky, *Die soziale Revolution*, 8, 53–54.

19. Eley, *Forging Democracy*, 142ff., 223ff.

20. Bernstein, "Revolutionen und Russland," 292.

21. Bernstein, Guesde, and Lafargue, *Gesellschaftliches und PrivatEigenthum*, 31; Guesde, "Lettre à Karl Marx à Londres," 44.

22. Bernstein, "Zusammenbruchstheorie und Colonialpolitik," 228; S. Bernstein, "Jules Guesde," 49–50.

23. Bernstein, "Utopismus und Eklekticismus," 174.

24. The wording is from the 1890 edition of his popular pamphlet *Collectivisme et revolution* (1879), quoted in Guesde, *AT*, 171n189.

25. Guesde, "Légalité et révolution"; Guesde, *Le Problème et la Solution*, 13; Guesde, *AT*, 169–73.

26. Jaurès, "Einleitung," 14–20, 29.

27. Jaurès, "Republik und Sozialismus," 57–58.

28. Groh, *Negative Integration und revolutionärer Attentismus*, 36.

29. Adler, "Beitrag in Debatte zum Arbeiterschutz," 295.

30. Adler, *ARB*, 6:27–28. See also Mommsen, "Victor Adlers Weg zum Sozialismus," 191.

31. Struve, "Die Marxsche Theorie der sozialen Entwicklung," 684.

32. Ibid.

33. Struve, "Introduction," xxxii–xxxiii (translated into German by A. Stelzig).

34. Plekhanov, "A New Champion of Autocracy," 419–20 (emphasis in the original). See also Van Ree, "Georgii Plekhanov and the Communist Manifesto."

35. Kolakowski, *Main Currents of Marxism,* 2:356–57. See also Davidshofer, *Marxism and the Leninist Revolutionary Model.*

36. Lenin, *Collected Works,* 8:103.

37. Ibid., 10:38.

38. Luxemburg, "Organisationsfragen," part 2, 535. The English translation is from Luxemburg, *The Rosa Luxemburg Reader,* 264. See also Kautsky's criticism of the Genevan émigrés in Kautsky to Adler (20 July 1905) in Adler, *Briefwechsel mit August Bebel und Karl Kautsky,* 464.

39. Luxemburg, "Organisationsfragen," part 1, 489–91. The English translations are from Luxemburg, *The Rosa Luxemburg Reader,* 253, 256.

40. Kolakowski, *Main Currents of Marxism,* 2:76–82; Grebing, "Rosa Luxemburg," 61–62; Nettl, *Rosa Luxemburg,* 1:364, 300; 2:756.

41. Kolakowski, *Main Currents of Marxism,* 2:82.

42. All of these metaphors are from Luxemburg, "Die Revolution in Rußland," 572–74. The English translations are from Luxemburg, *The Complete Works of Rosa Luxemburg,* 3:51–52.

43. Luxemburg, "Die Revolution in Rußland," 575ff. The English translations are from Luxemburg, *The Complete Works of Rosa Luxemburg,* 3:55ff.

44. One of the earliest references is Friedrich Schlegel's description of the French Revolution as a "total revolution," an "almost universal earthquake." Quoted in Koselleck, "Revolution," 738.

45. Bernstein, "Revolutionen und Russland," 291. See also Bernstein, "Ist der politische Streik in Deutschland möglich?," 33.

46. *MEW,* 23:15–16. The English translation is from *MECW,* 35:10. In the *Manifesto,* too, Marx and Engels used birth metaphors in various contexts to underscore the "natural" dynamics of social developments, for example, "But not only has the bourgeoisie forged the weapons that bring death to itself; it has also called into existence the men who are to wield those weapons—the modern working class—the proletarians" (*MECW,* 6:494).

47. Bernstein, Guesde, and Lafargue, *Gesellschaftliches und PrivatEigenthum,* 30–31. He used this metaphor throughout his life. See, for example, Bernstein, *Die deutsche Revolution,* 1.

48. Kautsky, "Einiges über die Berechtigung socialistischer Ideen," IISH, Kautsky-FA 2094, 13.
49. Kautsky, *Die soziale Revolution*, 13–15. German chancellor Bernhard von Bülow caricatured *The Social Revolution* as the "Baedeker for the future state." See Kautsky, [Self-Portrait], 137.
50. Luxemburg, *GW*, 1/2:377.
51. Quoted in Weber, *Der Gründungsparteitag der KPD*, 183–84. She described the subsequent conflicts within social democracy as the normal "baby steps" (*Kinderschritte*) of a young and slowly maturing social order.
52. Lenin, *Collected Works*, 8:111.
53. Plekhanov, "A New Champion of Autocracy," 420.
54. See Gay, *The Cultivation of Hatred*.
55. Fetscher, *Der Marxismus*, 696.
56. Melrose has aptly described the crucial relevance of theorizing about revolution within German social democracy as a "seemingly radical alibi." See Melrose, "*Das aufrechterhaltene scheinradikale Alibi*," 302. On the socialist or "marxiological" (Melrose) discursive community, see Wuthnow, *Communities of Discourse*; Melrose, "Agents of Knowledge."
57. Morina, "Marx' Prophezeiungen"; Steinberg, "Die Herausbildung des Revisionismus Bernsteins."
58. Lenin, *Collected Works*, 5:355 (emphasis in the original).
59. In a letter to Bernstein from 23 October 1898, Kautsky wrote that what bothered him most was not "your critique of Marxism, but your attempts to reconcile Marxism and anti-Marxism with one another." Quoted in Schelz-Brandenburg, *Eduard Bernsteins Briefwechsel mit Karl Kautsky*, 795.
60. Grebing, *Der Revisionismus*, 45. See also the correspondence between Adler, Bebel, Kautsky, Bernstein, and Auer in Adler, *Briefwechsel*, 242–312. On the question of party membership, see especially 309ff.
61. Melrose, "Agents of Knowledge," 20.
62. Lenin, *Collected Works*, 5:352–53n.
63. Luxemburg, "Die englische Brille." Luxemburg wrote that Bernstein's "English glasses" affected his perception like a concave mirror, turning everything he saw upside down. For the critique of émigrés, see Kautsky to Adler (20 July 1905), in Adler, *Briefwechsel*, 464–65. Additional references are in Morina, "Marx' Prophezeiungen," 103ff.
64. See the overviews in Grebing, *Der Revisionismus*, 11–45; Joll, *The Second International*, 77–105.

CHAPTER 13

1. Lenin, *Collected Works*, 31:27.
2. Figes, *A People's Tragedy*, 173ff.
3. Daly, "Police and Revolutionaries," 647.
4. Bebel, "Ein Buch über die Revolution in Rußland," 285.
5. Putnam, "P. B. Struve's View of the Russian Revolution of 1905," 469.
6. Kautsky, "Die zivilisierte Welt und der Zar," 614.
7. Ibid., 615.
8. Ibid., 615ff.
9. Kautsky, "Die Bauern und die Revolution," 671.
10. Lenin, *Collected Works*, 8:231–32.
11. Kautsky, "Die Bauern und die Revolution," 674.
12. Ibid., 675 (emphasis in the original).
13. Proclaiming the inevitability of this dissolution was the very purpose of the *Manifesto*, Marx and Engels wrote in the preface to the second Russian edition. See *MECW*, 24:426.
14. Marx to Zasulich (8 March 1881), in *MECW*, 46:71–72. Zasulich had previously written to Marx that his works were gaining popularity in Russia and that Russians who saw themselves as Marx's students and called themselves "Marxists" were asserting that the village commune was an "archaic form," doomed by history. See *MEW*, 19:242, 572n115.
15. The preface to the second Russian edition of the Manifesto was written in January 1882. See *MECW*, 24:426: "The Communist Manifesto had as its object the proclamation of the inevitably impending dissolution of modern bourgeois property. But in Russia we find, face to face with the rapidly developing capitalist swindle and bourgeois landed property, which is just beginning to develop, more than half the land owned in common by the peasants. Now the question is: can the Russian obshchina, a form of primeval common ownership of land, even if greatly undermined, pass directly to the higher form of communist common ownership? Or must it, conversely, first pass through the same process of dissolution as constitutes the historical development of the West? The only answer possible today is this: If the Russian Revolution becomes the signal for a proletarian revolution in the West, so that the two complement each other, the present Russian common ownership of land may serve as the starting point for communist development."
16. Sperber describes Marx's formulations about Russia as "tea leaves to be read" (*Karl Marx*, 535).

17. Kautsky, "Die Differenzen unter den russischen Sozialisten," 76–77. See also Kautsky, "Die Folgen des japanischen Sieges."

18. Bebel to Adler (16 September 1905) and Adler to Kautsky (17 July 1905), in Adler, *Briefwechsel*, 468, 461 (emphasis in the original).

19. See also Kautsky, "Die Folgen des japanischen Sieges," 461n1.

20. Kautsky, "Die russische Duma," 244–45.

21. On the history of this friendship, see Morina, "Marx' Prophezeiungen"; Steinberg, "Die Herausbildung des Revisionismus Bernsteins."

22. Bernstein, "Entwicklungsgang eines Sozialisten," 33, 37.

23. Bernstein to Adler (28 March 1899), in Adler, *Briefwechsel*, 306.

24. Bernstein, "Revolutionen und Russland," 289.

25. Ibid., 291–92.

26. Ibid., 293.

27. See Bernstein, *Der politische Massenstreik*; Bernstein, "Politischer Massenstreik und Revolutionsromantik"; as well as the documentation in Grunenberg, *Die Massenstreikdebatte*.

28. For Bernstein's criticism of Luxemburg, see Bernstein, "Politischer Massenstreik und Revolutionsromantik," 14. On Bolshevism after 1917, see Bernstein, "Die mechanische und die organische Idee der Revolutionsgewalt"; Bernstein, *Die Voraussetzungen des Sozialismus*, 54–64.

29. Kautsky to Adler (21 March 1899), in Adler, *Briefwechsel*, 304; Bernstein, "Die Menge und das Verbrechen," 229, 237.

30. Beller, *A Concise History of Austria*, 165.

31. On the voting reform of 1905–7, see Sutter and Bruckmüller, "Der Reichsrat," 77–90. On the role of Adler, see Meysels, *VictorAdler*, 129–39.

32. Adler to Bebel (23 September 1906), in Adler, *Briefwechsel*, 472.

33. Adler, *ARB*, 4:94. For Adler's views on political violence, see 4:72–73, 77–86.

34. Adler to Bebel (23 September 1906), in Adler, *Briefwechsel*, 471 (emphasis in the original).

35. Adler, *ARB*, 8:271–72.

36. Ibid., 8:273–74.

37. Pollatschek, "Victor Adlers Vermächtnis."

38. Bebel to Adler (30 May 1905), in Adler, *Briefwechsel*, 455.

39. Adler to Bebel (1 November 1898) and Adler to Kautsky (7 March 1899), in Adler, *Briefwechsel*, 268, 292.

40. Adler to Kautsky (17 July 1905), in Adler, *Briefwechsel*, 460–61.

41. Helmuth von Moltke, the Prussian chief of staff, had used this formulation to describe his military strategy in the war against Austria.

See Jena, *Georgi Walentinowitsch Plechanow*, 149. Lenin, too, adopted the same German words (*Getrennt marschieren, gemeinsam schlagen!*), but, unlike Plekhanov, he meant that only socialist groups—and not bourgeois parties—should "strike together." See Lenin, *Collected Works*, 8:164.

42. Kautsky, "Die Bauern und die Revolution," 672.

43. For example, P. Lepeshinski in 1905, as quoted (without attribution) in Jowtschuk and Kurbatowa, *Georgi Plechanow*, 199.

44. Lenin to Plekhanov (end of October 1905), in Lenin, *Collected Works*, 34:365. Both men were still in Geneva, but not on speaking terms.

45. The original Russian title was *Дневник соціальдемократа*, and it was published intermittently in Geneva between 1905 and 1911.

46. See a summary of the Bolshevik reactions in Jowtschuk and Kurbatowa, *Georgi Plechanow*, 200ff.

47. Plekhanov, "N. G. Chernyshevsky," 155.

48. Lenin, *Collected Works*, 8:336; Jowtschuk and Kurbatowa, *Georgi Plechanow*, 206ff.

49. Plekhanov, "The Proletarian Movement and Bourgeois Art," 417.

50. Jaurès, *Œuvres*, 10:451–52. For context on the Parisian conference in which Struve played a leading role, see Pipes, *Struve*, 363ff. Eighteen parties were invited, but only eight attended (including Struve's Union of Liberation). The Russian Social Democrats had initially intended to participate, but withdrew at the last minute—not least because they feared the majority influence of the Socialist Revolutionaries.

51. Jaurès, *Œuvres*, 10:454.

52. A male French worker's average daily wage was around four francs in 1900; his annual income was around one thousand francs. See Institut National de la Statistique, *Annuaire Statistique de la France* (1901), 308.

53. Candar, "Les socialistes français," 366–69. Jaurès's most important articles on the Russian revolution are reprinted in *Œuvres*, 10:451–575.

54. Harison, "The Paris Commune of 1871," 6, 20, 24.

55. Jaurès, *Œuvres*, 10:461.

56. Charles Bonnier used this term in *Le Socialiste* on 7 February 1904. Quoted in Candar, "Les socialistes français," 367.

57. Jaurès, *Œuvres*, 10:446.

58. Candar, "Les socialistes français," 370; Jaurès, *Œuvres*, 10:458ff.

59. Guesde, "Radicalisme et socialisme," 531–32.

60. Jaurès, *Œuvres*, 10:454ff.

61. Ibid., 10:464–66.

62. Candar, "Les socialistes français," 368.

63. Jaurès, *Œuvres*, 10:453, 487–91.

64. Ibid., 10:490.
65. Struve, "My Contacts and Conflicts with Lenin II," 84.
66. Struve, "My Contacts with Rodichev," 365–67; Struve, "My Contacts and Conflicts with Lenin II," 81–84.
67. Pipes, *Struve*, 271–72.
68. Ibid., 271–97.
69. Struve, "Betrachtungen," 7–8. For context, see Melnik, *Russen über Russland*, ix; Putnam, "P. B. Struve's View of the Russian Revolution of 1905."
70. Struve, "Betrachtungen," 11, 15.
71. Ibid., 4–6, 11–12, 14–15.
72. Quoted in Service, *Lenin*, 177 (emphasis in the original).
73. Lenin, *Collected Works*, 10:19.
74. Daly, "Police and Revolutionaries," 647–48; Service, Lenin, 175.
75. Lenin, *Collected Works*, 10:19.
76. Service, *Lenin*, 176. He delivered his first speech before a large party gathering in St. Petersburg (using the pseudonym Karpov) only in May 1906. See also the contemporary reports in Lenin, *Collected Works*, 10:407ff.
77. Ascher, *The Revolution of 1905*, 220–21. See also Krupskaya, *Memories of Lenin*, 99–106.
78. Service, *Lenin*, 176ff.
79. See Lenin to A.V. Lunacharsky (11 October 1905), in Lenin, *Briefe*, 2:27 (emphasis in the original); Lenin to an unknown recipient (April 1905), 2:31; as well as Lenin, *Collected Works*, 8:277ff. These texts included Marx's *Class Struggles in France, 1848 to 1850*, his and Engels's *Address of the Central Authority to the League*, and Engels's *Campaign for the German Imperial Constitution*, all written in 1850.
80. Lenin, *Collected Works*, 8:159 (emphasis in the original).
81. Krupskaya, *Memories of Lenin*, 86.
82. Lenin, *Collected Works*, 8:385.
83. Ibid., 8:276–92. The quotation is on 286.
84. Ibid., 8:284.
85. Ibid., 8:287–92.
86. Ibid., 8:71.
87. Lenin to the secretary of the office of the Committee of the Majority (29 January 1905) in Lenin, *Briefe*, 2:10; Lenin to S. I. Gusev (15 February 1905), 2:12 (emphasis in the original) Eighteen issues of *Vperyod* were published in Geneva through May 1905. The journal was regularly

smuggled into Russia, and some individual articles were disseminated as pamphlets.

88. Lenin to A. A. Bogdanov (10 January 1905) in Lenin, *Collected Works*, 8:44–45 (emphasis in the original).

89. Lenin to S. I. Gusev (20 February 1905), in Lenin, *Briefe*, 2:73.

90. Lenin to the Central Committee of the RSDLP (15 September 1905) in Lenin, *Briefe*, 2:68–69; Lenin to M. M. Essen (26 October 1905), 2:99.

91. Lenin, *Collected Works*, 9:414–15.

92. Ibid., 8:107, 154.

93. Krupskaya, *Memories of Lenin*, 105–6. It is notable that Krupskaya remembered these events only hazily ("Unless my memory deceives me, we returned on the very eve of the dispatch of the Semenov regiment to Moscow"), which suggests that she and Lenin did not immediately return to Moscow after the end of the party meeting. She wrote nothing else about their time in the city, with the exception of an anecdote about a Moscow worker, who tried in vain to persuade a soldier of the Semenov regiment not to shoot him.

94. Lenin to M. M. Essen (26 October 1905), in Lenin, *Briefe*, 2:100–101.

95. Lenin, *Collected Works*, 10:94; 11:173.

96. Weber, *Der Gründungsparteitag der KPD*, 87–136. Luxemburg argued that the working class was not yet politically "mature" enough to master the "greatest tasks of world history." The masses first had to be "schooled" to fulfill these tasks, acquiring the patience to make elections a "new instrument of revolutionary struggle." She was shocked by the party conference's decision not to participate in national elections. Luise Kautsky found her in one of the conference rooms, "deeply disappointed and bitter" that the majority of participants had "completely" pushed her aside. See IISH, Alexander Stein papers, "Rosa Luxemburg," 24–25. She was absent for part of the next day, and the conference report noted that she was "physically indisposed" (Weber, *Der Gründungsparteitag der KPD*, 224).

97. Lenin, *Collected Works*, 10:390.

98. Ibid., 8:232–33, 258.

99. Ibid., 10:92.

100. Ibid., 10:491–92.

101. Krupskaya, *Memories of Lenin*, 113ff.

102. Quoted in Service, *Lenin*, 186. See the original quote in Gorki, "V. I. Lenin," 262.

103. Lenin, *Collected Works*, 11:175–78.

104. In 1920, Lenin recalled the events of 1905–6: "All classes came out in the open. All programmatical and tactical views were tested by the action of the masses. . . . Without the 'dress rehearsal' of 1905, the victory of the October Revolution in 1917 would have been impossible" (*Collected Works*, 31:27). In 1906, his view was similar (*Collected Works*, 11:171–78).

105. Lenin, *Collected Works*, 10:432–33.

106. Nettl, *Rosa Luxemburg*, 1:36 (and also 9).

107. Luxemburg to Leo Jogiches (20 October and 1 November 1905), in Luxemburg, *GB*, 2:211, 228.

108. Luxemburg to Robert Seidel (15 August 1898), in Luxemburg, *GB*, 1:185–86. For an overview of this debate, see Fetscher, *Der Marxismus*, 117–81. Nettl writes that "Rosa Luxemburg's controlling doctrine was not democracy, individual freedom, or spontaneity, but participation." See Nettl, *Rosa Luxemburg*, 1:12–13, 34–36.

109. Luxemburg to Luise and Karl Kautsky (13 July 1900), in Luxemburg, *GB*, 1:494–95. The English translation is from Luxemburg, *The Letters of Rosa Luxemburg* (1978), 83 (emphasis in the original).

110. See, for example, Roland Holst-van der Schalk, *Rosa Luxemburg*, 15–16; Stein, "Rosa Luxemburg" (handwritten manuscript), IISH, Alexander Stein papers, 25. Hirsch borrows a phrase from Bebel, describing Luxemburg as a "pike in a pond of Social Democratic carp," soft-hearted and yet "breathtakingly bold" (*Rosa Luxemburg in Selbstzeugnissen*, 28ff., 36, 41). Frölich calls her a "fighter" and a "candle burning at both ends" (*Rosa Luxemburg*, 219–32). Flechtheim describes her "physical bravery" and "intellectual courage" (*Rosa Luxemburg zur Einführung*, 68ff.).

111. Luxemburg to Leo Jogiches (21 March 1895), in Luxemburg, *GB*, 1:56–57.

112. Winnig, *Der weite Weg*, 278–79. In his National Socialist text *Vom Proletariat zum Arbeitertum* (1933), Winnig placed the meeting in 1912, and he repeated the content of the conversation without the threat (132). Frölich also cited the anecdote in his memoirs, based on a newspaper article from 1920. He considered the story believable, despite Winnig's later rightward turn. According to Frölich, Luxemburg threatened Winnig that "in the revolution, we'll have to put you against the wall!" (IISH, Frölich papers, "Memoiren," 88–89). During the German Revolution of November 1918, Winnig served as minister plenipotentiary to the Baltic provinces, leading Luxemburg to remark that he should be jailed as a "Judas of the socialist movement." See Weber, *Der Gründungsparteitag der KPD*, 193–95.

113. Luxemburg to Leo Jogiches (17 October 1905) in Luxemburg, *GB*, 2:204.

114. See, for example, Nettl, *Luxemburg*, 1:334–35; 2:730ff.
115. Ibid., 1:314–15, 325ff; Luxemburg to Jogiches, 26/27 October 1905 and 1 November 1905, in Luxemburg, *GB*, 2:221, 229.
116. Luxemburg to Leo Jogiches (26–27 October and 27 October 1905), in Luxemburg, *GB*, 2:221, 224.
117. See her letters to Jogiches from 20 May, 2 June, 20 October, 1 November, 3 November, and 4 November 1905, in Luxemburg, *GB*, 2:103, 125, 209, 229–32 (emphasis in the original).
118. See her letters to Jogiches, especially between April and August 1905, in Luxemburg, *GB*, 2:80–81, 87–93, 101–2, 112, 116, 134, 159.
119. Luxemburg to Julius Bruhns (30 March 1905), in Luxemburg, *GB*, 2:77. Gretchen's well-known words in Goethe's *Faust* are "Meine Ruh' ist hin, mein Herz ist schwer" (My peace is gone, my heart is heavy).
120. See Luxemburg, *GW*, 1/2:575, 491ff., 519–22, 587–91.
121. Luxemburg, "Die Revolution in Rußland," 573. The English translation is from *CW*, 3:52.
122. Luxemburg to Leo Jogiches (7 May, 16–18 May, and 20 May 1905), in Luxemburg, *GB*, 2:91, 101, 103.
123. Luxemburg to Leo Jogiches (25 May and 29 May 1905), in Luxemburg, *GB*, 2:110 and 117.
124. See especially her letters to Jogiches from May and September–October 1905, in Luxemburg, *GB*, 2:84–86, 91, 96, 171ff., 199.
125. Luxemburg, *GW*, 1/2:479–80, 485–90.
126. Ibid., 1/2:531–32.
127. Ibid., 1/2:480–90; Luxemburg, "Die Revolution in Rußland," 572ff. The English translation is from *CW*, 3:56–58 (emphasis in the original).
128. Luxemburg, *GW*, 1/2:577; *CW*, 3:51.
129. Quoted in Weber, *Der Gründungsparteitag der KPD*, 179.
130. Luxemburg, *GW*, 1/2:531–32; *CW*, 3:111.
131. Luxemburg, *GW*, 1/2:542–43; Luxemburg to Jogiches (10 May 1905), in Luxemburg, *GB*, 2:94.
132. Luxemburg to Jogiches (16–18 May and 4 June 1905), in Luxemburg, *GB*, 2:101, 127.
133. Luxemburg to Luise and Karl Kautsky (2 January 1906), in Luxemburg, *GB*, 2:240–41. On the workers' organizations in Moscow, see Engelstein, *Moscow, 1905*.
134. Luxemburg to Luise and Karl Kautsky (5 February 1906), in Luxemburg, *GB*, 2:248. The English translation is from Luxemburg, *The Letters of Rosa Luxemburg* (2011), 228 (emphasis in the original).
135. With a focus on Łodz, see Marzec, "The 1905–1907 Revolution," 58ff.

136. Luxemburg to Luise and Karl Kautsky (5 February 1906), in Luxemburg, *GB*, 2:248–49. The English translation is from Luxemburg, *The Letters of Rosa Luxemburg* (1978), 83 (emphasis in the original).
137. Kolakowski, *Main Currents of Marxism*, 2:88.
138. Luxemburg, *GW*, 1/2:528. See also *GW*, 2:91–170, 344–77, 378–420.
139. Lenin, *Collected Works*, 8:61; Bernstein, "Politischer Massenstreik."
140. Luxemburg to Luise and Karl Kautsky (13 March 1906), in Luxemburg, *GB*, 2:249. The English translation is from Luxemburg, *The Letters of Rosa Luxemburg* (2011), 229.
141. Luxemburg to Luise and Karl Kautsky (13 March 1906), in Luxemburg, *GB*, 2:250, 256n64. The English translation is from Luxemburg, *The Letters of Rosa Luxemburg* (2011), 230.
142. On her meeting with Lenin, see Krupskaya, *Memories of Lenin*, 112; Luxemburg's letter to the Kautskys on 11 August 1906: "The general impression of disarray and disorganization, but above all, confusion in concepts and in tactics, has completely disgusted me. By God, the revolution is great and strong, if the Social Democrats don't foul it up!" Luxemburg, *The Letters of Rosa Luxemburg* (2011), 232.
143. Luxemburg to Mathilde and Emanuel Wurm (18 July 1906), in Luxemburg, *GB*, 2:250 (see also 259).
144. Nettl, *Rosa Luxemburg*, 1:322.

CONCLUSION

1. Shore, *Caviar and Ashes*, 8.
2. The term "voluntary elite" (*Willens-Elite*) is from Niethammer, "Die letzte Gemeinschaft," 21–23; see also Weisbrod, "Generation und Generationalität in der neueren Geschichte," 4.
3. Fleischer, *Der Marxismus in seinem Zeitalter*, 203.
4. Adler to Engels (15 June 1895), in Adler, *ARB*, 1:127–28 (emphasis in the original).
5. Engels to Bernstein (25 October 1881), in *MECW*, 46:147.
6. Geyer, *Lenin in der russischen Sozialdemokratie*, 36.
7. Berlin, *The Sense of Reality*, 7.
8. See Kroll, *Kommunistische Intellektuelle*, 9–10, 85–86; Shore, *Caviar and Ashes*, 9.
9. Puschnerat, *Clara Zetkin*, 12.

Bibliography

ARCHIVES

International Institute of Social History (IISH), Amsterdam
Victor Adler papers
Eduard Bernstein papers
Alexandre Bracke papers
Paul Frölich papers
Jules Guesde papers
Karl Kautsky papers
Kautsky family archive (Kautsky-FA)
Kleine Korrespondenz (from the SPD archives)
Rosa Luxemburg papers
Alexander Stein papers

Stiftung Parteien- und Massenorganisationen der DDR (SAPMO) im Bundesarchiv, Berlin-Lichterfelde
NY 4002/1, Teilnachlass Rosa Luxemburg

Verein für Geschichte der ArbeiterInnenbewegung (VGA), Vienna
Victor Adler Archive

Hoover Institution Archives, Stanford University
Petr Berngardovich Struve papers, 1890–1982

Schweizerisches Sozialarchiv
Ar 58.31.10, Bestand des Schweizerischen Arbeitersänger-Verbands

PUBLISHED SOURCES AND SECONDARY LITERATURE

Adler, Heinrich. "Im Elternhaus." In *Victor Adler im Spiegel seiner Zeitgenossen*, edited by Wanda Lanzer and Ernst Karl Herlitzka, 19–20. Vienna: Verlag der Wiener Volksbuchhandlung, 1968.

Adler, Victor. *Aufsätze, Reden und Briefe (ARB)*. Edited by Otto Bauer and Gustav Pollatschek. 11 vols. Vienna: Verlag der Wiener Volksbuchhandlung, 1924–29.

Adler, Victor. "Beitrag in Debatte zum Arbeiterschutz auf Brüsseler Kongress der II. Internationale 1891." In *Congrès international ouvrier socialiste tenu à Bruxelles du 16 au 23 août 1891*, edited by Michel Winock, 294–95. Geneva: Minkoff Reprint, 1977.

Adler, Victor. "Die Berufskrankheiten der Arbeiter." *Neue Zeit* 1, no. 2 (1883): 97–99.

Adler, Victor. *Briefwechsel mit August Bebel und Karl Kautsky: Sowie Briefen von und an Ignaz Auer, Eduard Bernstein, Adolf Braun, Heinrich Dietz, Friedrich Ebert, Wilhelm Liebknecht, Hermann Müller und Paul Singer*. Edited by Friedrich Adler. Vienna: Verlag der Wiener Volksbuchhandlung, 1954.

Adler-Gillies, Mira. "Cooperation or Collectivism: The Contest for Meaning in the French Socialist Movement, 1870–90." *French History* 28, no. 3 (2014): 385–405.

Adorno, Theodor W. "Engagement." In *"Ob nach Auschwitz noch sich leben lasse": Ein philosophisches Lesebuch*, edited by Rolf Tiedemann, 287–307. Frankfurt: Suhrkamp, 1997.

Akademisches Gymnasium Wien. *JahresBericht über das k.k. akademische Gymnasium in Wien: Für das Schuljahr 1873–74*. Vienna: Selbstverlag des k.k. akademischen Gymnasiums, 1874.

Alemann, Ulrich von, et al., eds. *Intellektuelle und Sozialdemokratie*. Opladen: Leske + Budrich, 2000.

Anderson, Benedict. *Imagined Communities: Reflections on the Origin and Spread of Nationalism*. Revised ed. London: Verso, 1991.

Anderson, Perry. *Considerations on Western Marxism*. London: Verso, 1976.

Angenot, Marc. *Jules Guesde, ou, La fabrication du Marxisme orthodoxe*. Montreal: CIADEST, 1997.

Die Arbeits- und Lebensverhältnisse der Wiener Lohnarbeiterinnen: Ergebnisse und stenographisches Protokoll der Enquete über Frauenarbeit abgehalten in Wien vom 1. März bis 21. April 1896. Vienna: Brand, 1897.

Arctander-O'Brien, William. *Novalis: Signs of Revolution*. Durham, NC: Duke University Press, 1995.

Arendt, Hannah. *On Revolution*. New York: Viking Press, 1963.

Arendt, Hannah. "Rosa Luxemburg." *Der Monat* 243 (1968): 28–40.

Arendt, Hannah. "Rosa Luxemburg: 1871–1919." In *Men in Dark Times*, 33–56. New York: Harcourt Brace Jovanovich, 1968.

Arendt, Hannah. *Vita activa oder vom tätigen Leben*. Munich: Piper, 2002.

Aron, Raymond. *The Committed Observer: Conversations with JeanLouis Missika and Dominique Wolton*. Chicago: Regnery Gateway, 1983.

Aron, Raymond. *The Opium of the Intellectuals*. New Brunswick, NJ: Transaction, 2006.

Aron, Raymond, and Milorad M. Drachkovitch, eds. *Marxism in the Modern World*. Stanford, CA: Stanford University Press, 1965.

Ascher, Abraham. *The Revolution of 1905*. Vol. 1: *Russia in Disarray*. Stanford, CA: Stanford University Press, 1988.

Aschmann, Birgit. *Gefühl und Kalkül: Der Einfluss von Emotionen auf die Politik des 19. und 20. Jahrhunderts*. Stuttgart: Steiner, 2005.

Auclair, Marcelle. *La Vie de Jean Jaurès, ou la France d'avant 1914*. Paris: Seuil, 1954.

Axelrod, Pavel Borisovic. "Das politische Erwachen der russischen Arbeiter und ihre Maifeier von 1891: Zum internationalen Arbeiterfeiertag." *Neue Zeit* 10, no. 28 (1892): 36–45.

Bandura, Albert. *Sozialkognitive Lerntheorie*. Stuttgart: Ernst Klett, 1979.

Baron, Samuel H. "The First Decade of Russian Marxism." *American Slavic & East European Review* 14, no. 3 (1955): 315–30.

Baron, Samuel H. *Plekhanov: The Father of Russian Marxism*. Stanford, CA: Stanford University Press, 1963.

Bartholmes, Herbert. *Bruder, Bürger, Freund, Genosse und andere Wörter der sozialistischen Terminologie: Wortgeschichtliche Beiträge*. Wuppertal: Hammer, 1970.

Bates, David. *Marxism, Intellectuals and Politics*. Basingstoke: Palgrave Macmillan, 2007.

Bebel, August. "Ein Buch über die Revolution in Rußland." *Neue Zeit* 23, no. 35 (1905): 284–86.

Bebel, August. *Aus meinem Leben*. Part 2. Stuttgart: Dietz, 1911.

Beller, Steven. *A Concise History of Austria*. New York: Cambridge University Press, 2006.

Beller, Steven. *Geschichte Österreichs*. Cologne: Böhlau, 2007.

Berger, Michael. *Karl Marx—Das Kapital: Eine Einführung*. Paderborn: Fink, 2013.

Berger, Peter L., et al. *Die gesellschaftliche Konstruktion der Wirklichkeit: Eine Theorie der Wissenssoziologie*. Frankfurt: Fischer, 2007.

Berger, Peter L., and Thomas Luckmann, *The Social Construction of Reality: A Treatise in the Sociology of Knowledge*. Garden City, NY: Doubleday, 1966.

Berger, Stefan. "Die europäische Arbeiterbewegung und ihre Historiker: Wandlungen und Ausblicke." *Jahrbuch für Europäische Geschichte* 6 (2005): 151–82.

Berger, Stefan. "Marxismusrezeption als Generationenerfahrung im Kaiserreich." In *Generationen in der Arbeiterbewegung*, edited by Klaus Schönhoven and Bernd Braun, 193–209. Munich: Oldenbourg, 2005.

Bering, Dietz. *Die Epoche der Intellektuellen 1898–2001: Geburt, Begriff, Grabmal*. Berlin: Berlin University Press, 2010.

Berlin, Isaiah. *Karl Marx: His Life and Environment.* Oxford: Oxford University Press, 1995.

Berlin, Isaiah. *Russian Thinkers.* New York: Penguin, 2008.

Berlin, Isaiah. *The Sense of Reality: Studies in Ideas and Their History.* London: Pimlico, 1997.

Bernstein, Eduard. *Die deutsche Revolution: Ihr Ursprung, ihr Verlauf und ihr Werk.* Berlin: Verlag für Gesellschaft und Erziehung, 1921.

Bernstein, Eduard. "Entwicklungsgang eines Sozialisten." In *Die Volkswirtschaftslehre der Gegenwart in Selbstdarstellungen,* edited by Felix Meiner, 1–58. Leipzig: Meiner, 1924.

Bernstein, Eduard. *Geschichte der Berliner Arbeiter-Bewegung.* Part 1: *Vom Jahre 1848 bis zum Erlaß des Sozialistengesetzes.* Berlin: Vorwärts, 1907.

Bernstein, Eduard. "Ist der politische Streik in Deutschland möglich?" *Sozialistische Monatshefte* 11, no. 1 (1905): 29–37.

Bernstein, Eduard. "Der Kampf der Sozialdemokratie und die Revolution der Gesellschaft." *Neue Zeit* 16, no. 18 (1898): 548–57.

Bernstein, Eduard. "Die mechanische und die organische Idee der Revolutionsgewalt." In *Die Befreiung der Menschheit,* edited by Ignaz Jezower, 110–15. Berlin: Bong, 1921.

Bernstein, Eduard. "Die Menge und das Verbrechen," *Neue Zeit* 16, no. 1 (1897–98): 229–37.

Bernstein, Eduard. *Der politische Massenstreik und die politische Lage der Sozialdemokratie in Deutschland: Zwölf Leitsätze über den politischen Massenstreik.* Breslau: Verlag der Volkswacht, 1905.

Bernstein, Eduard. "Politischer Massenstreik und Revolutionsromantik." *Sozialistische Monatshefte* 10, no. 1 (1906): 12–20.

Bernstein, Eduard. "Revolutionen und Russland." *Sozialistische Monatshefte* 11, no. 4 (1905): 289–95.

Bernstein, Eduard. *Sozialdemokratische Lehrjahre: Entwicklungsgang eines Sozialisten.* Berlin: Dietz, 1991.

Bernstein, Eduard. *Die Sozialisierung der Betriebe: Leitgedanken für eine Theorie des Sozialisierens: Vortrag gehalten von Eduard Bernstein im staatswissenschaftlichen Seminar der Universität Basel am 24. Februar 1919.* Basel: National-Zeitung, 1919.

Bernstein, Eduard. "Utopismus und Eklekticismus." In *Zur Geschichte und Theorie des Sozialismus,* edited by Eduard Bernstein, 171–79. Leipzig, 2005.

Bernstein, Eduard. *Von 1850 bis 1872: Kindheit und Jugendjahre.* Berlin: Reiss, 1926.

Bernstein, Eduard. *Die Voraussetzungen des Sozialismus und die Aufgaben der Sozialdemokratie.* Reinbek bei Hamburg: Rowohlt, 1969.

Bernstein, Eduard. "Vorwort." In *Die Kulturanschauung des Sozialismus: Ein Beitrag zum WirklichkeitsIdealismus*, by David Koigen, iii–xi. Berlin: Dümmlers, 1903.

Bernstein, Eduard. "Wie ich als Jude in der Diaspora aufwuchs." In *Ich bin der Letzte, der dazu schweigt*, edited by Ludger Heid, 76–86. Potsdam:Verlag für Berlin-Brandenburg, 2004.

Bernstein, Eduard. "Zusammenbruchstheorie und Colonialpolitik." In *Zur Geschichte und Theorie des Sozialismus*, edited by Eduard Bernstein, 218–48. Leipzig, 2005.

Bernstein, Eduard, and Friedrich Engels. *Eduard Bernsteins Briefwechsel mit Friedrich Engels*. Edited by Helmut Hirsch. Assen:Van Gorcum, 1970.

Bernstein, Eduard, Jules Guesde, and Paul Lafargue. *Gesellschaftliches und PrivatEigenthum: Ein Beitrag zur Erläuterung des sozialistischen Programms*, Hottingen-Zurich:Volksbuchhandlung, 1885.

Bernstein, Samuel. "Jules Guesde: Pioneer of Marxism in France." *Science & Society* 4, no. 1 (1940): 29–56.

Beyme, Klaus von. *Politische Theorien im Zeitalter der Ideologien 1789–1945*. Wiesbaden:Westdeutscher Verlag, 2002.

Beyme, Klaus von. *Sozialismus: Theorien des Sozialismus, Anarchismus und Kommunismus im Zeitalter der Ideologien 1789–1945*. Wiesbaden: Springer VS, 2013.

Billington, James H. *Fire in the Minds of Men: Origins of the Revolutionary Faith*. New York: Basic Books, 1980.

Blos, Wilhelm. "Ludwig Börne: Zur Säkularfeier seiner Geburt I." *Neue Zeit* 4, no. 6 (1886): 264–70.

Blos, Wilhelm. "Ludwig Börne: Zur Säkularfeier seiner Geburt II." *Neue Zeit* 4, no. 7 (1886): 326–33.

Blum, Léon. *Les Congrès Ouvriers et Socialistes Français*.Vol. 1. Paris: Bellais, 1901.

Blume, Ludwig. "Das Ideal des Helden und des Weibes bei Homer: Mit Rücksicht auf das deutsche Alterthum." In *JahresBericht über das k.k. akademische Gymnasium in Wien*, edited by Akademisches Gymnasium Wien, 1–51.Vienna: Selbstverlag des k.k. akademischen Gymnasiums, 1874.

Blumenberg, Werner. *Karl Kautskys literarisches Werk: Eine bibliographische Übersicht*. 's-Gravenhage: Mouton, 1960.

Böck, Susanne. "Entfernung von der bürgerlichen Welt: Emma und Victor Adler." *Homme: Zeitschrift für Feministische Geschichtswissenschaft* 7, no. 1 (1996): 90–96.

Börne, Ludwig. *Mittheilungen aus dem Gebiete der Länder und Völkerkunde*. Part 1. Offenbach: Brunet, 1833.

Bolingbroke, Henry St. John. "Letters on the Study and Use of History." In *The Works of the Late Right Honourable Henry St. John, Lord Viscount Bolingbroke*, vol. 3, edited by Henry St. John Bolingbroke, 313–467. London: Luke Hansaid & Sons, 1809.

Bonß, Wolfgang. *Die Einübung des Tatsachenblicks: Zur Struktur und Veränderung empirischer Sozialforschung*. Frankfurt: Suhrkamp, 1982.

Boswell, A. Bruce. *Poland and the Poles*. New York: Dodd, Mead, 1919.

Bouvier, Beatrix. "Karl Marx in der neueren Forschung." *Geschichte für heute* 1 (2018): 5–15.

Bracke-Desrousseaux, Alexandre Marie. "Cahier no. 6: 'Jules Guesde,' *Pages choisies*." *L'OURS* 7 (1970): 1–64.

Bracke-Desrousseaux, Alexandre Marie. "La Formation de Jules Guesde." *La Revue Socialiste* 20 (1948): 371–77.

Braskén, Kasper. *The International Workers' Relief, Communism, and Transnational Solidarity: Willi Münzenberg in Weimar Germany*. Basingstoke: Palgrave Macmillan, 2015.

Braun, Hermann. "Materialismus." In *Geschichtliche Grundbegriffe*, edited by Otto Brunner et al., vol. 3, 977–1019. Stuttgart: Klett-Cotta, 1982.

Braun, Leopold. "Jugenderinnerungen." In *Victor Adler im Spiegel seiner Zeitgenossen*, edited by Wanda Lanzer and Ernst Karl Herlitzka, 59–60. Vienna: Verlag der Wiener Volksbuchhandlung, 1968.

Braun, Wilhelm Alfred. *Types of Weltschmerz in German Poetry*. New York: Columbia University Press, 1905.

Braunthal, Julius. *Geschichte der Internationale*. Hannover: Dietz, 1961.

Braunthal, Julius. *Victor und Friedrich Adler: Zwei Generationen Arbeiterbewegung*. Vienna: Wiener Neustadt, 1965.

Brecht, Bertolt. "Kleines Organon für das Theater (1948)." In *Gesammelte Werke*, vol. 16, edited by Elisabeth Hauptmann, 660–708. Frankfurt: Suhrkamp, 1968.

Bronner, Stephen Eric. *A Revolutionary for Our Times: Rosa Luxemburg*. London: Pluto Press, 1981.

Bruckmüller, Ernst. *Parlamentarismus in Österreich*. Vienna: Öbv & hpt, 2001.

Bruckmüller, Ernst. *Sozialgeschichte Österreichs*. Vienna: Böhlau, 2001.

Brückweh, Kerstin, et al., eds. *Engineering Society: The Role of the Human and Social Sciences in Modern Societies, 1880–1980*. Basingstoke: Palgrave Macmillan, 2012.

Brügel, Ludwig. *Geschichte der österreichischen Sozialdemokratie*. Vol. 3. Vienna: Verlag der Wiener Volksbuchhandlung, 1922.

Burdorf, Dieter, et al., eds. *Metzler Literatur Lexikon: Begriffe und Definitionen*. Stuttgart: Metzler, 2007.

Camus, Albert. *The Rebel: An Essay on Man in Revolt*. Translated by Anthony Bower. New York: Vintage International, 1991.

Candar, Gilles. "Les socialistes français et la révolution de 1905." *Cahiers du Monde russe* 48, nos. 2–3 (2007): 365–77.

Candar, Gilles, and Jean-Jacques Becker, eds. *Histoire des Gauches en France*. Vol. 1. Paris: Découverte, 2004.

Carsten, Francis Ludwig. *Eduard Bernstein 1850–1932: Eine politische Biographie*. Munich: C. H. Beck, 1993.

Carver, Terrell. "Marx and Marxism." In *The Modern Social Sciences*, edited by Dorothy Ross and Theodore M. Porter, vol. 7, 183–202. Cambridge: Cambridge University Press, 2003.

Chernyshevsky, Nikolai. *What Is to Be Done?* Translated by Michael R. Katz. Ithaca, NY: Cornell University Press, 1989.

Colin, Nicole, and Franziska Schössler. *Das nennen Sie Arbeit? Der Produktivitätsdiskurs und seine Ausschlüsse*. Heidelberg: Synchron, 2013.

Colquitt, Jason A., Jeffrey A. LePine, and Raymond A. Noe. "Toward an Integrative Theory of Training Motivation: A Meta-Analytic Path Analysis of 20 Years of Research." *Journal of Applied Psychology* 85, no. 5 (2000): 678–707.

Compère-Morel, Adéodat Constant. *Jules Guesde—le socialisme fait homme, 1845–1922*. Paris: A. Quillet, 1937.

Congrès ouvrier français. *Séances du Congrès ouvrier socialiste de France, 3e session, tenue à Marseille du 20 au 31 octobre 1879*. Marseille: J. Doucet, 1879.

Conze, Werner. "Demokratie." In *Geschichtliche Grundbegriffe*, edited by Otto Brunner et al., vol. 1, 821–99. Stuttgart: Klett-Cotta, 1972.

Conze, Werner. "Proletariat, Pöbel, Pauperismus." In *Geschichtliche Grundbegriffe*, edited by Otto Brunner et al., vol. 5, 27–68. Stuttgart: Klett-Cotta, 1984.

Courtois, Stéphane, Marc Lazar, and Shmuel Trigano, eds. *Rigueur et Passion*. Paris: L'Age d'Homme, 1994.

Dahrendorf, Ralf, and Christoph Henning. "Karl Marx." In *Klassiker der Soziologie*, edited by Dirk Kaesler, 58–73. Munich: C. H. Beck, 2002.

Daly, Jonathan W. *Autocracy under Siege: Security Police and Opposition in Russia, 1866–1905*. DeKalb: Northern Illinois University Press, 1998.

Daly, Jonathan W. "Police and Revolutionaries." In *Imperial Russia, 1689–1917*, 637–54. Edited by Dominic Lieven. Cambridge: Cambridge University Press, 2006.

Davidshofer, William J. *Marxism and the Leninist Revolutionary Model*. Basingstoke: Palgrave Macmillan, 2014.

Dekker, Rudolf. *Childhood, Memory, and Autobiography in Holland: From the Golden Age to Romanticism*. Basingstoke: Macmillan, 2000.

Dekker, Rudolf. *Egodocuments and History: Autobiographical Writing in Its Social Context since the Middle Ages*. Hilversum: Verloren, 2002.

Derfler, Leslie. *Paul Lafargue and the Founding of French Marxism, 1842–1882*. Cambridge: Harvard University Press, 1991.

Derfler, Leslie. "Reformism and Jules Guesde: 1891–1904." *International Review of Social History* 12, no. 1 (1967): 66–80.

Deutscher, Isaac, and Tamara Deutscher. *Marxism in Our Time*. Berkeley, CA: Ramparts Press, 1971.

Deville, Gabriel. *Le Capital de Karl Marx: Aperçu sur le Socialisme Scientifique*. Paris: Flammarion, 1897.

Dill, Wolfgang, and Günter Dill. "Jean Jaurès." In *Klassiker des Sozialismus*, edited by Walter Euchner, vol. 2, 7–26. Munich: C. H. Beck, 1991.

Dilthey, Wilhelm. *Weltanschauungslehre: Abhandlungen zur Philosophie der Philosophie*. Leipzig: Teubner, 1991.

Dilthey, Wilhelm. "2. Literaturbrief (1876)." In *Zur Geistesgeschichte des 19. Jahrhunderts*, edited by Ulrich Hermann, 8–13. Göttingen: Vandenhoeck & Ruprecht, 1988.

Dilthey, Wilhelm. *Das Wesen der Philosophie*. Hamburg: Felix Meiner, 1984.

Dirsch, Felix. *Solidarismus und Sozialethik: Ansätze zur Neuinterpretation einer modernen Strömung der katholischen Sozialphilosophie*. Berlin: Lit, 2006.

Dohrn, Verena. *Jüdische Eliten im Russischen Reich: Aufklärung und Integration im 19. Jahrhundert*. Cologne: Böhlau, 2008.

Dommanget, Maurice. *L'Introduction du Marxisme en France*. Lausanne: Rencontre, 1969.

Dornheim, Andreas. "Sozialdemokratie und Bauern: Agrarpolitische Positionen und Probleme der SPD zwischen 1890 und 1948." *Jahrbuch für Forschungen zur Geschichte der Arbeiterbewegung* 2 (2003): 43–60.

Dostoevsky, Fyodor. *Dostoevsky: Letters and Reminiscences*. Translated by S. S. Koteliansky and J. Middleton Murry. London: Chatto & Windus, 1923.

Dostojewski, Fjodor M., and Volker Braun. *Rede über Puschkin am 8. Juni 1880 vor der Versammlung des Vereins "Freunde Russischer Dichtung."* Hamburg: Europäische Verlagsanstalt, 1992.

Dostoyevsky, Fyodor. *Demons*. Translated by Robert A. Maguire. London: Penguin, 2008.

Dowe, Dieter. *"Agitieren, organisieren, studieren!" Wilhelm Liebknecht und die frühe deutsche Sozialdemokratie*. Bonn: Friedrich-Ebert-Stiftung, 2000.

Draitser, Emil. *Techniques of Satire: The Case of Saltykov Ščedrin*. Berlin: De Gruyter, 1994.

Drake, Richard. *Apostles and Agitators: Italy's Marxist Revolutionary Tradition*. Cambridge, MA: Harvard University Press, 2003.

Droz, Jacques. *Der Einfluß der deutschen Sozialdemokratie auf den französischen Sozialismus (1871–1914)*. Opladen: Westdeutscher Verlag, 1973.

Droz, Jacques. *Histoire Générale du Socialisme*. Vol. 2: *De 1875 à 1918*. Paris: Presses Universitaires de France, 1974.

Droz, Jacques. "Romanticism in Political Thought." In *Dictionary of the History of Ideas: Studies of Selected Pivotal Ideas*, vol. 4: *Psychological Ideas in Antiquity—Zeitgeist*, edited by Philip Paul Wiener, 205–8. New York: Charles Scribner's Sons, 1973.

Droz, Jacques. *Die sozialistischen Parteien Europas: Frankreich*. Frankfurt: Ullstein, 1975.

Dühring, Eugen. *Kritische Geschichte der Nationalökonomie und des Socialismus*. Leipzig: Fues, 1879.

Eaton, Henry. "Marx and the Russians." *Journal of the History of Ideas* 41, no. 1 (1980): 89–112.

Ebert, Kurt. *Die Anfänge der modernen Sozialpolitik in Österreich: Die Taaffesche Sozialgesetzgebung für die Arbeiter im Rahmen der Gewerbeordnungsreform (1879–1885)*. Vienna: Verlag der Österreichischen Akademie der Wissenschaften, 1975.

Eckert, Georg, and Götz Langkau. *Wilhelm Liebknecht: Briefwechsel mit deutschen Sozialdemokraten*. Vol. 1: *1862–1878*. Assen: Van Gorcum, 1973.

Eisengarten, Oscar. "Englands industrielle Reservearmee." *Neue Zeit* 2, no. 4 (1884): 164–72.

Eley, Geoff. *Forging Democracy: The History of the Left in Europe, 1850–2000*. Oxford: Oxford University Press, 2002.

Eley, Geoff. "Intellectuals and the German Labor Movement," In *Intellectuals and Public Life: Between Radicalism and Reform*, edited by Leon Fink, Stephen T. Leonard, and Donald M. Reid, 74–96. Ithaca, NY: Cornell University Press, 1996.

Elias, Norbert. *Engagement und Distanzierung: Arbeiten zur Wissenssoziologie I*. Frankfurt: Suhrkamp, 1983.

Elias, Norbert. *Involvement and Detachment*. Edited by Michael Schröter. Oxford: Basil Blackwell, 1987.

Elkar, Rainer. "Young Germans and Young Germany." In *Generations in Conflict: Youth Revolt and Generation Formation in Germany, 1770–1968*, edited by Mark Roseman, 69–91. Cambridge: Cambridge University Press, 1995.

Engels, Friedrich. "Die Entwicklung des Sozialismus in Deutschland." *Neue Zeit* 10, no. 1 (1891–92): 580–89.

Engels, Friedrich. "Ein gerechter Tageslohn für ein gerechtes Tageswerk." In *Ausgewählte Werke in sechs Bänden*, edited by Institut für Marxismus-Leninismus beim ZK der SED, 478–81. Berlin: Dietz, 1988.

Engels, Friedrich. "Zur Kritik des sozialdemokratischen Programmentwurfes 1891." *Neue Zeit* 20, no. 1 (1902): 5–13.

Engels, Friedrich, and Karl Kautsky. *Friedrich Engels' Briefwechsel mit Karl Kautsky.* Edited by Benedikt Kautsky. Vienna: Danubia-Verlag, 1955.

Engelstein, Laura. *Moscow, 1905: WorkingClass Organization and Political Conflict.* Stanford, CA: Stanford University Press, 1982.

Epstein, Catherine. *The Last Revolutionaries: German Communists and Their Century.* Cambridge, MA: Harvard University Press, 2003.

Erikson, Erik H. *Identity and the Life Cycle.* New York: W. W. Norton, 1980.

Erikson, Erik H. "Youth—Fidelity and Diversity," *Daedalus* 117, no. 3 (1988): 1–24.

Euchner, Walter, ed. *Klassiker des Sozialismus.* Vol. 1: *Von Babeuf bis Plechanow.* Munich: C. H. Beck, 1991.

Euchner, Walter. *Klassiker des Sozialismus.* Vol. 2: *Von Jaurès bis Marcuse.* Munich: C. H. Beck, 1991.

Fetscher, Iring. *Grundbegriffe des Marxismus: Eine lexikalische Einführung.* Hamburg: Hoffmann, 1976.

Fetscher, Iring. *Karl Marx und der Marxismus: Von der Ökonomiekritik zur Weltanschauung.* Munich: Piper, 1985.

Fetscher, Iring. *Der Marxismus: Seine Geschichte in Dokumenten: Philosophie—Ideologie—Ökonomie—Soziologie—Politik.* Munich: Piper, 1989.

Feuerbach, Ludwig. *Das Wesen des Christentums.* 2 vols. Berlin: Akademie-Verlag, 1956.

Figes, Orlando. *A People's Tragedy: A History of the Russian Revolution.* New York: Viking, 1997.

Figes, Orlando. *Natasha's Dance: A Cultural History of Russia.* New York: Picador, 2002.

Fischer, Frank. "Victor Adler schreibt ein Gesuch." *ArbeiterZeitung* 120 (1958): 9.

Fischer, Wolfram. "Der Wandel der sozialen Frage in den fortgeschrittenen Industriegesellschaften." In *Das Soziale in der sozialen Marktwirtschaft,* edited by Karl Hohmann, 103–30. Stuttgart: Fischer, 1988.

Flechtheim, Ossip K. *Rosa Luxemburg zur Einführung.* Hamburg: Junius, 1985.

Fleischer, Helmut, ed. *Der Marxismus in seinem Zeitalter.* Leipzig: Reclam, 1994.

Foote, I. P. *SaltykovShchedrin's "The Golovlyovs": A Critical Companion.* Evanston, IL: Northwestern University Press, 1997.

Foucault, Michel. "Interview with Christian Panier and Pierre Watté." In *Wrong-Doing, Truth-Telling: The Function of Avowal in Justice,* 247–52. Translated by Stephen W. Sawyer. Chicago: University of Chicago Press, 2014.

Foucault, Michel. "The Political Function of the Intellectual." *Radical Philosophy* 17 (1977): 12–14.

Frevert, Ute. *Emotions in History: Lost and Found*. New York: Central European University Press, 2011.

Frevert, Ute. "Was haben Gefühle in der Geschichte zu suchen?" *Geschichte und Gesellschaft* 35, no. 2 (2009): 183–208.

Frölich, Paul. *Politische Autobiographie, 1900–1921*. Berlin: BasisDruck, 2013.

Frölich, Paul. *Rosa Luxemburg: Gedanke und Tat*. Frankfurt: Europäische Verlagsanstalt, 1967.

Führer, Karl, et al., eds. *Revolution und Arbeiterbewegung in Deutschland 1918–1920*. Essen: Klartext, 2013.

Fulbrook, Mary, and Ulinka Rublack. "In Relation: The 'Social Self' and Ego-Documents." *German History* 28, no. 3 (2010): 263–72.

Fuller, Michael B. *Echoes of Utopia: Studies in the Legacy of Marx*. Aldershot: Ashgate, 2000.

Furness, W. H. *Schiller's Song of the Bell: A New Translation*. Philadelphia, PA: C. Sherman, 1849.

G., L. "Rezension Jules Guesde, Essai de Catéchisme socialiste." *Die Zukunft: Socialistische Revue* 1 (1877–78): 463–64.

Gabely, Emerich. "Ueber Witterungsverhältnisse." In *Jahresbericht des K. K. OberGymnasiums zu den Schotten in Wien*, edited by K. K. Obergymnasium zu den Schotten Wien, 1–44. Vienna: Anton Schweiger & Comp., 1864.

Gaido, Daniel, and Manuel Quiroga. "A Forgotten Work by Rosa Luxemburg." *Capital & Class* 44, no. 3 (2020): 443–62.

Gall, Lothar. *Europa auf dem Weg in die Moderne: 1850–1890*. Munich: Oldenbourg, 2004.

Gay, Peter. *The Cultivation of Hatred*. New York, Norton, 1996.

Gay, Peter. *The Dilemma of Democratic Socialism: Eduard Bernstein's Challenge to Marx*. New York: Collier Books, 1962.

Gerber, Jan. *Karl Marx in Paris: Die Entdeckung des Kommunismus*. München: Piper, 2018.

Geyer, Dietrich. *Lenin in der russischen Sozialdemokratie: Die Arbeiterbewegung im Zarenreich als Organisationsproblem der revolutionären Intelligenz, 1890–1903*. Cologne: Böhlau, 1962.

Gilcher-Holtey, Ingrid. *Eingreifendes Denken: Die Wirkungschancen von Intellektuellen*. Weilerswist: Velbrück Wissenschaft, 2007.

Gilcher-Holtey, Ingrid. *Das Mandat des Intellektuellen: Karl Kautsky und die Sozialdemokratie*. Berlin: Siedler, 1986.

Gildea, Robert. *Children of the Revolution: The French, 1799–1914*. Cambridge, MA: Harvard University Press, 2008.

Gillis, John R. *Youth and History: Tradition and Change in European Age Relations, 1770–Present*. London: Academic Press, 1981.

Gleb, Albert J. "Activist Subjectivities and the Charisma of World Revolution." In *Germany 1916–23: A Revolution in Context*, edited by Klaus Weinhauer, Anthony McElligott, and Kirsten Heinsohn, 181–204. Bielefeld: Transcript, 2015.

Godart, Justin. "Un grand parlementaire: Jean Jaurès." *Cahiers Jaurès* 3, no. 189 (2008): 59–72.

Goldberg, Harvey. "Jean Jaurès and the Carmaux Strikes: The Coal Strike of 1892." *American Journal of Economics and Sociology* 17, no. 2 (1958): 167–78.

Goldberg, Harvey. *The Life of Jean Jaurès*. Madison: University of Wisconsin Press, 1962.

Goodwin, Jeff, and James M. Jasper. *Rethinking Social Movements: Structure, Meaning, and Emotion*. Lanham, MD: Rowman & Littlefield, 2003.

Goodwin, Jeff, James M. Jasper, and Francesca Polletta. *Passionate Politics: Emotions and Social Movements*. Chicago: University of Chicago Press, 2001.

Goodwin, Jeff, James M. Jasper, and Francesca Polletta. "The Return of the Repressed: The Fall and Rise of Emotions in Social Movement Theory." *Mobilization* 5 (2000): 65–84.

Gorham, Deborah. "The 'Maiden Tribute of Modern Babylon' Re-examined: Child Prostitution and the Idea of Childhood in Late-Victorian England." *Victorian Studies* 21, no. 3 (1978): 353–79.

Gorki, Maxim. "V. I. Lenin." In *V. I. Lenin i A. M. Gorki: Pisma, vospominaniia, dokumenty*, edited by Institut marksizma-leninizma, 238–78. Moscow: Izd-vo Akademii nauk SSSR, 1961.

Grebing, Helga. "Arbeiterbewegung und Gewalt." In *Arbeiterbewegung und politische Moral*, edited by Helga Grebing, 13–28. Göttingen: SOVEC, 1985.

Grebing, Helga. *Arbeiterbewegung: Sozialer Protest und kollektive Interessenvertretung bis 1914*. Munich: Deutscher Taschenbuchverlag, 1987.

Grebing, Helga. *Geschichte der deutschen Arbeiterbewegung: Von der Revolution 1848 bis ins 21. Jahrhundert*. Berlin: Vorwärts, 2007.

Grebing, Helga. "Jüdische Intellektuelle und ihre politische Identität in der Weimarer Republik." *Mitteilungsblatt des Instituts für soziale Bewegungen* 34 (2005): 11–23.

Grebing, Helga. "Die linken Intellektuellen und die gespaltene Arbeiterbewegung." In *Intellektuelle und Sozialdemokratie*, edited by Ulrich von Alemann et al., 79–89. Opladen: Leske + Budrich, 2000.

Grebing, Helga. *Der Revisionismus: Von Bernstein bis zum "Prager Frühling."* Munich: C. H. Beck, 1977.

Grebing, Helga. "Rosa Luxemburg." In *Klassiker des Sozialismus*, edited by Walter Euchner, vol. 1, 58–71. Munich: C. H. Beck, 1991.

Grebing, Helga, and Walter Euchner, eds. *Geschichte der sozialen Ideen in Deutschland: Sozialismus—katholische Soziallehre—protestantische Sozialethik: Ein Handbuch.* Essen: Klartext, 2000.

Grebing, Helga, Klaus Faber, and Richard Saage, eds. *Sozialdemokratie und Menschenbild: Historische Dimension und aktuelle Bedeutung.* Marburg: Schüren, 2012.

Grimmer, Ian. "'Moral Power' and Cultural Revolution: Räte geistiger Arbeiter in Central Europe 1918/19." In *Germany 1916–23: A Revolution in Context,* edited by Klaus Weinhauer, Anthony McElligott, and Kirsten Heinsohn, 205–28. Bielefeld: Transcript, 2015.

Groh, Dieter. *Negative Integration und revolutionärer Attentismus: Die deutsche Sozialdemokratie am Vorabend des Ersten Weltkrieges.* Frankfurt: Ullstein, 1974.

Grunenberg, Antonia. *Die Massenstreikdebatte: Beiträge von Parvus, Rosa Luxemburg, Karl Kautsky und Anton Pannekoek.* Frankfurt: Europäische Verlagsanstalt, 1970.

Guesde, Benoît, and Georges Bourgin. "Jules Guesde et sa Famille en 1873." *Bulletin of the International Institute for Social History* 3 (1939): 73–74.

Guesde, Jules. *Ausgewählte Texte (AT), 1867–1882.* Edited by Claude Willard. Berlin: Rütten & Loening, 1962.

Guesde, Jules. "Le Collectivisme Devant la 10e Chambre." In *Çà et Là,* edited by Jules Guesde, 153–83. Paris: Rivière, 1914.

Guesde, Jules. "Le Collectivisme: Discours." *L'Émancipation Ouvrière: Bulletin Mensuel de la Fédération nationale de l'Industrie textile,* 1, nos. 6–7 (1894): 1–2.

Guesde, Jules. *Collectivisme et Révolution.* Paris: Impr. de A. Reiff, 1879.

Guesde, Jules. "Le Droit des Déshérités." In *Quatre Ans de Lutte de Classe à la Chambre, 1893–1898,* edited by Jules Guesde, 200–18. Paris: Jacques, 1901.

Guesde, Jules. *Essai de Catéchisme Socialiste.* Brussels: H. Kistemaeckers, 1878.

[Guesde, Jules]. "Jules Guesde chez lui." *La Question Sociale* 4, no. 179 (1893): 1–2.

Guesde, Jules. "Légalité et révolution." *Le Socialisme,* nos. 1–2 (1907) : 1–2.

Guesde, Jules. "Lettre à Karl Marx à Londres, Mars ou Avril 1879." In *La Naissance du Parti Ouvrier Français,* edited by Claude Willard, 43–46. Paris: Éditions sociales, 1981.

Guesde, Jules. *Le Livre Rouge de la Justice Rurale: Documents pour servir à l'Histoire d'une République sans Républicains.* Geneva: V. Blanchard, 1871.

Guesde, Jules. *Le Problème et la Solution.* Lille: Socialiste, 1895.

Guesde, Jules. "De la Propriété: Lettre au sénateur Lampertico." In *Çà et Là,* edited by Jules Guesde, 1–30. Paris: Rivière, 1914.

Guesde, Jules. "Radicalisme et socialisme: Discours prononcé au banquet organisé par L'humanité, pour fêter les succès socialistes aux élections législatives de 1906." *La Nouvelle Revue Socialiste* 1, no. 8 (1926): 530–32.

Guesde, Jules. "Republique & Socialisme." *L'Egalité de Marseille,* 10 January 1873.

Guillaume, Jules. *L'Internationale: Documents et Souvenirs (1864–1878).* Vol. 3. Paris: Stock, 1909.

Günther, Dagmar. "Engagement und Elfenbeinturm: Zur politischen Dimension der Literatur in der frühen Bundesrepublik und in der IV. Republik Frankreichs." In *Neue Politikgeschichte,* edited by Ute Frevert and Heinz-Gerhard Haupt, 241–67. Frankfurt: Campus, 2005.

Gymnasium zu den Schotten Wien. *Jahresbericht des K. K. OberGymnasiums zu den Schotten in Wien.* Vienna: Anton Schweiger & Comp., 1863–70.

Habermas, Jürgen. "Der deutsche Idealismus der jüdischen Philosophen." In *PhilosophischPolitische Profile,* edited by Jürgen Habermas, 39–64. Frankfurt: Suhrkamp, 1991.

Habermas, Jürgen. "Heinrich Heine und die Rolle des Intellektuellen." In *Die Moderne: Ein unvollendetes Projekt,* edited by Jürgen Habermas, 130–58. Leipzig: Reclam, 1994.

Häberlen, Joachim C. *Vertrauen und Politik im Alltag: Die Arbeiterbewegung in Leipzig und Lyon im Moment der Krise 1929–1933.* Göttingen: Vandenhoeck & Ruprecht, 2013.

Häberlen, Joachim C., and Jake P. Smith. "Struggling for Feelings: The Politics of Emotions in the Radical New Left in West Germany, 1968–84." *Contemporary European History* 23, no. 4 (2014): 615–38.

Häberlen, Joachim C., and Russell Spinney. "Introduction: Emotions in Protest Movements in Europe since 1917." *Contemporary European History* 23, no. 4 (2014): 489–503.

Haimson, Leopold H. "Lenin's Revolutionary Career Revisited: Some Observations on Recent Discussions." *Kritika* 5, no. 1 (2004): 55–80.

Haimson, Leopold H. *The Russian Marxists and the Origins of Bolshevism.* Cambridge, MA: Harvard University Press, 1955.

Haine, W. Scott. *The World of the Paris Café: Sociability among the French Working Class, 1789–1914.* Baltimore, MD: Johns Hopkins University Press, 1996.

Hall, Joy H. "Gabriel Deville and the Abridgement of Capital." *Proceedings of the Western Society for French History* 10 (1982): 438–48.

Hamburg, Gary M. "Russian Political Thought, 1700–1917." In *Imperial Russia, 1689–1917,* 116–144. Edited by Dominic Lieven. Cambridge: Cambridge University Press, 2006.

Harison, Casey. "The Paris Commune of 1871, the Russian Revolution of 1905, and the Shifting of the Revolutionary Tradition." *History & Memory* 19, no. 2 (2007): 5–42.

Hartmann, Klaus. "Engagement." In *Historisches Wörterbuch der Philosophie*, vol. 2, edited by Joachim Ritter, 500. Basel: Schwabe, 1972.

Haumann, Heiko. *Geschichte Russlands*. Zurich: Chronos, 2003.

Haupt, Georges. "Zur Begriffsgeschichte des Wortpaares 'Marxist' und 'Marxismus.'" *Forschungen zur osteuropäischen Geschichte* 25 (1978): 108–20.

Haupt, Georges. "International Leading Groups in the Working-Class Movement." In *Aspects of International Socialism, 1871–1914*, edited by Georges Haupt, 81–100. Cambridge: Cambridge University Press, 1986.

Haupt, Georges. "Marx and Marxism." In *The History of Marxism*, edited by Eric Hobsbawm, 265–89. Brighton: Harvester Press, 1982.

Haupt, Georges. *Programm und Wirklichkeit: Die internationale Sozialdemokratie vor 1914*. Berlin: Luchterhand, 1970.

Haupt, Georges. "Die sozialistische Bewegung als soziologische Realität." In *Programm und Wirklichkeit: Die internationale Sozialdemokratie vor 1914*, edited by Georges Haupt, 116–205. Berlin: Luchterhand, 1970.

Haupt, Georges, ed. *Congrès Socialiste International Amsterdam 14–20 Août 1904*. Geneva: Minkoff, 1984.

Haupt, Georges, and Jean-Jacques Marie. *Makers of the Russian Revolution: Biographies of Bolshevik Leaders*. London: Allen & Unwin, 1974.

Haupt, Heinz-Gerhard. "Frankreich—Langsame Industrialisierung und republikanische Tradition." In *Europäische Arbeiterbewegung im 19. Jahrhundert*, edited by Jürgen Kocka, 39–76. Göttingen: Vandenhoeck & Ruprecht, 1983.

Haupt, Heinz-Gerhard, and Ernst Hinrichs. *Kleine Geschichte Frankreichs*. Bonn: Bundeszentrale für Politische Bildung, 2005.

Heid, Ludger. "'. . . schreiben mir, dem Juden und Sozialisten, als doppelte Pflicht vor . . .' Eduard Bernstein—eine Annäherung an sein Judentum." In *Ich bin der Letzte, der dazu schweigt*, edited by Ludger Heid, 13–56. Potsdam: Verlag für Berlin-Brandenburg, 2004.

Heine, Heinrich. *Poetry and Prose*. Edited by Jost Hermand and Robert C. Holub. New York: Continuum, 1982.

Henning, Christoph. *Philosophie nach Marx: 100 Jahre Marxrezeption und die normative Sozialphilosophie der Gegenwart in der Kritik*. Bielefeld: Transcript, 2005.

Henninger, Max. "Armut, Arbeit, Entwicklung: Zur Kritik der Marx'schen Begriffsbestimmungen." In *Über Marx hinaus*, edited by Marcel Van der Linden, Karl Heinz Roth, and Max Henninger, 335–62. Berlin: Assoziation A, 2009.

Henze, Valeska. "Jugendbilder und politische Transformation in Polen." In *Nationen und ihre Selbstbilder: Postdiktatorische Gesellschaften in Europa*, edited by Regina Fritz et al., 255–79. Göttingen: Wallstein, 2008.

Henze, Valeska. "Ode an die Jugend." (Adam Mickiewicz, 1820). Translated from the Polish. In *Nationen und ihre Selbstbilder: Postdiktatorische Gesellschaften in Europa*, edited by Regina Fritz et al., 278. Göttingen: Wallstein, 2008.

Hertfelder, Thomas. "Kritik und Mandat: Zur Einführung." In *Kritik und Mandat: Intellektuelle in der deutschen Politik*, edited by Gangolf Hübinger and Thomas Hertfelder, 11–29. Stuttgart: Deutsche Verlags-Anstalt, 2000.

Heter, Storm. "Sartre's Political Philosophy." In *The Internet Encyclopedia of Philosophy*. ISSN 2161-0002. https://iep.utm.edu/sartre-p/.

Hilger, Marie-Elisabeth, and Lucian Hölscher. "Kapital, Kapitalist, Kapitalismus." In *Geschichtliche Grundbegriffe*, edited by Otto Brunner et al., vol. 3, 399–454. Stuttgart: Klett-Cotta, 1982.

Hirsch, Helmut. *Rosa Luxemburg in Selbstzeugnissen*. Hamburg: Rowohlt, 2004.

Hobsbawm, Eric. *The Age of Empire*. New York: Vintage Books, 1989.

Hobsbawm, Eric. *The Age of Revolution 1789–1848*. New York: Vintage Books, 1996.

Hobsbawm, Eric. "The Fortunes of Marx' and Engels' Writings." In Hobsbawm, *The History of Marxism*, 327–44. Brighton: Harvester Press, 1982.

Hobsbawm, E. J. "Hannah Arendt on Revolution." In Hobsbawm, *Revolutionaries: Contemporary Essays*, 201–8. New York: Pantheon, 1973.

Hobsbawm, Eric. *The History of Marxism*. Brighton: Harvester Press, 1982.

Hobsbawm, Eric. *How to Change the World: Reflections on Marx and Marxism*. New Haven, CT: Yale University Press, 2011.

Hobsbawm, E. J. "Intellectuals and the Class Struggle." In Hobsbawm, *Revolutionaries: Contemporary Essays*, 245–66. New York: Pantheon, 1973.

Hobsbawm, Eric. "Marx, Engels and Politics." In Hobsbawm, *The History of Marxism*, 227–64. Brighton: Harvester Press, 1982.

Hobsbawm, E. J. *Revolutionaries: Contemporary Essays*. New York: Pantheon, 1973.

Hölscher, Lucian. *Weltgericht oder Revolution: Protestantische und sozialistische Zukunftsvorstellungen im deutschen Kaiserreich*. Stuttgart: Klett-Cotta, 1989.

Hoff, Jan. *Marx Global: Zur Entwicklung des internationalen MarxDiskurses seit 1965*. Berlin: Akademie Verlag, 2009.

Hohberg, Claudia. "Probleme der Entwicklung der Beziehungen zwischen der deutschen und russischen Arbeiterbewegungen in den 90er Jahren des Jahrhunderts: Zum Briefwechsel G. V. Plechanovs mit deutschen Sozialdemokraten." *Jahrbuch für Geschichte* 22 (1981): 227–49.

Holquist, Peter. "Violent Russia, Deadly Marxism? Russia in the Epoch of Violence, 1905–21." *Kritika* 4, no. 3 (2003): 627–52.

Hübinger, Gangolf. "Intellektuelle und Soziale Frage im Kaiserreich: Ein Überblick." In *Intellektuelle und Sozialdemokratie*, edited by Ulrich von Alemann et al., 29–42. Opladen: Leske + Budrich, 2000.

Hughes, Henry Stuart. *Consciousness and Society: The Reorientation of European Social Thought 1890–1930*. New York: Vintage Books, 1961.

Hugo, Victor. *Selected Poems of Victor Hugo: A Bilingual Edition*. Translated by E. H. Blackmore and A. M. Blackmore. Chicago: University of Chicago Press, 2001.

Hunt, Lynn. *Inventing Human Rights: A History*. New York: W.W. Norton, 2007.

Hunt, Lynn. *Politics, Culture, and Class in the French Revolution*. Berkeley: University of California Press, 1984.

Hunt, Tristram. *Marx's General: The Revolutionary Life of Friedrich Engels*. New York: Metropolitan Books, 2009.

Institut National de la Statistique et des Études Économiques. *Annuaire Statistique de la France*. Paris: Imprimerie nationale, 1878, 1898, 1901.

Jackson, John Hampden. *Jean Jaurès: His Life and Work*. London: Allen & Unwin, 1943.

Jaeger, Friedrich, and Jörn Rüsen. *Geschichte des Historismus: Eine Einführung*. Munich: Beck, 1992.

Jaeger, Hans. "Generationen in der Geschichte: Überlegungen zu einer umstrittenen Konzeption." *Geschichte und Gesellschaft* 3, no. 4 (1977): 429–52.

Jaurès, Auguste-Marie-Joseph-Jean. *La Question Religieuse et le Socialisme*. Edited by Michel Launay. Paris: Éditions de Minuit, 1959.

Jaurès, Jean. "Die nichtkonfessionelle Schule und die Freiheit des Geistes." In Jean Jaurès. Aus seinen Reden und Schriften, edited by Louis Lévy, 117–19. Wien: Verlag der Wiener Volksbuchhandlung, 1949.

Jaurès, Jean. *La Constituante (1789–1791)*. Paris: J. Rouff, 1901.

Jaurès, Jean. "Cours de Philosophie." *Europe: Revue Mensuelle* 36, nos. 354–55 (1958): 126–39.

Jaurès, Jean. *Cours de Philosophie: La Bienveillance dans les Jugements*. Edited by Jòrdi Blanc. Valence d'Albigeois: Vent Terral, 2005.

Jaurès, Jean. "Einleitung." In *Jean Jaurès: Socialistische Studien: Aus Theorie und Praxis*, edited by Albert Südekum, 7–48. Berlin: Socialistische Monatshefte, 1902.

Jaurès, Jean. "Die Entwicklung des ländlichen Eigentums." In *Jean Jaurès: Socialistische Studien: Aus Theorie und Praxis*, edited by Albert Südekum, 62–67. Berlin: Socialistische Monatshefte, 1902.

Jaurès, Jean. "Die idealistische Geschichtsauffassung: Diskussion zwischen Jean Jaurès und Paul Lafargue." *Neue Zeit* 13/2, no. 44 (1894): 545–57.

Jaurès, Jean. "Kleine Anfänge." In *Jean Jaurès: Socialistische Studien: Aus Theorie und Praxis*, edited by Albert Südekum, 68–73. Berlin: Socialistische Monatshefte, 1902.

Jaurès, Jean. "Notwendige Rückschau." In *Jean Jaurès: Socialistische Studien: Aus Theorie und Praxis*, edited by Albert Südekum, 78–84. Berlin: Socialistische Monatshefte, 1902.

Jaurès, Jean. *Œuvres Jean Jaurès (Œuvres)*. Edited by Madeleine Rebérioux and Gilles Candar. Vol. 1: *Les années de jeunesse (1859–1889)*. Paris: Fayard, 2009.

Jaurès, Jean. *Œuvres Jean Jaurès (Œuvres)*. Edited by Madeleine Rebérioux and Gilles Candar. Vol. 2: *Le Passage aux Socialisme*. Paris: Fayard, 2009.

Jaurès, Jean. *Œuvres Jean Jaurès (Œuvres)*. Edited by Madeleine Rebérioux and Gilles Candar. Vol. 10: *Laïcité et Unité*. Paris: Fayard, 2015.

Jaurès, Jean. "Les origines du socialisme allemand." In *Études Socialistes I: 1888–1897*, edited by Max Bonnafous, 49–111. Paris: Rieder, 1931.

Jaurès, Jean. *Préface aux Discours Parlementaires: Le Socialisme et le Radicalisme en 1885*. Paris: Slatkine, 1980.

Jaurès, Jean. "La Question religieuse." In *Action Socialiste*, edited by Jean Jaurès, 160–67. Paris: Bellais, 1899.

Jaurès, Jean. *De la Réalité du Monde Sensible*. Paris: Alcan, 1902.

Jaurès, Jean. "Republik und Socialismus." In *Jean Jaurès: Socialistische Studien: Aus Theorie und Praxis*, edited by Albert Südekum, 51–58. Berlin: Socialistische Monatshefte, 1902.

Jaurès, Jean. *Aus seinen Reden und Schriften (RS)*. Edited by Louis Lévy. Vienna: Wiener Volksbuchhandlung, 1949.

Jaurès, Jean. *Studies in Socialism*. Translated by Mildred Minturn. New York: Knickerbocker Press, 1906.

Jaurès, Jean. *Die Ursprünge des Sozialismus in Deutschland*. Frankfurt: Ullstein, 1974.

Jaurès, Jean, and Jules Guesde. *Zum Bruderzwist in Frankreich: Zwei Reden über die Taktik der Sozialdemokratie gehalten zu Lille am 27. November 1900*. Dresden: Sächsische Arbeiter-Zeitung, 1900.

Jena, Detlef. *Georgi Walentinowitsch Plechanow: Historischpolitische Biographie*. Berlin: Deutscher Verlag der Wissenschaften, 1989.

Jezower, Ignaz. *Die Befreiung der Menschheit: Freiheitsideen in Vergangenheit und Gegenwart*. Berlin: Bong, 1921.

Johnson, Chalmers. *Revolutionary Change*. Boston: Little, Brown, 1966.

Johnson, Paul. *A History of the Jews*. New York: Perennial Library, 1988.

Joll, James. *The Second International 1889–1914*. New York: Praeger, 1956.

Jones, Gareth Stedman. *Karl Marx: Greatness and Illusion*. Cambridge, MA: Harvard University Press, 2016.

Jowtschuk, Michail, and Irina Kurbatowa. *Georgi Plechanow: Eine Biographie*. Berlin: Dietz, 1983.

Judt, Tony. *Marxism and the French Left: Studies in Labour and Politics in France, 1830–1981*. Oxford: Clarendon Press, 1986.

Jung, Thomas. *Die Seinsgebundenheit des Denkens: Karl Mannheim und die Grundlegung einer Denksoziologie*. Bielefeld: Transcript, 2007.

Jung, Thomas, and Stefan Müller-Doohm. *Fliegende Fische: Eine Soziologie des Intellektuellen in 20 Porträts*. Frankfurt: Fischer, 2009.

Der Jungfrauentribut des modernen Babylon: Die Enthüllungen der "Pall Mall Gazette" in deutscher Bearbeitung. Berlin: Bartels, 1890.

Jureit, Ulrike. *Generationenforschung*. Göttingen: Vandenhoeck & Ruprecht, 2006.

Kaesler, Dirk. *Klassiker der Soziologie: Von Auguste Comte bis Norbert Elias*. Munich: C. H. Beck, 2002.

Kautsky, John H. "Classical Marxism and Its Social Science." In *Karl Kautsky and the Social Science of Classical Marxism*, edited by John H. Kautsky, 1–4. Leiden: Brill, 1989.

Kautsky, John H., ed. *Karl Kautsky and the Social Science of Classical Marxism*.

Kautsky, Karl. "Die Bauern und die Revolution in Rußland." *Neue Zeit* 23, no. 21 (1904): 670–77.

Kautsky, Karl. "Ein Brief über Bernstein an Plechanoff: Eine Reminiszenz zum fünfundsiebzigsten Geburtstag Eduard Bernsteins." *Der Kampf* 18, no. 1 (1925): 1–2.

Kautsky, Karl. "Darwin und Sozialismus." *Gleichheit*, nos. 42–45 (16, 23, 31 October and 6 November 1875): 1f.

Kautsky, Karl. "Die Differenzen unter den russischen Sozialisten." *Neue Zeit* 23, no. 29 (1905): 68–79.

Kautsky, Karl. *The Economic Doctrines of Karl Marx*. Translated by H. J. Stenning. London: A. & C. Black, 1925.

Kautsky, Karl. *Erinnerungen und Erörterungen*. The Hague: Mouton, 1960.

Kautsky, Karl. "Die Folgen des japanischen Sieges und die Sozialdemokratie." *Neue Zeit* 23, no. 41 (1905): 460–68.

Kautsky, Karl. "Friedrich Engels." In *Österreichischer ArbeiterKalender für das Schaltjahr 1888*, 29–47. Brünn: Volksbuchhandlung, 1887.

Kautsky, Karl. "Zum Gedächtnis Jean Jaurès." *Der Kampf* 12, no. 18 (1919): 501–6.

Kautsky, Karl. "Zum internationalen Kongreß." *Neue Zeit* 22, no. 2 (1903):
     577–85.
Kautsky, Karl. *Karl Marx' ökonomische Lehren*. Stuttgart: J. H. W. Dietz
     Nachf., 1912.
Kautsky, Karl. "Karl Marx' Tod." *Wahrheit* 3, no. 7 (1883): 1–2.
Kautsky, Karl. "Der Luxus im sozialistischen Staate." *Gleichheit* 28 (15, 22 July
     and 29, 30 August, 1876): 1f.
Kautsky, Karl. "Mein erster Aufenthalt in London." In Friedrich Engels and
     Karl Kautsky, *Friedrich Engels' Briefwechsel mit Karl Kautsky*, 17–34. Edited
     by Benedikt Kautsky. Vienna: Danubia-Verlag, 1955.
Kautsky, Karl. "Die Parteien und die Wissenschaft." *Vorwärts*, no. 116 (1877): 1.
Kautsky, Karl. "Das Proletariat." In *Österreichischer ArbeiterKalender für das Jahr
     1879*, 52–57. Brünn, 1879.
Kautsky, Karl. "Die Rebellionen in Schillers Dramen." *Neue Zeit* 23, no. 31
     (1904–5): 133–53.
Kautsky, Karl. *The Road to Power*. Translated by A. M. Simons. Chicago:
     Samuel A. Bloch, 1909.
Kautsky, Karl. "Die russische Duma." *Neue Zeit* 24, no. 34 (1906): 241–45.
Kautsky, Karl. [Self-Portrait]. In *Die Volkswirtschaftslehre der Gegenwart in
     Selbstdarstellungen*, edited by Felix Meiner, 117–53. Leipzig: Meiner, 1924.
Kautsky, Karl. *The Social Revolution*. Translated by A. M. Simons and May
     Wood Simons. Chicago: Charles H. Kerr, 1902.
Kautsky, Karl. "Ein sozialdemokratischer Katechismus." *Neue Zeit* 12, no. 12
     (1894): 361–69.
Kautsky, Karl. "Ein sozialdemokratischer Katechismus." *Neue Zeit* 12, no. 13
     (1894): 402–10.
Kautsky, Karl. *Die soziale Revolution*. Berlin: Vorwärts, 1904.
Kautsky, Karl. *Sozialreform und soziale Revolution*. Berlin: Vorwärts, 1907.
Kautsky, Karl. "Die Sprache unserer Presse: Aus Börnes 'Briefe aus Paris.'"
     Vorwärts 105 (1878): 2–3.
Kautsky, Karl. *Terrorismus und Kommunismus: Ein Beitrag zur Naturgeschichte
     der Revolution*. Berlin: Verlag Neues Vaterland, 1919.
Kautsky, Karl. "An unsere Leser!" *Neue Zeit* 1, no. 1 (1883): 1–8.
Kautsky, Karl. "Viktor Adler: Erinnerungsblätter zu seinem 60. Geburtstag."
     Neue Zeit 30, no. 38 (1912): 417–27.
Kautsky, Karl. "Vorgeschichte meiner Beziehungen zu Engels." In Friedrich
     Engels and Karl Kautsky, *Friedrich Engels' Briefwechsel mit Karl Kautsky*,
     1–11. Edited by Benedikt Kautsky. Vienna: Danubia-Verlag, 1955.
Kautsky, Karl. *Der Weg zur Macht: Politische Betrachtungen über das Hineinwachsen
     in die Revolution*. Berlin: Vorwärts, 1909.

Kautsky, Karl. "Die zivilisierte Welt und der Zar." *Neue Zeit* 23, no. 19 (1904): 614–17.

Kautsky, Minna. "Ein Proletarierkind." Part 2. *Neue Welt* 1, no. 40 (1876): 378–79.

Kautsky, Minna. "Ein Proletarierkind." Part 3. *Neue Welt* 1, no. 41 (1876): 390–91.

Kennan, George. *Siberia and the Exile System.* Vol. 1. New York: Century, 1891.

Keßler, Mario. *Ruth Fischer—Ein Leben mit und gegen Kommunisten (1895–1961).* Cologne: Böhlau, 2013.

Kingston-Mann, Esther. "Marxism and Russian Rural Development: Problems of Evidence, Experience, and Culture." *American Historical Review* 86, no. 4 (1981): 731–52.

Knoblauch, Hubert. *Wissenssoziologie.* Konstanz: UVK, 2005.

Kocka, Jürgen. *Europäische Arbeiterbewegung im 19. Jahrhundert: Deutschland, Österreich, England und Frankreich im Vergleich.* Göttingen: Vandenhoeck & Ruprecht, 1983.

Kocka, Jürgen. "Das europäische Muster und der deutsche Fall." In *Bürgertum im 19. Jahrhundert*, edited by Jürgen Kocka, 9–84. Göttingen: Vandenhoeck & Ruprecht, 1995.

Kocka, Jürgen, and Jürgen Schmidt. *Arbeiterleben und Arbeiterkultur: Die Entstehung einer sozialen Klasse.* Bonn: Dietz, 2015.

Koebner, Thomas, Rolf-Peter Janz, and Frank Trommler. *Mit uns zieht die neue Zeit: Der Mythos Jugend.* Frankfurt: Suhrkamp, 1985.

Koenen, Gerd. *Utopie der Säuberung: Was war der Kommunismus?* Frankfurt: Fischer, 2000.

Kolakovsky, Leszek. "On Marxism, Christianity, and Totalitarianism." In *Totalitarianism and Political Religions*, edited by Hans Maier, 342–48. Translated by Wolfgang Grycz. London: Routledge, 2004.

Kolakowski, Leszek. *Main Currents of Marxism.* Translated by P. S. Falla. Vol. 1: *The Founders.* Oxford: Oxford University Press, 1978.

Kolakowski, Leszek. *Main Currents of Marxism.* Translated by P. S. Falla. Vol. 2: *The Golden Age.* Oxford: Oxford University Press, 1978.

Koller, Christian. "Soziale Bewegungen: Emotion und Solidarität." In *Theoretische Ansätze und Konzepte der Forschung über soziale Bewegungen in der Geschichtswissenschaft*, edited by Jürgen Mittag, 403–22. Essen: Klartext, 2014.

Korolenko, Wladimir. *Die Geschichte meines Zeitgenossen.* Berlin: Dietz, 1947.

Koropeckyj, Roman Robert. *Adam Mickiewicz: The Life of a Romantic.* Ithaca, NY: Cornell University Press, 2008.

Korsch, Karl. *Die materialistische Geschichtsauffassung und andere Schriften.* Edited by Erich Gerlach. Frankfurt: Europäische Verlagsanstalt, 1971.

Koselleck, Reinhart. "*Begriffgeschichte* and Social History." In *Futures Past: On the Semantics of Historical Time*, 75–91. Translated by Keith Tribe. New York: Columbia University Press, 2004.

Koselleck, Reinhart. "Begriffsgeschichte und Sozialgeschichte." In Koselleck, *Vergangene Zukunft*, 107–29. Frankfurt: Suhrkamp, 1979.

Koselleck, Reinhart. "'Erfahrungsraum' und 'Erfahrungshorizont': Zwei historische Kategorien." In Koselleck, *Vergangene Zukunft*, 349–75. Frankfurt: Suhrkamp, 1979.

Koselleck, Reinhart. "Einleitung." In *Geschichtliche Grundbegriffe*, edited by Otto Brunner et al., vol. 1, xiii–xxvii. Stuttgart: Klett-Cotta, 1972.

Koselleck, Reinhart. "Die Geschichte der Begriffe und Begriffe der Geschichte." In *Begriffsgeschichten*, edited by Reinhart Koselleck et al., 56–76. Frankfurt: Suhrkamp, 2006.

Koselleck, Reinhart. "Geschichte, Geschichten und formale Zeitstrukturen." In Koselleck, *Vergangene Zukunft*, 130–43. Frankfurt: Suhrkamp, 1979.

Koselleck, Reinhart. "Historia Magistra Vitae: Über die Auflösung des Topos im Horizont neuzeitlich bewegter Geschichte." In Koselleck, *Vergangene Zukunft*, 38–66. Frankfurt: Suhrkamp, 1979.

Koselleck, Reinhart. "Historia Magistra Vitae: The Dissolution of the Topos into the Perspective of a Modernized Historical Process." In *Futures Past: On the Semantics of Historical Time*, 26–42. Translated by Keith Tribe. New York: Columbia University Press, 2004.

Koselleck, Reinhart. "Introduction and Prefaces to the Geschichtliche Grundbegriffe." Translated by Miichaela Richter. *Contributions to the History of Concepts* 6, no. 1 (2011): 1–37.

Koselleck, Reinhart. "Revolution: Rebellion, Aufruhr, Bürgerkrieg." In *Geschichtliche Grundbegriffe*, edited by Otto Brunner et al., vol. 5, 653–788. Stuttgart: Klett-Cotta, 1984.

Koselleck, Reinhart. *Vergangene Zukunft: Zur Semantik geschichtlicher Zeiten.* Frankfurt: Suhrkamp, 1979.

Koselleck, Reinhart, et al. "Geschichte, Historie." In *Geschichtliche Grundbegriffe*, edited by Otto Brunner et al., vol. 2, 593–717. Stuttgart: Klett-Cotta, 1975.

Koven, Seth. *Slumming: Sexual and Social Politics in Victorian London.* Princeton, NJ: Princeton University Press, 2006.

Kramme, Monika Maria. "Anmerkungen zur zerbrochenen Einheit der Geschichte der Arbeiterschaft und Geschichte des Marxismus." *Archiv für Sozialgeschichte* 24 (1984): 593–604.

Krobb, Florian. "'Die Kunst der Väter todtet das Leben der Enkel': Decadence and Crisis in Fin-de-Siècle German and Austrian Discourse." *New Literary History* 35, no. 4 (2004): 547–62.

Kroll, Thomas. *Kommunistische Intellektuelle in Westeuropa: Frankreich, Österreich, Italien und Großbritannien im Vergleich (1945–1956)*. Cologne: Böhlau, 2007.

Kropotkin, Petr Alekseevich. *Memoiren eines Revolutionärs*. Frankfurt: Insel, 1969.

Krupskaya, Nadezhda. *Memories of Lenin*. London: Lawrence & Wishart, 1942.

Kuhn, Annette. "Exkurs—christlich-sozial." In *Geschichtliche Grundbegriffe*, edited by Otto Brunner et al., vol. 5, 815–20. Stuttgart: Klett-Cotta, 1984.

Kupfer, Torsten. *Geheime Zirkel und Parteivereine: Die Organisation der deutschen Sozialdemokratie zwischen Sozialistengesetz und Jahrhundertwende*. Essen: Klartext, 2003.

Lampertico, Fedele. *Economia Dei Popoli e Degli Stati: Introduzione*. Milan: Treves, 1874.

Langewiesche, Dieter, and Klaus Schönhoven. "Arbeiterbibliotheken und Arbeiterlektüre im Wilhelminischen Deutschland." *Archiv für Sozialgeschichte* 16 (1976): 135–204.

Lanzer, Wanda, and Ernst Karl Herlitzka, eds. *Victor Adler im Spiegel seiner Zeitgenossen*. Vienna: Verlag der Wiener Volksbuchhandlung, 1968.

Lasky, Melvin J. *Utopia and Revolution*. New Brunswick, NJ: Transaction, 2004.

Lassalle, Ferdinand. *Herr BastiatSchulze von Delitzsch, der ökonomische Julian, oder: Capital und Arbeit*. Berlin: R. Schlingmann, 1864.

Lehnert, Detlef. *Reform und Revolution in den Strategiediskussionen der klassischen Sozialdemokratie: Zur Geschichte der deutschen Arbeiterbewegung von den Ursprüngen bis zum Ausbruch des 1. Weltkriegs*. Bonn: Neue Gesellschaft, 1977.

Lembcke, Oliver W., and Florian Weber. "Emotion und Revolution: Spurenlese zu einer Theorie der affektiven Grundlagen politischer Ordnungen." *Österreichische Zeitschrift für Politikwissenschaft* 39, no. 2 (2010): 171–86.

Lembcke, Oliver W., and Florian Weber. "Leidenschaft, Affekt und Gefühl bei Max Weber—eine politiktheoretische skizze." In *Emotionen und Politik: Begründungen, Konzeptionen und Praxisfelder politikwissenschaftlicher Emotionsforschung*, edited by Karl-Rudolf Korte, 91–112. Baden-Baden: Nomos, 2015.

Lenin, Vladimir I. *Collected Works*. 45 vols. Moscow: Progress Publishers, 1960–72.

Lenin, Wladimir I. *Absender, Wl. Uljanow: Briefe W. I. Lenins an seine Mutter*. Berlin: Dietz, 1965.

Lenin, Wladimir I. *Briefe*. Vol. 1: *1893–1904*. Berlin: Dietz, 1967.

Lenin, Wladimir I. *Briefe*. Vol. 2: *1905–November 1910*. Berlin: Dietz, 1967.

Lenin, Wladimir I. *Briefe*. Vol. 10: *Briefe an die Angehörigen, 1893–1922*. Berlin: Dietz, 1976.

Leo, Per. *Der Wille zum Wesen: Weltanschauungskultur, charakterologisches Denken und Judenfeindschaft in Deutschland, 1890–1940.* Berlin: Matthes & Seitz, 2013.

Leon, Daniel De. "Flashlights of the Amsterdam International Socialist Congress, 1904." In *Congrès Socialiste International Amsterdam 14–20 Août 1904,* edited by Georges Haupt, 1081–242. Geneva: Minkoff, 1984.

Leonards, Chris, and Nico Randeraad. "Transnational Experts in Social Reform, 1840–1880." *International Review of Social History* 55, no. 2 (2010): 215–39.

Lepsius, M. Rainer. "Interessen und Ideen: Die Zurechnungsproblematik bei Max Weber." In *Interessen, Ideen und Institutionen,* edited by M. Rainer Lepsius, 31–43. Opladen: Westdeutscher Verlag, 1990.

Lepsius, M. Rainer. "Kritik als Beruf." In *Interessen, Ideen und Institutionen,* edited by M. Rainer Lepsius, 270–85. Opladen: Westdeutscher Verlag, 1990.

Lethen, Helmut, Birte Löschenkohl, and Falko Schmieder, eds. *Der sich selbst entfremdete und wiedergefundene Marx.* Paderborn: Wilhelm Fink, 2010.

Levin, Mark R. *American Marxism.* New York: Simon & Schuster, 2021.

Lévy, Alain. "Nouveaux regards sur la formation religieuse de Jean Jaurès." *Cahiers Jaurès* 2 (2001): 8–22.

Lichtheim, George. *From Marx to Hegel.* New York: Herder and Herder, 1971.

Lichtheim, George. *Marxism, an Historical and Critical Study.* New York: Columbia University Press, 1982.

Lichtheim, George. *The Origins of Socialism.* New York: Praeger, 1969.

Lichtheim, George. "Socialism and the Jews." In *Collected Essays,* edited by George Lichtheim, 413–57. New York: Viking Press, 1973.

Liebknecht, Wilhelm. *Wissen ist Macht—Macht ist Wissen.* Leipzig: Verlag der Genossenschaftsbuchdruckerei, 1873.

Lindenberg, Daniel. *Le Marxisme Introuvable.* Paris: Calmann-Lévy, 1975.

Linse, Ulrich. "'Propaganda der Tat' und 'Direkte Aktion': Zwei Formen anarchistischer Gewaltanwendung." In *Sozialprotest, Gewalt, Terror,* edited by Wolfgang J. Mommsen and Gerhard Hirschfeld, 237–69. Stuttgart: Klett-Cotta, 1982.

Loewy, Michael. *Marxisme et Romantisme Révolutionnaire: Essais sur Lukács et Rosa Luxemburg.* Paris: Le Sycomore, 1979.

Loewy, Michael. "Romantik." In *Kritisches Wörterbuch des Marxismus,* vol. 6: *Pariser Kommune bis Romantik,* edited by Wolfgang Fritz Haug, 1152–54. Berlin: Argument, 1987.

Lorm, Hieronymus. *Gedichte.* Dresden: Minden, 1894.

Lubbock, John. *Die Entstehung der Civilisation und der Urzustand des Menschengeschlechtes. Erläutert durch das innere und äussere Leben der Wilden.* Jena: Hermann Costenoble, 1875.

Luxemburg, Rosa. *Die Akkumulation des Kapitals*. Berlin:Vorwärts, 1913.

Luxemburg, Rosa. "Adam Mickiewicz." *Leipziger Volkszeitung*, 24 December 1898, Beilage, 1.

Luxemburg, Rosa. *The Complete Works of Rosa Luxemburg (CW)*. 3 vols. Edited by Peter Hudis et al. London:Verso, 2013–19.

Luxemburg, Rosa. *Einführung in die Nationalökonomie*. Edited by Paul Levi. Berlin: Laub, 1925.

Luxemburg, Rosa. "Einleitung." In *Die Geschichte meines Zeitgenossen*, by Wladimir Korolenko, 5–37. Berlin: Dietz, 1947.

Luxemburg, Rosa. "Die englische Brille." *Leipziger Volkszeitung*, 10 May 1899, 1–2.

Luxemburg, Rosa. *Gesammelte Briefe (GB)*. 2 vols. Edited by Annelies Laschitza and Günter Radczun. Berlin: Dietz, 1984.

Luxemburg, Rosa. *Gesammelte Werke (GW)*. 5 vols. Edited by the Institut für Marxismus-Leninismus beim ZK der SED. Berlin: Dietz, 1974.

Luxemburg, Rosa. "Gleb Uspenski." In *Rosa Luxemburg: Schriften über Kunst und Literatur*, edited by Marlen M. Korallov, 14–19. Dresden:Verlag der Kunst, 1972.

Luxemburg, Rosa. *The Letters of Rosa Luxemburg*. Edited by Stephen Eric Bronner. Boulder, CO:Westview Press, 1978.

Luxemburg, Rosa. *The Letters of Rosa Luxemburg*. Edited by Georg Adler, Peter Hudis, and Annelies Laschitza. Translated by George Shriver. London:Verso, 2011.

Luxemburg, Rosa. "Organisationsfragen der russischen Sozialdemokratie." Part 1. *Neue Zeit* 22, no. 42 (1903): 484–92.

Luxemburg, Rosa. "Organisationsfragen der russischen Sozialdemokratie." Part 2. *Neue Zeit* 22, no. 43 (1903): 529–35.

Luxemburg, Rosa. "Das Problem der 'hundert Völker.'" *Neue Zeit*, 23, no. 20 (1905): 643–46.

Luxemburg, Rosa. "Rezension Franz Mehring 'Schiller: Ein Lebensbild für deutsche Arbeiter.'" *Neue Zeit* 23, no. 31 (1904–5): 163–65.

Luxemburg, Rosa. "Die Revolution in Rußland." *Neue Zeit* 23, no. 18 (1904–5): 572–77.

Luxemburg, Rosa. *The Rosa Luxemburg Reader*. Edited by Peter Hudis and Kevin B. Anderson. New York: Monthly Review Press, 2004.

Luxemburg, Rosa. *Selected Political and Literary Writings*. Pontypool: Merlin Press, 2009.

Luxemburg, Rosa. "Der Sozialismus in Polen." *Sozialistische Monatshefte* 10, no. 10 (1897): 547–56.

Maderthaner, Wolfgang. "Victor Adler." In *Victor Adler—Friedrich Engels*, edited by Gerd Callesen and Wolfgang Maderthaner, ix–xvii. Berlin: Akademie-Verlag, 2011.

Maderthaner, Wolfgang. "Victor Adler und die Religion des Ästhetischen: Bemerkungen zur Wagner-Rezeption im Wien des ausgehenden 19. Jahrhunderts." *Jahrbuch des Vereins für Geschichte der Stadt Wien* 66 (2010): 105–17.

Maier, Hans, ed. *"Totalitarismus" und "politische Religionen."* Paderborn: Schöningh, 1996.

Malia, Martin. *The Soviet Tragedy: A History of Socialism in Russia, 1917–1991.* New York: Free Press, 1994.

Malon, Benoît. "Le Collectivisme en France de 1875 à 1879." *La Revue Socialiste* 2, no. 19 (1886): 990–1016.

Man, Hendrik de. *Zur Psychologie des Sozialismus.* Bonn: Hohwacht, 1976.

Mannheim, Karl. *Ideologie und Utopie.* Frankfurt: Klostermann, 1985.

Mannheim, Karl. *Ideology and Utopia.* Translated by Louis Wirth and Edward Shils. New York: Harcourt, Brace, 1936.

Mannheim, Karl. "The Problem of the Intelligentsia: An Enquiry into Its Past and Present Role." In *Essays on the Sociology of Culture*, edited by Ernest Manheim, 91–170. London: Routledge & Kegan Paul, 1956.

Marx, Karl. "Der Bürgerkrieg in Frankreich: Adresse des Generalraths der internationalen Arbeiterassoziation." In *Ausgewählte Werke in sechs Bänden*, edited by Institut für Marxismus-Leninismus beim ZK der SED, vol. 4, 51–102. Berlin: Dietz, 1988.

Marx, Karl. *Early Political Writings.* Edited and translated by Joseph O'Malley. Cambridge: Cambridge University Press, 1994.

Marx, Karl. *The Ethnological Notebooks of Karl Marx: Studies of Morgan, Phear, Maine, Lubbock.* Edited by Lawrence Krader. Assen:Van Gorcum, 1974.

Marx, Karl. "Randglossen zum Programm der deutschen Arbeiterpartei." In *Ausgewählte Werke in sechs Bänden*, edited by Institut für Marxismus-Leninismus beim ZK der SED, vol. 4, 382–415. Berlin: Dietz, 1988.

Marx, Karl, and Friedrich Engels. *Collected Works (MECW).* 50 vols. London: Lawrence & Wishart, 1975–2005.

Marx, Karl, and Friedrich Engels. *The Communist Manifesto.* Edited by Gareth Stedman Jones. London: Penguin Books, 2002.

Marx, Karl, and Friedrich Engels. *Werke (MEW).* 43 vols. Berlin: Dietz, 1956–90.

Marx, Karl, Friedrich Engels, and Ferdinand Lassalle. *Aus dem literarischen Nachlass von Karl Marx, Friedrich Engels und Ferdinand Lassalle: Von März 1841 bis März 1844.* Edited by Franz Mehring. Stuttgart: Dietz, 1902.

Marzec, Wiktor. "The 1905–1907 Revolution in the Kingdom of Poland: Articulation of Political Subjectivities among Workers." *Contention: The Multidisciplinary Journal of Social Protest* 1, no. 1 (2013): 53–72.

Mayer, Robert. "Plekhanov, Lenin and Working-Class Consciousness." *Studies in East European Thought* 49, no. 3 (1997): 159–85.

McKinsey, Pamela Sears. "The Kazan Square Demonstration and the Conflict between Russian Workers and Intelligenty." *Slavic Review* 44, no. 1 (1985): 83–103.

Mehring, Franz. *Bis zum Erfurter Programm.* Stuttgart: Dietz, 1913.

Mehring, Franz. *Aus dem literarischen Nachlass von Karl Marx, Friedrich Engels und Ferdinand Lassalle, 1849 bis 1862.* Stuttgart: 1902.

Mehring, Franz. *Schiller: Ein Lebensbild für deutsche Arbeiter.* Leipzig:Verlag der Leipziger Buchdruckerei, 1905.

Melnik, Josef, ed. *Russen über Russland: Ein Sammelwerk.* Frankfurt: Rütten & Loening, 1906.

Melrose, Jamie. "Agents of Knowledge: Marxist Identity Politics in the Revisionismusstreit." *History of European Ideas* 42, no. 8 (2016): 1069–88.

Melrose, Jamie. "*Das aufrechterhaltene scheinradikale Alibi*: The Golden Age of Social Democratic Marxism Reconsidered." *Journal of Labor & Society* 18, no. 2 (2015): 291–305.

Mergel, Thomas. "Marx, Engels und die Globalisierung." *Zeithistorische Forschungen/Studies in Contemporary History* 6, no. 2 (2009): 276–89.

Mermeix. *La France Socialiste: Notes d'Histoire Contemporaine.* Paris: Fetscherin & Chuit, 1886.

Meyer, Conrad Ferdinand. "Huttens letzte Tage." In *Sämtliche Werke in zwei Bänden*, vol. 2, edited by Conrad Ferdinand Meyer, 8–452. Munich: Winkler, 1968.

Meyer, Hermann Julius, ed. *Meyers Grosses KonversationsLexikon.* Leipzig: Bibliographisches Institut, 1905.

Meyer,Thomas. "Eduard Bernstein (1850–1932)." In *Klassiker des Sozialismus*, edited by Walter Euchner, vol. 2, 203–217. Munich: C. H. Beck, 1991.

Meysels, Lucian O. *Victor Adler: Die Biographie.* Vienna: Amalthea, 1997.

Michler,Werner. "Zwischen Minna Kautsky und Hermann Bahr: Literarische Intelligenz und österreichische Arbeiterbewegung vor Hainfeld (1888)." In *Literarisches Leben in Österreich 1848–1890*, edited by Klaus Amann et al., 94–137. Vienna: Böhlau, 2000.

Miersch, Klausjürgen. *Die Arbeiterpresse der Jahre 1869 bis 1889 als Kampfmittel der österreichischen Sozialdemokratie.* Vienna: Europa-Verlag, 1969.

Mittag, Jürgen: *Biografische Ansätze zur Geschichte der Arbeiterbewegung im 20. Jahrhundert.* Bochum: Klartext, 2011.

Mittag, Jürgen. *Theoretische Ansätze und Konzepte der Forschung über soziale Bewegungen in der Geschichtswissenschaft.* Essen: Klartext, 2014.

Mommsen, Hans. "Victor Adlers Weg zum Sozialismus." In *Arbeiterbewegung und nationale Frage: Ausgewählte Aufsätze*, edited by Hans Mommsen, 180–94. Göttingen: Vandenhoeck & Ruprecht, 1979.

Morat, Daniel. "Intellektuelle und Intellektuellengeschichte." Version: 1.0. *Docupedia-Zeitgeschichte*, 20 November 2011. http://docupedia.de/zg/intellektuelle_und_intellektuellengeschichte?oldid=106435.

Morina, Christina. "'Marx' Prophezeiungen auf dem Prüfstand seiner Erben: Eine ideen- und erfahrungsgeschichtliche Annäherung an Eduard Bernstein und Karl Kautsky." In *Prüfstein Marx: Zu Edition und Rezeption eines Klassikers*, edited by Michael Ploenus and Matthias Steinbach, 93–112. Berlin: Metropol, 2013.

Morina, Christina. "'Sowie ich den Erdgeruch von Proletariern spüre . . .': Politische Ideengeschichte als Erfahrungsgeschichte." In *Biografische Ansätze zur Geschichte der Arbeiterbewegung im 20. Jahrhundert*, edited by Jürgen Mittag, 73–88. Bochum: Institut für soziale Bewegungen, 2011.

Morina, Christina. "Szenen einer marxistischen Familie: Historischer Streifzug durch die vernetzte Lebenswelt führender Marxisten, 1871–1917." *Perspektiven ds. Zeitschrift für Gesellschaftsanalyse und Reformpolitik* 27, no. 2 (2010): 55–69.

Moss, Bernard H. *The Origins of the French Labor Movement, 1830–1914: The Socialism of Skilled Workers*. Berkeley: University of California Press, 1976.

Mosse, George L. *The Crisis of German Ideology: Intellectual Origins of the Third Reich*. New York: Grosset & Dunlap, 1971.

Muller, Jerry Z. *The Mind and the Market: Capitalism in Western Thought*. New York: Anchor Books, 2003.

Negri, Antonio. *Factory of Strategy: Thirty Three Lessons on Lenin*. New York: Columbia University Press, 2015.

Nettl, J. P. *Rosa Luxemburg*. 2 vols. London: Oxford University Press, 1966.

Neusüß, Christel. *Die Kopfgeburten der Arbeiterbewegung oder Die Genossin Luxemburg bringt alles durcheinander*. Hamburg: Rasch und Röhring, 1985.

Niethammer, Lutz. "Die letzte Gemeinschaft: Über die Konstruierbarkeit von Generationen und ihre Grenzen." In *Historische Beiträge zur Generationsforschung*, edited by Bernd Weisbrod, 13–38. Göttingen: Wallstein, 2009.

Nietzsche, Friedrich: *Richard Wagner in Bayreuth, Der Fall Wagner, Nietzsche contra Wagner*. Stuttgart: Reclam, 1973.

Nieuwenhuis, Ferdinand Domela. "César de Paepe (1841–1890)." *Neue Zeit* 9, no. 24 (1890–91): 759–66.

Nipperdey, Thomas. *Arbeitswelt und Bürgergeist*. Munich: C. H. Beck, 1998.

Nolte, Ernst. "Diktatur." In *Geschichtliche Grundbegriffe*, edited by Otto Brunner et al., vol. 1, 900–924. Stuttgart: Klett-Cotta, 1972.

Nossig-Prochnik, Felicie. "Die soziale Frage auf der französischen Bühne." *Neue Zeit* 16, no. 20 (1898): 625–29.

Nuttil, Paul. "Ein Weg zu Gott auf Grundlage festgestellter Ergebnisse der neueren Naturwissenschaft." *Jahresbericht des K. K. OberGymnasiums zu den Schotten in Wien*, 3.Vienna, 1864: III-51.

Obermayer-Marnach, Eva, and Leo Santifaller, Leo. *Österreichisches Biographisches Lexikon: 1815–1950.* Graz: Böhlau, 1965.

Opitz, Michael. "Engagierte Literatur." In *Metzler Lexikon Literatur*, edited by Dieter Burdorf et al., 190. 3rd ed. Stuttgart: Metzler, 2007.

Osborne, John. *Vom Nutzen der Geschichte: Studien zum Werk Conrad Ferdinand Meyers.* Paderborn: Igel Verlag Wissenschaft, 1994.

Osterhammel, Jürgen. *The Transformation of the World: A Global History of the Nineteenth Century.* Translated by Patrick Camiller. Princeton, NJ: Princeton University Press, 2014.

Österreichischer ArbeiterKalender für das Schaltjahr 1888. Volksfreund: Brünn, 1887.

Pankoke, Eckart. *Sociale Bewegung, sociale Frage, sociale Politik: Grundfragen der deutschen Socialwissenschaft im 19. Jahrhundert.* Stuttgart: Klett, 1970.

Paris, Rainer. "Leidenschaft—Eine Skizze." *Berliner Debatte Initial* 12, no. 1 (2001): 135–38.

Peillon, Vincent. *Jean Jaurès et la Religion Socialisme.* Paris: Grasset, 2000.

Pernerstorfer, Engelbert. "Aus jungen Tagen." In *Victor Adler im Spiegel seiner Zeitgenossen*, edited by Wanda Lanzer and Ernst Karl Herlitzka, 139–43. Vienna: Verlag der Wiener Volksbuchhandlung, 1968.

Perrot, Michelle. "Le Premier Journal Marxiste Français: 'L'Égalité' de Jules Guesde (1877–1883)." *L'Actualité de l'Histoire* 28 (1959): 1–26.

Perrot, Michelle, and Claude Willard. "Le Mouvement socialiste en France (1893–1905): Les Guesdistes." *Annales: Économies, Sociétés, Civilisations* 22, no. 3 (1967): 701–10.

Piaget, Jean, Lorenz Häfliger, and Bärbel Inhelder. *Die Psychologie des Kindes.* Stuttgart: Klett-Cotta, 2009.

Pierson, Stanley. *Marxist Intellectuals and the Working Class Mentality in Germany, 1887–1912.* Cambridge, MA: Harvard University Press, 1993.

Piketty, Thomas. *Capital in the Twenty-First Century.* Translated by Arthur Goldhammer. Cambridge, MA: Belknap Press, 2014.

Pinkert-Sältzer, Inge, ed. *German Songs: Popular, Political, Folk, and Religious.* New York: Continuum, 1997.

Pipes, Richard. "The Origins of Bolshevism: The Intellectual Evolution of Young Lenin." In *Revolutionary Russia*, edited by Richard Pipes, 33–66. Cambridge, MA: Harvard University Press, 1968.

Pipes, Richard. *Struve: Liberal on the Left, 1870–1905*. Cambridge, MA: Harvard University Press, 1970.

Plaggenborg, Stefan. *Experiment Moderne: Der sowjetische Weg*. Frankfurt: Campus, 2006.

Plamper, Jan. *Geschichte und Gefühl: Grundlagen der Emotionsgeschichte*. Munich: Siedler, 2012.

Plechanow, Georgij W. "Über die Anfänge der Lehre vom Klassenkampf." Part 2. *Neue Zeit* 21, no. 10 (1902): 292–305.

Plechanow, Georgij W. "Die Anfänge der sozialdemokratischen Bewegung in Rußland." *Volksstaat* 25, no. 76 (1909).

Plechanow, Georgij W. "Dialektik und Logik." In Plechanow, *Grundprobleme des Marxismus*, 120–31. Berlin: Dietz, 1958.

Plechanow, Georgij W. *Grundprobleme des Marxismus*. Berlin: Dietz, 1958.

Plechanow, Georgij W. "Zu Hegels sechzigstem Todestag." *Neue Zeit* 10, nos. 7–8 (1892): 198–203, 273–82.

Plechanow, Georgij W. "Karl Marx und Leo Tolstoi." In *L. N. Tolstoj im Spiegel des Marxismus*, by Wladimir Lenin und Georgij W. Plechanow, 89–112. Vienna: Verlag für Literatur und Politik, 1928.

Plechanow, Georgij W. "Die sozialpolitischen Zustände Rußlands im Jahre 1890." Part 11. *Neue Zeit* 9.2, nos. 47–52 (1890–91): 661–68, 691–96, 731–39, 765–70, 791–800, 827–34.

Plechanow, Georgij W. *N. G. Tschernischewsky: Eine literarhistorische Studie*. Stuttgart: Dietz, 1894.

Plekhanov, Georgi. *The Development of the Monist View of History*. Translated by Andrew Rothstein. Moscow: Foreign Languages Publishing House, 1956.

Plekhanov, Georgi. "Fundamental Problems of Marxism." In *Selected Philosophical Works*, vol. 3, edited by Georgij W. Plechanow, 117–83. Honolulu: University Press of the Pacific, 2004.

Plekhanov, Georgi. "Karl Marx." In *Selected Philosophical Works*, vol. 2, edited by Georgij W. Plechanow, 672–78. Honolulu: University Press of the Pacific, 2004.

Plekhanov, Georgi. "N. G. Chernyshevsky." In *Selected Philosophical Works*, vol. 4, 65–156. Honolulu: University Press of the Pacific, 2004.

Plekhanov, Georgi. "A New Champion of Autocracy, or Mr. L. Tikhomirov's Grief." In *Selected Philosophical Works*, vol. 1, edited by Georgij W. Plechanow, 411–50. Honolulu: University Press of the Pacific, 2004.

Plekhanov, Georgi. "Notes to Engels' Book *Ludwig Feuerbach*." In *Selected Philosophical Works*, vol. 1, edited by Georgij W. Plechanow, 427–76. Honolulu: University Press of the Pacific, 2004.

Plekhanov, Georgi. "Our Differences." In *Selected Philosophical Works,* vol. 1, edited by Georgij W. Plechanow, 107–352. Honolulu: University Press of the Pacific, 2004.

Plekhanov, Georgi. "The Proletarian Movement and Bourgeois Art." In *Selected Philosophical Works*, vol. 5, 398–417. Honolulu: University Press of the Pacific, 2004.

Plekhanov, George. *The Role of the Individual in History.* New York: International Publishers, 1940.

Plekhanov, Georgi. "So-called Religious Seekings in Russia: Three Articles 1909." In *Selected Philosophical Works,* vol. 3, edited by Georgij W. Plechanow, 306–413. Honolulu: University Press of the Pacific, 2004.

Plekhanov, Georgi. "Socialism and Political Struggle." In *Selected Philosophical Works,* vol. 1, edited by Georgij W. Plechanow, 47–106. Honolulu: University Press of the Pacific, 2004.

Plekhanov, Georgii Valentinovich. *Sochineniia* [Collected works]. Edited by Institut K. Marksa and F. Engelsa. Vol. 1. Moscow: Gosudartstvennoe izdatel'stvo, 1923.

Plekhanov, Georgii Valentinovich. *Sochineniia* [Collected works]. Edited by Institut K. Marksa and F. Engelsa. Vol. 3. Moscow: Gosudartstvennoe izdatel'stvo, 1923.

Plekhanov, Georgii Valentinovich. В. Г. Белинскии. Речь, произнесенная весною 1898 года по случаю пятидесятилетия со дня смерти Белинского на русских собраниях в Женеве, Цюрихе и Берне [W. G. Belinsky, speech given in the spring of 1898 on the 50th anniversary of his death, at Russian gatherings in Geneva, Zurich, and Bern]. In Plekahnov, *Sochineniia,* vol. 10, 317–49. Moscow: Gosudartstvennoe izdatel'stvo, 1923.

Plekhanov, Georgii Valentinovich. Закон экономического развития общества и задачи социализма в Россиип [The law of economic development in society and the problems of socialism in Russia]. In Plekahnov, *Sochineniia,* vol. 1, 56–74. Moscow: Gosudartstvennoe izdatel'stvo, 1923.

Plekhanov, Georgii Valentinovich. Русский рабочий в революционном движении [The Russian workers and the revolutionary movement]. In Plekahnov, *Sochineniia,* vol. 3, 121–205. Moscow: Gosudartstvennoe izdatel'stvo, 1923.

Polexe, Laura. *Netzwerke und Freundschaft: Sozialdemokraten in Rumänien, Russland und der Schweiz an der Schwelle zum 20. Jahrhundert.* Göttingen: V & R Unipress, 2011.

Pollatschek, Gustav. "Victor Adlers Vermächtnis." *Arbeiter-Zeitung,* 24 June 1932, 1–2.

Pomper, Philip. *Lenin's Brother: The Origins of the October Revolution*. New York: W. W. Norton, 2010.

Pomper, Philip. *The Russian Revolutionary Intelligentsia*. New York: Crowell, 1970.

Popper, Karl. *Lesebuch: Ausgewählte Texte zu Erkenntnistheorie, Philosophie der Naturwissenschaften, Metaphysik, Sozialphilosophie*. Tübingen: Mohr, 1995.

Porter, Theodore M. *Karl Pearson: The Scientific Life in a Statistical Age*. Princeton, NJ: Princeton University Press, 2004.

Potresov, Alexander. "Lenin: Versuch einer Charakterisierung." *Die Gesellschaft* 2 (1927): 405–18.

Prochasson, Christophe. *Les Intellectuels et le Socialisme: XIXe–XXe siècle*. Paris: Plon, 1997.

Prochasson, Christophe. "L'invention du Marxisme Français." In *Histoire des Gauches en France*, edited by Gilles Candar and Jean-Jacques Becker, vol. 1, 426–43. Paris: Découverte, 2004.

Puschnerat, Tânia. *Clara Zetkin—Bürgerlichkeit und Marxismus: Eine Biographie*. Essen: Klartext, 2003.

Putnam, George. "P. B. Struve's View of the Russian Revolution of 1905." *Slavonic and East European Review* 45, no. 105 (1967): 457–73.

Puttkamer, Joachim von. *Fabrikgesetzgebung in Russland vor 1905: Regierung und Unternehmerschaft beim Ausgleich ihrer Interessen in einer vorkonstitutionellen Ordnung*. Cologne: Böhlau, 1996.

Quante, Michael. "Die fragile Einheit des Marxschen Denkens: Neuere Literatur zur Philosophie von Karl Marx." *Zeitschrift für philosophische Forschung* 60, no. 4 (2006): 590–608.

Quante, Michael, and David P. Schweikard, eds. *Marx-Handbuch: Leben—Werk—Wirkung*. Stuttgart: J. B. Metzler, 2016.

Rabinowitz, Sonja. *Zur Entwicklung der Arbeiterbewegung in Rußland bis zur großen Revolution von 1905*. Berlin: Springer, 1914.

Raphael, Lutz. "Embedding the Human and Social Sciences in Western Societies, 1880–1980: Reflections on Trends and Methods of Current Research." In *Engineering Society: The Role of the Human and Social Sciences in Modern Societies, 1880–1980*, edited by Kerstin Brückweh et al., 41–58. Basingstoke: Palgrave Macmillan, 2012.

Raphael, Lutz. "Die Verwissenschaftlichung des Sozialen als methodische und konzeptionelle Herausforderung für eine Sozialgeschichte des 20. Jahrhunderts." *Geschichte und Gesellschaft* 22, no. 2 (1996): 165–93.

Rappoport, Charles. "Jules Guesde und die französische Arbeiterbewegung." Part 1. *Neue Zeit* 26, no. 14 (1907): 469–76.

Rappoport, Charles. "Jules Guesde und die französische Arbeiterbewegung."
Part 2. *Neue Zeit* 26, no. 15 (1907): 512–21.

Rattner, Josef, and Gerhard Danzer. *Die Junghegelianer: Porträt einer progressiven Intellektuellengruppe.* Würzburg: Königshausen & Neumann, 2005.

Rebérioux, Madeleine. "Jean Jaurès et le Marxisme." In *Histoire du Marxisme Contemporain*, edited by Dominique-Antoine Grisoni, vol. 3, 205–45. Paris: Union générale d'éditions, 1977.

Rebérioux, Madeleine. "Le socialisme Français de 1871 à 1914." In *Histoire Générale du Socialisme*, vol. 2: *De 1875 à 1918,* edited by Jacques Droz, 133–236. Paris: Presses Universitaires de France, 1974.

Resis, Albert. "Das Kapital Comes to Russia." *Slavic Review* 29, no. 2 (1970): 219–37.

Ringer, Fritz K. "Die Zulassung zur Universität." In *Geschichte der Universität in Europa*, edited by Walter Rüegg, 199–226. Munich: C. H. Beck, 2004.

Ritsert, Jürgen. *Ideologie: Theoreme und Probleme der Wissenssoziologie.* Münster: Westfälisches Dampfboot, 2002.

Ritter, Gerhard A. *Soziale Frage und Sozialpolitik in Deutschland seit Beginn des 19. Jahrhunderts.* Leverkusen: Leske + Budrich, 1998.

Ritter, Gerhard A., and Klaus Tenfelde. *Arbeiter im Deutschen Kaiserreich: 1871 bis 1914.* Bonn: Dietz, 1992.

Röder, Petra. *Utopische Romantik, die verdrängte Tradition im Marxismus: Von der frühromantischen Poetologie zur marxistischen Gesellschaftstheorie.* Würzburg: Königshausen + Neumann, 1982.

Rohrwasser, Michael. "Religions- und kirchenähnliche Strukturen im Kommunismus und Nationalsozialismus und die Rolle des Schriftstellers." In *"Totalitarismus" und "politische Religionen,"* edited by Hans Maier, 384–400. Paderborn: Schöningh, 1996.

Roland Holst-van der Schalk, Henriette: *Rosa Luxemburg: Ihr Leben und Wirken.* Zurich: Jean Christophe-Verlag, 1937.

Roseman, Mark. "Generationen als 'Imagined Communities': Mythen, generationelle Identitäten und Generationenkonflikte in Deutschland vom 18. bis zum 20. Jahrhundert." In *Generationen: Zur Relevanz eines wissenschaftlichen Grundbegriffs*, edited by Ulrike Jureit, 180–99. Hamburg: Hamburger Edition, 2005.

Roseman, Mark, ed. *Generations in Conflict: Youth Revolt and Generation Formation in Germany, 1770–1968.* Cambridge: Cambridge University Press, 1995.

Rotter, Julian B. *Social Learning and Clinical Psychology.* Englewood Cliffs, NJ: Prentice-Hall, 1954.

Rucht, Dieter. "Zum Stand der Forschung zu sozialen Bewegungen." In *Theoretische Ansätze und Konzepte der Forschung über soziale Bewegungen in der Geschichtswissenschaft*, edited by Jürgen Mittag, 61–88. Essen: Klartext, 2014.

Saage, Richard. *Industrielle Revolution und Technischer Staat im 19. Jahrhundert.* Münster: Lit, 2002.

Saage, Richard. *Zwischen Darwin und Marx: Zur Rezeption der Evolutionstheorie in der Deutschen und der Österreichischen Sozialdemokratie vor 1933/34.* Cologne: Böhlau, 2012.

Safranski, Rüdiger. *Romantik: Eine deutsche Affäre.* Munich: Hanser, 2007.

Sand, George. *Novels.* Vol. 6: *The Sin of Monsieur Antoine (Vol. 2).* Boston: Jefferson Press, 1902.

Sandgruber, Roman. *Die Anfänge der Konsumgesellschaft. Konsumgüterverbrauch, Lebensstandard und Alltagskultur in Österreich im 18. und 19. Jahrhundert.* Vienna: Verlag für Geschichte und Politik, 1982.

Sartre, Jean-Paul. "Why Write?" In *What Is Literature?*, edited by Jean-Paul Sartre, 38–66. Translated by Bernard Frechtman. New York: Philosophical Library, 1949.

Schacherl, Michael. "Einleitung." In *Victor Adler über Arbeiterschutz und Sozialreform*, edited by Otto Bauer et al., 3–7. Vienna: Wiener Volksbuchhandlung, 1925.

Schelsky, Helmut. *Die Arbeit tun die anderen: Klassenkampf und Priesterherrschaft der Intellektuellen.* Opladen: Westdeutscher Verlag, 1975.

Schelz-Brandenburg, Till, ed. *Eduard Bernsteins Briefwechsel mit Karl Kautsky (1895–1905).* Frankfurt: Campus, 2003.

Schickl, Sebastian D. *Universalismus und Partikularismus: Erfahrungsraum, Erwartungshorizont und Territorialdebatten in der diskursiven Praxis der II. Internationale 1889–1917.* St. Ingbert: Röhrig Universitätsverlag, 2012.

Schieder, Wolfgang. *Karl Marx als Politiker.* Munich: Piper, 1991.

Schieder, Wolfgang. "Sozialismus." In *Geschichtliche Grundbegriffe*, edited by Otto Brunner et al., vol. 5, 923–96. Stuttgart: Klett-Cotta, 1984.

Schiller, Friedrich. *Wallenstein: A Dramatic Poem.* Translated by Flora Kimmich. Cambridge, UK: Open Books. https://books.openedition.org/obp/3851.

Schmidt, Jürgen. *August Bebel: Kaiser der Arbeiter: Eine Biografie.* Zurich: Rotpunktverlag, 2013.

Schmitt, Carl. *Politische Romantik.* Munich: Duncker & Humblot, 1925.

Schönhoven, Klaus, and Bernd Braun, eds. *Generationen in der Arbeiterbewegung.* Munich: Oldenbourg, 2005.

Schopenhauer, Arthur. *The World as Will and Representation.* Vol. 1. Translated by E. F. J. Payne. New York: Dover, 1969.

Schultz, Helga. *Europäischer Sozialismus—immer anders.* Berlin: BWV, 2014.

Schulze-Delitzsch, Hermann. *Capitel zu einem deutschen Arbeiterkatechismus: Sechs Vorträge vor dem Berliner Arbeiterverein*. Leipzig: Keil, 1863.

Schütz, Alfred. *The Phenomenology of the Social World*. Translated by George Walsh and Frederick Lehnert. Evanston, IL: Northwestern University Press, 1967.

Schütz, Alfred. *Der sinnhafte Aufbau der sozialen Welt: Eine Einleitung in die verstehende Soziologie*. Konstanz: UVK Verlagsgesellschaft, 2004.

Schütz, Alfred, and Thomas Luckmann. *Strukturen der Lebenswelt*. Stuttgart: UTB, 2003.

Schwarz, Werner Michael, Margarethe Szeless, and Lisa Wögenstein. "Bilder des Elends in der Großstadt (1830–1930)." In *Ganz unten: Die Entdeckung des Elends*, edited by Werner Michael Schwarz, Margarethe Szeless, and Lisa Wögenstein, 9–17. Vienna: Brandstätter, 2007.

Schwarz, Werner Michael, Margarethe Szeless, and Lisa Wögenstein, eds. *Ganz unten: Die Entdeckung des Elends*. Vienna: Brandstätter, 2007.

Sensales, Alfredo. "The Catholic Organicism of Fedele Lampertico." In *Humanism and Religion in the History of Economic Thought*, edited by Daniela Parisi Acquaviva und Stefano Solari, 188–224. Milan: Angeli, 2010.

Service, Robert. *Lenin: A Biography*. Cambridge, MA: Harvard University Press, 2000.

Shore, Marci. *Caviar and Ashes: A Warsaw Generation's Life and Death in Marxism, 1918–1968*. New Haven, CT: Yale University Press, 2006.

Siljak, Ana. *Angel of Vengeance: The Girl Who Shot the Governor of St. Petersburg and Sparked the Age of Assassination*. New York: St. Martin's Press, 2008.

Soulé, Louis. *La Vie de Jaurès, 1859–1892*. Paris: Émancipatrice, 1921.

Sperber, Jonathan. *Karl Marx: A Nineteenth-Century Life*. New York: Liveright, 2013.

Stadler-Labhart, Verena. *Rosa Luxemburg an der Universität Zürich 1889–1897*. Zurich: Rohr, 1978.

Stead, William T. *The Maiden Tribute of Modern Babylon: The Report of Our Secret Commission*. Charleston, SC: Lowood Press, 2011.

Steenson, Gary P. *After Marx, before Lenin: Marxism and Socialist Working Class Parties in Europe, 1884–1914*. Pittsburgh, PA: University of Pittsburgh Press, 1991.

Steenson, Gary P. "Early Assumptions, Preconceptions and Prejudices." In *Karl Kautsky and the Social Science of Classical Marxism*, edited by John H. Kautsky, 33–43. Leiden: Brill, 1989.

Steenson, Gary P. *Karl Kautsky, 1854–1938: Marxism in the Classical Years*. Pittsburgh, PA: University of Pittsburgh Press, 1978.

Steger, Manfred B. *The Quest for Evolutionary Socialism: Eduard Bernstein and Social Democracy*. Cambridge: Cambridge University Press, 1997.

Stein, Ludwig. *Aus dem Leben eines Optimisten*. Berlin: Brückenverlag, 1930.

Steinbach, Günther. "Engelbert Pernerstorfer." In *Werk und Widerhall*, edited by Norbert Leser, 274–84. Vienna: Verlag der Volksbuchhandlung, 1964.

Steinbach, Matthias. *Ökonomisten, Philanthropen, Humanitäre: Professorensozialismus in der akademischen Provinz.* Berlin: Metropol, 2008.

Steinberg, Hans-Josef. "Die Herausbildung des Revisionismus Bernsteins im Lichte des Briefwechsels Bernstein-Kautsky." In *Bernstein und der demokratische Sozialismus*, edited by Horst Heimann and Thomas Meyer, 37–46. Berlin: Dietz, 1978.

Steinberg, Hans-Josef. "Karl Kautsky und Eduard Bernstein." In *Deutsche Historiker*, edited by Hans-Ulrich Wehler, vol. 1, 53–62. Göttingen: Vandenhoeck & Ruprecht, 1973.

Strobel, Georg W. *Die Partei Rosa Luxemburgs, Lenin und die SPD: Der polnische "europäische" Internationalismus in der russischen Sozialdemokratie.* Wiesbaden: Franz Steiner, 1974.

Struve, Peter. "Betrachtungen über die russische Revolution." In *Russen über Russland*, edited by Josef Melnik, 1–15. Frankfurt: Rütten & Loening, 1906.

Struve, Petr B. *Collected Works.* Vol. 1: *First Writings, 1892–1895*, and Vol. 3: *Revisionism, 1898–1900.* Edited by Richard Pipes. Ann Arbor, MI: University Microfilms, 1970.

Struve, Peter von. "Die Marxsche Theorie der sozialen Entwicklung: Ein kritischer Versuch." *Archiv für soziale Gesetzgebung und Statistik* 14 (1899): 658–704.

Struve, Petr B. "Introduction to Karl Marx, Capital" [in Russian]. In *Collected Works*, vol. 3: *Revisionism, 1898–1900*, edited by Richard Pipes, xxvii–xxxiv. Ann Arbor, MI: University Microfilms, 1970.

Struve, Peter. "Ivan Aksakov." *Slavonic Review* 2, no. 6 (1924): 514–18.

Struve, Peter. "Leo Tolstoj." *Jahrbücher für Kultur und Geschichte der Slaven* 9, nos. 1–2 (1933): 5–36.

Struve, Peter. "My Contacts and Conflicts with Lenin I." *Slavonic Review* 12, no. 36 (1934): 573–95.

Struve, Peter. "My Contacts and Conflicts with Lenin II." *Slavonic Review* 13 (1934): 66–84.

Struve, Peter. "My Contacts with Rodichev." *Slavonic Review* 12, no. 35 (1934): 347–67.

Struve, Peter von. "Zwei bisher unbekannte Aufsätze von Karl Marx aus den vierziger Jahren: Ein Beitrag zur Entstehungsgeschichte des wissenschaftlichen Sozialismus." *Neue Zeit* 14, no. 27 (1895): 4–11, 48–55.

Stuart, Robert. *Marxism at Work: Ideology, Class, and French Socialism during the Third Republic.* Cambridge: Cambridge University Press, 1992.

Südekum, Albert, ed. *Jean Jaurès: Socialistische Studien: Aus Theorie und Praxis.* Berlin: Socialistische Monatshefte, 1902.

Sutter, Berthold, and Ernst Bruckmüller. "Der Reichsrat, das Parlament der westlichen Reichshälfte Österreich-Ungarns (1861–1918)." In *Parlamentarismus in Österreich*, edited by Ernst Bruckmüller, 60–109. Vienna: Öbv & hpt, 2001.

Swaan, Abram de. *Der sorgende Staat: Wohlfahrt, Gesundheit und Bildung in Europa und den USA der Neuzeit.* Frankfurt: Campus, 1993.

Symmachos [Karl Kautsky]. "Die soziale Frage vom Standpunkt des Kopfarbeiters aus betrachtet." *Der Volksstaat*, nos. 109–116 (17, 22, 24, 29 September and 1, 6, 8 October 1875): 1.

Symmachos [Karl Kautsky]. "Der Kampf um's Dasein in der Menschenwelt." *Vorwärts*, nos. 38–42 (30 March and 1, 6, 8, 11 April 1877): 1–2.

Tacke, Charlotte. "Von der Zweiten Republik bis zum Ersten Weltkrieg (1848– 1914)." In *Kleine Geschichte Frankreichs*, edited by Heinz-Gerhard Haupt and Ernst Hinrichs, 311–60. Bonn: Bundeszentrale für Politische Bildung, 2005.

Tennstedt, Florian. "Arbeiterbewegung und Familiengeschichte bei Eduard Bernstein und Ignaz Zadek." *Internationale Wissenschaftliche Korrespondenz zur Geschichte der deutschen Arbeiterbewegung.* 18, no. 4 (1982): 451–81.

Ternes, Bernd. *Karl Marx: Eine Einführung.* Konstanz: UTB, 2008.

Tolstoï, Lyof N. *The Novels and Other Works of Lyof N. Tolstoï.* Vol. 1: *Essays, Letters, Miscellanies.* New York: Charles Scribner's Sons, 1913.

Tolstoy, Leo. "On Popular Education." In *Fables for Children*, edited and translated by Leo Wiener, 251–326. Boston: Dan Estes, 1904.

Tucker, Robert C. "Marxism—Is It Religion?" *Ethics* 68, no. 2 (1958): 125–30.

Uspensky, G. I., and A. N. Terpigoriew. *Verlumpung der Bauern und des Adels in Russland.* Edited by H. von Samson-Himmelstjerna. Leipzig: Duncker & Humblot, 1892.

Van der Linden, Marcel. *Workers of the World: Essays toward a Global Labor History,* Leiden: Brill, 2008.

Van der Linden, Marcel, and Karl Heinz Roth. "Einleitung." In *Über Marx hinaus*, edited by Marcel Van der Linden, Karl Heinz Roth, and Max Henninger, 7–28. Berlin: Assoziation A, 2009.

Van der Linden, Marcel, Karl Heinz Roth, and Max Henninger, eds. *Über Marx hinaus: Arbeitsgeschichte und Arbeitsbegriff in der Konfrontation mit den globalen Arbeitsverhältnissen des 21. Jahrhunderts.* Berlin: Assoziation A, 2009.

Van Ree, Erik. "Georgii Plekhanov and the Communist Manifesto: The Proletarian Revolution Revisited." *Revolutionary Russia* 26, no. 1 (2013): 32–51.

Van Ree, Erik. "German Marxism and the Decline of the Permanent Revolution, 1870–1909." *History of European Ideas* 38, no. 4 (2011): 570–89.

Vasold, Georg. "'Die vielen stillen und lauten Tragödien des Großstadtlebens': Elendsdarstellungen von Käthe Kollwitz." In *Ganz unten: Die Entdeckung des Elends*, edited by Werner Michael Schwarz, Margarethe Szeless, and Lisa Wögenstein, 139–47. Vienna: Brandstätter, 2007.

Venturi, Franco. *Roots of Revolution: A History of the Populist and Socialist Movements in 19th Century Russia.* Translated by Francis Haskell. London: Phoenix, 2001.

Verheyen, Nina. "Geschichte der Gefühle." Version: 1.0. *Docupedia-Zeitgeschichte*, 18 June 2010. https://docupedia.de/zg/Geschichte_der_Gef%C3%BChle.

Ville de Castres, Musée Jaurès, and Gaston M. Poulain. *Exposition du Centenaire de la Naissance de Jaurès.* Castres: Musée Jaurès, 1959.

Vogt, Linda. *Eingreifendes Denken in der Literatur: Überlegungen zu dem Begriffsgegensatz Engagement—Autonomie.* Erlangen, 2016. http://www.eingreifendes-denken.phil.uni-erlangen.de/download.html.

Volkogonov, Dimitri. *Lenin: Life and Legacy.* London: HarperCollins, 1994.

Walker, Barbara. "On Reading Soviet Memoirs: A History of the 'Contemporaries' Genre as an Institution of Russian Intelligentsia Culture from the 1790s to the 1970s." *Russian Review* 59, no. 3 (2000): 327–52.

Walkowitz, Judith R. *City of Dreadful Delight: Narratives of Sexual Danger in Late Victorian London.* London: Virago, 2011.

Walther, Rudolf. "Marxismus." In *Geschichtliche Grundbegriffe*, edited by Otto Brunner et al., vol. 3, 937–76. Stuttgart: Klett-Cotta, 1982.

Walzer, Michael. *Exodus and Revolution.* New York: Basic Books, 1985.

Weber, Florian. "Von den klassischen Affektenlehren zur Neurowissenschaft und zurück: Wege der Emotionsforschung in den Geistes- und Sozialwissenschaften." *Neue Politische Literatur* 53 (2008): 21–42.

Weber, Hermann. *Der Gründungsparteitag der KPD. Protokoll und Materialien.* Frankfurt: Europäische Verlagsanstalt, 1969.

Weber, Max. *Weber: Political Writings.* Edited and translated by Peter Lassman and Ronald Speirs. Cambridge: Cambridge University Press, 1994.

Weber, Max. *Politik als Beruf.* Stuttgart: Reclam, 1992.

Wehler, Hans-Ulrich. *Das Deutsche Kaiserreich 1871–1918.* Göttingen: Vandenhoeck & Ruprecht, 1994.

Wehler, Hans-Ulrich. *The German Empire: 1871–1918.* Translated by Kim Traynor. Providence, RI: Berg, 1985.

Weinhauer, Klaus, Anthony McElligott, and Kirsten Heinsohn, eds. *Germany 1916–23: A Revolution in Context.* Bielefeld: Transcript, 2015.

Weisbrod, Bernd. "Generation und Generationalität in der neueren Geschichte." *Aus Politik und Zeitgeschichte* 8 (2005): 3–9.

Welskopp, Thomas. "'Arbeiterintellektuelle,' 'sozialdemokratische Bohemiens' und 'Chefideologen': Der Wandel der Intellektuellen in der frühen deutschen Sozialdemokratie: Ein Fallbeispiel." In *Intellektuelle und Sozialdemokratie*, edited by Ulrich von Alemann et al., 43–58. Opladen: Leske + Budrich, 2000.

Welskopp, Thomas. *Das Banner der Brüderlichkeit: Die deutsche Sozialdemokratie vom Vormärz bis zum Sozialistengesetz*. Bonn: Dietz, 2000.

Welskopp, Thomas. "Generation Bebel." In *Generationen in der Arbeiterbewegung*, edited by Klaus Schönhoven and Bernd Braun, 51–68. Munich: Oldenbourg, 2005.

Wendel, Friedrich. *Der Sozialismus in der Karikatur von Marx bis MacDonald: Ein Stück Kulturgeschichte*. Berlin: Dietz, 1924.

Wenzel, Uwe Justus. *Der kritische Blick: Über intellektuelle Tätigkeiten und Tugenden*. Frankfurt: Fischer, 2002.

White, James D. *Lenin: The Practice and Theory of Revolution*. Basingstoke: Palgrave, 2001.

Willard, Claude. "Einführung." In *Ausgewählte Texte, 1867–1882*, by Jules Guesde, 5–69. Berlin: Rütten & Loening, 1962.

Willard, Claude. *Les Guesdistes: Le Mouvement Socialiste en France (1893–1905)*. Paris: Éditions sociales, 1965.

Willard, Claude. *Jules Guesde, l'apôtre et la loi*. Paris: Éditions Ouvrieres, 1991.

Willard, Claude, ed. *La Naissance du Parti Ouvrier Français: Correspondence inédite de Paul Lafargue, Jules Guesde et al.* Paris: Éditions sociales, 1981.

Winkler, Martina. "Rulers and Ruled, 1700–1917." *Kritika* 12, no. 4 (2011): 789–806.

Winnig, August. *Der weite Weg*. Hamburg: Hanseatische Verlagsanstalt, 1932.

Winock, Michel. *Das Jahrhundert der Intellektuellen*. Konstanz: UVK, 2007.

Winterberg, Yury, and Sonya Winterberg. *Kollwitz: Die Biografie*. Munich: Bertelsmann, 2015.

Wistrich, Robert S. "Eduard Bernstein and the Jewish Problem." *Jahrbuch des Instituts für Deutsche Geschichte* 8 (1979): 243–56.

Wistrich, Robert S. *Revolutionary Jews from Marx to Trotsky*. New York: Barnes & Noble, 1976.

Wistrich, Robert S. "Rosa Luxemburg: The Polish-German-Jewish Identities of a Revolutionary Internationalist." *Leo Baeck Institute Year Book*, 57, no. 4 (2012): 239–66.

Wistrich, Robert S. *Socialism and the Jews*. London: Associated University Presses, 1982.

Wistrich, Robert S. "Victor Adler: A Viennese Socialist against Philosemitism." *Wiener Library Bulletin* 27, no. 32 (1974): 26–33.

Julius Wolf. [Selbstdarstellung]. In *Die Volkswirtschaftslehre der Gegenwart in Selbstdarstellungen*, edited by Felix Meiner, 209–47. Leipzig: Felix Meiner, 1924.

Wolf, Julius. [Self-Portrait]. In *Die Volkswirtschaftslehre der Gegenwart in Selbstdarstellungen*, edited by Felix Meiner, 209–47. Leipzig: Felix Meiner, 1924.

Wolfe, Bertram D. "Leninism." In *Marxism in the Modern World*, edited by Raymond Aron and Milorad M. Drachkovitch, 47–89. Stanford, CA: Stanford University Press, 1965.

Wondratsch, Irene. "Zur sozialen Lage der Arbeiterschaft im 19. Jahrhundert am Beispiel der Wienerberger Ziegelarbeiter." *Zeitgeschichte* 9, no. 2 (1981): 52–70.

Wood, Ellen Meiksins. "Politics and the Communist Manifesto." *Against the Current* 72, January–February 1998. https://www.solidarity-us.org/node/1151.

Wortman, Richard. *The Crisis of Russian Populism*. London: Cambridge University Press, 1967.

Wuthnow, Robert. *Communities of Discourse: Ideology and Social Structure in the Reformation, the Enlightenment, and European Socialism*. Cambridge, MA: Harvard University Press, 1989.

Zelnik, Reginald E. *Labor and Society in Tsarist Russia: The Factory Workers of St. Petersburg, 1855–1870*. Stanford, CA: Stanford University Press, 1971.

Zelnik, Reginald E. "Russian Workers and Revolution." In *Imperial Russia, 1689–1917*, edited by Dominic Lieven, 617–36. Cambridge: Cambridge University Press, 2006.

Zelnik, Reginald E. *Workers and Intelligentsia in Late Imperial Russia: Realities, Representations, Reflections*. Berkeley: University of California Press, 1999.

Zetkin, Ossip. *Charakterköpfe aus der französischen Arbeiterbewegung*. Berlin: Berliner Volkstribüne, 1889.

Zévaès, Alexandre. *Jules Guesde, 1845–1922*. Paris: Rivière, 1928.

Zomeren, M., T. van Postmes, and R. Spears. "Toward an Integrative Social Identity Model of Collective Action: A Quantitative Research Synthesis of Three Socio-Psychological Perspectives." *Psychological Bulletin* 134, no. 4 (2008): 504–35.

Index

For the benefit of digital users, indexed terms that span two pages (e.g., 52–53) may, on occasion, appear on only one of those pages.